FABRIZIO PLESSI · OPUS VIDEO SCULPTURE

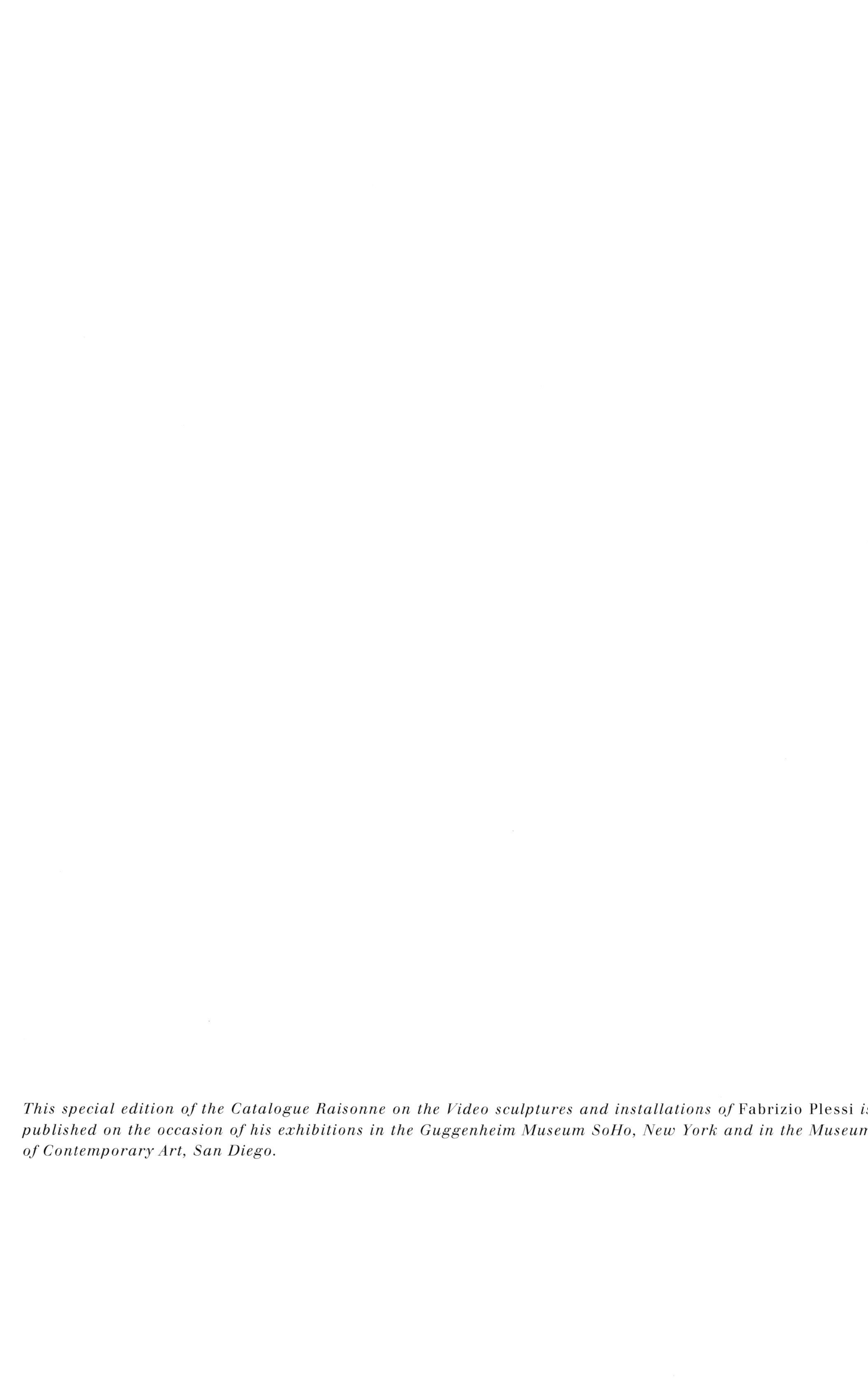

This special edition of the Catalogue Raisonne on the Video sculptures and installations of Fabrizio Plessi *is published on the occasion of his exhibitions in the Guggenheim Museum SoHo, New York and in the Museum of Contemporary Art, San Diego.*

FABRIZIO PLESSI

GUGGENHEIM MUSEUM SOHO, NEW YORK
JUNE 16 - SEPTEMBER 20, 1998

MUSEUM OF CONTEMPORARY ART, SAN DIEGO
NOVEMBER 8, 1998 - JANUARY 31, 1999

CHORUS - VERLAG

IMPRESSUM

This special edition of the Catalogue Raisonné on the video sculptures and installations is published on the occasion of the exhibitions of Fabrizio Plessi in the Guggenheim Museum SoHo in New York and the Museum of Contemporary Art in San Diego.

These extraordinary exhibitions could not have been possible without the generous support of the sponsor Aloys F. Dornbracht GmbH & Co. KG, Iserlohn/Germany who enabled also to produce this catalogue. We are most grateful.

We also thank the Italian Cultural Institute *Istituto Italiano di Cultura* in New York and its director Gioacchino Lanza Tomasi for supporting this book.

A special thank is due to Carlo Ansaloni who realised all the installations of Fabrizio Plessi and coordinated his shows since many years.

For the production of this publication have been included:

Prefaces:	Marco Caselli · Ferrara	Lay out:
Hugh M. Davies · San Diego	Thomas Clocchiatti · Perugia	Dorothea van der Koelen · Mainz
Andreas Dornbracht · Iserlohn	Zeno Colantoni · Roma	Martin van der Koelen · München
John G. Hanhardt · New York	Pere Colom · Barcelona	
Heinrich Klotz · Karlsruhe	Uli Deck · Karlsruhe	Type:
	Alberto Favretto · Venezia	Walbaum-Antiqua
Text:	Heinrich Fischer · Graz	
Dorothea van der Koelen · Mainz	Claudio Franzini · Venezia	Paper:
	Gert Heide · Graz	BVS matt weiß, 170 g/qm,
Work data and appendix:	Rainer Hoeft · Köln	100% chlorfrei, gestrichen
Martin van der Koelen · München	Mimmo Jodice · Napoli	Bilderdruck der Papierfabrik
	Benjamin Katz · Köln	Scheufelen · Lenningen
Translations:	Hermann Lilienthal · Bonn	
Heinz Bartkowski · Aschaffenburg	Hans-Georg Merkel · Landau	Reproductions:
Gabi Gappmayr · Innsbruck	Giuseppe Molteni · Milano	Digital Prisma · Bad Sobernheim
Jörg Schepers · Perugia	Roberta Motta · Milano	Schoell Reprotechnik · Mainz
	Helge Mundt · Hamburg	Engelhardt & Bauer · Karlsruhe
Photographs:	Monika Nicolic · Kassel	
Archives Plessi · Venezia	Theo de Nooij · Den Haag	Total production:
Archives Weisser Raum · Hamburg	Luciano Romano · Roma	Engelhardt & Bauer Druck- und
Yves Breton · Paris	Ursula Rudischer · Mainz	Verlagsgesellschaft · Karlsruhe
Susanne Brügger · Köln	Andreas Sauer · Heidelberg	
Christian Buck · Heidelberg	Nic Tenwiggenhorn · Düsseldorf	*Printed in Germany*
Angel Carrera · Valencia	Wolfgang Wössner · Wien	ISBN 3-931876-10-1

CONTENTS

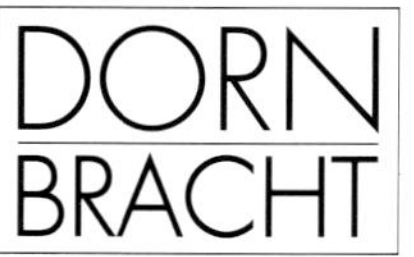

This exhibition is sponsored by Dornbracht.

EINLEITENDE WORTE

von Andreas Dornbracht
Geschäftsführer Aloys F.
Dornbracht Armaturenfabrik

Die Ausstellung des Medienkünstlers Fabrizio Plessi im Guggenheim Museum SoHo verweist auf ein Element, das den meisten von uns in seiner ursprünglichen Kraft und seiner essentiellen Bedeutung im Alltag längst nicht mehr bewußt ist: das Wasser. Wasser als Elixier des Lebens, Quelle immer neuer Inspiration für den Künstler und zugleich Inhalt täglicher Rituale, wie dem des Waschens, der Reinigung.

Als Hersteller von Design-Armaturen hat Dornbracht einen ausgeprägten Bezug zu diesem Ritual des Waschens und dem Element Wasser. Mit dem Anspruch, kulturelle Relevanz zu dokumentieren, sehen wir es als unternehmerische Aufgabe an, uns mit zeitgenössischen Interpretationen von Kultur im Bad auseinanderzusetzen.

Bereits in der Vergangenheit schufen international renommierte Fotografen und Künstler für unser Projekt *Statements* Arbeiten, die weit über die Branche hinaus Anerkennung fanden und in mehreren Ausstellungen gezeigt wurden.

Auch hier fördert Dornbracht mit den Ausstellungen Fabrizio Plessis im Guggenheim Museum SoHo und im Museum of Contemporary Art, San Diego, die Anerkennung für das Werk eines Künstlers, der, wie wir, Wasser in seiner Transparenz und Erscheinungsvielfalt als ästhetische Herausforderung begreift.

Der vorliegende Katalog vermittelt Idee und Anliegen des Künstlers und dokumentiert seine gesamten Video-Skulpturen und -Installationen.

Ich wünsche allen Besuchern ein schönes und bereicherndes Kunsterlebnis mit Fabrizio Plessi.

FOREWORD

by Andreas Dornbracht
Managing Director of Aloys F.
Dornbracht Fitting Factory

The exhibition of the works of media artist Fabrizio Plessi at the Guggenheim Museum SoHo, adresses an element which, despite its natural potency and the essential role it plays in everyday life, most of us tend to take for granted: water. Water as the elixir of life. The source of endless inspiration for artists, and at the same time an essential part of our daily rituals surrounding washing and cleaning.

Dornbracht as a manufacturer of designer bathroom fixtures, has a particular relationship with the ritual of washing and the element of water. With the aim of documenting works of cultural relevance, we at Dornbracht see it as our corporate obligation to concern ourselves with contemporary expressions of bathroom culture.

In the past, internationally renowned photographers and artists created works for Dornbracht's Statements *project, which achieved recognition far beyond the confines of our industrie and which were displayed at a number of exhibitors.*

Here too, with these exhibitions of Fabrizio Plessi's works at the Guggenheim Museum SoHo and the Museum of Contemporary Art, San Diego, Dornbracht is promoting the recognition of an artist who expresses in his work the vision of water which Dornbracht shares: water as an aesthetic challenge in its transparency and all its various forms.

This catalog presents the artist's ideas and concerns, and documents the body of his work in video sculpture and video installation.

I would like to wish all visitors a pleasant and enriching artistic experience with the works of Fabrizio Plessi.

INTRODUZIONE

di Andreas Dornbracht
Gerente della fabbrica di
rubinetterie è Aloys F. Dornbracht

La mostra dell'artista dei media Fabrizio Plessi al Guggenheim Museum SoHo, rimanda ad un elemento la cui forza primordiale ed il cui significto essenziale sfuggono oramai, nella vita quotidiana, alla ricezione cosciente della maggior parte di noi: l'acqua. L'acqua come elisir di vita, fonte di sempre nuova ispirazione per l'artista ed al contempo soggetto di riti quotidiani come quello della pulizia e del lavarsi.

Produttrice di rubinetterie d'alto design, la Dornbracht ha uno spiccato rapporto con il rito della pulizia e con l'elemento acqua. Volendo documentare l'essenzialità di questo aspetto culturale, come azienda pensiamo sia nostro compito primario occuparci delle attuali interpretazioni della cultura del bagno. Già in passato fotografi ed artisti rinomati a livello internazionale hanno creato per il nostro progetto *Statements* opere che, apprezzate ben oltre i confini del settore, sono state esposte in più di una mostra. Anche nel caso attuale la Dornbracht promuove, con gli esposizioni di Fabrizio Plessi al Guggenheim Museum SoHo e al Museum of Contemporary Art, San Diego, il riconoscimento dell'opera di un artista che, al pari di noi, interpreta l'elemento acqua, con la sua trasparenza e molteplicità d'aspetti, come una vera sfida estetica.

Questo catalogo vuole trasmettere il concetto, e le intenzioni dell'artista, é documentazione di tutte le sue sculture video e installazioni video.

Auguro a tutti i visitatori una magnifica ed intensa esperienza artística in compagnia di Fabrizio Plessi.

THE ART OF FABRIZIO PLESSI
by John G. Hanhardt
Senior Curator, Film and Media
Arts, Solomon R. Guggenheim
Museum, New York

It is a happy coincidence that this catalogue raisonné of Fabrizio Plessi's video sculptures and installations is being issued at the same time as his first one-artist exhibition in the United States. The Guggenheim Museum is presenting Plessi's work as part of 'Mapping the Media Arts', an ongoing exhibition program which seeks to describe and respond to the history and contemporary developments in the media arts. The Plessi exhibition also inaugurates a new series, 'European Perspectives on the Media Arts', which looks to recognize key artists, themes, and projects in the history of media art practises in Europe. In this case ZKM / Center for Art and Media Karlsruhe and its director Heinrich Klotz have chosen to present the installati-

ons of the Italian artist Fabrizio Plessi. It is another step in the continuing efforts of the Guggenheim Museum to provide global perspectives on the media arts by inviting curators, theorists, and institutions to present work that they feel deserves wider recognition and in-depth consideration in the history of the media arts.

Located in Karlsruhe, Germany, ZKM is a leading exhibition and educational center devoted to developments in the arts through new media and interactive technologies. Heinrich Klotz and Thomas Krens, director of the Guggenheim Museum, have forged a relationship between the two instituitons which resulted in the exhibition Mediascape presented at the Guggenheim Museum SoHo in 1996. Fabrizio Plessi, who began his career in

the early 1970s and is best known for his large-scale video installations featured in international European art exhibitions and included in museum collections, is being represented with four of his major installation pieces: Bronx (1986), Roma (1988), Cristalli Liquidi (1993), and Movimenti Catodici Barocchi (1996). This extraordinary exhibition could not have been possible without the generous support of our sponsor Aloys F. Dornbracht GmbH & Co. KG. We are also most grateful to Andreas Dornbracht, Managing Director, for his leadership and commitment to this project.

As one walks through the galleries and encounters each of Plessi's installations, one is immediately impressed by the theatrical presentation of his

materials and the grand scale of representation. At the heart of each work is the moving image, presented through the video monitor, which, through the recorded image, captures and infuses the work with the ebb and flow of the natural elements. Primary elements - fire and water - harnessed by the electronic signal, are combined with the materials of the built environment on a spectacular scale. Plessi's projects demonstrate an attention to the detail of physical materials combined with the power of the recorded image to evoke the distance of cultural history and nearness of personal memory. In addition, Plessi explores how the materials of ancient and contemporary history combine through the presentness of the moving image to orchestrate a total, enveloping impression that conjures a celebration of the pleasures of the real.

The distinctive features shared by Bronx, Roma, Cristalli Liquidi, and Movimenti Catodici Barocchi are an interplay between different material histories recoded and articulated through the spectacle of the multimedia installation: in Roma, a ring of monitors display the flowing waters of the Tiber River in a formation evoking the circular sign of the eternal return of Rome's past; Bronx suggests the violence of an industrial past and the struggle for a urban future as shovels penetrate the electronic flow of monitor screens; Cristalli Liquidi captures the Romantic imagination and luminosity of Venice's architecture and canals in an installation in which bukkets housing video monitors seem to capture an infinite supply of water poured out from delicate glasses suspended from the ceiling; Movimenti Catodici Barocchi removes the Baroque architectural

form from its rooted place in the past and suspends it in the present, as virtual flames lapping out from video monitors appear to threaten their wooden architectural framework.

Plessi, whose career began within the conceptual and performative strategies of the early 1970s, was later to develop a distinctive body of work articulated in his plans, drawings, and installation pieces. In Plessi's hands, video went from being a conceptual recording medium to being a means to expand the installation as a virtual environment by allowing the introduction of movement and the forces of the natural world into his meta-architectural projects. Plessi's drawings and plans describe a poetic and visual imagination that became the basis for an operatic spectacle of presentation, creating a multitextual mise-en-scène which we encounter as we look at and move about his installations. Plessi's art is filled with the dark echoes of Romanticism and an engagement with the aesthetics of light and color, sensory and emotional impressions. Plessi's works from the 1980s show a commonality with early postmodern strategies of combining historical styles and references to convey less an ironic sense of history than a personal meditation on historical loss, evoked by the rhetorical manipulation of architecture as history.

Plessi's importance to the history of video art practices in Italy and his development of the large-scale installation seen as a fully developed, theatrical mise-en-scène have uniquely positioned him and place his work in a compelling dialogue with that of other artists and art movements. Plessi's treatment of the exhibiti-

on space and manipulations of scale can be seen in relation to architecturally referenced pieces from the 1980s by Nam June Paik such as My Faust (1989-1991) and other earlier, metaphorical Paik installations including TV Garden (1973). In the United States, the treatment of place and landscape through installation practises has been a distinctive element in the history of installation art practices. An exhibition organized in 1988 by William D. Judson, Curator at the Carnegie Museum, entitled American Landscape Video: The Electronic Grove, *identified a selection of installations by Dara Birnbaum, Frank Gillette, Doug Hall, Mary Lucier, Rita Myers, Steina Vasulka, and Bill Viola that engaged the complex of history, memory, and place. Plessi's work clearly engages similar and related issues within the context of European cultural history. The differences and similarities between these artists and themes highlights the need to open up a greater dialogue between different media art histories and examine the shared references as well as divergences of these various cultural histories. In Plessi's art, the city of Venice - the site of his home and studio - functions as a major cultural inspiration and influence: the city as a work of sculpture, a celebration of the spectacle of aesthetics held together by a civic struggle to maintain its viability and preserve its past. Plessi's art is about the need to conserve, cherish, and celebrate the materials of culture and in the process to create new memories for the future. Plessi's work, like the city of Venice, celebrates the possibility of a poetics of art that captures the past in a self-reflexive present.*

FABRIZIO PLESSI
by Hugh M. Davies
Director, Museum of
Contemporary Art, San Diego

I am sure that were some wonderful works in the 1993 Venice Biennale. But well beyond the biannual bombast of the Giardini and the officially sponsored Olympian artistic efforts to outspend and outshine national opposition, by far the most memorable work occurred in the Café Florian. Not surprisingly, Cristalli liquidi, *a knowingly succinct and delicately moving site-specific work, situated in the very heart of the city, was the product of native son, Fabrizio Plessi.*

At the invitation of the café, Plessi cordoned off one of the small, elegant, rococo rooms, which face the Piazza San Marco. In what is probably the oldest continually operating café in the world, these delicately muraled and mirrored chambers, with their slight furniture and crimson-cushioned banquettes, are redolent with centuries of gentle conversation. The continuing tinkle of fine china, the crisp, haughty attire of the waiters, the lilting strains of the string quartet, while quaintly anachronistic, are deeply reassured and entirely appropriate to La Serenissima.

Into this refined environment Plessi inserted two elements: above, five hundred beautifully hand-crafted, clear crystal Murano glasses hanging like a peel of celestial bells from a rack mounted on the ceiling; and, below, fourteen industrially-fabricated, opaque, galvanized zinc buckets. Each bucket contained a circular masked video monitor. Intermittently, a simulated drop of water landed in the buckets - the 'plop' followed by concentric ripples across the surface of the screens. The contrast of crystal and zinc, the mirrored placement of reflected vessels - liquid streams of aqua above and electrons below - created a vertical, spatial tension, a charged gap between ancient and modern. The agonizing wait for the descending drop adding a temporal and sonic dimension. The syncopated sound of drops, the arrhythmic heartbeat of the water-bound city. The glasses forming a fabulous Venetian chandelier, the very apex and emblem of a rarified, opulent, privileged room - the utilitarian buckets evoking the common public space of the ubiquitous canal. The water table below the table, as it were - the constant reminder of aquatic erosion that continually threatens this otherwise timeless city, the liquid symbol of flux and the fugitive.

It is clear that Plessi is not a video artist. He merely uses the medium as one of many to create his compelling environments. But he is a Venetian artist while very much a man of the world. Water is the constant in all his work. I like to think of him with Veronese, with Longhi, even with Thomas Mann. His is a rich, humanistic and sensual art that embodies timeless qualities and themes in concert with his modern materials and observations. We at the Museum of Contemporary Art are deeply honored to exhibit his important work and to introduce Fabrizio Plessi to new audiences in California and the United States.

FABRIZIO PLESSI
von Heinrich Klotz
Leiter des Museums für Neue Kunst
im ZKM / Zentrum für Kunst und
Medientechnologie, Karlsruhe

FABRIZIO PLESSI
by Heinrich Klotz
director of the Museum of New
Art in the ZKM / Center for Art
and Media, Karlsruhe

FABRIZIO PLESSI
di Heinrich Klotz
direttore del museo per arte
nuova al ZKM / Centro per arte e
media, Karlsruhe

Auf einem Monitor sind einige blaue Neonbuchstaben aufgereiht, die ein nur schwer entzifferbares Wort in Spiegelschrift wiedergeben. Die darunterstehende Mattscheibe aber zeigt die Reflexion dieser Neonbuchstaben und man liest das sich im Wasser spiegelnde nun entzifferbare Wort ›Wasser‹. Das Videowasser im Monitor entschlüsselt das entstellte Wort der Neonbuchstaben, so als benötige man zur Erkenntnis der Wirklichkeit Videokamera und Monitor. Aber wir wissen, daß das reflektierte Wort im Monitor nicht wirklich ein Reflex ist, sondern die Videoaufnahme des im Wasser reflektierten Wortes ›Wasser‹.

Auf einem auf Räder gesetzten beweglichen Monitor sieht man ein Glas mit Flüssigkeit. Es fährt auf einen realen Ventilator zu, der ringsum die Luft in Bewegung setzt. Je näher der Monitor auf den Ventilator zufährt, desto stärker gerät die Flüssigkeit im Glas in Bewegung bis sie, dicht vor dem Ventilator - überschwappt. Wie aber kann der Ventilator als Teil unserer dreidimensionalen Wirklichkeit das Wasser im Glase auf der Mattschei-

On a monitor some blue neon letters which represent a hardly decipherable word in mirror writing are strung together. The monitor below, however, shows the reflection of these neon letters and one can now decipher the word 'water' which is reflected in the water. The videowater on the monitor deciphers the distorted word in neon letters, as if the videocamera and the monitor were necessary elements for the recognition of reality. But we know that the reflected word on the monitor is not really a reflection but the video representation of the word 'water' reflected in the water.

On a mobile monitor on wheels there is a glass filled with liquid. It drives towards a real ventilator, which starts moving the air. The closer the monitor gets to the ventilator, the more the liquid in the glass starts to move, until it splashes over, just before reaching the ventilator. How can the ventilator as being part of our three-dimensional world set into motion the water in the glass on the monitor? Only

Su di un monitor sono allineate alcune lettere blu al neon che riproducono in modo rovesciato una parola appena decifrabile. Lo schermo televisivo posto al di sotto mostra però il riflesso di tali lettere e si legge, adesso in maniera chiara, la parola ›Water‹ rispecchiata nell'acqua. L'acqua video del monitor svela la parola alterata, quasi si avesse bisogno della videocamera e del monitor per la conoscenza della realtà. Sappiamo però che la parola riflessa nel monitor non è realmente un riflesso ma una videoregistrazione della parola ›Water‹ rispecchiata nell'acqua.

Un monitor mobile su ruote mostra un bicchiere contenente un liquido. Il monitor si muove in direzione di un ventilatore reale che muove l'aria tutt'intorno (*Water Wind*, 1984). Man mano che il monitor si avvicina al ventilatore, il liquido del bicchiere inizia ad agitarsi fino a traboccare in prossimità del ventilatore. Ma come riesce il ventilatore, quale parte integrante della nostra realtà tridi-

be in Bewegung setzen? Das kann nur Fabrizio Plessi.

Die berühmte Installation *Roma*, die Plessi auf der documenta 8 in Kassel zum ersten Mal der Öffentlichkeit vorstellte, gab ebenfalls ein ganz ähnliches Rätsel auf: Auf 36 im Dreiviertelkreis aufgestellten, nach oben gerichteten Monitoren fließt - quasi durch die Kästen hindurch - ein unaufhörlich strudelnder Wasserstrom. Am Kopf des Dreiviertelkreises steht ein großes Förderband, das schräg nach unten auf den mittleren Monitor herabführt. Obwohl das Band läuft, sieht man auf ihm keinen Stein, der unten ins Wasser fallen könnte, sozusagen in den Monitor hinein. Aber man hört den Stein, der in unregelmäßigen Abständen ins Monitorwasser hineinplumpst. Und wenn man dann hingeht und in den Monitor hineinblickt, sieht man tatsächlich den Stein ins Wasser fallen. Er fällt vom laufenden Förderband herab auf dem kein Stein befördert wird, und plumpst laut hinein in den Wasserfluß. Kein Zweifel - hier geschieht ein Wunder.

Ich habe Besucher vor diesem Wasserkreis stehen sehen, die geradezu abwesend und verklärt auf den unsichtbaren, sichtbaren Stein blickten, der da ins Wasser fiel.

Plessi, dieser mediale Wasserkünstler, hat viele solcher Wunder vollbracht, etwa die beiden Volkswagen, die zwar im Trockenen stehen, auf deren Windschutzscheiben jedoch der Regen niederprasselt und die Scheibenwischer vehement hin- und herfahren: Es sind zwei Monitore hinter der Scheibe, auf denen sich der Regen abspielt.

Oder das große Mühlrad, das von einem Wasserstrom angetrieben wird und sich dreht. Tatsächlich sprudelt unten, wo das Was-

Fabrizio Plessi succeeds in doing this.

The famous installation Roma, *presented to the public by Plessi for the first time at the documenta 8 in Kassel, presented a similar riddle: On 36 upright monitors arranged in a three-quarter-circle a continually swirling waterstream virtually floats through the boxes. At the top of the threequarter-circle there is a big conveyor belt leading diagonally down to the middle monitor. Even though the belt is in motion, no stone can be seen there that could fall into the water or, more exactly, into the monitor. There is however the sound of a stone going splash into the monitor water at irregular intervals. And when one comes close to look on the monitor, one really sees the stone tumbling down into the water. It falls from the belt in motion, which carries no stone, and with a big splash it tumbles down into the floating water. There is no doubt about it. - It is a miracle.*

I have seen visitors, standing in front of this water circle, who were looking in a somehow absent-minded and enchanted way at the invisible and at the same time visible stone that fell into the water.

Plessi, this media water artist, has worked a lot of these miracles, such as for example the two volkswagen which stand in the dry, on the windshield of which though the rain drums and the windshield wipers energetically move back and forth. Behind the window there are two monitors where the rain takes place.

Or the big millwheel, which is driven by a water stream and which rotates. At the point where the water falls down from the shovels it bubbles and disap-

mensionale, a muovere l'acqua del bicchiere sul monitor? Lo sa solo Fabrizio Plessi.

Anche la famosa installazione *Roma*, presentata per la prima volta al pubblico alla documenta 8 di Kassel (Germania), propone un simile mistero: in trentasei televisori disposti in tre quarti di cerchio con i monitors rivolti verso l'alto scorre incessante - quasi li attraversasse - uno spumeggiante torrente d'acqua. Alle estremità del cerchio si trova un grande nastro trasportatore che, inclinato verso il basso, punta sul monitor centrale. Sebbene il nastro si muova, non si vede alcun sasso che possa cadere in acqua o, per così dire, nel monitor. Eppure, ad intervalli irregolari, si ode un sasso piombare nell'acqua del monitor. E se poi si getta uno sguardo nel monitor, si scorge il sasso che cade veramente in acqua. Esso scende dal nastro in movimento che non trasporta nessun sasso e precipita rumorosamente nel flusso d'acqua. Senza dubbio, un miracolo.

Ho osservato spettatori di fronte a questo specchio d'acqua guardare, quasi assenti ed incantati, il sasso invisibile, che poi visibile davanti ai loro occhi cade nell'acqua.

Plessi, questo artista mediale dell'acqua, ha compiuto tanti di siffatti miracoli, come ad esempio i due maggiolini Volkswagen, che si trovano sì all'asciutto, ma sul parabrezza batte la pioggia mentre i tergicristalli si muovono con veemenza: tutto ciò accade su due monitors posti dietro il vetro della macchina (*Wasserwagen*, 1981).

O anche la grande ruota del mulino (*Tempo Liquido*, 1989) che gira sotto la spinta di un

ser aus den Schaufeln herabfällt, ein Strom hervor, der in einer Entfernung von einigen Metern wieder im Boden verschwindet. So weit, so gut. Doch die Irritation wächst bis zum sprachlosen Staunen, wenn man erkennt, daß die Schaufeln des Rades von Monitoren gebildet werden, von denen das Wasser - nicht wirklich - sondern als bewegtes Videobild - herabsprudelt. Alles ist wirklich, nur das Wasser, das antreibt und das Rad zum Drehen bringt, ist eine bloße Täuschung, ist ein elektronisches Bild.

Nahezu alle Arbeiten des Künstlers haben auf vielfältige Weise das große Thema der Künste zum Inhalt, das Thema von Wirklichkeit und Täuschung, von Schein und Sein, von Realität und Fiktion. Immer stellt sich die Frage erneut: Wo beginnt der Schein und was ist die Realität? Plessi scheint zu antworten: Dort, wo wir die Wirklichkeit erwarten, dort ist sie gerade nicht, dort ist medialer Schein, dort geschehen die Wunder der Fiktion. Und wenn wir vom Schein fortgerissen werden und vermeinen, überall Fiktionen zu erkennen, dann stoßen wir auf die harte Materialität des Wirklichen.

Fabrizio Plessi ist unter den bedeutenden Medienkünstlern der Gegenwart derjenige, der es wie kein anderer versteht, auf dem schmalen Grat zwischen Schein und Wirklichkeit zu balancieren. Die Avantgarde der Moderne hat gefordert, daß Kunst und Leben, also Schein und Sein, miteinander identisch werden sollen. Der Fortschritt der Kunst, so haben sie fast alle gemeint, bestünde darin, die Kunst in das Leben hinein zu entgrenzen. Plessi tut dies gerade nicht. Er treibt die Fiktion weit in die Realität vor. Doch er hält inne und stoppt knapp vor dem Umkippen in die Wirklichkeit ab, hält

pears at a distance of a few meters. So far, so good. The confusion turns more and more into speechless astonishment, when one realizes that the shovels of the wheel are realized by monitors from where the water bubbles down, not really, but as an animated video image. Everything is real, only the water which drives the wheel and makes it rotate is a pure illusion, an electronic image.

Almost all the works of this artist deal in various ways with one of the great artistic themes, that is the theme of reality and illusion, of appearance and reality, of reality and fiction. It is always the question of where the appearance sets in and the question of what is real? Plessi seems to answer: Reality is not where we expect it to be, it is only the illusion of the media. These are miracles of fiction. And when we are driven away by mere illusion and think we would always perceive appearances, then we are confronted with the hard materiality of reality.

Among the important media artists of today Fabrizio Plessi is the one who understands like no-one else to achieve a balance between appearance and reality. The avantgarde of modern art has claimed that art and life, that is appearance and reality, should become identical. They have said that a step forward in art would consist in opening up art towards life. This is eactly what Plessi does not do. He pushes the illusion far forward towards reality. He stops however just before it turns into reality. He records the appearance when it is still illusion and creates a dramatic interference with reality. This balancing act between an illusionary taking-for-

torrente d'acqua. L'acqua in realtà sgorga in basso dalle pale del mulino e a distanza di pochi metri scompare nel pavimento. Fin qui tutto bene. Ma l'irritazione si trasforma in stupore quando ci si accorge che le pale sono fatte di monitors dai quali fuoriesce acqua non vera, ma come immagine video in movimento. Tutto è reale, solo l'acqua che muove la ruota e la fa girare si rivela una semplice illusione, un'immagine elettronica.

Quasi tutti lavori dell'artista hanno, in modo diverso, il grande tema delle arti quale argomento: il tema della realtà e dell'illusione, dell'essere e dell'apparenza, del reale e della finzione. Ogni volta ci si pone il quesito: dove inizia l'apparenza e che cos'è la realtà? Plessi sembra rispondere: la realtà non si trova lì dove ce l'aspettiamo, perché lì è apparenza mediale, lì si compiono i miracoli. E nel momento in cui veniamo trascinati dall'apparenza, convinti di riconoscere dappertutto la finzione, ci scontriamo con la dura materialità del reale.

Fra gli importanti artisti mediali contemporanei Fabrizio Plessi come nessun altro sa stare in bilico fra apparenza e realtà. L'avanguardia dell'arte moderna pretendeva di rendere identiche fra di loro arte e vita e cioè apparenza e essere. In tanti hanno pensato che il progresso dell'arte consistesse nello sconfinare dell'arte nella vita. Plessi no, egli spinge la finzione dentro la realtà per fermarsi appena prima del ribaltamento nel reale; egli fissa la finzione quando ancora è apparenza e la fa incontrare drammaticamente con la realtà. Tale equilibrio fra l'illusorio credere-per-vero e la

9

die Fiktion fest, wo sie noch Schein ist und läßt sie dramatisch auf die Wirklichkeit treffen. Dieser Balanceakt zwischen täuschendem Für-wahr-halten und Wahrheit des Wirklichen, dieses spannungsvolle Verhältnis von Schein und Sein ist der Boden, auf dem mit der Fiktion die Poesie entsteht. Es ist das Schöne, es ist der poetische Augenblick, in dem wir erkennen, daß das kräftig antreibende Wasser auf dem Mühlrad nur Schein ist und daß das Mühlrad sich trotzdem dreht.

So also können wir sagen, Plessis Kunst besteht darin, die Täuschung im Moment des Auftreffens auf die Wirklichkeit zu erhalten, also, um es allgemeiner zu formulieren - eine fast wahre Geschichte zu erzählen.

Tatsächlich erzählt Plessi Geschichten, die Geschichte von der Annäherung eines Wasserglases an den Ventilator, die Geschichte der Neonbuchstaben, die sich erst in der Umkehrung der fiktiven Reflexion entziffern, die Geschichte vom Stein auf dem Förderband, der fiktiv ins Medienwasser fällt und so fort. Alles dies sind Geschichten, sind narrative Fiktionen. Die Videokunst gibt uns die Möglichkeit, aus der Abstraktion der modernen Malerei auszubrechen und an die Stelle autonomer Formen den erzählenden Schein, die narrative Fiktion zu setzen. Mit dem Wechsel der Gattungen von der Malerei zur Videoinstallation erhält das gegenständlich erzählende Bild neuen Auftrieb, und es gelingt uns, mit diesem neuen Mittel, der Medienkunst, nie gesehene, nie gehörte Geschichten zu erzählen, also Darstellungsmodi zu entwickeln, die erst mit Hilfe der Videokamera möglich geworden sind, Fiktionen, die im Bereich der traditionellen Künste nicht mehr geglaubt wurden, sind nun erlaubt. Was wir mit

true and the truth of reality, this exciting relationship between appearance and reality is the base where, by means of fiction, poetry has its origin. It is the beautiful, the poetical moment, when we realize that the water is only illusion and that the millwheel rotates just the same.

We can therefore say that Plessi's art consists in capturing the illusion in the moment of its interference with reality, or to put it more generally, in telling us an almost true story.

In fact, Plessi tells stories, the story of an approach of a glass of water towards a ventilator, the story of the neon letters which are only decipherable in the inversion of a ficticious reflection, the story of the stone on the conveyor belt, which apparently falls into the monitor water and so on. These are all stories, narrative fictions. Video Art gives us the possibility to escape from the abstraction of modern painting and to replace autonomous forms by narrative appearance or fiction. The change from the genre of painting to video installation gives a new impetus to the narrative and figurative aspect. This new means of expression makes it possible to tell never-heard and never-seen stories, to develop new ways of representation which have only become possible because of the video camera and to present fictions that have no longer been credible in the traditional arts. Everything we could no longer express by means of traditional concepts now has a new language.

The concepts of Plessi's video fictions are quite varied. He also deals with other themes than the above-mentioned water

verità della realtà, questo rapporto teso fra apparenza ed essere costituisce il terreno sul quale nasce, con la finzione, la poesia. È il bello, è il momento poetico, nel quale comprendiamo che la potente acqua che mette in moto la ruota del mulino è solamente apparenza che nondimeno fa girare la ruota.

Possiamo quindi affermare che l'arte di Plessi consiste nel mantenere l'illusione nel momento dell'incontro con la realtà o, per dirlo in maniera più generale, nel raccontare una storia quasi vera.

Infatti, Plessi racconta storie, la storia dell'avvicinarsi di un bicchier d'acqua al ventilatore, la storia delle lettere al neon che si decifrano solamente attraverso il rovesciamento del riflesso fittizio, la storia del sasso sul nastro trasportatore che cade nell'acqua mediale e così via. Tutte queste sono storie, finzioni narrative. La videoarte ci permette di evadere dall'astrazione della pittura moderna e di sostituire forme autonome con l'apparenza e la finzione narrativa. Con il passaggio dalla pittura alla videoinstallazione l'immagine oggettivo-narrativa riceve un nuovo impulso e si è in grado, con tale nuovo mezzo - l'arte mediale - di raccontare storie mai viste né sentite, di sviluppare quindi modalità di rappresentazione divenute possibili soltanto coll'ausilio della videocamera. Finzioni non accettate nell'ambito delle arti tradizionali sono ora permesse. Quello che non eravamo capaci di dire con le arti tradizionali giunge adesso ad un nuovo linguaggio.

I contenuti delle videofinzioni di Plessi sono multiformi. Anche quando va oltre la temati-

den Mitteln der herkömmlichen
Künste nicht mehr sagen konnten,
gelangt nun zu neuer Sprache.

Die Inhalte von Plessis Videofik-
tionen sind vielgestaltig. Auch wenn
er andere Themen intoniert, nicht
nur bei den hier in den Vordergrund gestellten Wasserthemen, so
sucht Plessi immer wieder das
spannungsvolle, manchmal sogar
tautologische Verhältnis zwischen
Schein und Sein in den Vordergrund
zu stellen. Seine Arbeit *Schrank des
Architekten* besteht aus schweren,
rostfarbenen Cortenstahlgestellen,
die in den unteren Regalteilen
säuberlich aufgestapelte Ziegel
tragen, blaßrote, bereits verwendete
und vom Mörtel befreite Backsteine
türmen sich zu unregelmäßiger
Höhe auf. Darüber aber, auf einer
zweiten Regalebene, sitzen ebensol-
che Ziegelwände - als Monitorbilder. Der blasse Schein des Matt-
scheibenimages kontrastiert mit der
anfaßbaren Präsenz der Ziegel, eine
durch Kontrast intensivierte Realität. Das bewegte Bild ist hier still-
gestellt, so still wie die lagernde
Ziegelwand. Bewegungslos verweist
das Abbild auf die unnachgiebige
Gegenwart des Wirklichen. Der
Stein stellt das bewegte Bild still.

Eine der jüngsten Arbeiten von
Plessi, die 1990 entstandene Videoskulptur *Proibito* ist wiederum eine
solche Regalwand aus Cortenstahl,
ein, so könnte man sagen, ›Schrank
des Meeres‹. Hinter einer quasi von
Brettern venagelten Wand öffnet
sich oben der Blick auf das Meer,
und man sieht über den gedunkel-
ten oder von Wasser und Sonne
ausgebleichten Planken, die umbre-
chenden Wellen auf den Strand
auflaufen. Hier ist Plessis Spiel mit
der Täuschung in den Wellen
verebbt und die Unendlichkeit des
Meeres bricht über der physischen
Nähe der Bretterwand über uns
herein. Wir sind gewohnt, bewegte
Bilder als Fernsehbilder zu erleben
und wir haben die Neigung, die

*concepts, but he always tries to
concentrate on the exciting
though sometimes even tautological relationship between
appearance and reality. His
work* The Architect°s Cabinet
*consists of heavy, russet Cor-
ten-steel racks which carry
properly layered bricks on the
lower shelves. Pale red bricks,
which have already been used
and which have been cleaned
from mortar, are piled up in
different heights. At the top of
these bricks there is a second
shelf with similar bricks in
layers - but these bricks are
only video images. The pale
glow of the monitor image
contrasts with the direct
presence of the bricks, a reality
which is intensified through
this contrast. The animated
image stands idle such as the
piled up bricks. The motionless
image refers to the inflexible
presence of reality. The stone
stops the animated image.*

*One of Plessi's most recent
work, his video sculpture*
Proibito *from 1990, consists
again of shelves made of Cor-
ten-steel, one might call it a
'cabinet of the sea'. Behind a
wall apparently covered with
boards, one can perceive the
sea and over the planks which
are darkened or bleached by
the water and the sun one sees
the breaking waves running in
the beach. In this case Plessi's
game of illusion has subsided
and the infinity of the sea
descends upon us over the
physical proximity of the
shelves.*

*We are used to experience
animated images only as
images on television and we
tend to regard the animated
images on the monitors with
the same scepticism of a satia-
ted experience of images, as it*

ca dell'acqua egli cerca sempre
di mettere in risalto il rapporto,
pieno di tensione e a volte
tautologico, fra apparenza ed
essere. La sua opera *Armadio
dell'Architetto* (1990) è costituita
da una struttura d'acciaio pe-
sante di color ruggine che
contiene mattoni accatastati
accuratarmente nella parte
inferiore; materiale laterizio
usato, liberato dal cemento e di
color rosaceo si erge ad altezza
irregolare. In alto, su un altro
piano, si vedono - come immagini dei monitors - altre pareti
uguali di mattoni. La pallida
apparenza dell'immagine dello
schermo si contrappone alla
presenza tangibile dei mattoni,
una realtà intensificata attraverso il contrasto. L'immagine in
movimento è qui ferma, immobile, come la parete dei mattoni.
Immobile, l'immagine riprodotta
rimanda alla presenza intransi-
gente del reale. Il mattone
ferma l'immagine in movimento.

Una delle opere più recenti
di Plessi, la videoscultura
Proibito realizzata nel 1990, è
ancora una parete a scaffale di
acciaio, un ›armadio del mare‹,
così protrebbe dirsi. Dietro una
parete quasi interamente coperta di tavole di legno inchiodate,
si apre in alto la vista sul mare
e sopra tale steccato scurito o
sbiadito dall'acqua e dal sole si
intravedono le onde che
s'infrangono sulla spiaggia. Qui
il gioco con l'illusione di Plessi
si spegne nelle onde e l'infinità
del mare si riversa su di noi
attraverso la vicinanza fisica
della parete di tavole.

Siamo avvezzi a vivere immagini in movimento come immagini televisive; siamo portati
dunque a confrontarci con le
immagini in movimento dei
monitors con lo stesso scetticis-
mo di una ipernutrita esperien-

bewegten Bilder auf Monitoren mit derselben Skepsis einer überfütterten Bilderfahrung zu begegnen, wie wir nun einmal nach täglich vierstündigem Fernsehen - dem statistischen Durchschnitt in Deutschland - auf bewegte Bilder überdrüssig reagieren. Doch Plessis Bilder sind keine Fernsehbilder; sie sind - mit den gleichen technischen Mitteln hervorgebracht - Gegenerklärungen gegen die üblichen Bilder der TV-Welt. Das vom Stein stillgestellte Monitorbild der Ziegel ist kein Fernsehbild, ebensowenig wie der ins Wasser fallende Stein, der immer wieder fällt, oder das Meer, das immer wieder anbrandet. Es sind Gegenbilder, poetische Entgegnungen gegen die Konsumbilder von SAT 1 und RTL Plus.

Auch die Videokunst operiert wie alle Kunst mit den technischen Mitteln des Alltags. Sie flieht nicht in ein Land des Goldmosaiks, sondern sie nimmt, was alltäglich greifbar ist. Aber sie verwandelt das banal Greifbare und rückt uns das immer schon Gesehene, aber nie Begriffene ins Blickfeld.

happens after four hours of TV a day - such is the statistic average in Germany. We are weary of such a lot of animated images. Plessi's images are no TV images. They are rather statements against the usual images of the world of TV, created however with the same technical means. All these works, the monitor image of the brick stopped by the stone, the stone which plunges again and again into the water and the sea with its breakers, are no TV images. These are all statements, poetical replies to the images of consumption on SAT 1 and RTL plus.

Such as art in general, Video Art also works with the technical means of everyday life. It does not escape in a land of gold mosaic, but takes all that is commonly available. Yet, the banal objects of everyday life are transformed and everything we have already seen but not really reflected becomes the focus of attention.

za televisiva, con la stessa satura reazione al consumo quotidiano di televisione (quattro ore al dì è la media statistica in Germania). Ma le immagini di Plessi non sono quelle della televisione; esse - prodotte con gli stessi mezzi tecnici - sono controdichiarazioni alle abituali immagini del mondo della TV. L'immagine del mattone del monitor fermata dalla pietra non è un'immagine televisiva come non lo è il sasso che cade di continuo nell'acqua o il mare che continuamente si infrange. Esse sono controimmagini, risposte poetiche alle immagini di consumo della televisione privata.

Come tutta l'arte, anche la videoarte adopera i mezzi tecnici della vita quotidiana. Essa non fugge nel mondo del mosaico d'oro, bensì fa uso di ciò che il quotidiano offre a portata di mano, trasformandolo, e pone nel nostro campo visivo il già da sempre visto ma mai compreso.

VORWORT

von Dorothea van der Koelen

»Fabrizio Plessis großes Thema heißt ›Wasser‹. Wasser ist seine Obsession in jeder nur denkbaren Dimension, in allen Erscheinungsformen und Funktionen. Er umkreist es immer wieder in seiner Arbeit, er läßt sich von ihm herausfordern, er fürchtet es, er spielt mit ihm, er verwandelt und bearbeitet es. Und er macht immer neue, überraschende Vorschläge, wie mit ihm umzugehen sei. Seinem von 1968 bis heute entstandenen Werk hat er den Oberbegriff *Acquabiografico* gegeben. Damit ist ausgedrückt, daß seine künstlerischen Aktivitäten inhaltlich ausschließlich auf das Thema Wasser gerichtet sind, und zudem verweist das hinzugefügte Wort ›biografico‹ auf die von Plessi angestrebte enge Verknüpfung des an sich zunächst abstrakten Themas Wasser mit dem eigenen Leben, mit der eigenen Geschichte, mit der bewußt gewordenen täglichen Umwelt.« (Jens Christian Jensen, in: Katalog Kunsthalle zu Kiel, Kiel 1977)

Nach seinem Studium an der Akademie der Schönen Künste in Venedig beginnt der 1940 in Reggio Emilia geborene Wahl-Venezianer Fabrizio Plessi, systematisch ein Werk zu entwickeln, in dem Wasser die Hauptrolle spielt. Es ist mit eigenen existentiellen, biographischen Erfahrungen verknüpft und wird zum Ausdruck einer weitreichenden visuellen und intellektuellen Dimension. Dabei ist die Vielseitigkeit der optischen, der visuellen Präsenz seiner Ideen, der Umsetzung in bildnerische Wahrnehmungsformen nicht weniger faszinierend als die Bedeutungskomplexität und die vielfältigen Bezugsmöglichkeiten. Es gibt so viele Perspektiven, Möglichkeiten,

PREFACE

von Dorothea van der Koelen

"Fabrizio Plessi's great theme is 'water'. Water, in every conceivable dimension, in all forms and functions, is his obsession. Again and again he circles it in his work, he accepts its challenge, he fears it, plays with it, changes and works on it. And he makes ever new, surprising suggestions on how to deal with it. He calls his work, from 1968 until today, Acquabiografico. Thus he indicates that his artistic activities are solely dealing with the subject of 'water', and the addition of the word 'biografico' points to the desired close connection of the - in itself at first abstract - subject of water with his own life, his personal history, the cognisance of his daily environment." (Jens Christian Jensen, in: catalogue Kunsthalle zu Kiel, Kiel 1977)

After his studies at the Academy of Fine Arts in Venice Fabrizio Plessi, the Venetian-by-choice, born in 1940 in Reggio Emilia, begins to systematically develop his work in which water plays the main role. It is tied to his own existential, biographic experiences, and becomes expression of a far-reaching visual and intellectual dimension. In this, the complexity of the optical, visual presence of his ideas, of the transformation into pictorial visual forms, is not less fascinating than the complexity of meaning and the multiple potential of references. There are so many perspectives, possibilities, ways and forms of expression to approach Fabrizio Plessi's work that only a small section can be mentioned here, without being able to fully describe or analyse each relevant work. The explanations given here are meant to be understood as only one of many possible aspects under which Plessi's work

PREFAZIONE

von Dorothea van der Koelen

»Il grande tema di Fabrizio Plessi è l'acqua. L'acqua, in ogni dimensione immaginabile, in ogni forma e funzione, è la sua ossessione. Egli le gira intorno in ogni momento del suo lavoro, ci gioca, la modula e la elabora, la teme e nello stesso momento viene da essa provocato, giungendo sempre a manipolarla in nuove soprendenti proposte. Alla sua opera realizzata dal 1968 fino ad oggi ha dato il titolo *Acquabiografico*, intendendo così esprimere che la sua attività artistica si concentra esclusivamente sul tema dell'acqua; il suffisso ›biografico‹ indica inoltre il voluto stretto collegamento del concetto - in sé astratto - dell'acqua con la propria vita, con la propria storia e con l'ambiente quotidiano.« (Jens Christian Jensen, in: catalogo Kunsthalle zu Kiel, Kiel 1977)

Dopo i suoi studi presso l'Accademia delle Belle Arti di Venezia, Fabrizio Plessi, nato a Reggio Emilia nel 1940 e residente per scelta nella città lagunare, inizia a sviluppare sistematicamente un'opera nella quale l'acqua assume un ruolo predominante. Essa è collegata direttamente con le proprie esperienze biografiche ed esistenziali e diventa espressione di una vasta dimensione visuale e intellettuale. La complessità della presenza ottica, visuale delle sue idee e la loro trasformazione in forme di percezione visive non sono meno affascinanti rispetto alla complessità dei significati e dei riferimenti. L'opera di Plessi offre modi, possibilità, prospettive e forme espressive così innumerevoli per avvicinarsi ad essa che in

13

Wege und Ausdrucksformen, sich dem Werk Fabrizio Plessis zu nähern, daß hier im folgenden nur immer ein kleiner Ausschnitt genannt werden kann, ohne das jeweilige Werk erschöpfend zu beschreiben oder analysieren zu wollen. Die Hinweise, die hier gegeben werden, sollen nur als einer von vielen möglichen Blickwinkeln verstanden werden, aus denen man das Werk Plessis betrachten, verstehen und lieben kann.

1968 beginnt Plessis Weg zum Wasser. Ein langer, vielseitiger und oft schwieriger Weg, der noch längst nicht zu Ende gegangen ist. Zunächst arbeitet Fabrizio Plessi zeichnerisch in Projektskizzen

can be seen, understood, and loved.

Plessi's way to water begins in 1968. It is a long, multifaceted and often difficult road that has by far not reached its end yet. In the beginning, Fabrizio Plessi draws up project-sketches and collages, he takes notes of actions and performances with water, and conceives his first neon installations in the middle of the seventies. His first project for a video-sculpture originates in 1968, called Water TV previsioni del tempo, *meaning 'weather forecast'. In this concept, a monitor can be seen, a TV set from which a strong jet of water flows towards the spectator. His project-*

seguito ne viene proposta solo una selezione, senza voler descrivere ed analizzare in maniera esauriente ogni singolo lavoro. Le indicazioni suggerite vogliono essere intese solamente quale una fra molteplici angolazioni possibili dalle quali si può osservare, comprendere e amare l'œuvre di Fabrizio Plessi.

Il cammino di Plessi verso l'acqua ha inizio nel 1968: un cammino lungo, variegato, spesso difficile e certamente non ancora giunto a termine. Inizialmente Fabrizio Plessi disegna schizzi per progetti e collages, annota azioni e perfor-mances con acqua e, verso la

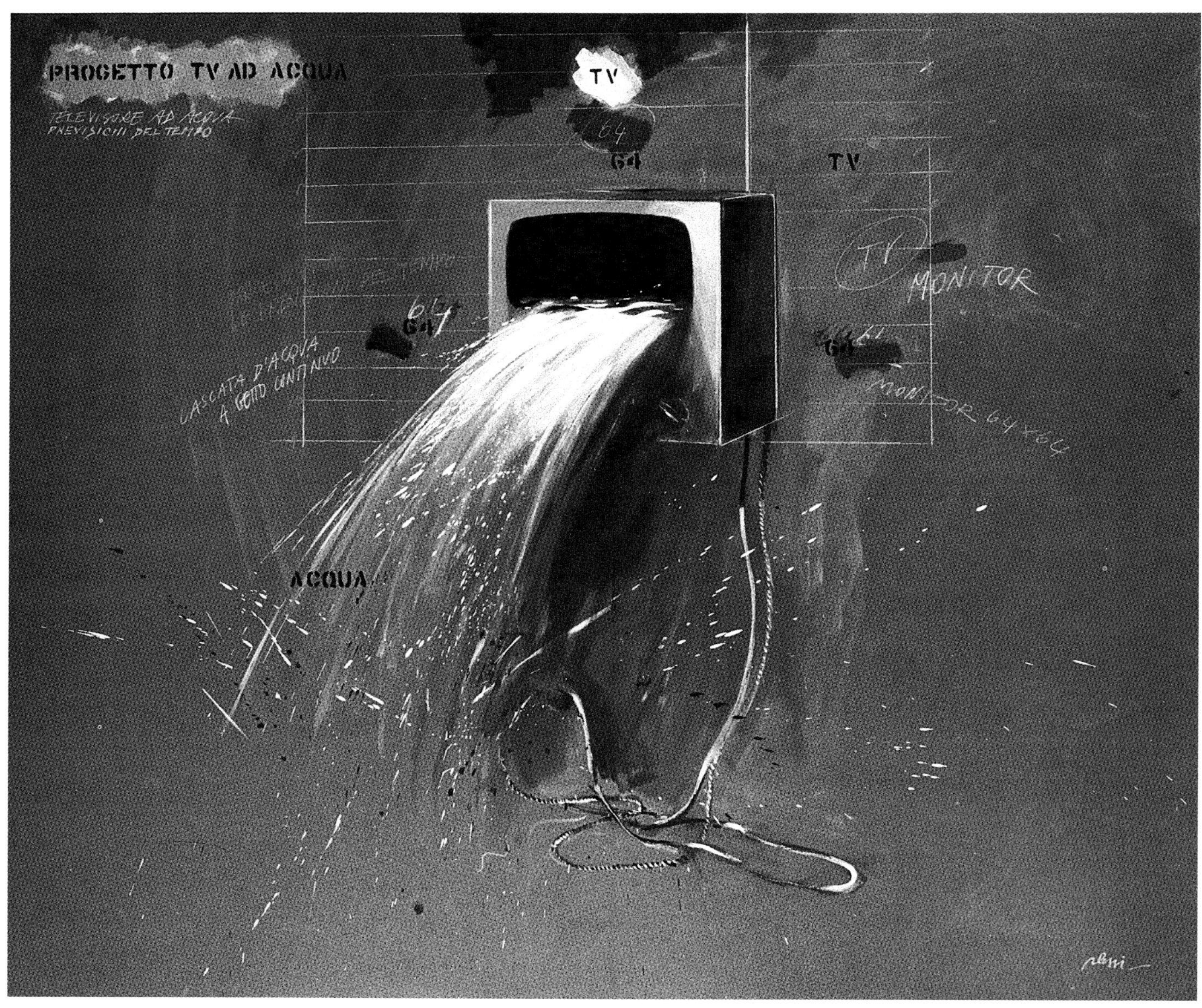

14

und Collagen, er notiert Aktionen
und Performances mit Wasser,
konzipiert seine ersten Neoninstallationen in der Mitte der 70er
Jahre. 1968 entsteht auch sein
erstes Projekt für eine Videoskulptur *Water TV previsioni del tempo*,
was in der Übersetzung soviel
bedeutet wie ›Wettervorhersage‹.

Zu sehen ist auf dem Konzept
ein Monitor, ein Fernseher, aus
dem dem Betrachter Wasser in
einem großen Strahl entgegenströmt. Seine Projektskizzen sind
vielfältig und oftmals paradox,
was das Erscheinungsbild angeht,
denn seine normalen materialen
Eigenschaften, physikalische und
chemische Gesetze, scheinen
gelegentlich außer Kraft gesetzt.
Dabei arbeitet Plessi schon deshalb in hohem Maße konzeptuell,
weil damit seiner Phantasie - im
Sinne der Realisierbarkeit - keine
Grenzen gesetzt sind.

*sketches are manifold and often
paradox in regard to their appearance, because the usual
material qualities, the laws of
physics and chemistry sometimes
seem to be broken. Yet Plessi
works mostly conceptual, to
avoid - in regard to their realisation - being confronted with
boundaries. Thus, in the early
seventies, projects are created
like the* Huge Sponges for the
State of Emergency in Case of
Flooding in Venice *that can dry
up the channel, lagoon and
flooded Marcus Square in seconds. It can be well understood that
Fabrizio Plessi never got permission by the state of Veneto to
realise his project. Many of his
actions and performances were
prepared in project-sketches, like*
Sawing a Lake in two Equal
Parts *in 1975, when Plessi used a
simple saw to saw Lake Stichter*

metà degli anni settanta, concepisce le sue prime installazioni
neon. Il 1968 segna anche la
nascita del primo progetto per
una videoscultura, *Water TV
previsioni del tempo*: il monitor
di un televisore dal quale fuoriesce un getto d'acqua in
direzione dello spettatore. Gli
schizzi di Plessi sono molteplici
e in apparenza spesso paradossali in quanto sembrano ignorare le normali caratteristiche
materiali e le leggi della fisica e
della chimica. Già per questo
Plessi lavora in modo estremamente concettuale per lasciare
libertà assoluta, nel senso della
realizzabiltà, alla sua fantasia.
Così hanno origine, nei primi
anni settanta, quei progetti che
riescono a prosciugare i canali,
la laguna e la piazza allagata di
S. Marco, come ad esempio le
giganti *Spugne per l'emergenza*

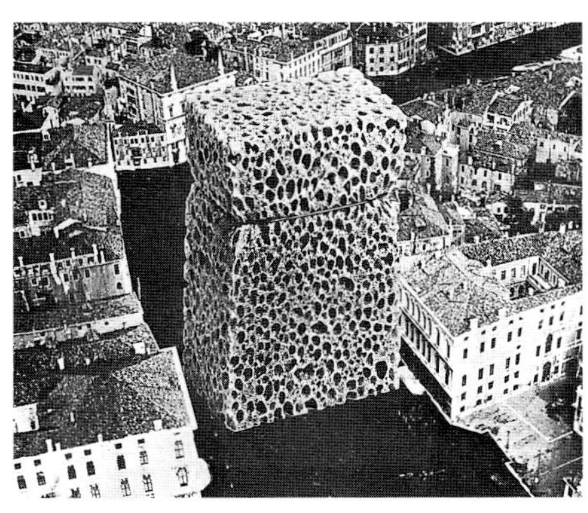

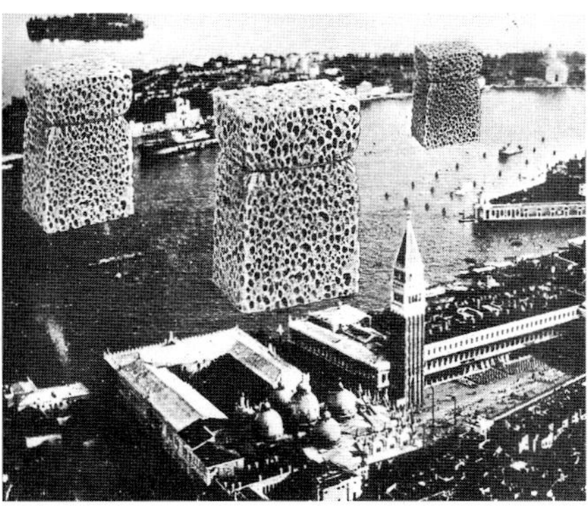

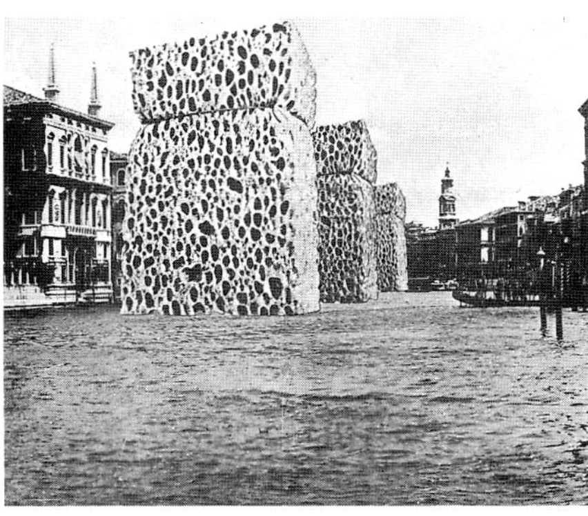

So entstehen in den frühen
70er Jahren Projekte, beispielsweise die riesigen *Schwämme für
den Ausnahmezustand im Fall von
Hochwasser in Venedig*, die den
Kanal, die Lagune und den überschwemmten Markusplatz in
sekundenschnelle trockenzulegen
vermögen. Einleuchtend, daß
Fabrizio Plessi vom Staate Veneto
keine Genehmigung erhalten hat,
sein Projekt zu realisieren. Auch
viele Aktionen und Performances
werden in Projektskizzen vorbereitet, wie beispielsweise *Einen*

into two exactly equal parts, or
The Holes in the Water, *in 1973,
when Plessi drove 300 holes -
with hammer and nail - at a
distance of one meter each into
the surface of the River Seine.
Here, too, the events* 100 Water
Pieces, *where the artist cut a jet
of tab-water into 100 of equal
length of one minute, as well as*
To Walk on Water *(1975), that
was recorded on video-tape, must
be named. Often, these events and
actions are only documented in
series of photos, and sometimes,*

d'acqua alta a Venezia. E, ovvio
che la Regione del Veneto ha
negato il permesso di realizzare
il progetto. Anche altre azioni e
performances saranno preparate
in una serie di schizzi progettuali, come *Tagliare un lago in
due parti uguali* (1975), in cui
Plessi divide con una sega
comune il lago di Stichter in due
parti esattamente uguali, o
Buchi nell'acqua del 1973, ove
Plessi effettua, munito di martello e chiodo, 300 fori ad una
distanza di un metro l'uno

See in zwei gleiche Teile sägen von
1975, als Fabrizio Plessi mit einer
einfachen Säge den Stichtersee in
zwei genau gleiche Teile durch-
sägte, oder *Die Löcher im Wasser*
von 1973, als Plessi mit einem
Hammer und einem Nagel 300 Löcher im Abstand von je einem
Meter in die Oberfläche der Seine
einschlug.

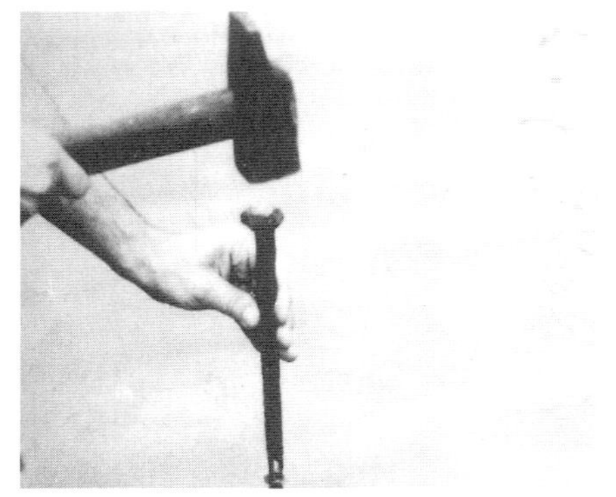

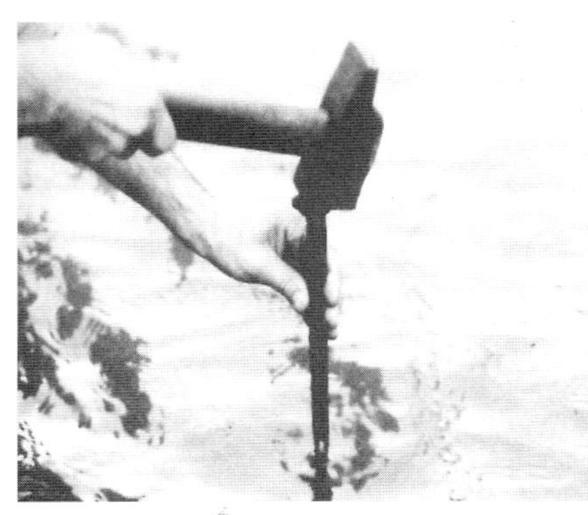

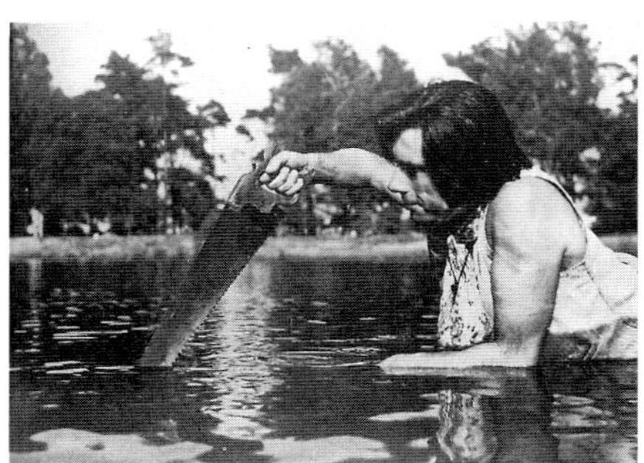

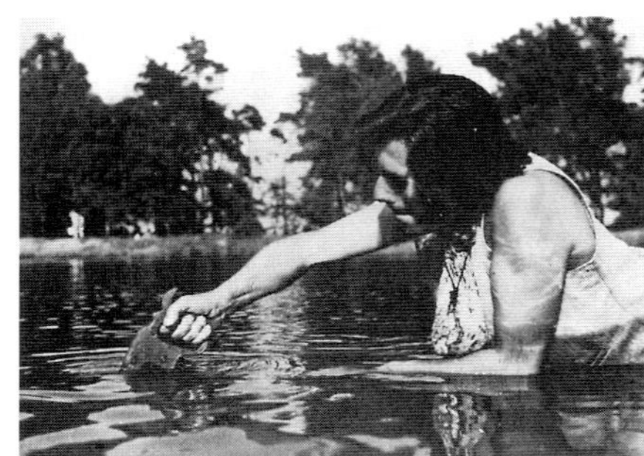

Auch die Aktion *100 Wasserstücke*, als der Künstler mit einer
Küchenschere einen Wasserstrahl
aus einem Wasserhahn in 100
gleichlange Stücke von je einer
Minute geschnitten hat, oder die
Aktion *Auf dem Wasser gehen* von
1975, die in einem Videotape
festgehalten wurde, sind hier zu

*the project is accompanied by
experimental video films that at
first are presented at film-bienna-
les, and only later as exhibits and
performances, as for example in
the Museum Folkwang in Essen at
the end of the seventies. They can
be regarded as the actual forerun-
ners of the video sculptures.*

dall'altro nello specchio d'acqua
del fiume Senna; o come
l'azione *100 pezzi d'acqua*, nella
quale l'artista taglia con le
forbici da cucina un getto
d'acqua di un rubinetto in cento
pezzi uguali della lunghezza di
un minuto o, ancora, quella
intitolata *Camminare sull'acqua*
del 1975, registrata in un video-
tape. Nella maggior parte dei
casi le azioni sono documentate
solamente attraverso fotografie.
Occasionalmente si realizzano
videofilms sperimentali, che
inizialmente verrano presentati
ai festivals cinematografici e
poi, verso la fine degli anni
settanta, in performances o in
musei, come per esempio il
Folkwang-Museum di Essen in
Germania e che sono da considerare di fatto precursori delle
videosculture.

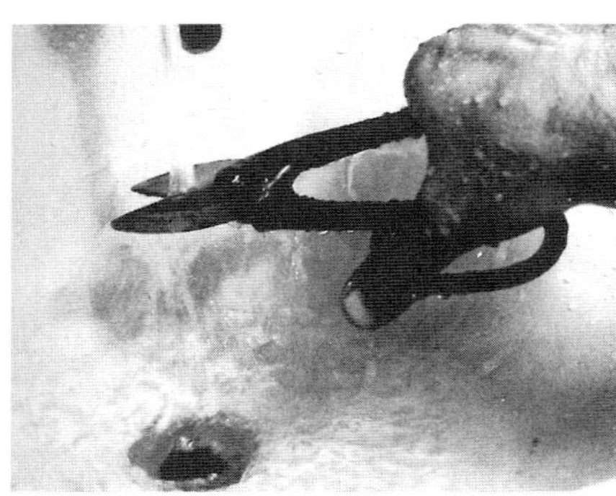

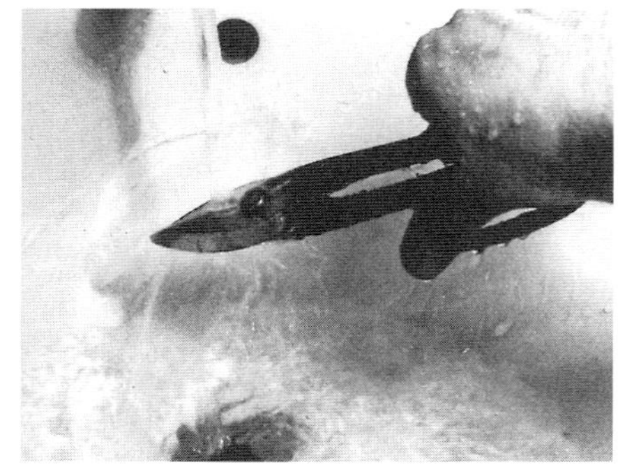

nennen. Oftmals sind diese Hand-
lungen und Aktionen nur in
Fotoserien dokumentiert, gelegentlich entstehen zum Thema
auch experimentelle Videofilme,
die zunächst auf Film-Biennalen
und erst später, zum Beispiel im
Folkwang-Museum Essen, Ende
der 70er Jahre als Ausstellungs-

*After the 1968 TV project that -
how could it ? - was never realised, the sculpture* Gabbia d'acqua
*- meaning cage for water - shown
at the Biennale in Venice in 1972,
represents a first water-sculpture
in which the element itself is
present and plays the central role.
Within a pyramidal construction*

Dopo il progetto *Water TV* del
1968, che per ovvi motivi non è
mai stato realizzato, l'opera
Gabbia d'acqua, esposta alla
Biennale di Venezia nel 1972,
rappresenta la prima scultura
d'acqua, nella quale l'elemento
proprio, realmente presente,
occupa il ruolo centrale. In una
struttura piramidale di ferro è
appesa ad una catena una gabbia piena d'acqua. L'acqua è
blu, ma col passare del tempo il
colore svanisce. Solamente dopo
un movimento, che agita il
liquido, il colore blu ritorna per
poi scomparire nuovamente. La

stücke und Performances präsentiert werden. Sie sind als die eigentlichen Vorläufer der Videoskulpturen anzusehen.

Nach dem TV-Projekt von 1968, das übrigens niemals - in welcher Weise auch? - realisiert wurde, stellt die Skulptur *Gabbia d'acqua*, zu deutsch: *Käfig des Wassers*, die 1972 auf der Biennale in Venedig präsentiert wurde, eine erste Wasserskulptur dar, bei der das Element, real vorhanden, selbst die zentrale Rolle spielt. In einer Pyramidenkonstruktion aus Stahl, bei der auf die Seitenwände und den Boden verzichtet wurde, hängt ein Käfig schwebend und sich bewegend an einer Kette über einem Flaschenzug, vom Boden abgehoben, gefüllt mit Wasser. Das Wasser ist blau. Doch die Färbung nimmt mit zunehmender Zeit ab. Erst wenn eine erneute Bewegung erfolgt und das Wasser in dem Käfig durcheinandergerüttelt wird, kommt die blaue Farbe wieder zustande. Nach einer gewissen Zeit verschwindet sie wieder. Diese Skulptur ist insofern besonders interessant, als sie nicht nur die erste Wasserskulptur, sondern in gewisser Weise auch eine Zeitskulptur darstellt, das andere große Thema Fabrizio Plessis.

Wenig später entsteht das Projekt *Water*, eine auf den Kopf gestellte Neonschrift aus den Buchstaben ›WATER‹ spiegelt sich im Wasser und läßt so das Wort wieder lesbar werden. Ende der 70er Jahre realisiert Plessi dieses Projekt großformatig in Duisburg am Bertasee auf Einladung des Lehmbruck-Museums. Idee und Realisierung prägen unmittelbar die nahezu zeitgleich entstehende Videoskulptur *Water* (cat. 76002), bei der die spiegelbildliche Darstellung der Neonbuchstaben nicht in realem, sondern in elektronischem Wasser auf einem

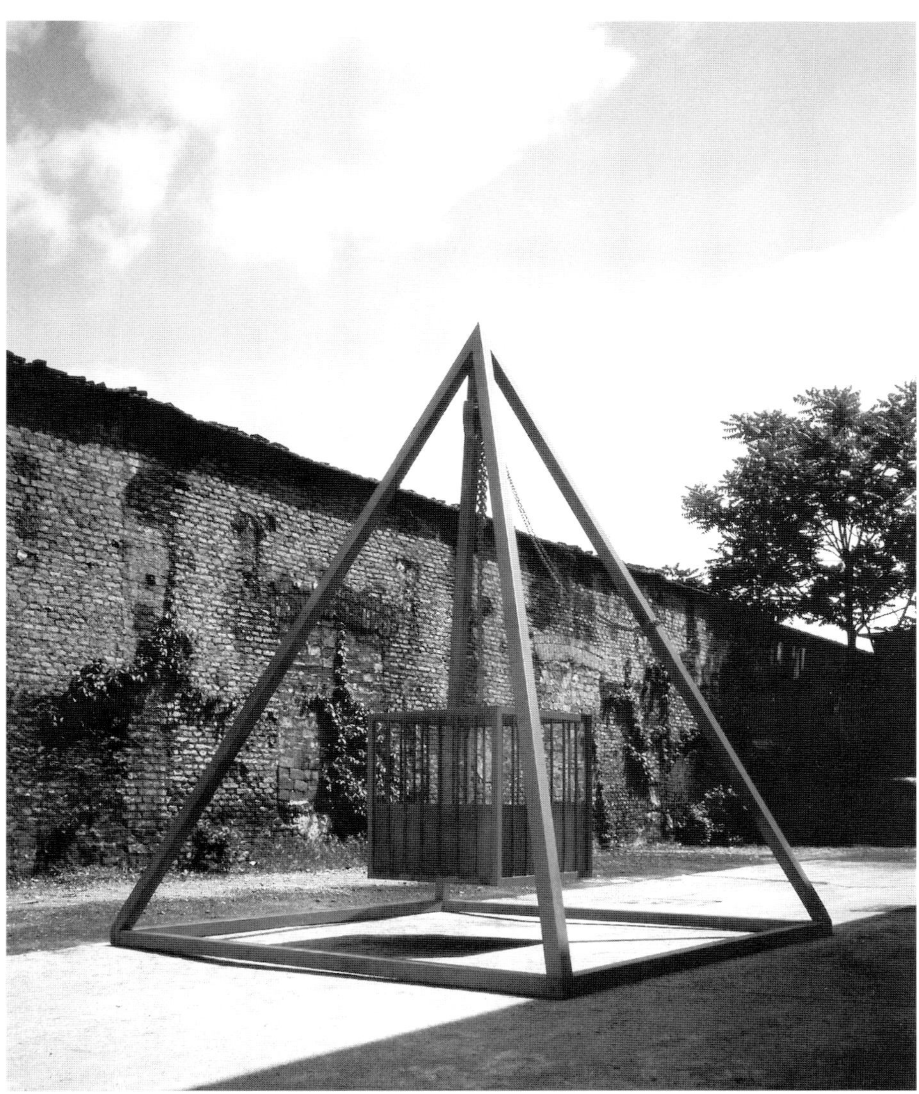

of steel that has neither sides nor bottom a cage filled with water hangs pending and swinging on a chain, lifted above the ground by a pulley. The water is blue. But the colour fades with time. Only when a new movement is created and the water in the cage is shaken the blue colour returns. After a certain time it fades again. Especially interesting in this sculpture is that it not only is the first water sculpture, but to a certain degree also a time sculpture, the other great theme in Plessi's work.

Soon thereafter the project Water *is created; neon-letters forming the word 'WATER' and turned upside down are mirrored in the water, thus making the*

particolarità di quest'opera sta nel fatto che non solo rappresenta la prima scultura d'acqua, ma anche la prima scultura del tempo, un tematica altrettanto centrale per Fabrizio Plessi.

Poco più tardi nasce il progetto *Water* (cat. 76002), nel quale la parola ›WATER‹ capovolta, scritta con tubi al neon, si riflette sulla superficie dell'acqua per risultare di nuovo leggibile. Alla fine degli anni settanta Plessi, su invito del Museo Lehmbruck, lo realizza in grandi dimensioni a Duisburg in Germania presso il Lago di Berta. L'idea del progetto influenza direttamente la quasi contemporanea concretizzazione della videoscultura *Water*, in

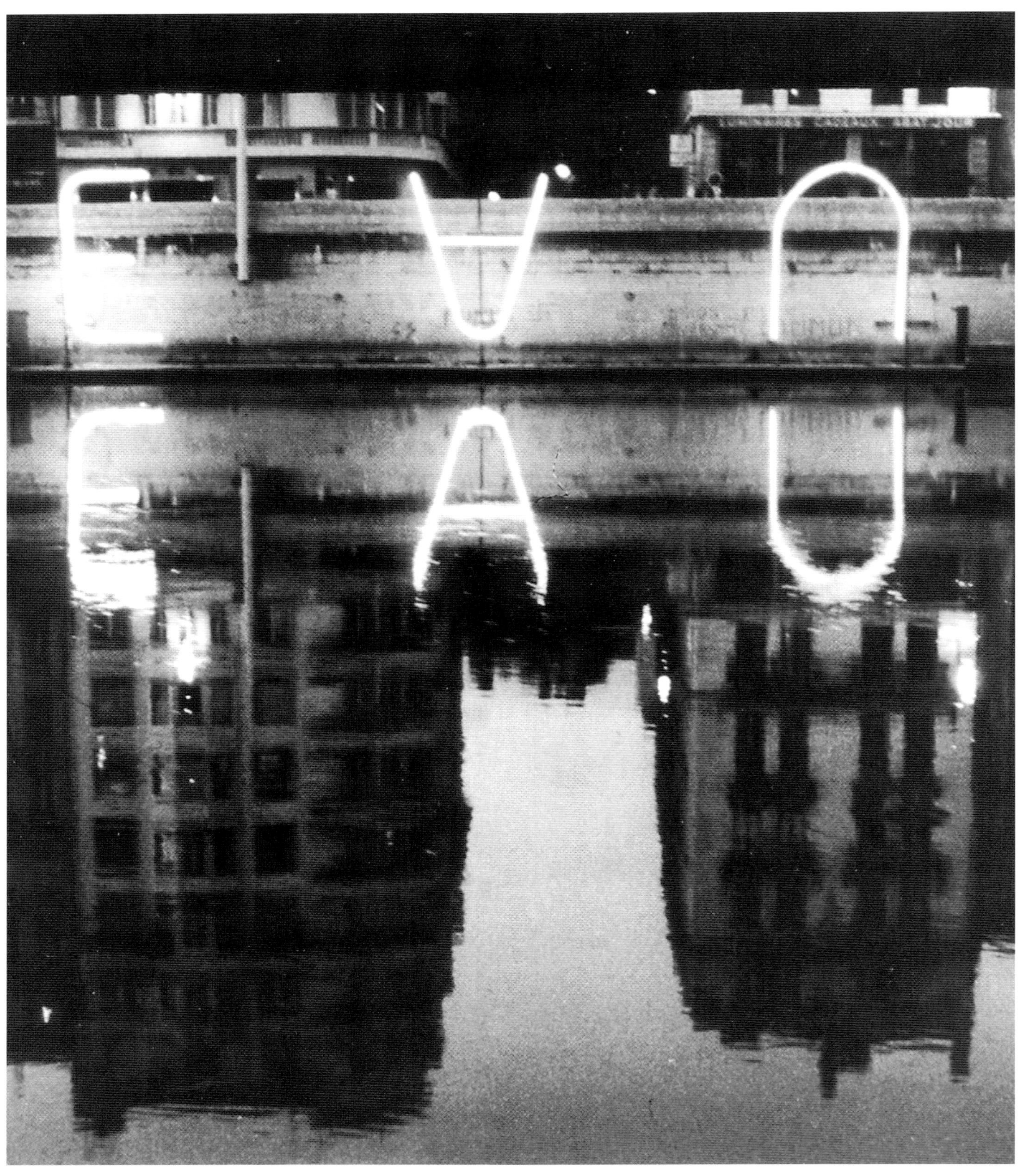

Bildschirm-Monitor zu sehen ist.
Die Neoninstallation *Water* modifiziert sich zu der französischen
Variante *Eau*, bei welchem drei
riesige Neonbuchstaben, jeweils
15 m hoch und insgesamt 40 m
auseinandergezogen, am Ufer der

word legible. At the invitation of
the Museum Lehmbruck in Duis-
burg, Plessi realises this project in
large scale on Lake Berta at the
end of the seventies. Idea and
realisation directly influence his
video sculpture Water *(cat.*

cui l'immagine speculare è
riflessa non più nell'acqua reale
ma in quella elettronica del
monitor di un televisore.
L'installazione ai tubi al neon
Water si modifica nella variante
francese *Eau*, dove le tre lettere

Rhone in Lyon auf den Kopf gestellt angebracht sind und sich nun seitenrichtig uns lesbar im Wasser spiegeln. Zur selben Zeit, im Jahre 1982, produziert Frigo in Lyon auch die Serie *Underwater*, eine Serie von insgesamt 12 experimentellen Videofilmen von Fabrizio Plessi, von denen einige später in Form von Videoskulpturen wieder erscheinen. Bei *Water Wind* wird eine Videoskulptur in Funktion gefilmt, dokumentiert und in Details präsentiert. Das Neonwort ›WATER‹ tritt - zu ›ART‹ modifiziert - in Videoinstallationen wieder auf, und *Wipers*, ein Scheibenwischerprogramm wird zum Bestandteil der Videoskulptur *Wasserwagen* (cat. 81005). Auch *Liquid Movie* kommt in der Serie *Underwater* bereits vor, die meisten anderen Filme aus dieser Serie sind selbständige, experimentelle Filme, die im Zusammenhang mit den Performances und Aktionen aus dieser Zeit stehen.

Nach seinen zahlreichen Aktionen mit Wasser, seinen Performances, den Projektskizzen, Zeichnungen und Collagen, den ersten Neoninstallationen mit *Reflecting Water*, den experimentellen Filmen aus der Frigo-Serie *Underwater* und den Skulpturen, wie der in Venedig, beginnt die eigentliche Phase seiner Videoinstallationen mit der Videoskulptur *Mare orrizontale* von 1976. Bis in die Mitte der 80er Jahre sind es mehr oder weniger plastische, freistehende Realisationen seiner skulpturalen Ideen mit Video und Monitor. Mit der umfangreichen Ausstellung in Mailand, in der Rotonda della Besana 1985, geht die Tendenz von der Videoskulptur zu ganzen Videoinstallationen und Videoräumen hin. Unmittelbar darauf entsteht *Bronx* (cat. 85003), gezeigt auf der Biennale in Venedig 1986; der beeindruk-

76002), created almost simultaneously, showing the mirrored reflection of the neon letters not in real but electronic water on a TV monitor. The neon installation Water *is then modified in the French version* Eau, *in which three huge neon letters, each 15 m high and spread over a distance of 40 m, are fixed upside down along the shore of the river Rhone in Lyon, their reflection in the water making the word legible. At the same time, in 1982, Frigo in Lyon produces the series* Underwater, *twelve experimental video films by Fabrizio Plessi, some of which are later shown as video sculptures. In* Water Wind *a video sculpture is filmed in function, documented and presented in detail. The neon-word 'WATER' - modified to 'ART' - re-appears in video installations, and* Wipers, *a windshield wipers program, becomes part of the video sculpture* Wasserwagen (cat. 81005). Liquid Movie, *too, is known from the series* Underwater, *whereas most other films from this series are independent experimental films that are related to the performances and events of the time. After his numerous actions with water, his performances, the project sketches, drawings and collages, the first neon installations with* Reflecting Water, *the experimental films of the Frigo series* Underwater, *and sculptures like the one in Venice, the specific phase of Plessi's video installations begins with the video sculpture* Mare orrizontale (cat. 76001) *of 1976. Up to the middle of the eighties, it comprises more or less sculpture-like, free-standing realisations of his sculptural ideas with video and TV-monitor. Beginning with the representative exhibition in the Rotonda della Besana in Milan in 1985, there is a tendency to move from video*

capovolte, che hanno un'altezza di 15 metri e una larghezza complessiva di 40 metri e sono installate lungo le rive del Rodano presso Lione, si riflettono nell'acqua del fiume. Nello stesso periodo, nel 1982, Frigo a Lione produce la serie Underwater, dodici videofilms sperimentali di Fabrizio Plessi, di cui alcuni saranno più tardi intergrati in videosculture. In *Water Wind* viene filmata, documentata e presentata nei dettagli una videoscultura in funzione. La scritta ai tubi al neon ›WATER‹ ricompare, trasformata in ›ART‹, in altre videoinstallazioni e *Wipers*, programma per un tergicristallo, diventa parte intergrante della videoscultura *Wasserwagen* (cat. 81005). Anche *Liquid Movie* viene già anticipata in *Underwater*, la maggior parte degli altri films di questa serie sono invece films autonomi e sperimentali, che nascono nel contesto di performances e azioni di quel periodo.

In seguito alle sue numerose azioni con l'acqua, alle performances, agli schizzi progettuali, ai disegni e collages, alle prime installazioni al neon con *Reflecting Water*, ai films sperimentali e alla serie di Frigo *Underwater* e alle sculture, come quella di Venezia, ha inizio la fase delle videoinstallazioni vere e proprie con la videoscultura *Mare Orizzontale* (cat. 76001) del 1976. Tale fase è per lo più caratterizzata, fino alla metà degli anni ottanta, dalla conversione delle proprie idee in realizzazioni sculturali con video e monitors. Con la grande mostra personale nella Rotonda della Besana a Milano nel 1985 si verifica un cambiamento di tendenza dalla videoscultura verso videoinstallazioni e video-ambienti complessi. Seguono

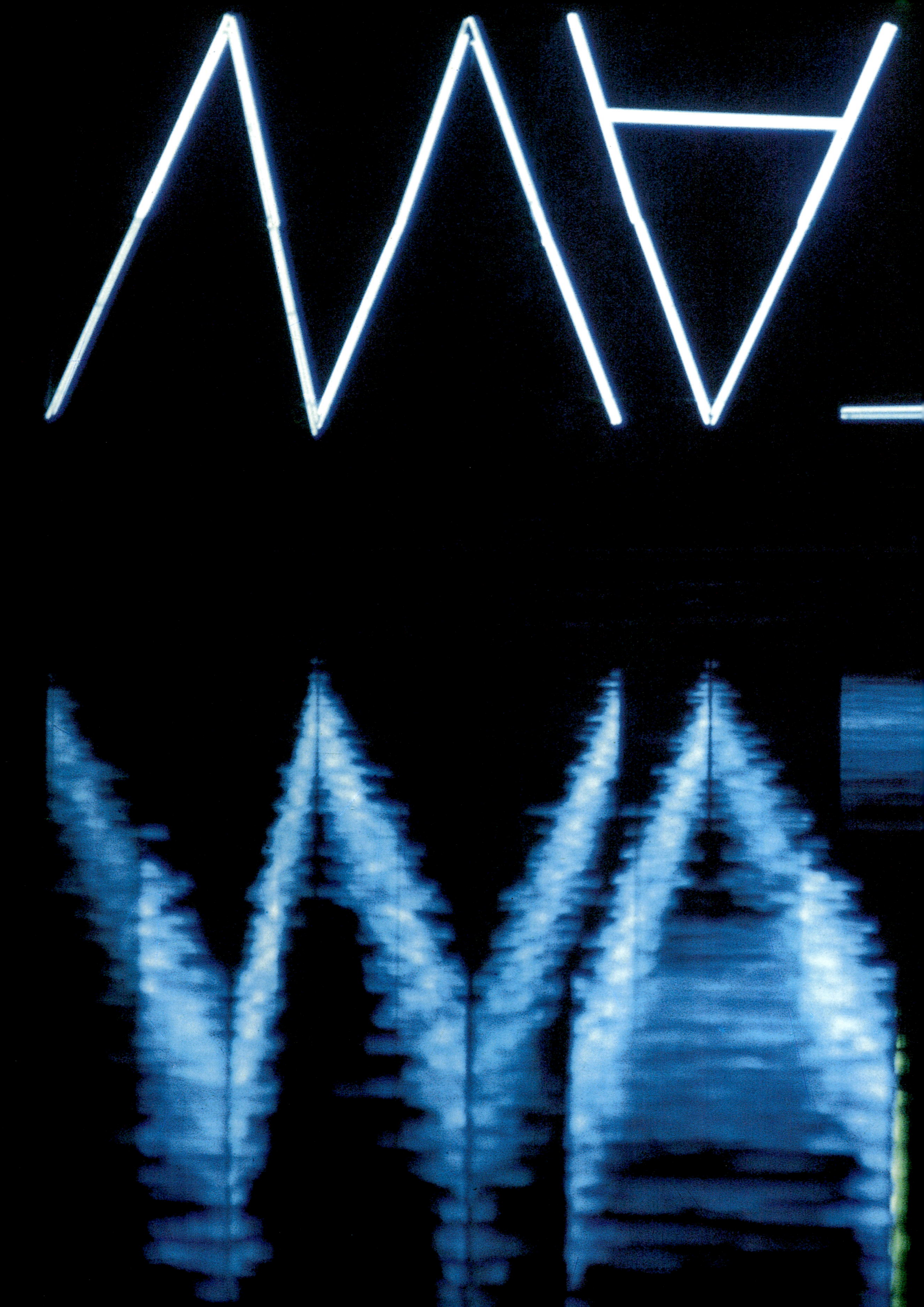

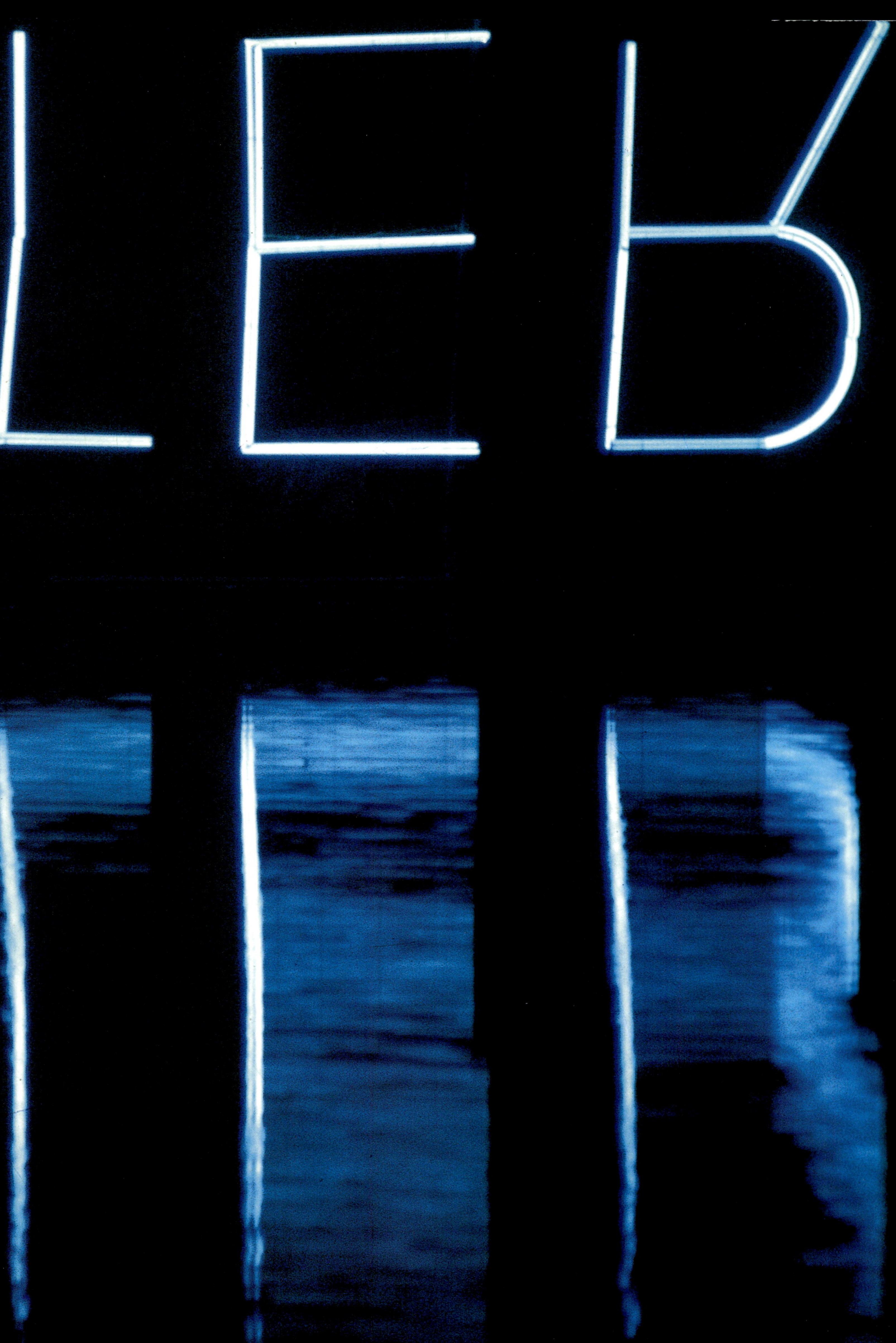

kende Raum *Roma* (cat. 87002) in Kassel im Apollon-Saal der Orangerie 1987, das raumumfassende Gestaltungsprinzip und Environment *Videoland* (cat. 87003) in Bologna 1987, *Materia Prima* (cat. 89005) in Köln und schließlich die ganze Serie der *Armadi*, der Räume für die Ausstellung in seiner Heimat- und Geburtsstadt Reggio Emilia.

Zu Beginn der 90er Jahre, spätestens aber mit dem *Raum der Wörter* (cat. 92003) in der Akademie in Berlin beginnt Fabrizio Plessis Interesse an der Geschichte, an den Wurzeln der Vergangenheit, an den Bindungen zu Vor- und Frühzeit, Anliegen, Ausdruck und Inhalt seiner Videoinstallationen und Skulpturen zu werden. Eine *Elektronische Ruine* (cat. 95001), ein *Elektronisches Aquädukt* (cat. 96004), der *Fluß der Geschichte* (cat. 96002) werden plötzlich wichtig und zugleich entstehen die großen, städtebezogenen Projekte und zwar Städte, die auf der ganzen Welt verteilt sind, seine *Progetti del Mondo*. Dazu gehören skulpturale Präsentationen wie *Cairo-Cairo*, aber auch die großen Videoinstallationen wie *Paris-Paris* (cat. 94001), *Fez-Fez* (cat. 96003) oder *Bombay-Bombay* (cat. 91001). Die jüngste Arbeit von 1998, die im letzten Moment noch in dieses Werkverzeichnis der Videoskulpturen und -Installationen aufgenommen werden konnte, *Das Floß der Kunst* (cat. 98001), das im Kunsthistorischen Museum in Wien gezeigt wird, weist darauf hin, daß Plessis Interesse und Neigung zur Anbindung an die Geschichte, an Vergangenheit und damit vielleicht auch an Zukunft noch längst nicht erloschen ist.

sculpture to complete video installations and video rooms. Immediately after, he creates Bronx *(cat. 85003), shown at the Biennale in Venice in 1986, followed by the impressive space* Roma *(cat. 87002) in the Apollo hall of the Orangery in Kassel in 1987, the spacious formative principle and environment* Videoland *(cat. 87003) in Bologna in 1987,* Materia Prima *(cat. 89005) in Cologne, and finally the whole series of* Armadi, *the rooms for the exhibition in his hometown Reggio Emilia. At the beginning of the nineties, and certainly with his* Room of Words *(cat. 92003) at the Berlin Academy, Fabrizio Plessi's interest in history, in the roots of the past, their connections to pre- and early history begins to become the centre of attention, expression and content of his video installations and sculptures. Suddenly, an* Electronic Ruin *(cat. 95001), an* Electronic Aqueduct *(cat. 96004), the* River of History *(cat. 96002) become important, and, at the same time, the great city projects are created, referring to cities all over the world: his* Progetti del Mondo. *They include sculptural presentations like* Cairo-Cairo *(cat. 91001), as well as the great video installations* Paris-Paris *(cat. 94001),* Fez-Fez *(cat. 96003), and* Bombay-Bombay *(cat. 91001). The* Raft of Art *(cat. 98001), his latest work of 1998, shown at the Museum of the History of Art in Vienna, which at the last minute could be included in this œuvre-list of video sculptures and -installations, demonstrates that Plessi's interest in and affinity to association with history, the past and, by doing so, perhaps to the future, has not at all been extinguished.*

immediatamente *Bronx* (cat. 85003), esposta alla Biennale di Venezia nel 1986, l'ambiente affascinante *Roma* (cat. 87002) della Sala di Apollo nella Orangerie di Kassel del 1987, l'environment *Videoland* (cat. 87003) di Bologna del 1987, *Materia Prima* (cat. 89005) di Colonia e infine l'intera serie degli *Armadi* e degli ambienti per la mostra nella sua città natale Reggio Emilia.

Dall'inizio degli anni novanta e non più tardi di *Raum der Wörter* (cat. 92003) dell'Accademia di Berlino, l'interesse di Fabrizio Plessi per la storia, le radici del passato e per i rapporti con l'età arcaica e con la preistoria diventa impegno, espressione e contenuto delle sue videoinstallazioni e sculture. Aquistano importanza adesso *Rovina Elettronica* (cat. 95001), *Acquedotto Elettronico* (cat. 96004), *Il Fiume della Storia* (cat. 96002) e contemporaneamente nascono i suoi lavori legati a città di tutto il mondo: i *Progetti del Mondo*, di cui fanno parte le opere sculturali comme *Cairo-Cairo* (cat. 91001), così come le grandi videoinstallazioni *Paris-Paris* (cat. 94001), *Fez-Fez* (cat. 96003) o *Bombay-Bombay* (cat. 91001). Il lavoro più recente del 1998, *L'Arca dell'Arte* (cat. 98001), che solo all'ultimo minuto si è potuto inserire nel presente catalogo delle opere di Plessi e che è esposta al Kunsthistorisches Museum di Vienna, è una dimostrazione che l'interesse e la tendenza dell'artista verso un legame con la storia, il passato e così forse anche con il futuro non si sono affatto esauriti.

ZU DIESEM OPUS

In dieses vorliegende Œuvre-Verzeichnis wurden alle Videoinstallationen und Skulpturen aufgenommen, von denen Fotomaterial und die wichtigsten Daten erhältlich waren. Wurden einzelne Videoskulpturen zu anderer Zeit, also später an anderem Ort, nochmals reinstalliert, finden sich auf der Titelseite zu jedem Werk die entsprechenden Ausstellungsorte und Ausstellungsinstitute, nach der Reihenfolge der Ausstellungen durchnumeriert. Hat sich eine Videoinstallation aber aufgrund des Ausstellungsraums beispielsweise in der Präsentation oder in der gedanklichen Konzeption des Künstlers verändert, wurde sie unter einer neuen Nummer in dieses Œuvre-Verzeichnis mit aufgenommen, wie die verschiedenen Versionen von *Bombay-Bombay* beispielsweise. Es wurde versucht, die Informationen über die einzelnen Videoskulpturen so ausführlich wie möglich zu erfassen, aber viele Fragen mußten aufgrund verlorengegangenen Informations- und Dokumentationsmaterials leider offenbleiben. Dennoch hoffen wir, mit der Form und Struktur des vorliegenden Bandes das Werk Fabrizio Plessis übersichtlich, visuell attraktiv und zugleich mit wissenschaftlichem Anspruch dokumentiert zu haben. Wir danken allen, die am Zustandekommen dieses ›Opus‹ mitgewirkt haben, in erster Linie Fabrizio Plessi, der unermüdlich Fotos und Publikationen für uns heraussuchte, Dokumentationsmaterial zur Verfügung stellte und unsere nie enden wollenden Fragen beantwortete, und seiner Frau Carla, für ihre liebenswürdige und wertvolle Unterstützung. Auch danken wir sehr herzlich Philip Rylands, dem Direktor der Fondation Peggy Guggenheim in Venedig, für seinen Enthusiasmus, mit dem er das Ganze vorangetrieben hat, sowie allen anderen, die unser Projekt mitgetragen und unterstützt haben.

die Herausgeber

ABOUT THIS OPUS

The catalogue raisonné presented here lists all video installations and sculptures of which photographic material and the most relevant data could be obtained. If video sculptures were re-installed later at another place, the title-page to each work indicates the different exhibition sites and institutes, numbered according to the sequence of exhibitions. Has, however, a video installation - because of the exhibition space - been altered in its presentation or in the mental concept of the artist, it has been included in this œuvre-list under a new number, as, for example, the different versions of Bombay-Bombay. It was attempted to collect as much information as possible on each video sculpture, but, unfortunately, many questions had, because of lost information- and documentation material - to remain unanswered. Nevertheless we hope to have documented, in form and structure of the volume presented here, the work of Fabrizio Plessi clearly, comprehensively, visually attractive, and, at the same time, with scientific accuracy. We thank everyone who has participated in completing this 'opus', first of all Fabrizio Plessi, who has untiringly searched for photos and publications for us, given us access to documenting material, and answered our never-ending questions and his wife Carla for her most gentle and valuable help in many questions. Also we thank very deeply Philip Rylands, the director of the Peggy Guggenheim Foundation in Venice for his enthusiasm, which carried the whole and all those who supported our project.

publishers

SUL QUEST'OPUS

Nel presente catalogo ragionato sono state inserite tutte le videoinstallazioni e sculture di cui si è potuto ottenere del materiale documentario, fotografie e dati più importanti. Qualora una videoscultura fosse stata esposta in luoghi e tempi diversi, i nomi delle città e delle istituzioni saranno elencati in ordine cronologico delle mostre nella pagina introduttiva di ogni singola opera numerata. Se invece una videoinstallzione ha subìto una modifica nella presentazione o nell'intento concettuale dell'artista, per esempio a causa delle specifiche caratteristiche del luogo d'esposizione, la si può trovare inserita nel catalogo con un nuovo numero: si vedano, ad esempio, le differenti versioni di *Bombay-Bombay*. Si è cercato di raccogliere più informazioni possibili per ogni singola opera, ma, purtroppo, qualche vuoto non si è colmato a causa della perdita di materiale informativo e documentativo. Tuttavia ci auguriamo d'aver presentato l'opera di Fabrizio Plessi, attraverso la forma e la struttura del presente volume, in maniera perspicua, attraente e, nello stesso tempo, scientificamente corretta. Ringraziamo tutti coloro che hanno contribuito alla realizzazione di questo opus, prima di tutti Fabrizio Plessi che, instancabile, ci ha messo a disposizione fotografie, pubblicazioni e materiale documentativo del suo archivio e che ha risposto alle nostre interminabili domande, e Carla Plessi per la gentile e prezioa collaborazione a quest'opera. Anche Philip Rylands, direttore della Fondazione Peggy Guggenheim di Venezia per l'entusiasmo con cui a portato avanti questo progetto e tutti gli altri che hanno condiviso e appoggiato i nostri sforzi.

gli editori

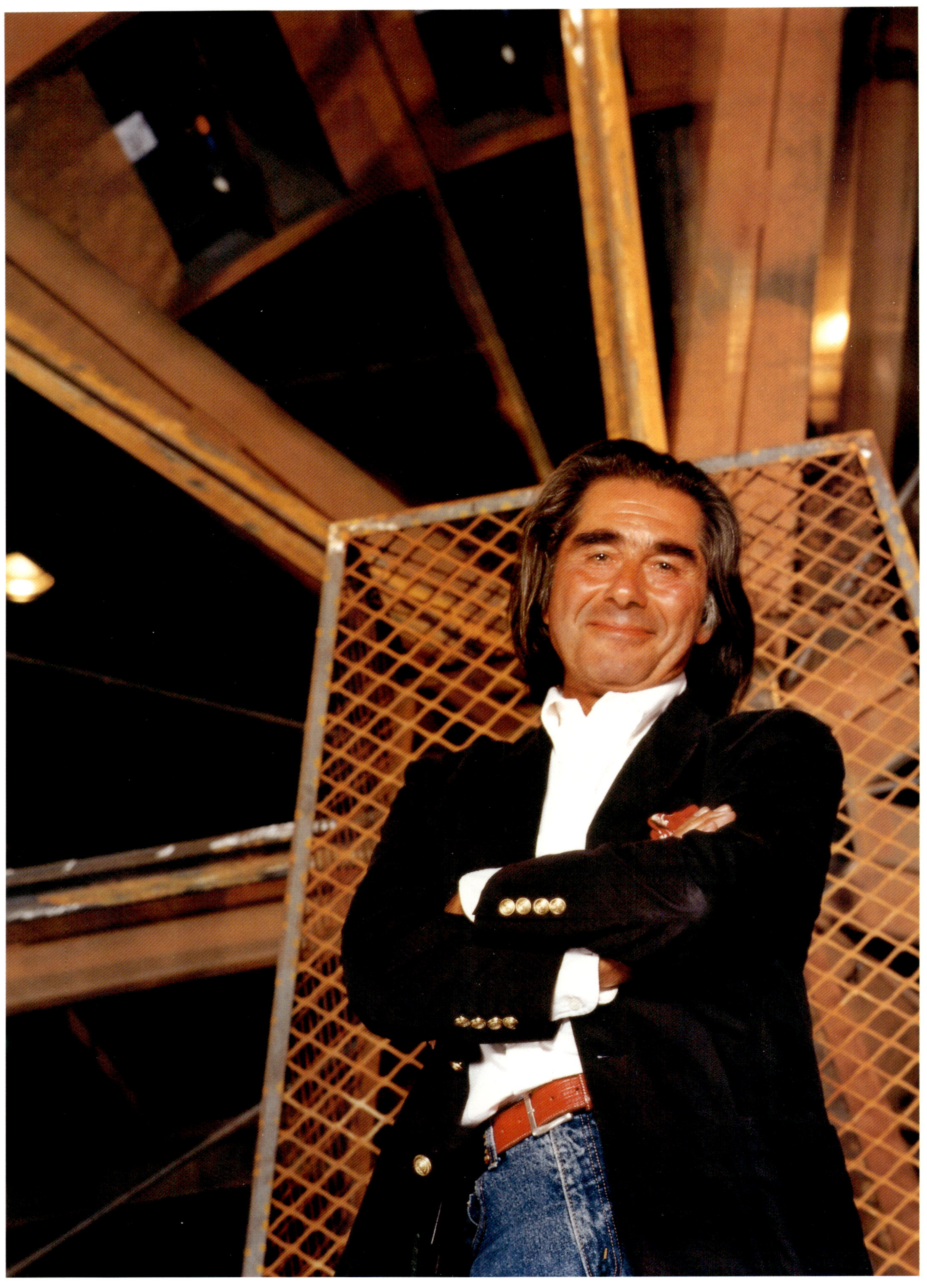

CATALOGUE

MARE ORIZZONTALE

76001

VILLENEUVE D'ASCQ 1984
Musée du Nord
76001.1

MILANO 1985
Rotonda della Besana
76001.2

ROMA 1987
RAI uno, ›Immagina‹
76001.3

MADRID 1988
Museo Español de Arte Contemporaneo
76001.4

LINZ 1988
Neue Galerie der Stadt Linz
76001.5

DORTMUND 1993
Museum am Ostwall
76001.6

HORIZONTALES MEER
Videoskulptur 1976
Holzkonstruktion, gespannter
Stahldraht, Sand (nicht bei allen
Präsentationen), 2 Monitore,
2 Videorecorder, 2 bespielte
Kassetten, Tonaufzeichnung

HORIZONTAL SEA
Video sculpture 1976
Wooden structure, wire, sand (not
all presentations), 2 monitors,
2 video recorders, 2 recorded video
cassettes

MARE ORIZZONTALE
Videoscultura 1976
Struttura in legno, filo teso in
ferro, sabbia, 2 monitors, 2 vhs,
2 cassette registrate, sonoro

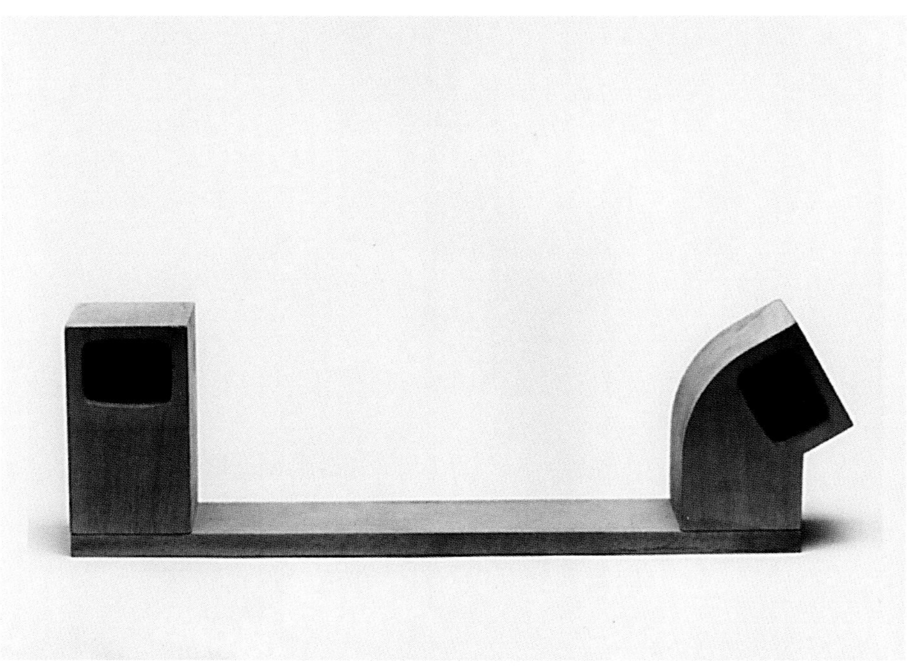

Mare Orizzontale gilt als die
erste Videoskulptur Fabrizio Plessis,
die nicht im Stadium des Projektes
verbleibt, sondern bereits 1976
realisiert wird. Sie besteht aus zwei
Monitoren, die in Holzgehäuse
eingebaut sind und einen Film über
eine Meereshorizontlinie zeigen
mit Wasser, das in Bewegung ist.
Einer der beiden Monitore ist
schräg gestellt. Auf diesem verläuft
die Wasserlinie diagonal zur
Position des Monitors, auf die
gesamte Konstruktion jedoch
bezogen, bleibt der Wasserspiegel
ebenso horizontal wie auf dem
anderen, herkömmlich präsentierten Monitor. Es scheint beinahe,
als sei das Wirkungsprinzip der
Wasserwaage hier versinnbildlicht,
die, ungeachtet ihrer Position und
Lage, immer eine Waagrechte
anzeigt - eine Horizontale eben.

Mare orrizontale *is conside-*
red to be Fabrizio Plessi's first
video sculpture that did not
remain in the stage of project,
but was realised as early as
1976. It consists of two moni-
tors built into wooden casings
and showing a film of an ocean
horizon with water in motion.
One of the two monitors is
positioned askew. On it, the
water line runs diagonally to
the positioning of the monitor,
yet, in looking at the whole
composition, the water level
remains as horizontal as on the
other, conventionally presented
monitor. It almost seems as if
the principle of the water-level
that, irrelevant of position and
state, always indicates the
parallel - the horizontal - is
symbolised here.

Mare Orizzontale è considerata
la prima videoscultura di Fabrizio
Plessi, che non si è fermata alla
fase di sola progettazione, ma che
è già stata realizzata nel 1976.
Consiste in due monitors inseriti
in una struttura di legno che
presentano un filmato dell'oriz-
zonte del mare. Uno dei due
monitors è fissato in una posizione obliqua e la linea d'acqua
corre diagonalmente sullo schermo; rispetto alla costruzione
intera il livello dell'acqua mantiene però la sua posizione orizzontale, esattamente come quella
dell'altro monitor. Sembra quasi
una rappresentazione simbolica
del principio di una livella a bolla
d'aria che, indipendentemente
dalla sua posizione, indica sempre una retta, un'orizzontale
appunto.

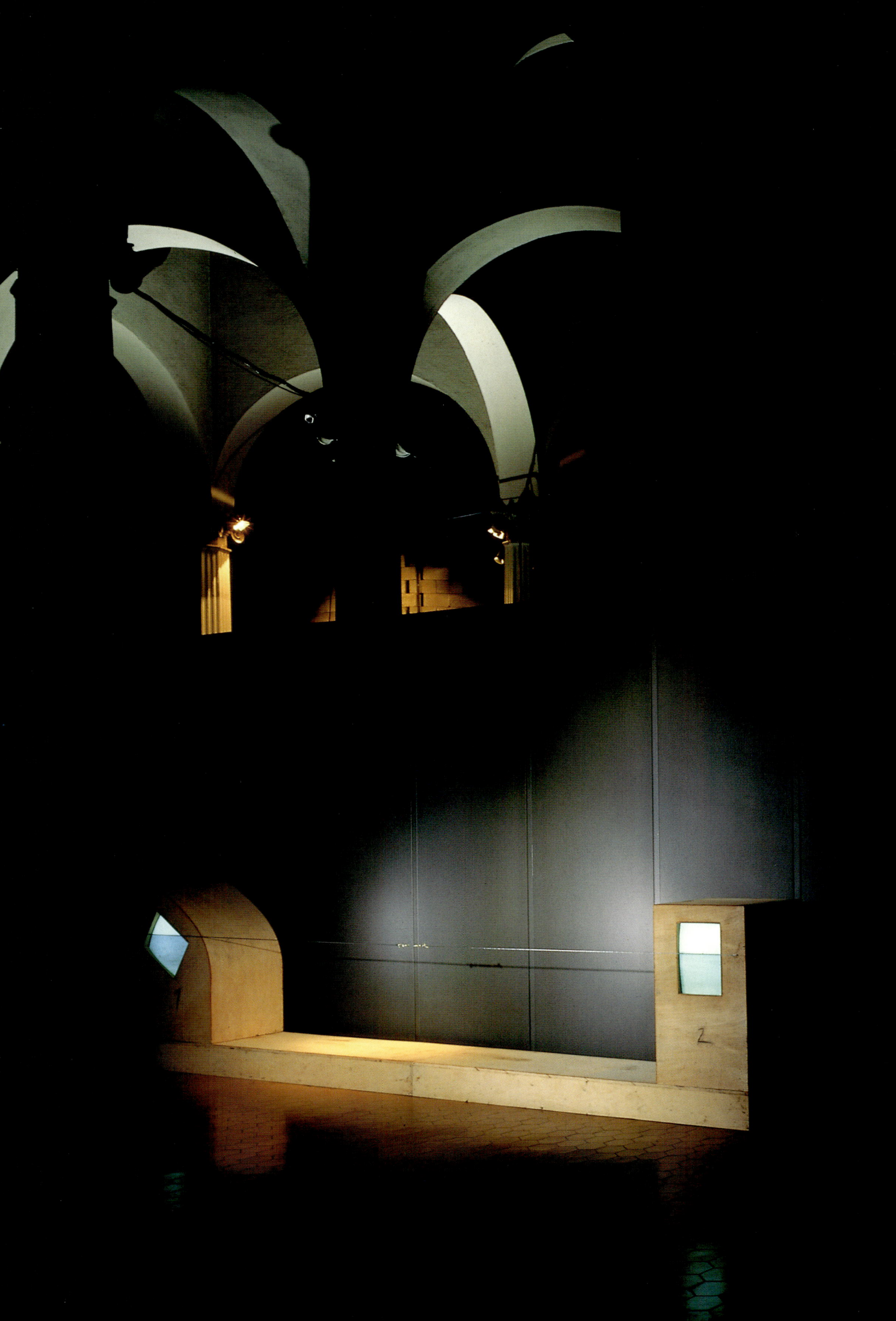

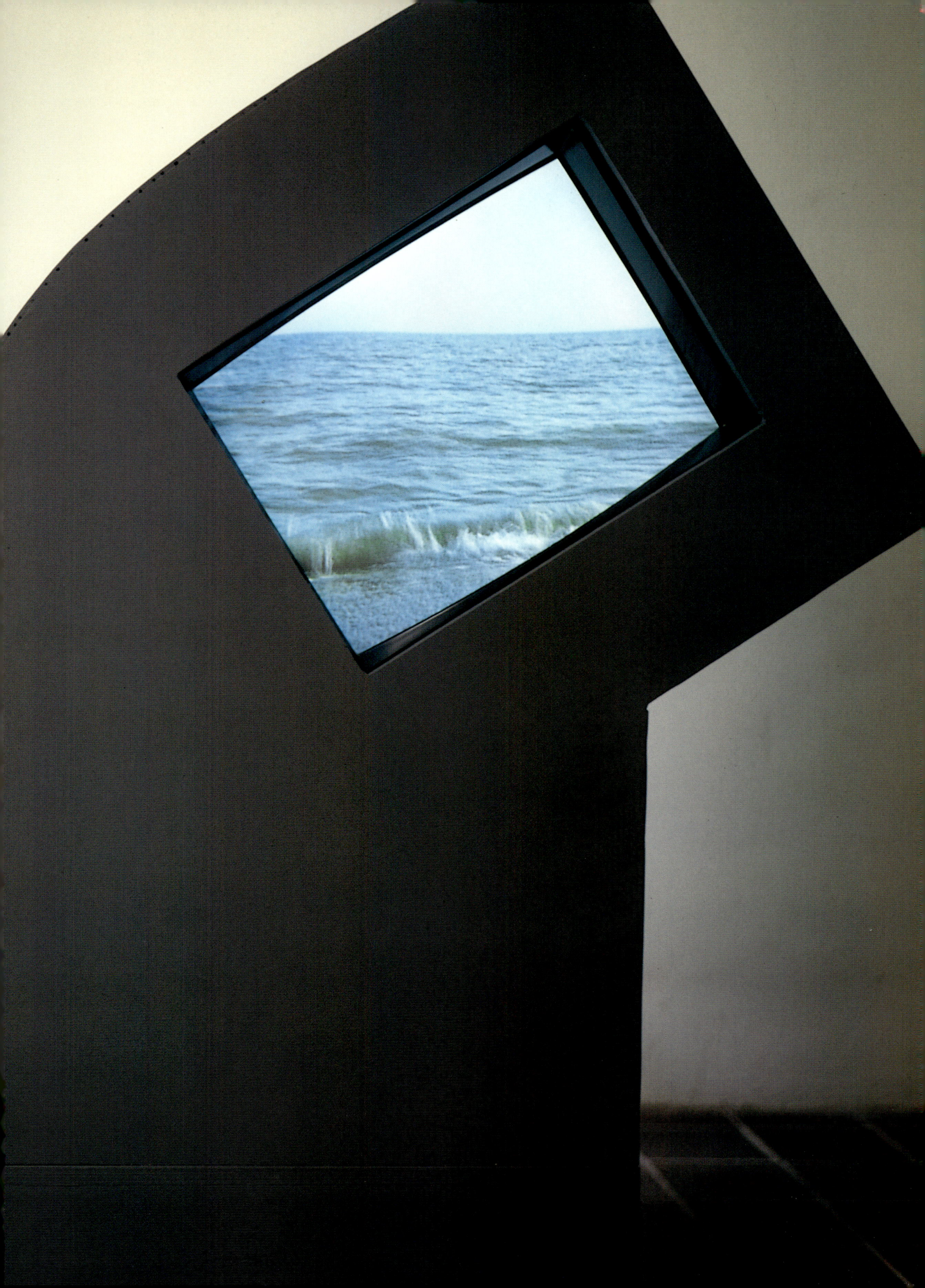

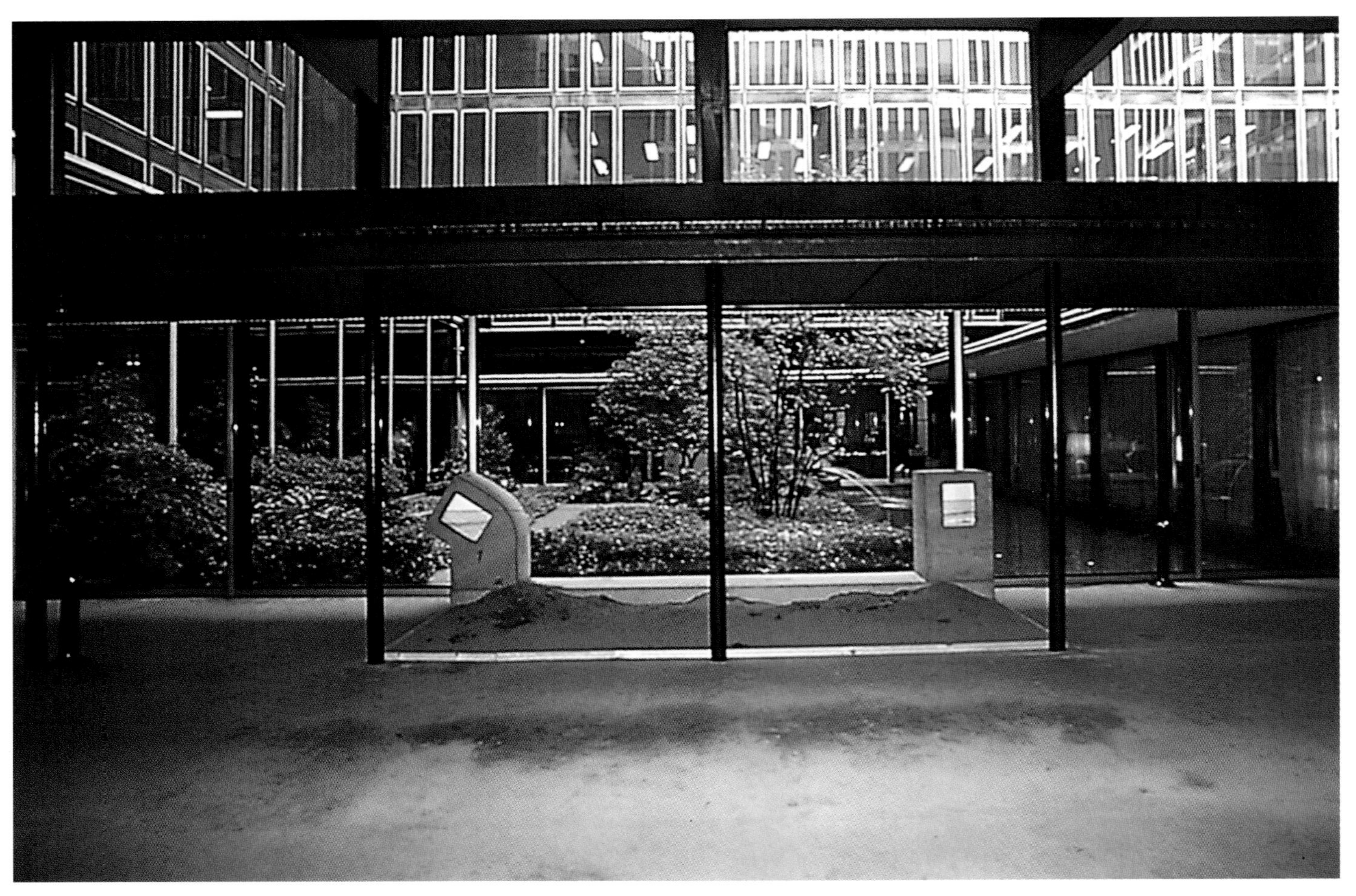

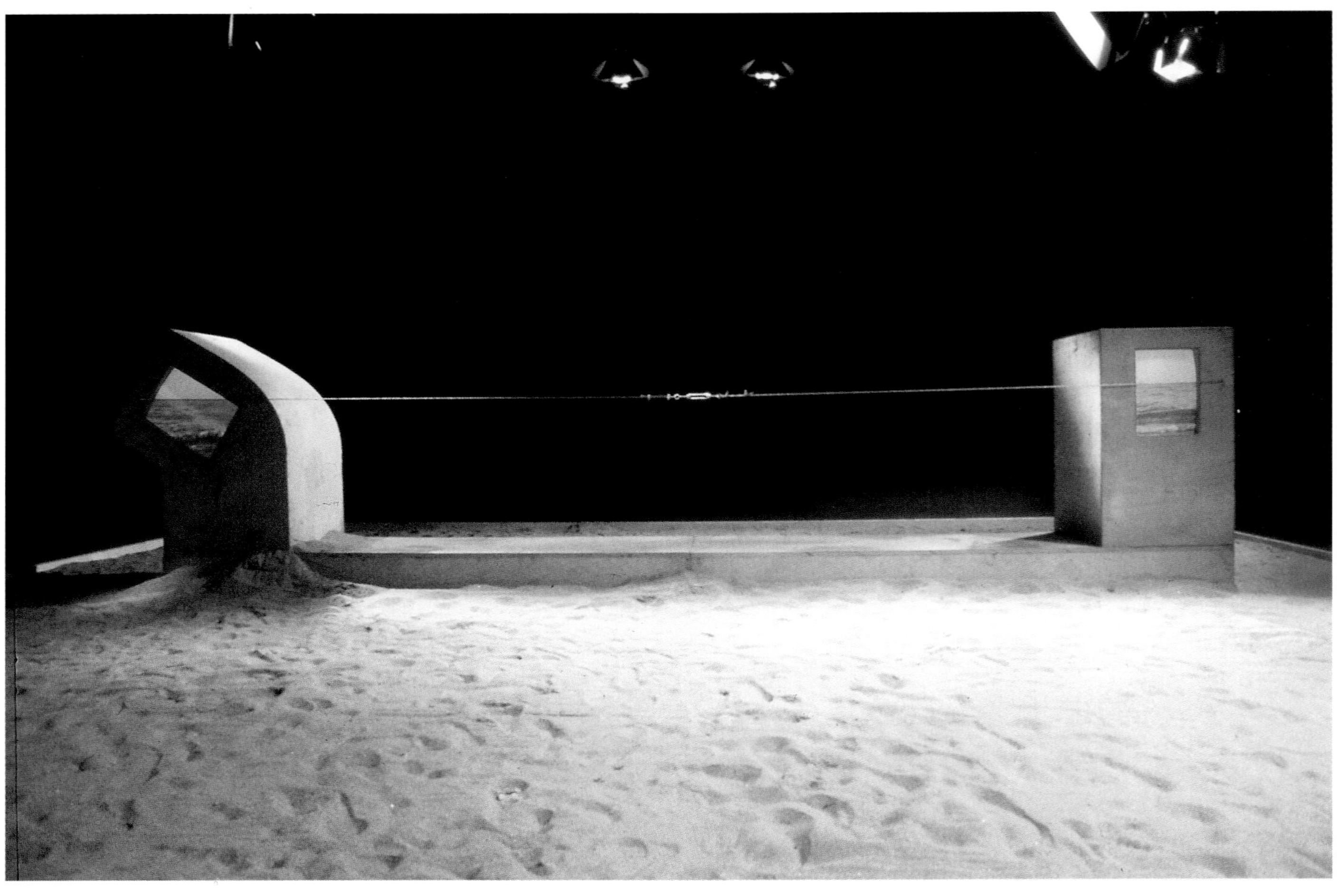

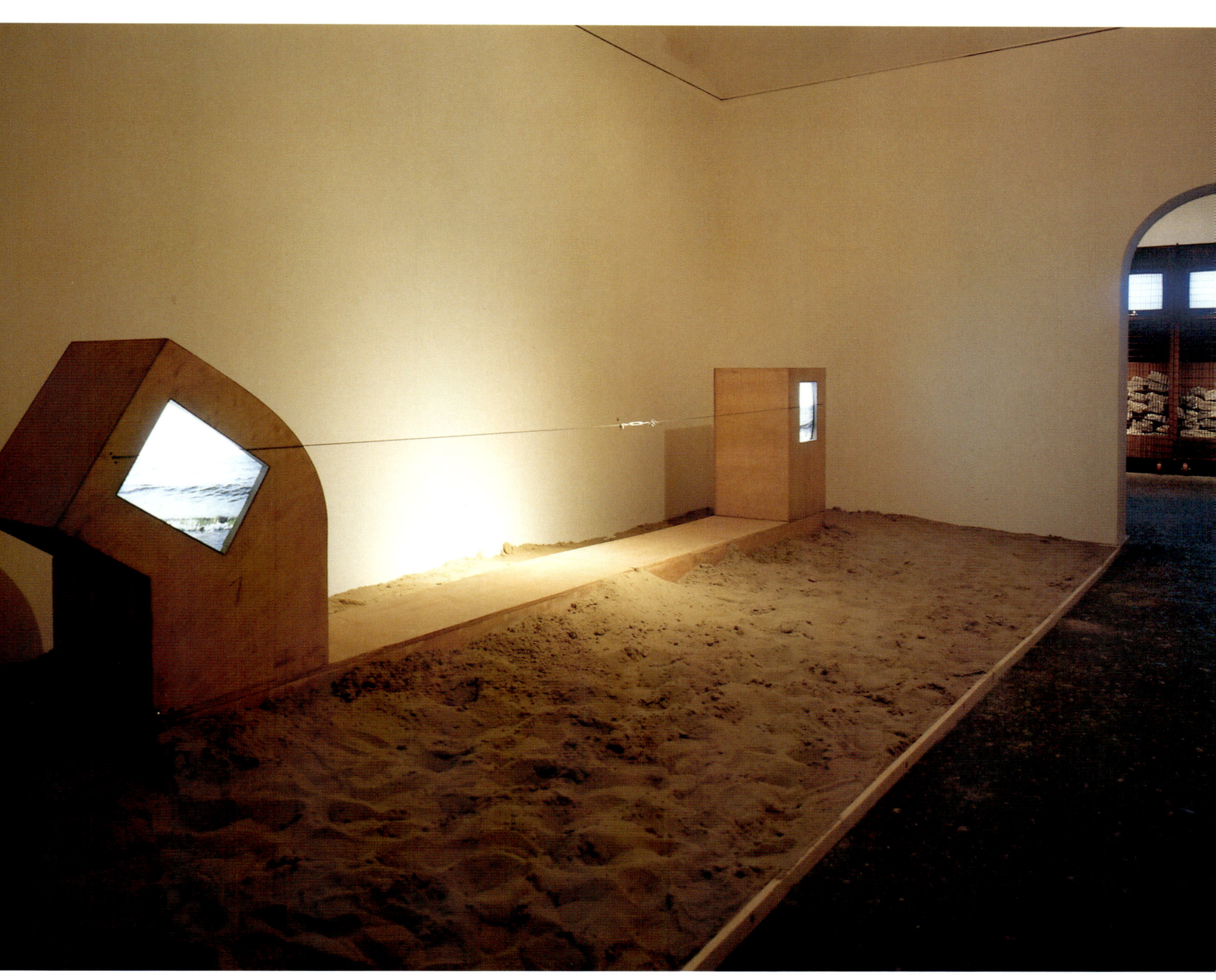

WATER

76002

ESSEN 1979
FOLKWANG MUSEUM
76002.1

VENEZIA 1984
XLI BIENNALE DI VENEZIA
76002.2

MILANO 1985
ROTONDA DELLA BESANA
76002.3

WASSER
Videoinstallation 1976
Leinwand (ab 1984), Neon,
Monitor, bespielte Kassette,
Tonaufzeichnung

WATER
Video installation 1976
Canvas (since 1984), neon,
monitor, video recorder, recorded
video cassette, soundrecording

ACQUA
Videoinstallazione 1976
Tela (da 1984), ferro, neon,
1 monitor, 1 vhs, 1 cassetta
registrata, sonoro

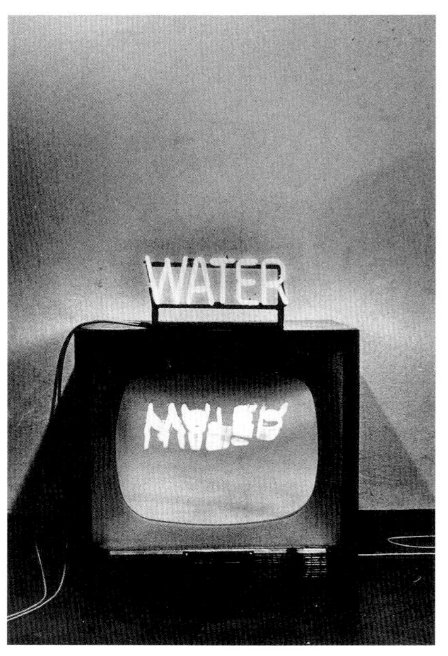

Fabrizio Plessi, der 1940 in Reggio Emilia gebürtige Italiener, hat nicht umsonst in Venedig, der Stadt des Wassers, sein Studium an der Akademie der schönen Künste absolviert. Spätestens seit 1968 ist Wasser das Hauptmotiv seiner Arbeit geworden, das Thema, dem er einen Großteil seines künstlerischen Engagements gewidmet hat. Nicht allein die zahlreichen Projektskizzen, Zeichnungen und Collagen seiner Performances und Aktionen mit Wasser, seine experimentellen Filme, wie die Serie *Underwater*, sondern auch die meisten seiner Videoskulpturen befassen sich mit diesem Sinnbild ewigen Entstehens und Vergehens. »Wasser ist seine Obsession, in jeder nur denkbaren Dimension, in allen Erscheinungsformen und Funktionen. Er umkreist es immer wieder in seiner Arbeit. Er läßt

Fabrizio Plessi, the Italian born in 1940 in Reggio Emilia, has had good reasons to study at the Academy of Fine Arts in Venice, the city of water. Certainly from 1968 onwards, water has become the main subject of his work, the theme to which he has dedicated most of his artistic engagement. Not only the numerous project sketches, drawings and collages of his performances and actions with water, his experimental films - like the series Underwater *- but also most of his video sculptures deal with this symbol of eternal creation and vanishing. "Water, in every conceivable dimension, in all forms and functions, is his obsession. Again and again he circles it in his work, he accepts its challenge, he fears it, plays with it, changes and works on it.*

Fabrizio Plessi, nato a Reggio Emilia nel 1940, non ha portato invano a termine gli studi all'Accademia delle Belle Arte di Venezia, la città dell'acqua. Al più tardi dal 1968 l'acqua diventa il motivo principale del suo lavoro, il tema al quale ha dedicato il maggior tempo della sua attività artistica. Non solo i numerosi schizzi progettuali, disegni e collages delle sue performances e azioni con l'acqua e i films sperimentali, come la serie *Underwater*, ma anche la maggior parte delle sue videosculture si occupano di questo simbolo dell'eterno ciclo del sorgere e svanire. »L'acqua, in ogni dimensione immaginabile, in ogni forma e funzione, è la sua ossessione. Egli le gira intorno in ogni momento del suo lavoro, ci gioca, la modula e la

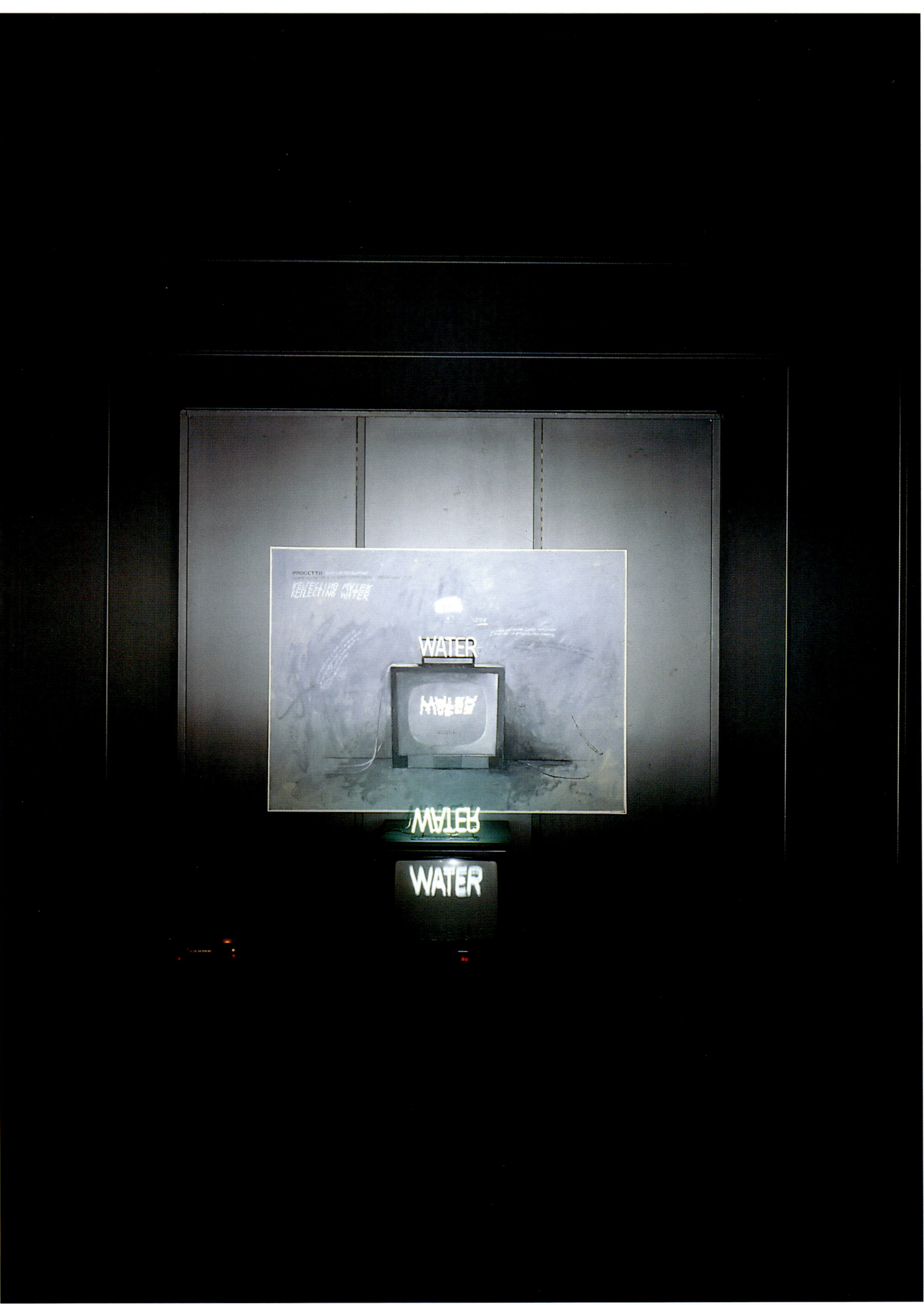
PROGETTO
REFLECTING WATER
WATER
WATER

sich von ihm herausfordern. Er fürchtet es. Er spielt mit ihm. Er verwandelt und bearbeitet es. Und er macht immer neue überraschende Vorschläge, wie mit ihm umzugehen sei«, schreibt Jens Christian Jensen in seinem Ausstellungskatalog. (Kunsthalle zu Kiel, Kiel 1977)

Die Videoskulptur *Water*, bestehend aus dem Wort ›WATER‹, leuchtend in Neonbuchstaben auf einen Fernsehapparat gestellt, in dem Wasser zu sehen ist. Dort scheint sich das Neonwort, als Reflex zu spiegeln, seitenverkehrt und auf den Kopf gestellt. Diese erste Version von 1976 wird 1984 für die Präsentation auf der Biennale in Venedig noch um ein Gemälde erweitert, auf dem genau die eben beschriebene Konstellation malerisch zu sehen ist Diese frühe Videoskulptur steht in Zusammenhang mit seinen Inszenierungen in Duisburg und Lyon, wo er die Worte ›WATER‹ beziehungsweise ›EAU‹ in Neonbuchstaben und überdimensionierter Größe an den Rand eines Sees oder eines Flusses auf dem Kopf stehend plaziert hat, so daß sich in dem realen Wasser die Worte in richtiger Schreibweise, doch leicht verschwommen, lesen lassen.

Das o.g. Werk nimmt im gesamten Œuvre Fabrizio Plessis eine Schlüsselrolle ein. Es weist nicht nur auf das Hauptthema seiner Arbeit hin, sondern auch auf das Phänomen, daß Fabrizio Plessi weniger technisch orientierter Videokünstler als vielmehr Maler, oder besser Zeichner, und Bildhauer ist, der Film, Video und Monitore als Medium zur Umsetzung seiner bildnerischen Ideen gewählt hat. Er selbst sagt: »Ich habe immer die Elektronik, oder genauer gesagt, das Fernsehen als nichts anderes angesehen, als ein Material. Ein beliebiges Material, mehr oder weniger wie das Eisen, die Kohle, das Stroh oder der Marmor.« (Katalog Museum Ludwig, Köln 1993)

And he makes ever new, surprising suggestions on how to deal with it" writes Jens Christian Jensen in his exhibition catalogue. (Catalogue, Kunsthalle Kiel, 1977)

When he, in 1974, finally creates his first video text it does not take long until the tape Acquabiografico *appears, a biography of water, a hymn to water, lastingly expressing his obsession.*

The video sculpture Water, *consisting of the word 'WATER', stands in bright neon letters on a TV monitor showing water, in which the neon word - upside down and sides vice-versa - seems to be mirrored. This first version of 1974 is later, for the presentation at the Biennale in Venice in 1984, increased by adding a painting which shows exactly the just described constellation.*

This early video sculpture is connected closely to his staging of the words 'WATER' and 'EAU' in oversized neon letters in Duisburg and Lyon, where he placed them upside down on the shores of a lake or river so that the words become legible in real water, though slightly diffused.

The above-mentioned work plays a key role in all of Plessi's œuvre. It not only points to the main theme of his work, but also to the phenomenon that Fabrizio Plessi is less technically oriented video artist than painter, better graphic artist and sculptor who has chosen film, video and TV monitor as media to transport his ideas. He himself says: "I have always regarded electronic media, and more precisely television, as nothing other than a material, a common and ordinary material, more or less like iron, coal, straw or marble." (Catalogue Museum Ludwig, Köln 1993)

elabora, la teme e nello stesso momento l'acqua lo provoca, giungendo sempre a manipolarla in nuove soprendenti proposte«, annota Jens Christian Jensen (catalogo Kunsthalle zu Kiel 1977).

La videoscultura *Water* è costituita dalla parola ›Water‹ scritta con tubi al neon posizionati su di un televisore che fa vedere uno specchio d'acqua nel quale apparentemente si riflette la parola al neon rovesciata e capovolta. Questa prima versione del 1976 verrà poi ampliata da un dipinto per quella della Biennale di Venezia del 1984, che rappresenta la stessa costellazione. Tale videoscultura, una fra le prime, è strettamente collegata con le opere di Duisburg e Lione, dove le rispettive parole ›WATER‹ e ›EAU‹, scritte in lettere superdimensionali capovolte di tubi al neon e piazzate lungo le rive di un lago o di un fiume, si riflettono nell'acqua reale in maniera leggibile ma sfuocata.

L'opera occupa una posizione chiave nell'intera œuvre di Fabrizio Plessi, in quanto non solo presenta il tema principale del suo lavora ma sottolinea anche il fatto che egli non si considera tanto un videoartista orientato verso la tecnica, quanto un pittore, o meglio disegnatore e scultore, che impiega film, video e monitors quale medium per la concretizzazione delle sue idee figurative. Plessi: »Io ho sempre considerato l'elettronica e più precisamente la televisione, nient'altro che un materiale, un materiale qualsiasi, più o meno come il ferro, il carbone, la paglia o il marmo.« (catalogo Museum Ludwig, Colonia 1993)

REFLECTING WATER

79001

ESSEN 1979
Folkwang Museum
79001.1

VILLENEUVE D'ASCQ 1984
Musée du Nord
79001.2

MILANO 1985
Rotonda della Besana
79001.3

BOLOGNA 1986
Galleria d'Arte Moderna
79001.4

REFLEKTIERENDES WASSER
Videoinstallation 1979
Stahlbecken, Petroleum, Neon,
2 Monitore, 2 Videorecorder,
2 bespielte Kassetten

Die Installation *Reflecting Water* basiert unmittelbar auf den Erfahrungen der vorangegangenen Arbeiten mit Neon. Doch hier wird nicht nur das Ergebnis präsentiert, sondern der Vorgang des Reflektierens selbst thematisiert. Zwei Monitore sind einander frontal gegenübergestellt, verbunden durch einen kleinen Kanal, der mit Petroleum gefüllt ist. Über dem einen Monitor befindet sich die Neonschrift ›WATER‹ auf den Kopf gestellt, über dem anderen Monitor als Äquivalent das Wort ›REFLECTING‹. In den beiden Monitoren ist jeweils ein Film zu sehen, in dem die Neonworte auf einer Wasseroberfläche gespiegelt und daher richtig herum zu lesen sind, aber wegen der Unruhe des Wassers leicht bewegt und verzerrt werden. Über die Idee des Films hinaus spiegeln sich die beiden Neonschriften nochmals in dem Petroleumkanal, der die beiden Monitore verbindet.

Es wird bei dieser Arbeit auf die Idee des Wassers, die Kategorie des Reflektierens verwiesen, womit die ganze Konstruktion aus seinem realen Zusammenhang in eine übergeordnete Gesetzmäßigkeit transponiert wird.

REFLECTING WATER
Video installation 1979
Neon, iron basin, kerosene,
2 monitors, 2 video recorders,
2 recorded video cassettes

The installation Reflecting Water *is based directly on the experiences with the above-mentioned neon work. Here, however, not only the result is presented, but the process of reflection itself is the theme. Two monitors are positioned face to face, connected by a small channel filled with kerosene. Above one monitor the neon writing 'WATER' is fixed, upside down, above the other - as equivalent - the word 'REFLECTING'. Both monitors show a film in which the respective neon words are mirrored on the surface of water, thus legible correctly, although - because of the water's movement - in slight motion and diffusion. Transgressing the idea of the film, the two neon writings again are reflected in the kerosene channel connecting the two monitors.*

In this work, the idea of water, the category of reflection, is pointed out, conveying the whole construction from its real context to a superior legitimacy.

ACQUA RIFLETTANTE
Videoinstallazione 1979
Vasca in ferro, petrolio, neon,
2 monitors, 2 vhs, 2 casette
registrate

L'installazione *Reflecting Water* si basa direttamente sulle esperienze dei precedenti lavori col neon, senza limitarsi alla presentazione di risultati ma tematizzando il processo proprio del riflettere. Due monitors sono collegati da un canale riempito di petrolio. Al di sopra di un monitor si trova la scritta al neon ›WATER‹ e al di sopra dell'altro ›REFLECTING‹ capovolte. In ambedue i monitors si vede un filmato nel quale appaiono rispettivamente le due parole leggermente sfuocate a causa della superficie dell'acqua e leggibili che a loro volta si riflettono nella superficie del petrolio del canale che collega i due monitors.

L'opera rimanda al concetto di acqua, alla categoria del riflettere, trasponendo l'intera costruzione dal suo reale contesto ad una regolarità superiore.

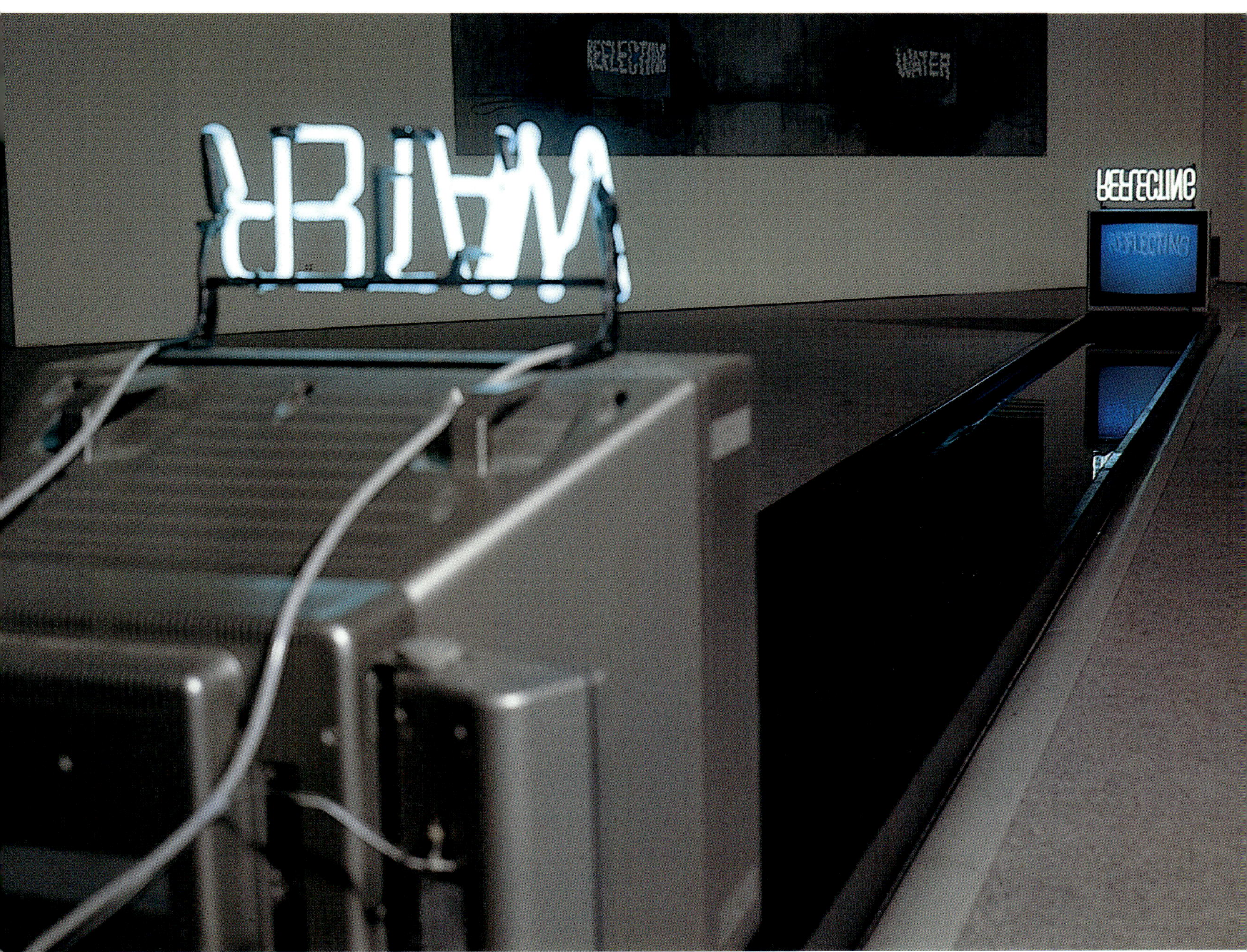

ARCO LIQUIDO

81001

FERRARA 1988
MUSEO PALAZZO DEI DIAMANTI
81001.1

PALMA DE MALLORCA 1989
PALAU SOLLERIC
81001.2

KÖLN 1997
GALERIE DOROTHEA VAN DER KOELEN, ART COLOGNE
81001.3

FLÜSSIGER BOGEN
Videoskulptur 1981
Eisenkonstruktion,
Industriegitter, Neon, Glaserkitt,
2 Monitore, 2 Videorecorder,
2 bespielte Kassetten

LIQUID ARCH
Video sculpture 1981
Neon, iron, metal grid, putty,
2 monitors, 2 video recorders,
2 recorded video cassettes

ARCO LIQUIDO
Videoscultura 1981
Ferro, grigliato industriale, neon,
stucco, 2 monitors, 2 vhs,
2 cassette registrate

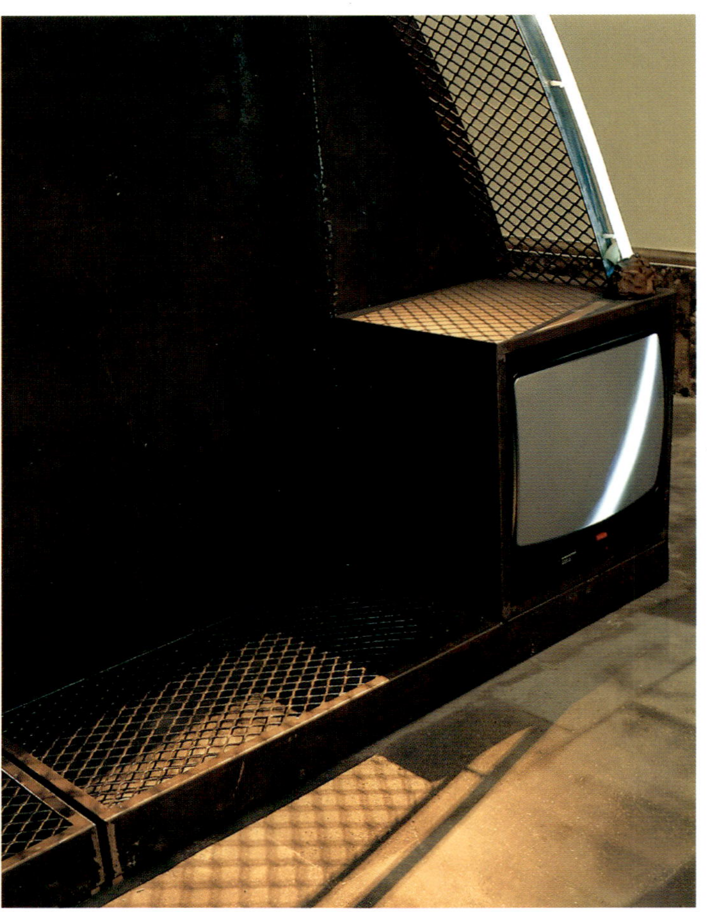

Die Erfahrungen der Lichtre-
flexionen macht sich Fabrizio
Plessi zu eigen, wenn er die
Reflexion eines halbkreisförmigen
Neonbogens scheinbar über zwei
Monitore bis auf den vor der
Skulptur befindlichen Boden
führt, so daß sich im gesamten
Bild der Kreislauf wieder schließt.
Interessanterweise lautet der
Titel der Arbeit nicht etwa ›Licht-
bogen‹, sondern *Arco Liquido*, also

His experiences with light
reflection enable Fabrizio Plessi
to seemingly draw the reflection
of a half-circle neon arch via two
monitors to the ground before
the sculpture, thus closing the
circle within the complete work.
It is interesting to note that the
work's title is not - as expected -
'Arch of Light' but Arco Liquido,
that is Liquid Arch, *pointing to*
the fact that not only water but

Fabrizio Plessi si appropria
delle esperienze con i riflessi di
luce quando conduce apparentemente attraverso due monitors
il riflesso di un semicerchio al
neon, posizionato su di loro,
fino al pavimento sul quale
poggia la scultura, ottenendo la
chiusura del cerchio. Curiosamente l'opera non è intitolata
›Arco di luce‹ ma *Arco Liquido*,
il che suggerisce che oltre

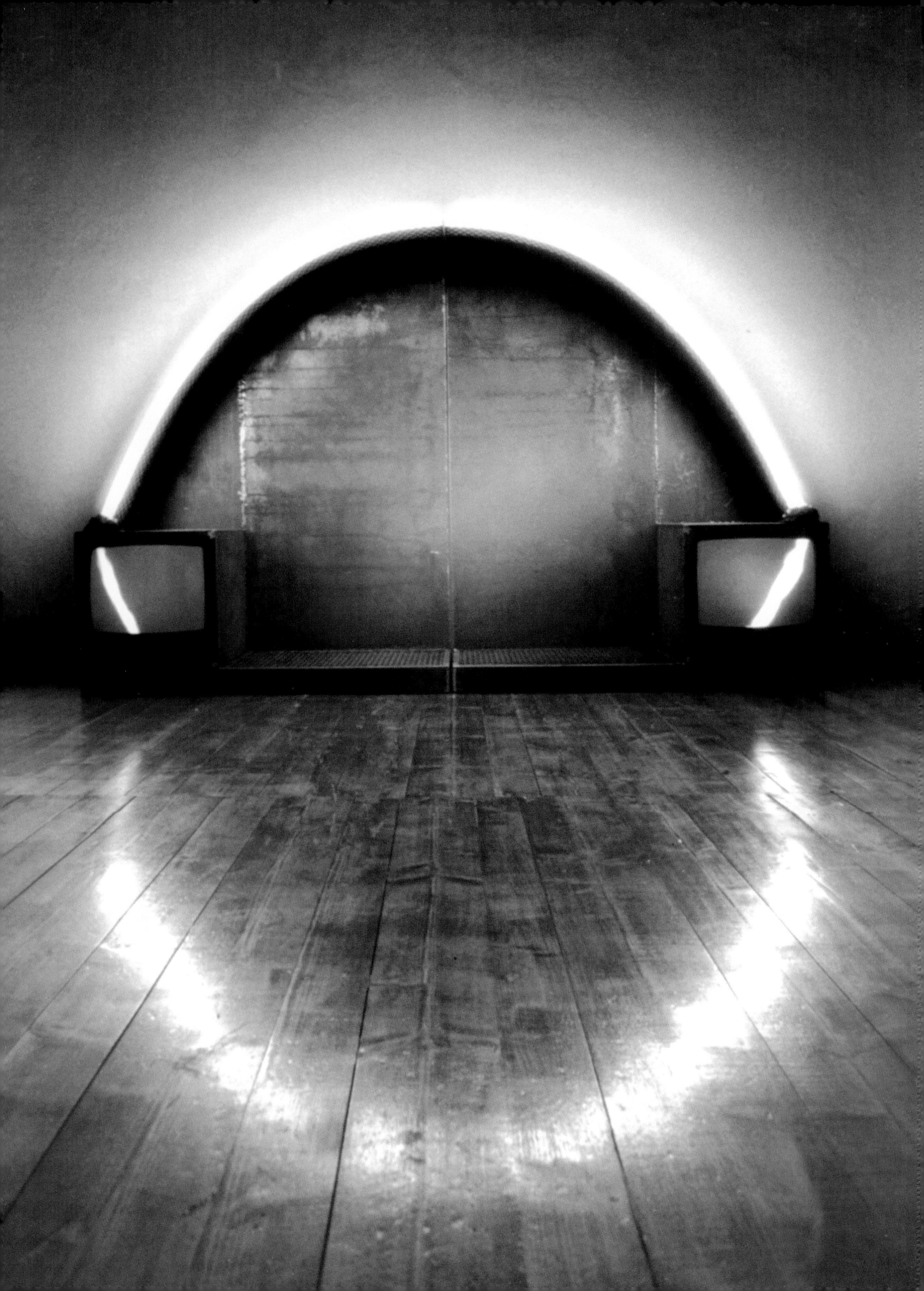

Flüssiger Bogen, und weist so darauf hin, daß nicht nur Wasser, sondern auch Strom, Licht, mithin Energie, fließen kann. Daß sich auch hier der Lichtbogen im Wasser spiegelt, verflüssigt, und damit aus der starren, geometrischen Form seiner Materie in eine immaterielle Dimension modifiziert, gibt dem tektonischen Prinzip, dem archaischen Rundbogen, der wie ein Architekturgebilde erscheint, wie ein Tor, eine Pforte, oder ein Fenster, eine instabile Dimension. Vielleicht möchte Fabrizio Plessi mit dieser Arbeit die bestehenden Normen, die herrschenden Hierarchien, die Architekturgesetzmäßigkeiten, die Gravitation, außer Kraft setzen, oder doch zumindest in Frage stellen. Denn die auf den ersten Blick so stabile Stahlbasis der Gehäuse mit den Monitoren und die Stahlplatte der Rückwand, die der ganzen Konstruktion Halt gibt, scheint durch das Licht an Stabilität zu verlieren, instabil zu werden und verweist damit auf das spätere Werk von 1984 *Soft Steel* (84001).

electricity, light, thus energy can flow. That here, too, the arch of light is reflected in water, liquidized, thus modified from its fixed geometric material form to an immaterial one adds an unstable dimension to the tectonic principle, the archaic arch that appears to be an architectural structure like a gate, a port, or a window. Perhaps Fabrizio Plessi wants to abolish the existing norms with this work, the ruling hierarchies, the laws of architecture and gravity, or at least question them. For the - at first glance - stable steel base of the monitor-casings as well as the steel back-plate that seem to give strength to the whole construction appear to lose stability, become unstable because of the light, thus indicating his later work of 1984, Soft Steel *(84 001)*

l'acqua possono scorrere anche la corrente elettrica, la luce e quindi l'energia. Il fatto che anche qui l'arco di luce si rifletta nell'acqua, si liquefaccia e, di conseguenza, esca dalla forma rigida e geometrica della sua materia per trasformarsi in una dimensione immateriale, conferisce una dimensione instabile al principio tettonico, all'arco arcaico, che appare come una struttura architettonica, come una porta o una finestra. Forse Fabrizio Plessi intende con quest'opera neutralizzare o per lo meno mettere in dubbio le norme esistenti, le gerarchie dominanti, i principì architettonici e la gravitazione. Il grigliato industriale che funge, a prima vista, da solida base dei contenitori dei monitors e la lastra di ferro della parete posteriore che garantisce la stabilità dell'insieme, sembrano perdere la loro solidità a causa della luce, anticipando il concetto dell'opera più tarda di *Soft Steel* del 1984 (cat. 84001).

WATER WIND I

81002

LYON 1981
FRIGO
81002.1

WASSER WIND I
Videoinstallation 1981
Ventilator, Heuhaufen, Monitor,
Videorecorder, bespielte Kassette

WATER WIND I
Video installation 1981
Fan, haycock, monitor, video
recorder, recorded video cassette

ACQUA VENTO I
Videoinstallazione 1981
Ventilatore, mucchio di fieno,
monitor, vhs, cassetta registrata

Bei *Water Wind*, der ersten von insgesamt vier Versionen dieser Idee, ist neben Wasser auch Wind zum Thema geworden; in späteren Video-Skulpturen und -Installationen wird man dann auch Feuer und Erde wiederfinden. Insgesamt betrachtet sind es also die ›Vier Elemente‹, die in der Performance *Two and Two* von 1976/77, bei der vier akustisch-optische Aktionen in freier Beziehung zu den Elementen Erde, Feuer, Wasser, Luft stehen, ihren Ursprung finden.

Die Präsentation besteht im wesentlichen aus zwei Elementen: aus einem, auf den Rücken gelegten Monitor, bei dem die Bildfläche nach oben zeigt, eingebaut in einen Heuhaufen, und bespielt mit einem Film, der Wasser in Bewegung zeigt, und einem Ventilator, auf der anderen Seite des Raumes, der die Bewegung des Wassers hervorzurufen scheint, so als wäre das Wasser ohne den Ventilator still, ruhig und unbewegt und würde seine Gestalt nur durch den Einfluß des Windes verändern.

Hieran knüpft sich die Überlegung, wann, unter welchen Umständen und aufgrund welcher Phänomene Wasser für uns als solches erkennbar ist. Wasser kann die unterschiedlichsten Farben haben: Blau wie der Himmel, Grün wie die Pflanzen und Algen, die darin schwimmen und sich bewegen, glitzernd wie Gold oder Edelsteine, es kann eine ganz glatte und ruhige Oberfläche besitzen, es kann sprudeln wie bei einem Springbrunnen,

In Water Wind, *the first of four versions of this idea, wind has, beside water, become the subject; in later video sculptures and -installations fire and earth will be found, too. Seen as a whole, it is the 'Four Elements' that originate in the performance* Two and Two *of 1976/77, in which four acoustic-optic actions are freely related to the elements earth, fire, water and air.*

The presentation consists mainly of two elements: one is a monitor, lying on the back, screen upwards, built into a haystack, showing a film of water in motion, the other a ventilator on the other side of the room that seems to create the water's motion, giving the impression that, without the ventilator, the water would be still, calm and motionless and would only change its state through the influence of the wind.

Connected to this is the thought when, under which circumstances and because of which phenomenons water as such can be recognised by us. Water can have many different colours: blue as the sky, green as plants and algae that float and live in it, glittering as gold or jewels, it can have a completely smooth and calm surface, it can bubble as a spring, flow as a river, it can build up to waves as in the sea, and it can fall as raindrops from the sky. And we are always

Nella prima delle quattro versioni di Water Wind si aggiunge la tematica del vento a quella dell'acqua, che in altre videosculture e installazioni successive saranno completate da quelle del fuoco e della terra. Così si ottengono i quattro elementi, che già trovano origine nella performance *Two and Two* del 1976/77, dove quattro azioni acustico-ottiche creano un libero rapporto con gli elementi terra, fuoco, acqua e aria.

L'opera è costituita principalmente da due componenti: un monitor, con lo schermo rivolto verso l'alto e inserito in un pagliaio che fa vedere l'acqua in movimento, e un ventilatore, posizionato nel lato opposto della sala che sembra provocare il movimento dell'acqua, come se essa senza il ventilatore fosse calma ed immobile e cambiasse fisionomia con il vento.

Il concetto dell'installazione si allaccia al seguente quesito: in quale circostanza e con quali criteri l'acqua sia riconoscibile come tale. L'acqua può acquisire i più differenti colori e fisionomie, blu come il cielo, verde come le piante e le alghe, scintillante come oro o pietre preziose, può essere piatta e calma, può zampillare come in una fontana, può scorrere come il fiume, può trasformarsi in onde del mare e può cadere

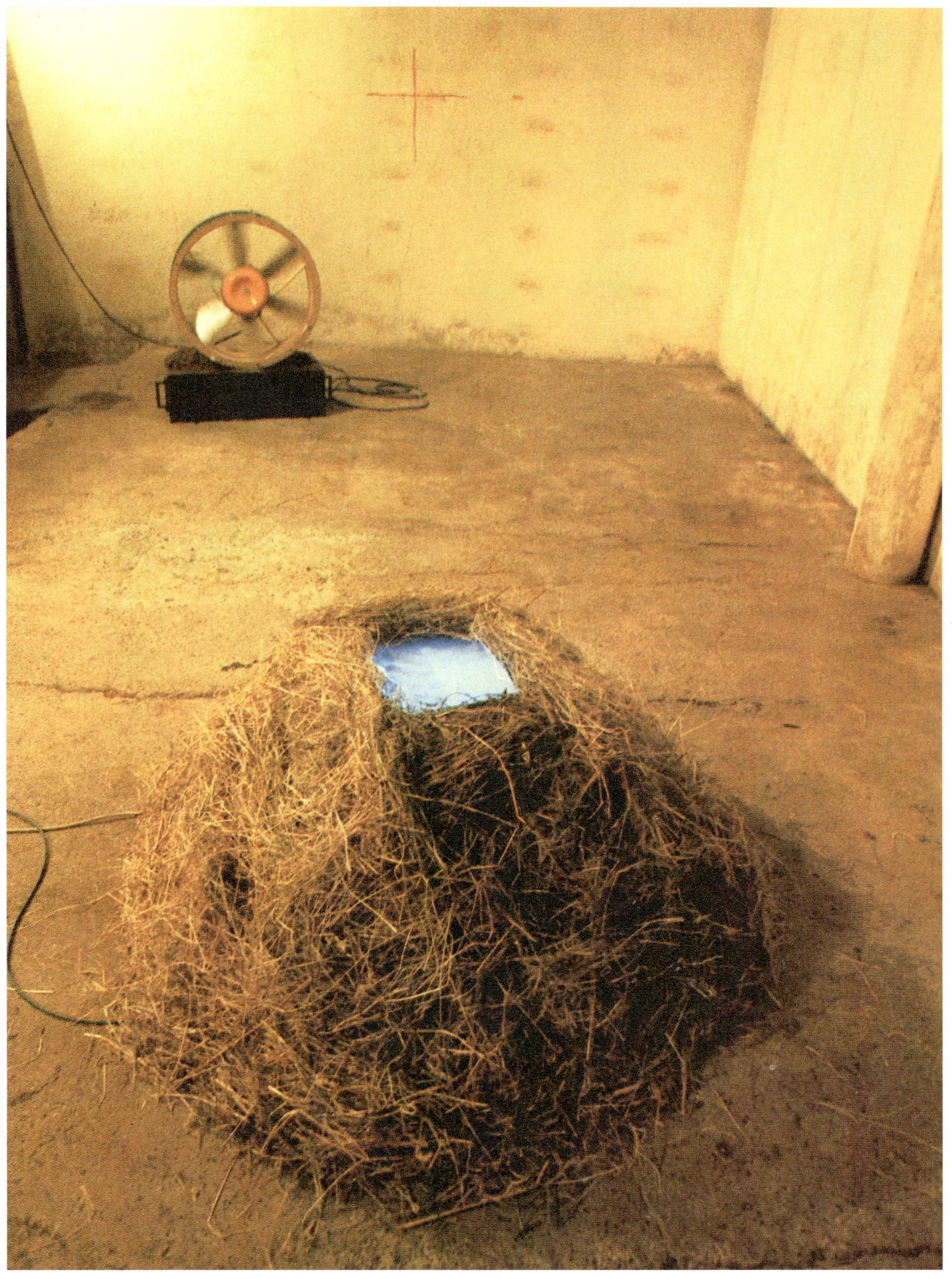

es kann fließen wie im Fluß, es kann sich zu Wellen auftürmen wie am Meer, und es kann als Regentropfen vom Himmel fallen. Und immer sind wir uns gewiß, daß es sich um Wasser handelt.

Was ist es also, das diese Gewißheit ausmacht, wenn doch seine Erscheinungsweisen so unterschiedlich sind? René Descartes hat sich, bei seiner analytischen Untersuchung darüber, was zur ganz deutlichen Erkenntnis eines Körpers erforderlich erscheint, ein Stück Bienenwachs vorgenommen. Er hat seine Beschaffenheit untersucht, den Duft, Farbe, Gestalt, Größe, Biegsamkeit, Härte etc. und festgestellt, daß alle diese Eigenschaften deutlich erkennbar und klar benennbar sind. Doch kaum kommt das Bienenwachs dem Feuer nahe, verändern sich alle diese Eigenschaften, die eben noch so klar und deutlich benennbar und erkennbar waren. Und es stellt sich die Frage: »Bleibt es nun noch dasselbe Stück Wachs?« (Descartes: *Meditationen*, Kap. 2) Er stellt fest, daß alles, was er mit den Sinnen wahrnehmen konnte, sich verändert hat, nur das Wachs selbst ist geblieben. Dies bringt ihn zu der Erkenntnis, daß der Begriff des Wachses, ungeachtet der unzähligen Möglichkeiten seiner Erscheinung, immer gleich gültig ist, denn »So muß ich schließlich gestehen, daß ich mir nicht einmal bildhaft vorstellen kann, was dieses Stück Wachs hier ist, sondern es allein durch den Geist auffasse.« (ebd.)

Es wird in dieser Videoskulptur von Fabrizio Plessi nicht nur auf die Beziehung zwischen Wasser und Wind verwiesen, sondern zugleich auf den Begriff des Wassers, der, wie wir eben bei dem Wachsbeispiel von Descartes gesehen haben, unabhängig von seiner momentanen Erscheinungsweise von seiner sinnlichen Wahrnehmbarkeit, als Begriff gültig bleibt.

certain that it is water.

What is it, then, that gives us this certainty when all these modes of existence are so different? In his analysis of what is necessary to clearly recognise a body, René Descartes has taken a piece of bee-wax. He examined its composition, smell, colour, shape, size, flexibility, hardness etc. and remarked that all these characteristics are clearly recognisable and can be named. Yet, as soon as bee-wax comes close to fire all these characteristics that only a moment ago could be listed and observed so clearly and definitely, change. And the question arises: "Is it still the same piece of wax?" (Descartes: Meditationes, chap. 2) He concludes that everything he could realise with his senses has changed, only the wax has remained, and this leads him to the cognition that the concept of wax is always equally valid, notwithstanding its innumerable modes of appearance, for: "So I have to admit that I can not even imagine what this piece of wax is, but can only conceive it in my mind." (Descartes, loc.cit.)

In this video sculpture, Fabrizio Plessi not only points to the relation between water and wind but at the same time to the concept of water that, as just seen in Descartes' wax-example, remains valid as a concept, independent from its momentary state and sensual perceptibility.

This video sculpture became main agent in the film Water Wind *from the series* Underwater *that was produced by Frigo in Lyon in 1982.*

come pioggia dal cielo. Sempre però siamo certi che si tratta dell'acqua.

Cos'è che ci rende così sicuri che si tratti veramente di acqua, se essa cambia di continuo il suo aspetto? René Descartes, nel suo tentativo analitico di stabilire che cosa determini il riconoscimento esatto di un corpo, ha osservato, dopo aver analizzato consistenza, odore, colore, forma, dimensioni, fessibilità e solidità di un blocco di cera d'api, che tutte queste caratteristiche sono inequivocalmente riconoscibili e classificabili. Ma appena la cera d'api viene avvicinata dal fuoco, tutte le caratteristiche appena definite si modificano. Sorge spontanea la domanda: ci troviamo ancora di fronte allo stesso blocco di cera? (cfr. René Descartes: *Meditazioni*, capitolo 2) Descartes afferma che tutto ciò che si percepisce con i sensi si è modificato, mentre la cera è rimasta tale, e giunge alla conclusione che il concetto di cera resta invariato, indipentemente dalle innumerevoli possibilità del suo apparire, ammettendo che non è quindi l'immagine ma soltanto la mente che fa comprendere che cosa è un blocco di cera. (cfr. ibid.) Fabrizio Plessi, nella sua videoscultura, non fa semplicemente riferimento al rapporto fra acqua e vento, ma al tempo stesso anche al concetto di acqua che, come si è visto nell'esempio di Descartes, rimane valido indipendentemente dalla sua contingente apparenza e dalla sua percezione sensuale.

La videoscultura fu l'attore principale del film *Water Wind* della serie *Underwater* realizzato da Frigo a Lione nel 1982.

50

WATER WIND II

81003

MILANO 1981
Triennale di Milano
81003.1

WASSER WIND II
Videoinstallation 1981
Ventilator, mehrere Heuhaufen,
6 Monitore, Videorecorder,
bespielte Kassette

WATER WIND II
Video installation 1981
Fan, haycocks, 6 monitors, video recorder, recorded video cassette

ACQUA VENTO II
Videoinstallazione 1981
Ventilatore, mucchi di fieno,
6 monitors, vhs, cassetta registrata

Die zweite Version von *Water Wind* zeigt eine ähnliche Konstruktion wie die eben beschriebene, nur quantifiziert sie den Grundgedanken. Zu sehen sind eine größere Anzahl von Monitoren, alle mit der Bildfläche nach oben gerichtet, in einzelne kleine Heuhaufen eingebettet. Ein Ventilator im Hintergrund scheint die Bewegung des Wassers auf der Filmoberfläche zu erzeugen. Der Wind ist real spürbar, doch kann er keinen Einfluß auf das Wasser nehmen, denn das Wasser ist imaginär und immateriell. Vorstellung und Realität vermischen sich miteinander, verschwimmen hier.

The second version of Water Wind *shows a construction similar to the one described above, only quantifying the basic idea. It consists of a greater number of monitors, all with the screens upwards, embedded in single small haystacks. A ventilator in the background seems to create the motion on the surface of the filmed water. One can sense real wind, yet it cannot have any influence on the water, for it is imaginary and immaterial. Here, idea and reality mix, diffuse.*

La seconda versione di *Water Wind* presenta una struttura simile rispetto alla prima, amplificando però il concetto di base con un maggior numero di monitors. Un ventilatore sembra agitare l'acqua degli schermi; il vento è realmente percepibile ma non può interferire sull'acqua, perchè immaginaria e immateriale. Immaginazione e realtà si mescolano, si confondono.

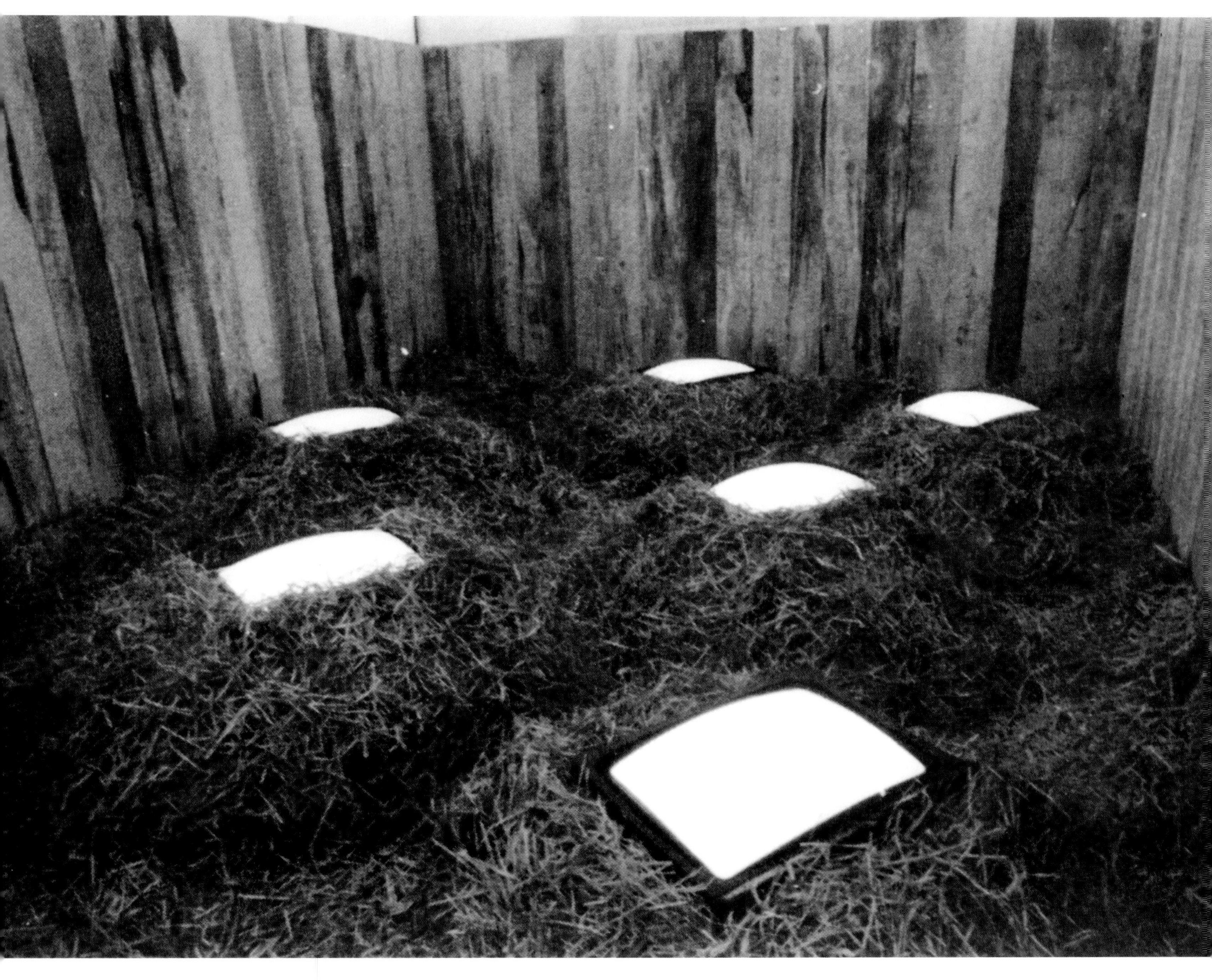

LIQUID MOVIE

81004

HEIDELBERG 1981
HEIDELBERGER KUNSTVEREIN
81004.1

MILANO 1985
ROTONDA DELLA BESANA
81004.2

FLÜSSIGER FILM
Videoinstallation 1981
Stahlgerüst, Filmleinwand,
Filmprojektion, 18 Monitore,
Videorecorder, bespielte Kassette

LIQUID MOVIE
Video installation 1981
Steel structure, film screen, film
show, 18 monitors, video recorder,
recorded video cassette

FILM LIQUIDO
Videoinstallazione 1981
Struttura metallica, schermo,
proiezione dei film, 18 monitors,
vhs, cassetta registrata

Liquid Movie ist der Name einer Videoskulptur, bei der der gleichnamige Film aus der Serie *Underwater* (s.o.) in die gesamte Präsentation integriert ist. In der Mitte des Gesamten ist eine Filmleinwand aufgespannt, umringt von 18 Monitoren, die rechteckig angeordnet sind. Alles ist in Dunkel gehüllt. Der Film zeigt eine Tänzerin in Bewegung. Auf den Monitoren sieht man, wiederum als bewegter Film, einen Ausschnitt: die Beine der Tänzerin, oder genauer, nur ein kleines Stück davon, die in Bewegung sind und daher ihre Form und Haltung ständig verändern. Obgleich der Betrachter den Zusammenhang zwischen den Monitoren und dem auf der Filmleinwand Dargestellten schnell herstellen kann, werden die sichtbaren Bildausschnitte auf den Monitoren zu einer abstrakten Form, deren Inhaltlichkeit sich auch aufgrund der Vervielfältigung, der Quantifizierung im Sinne eines gesamten Struktureindrucks aufhebt.

Liquid Movie *is the title of a video sculpture in which the film of the same title from the series* Underwater *(s.a.) is integrated into the presentation. In the centre of the installation a projection screen is erected, surrounded by 18 monitors arranged in a rectangular shape. Everything is in darkness. The film shows a dancer in motion. The monitors show - also as motion picture - a section: the dancer's legs, or, to be more exact, only a part of these, moving and therefore constantly changing their shape and position. Although the spectator can quickly recognise the connection between what is shown on the monitors and on the screen, the visible sections on the monitors soon take on an abstract form the content of which is lost because of the multiplication, the quantification in the sense of a total structural impression.*

Liquid Movie è il titolo di una videoscultura nella quale è inserito l'omonimo film della serie Underwater (v.s.). In un ambiente oscurato è collocato uno schermo cinematografico centrale circondato da 18 monitors esposti in un rettangolo. Il filmato presenta una danzatrice in movimento, mentre i monitors mostrano un dettaglio delle gambe della danzatrice sempre in movimento, che di conseguenza cambiano continuamente forma e posizione. Sebbene lo spettatore possa ricostruire immediatamente la correlazione tra le immagini dello schermo e quelle dei monitors, queste ultime si trasformano in una forma astratta il cui contenuto viene neutralizzato a causa della moltiplicazione, della quantificazione nel senso di una impressione strutturale totale.

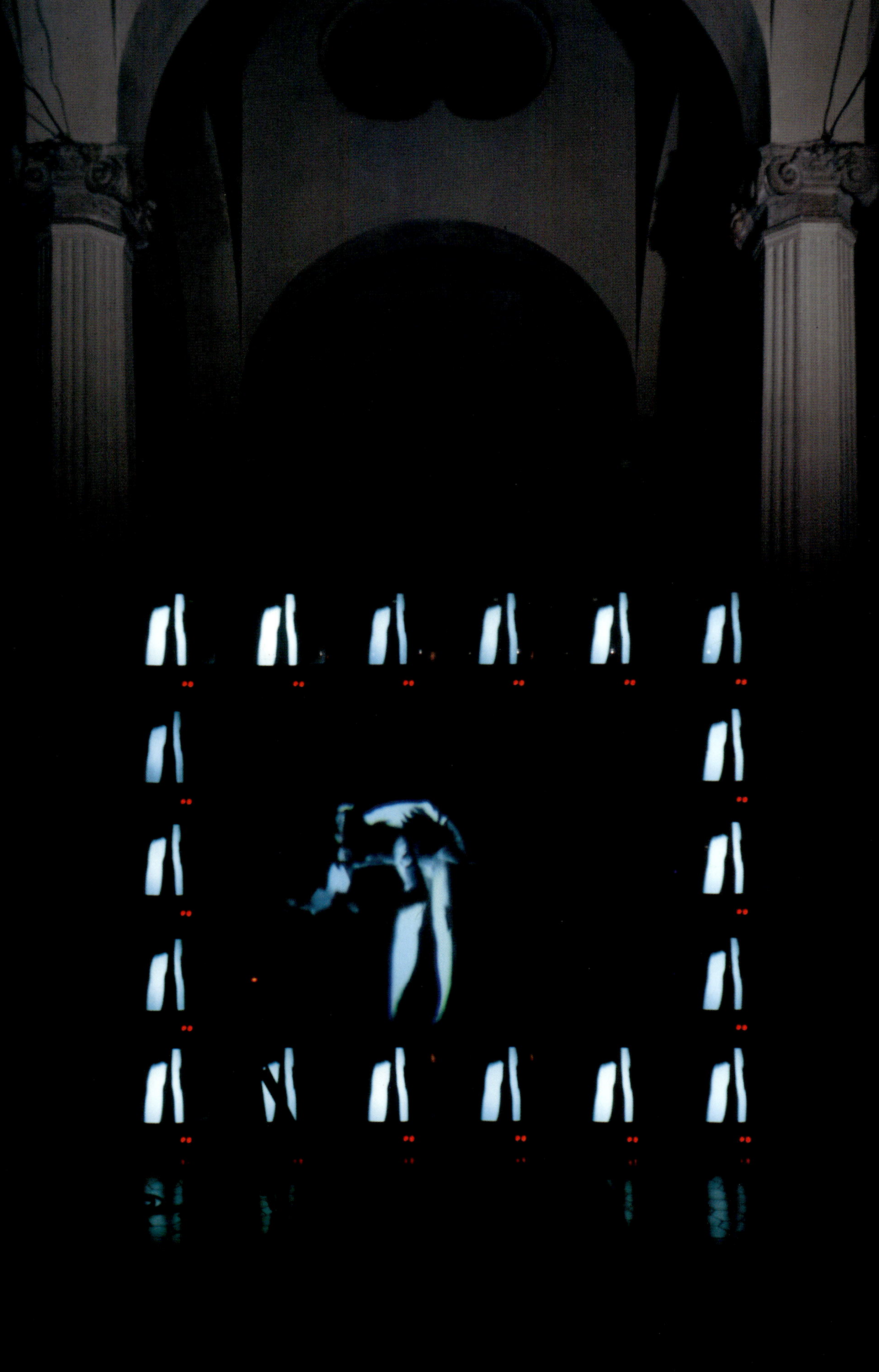

WASSERWAGEN

81005

LINZ 1988
NEUE GALERIE DER STADT LINZ
81005.1

ROMA 1988
RAI UNO ›IMMAGINA‹
81005.2

BARCELONA 1992
FUNDACIÓ JOAN MIRÓ
81005.3

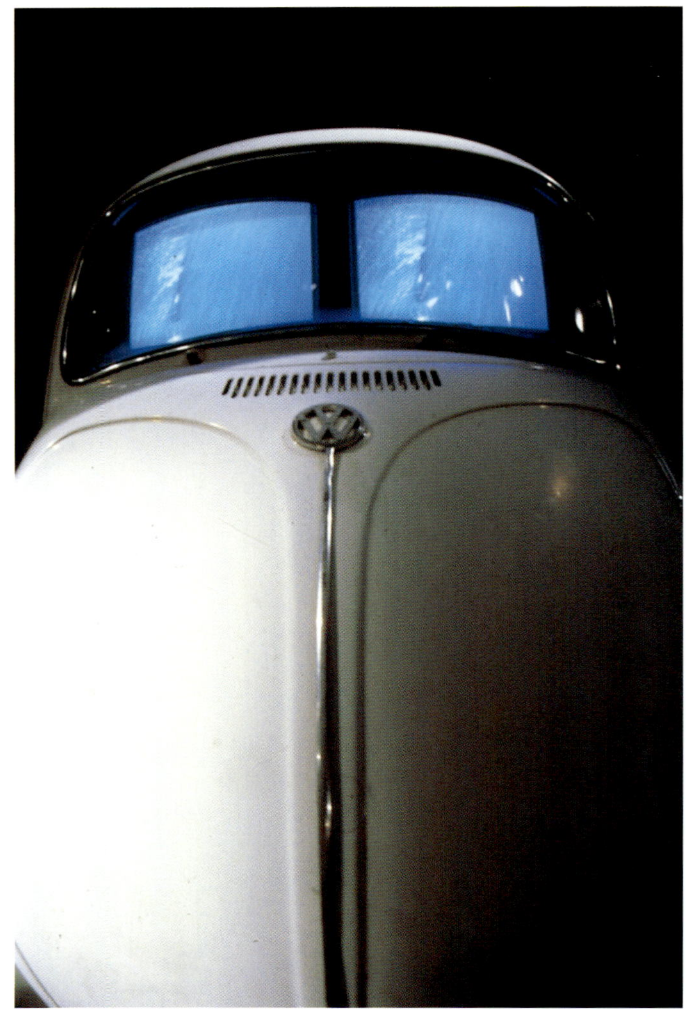
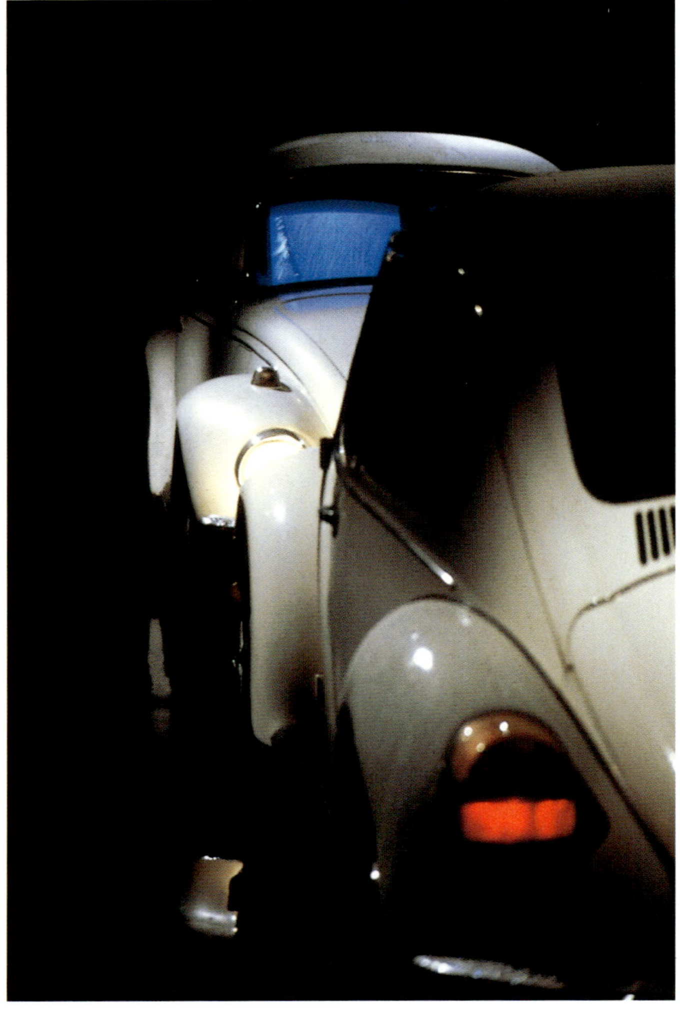

Zwei Fahrzeuge des Typs
VW Käfer sind einander frontal
gegenüber plaziert. Anstelle der
Windschutzscheibe sind jeweils
zwei Monitore eingebaut, die
Scheibenwischer in Aktion zeigen.
Versuchend, das Regenwasser, das
scheinbar auf die Windschutzscheibe tropft, wegzuwischen, um

Two VW Beetle automobiles
are placed opposite each other.
Instead of the windshields two
monitors each, showing winds-
hield wipers in action, have been
built in, trying to wash away the
raindrops that seem to fall on
the windshield, to allow vision.
The electronic windshield

Due automobili del tipo VW
Maggiolino sono posizionate
una di fronte all'altra. I tergicristalli sono stati sostituiti
da due monitors che presentano
i tergicristalli in movimento nel
tentativo di tergere la pioggia
che apparentemente cade sul
parabrezza. I tergicristalli

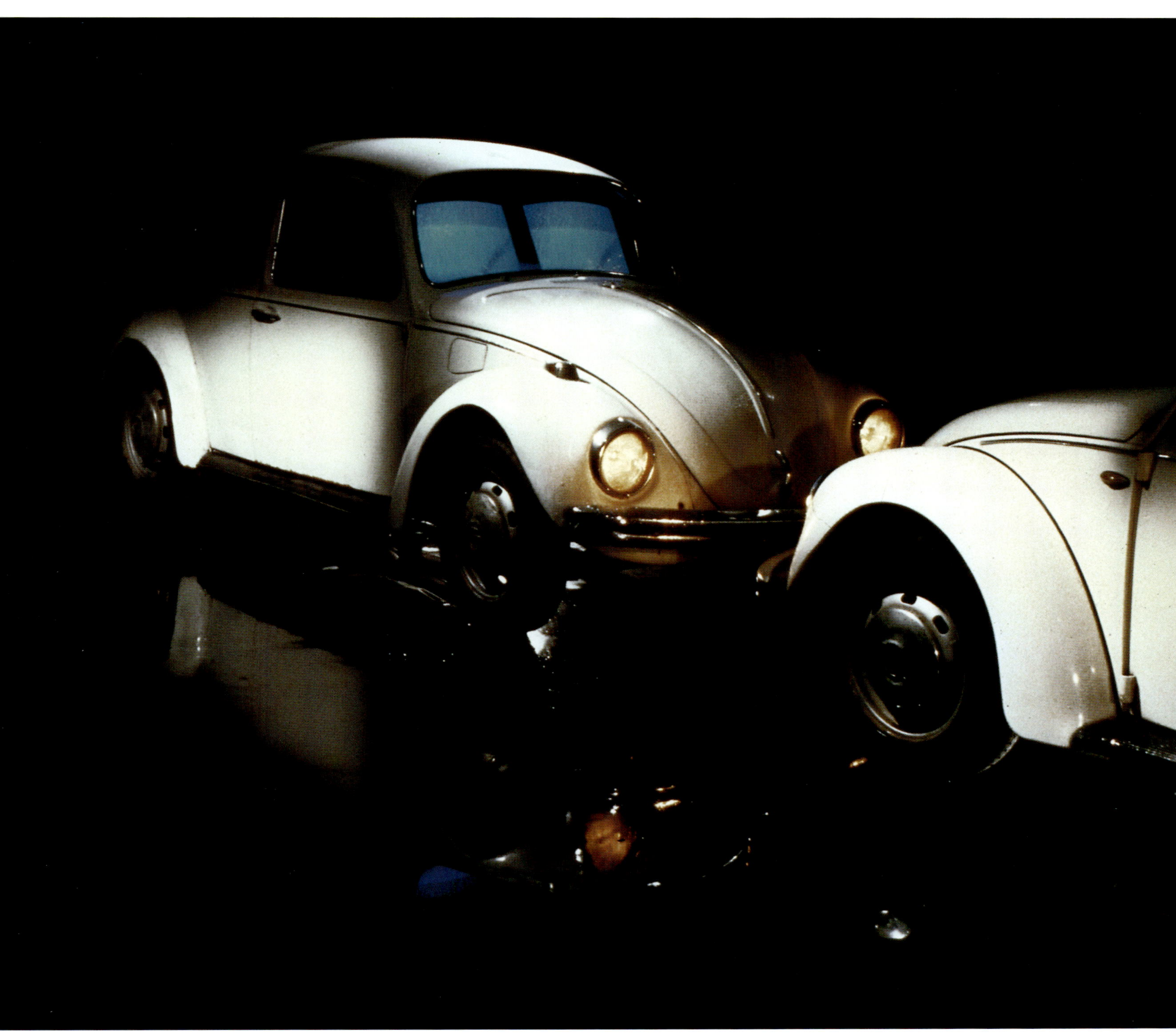

einen Durchblick zu ermöglichen.
Die elektronischen Scheibenwischer erzeugen zusammen mit den
leuchtenden Scheinwerfern einen
Realitätseindruck, der so überzeu-
gend wird, daß die beiden Fahrzeuge beinahe zum Leben erweckt zu
sein scheinen. Ja, man kann sich
sogar des Eindrucks nicht erweh-
ren, als hätte man mit den beiden
Autos, den *Wasserwagen*, Wesen
vor sich, die in einer wie auch
immer gearteten Beziehung zueinander stünden. Es ist die einzige
Videoinstallation, bei der Fahrzeuge eine Rolle spielen.

wipers, together with the tur-
ned-on headlights, create such
an impression of reality that the
two vehicles seem to have
almost come alive. One can even
hardly resist the impression
that with these two cars, the
Water Cars, *one is confronted*
with two beings that stand in a
- whatever kind of - relation to
each other. It is the only video
installation in which cars play
a part.

elettronici producono, insieme
ai fari accesi, una impressione
reale così convincente che le
due macchine, *Wasserwagen*,
sembrano quasi portate in vita
o, anzi, esseri che vivono una
relazione enigmatica fra di
loro. La videoinstallazione è
l'unica nell'opera di Plessi che
fa uso di automobili.

LIQUID GRAVITY CENTER

82001

FERRARA 1982
MUSEO PALAZZO DEI DIAMANTI
82001.1

MÜNCHEN 1983
STÄDTISCHE GALERIE IM LENBACHHAUS
82001.2

VILLENEUVE D'ASCQ 1984
MUSÉE DU NORD
82001.3

MILANO 1985
ROTONDA DELLA BESANA
82001.4

ROMA 1987
RAI UNO, ›IMMAGINA‹
82001.5

MADRID 1988
MUSEO ESPAÑOL DE ARTE CONTEMPORANEO
82001.6

FLÜSSIGES
GRAVITATIONSZENTRUM
Videoinstallation 1982
Erde, Kieselsteine, 1 Monitor,
Videorecorder, Kassette; später
erweitert: Förderband, Dreh-
scheibe, zusätzliche Monitore

LIQUID GRAVITY CENTER
Video installation 1982
Earth, stones, 1 monitor, recorder,
cassette; subsequently extented:
conveyor belt, rotating platform,
additional monitors

CENTRO LIQUIDO DI
GRAVITAZIONE
Videoinstallazione 1982
Terra, sassi, 1 monitor, vhs,
cassetta, sonoro; dopo variazioni
amplificati: montacarichi,
meccanica rotante, 36 monitors

Ähnlich wie bei *Liquid Movie* sind auch hier bei *Liquid Gravity Center* Bestandteile autarker separater Videotapes aus der Serie *Underwater* (s.o.), hier mit dem Titel *Up Down* von 1982, in das Environment integriert, wobei sich die Präsentationsform im Laufe verschiedener Ausstellungen, an verschiedenen Ausstellungsorten mehrfach verändert hat. Die ursprüngliche erste Version, präsentiert in Ferrara, kommt noch ohne die aufrecht stehenden zusätzlichen Monitore mit dem Film *Up Down* aus. Auch gibt es noch kein Förderband wie bei der Präsentation in der Rotonda della Besana in Mailand, welche die imaginären Steine, ähnlich wie bei der späteren Roma-

Similar to Liquid Movie, Liquid Gravity Centre *also integrates parts of self-sufficient separate video tapes from the series* Underwater *(s.a.), here entitled* Up Down, *of 1982, undergoing several changes in presentation in the course of different exhibitions at different exhibition sites. The original first version, presented in Ferrara, does without the upright positioned additional monitors showing the film* Up Down. *Neither is there a conveyor-belt - as in the show in the Rotonda della Besana in Milan - that could, as in the later work* Roma *in* Kassel, *transport imaginary*

Così come in *Liquid Movie*, anche *Liquid Gravity Center* integra frammenti di videotapes autonomi della serie *Underwater* cambiando l'insieme secondo i luoghi diversi delle esposizioni. La versione originale, presentata a Ferrara, fa ancora a meno dei monitors aggiuntivi con il filmato *Up Down*, nonchè dello montacarichi presente alla mostra della Rotonda della Besana a Milano che, come in *Roma* nella versione di Kassel, trasporta i sassi immaginari al centro del liquido gravitazionale.

L'elemento base di questa videoscultura è posizionato in maniera concentrica. Al centro

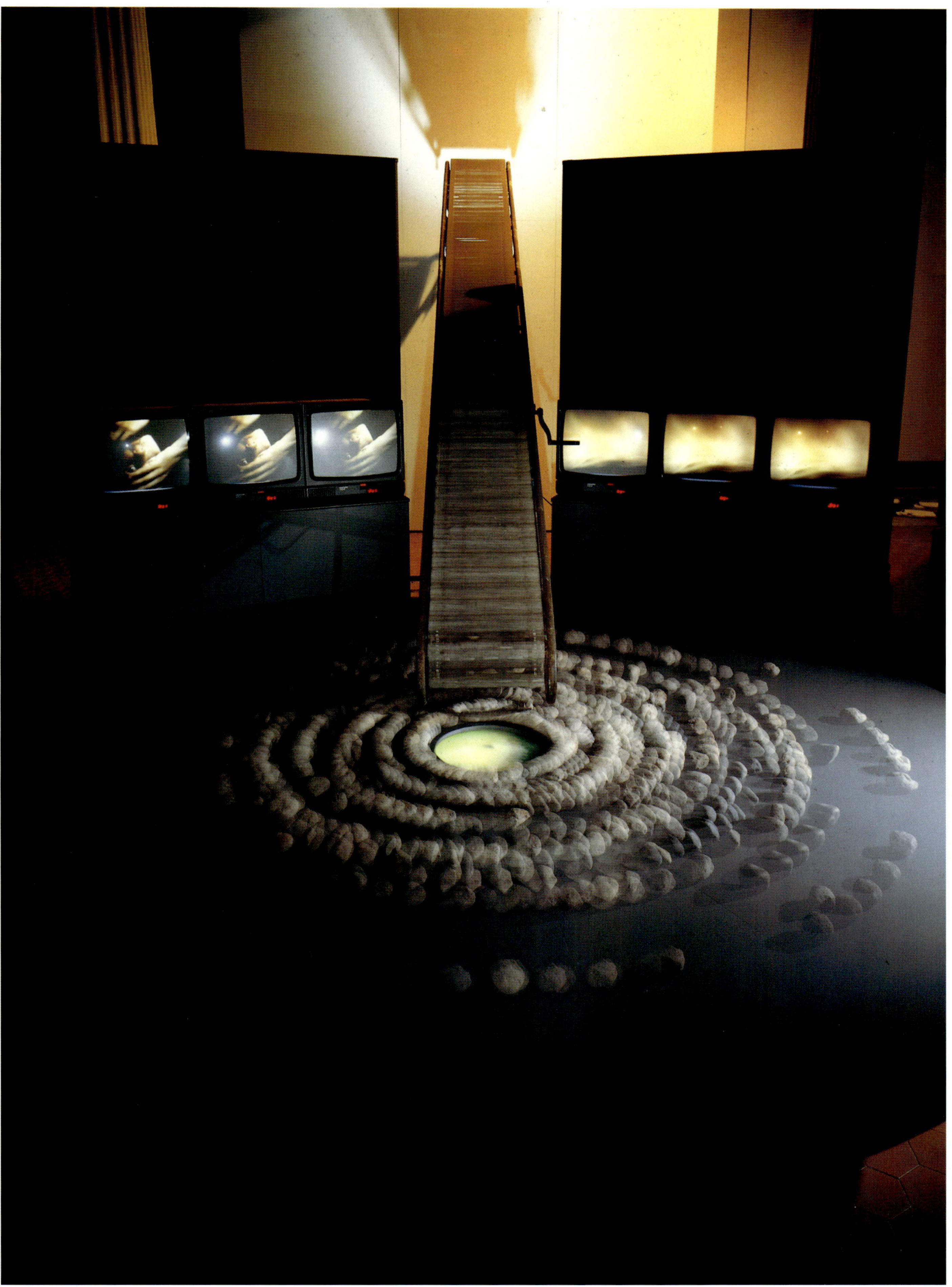

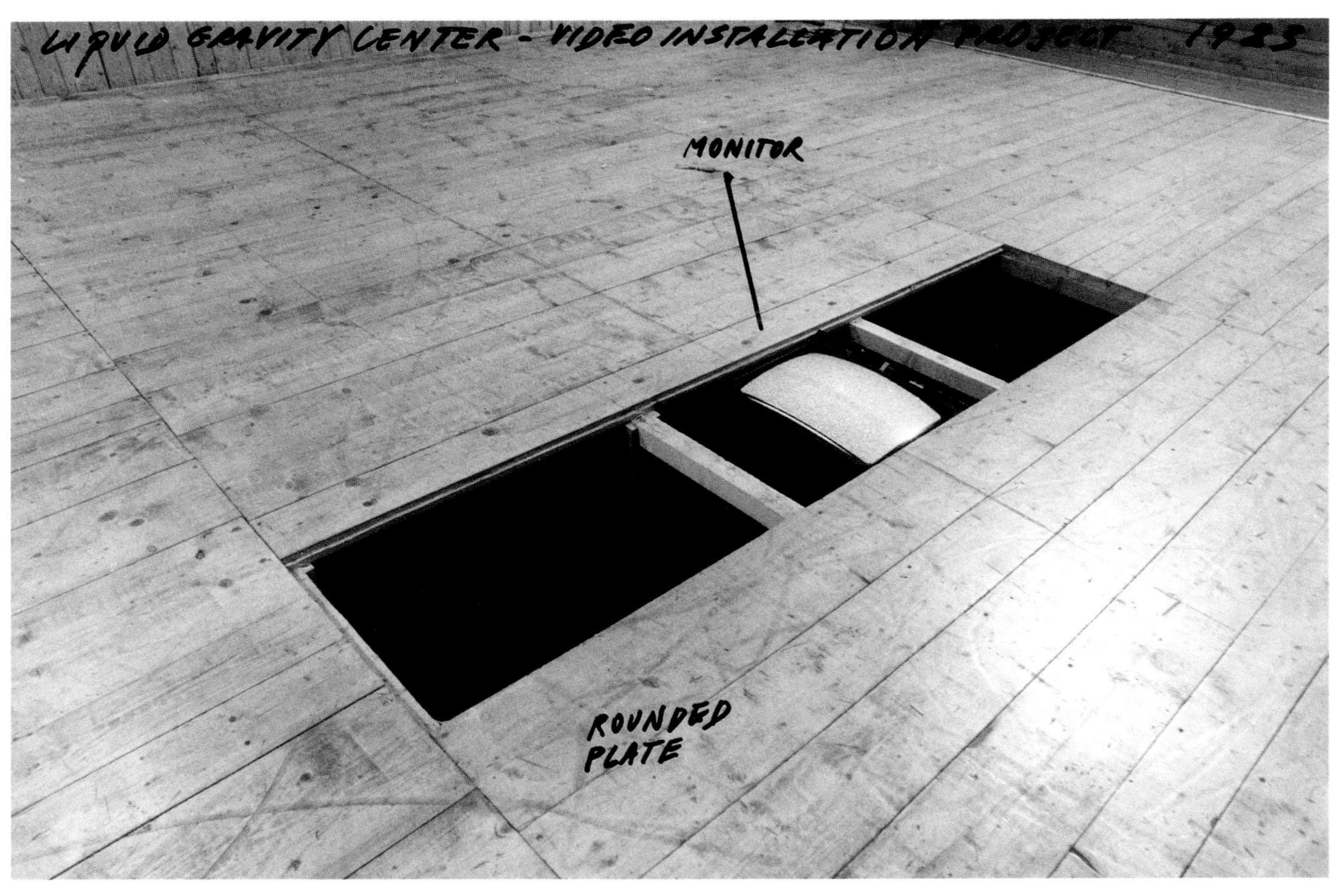

LIQUID GRAVITY CENTER - VIDEO INSTALLATION PROJECT 1983
MONITOR
ROUNDED
PLATE

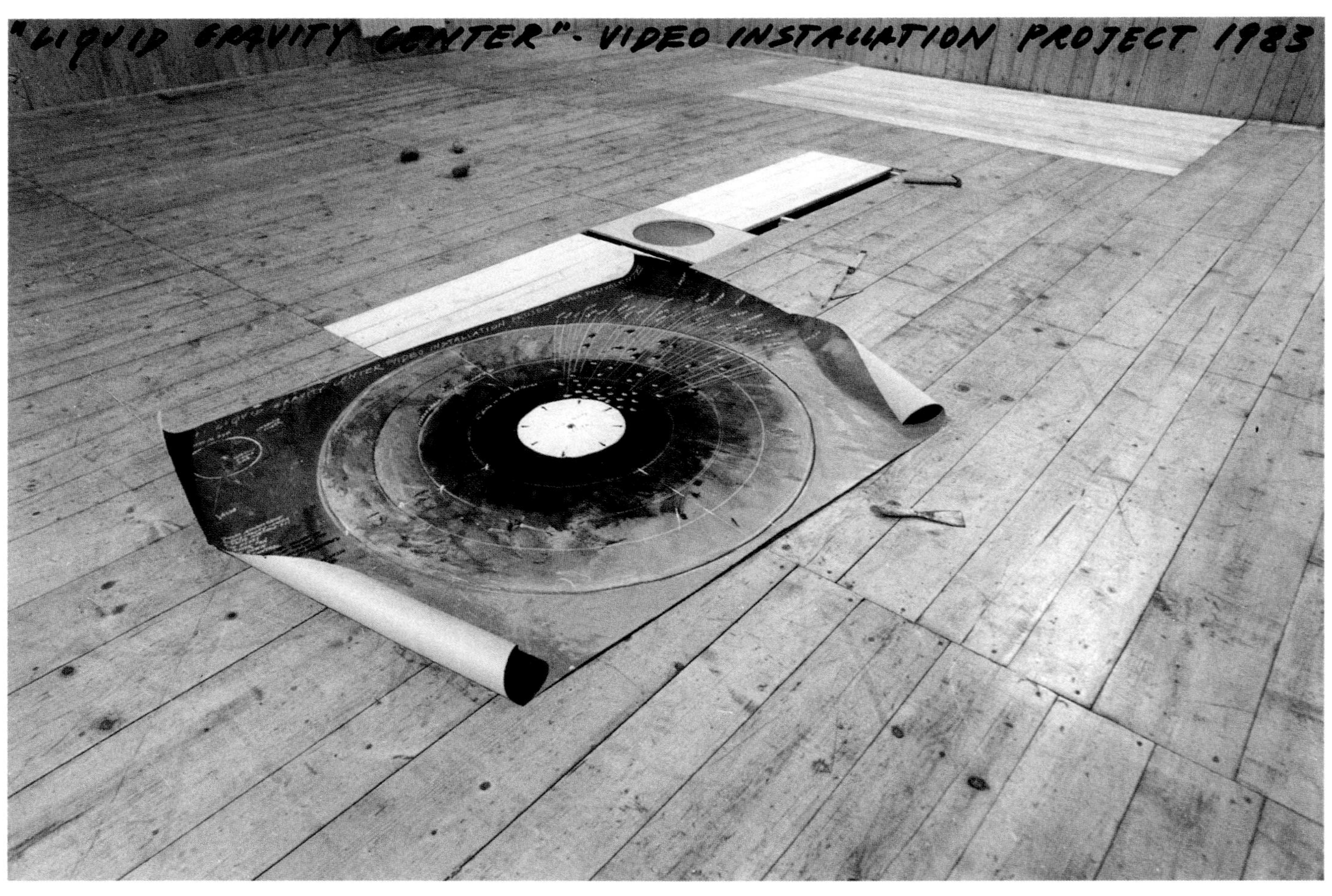

"LIQUID GRAVITY CENTER" - VIDEO INSTALLATION PROJECT 1983

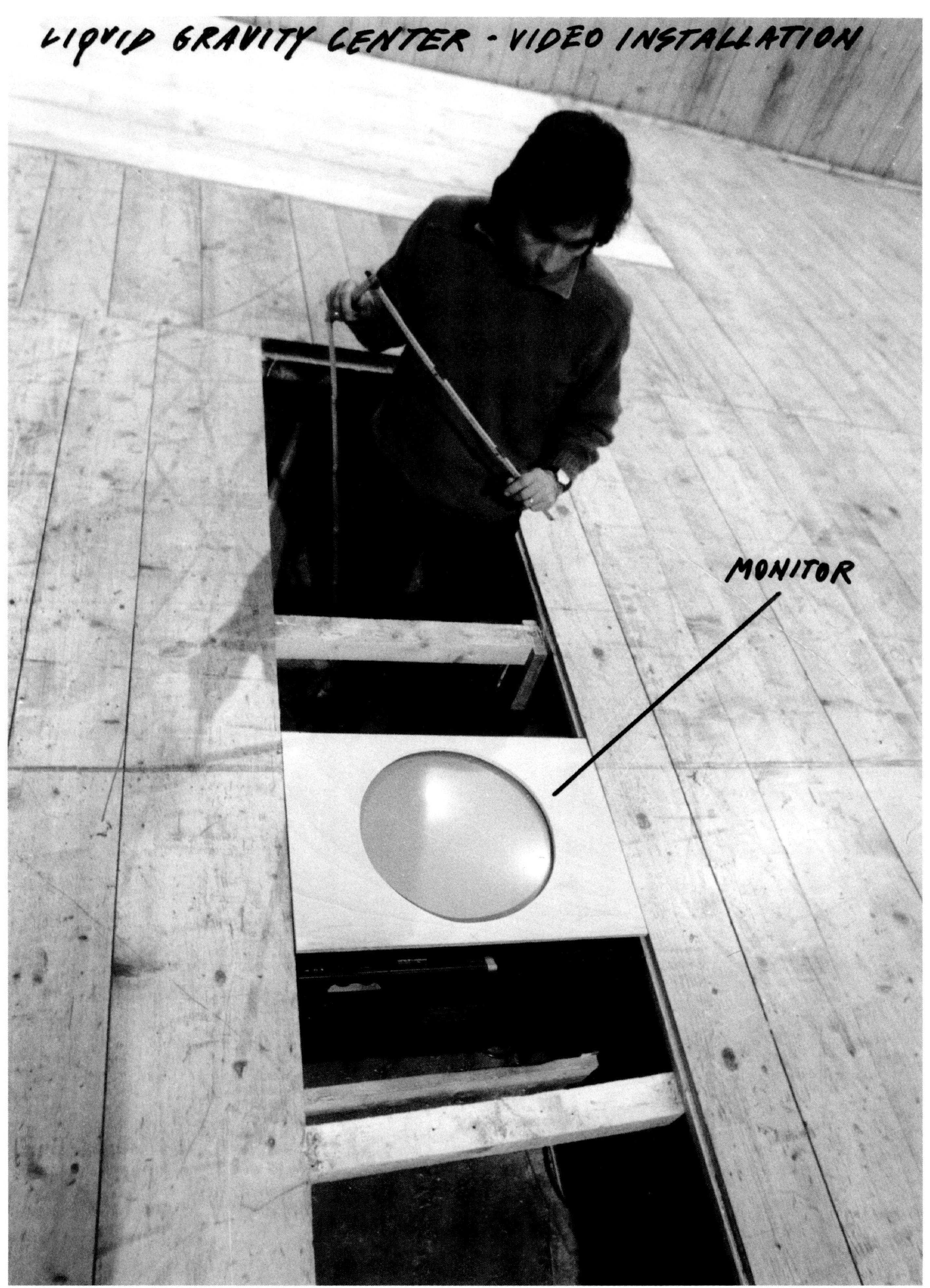
MONITOR

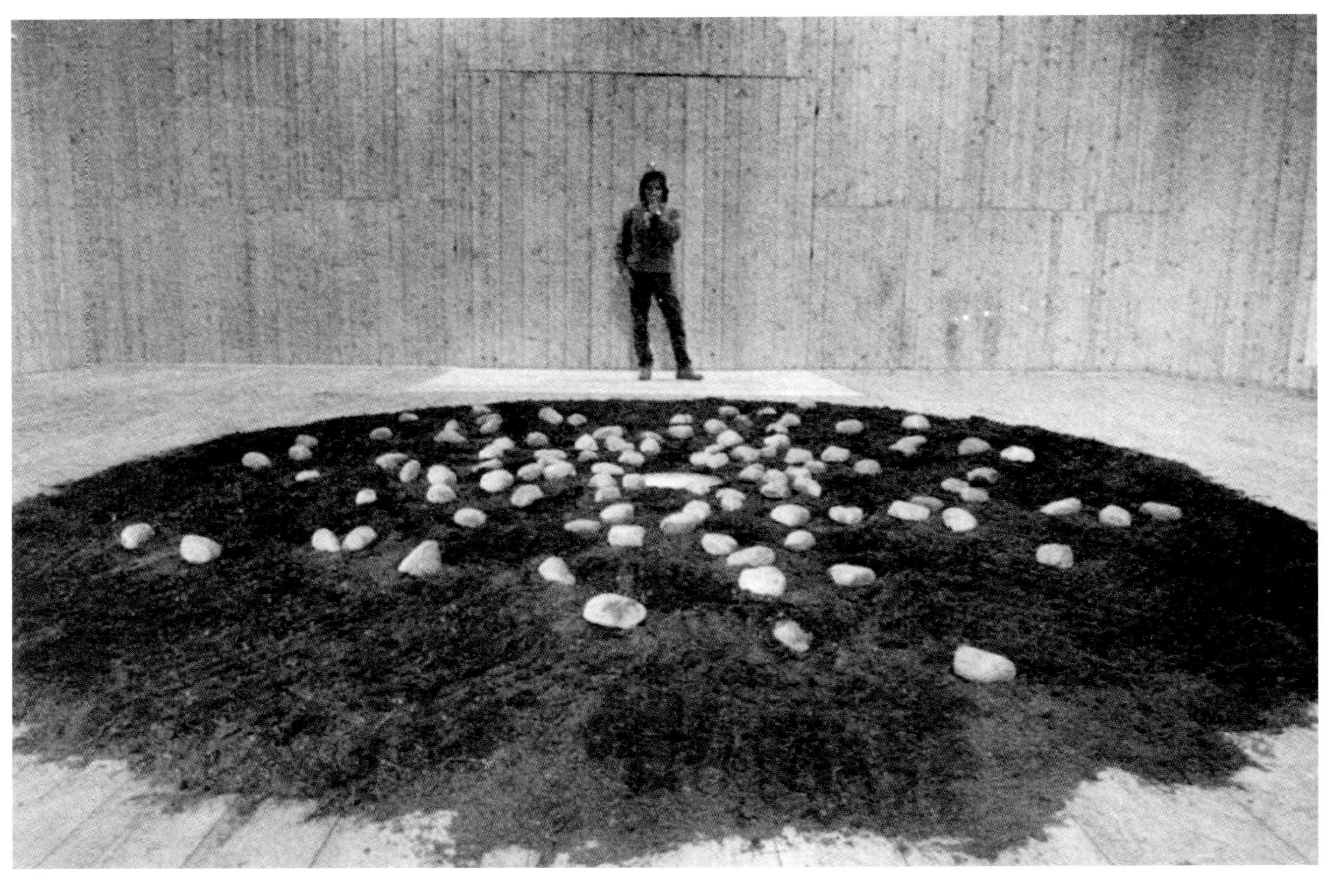

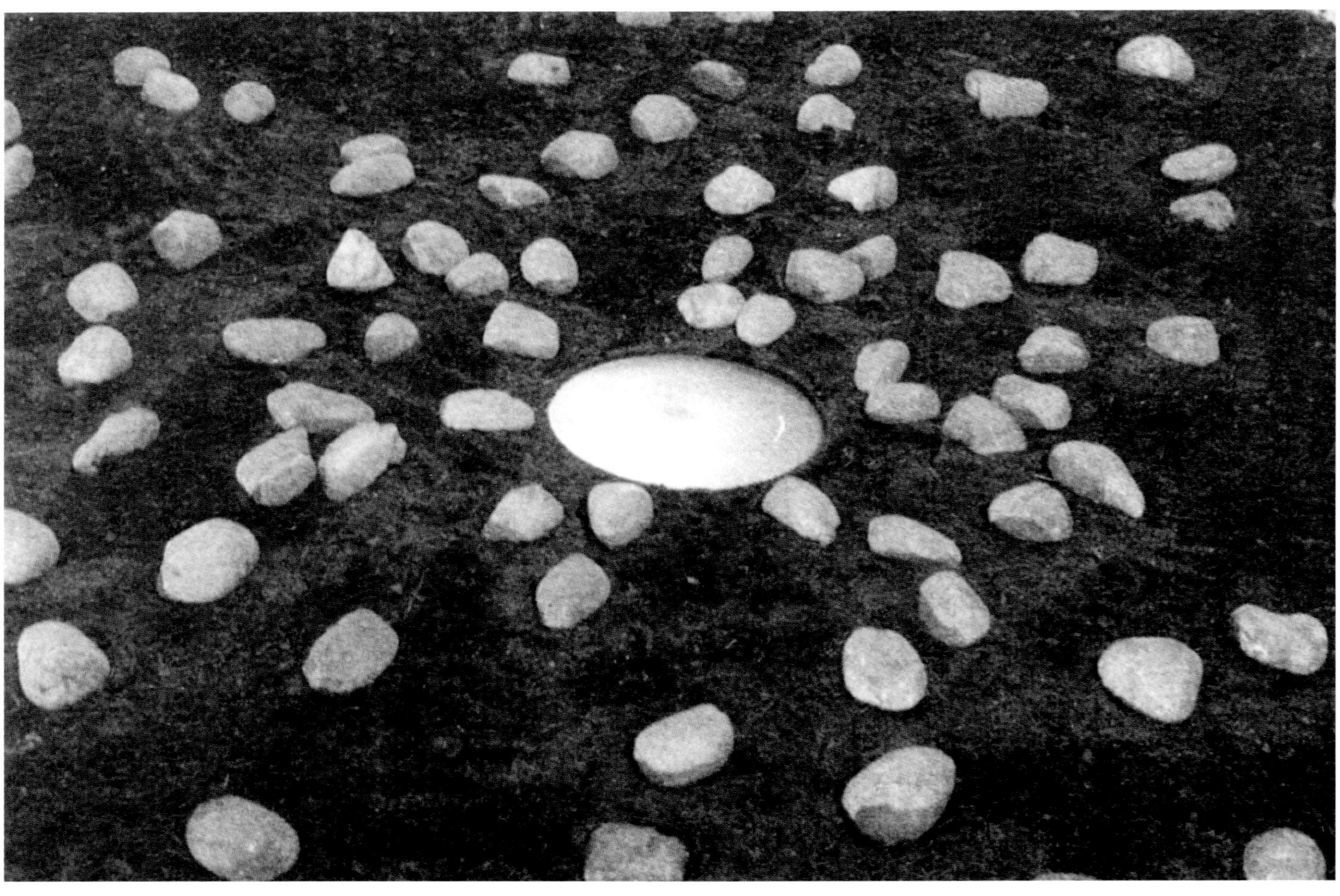

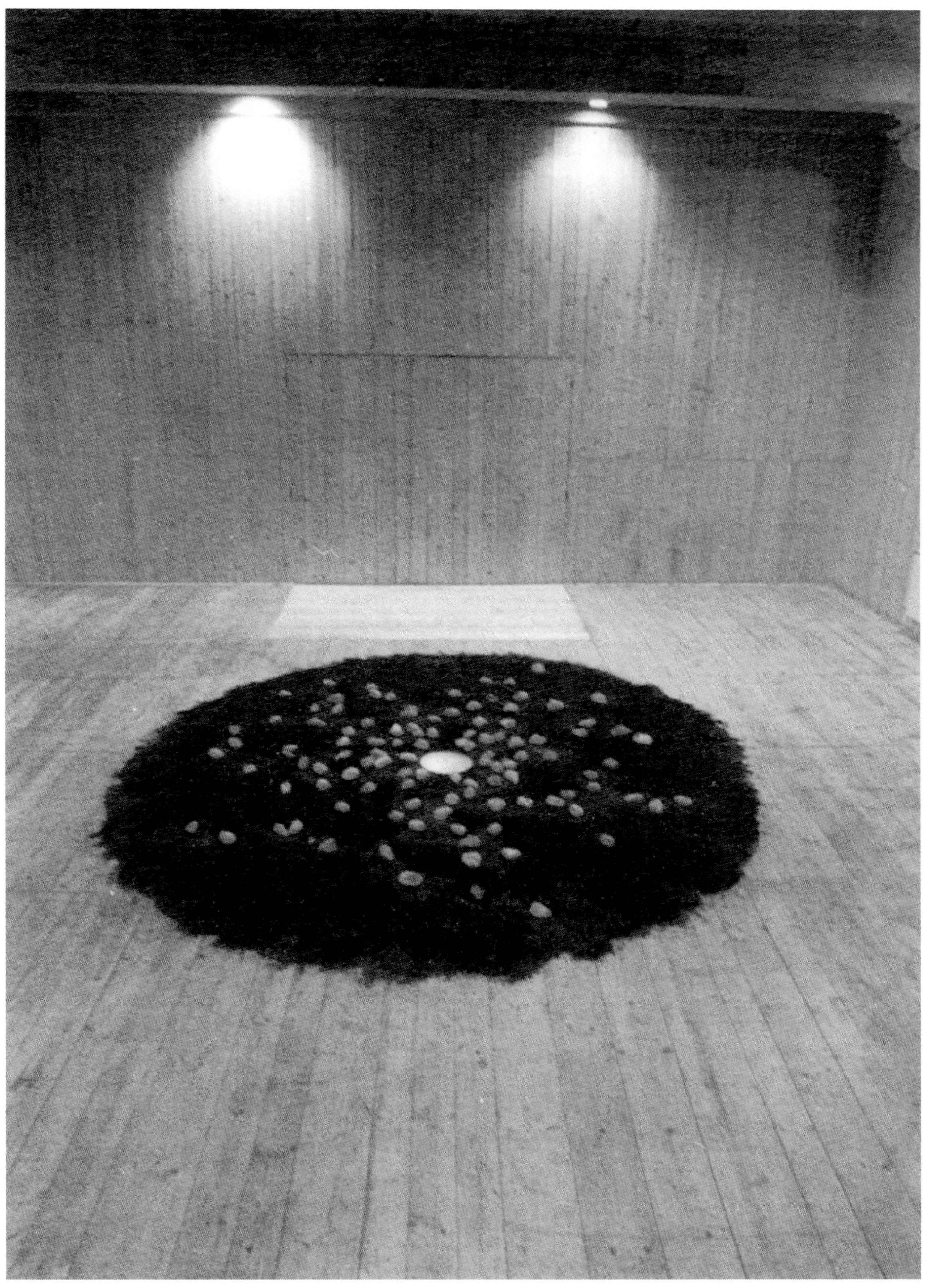

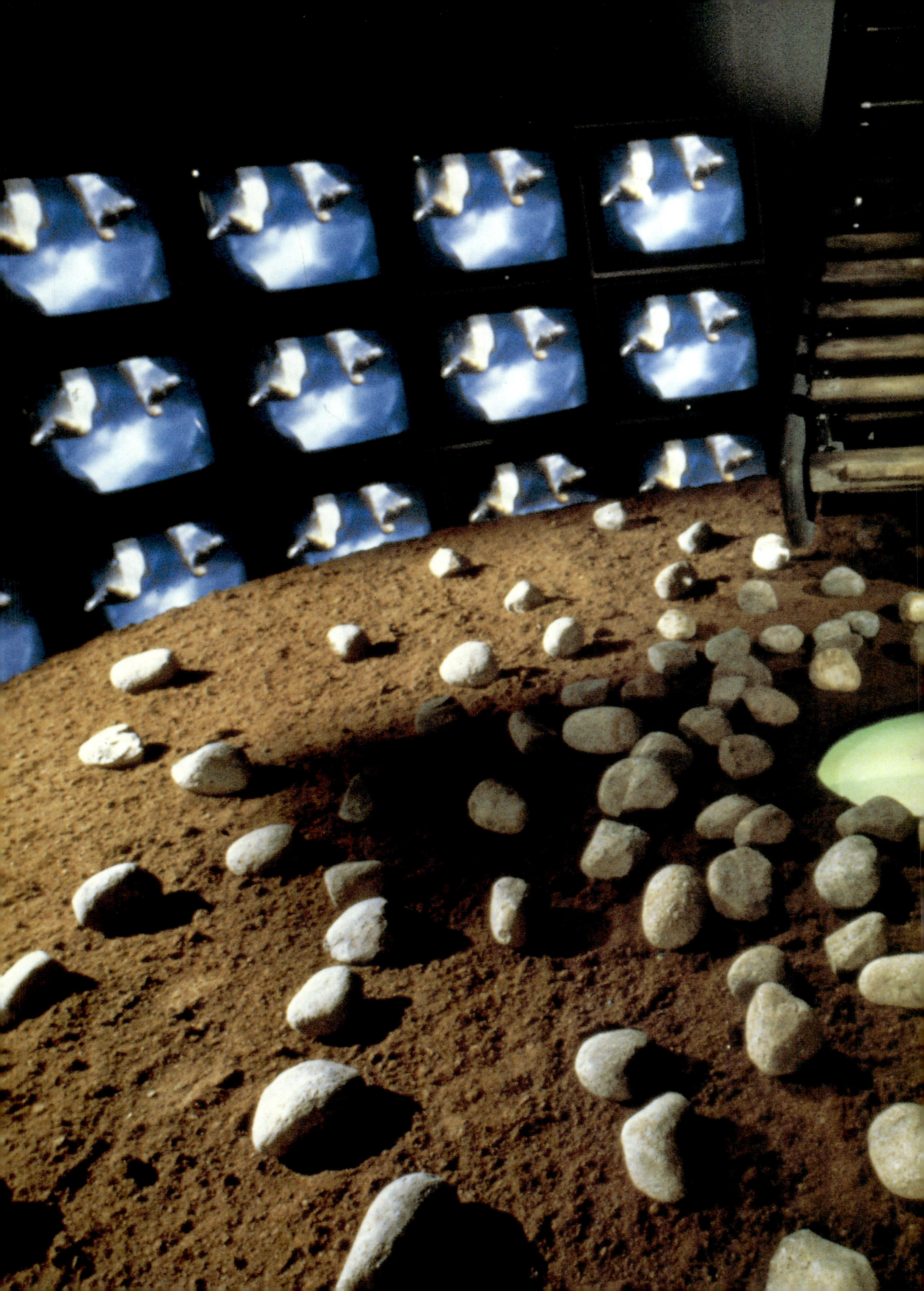

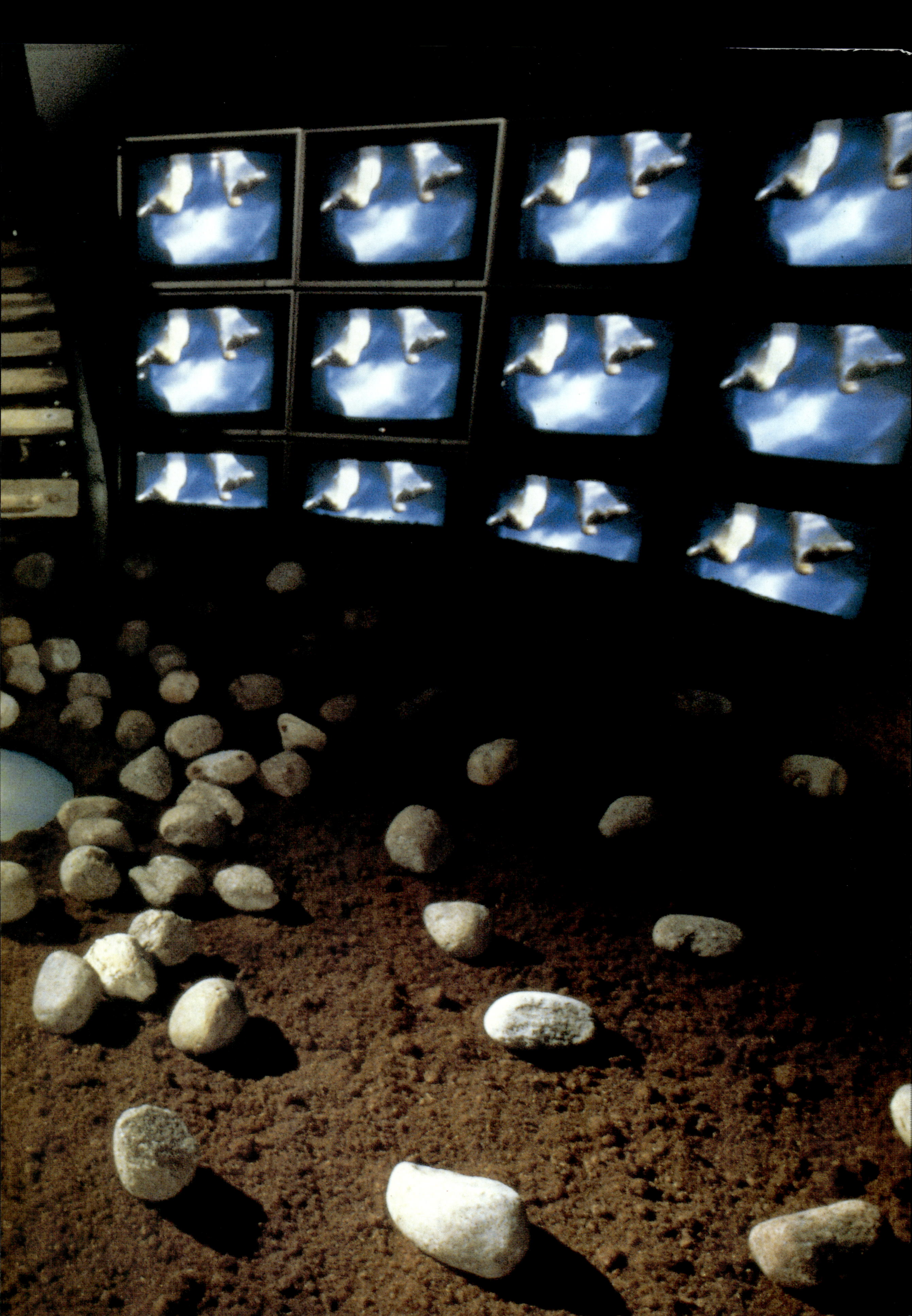

Arbeit von Kassel, in das flüssige Gravitationszentrum transportieren könnte.

Das Basiselement dieser Videoskulptur ist konzentrisch aufgebaut. In der Mitte befindet sich ein in den Boden eingelassener, mit dem Bildschirm nach oben weisender Monitor, dessen Umgebung weiträumig mit einer kreisförmig angelegten Erdschicht bedeckt ist. Auf dieser Erdschicht liegen ungeordnet verstreut, doch zum Zentrum hin dichter werdend, eine Reihe großformatiger Kieselsteine. Der Monitor zeigt, wie kaum anders zu erwarten, Wasser. Doch alle drei Sekunden scheint wie magisch oder durch Gravitation angezogen, einer der umliegenden Steine in das immaterielle Wasser, das flüssige Gravitationszentrum, zu fallen und erzeugt eine Wellenbewegung. Über das Förderband - bei den späteren Versionen - scheinen unaufhörlich weitere imaginäre Steine anzukommen, die dann in das elektronische Wasser plumpsen.

Bei einer weiteren Präsentation ist die Erdoberfläche durch eine kreisrunde, sich drehende Holzscheibe ersetzt worden, und es erscheinen bereits die ersten Monitore mit dem Film *Up Down*. Eine spätere Aufstellung, wohl bis dato die jüngste, zeigt das Ambiente, umgeben von zahlreichen Monitoren, bei denen alles ununterbrochen in Bewegung zu sein scheint. Das Gravitationsfeld zieht alle Energien zum Zentrum hin und setzt alle anderen Kräfte außer Kraft. Die Gravitation ist eine gesetzmäßige Kraft oder Energie, die - wie Eigenschaften oder Dispositionen - selbst nicht sichtbar ist, sondern nur durch ihre Wirkung erkannt werden kann. Eine Kraft, die auf alle Gegenstände wirkt, die eine raumzeitliche Ausdehnung haben.

stones into the liquid gravity centre.

The basic element of this video sculpture is built up concentrically. In its centre, a monitor is embedded in the ground, screen up, its surroundings widely covered with circular layers of soil. Without order, though closer together towards the centre, a number of large rhinestones is placed on the soil. The monitor shows, as can be expected, water. Every three seconds, however, one of the stones seems to drop - magically or pulled by gravitation - into the immaterial water, the liquid centre of gravity, thereby creating waves. In later versions, more and more imaginary stones seem to permanently come down the conveyor-belt, dropping into the electronic water.

In another presentation, the soil is replaced by a circular, turning wooden disk, and the first monitors showing the film Up Down *are added. A later exhibition, up to now probably the latest, shows the ambience surrounded by numerous monitors giving the impression of permanent motion. The field of gravity draws all energies to the centre, eliminating all other forces.*

Gravity itself is a force or energy following natural law, itself - like characteristics or dispositions - not visible, only recognisable through its effects, a force that works on everything that has space/time extend.

si trova un monitor, inserito nel pavimento con lo schermo rivolto verso l'alto, attorno al quale si estende un cerchio costituito da uno strato di terra. Su di esso sono distribuiti, in maniera disordinata ma in numero crescente verso il centro, dei grandi ciottoli. Il monitor presenta, come ovvio, l'acqua. Ma come per magia o attratto dalla forza di gravità ogni tre secondi uno dei sassi vicini sembra cadere nell'acqua immateriale, nel centro del liquido gravitazionale, e provoca un movimento ondoso. Dallo montacarichi - presente nelle versioni successive - arrivano apparentemente altri sassi che precipitano nell'acqua elettronica.

In un'altra versione lo strato di terra è sostituito da un disco ruotante di legno e compaiono i primi monitors con il filmato *Up Down*. Una successiva e più recente versione presenta un ambiente circondato da numerosi monitors in cui tutto sembra in continuo movimento. Il campo gravitazionale attrae tutte le energie verso il suo centro annullando tutte le altre forze.

La gravitazione è una forza, un'energia che è in sé - per disposizione e proprietà - invisibile e riconoscibile solo attraverso l'effetto esercitato su tutta la materia che possiede una dimensione spazio-temporale.

WATER WIND III

83001

GRENOBLE 1983
MUSÉE DE GRENOBLE
83001.1

WASSER WIND III
Videoinstallation 1983
Windmaschine, Kohlehaufen,
30 Monitore, Videorecorder,
bespielte Kassetten

WATER WIND III
Video installation 1983
Heaps of coal, 30 monitors, video
recorder, recorded video cassettes

ACQUA VENTO III
Videoinstallazione 1983
Macchina di vento, mucchi di
carbone, 30 monitors, vhs,
cassette registrate

Die dritte Version von *Water Wind* zeigt eine große Anzahl von Monitoren, wie bisher mit der Bildschirmfläche nach oben auf den Rücken gelegt, doch diesmal nicht in Heu, sondern in kleine Haufen von Kohlestücken eingebettet. Am Ende des langgestreckten Raumes in Grenoble befindet sich ein Ventilator, der das elektronische Wasser auf den Monitoren durch seinen Wind in Bewegung zu bringen scheint.

The third version of Water Wind *shows a large number of monitors, as before with screens upwards on their back, this time, however, not embedded in hay but in small piles of pieces of coal. At the end of the long room in Grenoble a ventilator is positioned that seems to move the electronic water on the screens with its airflow.*

La terza versione di *Water Wind* è costituita da un grande numero di monitors con gli schermi sempre rivolti verso l'alto ma non più inseriti in un pagliaio bensì in piccoli mucchi di carbone. Alla fine del lungo corridoio della mostra a Grenoble si trova il ventilatore che apparentemente agita con il suo vento l'acqua elettronica dei monitors.

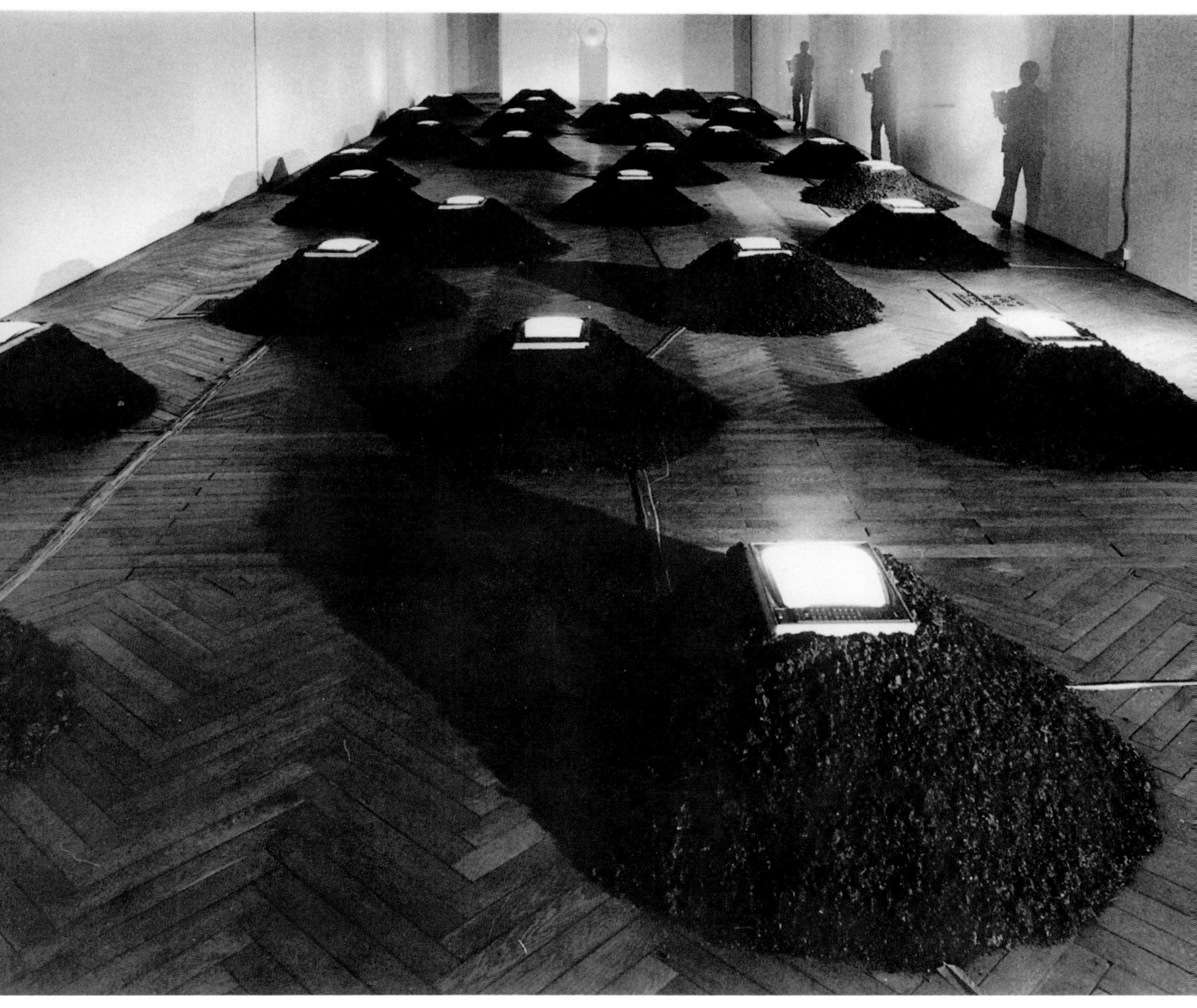

SOFT STEEL

84001

VILLENEUVE D'ASCQ 1984
Musée du Nord
84001.1

WEICHER STAHL
Videoinstallation 1984
Struktur aus Holz und Stahl,
Element aus Gußeisen, Eisenrohr,
1 Monitor, Videorecorder,
bespielte Kassette

SOFT STEEL
Video installation 1984
Structure of wood and steel, cast-
iron element, iron tube, 1 monitor,
video recorder, recorded video
cassette

ACCIAIO MOLLE
Videoinstallazione 1984
Struttura in legno, acciaio,
elemento in ghisa, pala di ferro,
1 monitor, vhs, cassetta registrata

Ähnlich wie bei dem *Arco Liqui-do*, dem *Flüssigen Bogen*, wird hier eine starre Materie in der Oberfläche des Wassers im Bildmonitor scheinbar verflüssigt: *Soft Steel.* Der Monitor ist mit Stahlplatten umstellt, er selbst scheint auf dem Kreissegment einer Stahlplatte zu stehen. In seiner Umgebung sind weitere Fragmente von einem denkbaren Kreis in Stahl um ihn herum gruppiert.

Erste Skizzen und Zeichnungen aus dem Jahre 1981 finden sich noch unter dem Titel *Sulla Riflessione (Über die Reflexion).* Doch darf diese Videoskulptur bereits als vorausschauend auf das zeitlich bald folgende Environment *Bronx* und die Videoskulptur *Winner* verstanden werden.

Here, similar to Arco Liquido, *the* Liquid Arch, *inflexible matter on the screen's water surface seems to be liquidified:* Soft Steel. *The monitor itself is surrounded by steel plates, and seems to stand on a circular segment of a steel plate. Around it, further fragments of an imaginable circle of steel are placed.*

First sketches and drawings from the year 1981 can be found under the title Sulla riflessione (On Reflection). *This video sculpture may, however, be considered as a preview of the soon to follow environment* Bronx *as well as the video sculpture* Winner.

Come in *Arco Liquido* anche in *Soft Steel* una materia rigida viene apparentemente liquefatta nella superficie dell'acqua di un monitor. Quest'ultimo è circondato da lastre di acciaio e sembra appoggiato su di un segmento di cerchio di un'altra lastra di acciaio. Nelle sue vicinanze sono raggruppati ulteriori segmenti di un immaginabile cerchio d'acciaio.

Primi schizzi e disegni del 1981 per il progetto sono ancora subordinati al titolo *Sulla riflessione,* ma si può già considerare questa videoscultura come anticipatrice del successivo environment *Bronx* e della videoscultura *Winner.*

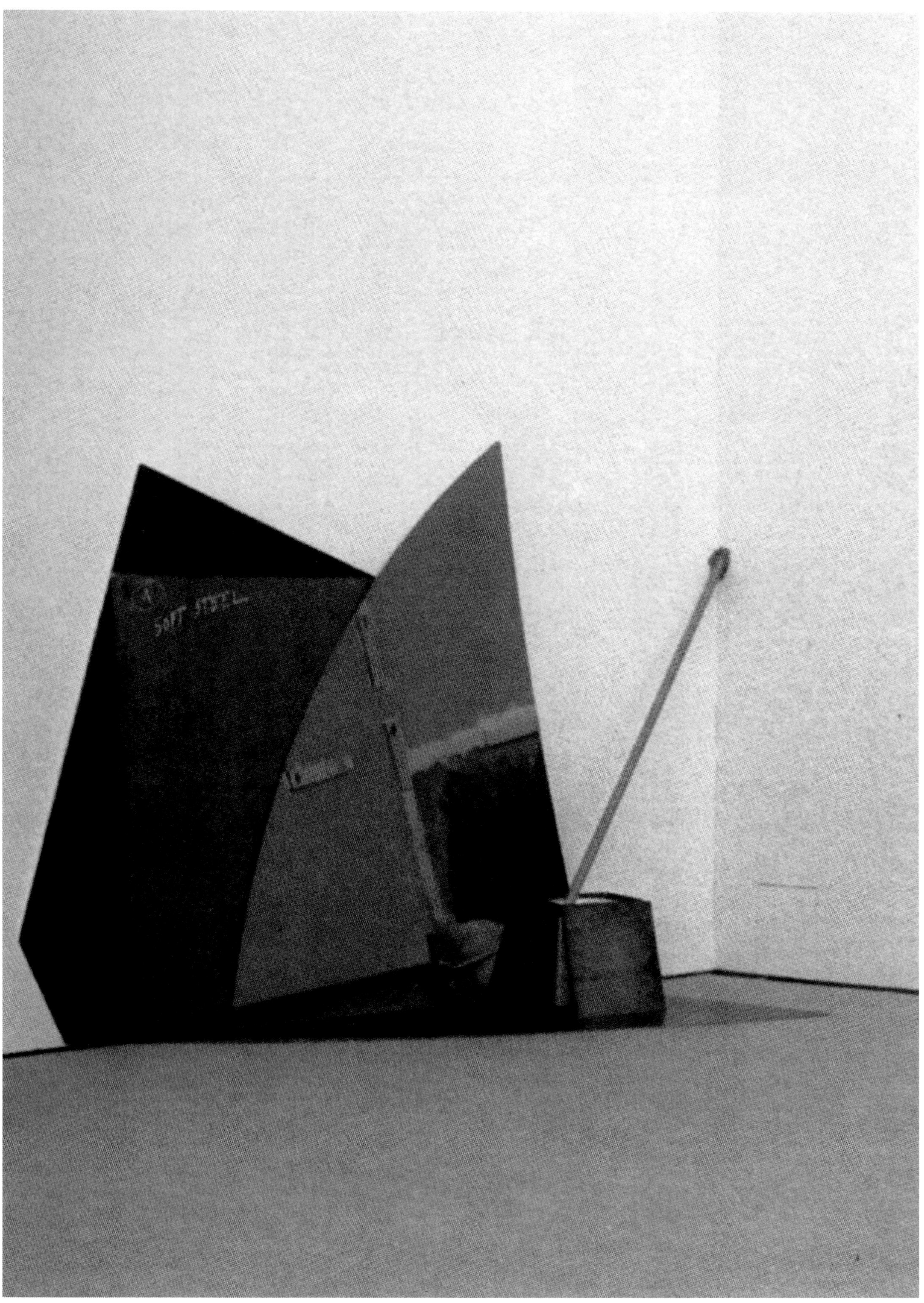

SOFT STEEL

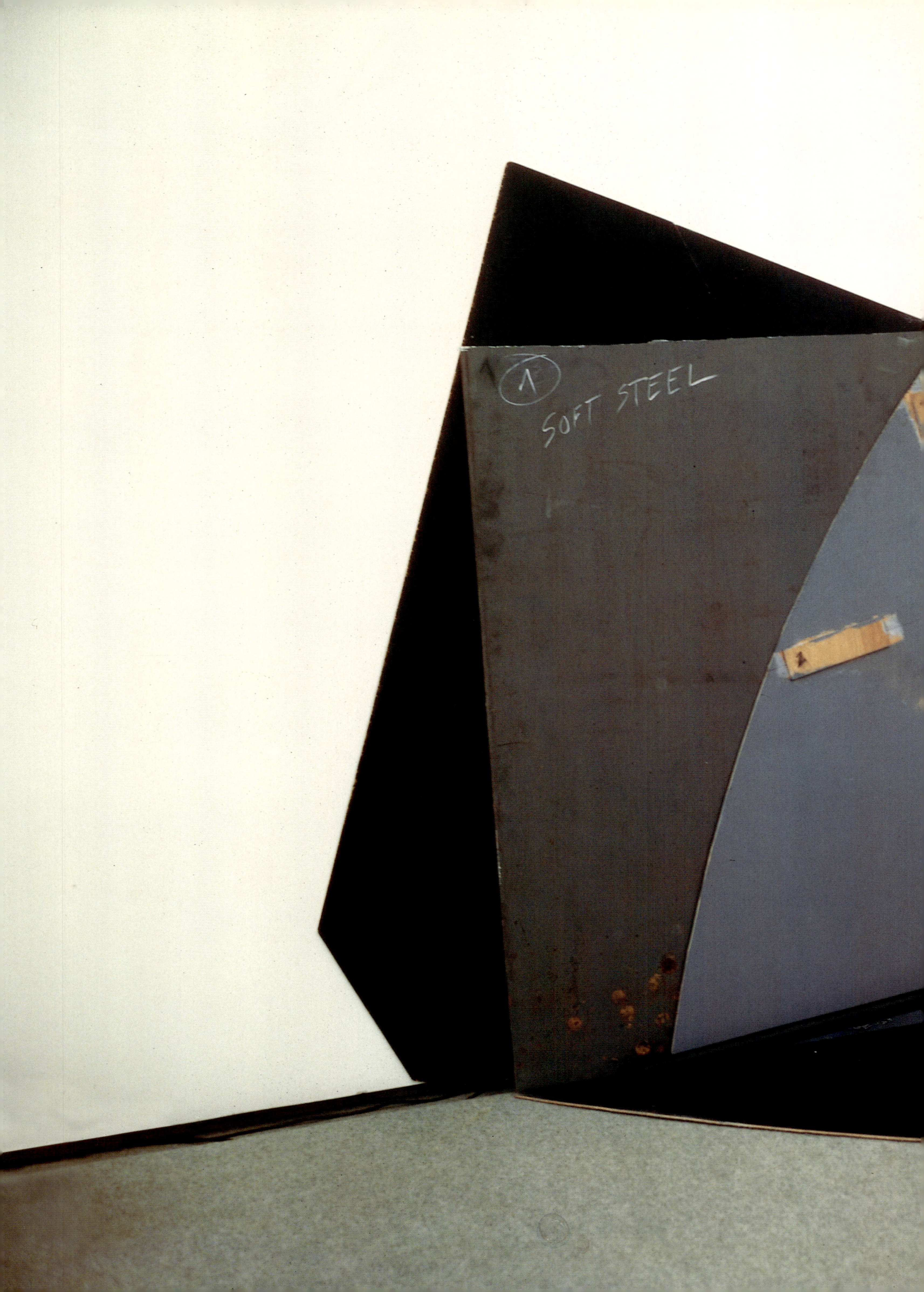

SOFT STEEL

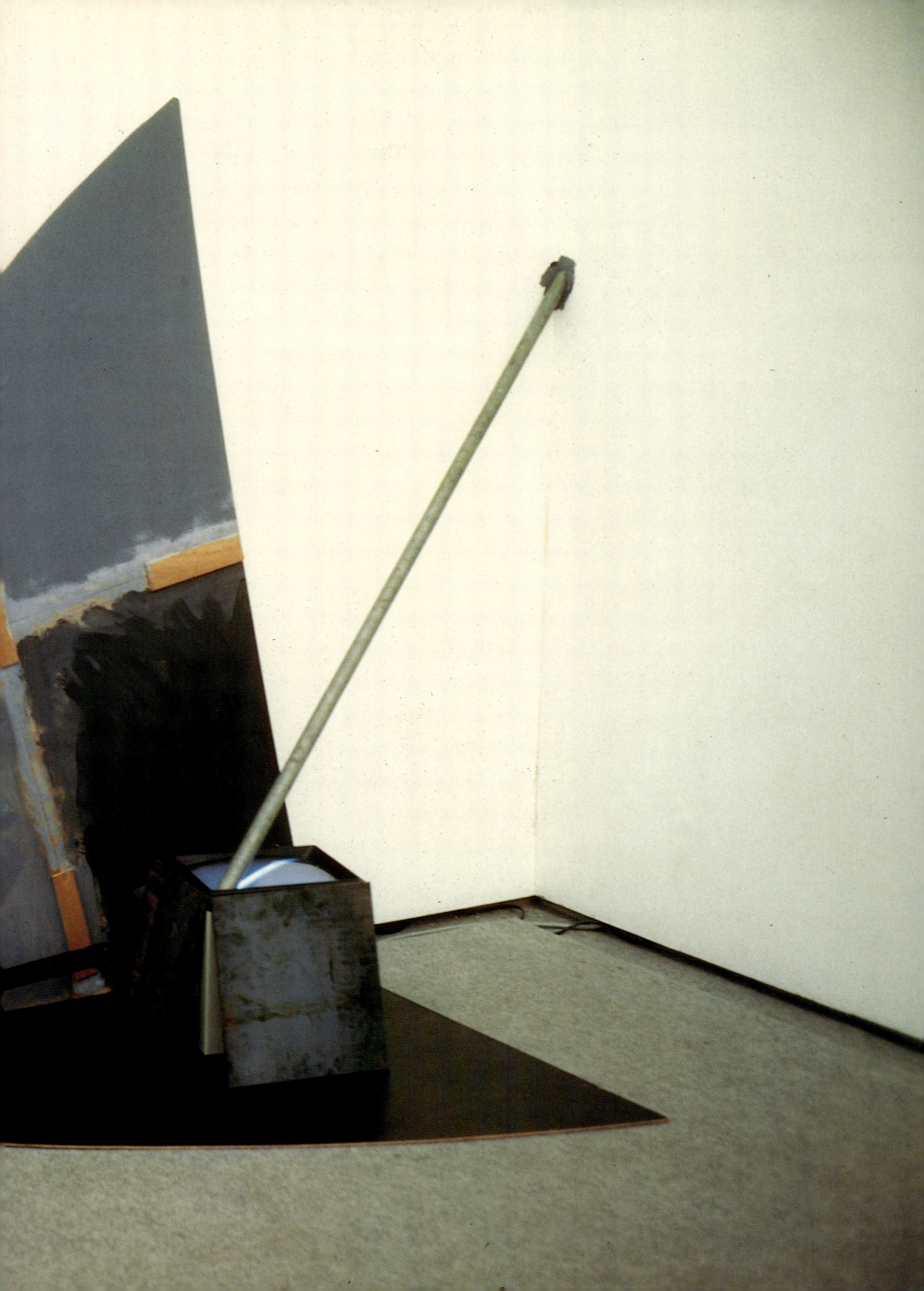

WATER WIND IV

84002

VILLENEUVE D'ASCQ 1984
Musée du Nord
84002.1

FERRARA 1984
Museo Palazzo dei Diamanti
84002.2

MILANO 1985
Rotonda della Besana
84002.3

MADRID 1988
Museo Español de Arte Contemporaneo
84002.4

DORTMUND 1993
Museum am Ostwall
84002.5

WASSER WIND IV
Videoskulptur 1984
Holzkonstruktion, Ventilator,
mechanische Teile, Monitor,
Videorecorder, bespielte Kassette,
Tonaufzeichnung

WATER WIND IV
Video sculpture 1984
Wood, mechanical parts, monitor,
video recorder, recorded video
cassette, soundrecording

ACQUA VENTO IV
Videoscultura 1984
Legno, ventilatore, parte
meccanica in movimento,
1 monitor, 1 vhs, 1 cassetta
registrata e sincronizzata sul
movimento, sonoro

Die vierte und bis dato letzte Version von *Water Wind* zeigt ein inzwischen durchgreifend verändertes Präsentationsbild. Zu sehen ist eine Rampe mit einer Schiene, auf der sich ein hölzernes Gehäuse mit eingebautem, vertikal gesetzten Monitor auf und ab bewegt. Auf der dem Bildschirm gegenüberliegenden Seite ist ein Ventilator angebracht. In einer bestimmten zeitlichen Abfolge bewegt sich das Gehäuse mit dem Bildschirm-Monitor auf den Ventilator zu. Zu sehen ist ein Wasserglas, dreiviertel gefüllt mit Wasser. Je näher sich der Monitor über die schräge Rampe dem laufenden Ventilator entgegen bewegt, ihm näher kommt, desto mehr wird das elektronische Wasser im Trinkglas in Unruhe versetzt. Ein realer Wind scheint auf das Abbild der Realität zu wirken. Ein außenstehendes Element modifiziert das elektronische Abbild. Sobald sich das elektronische Wasser in dem Trinkglas auf dem Monitor von dem Ventilator weg bewegt, kehrt wieder Ruhe im Glas ein, so, als sei niemals eine Bewegung gewesen, als sei nichts geschehen.

The fourth and, up to now, latest version of Water Wind *is presented in a thoroughly changed form. It shows a ramp with a rail on which a wooden box with a built-in, vertically positioned monitor moves up and down. A ventilator is placed opposite to the screen. In fixed sequences the casing with the TV monitor moves towards the ventilator. A glass, three-quarters filled with water, can be seen. The closer the monitor approaches the ventilator, the more the water in the glass moves. A real wind, an element from without, seems to work on the image of reality, and to modify it. As soon as the electronic water in the glass on the monitor moves away from the ventilator again, quiet returns to the glass, so as if there had never been any motion, as if nothing had happened.*

La quarta e finora ultima versione di *Water* si presenta in una maniera decisamente modificata. Sul binario di una rampa inclinata si muove una scatola di legno con, al suo interno, un monitor verticale che presenta un bicchiere d'acqua riempito per tre quarti. Al lato opposto dello schermo è collocato un ventilatore. Con una certa sequenza temporale la scatola lignea con il monitor si avvicina al ventilatore. Più il monitor si avvicina al ventilatore, più risulta agitata l'acqua elettronica del bicchiere. Un vento reale sembra agire su di una immagine della realtà; un elemento esteriore modifica l'immagine elettronica. Appena l'acqua elettronica del bicchiere nel monitor si allontana dal ventilatore essa si calma come se non ci fosse mai stato movimento, come se niente fosse successo.

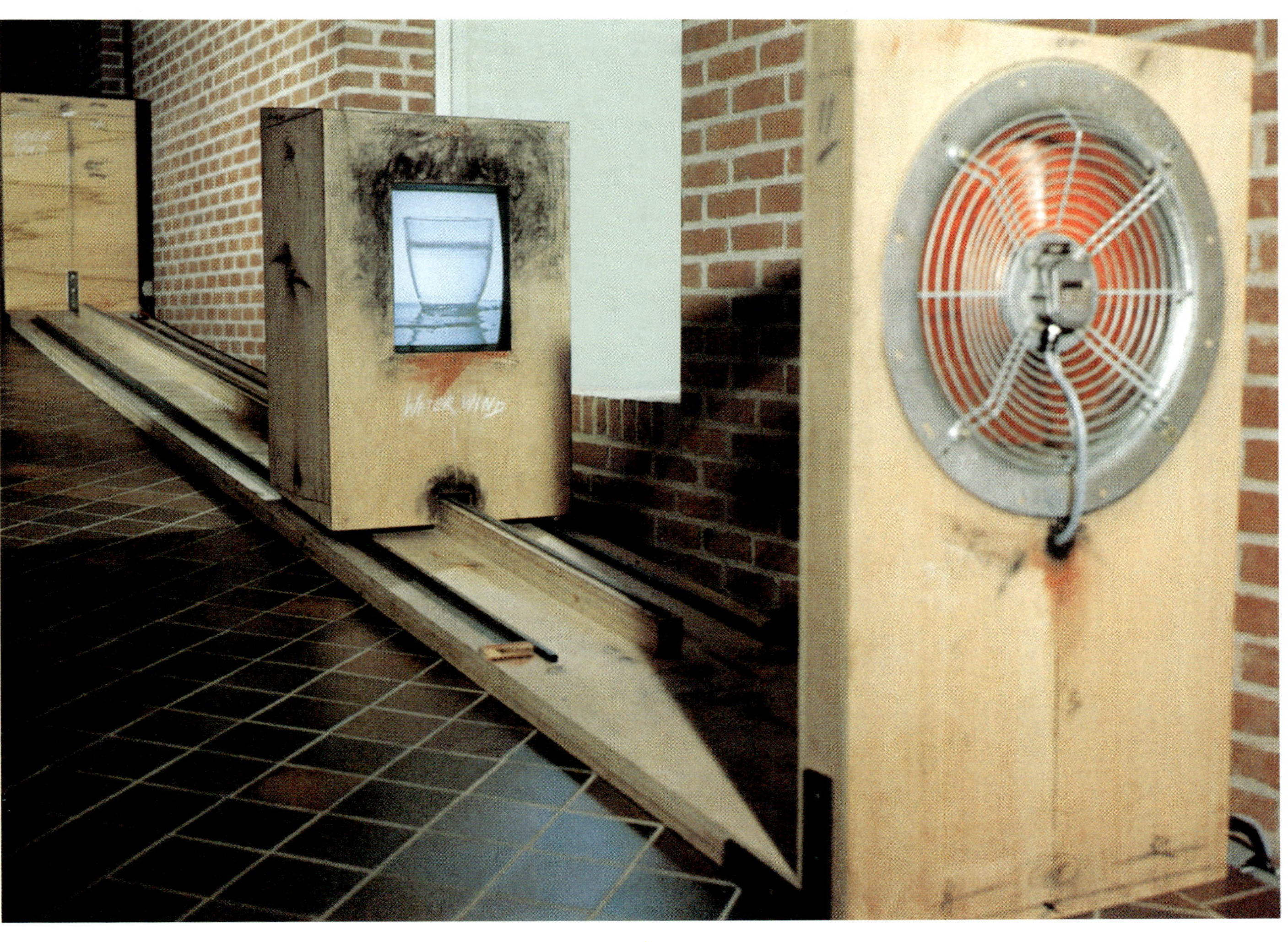

WATER WIND

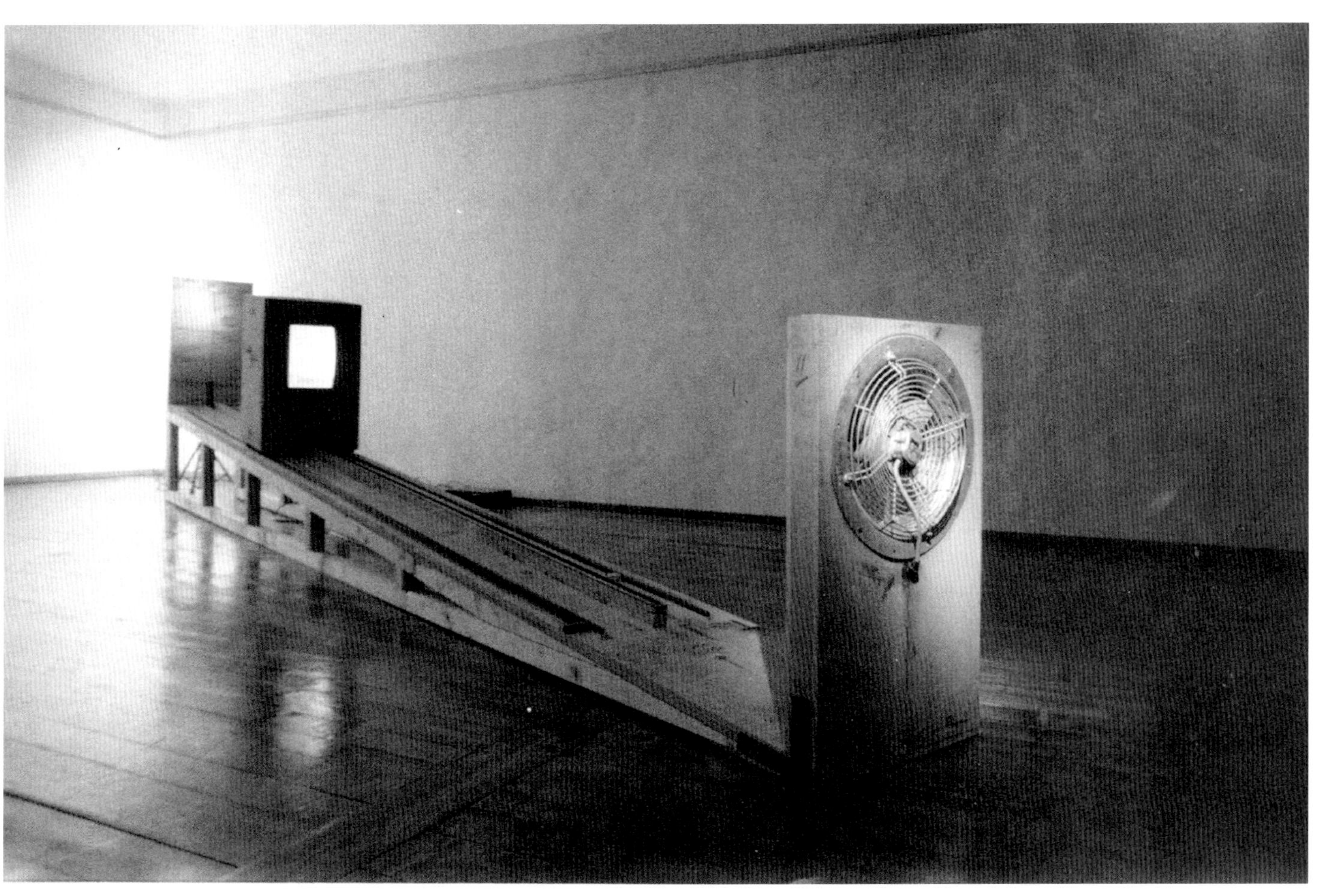

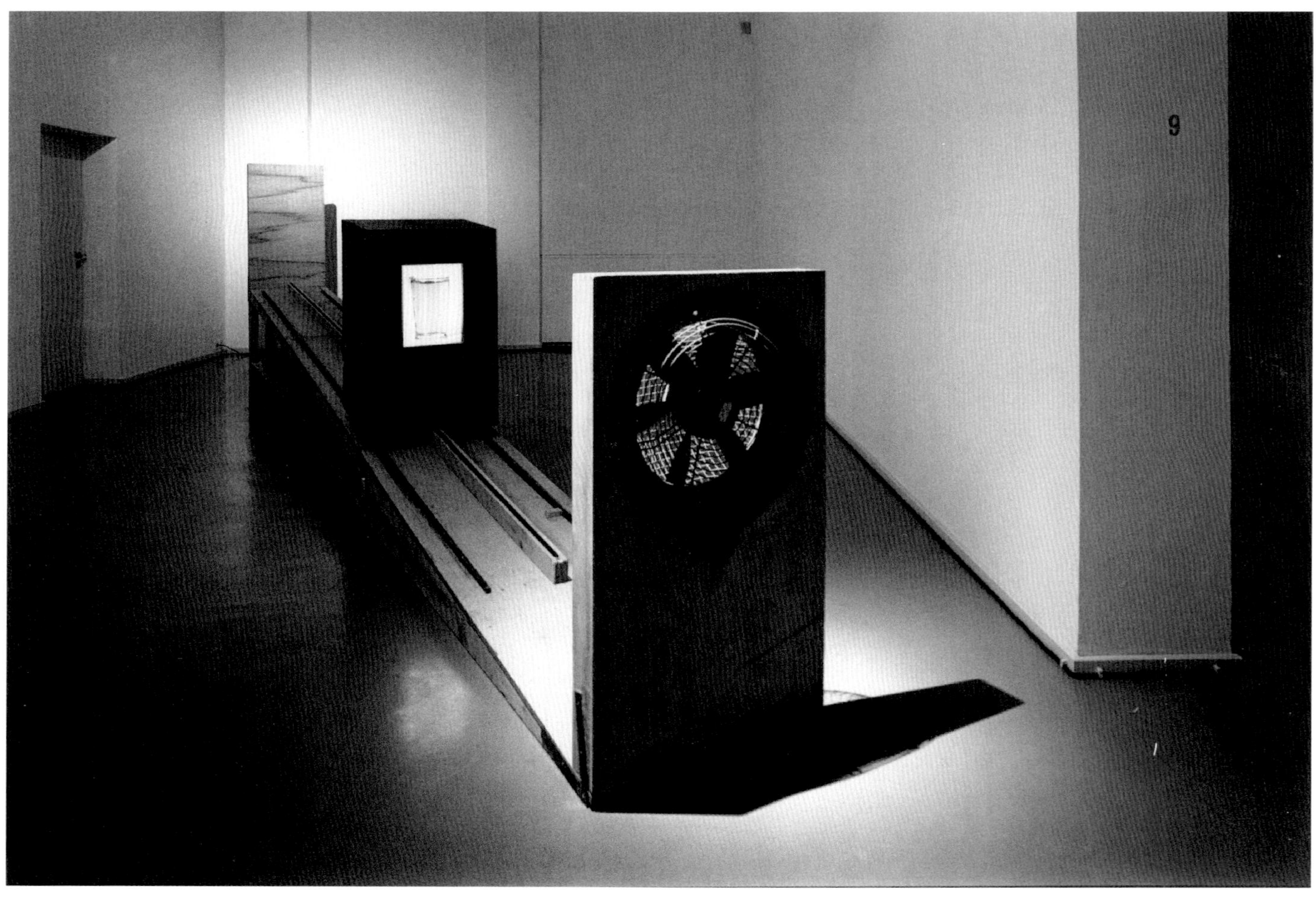

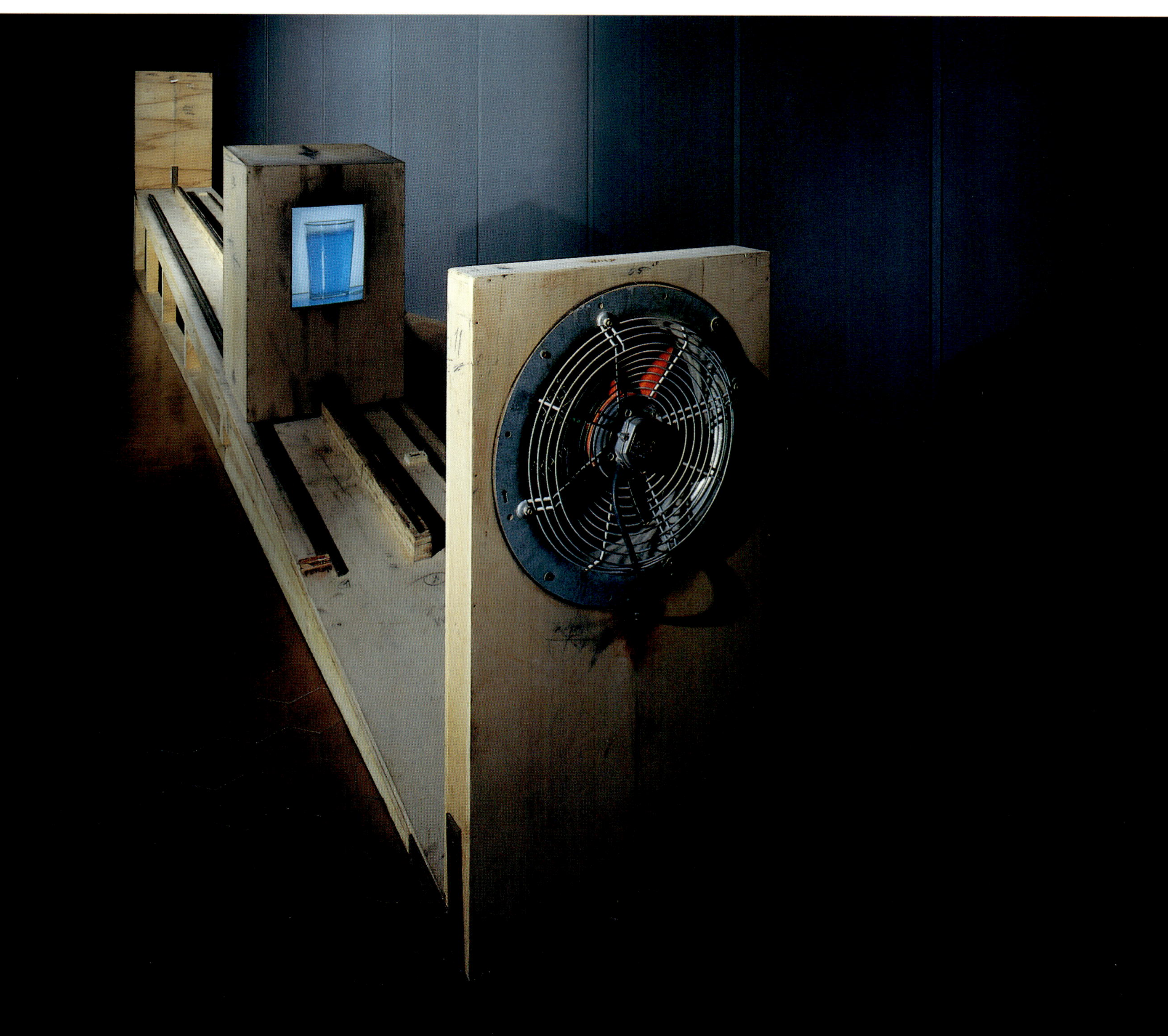

VIDEO GOING

84003

VILLENEUVE D'ASCQ 1984
Musée du Nord
84003.1

MILANO 1985
Rotonda della Besana
84003.2

VIDEO GOING
Videoinstallation 1984
Runde Stahlpiste (∅ 600 cm),
2 Gehäuse aus Holz und Stahl mit
mechanischem Antrieb, die sich
selbständig auf der Piste bewegen,
2 Monitore, 2 Videorecorder mit
drahtloser Übertragung, Kassetten

VIDEO GOING
Video installation 1984
Platform of steel elements,
2 structures of wood and steel with
automatic motion, 2 monitors,
2 video recorders, wireless
transmission, cassettes

VIDEO CAMMINANDO
Videoinstallazione 1984
Pista magnetica in ferro,
2 televisori robotizzati, strumenti
d'alimentazione, strutture in
legno e in ferro, mecchaniche di
movimento, cassette registrate,
trasmissione via etere

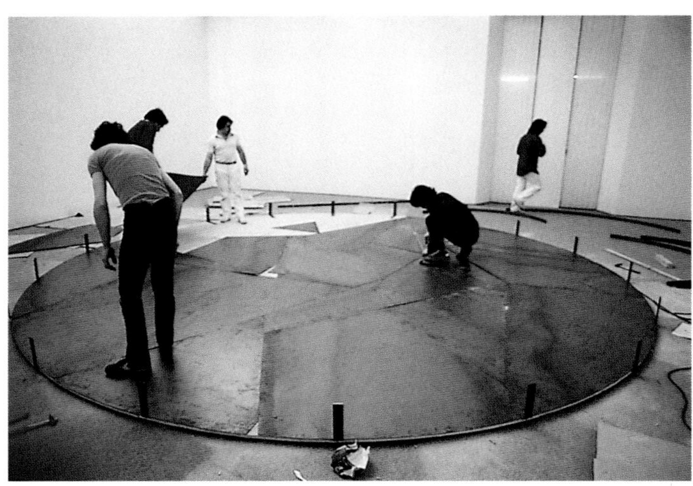
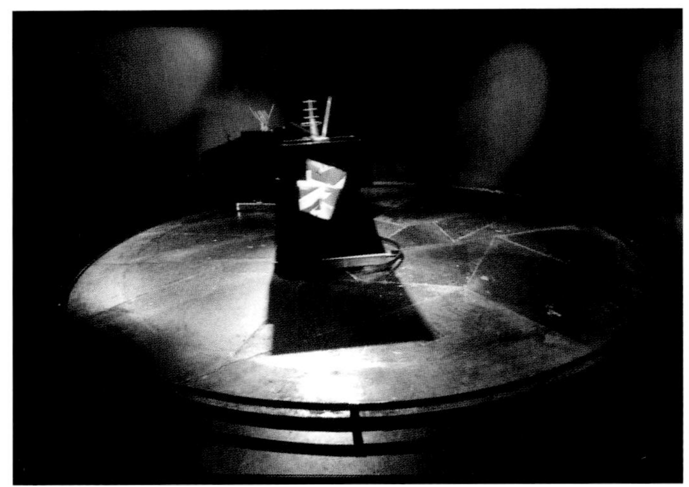

Auf einer kreisrunden Stahlplatte, zusammengesetzt aus mehreren einzelnen Elementen, sind zwei Monitore in postmodernen und zugleich futuristisch anmutenden Gehäusen präsentiert. Sie erscheinen wie zwei roboterartige Wesen und tatsächlich bewegen sie sich selbständig auf ihrer Plattform - *Video Going*. In den beiden Monitoren läuft zeitversetzt ein komplexes Programm kubistisch aufgelöster Wasserfälle ab, so daß das an sich weiche, veränderliche Wasser, das keine feste Form besitzt, plötzlich einen konstruktiven Charakter bekommt. Wegen der ständigen Positionsänderung der Roboter-Monitore kann der Betrachter jeweils nur eine Momentaufnahme einer kubistischen Bewegung sehen.

On a circular steel plate, combined from several elements, two monitors are presented in casings that appear post-modern and at the same time futuristic. They look like two robot-like beings, and indeed, they are moving automatically on the platform - Video Going. The two monitors show, at different times, a complex program of cubism-like dissolved waterfalls, so that the in itself soft, variable water that has no fixed form, all of a sudden takes on constructive characteristics. The robot monitors change continuously their position, so that the spectator can only get a glimpse of a cubist movement at a time.

The reference to cubism is relevant here, because it contains

Su di una lastra d'acciaio circolare composta da vari elementi singoli vengono presentati due monitors inseriti in strutture postmoderne e, nello stesso momento, futuristiche che appaiono come esseri robot e davvero camminano sulla loro pista - *Video Going*. Sugli schermi si vede un complesso programma di cascate stilizzate in forme cubistiche, in modo tale che l'acqua, in sè morbida, mutabile e senza forme rigide, acquista un carattere costruttivo. In causa del cambiamento permanente delle posizioni dei monitors robot, lo spettatore riesce a vedere solamente un'istantanea di un movimento cubista.

Il riferimento al cubismo è

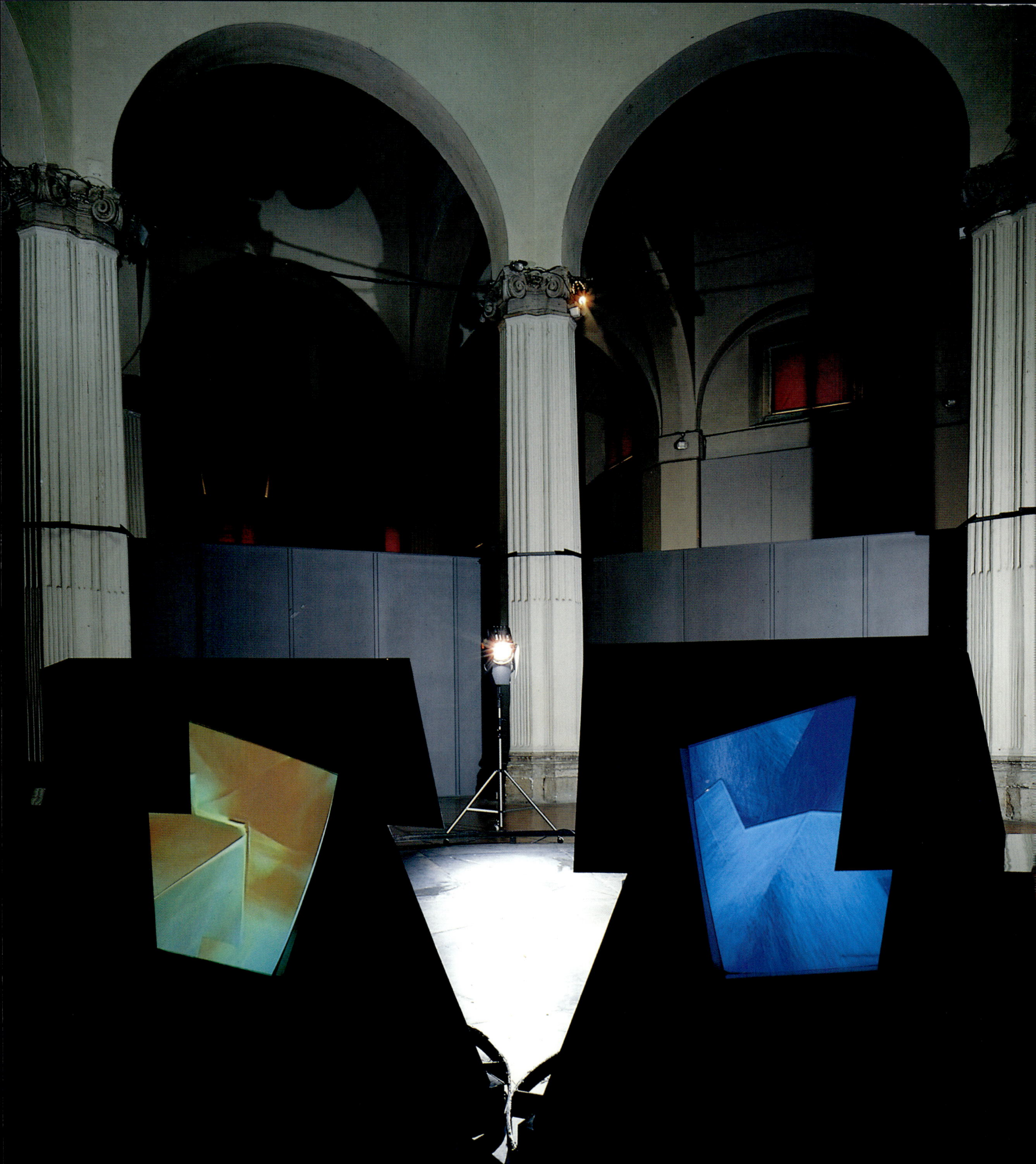

Der Hinweis auf den Kubismus ist schon deshalb wichtig, da dort der Ursprung für das Thema ›Bewegung in der Kunst‹ liegt. Zu Beginn des 20. Jahrhunderts (1909 erschien das erste futuristische Manifest) steht die Auflösung bestehender bildnerischer Prinzipien zugunsten einer dynamischen Veränderbarkeit von Formen und Konstellationen im Vordergrund. Bewegung und Bewegtheit werden in den Manifesten als universelle Dynamik thematisiert und manifestieren sich in Bildtiteln wie bei der 1913 entstandenen Skulptur von Umberto Boccioni *Urformen der Bewegung im Raum*. Wenige Jahre später, um 1911, hat sich aus dem Futurismus der analytische Kubismus entwickelt, bei dem vor allem der Begriff der Simultaneität, der Gleichzeitigkeit unterschiedlichster Formen, Elemente und Prinzipien innerhalb eines bildnerischen Geschehens in den Mittelpunkt rückt. Neben dem französischen Kubismus hat sich daraus um 1913 der russische Konstruktivismus und unmittelbar darauf 1915 der Suprematismus Kasimir Malewitschs entwickelt.

Die ersten Skizzen mit futuristisch-kubistisch ausgeschnittenen Gehäusen von Fernsehmonitoren findet man in dem Projekt *Reflecting Water*, in dem ein gezackter Neonbogen, ähnlich wie bei *Arco Liquido*, sich als Bildspiegelung in den gezackten Monitoren fortsetzt.

the roots of the subject 'Movement in Art'. At the beginning of the twentieth century (the first futuristic manifesto appears in 1909) the dissolution of existing pictorial principles in favour of dynamic variations of forms and constellations comes to the fore. Motion and emotion are discussed in manifestos as universal dynamics, and appear in titles of works, as in Umberto Boccioni's sculpture of 1913, Original Forms of Motion in Space. *A few years later, around 1911, analytic cubism has developed from futurism, centring mainly around the term simultaneity, the occurrence of different forms, elements and principles within an imaginal process at the same time. Beside French cubism, around 1913 Russian constructivism and, in 1915, Kasimir Malewitsch's suprematism evolved from it.*

The first sketches of cubufuturistic cut-outs of TV-monitor cases can be found in the project Reflecting Water, *in which an indented neon arch - similar to* Arco Liquido, *continues as reflection on the indented monitors.*

importante per il fatto che in esso ha origine la tematica del movimento nell'arte. All'inizio del XX secolo (nel 1909 fu pubblicato il primo manifesto programmatico dei futuristi) si assiste alla negazione dei principì figurativi esistenti a favore della modifica dinamica delle forme e costellazioni. Movimento e mobilità vengono definiti, nei manifesti, come dinamica universale e si concretizzano nei titoli delle opere, come per la scultura *Forme uniche della continuità nello spazio* realizzata da Umberto Boccioni nel 1913. Intorno al 1911 nasce dal futurismo il cubismo analitico che pone al centro della sua attenzione soprattutto il concetto della simultaneità delle forme, degli elementi e dei principì più variegati nella raffigurazione figurativa. Accanto al cubismo francese si sviluppa, intorno al 1913, il costruttivismo russo e immediatamente dopo, nel 1915, il suprematismo di Kazimir Malevic.

I primi schizzi con scatole di monitors di taglio cubistafuturistico si ritrovano nel progetto *Reflecting Water* dove un arco al neon dentellato, simile a quello di *Arco Liquido*, si estende nel riflesso dei monitors altrettanto dentellati.

CASABLANCA

84004

VILLENEUVE D'ASCQ 1984
Musée du Nord
84004.1

MILANO 1985
Rotonda della Besana
84004.2

ROMA 1987
RAI uno, ›Immagina‹
84004.3

CASABLANCA
Videoinstallation 1984
2 Holzgehäuse, Sand, Spielzeug-
flugzeug und -Palme, Kaffeehaus-
möbel, 2 Monitore, 2 Videorecorder, 2 bespielte Kassetten,
synchron ablaufend,
Tonaufzeichnung

CASABLANCA
Video installation1984
2 wooden cases, sand, toy-plane
and toy-palm, furniture (not all
presentations), 2 monitors, 2 video
recorders, wireless transmission,
recorded video cassettes,
soundrecording

CASABLANCA
Videoinstallazione 1984
Struttura in legno dipinto, sabbia,
mobili (presentazione RAI),
aeroplano e palma giocattolo,
2 monitors, 2 vhs, 2 cassette in
sincrono registrate, sonoro

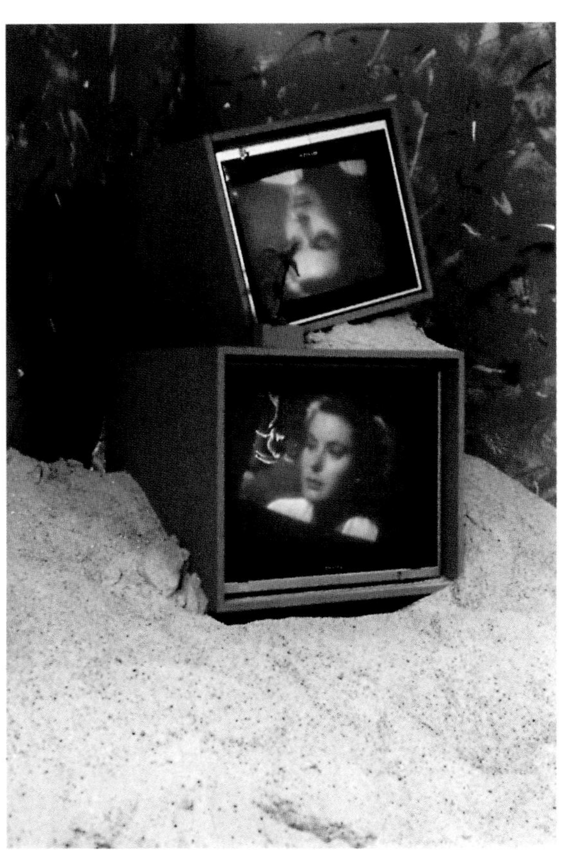

Casablanca baut unmittelbar
auf dem konstruktivistisch-
futuristischen Grundkonzept der
Arbeit *Video Going* auf und impliziert zugleich eine romantische
Dimension. In einem kaffeehaus-
artigen Ambiente mit Tischen,
Stühlen und einem Ventilator,
sind auf einem der Tische in
einem Sandhaufen eingebettet,
zwei Monitore übereinander
gestellt. Der obere Monitor steht
nicht nur auf dem Kopf, sondern
ist zudem auf die Spitze gestellt,

Casablanca *is directly based*
on the constructivist-futuristic
concept of Video Going, *and at*
the same time implies a romantic
dimension. In a coffee-house-like
ambient with tables, chairs, and
a ventilator, two monitors are
placed, one above the other, on
one of the tables, embedded in a
heap of sand. The monitor on top
is not only placed upside down,
but also on one corner, giving
the whole construction an air of
instability. On this monitor, one

Casablanca fa direttamente
riferimento al concetto costrut-
tivista-futurista di *Video Going*
ed introduce al tempo stesso
una dimensione romantica. In
una specie di ambiente da caffè
si trovano sedie, tavoli e un
ventilatore. Su uno dei tavoli
sono appoggiati, uno sopra
l'altro ed adagiati nella sabbia,
due monitors. Quello superiore,
capovolto, poggia solo su di un
angolo, conferendo all'insieme
un'impressione di instabilità, e

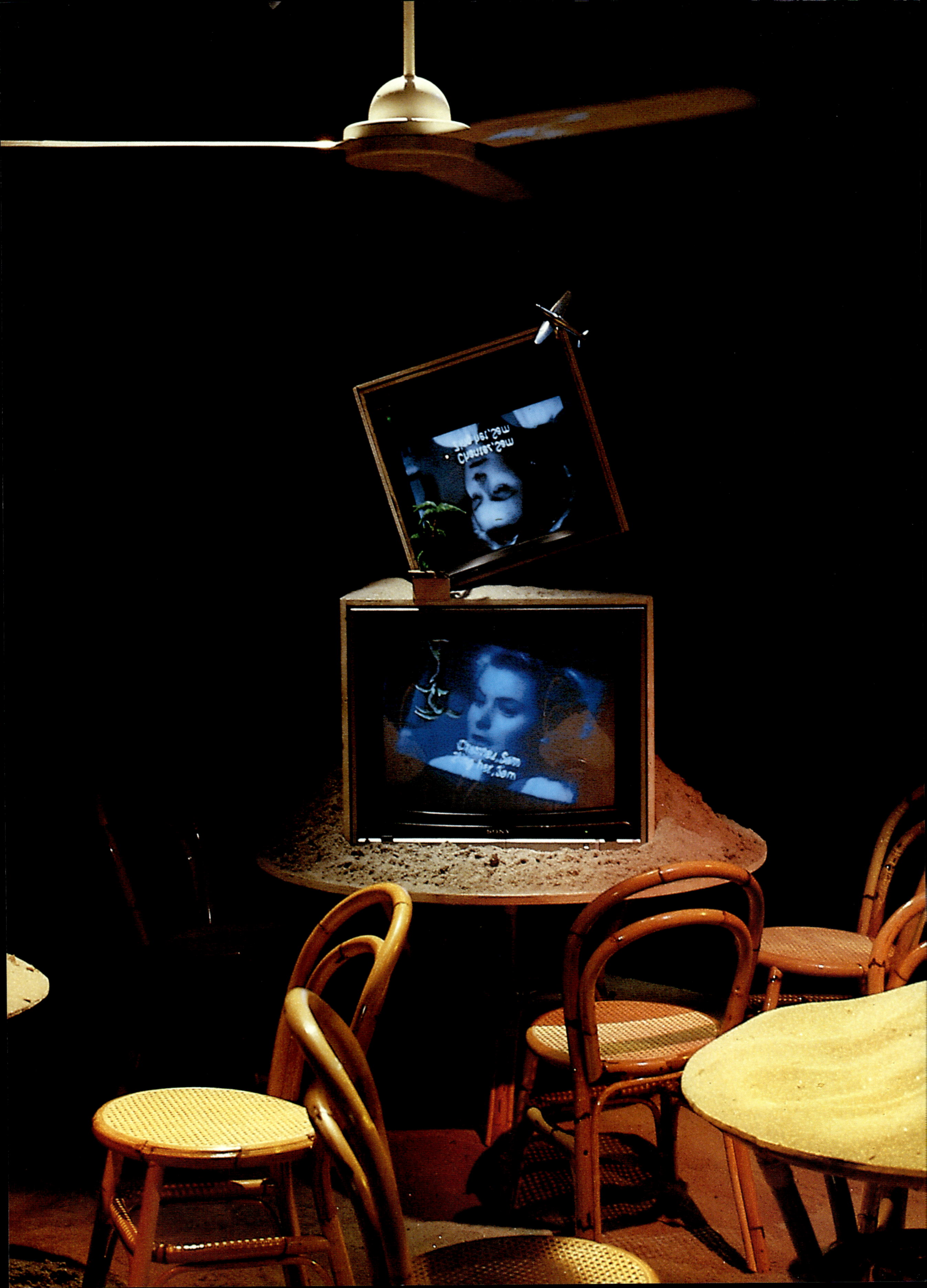

was der ganzen Konstruktion eine Instabilität verleiht. In dem oberen Monitor sieht man eine der entscheidenden Szenen aus dem Film *Casablanca* mit der weiblichen Hauptfigur, der berühmten Ingrid Bergmann, darunter ein seitenverkehrter Sprachtext zur Szene. Die oben dargestellte Situation scheint sich in dem unteren Monitor zu spiegeln, obwohl auch hier nur ein Film abläuft, denn zu sehen ist die gleiche Schräglage der Figur, nur mit dem Unterschied, daß der Bildtext jetzt lesbar wird. Das Programm des oberen kleineren Monitors spiegelt sich seitenrichtig in dem darunter befindlichen großen Monitor. Eine Art Collage aus Realität und Vorstellung entsteht hier, die dem Betrachter eine große Assoziationsvielfalt ermöglicht.

of the key scenes of the movie Casablanca, *featuring the famous Ingrid Bergmann, can be seen, with the text to this scene below it in mirrorwriting. This scene seems to be mirrored on the monitor below, although here, too, a film is shown that pictures the same askew position of the actress, the only difference being the fact that the text is legible now. The upper, smaller monitor's program is mirrored in the bigger monitor below it. A sort of collage of reality and imagination is thus created here, offering the spectator a wide variety of associations.*

mostra una scena centrale del film *Casablanca* con la famosa attrice Ingrid Bergmann, sotto alla quale si leggono dei sottotitoli rovesciati. La scena sembra riflettersi nel monitor inferiore con la stessa inclinazione delle immagini, ma con la differenza che adesso le immagini e i sottotitoli risultano leggibili. Il programma del monitor più piccolo superiore si riflette, adesso in posizione normale, in quello più grande inferiore costruendo una sorta di collage fra realtà e immaginazione e suggerendo allo spettatore una molteplicità di associazioni.

NARCISO

85001

MILANO 1985
Rotonda della Besana
85001.1

NARZISS
Videoskulptur 1985
Holz, Neon, Pendel- und
Synchronisierungsmechanismus,
Monitor, Videorecorder, bespielte
Kassette
300 x 260 x 60 cm

NARCISSUS
Video sculpture 1985
Wood, neon, mechanical parts,
monitor, video recorder, recorded
video cassettes
300 x 260 x 60 cm

NARCISO
Videoscultura 1985
Struttura in legno, pendolo al
neon, strumento meccanico,
1 monitor, vhs, cassetta registrata,
movimenti in esatta sincronia con
la cassetta video
300 x 260 x 60 cm

In eine pyramidenartige Dreieckkonstruktion aus Holz ist auf der Unterseite ein liegender Monitor eingebaut. Von der oberen Spitze heran schwingt ein Neonstab wie ein Pendel von rechts nach links. Jedesmal, wenn der Neonstab den Monitor passiert, scheint er das elektronische Wasser im Monitor zu erleuchten und spiegelt sich darin. Sobald der Stab wieder zurück auf die andere Seite schwingt, verschwindet auch die leuchtende Erscheinung auf dem Monitor. Alle Bewegungen finden in exaktem Synchronismus mit der Videokassette statt.

Auch hier gibt es bereits 1981 Vorzeichnungen und Projektskizzen für ein Neonpendel, das sich jedesmal im elektronischen

Built into a pyramid-like triangular wooden construction, a monitor, lying on its back, is positioned at its bottom. Hanging from the top, a neon staff swings - pendulum-like - from right to left. Every time the neon staff passes the monitor, it seems to illuminate the electronic water in the monitor, and is mirrored in it. As soon as it swings back to the other side, the shiny apparition on the monitor disappears. All movements take place in exact synchrony with the video cassette.

Here, too, first drawings and project-sketches for a neon pendulum reflecting in electronic water every time it passes the monitor exist as early as 1981; at that time, however, under the

Nella base di una costruzione triangolare lignea è inserito, lateralmente, un monitor che fa vedere una superficie d'acqua. Dalla punta superiore della costruzione oscilla da destra a sinistra, come un pendolo, un'asta al neon. Ogni qual volta l'asta passa sopra il monitor essa si riflette nell'acqua elettronica e sembra illuminarla. Appena l'asta si muove verso l'altro lato scompare anche l'immagine illuminata del monitor. Tutti i movimenti sono coordinati in perfetta sincronia con la videocassetta.

Anche in questo caso esistono già, con il titolo *Reflecting Water*, schizzi preparatori precedenti del 1981 per un pendolo al neon che si riflette

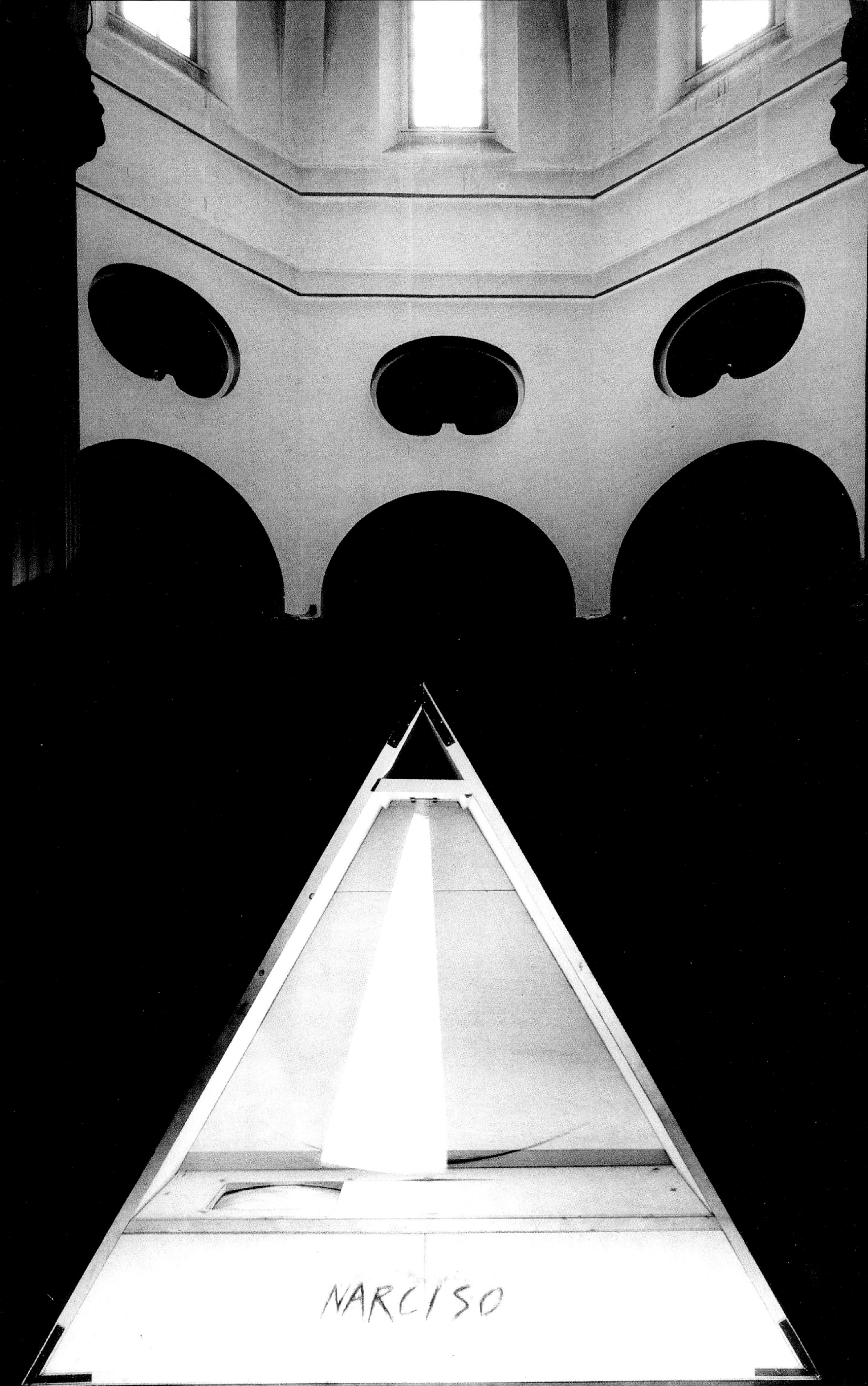
NARCISO

Wasser widerspiegelt, wenn es den Monitor passiert; doch seinerzeit, 1981, noch unter dem Titel *Reflecting Water* und ohne das dreieckige Holzgehäuse um die gesamte Konstruktion. Die Faszination, die von dem leuchtenden Neonstab ausgeht, besteht vor allem in der Fähigkeit ohne eine direkte Berührung, durch reine Magie, den ruhenden, scheinbar leblosen Monitor zum Leben zu erwecken. Daß der *Narziß*, hier der Neonstab, wie der Titel schon ankündigt, aus reiner Selbstverliebtheit in der Bewegung innehalten könnte, um sich an seinem eigenen Spiegelbild zu ergötzen, erhöht die Dramatik zusätzlich; zumal sich das Lichtpendel sehr langsam bewegt.

Physikalische Zusammenhänge und menschliche Eigenschaften werden hier in ein koinzidentes Verhältnis gebracht.

title Reflecting Water, *without the triangular housing around the whole construction. The fascination emanating from the shining neon staff is mainly caused by its ability to enliven the seemingly lifeless, resting monitor without direct contact, through sheer magic. That* Narcissus, *here the neon staff, could, as the title indicates, stop in his motion out of pure self-worship to indulge in his own reflection only heightens the tension, especially since the light pendulum moves dramatically slow.*

Physical contexts and human characteristics are here brought into a coincided relation.

nell'acqua elettronica di un monitor, ma ancora priva della struttura lignea. Il fascino emanato dall'asta al neon consiste soprattutto nella capacità di attivare senza sollecitazioni esterne dirette, come per pura magia, il monitor apparentemente senza vita. Il fatto che *Narciso*, cioè l'asta al neon, possa fermarsi nel suo movimento a causa del suo autocompiacimento, per deliziarsi nella propria immagine, incrementa ulteriormente la drammaticità, tanto più che il pendolo di luce si muove molto lentamente.

Leggi di fisica e caratteristiche umane vengono qui unite in una relazione coincidente.

MARE DI MARMO

85002

MILANO 1985
ROTONDA DELLA BESANA
85002.1

BOLOGNA 1987
GALLERIA D'ARTE MODERNA
85002.2

ZARAGOZA 1988
PALACIO SÁSTAGO
85002.3

HUMLEBAEK 1989
LOUISIANA MUSEUM
85002.4

PERUGIA 1995
ROCCA PAOLINA
85002.5

MEER AUS MARMOR
Videoinstallation 1985
Windmaschine, Travertinplatten,
100 Monitore (spätere Präsentation: 80), 2 Videorecorder,
2 bespielte Kassetten

SEA OF MARBLE
Video installation 1985
800 travertine slabs, wind
machine, 100 monitors (subsequent
presentation: 80), video recorder,
recorded video cassette

MARE DI MARMO
Videoinstallazione 1985
Lastre di travertino, macchina del
vento, 100 monitors (Perugia: 80),
vhs, cassetta registrata

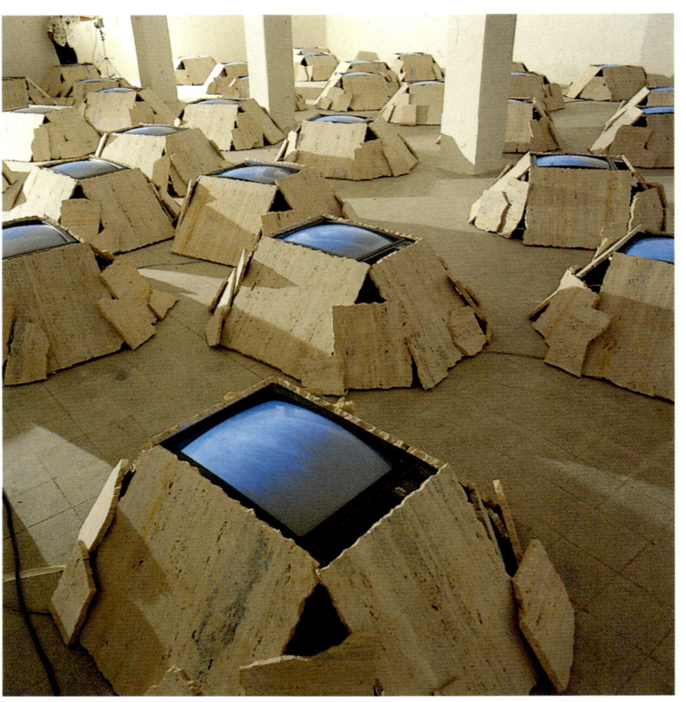

Wenn Fabrizio Plessi bis in die
Mitte der 80er Jahre bei seinen,
zum Teil durchaus raumgreifenden, Präsentationen noch eher im
Bereich der Videoskulptur geblieben ist, so finden wir mit *Mare di
Marmo* erstmalig eine Videoinstallation im Sinne eines raumumfas-
senden Environments vor. Es
handelt sich nicht um einzelne
Monitore, die in einer wie auch
immer gearteten Beziehung
zueinander stehen, sei es aufgrund des Filmes, der in ihnen
abläuft oder sei es aufgrund der
Konstellation, die sie zueinander
einnehmen. Hier hebt sich der
Monitor als Einzelelement im

While Fabrizio Plessi worked
up to the middle of the eighties
mainly with video sculptures,
though often presented on a
large scale, we encounter, in
Mare di Marmo, *the first video*
installation in the sense of a
spacious environment. Here we
are not dealing with single
monitors, being connected in
whatever kind of relation to each
other - be it because of the film
shown on them, be it the constel-
lation they are in. The monitor
now recedes as single element in
favour of the structural impressi-
on. Separate waters turn into
rivers, become a sea, flowing in

Se Fabrizio Plessi si è orientato, fino alla metà degli anni
ottanta, prevalentemente verso
la forma espressiva della videoscultura, troviamo in *Mare di
Marmo* per la prima volta una
videoinstallazione intesa come
environment spaziale. Qui non
si tratta più di singoli monitors
rapportati in qualche modo fra
di loro, attraverso i films o la
loro costellazione, ma del monitor che, come elemento singolo,
si neutralizza nel senso
dell'impressione strutturale.
L'acqua singola viene moltipli-
cata e si trasforma in un mare
nel marmo. Il movimento

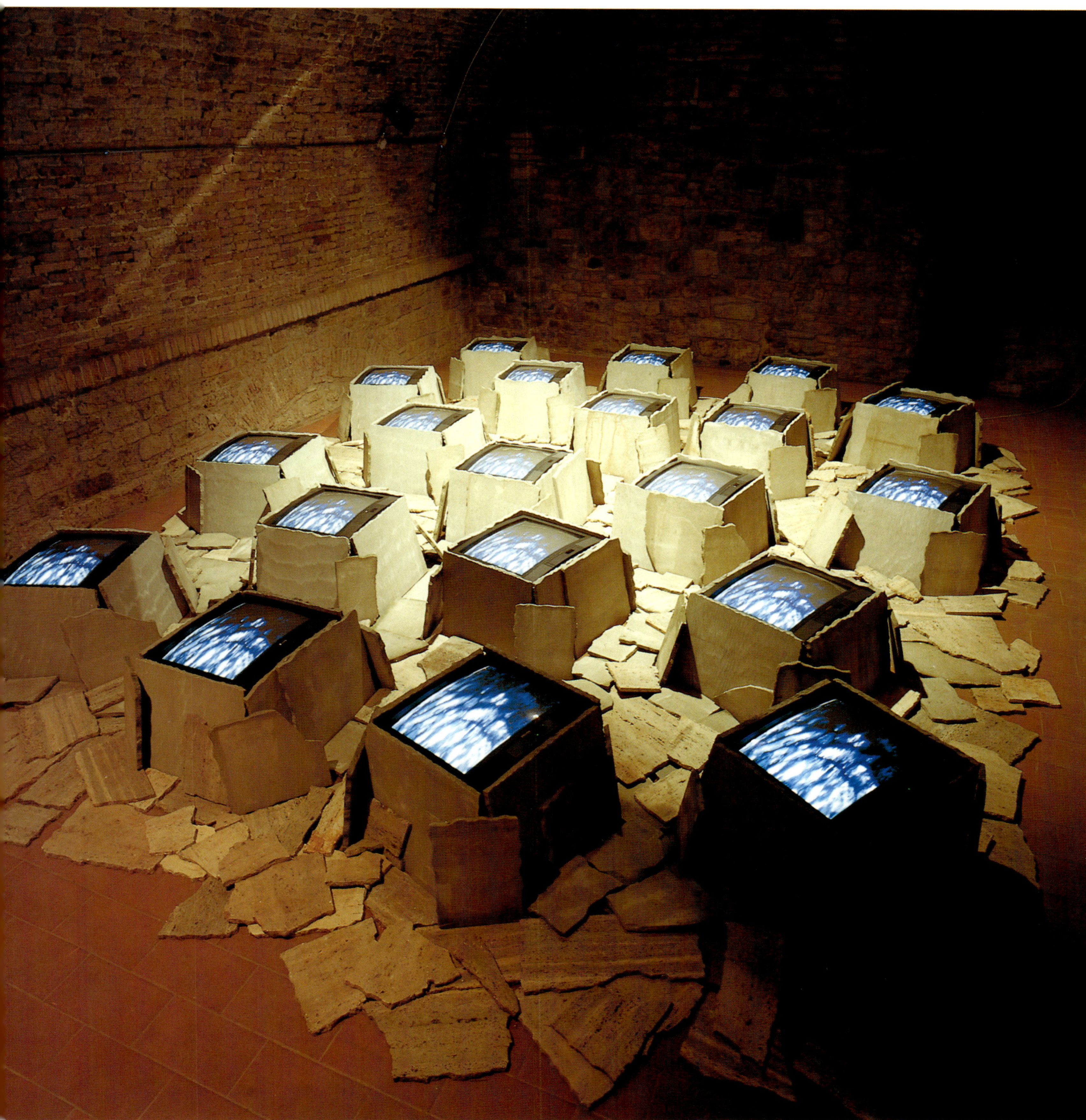

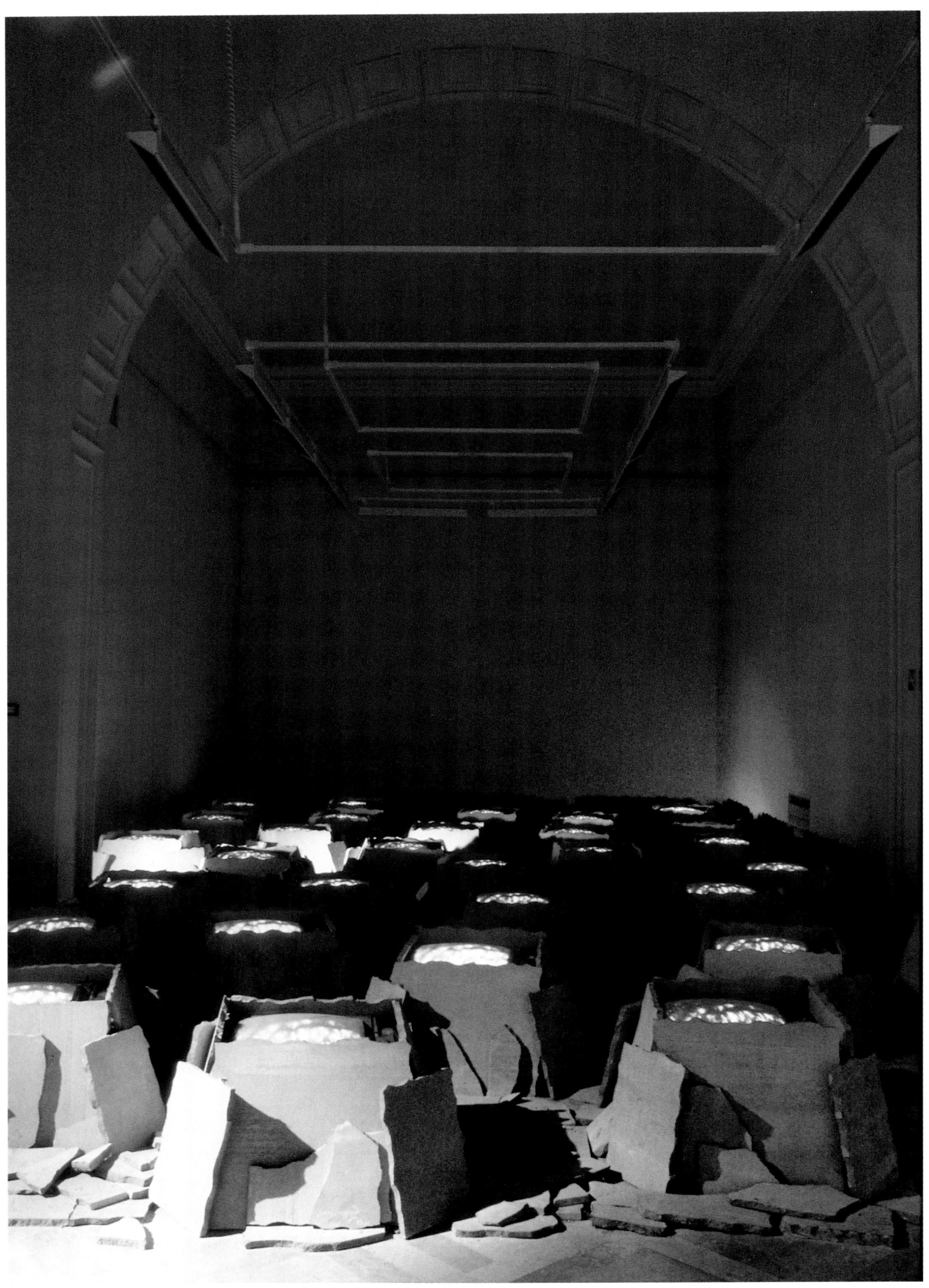

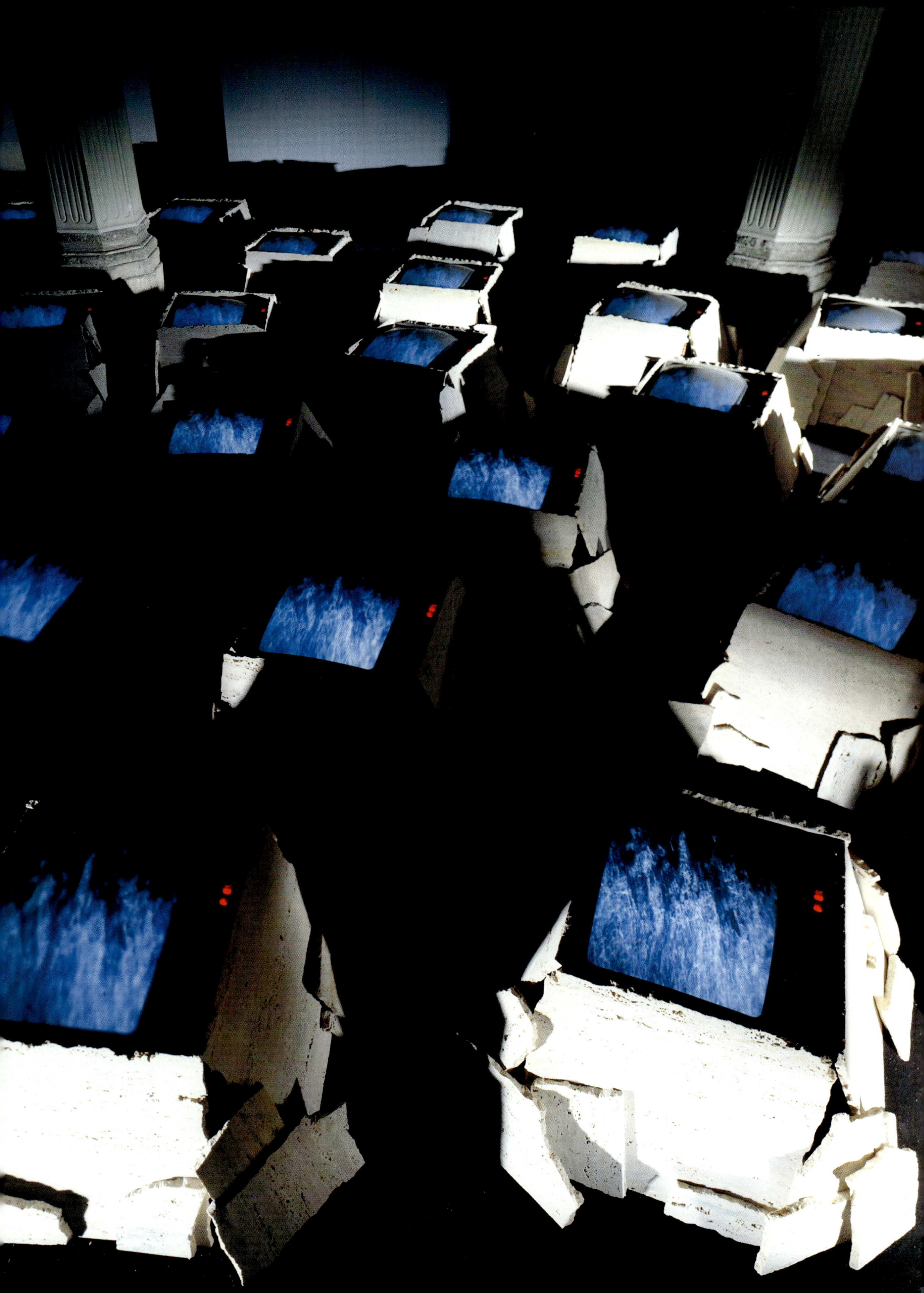

Sinne des Struktureindrucks auf.
Einzelne Wasser werden zu
Gewässer, werden zu einem Meer,
das in einem Meer aus Marmor
fließt. Die Bewegung des Wassers
auf den Monitoren scheint durch
eine Windmaschine hervorgeru-
fen, die eine reale Luftbewegung
erzeugt. Das elektronisch simu-
lierte Meer in den Monitoren
schlägt Wellen und kräuselt sich.
Und wieder ist es ähnlich und
vergleichbar mit dem Bau der
Windkonstruktionen der frühen
80er Jahre, bei denen ein realer
Initiator, ein natürliches außenstehendes Element, ein elektronisches Monitorbild, modifiziert.

dell'acqua dei monitors sembra
essere provocato da una macchina del vento, che produce una
corrente d'aria reale. Il mare
simulato nei monitors ondeggia
e si increspa. E ancora troviamo
un'analogia e una similtudine
con costruzioni del vento dei
primi anni ottanta, nelle quali
un iniziatore reale, un elemento
esterno modifica l'immagine
elettronica di un monitor.

BRONX

85003

MILANO 1985
Rotonda della Besana
85003.1

VENEZIA 1986
XLII Biennale di Venezia
85003.2

CAVAILLON 1987
Centre Culturel
85003.3

ROMA 1987
RAI uno, ›Immagina‹
85003.4

MADRID 1988
Museo Español de Arte Contemporaneo
85003.5

DORTMUND 1993
Museum am Ostwall
85003.6

KARSRUHE 1997
Zentrum für Kunst und Medientechnologie
85003.7

NEW YORK 1998
Guggenheim Museum Soho
85003.8

SAN DIEGO 1998
Museum of Contemporary Art La Jolla
85003.9

BRONX
Videoinstallation 1985
Strukturen aus rostigen
Eisenplatten, 26 Schaufeln,
Eisengitter, 26 Monitore,
2 Videorecorder, 2 bespielte
Kassetten, Tonaufzeichnung
740 x 880 cm

BRONX
Video installation 1985
Structures of rusty iron plates,
26 shovels, iron lattice,
26 monitors, video recorder,
recorded video cassette,
soundrecording
740 x 880 cm

BRONX
Videoinstallazione 1985
Struttura in ferro, lastre di ferro
arrugginito, 26 pale agricole,
grigliato industriale, 26 monitors,
2 vhs, cassette registrate
740 x 880 cm

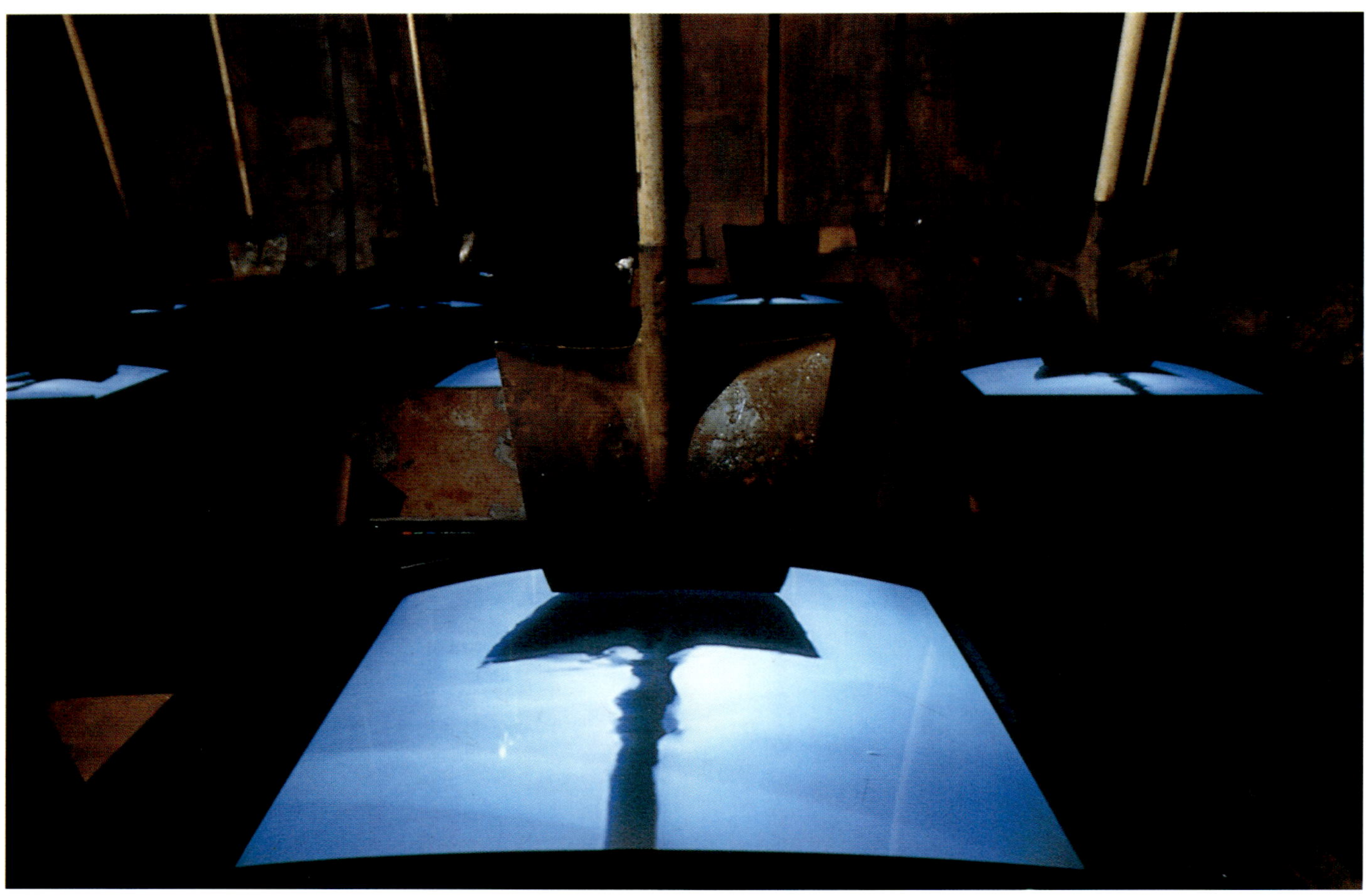

Die Videoinstallation *Bronx*, die
auf der 42. Biennale in Venedig,
schon aufgrund seiner Präsentation
in einem abgetrennten, eigens in
die Ausstellungsfläche eingebauten
Raum, großes Aufsehen erregte,
basiert auf einer Projektstudie,
einer Zeichnung von 1981 mit dem
Titel *Sulla Riflessione (Über die
Reflexion)*. Bei diesem frühen
Projekt für eine Videoskulptur ist
ein einzelner Monitor mit dem
Bildschirm nach oben gerichtet
zwischen vier Platten aus rostrotem
Stahl gestellt. Ein auf die Bild-

The video installation Bronx
*that drew great attention at the
42nd Biennale in Venice - if only
because of its presentation in a
separate, especially built-in room
in the exhibition hall - is based
on a project study, a drawing of
1981 entitled* Sulla riflessione
(On Reflection). *In this early
project for a video sculpture, a
single monitor is placed - screen
turned upwards - between four
plates of stainless steel. A vertical element, standing on the
screen, is reflected in the*

La videoinstallazione *Bronx*,
esposta allaXLII Biennale di
Venezia dove ha suscitato grande
stupore, e non solo per il modo
inconsueto della sua presentazione in uno spazio appartato, si
basa su di uno studio progettuale
per una videoscultura, un disegno
del 1981 dal titolo *Sulla riflessione*
dove un singolo monitor, con lo
schermo rivolto verso l'alto, è
cicondato da quattro lastre di
ferro di color ruggine. Un elemento verticale non ancora iden-
tificabile, posizionato sullo

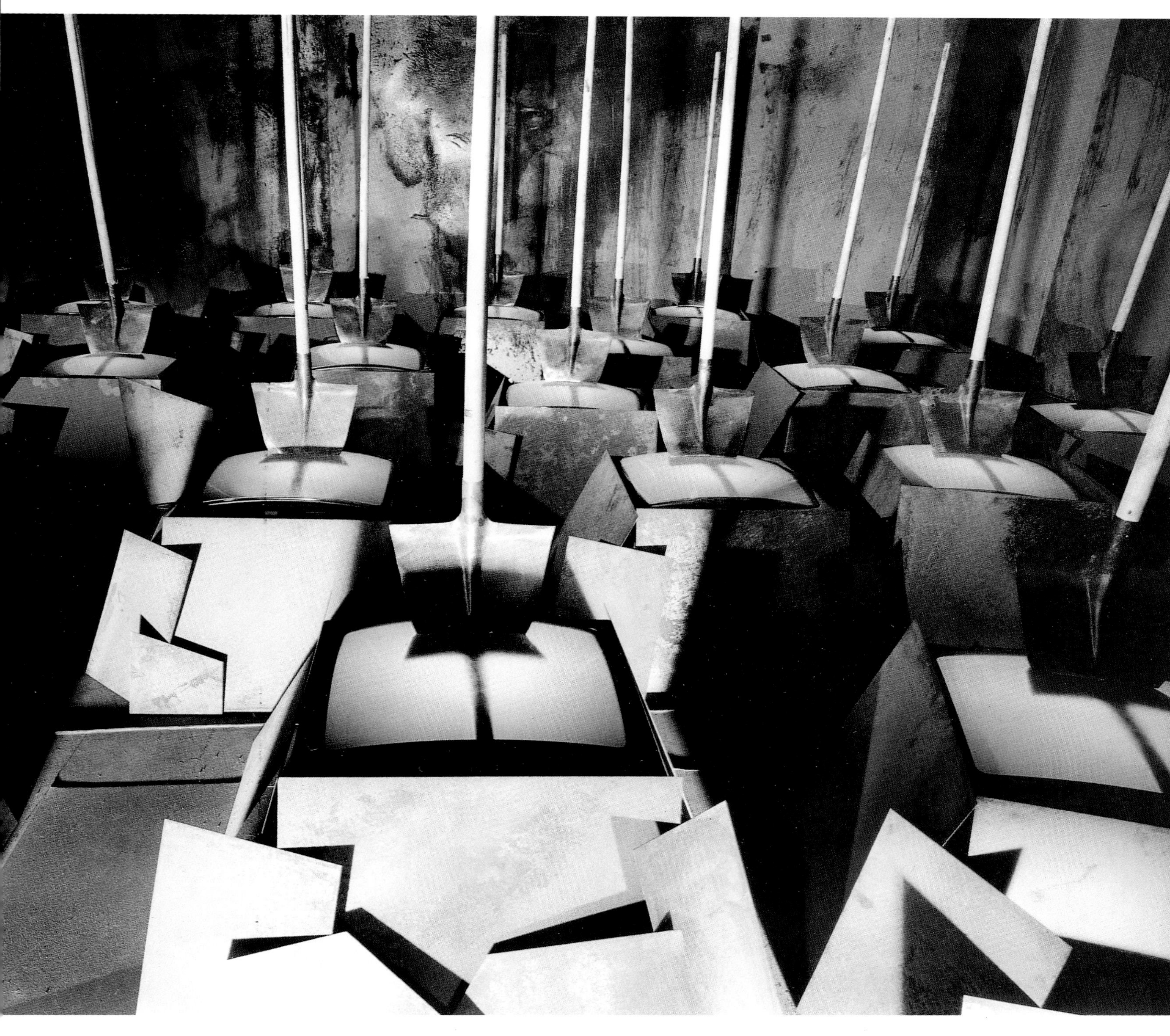

schirmseite gestelltes vertikales Element spiegelt sich im elektronischen Wasser des Monitors. Doch dieses Element ist noch nicht näher identifizierbar. Dagegen verweist eine Zeichnung von 1972 mit dem Titel *Buco nell'acqua* ganz unmittelbar auf die in *Bronx* wiederkehrenden Schaufeln. Bei diesem frühen Projekt spielen Monitore und

monitor's electronic water. This element is, however, not yet identifiable, whereas a drawing of 1972, entitled Buco nell'acqua *points directly to the shovels reappearing in* Bronx. *In this early project, monitors and video films do not yet play a part. Yet the shovel's grip is constructed from a neon staff. The drawn project of 1972 is closely connec-*

schermo, si riflette nell'acqua elettronica del monitor. Un disegno del 1972 dal titolo *Buco nell'acqua*, invece, già anticipa le pale che poi ritornano in *Bronx*. In questo precoce progetto monitors e videofilms non rivestono ancora importanza, mentre il manico della pala è costituito da un'asta al neon. Il disegno del progetto del 1972 è strettamente

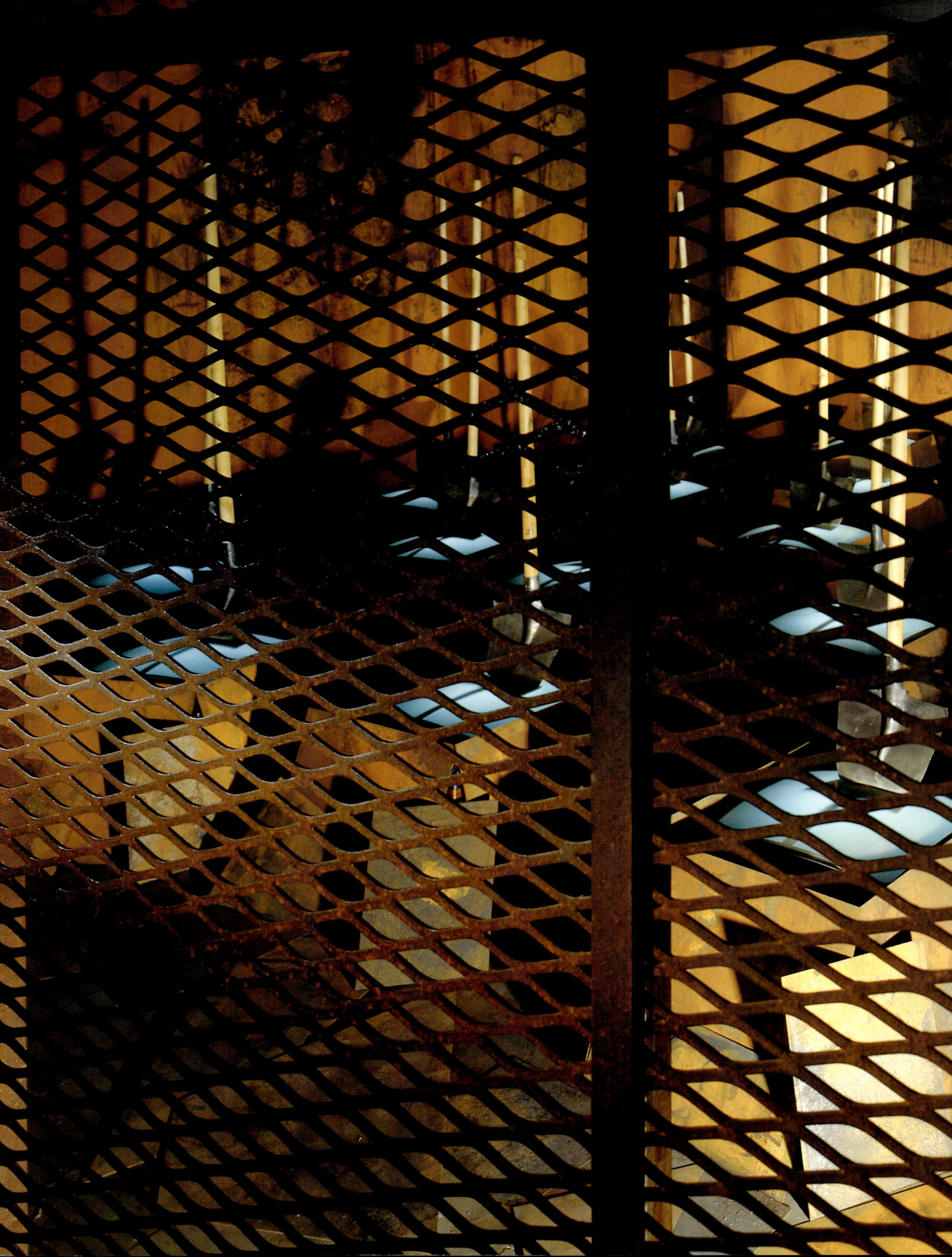

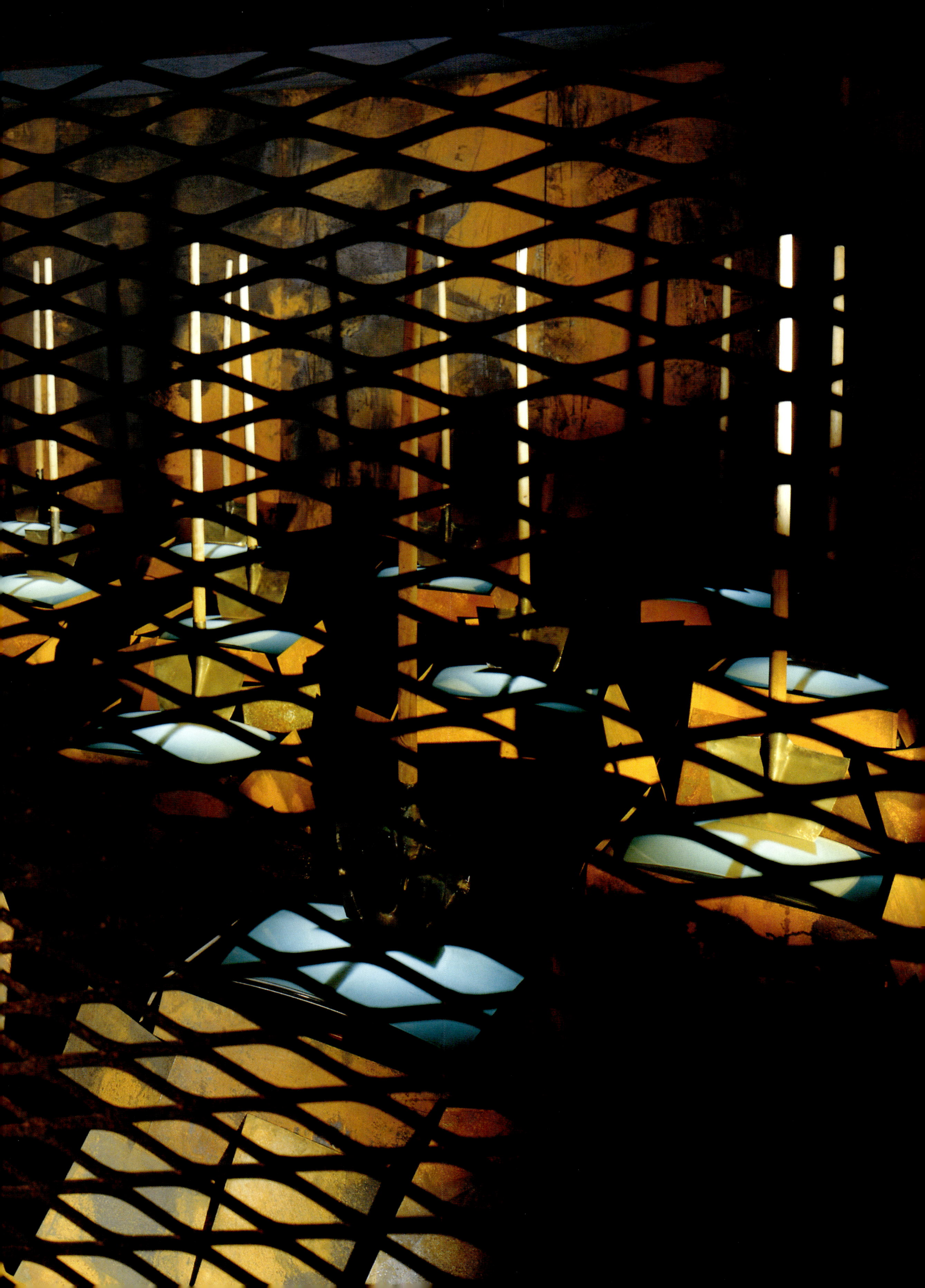

Videofilme noch keine Rolle. Doch der Griff der Schaufel ist aus einem Neonstab konstruiert. Das gezeichnete Projekt von 1972 hängt zusammen mit den zeitgleichen Aktionen mit Wasser, die Plessi zu dieser Zeit ausgeführt und fotografisch oder in Filmen dokumentiert hat. Dazu gehört die Aktion *Einen See in zwei gleiche Teile sägen* von 1975 ebenso wie *100 Wasserstücke*, oder *Löcher im Wasser*, um nur ein paar Beispiele zu nennen.

Bei der Videoinstallation *Bronx* ist es die gleiche Idee, wie seinerzeit bei den Aktionen, nämlich mit einem Werkzeug - damals einer Schere, einem Nagel, einer Säge, hier jetzt mit einer Schaufel - Löcher in das Wasser zu graben. Das visuelle Ergebnis der Präsentation einer großen Anzahl von Monitoren mit einer großen Anzahl von darin steckenden Schaufeln, die sich in der Wasseroberfläche spiegeln, irritiert den Betrachter, denn die Schaufeln versinken nicht im Wasser, wie man erwarten würde, sondern sie spiegeln sich darin, wie der Lichtstrahl des Narziß. Verwunderung stellt sich darüber ein, daß eine flüssige Materie, die flexibel, veränderlich und instabil zu sein scheint, einen Gegenstand, bestehend aus stabiler Materie, zu halten, zu tragen vermag.

Aber die Installation *Bronx* hat auch etwas Bedrohliches an sich. Zunächst einmal sind dort Gitter, ein Vorgriff auf die späteren Schranktüren, die, von außen betrachtet, den Zugriff verwehren und von innen betrachtet, den Ausweg verschließen. Einem Aufstand gleich weisen die Schaufeln mit ihren Stielen nach oben, werden zu (menschlichen) Wesen, die zur Wehr, zur Gegenwehr, entschlossen scheinen. So wird die ganze Installation zu einem Sinnbild für die Gefährdung des Menschen durch den Menschen, bezogen auf den Stadtteil Bronx in New York.

ted to the actions with water of the same period which Plessi executed, photographed and documented on film at that time. These include the event To Saw a Lake into two Equal Parts, *of 1975, as well as* 100 Water Pieces, *when Plessi used regular kitchen scissors to cut a jet of tab water into 100 pieces of equal length of one minute, or* Holes in the Water, *where the artist used hammer and nail to drive 300 holes - at a distance of one metre each - into the surface of the river Seine, to mention but a few examples.*

The video installation Bronx *is based on the same idea as in the events, that is to use a tool - at that time scissors, a nail, a saw, now a shovel - to dig holes in the water. The visual result of a presentation of a number of monitors with a great number of shovels in them, reflecting on the water's surface, irritates the spectator because the shovels do not - as expected - sink into the water but mirror in it, like* Narcissus' *light beam. One is amazed that liquid matter that seems to be flexible, variable and unstable is able to hold, to carry an object of stable matter.*

But the installation Bronx *has something threatening in it, too. First, there are gratings - an indication of the later cabinet doors - which, looked at from the outside, deny access and, from the inside, restrict exit. Resembling a revolt, the shovels erect their handles upwards, become (human) beings that seem determined to resist, to attack. So the whole installation becomes a symbol of the threat of humans by humans, referring to the Bronx district in New York.*

collegato con le azioni coll'acqua, che Plessi in quel periodo realizza, fotografa o documenta attraverso filmati, come per esempio l'azione *Tagliare un lago un due parti uguali* del 1975 o quella di *100 pezzi d'acqua*, nella quale l'artista taglia con forbici da cucina un getto d'acqua di un rubinetto in cento pezzi uguali di una lunghezza di un minuto ciascuno o, ancora, *Buchi nell'acqua*, dove Plessi effettua, munito di martello e chiodo, 300 fori ad una distanza di un metro l'uno dall'altro nello specchio d'acqua del fiume Senna.

Nella videoinstallazione *Bronx* è presente la stessa idea delle azioni precedenti, e cioè forare con un utensile - con le forbici, un chiodo o una sega prima, con una pala poi - la superficie dell'acqua. Il visibile effetto finale della presentazione di un gran numero di monitors con un altrettanto grande numero di pale, conficcate in essi e riflesse dall'acqua, provoca irritazione nello spettatore, perchè le pale non affondano nel liquido, come ci si potrebbe aspettare, bensì si riflettono, come il raggio di luce di Narciso. Si rimane perplessi per il fatto che una materia liquida, in apparenza flessibile, mutevole e instabile, possa reggere e trattenere un oggetto di materia solida.

Ma l'installazione Bronx trasmette qualcosa di minaccioso. Innanzitutto si vede una grata, un'anticipazione delle più tarde porte degli *Armadi*, che vista da fuori precludono l'accesso e da dentro l'uscita. Simile ad una insurrezione i manici delle pale sono rivolti verso l'alto e diventano esseri (umani) decisi a difendersi. Così l'intera installazione, riferita al quartiere Bronx di New York, si trasforma nella metafora della minaccia dell'uomo all'uomo.

WATER DESERT

85004

VENEZIA 1990
STUDIO BARNABÓ
85004.1

DORTMUND 1993
MUSEUM AM OSTWALL
85004.2

PERUGIA 1995
ROCCA PAOLINA
85004.3

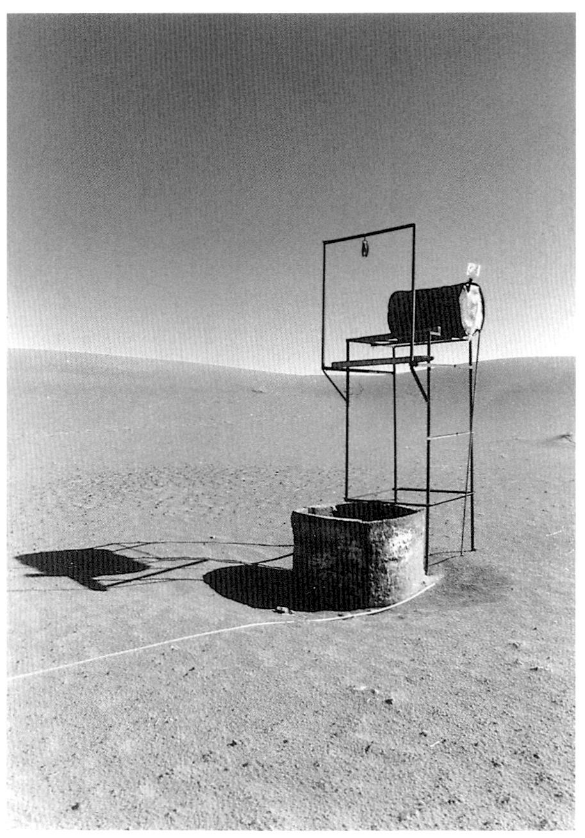

Eine Bedrohung ganz anderer Art sieht Fabrizio Plessi, wenn das Wasser auszubleiben scheint. So hat er ein Rettungsprinzip nachgebaut - basierend auf einem Foto, das er selbst in der Wüste von einer Konstruktion, die er dort vorfand, aufgenommen hat. Nur gibt es auf dem Grunde des Brunnen seiner Videoskulptur *Water Desert* (*Wasserwüste*) kein reales Wasser, sondern einen

A threat of a totally different kind is seen by Fabrizio Plessi in the seeming absence of water. Therefore he has reconstructed a means of rescue - based on a photo he took of a construction he found in the desert. Only, at the bottom of the well in his video sculpture Water Desert *there is no real water but a monitor that makes sparkling water electronically visible.*

Una minaccia di tutt'altro tipo intravede Plessi nella possibilità di mancanza d'acqua e, di conseguenza, egli ricostruisce un principio di salvataggio, basandosi su una foto scattata da lui stesso di una costruzione nel deserto. Solo che, sul fondo del pozzo della sua videoscultura *Water Desert*, non c'è acqua reale, ma un monitor dal quale si vede sgorgare acqua elettronica.

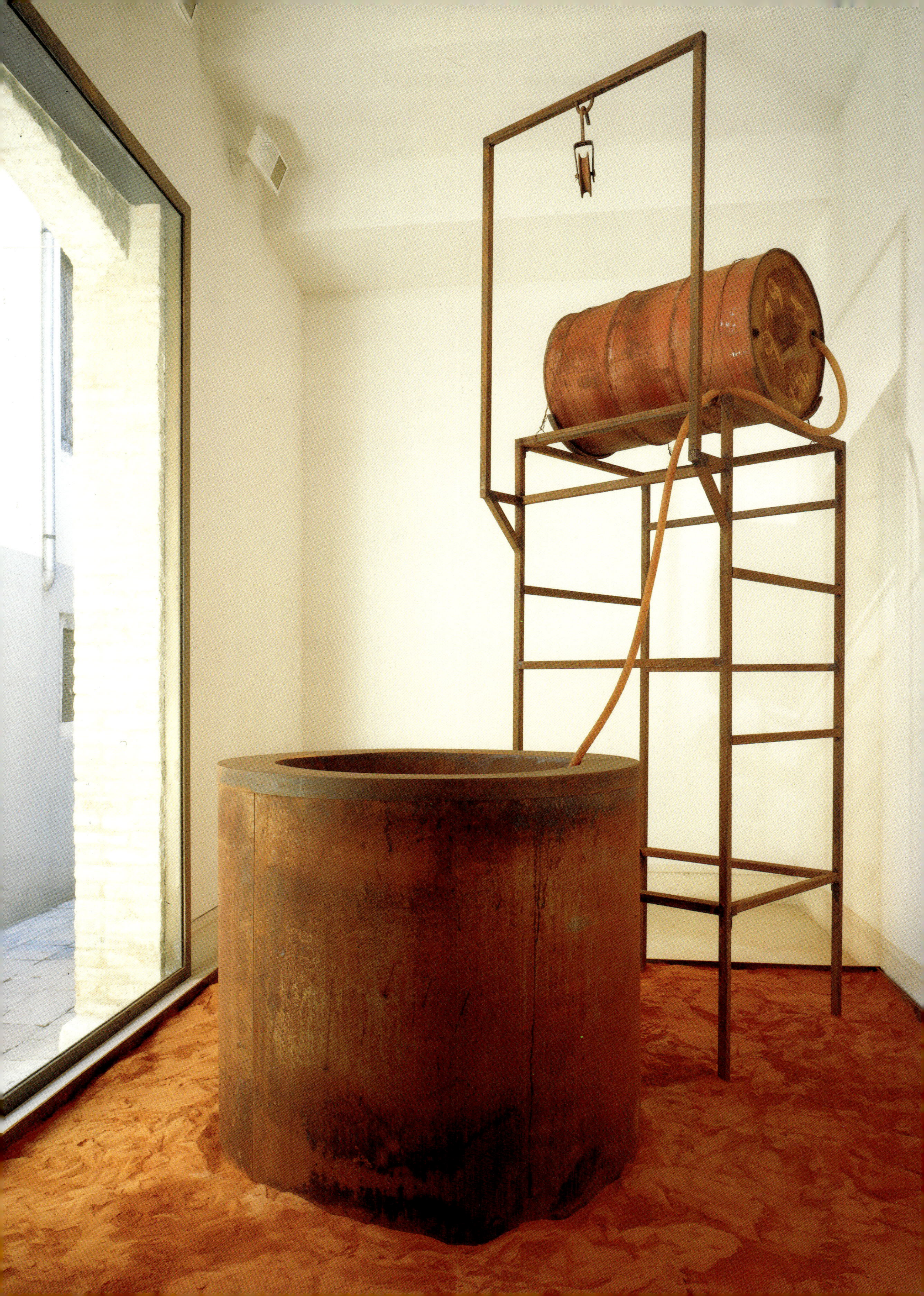

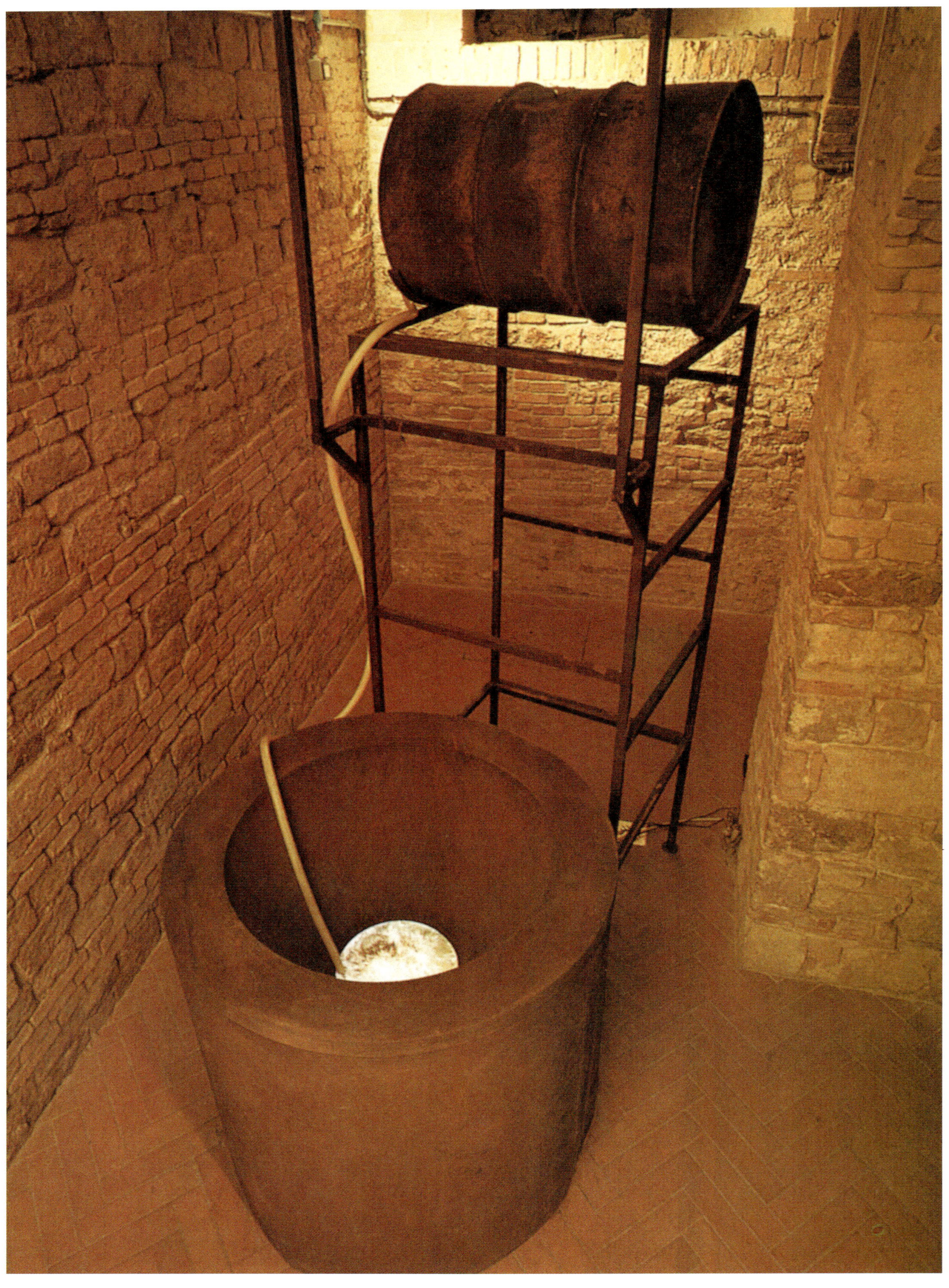

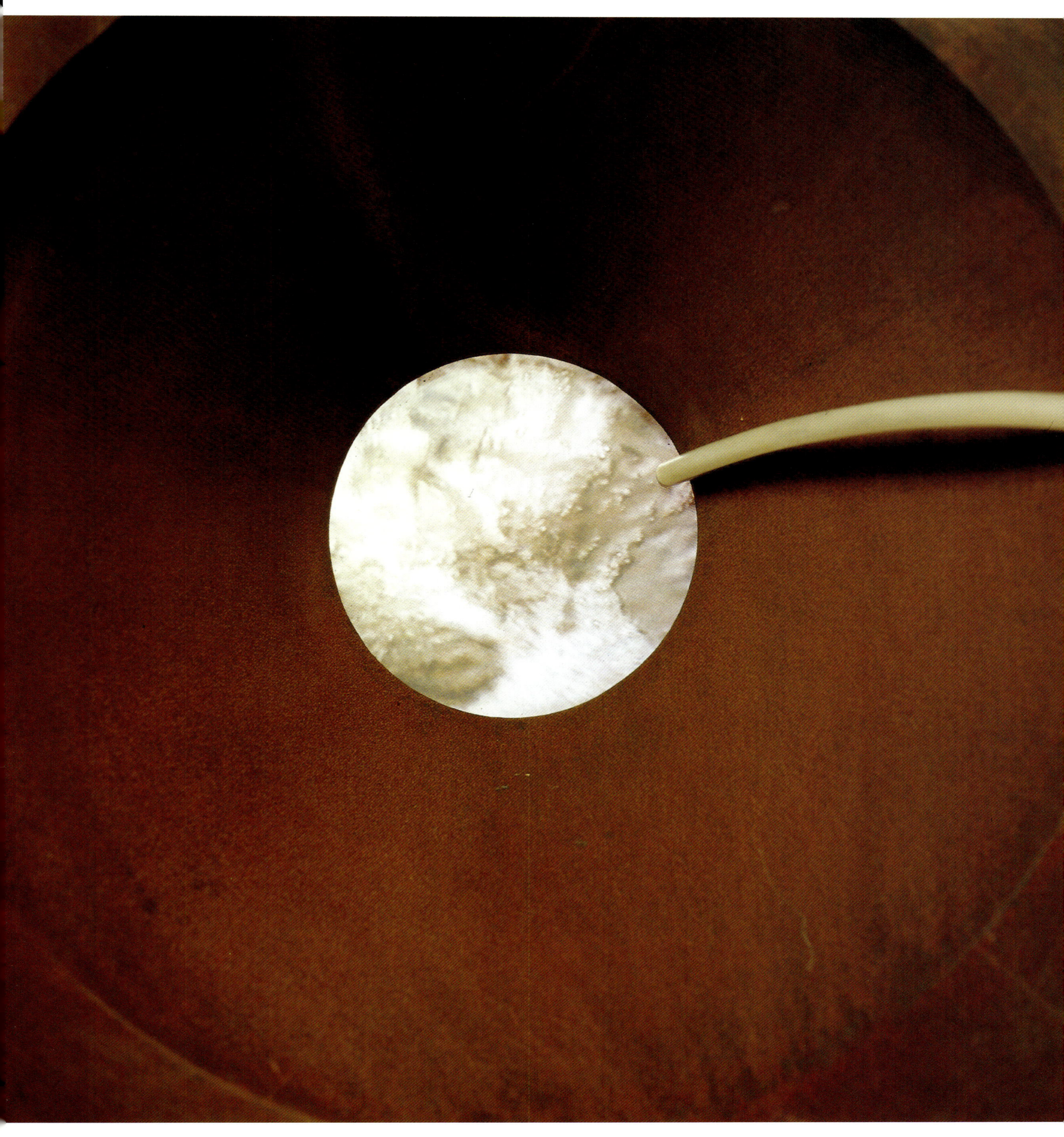

Monitor, der sprudelndes Wasser elektronisch sichtbar werden läßt.

Neben den Reminiszenzen italienischer Arte Povera - aufgrund der verwendeten Materialien, wie beispielsweise der verrosteten Tonne - lebt diese Arbeit aus dem Dialog der Gegensätze. Der Kontrast des unendlichen Wüsteneindrucks mit der endlichen Menge von Wasser macht dieses als Mangelware um so kostbarer. Während es in Venedig gelegentlich zuviel des Guten davon gibt, so viel zu viel, daß Plessi in den frühen 70er Jahren Projekte, Entwürfe und Vorschläge erfunden und ausgearbeitet hat, wie beispielsweise den *Schwamm für den Ausnahmezustand im Fall von Hochwasser* in Venedig. Diese Pläne und Konzepte haben aufgrund ihrer wissenschaftlich anmutenden Detailgenauigkeit Realitätscharakter und sind dennoch in den seltensten Fällen zu realisieren, zu verwirklichen. Doch gerade die Ideenskizze, die seiner Phantasie freien Lauf läßt, in der Unmögliches möglich werden kann und bildnerisch dargestellt zur Realität, liegt Fabrizio Plessi sehr, denn »Der Künstler ist ein Erfinder von Ideen, die sich visuell realisieren lassen« (Günther Uecker).

Interessant ist bei dieser Arbeit *Water Desert* auch, daß zum ersten Mal ein Monitor so in ein Gehäuse eingebaut ist, daß er selbst von seiner Form her kaum noch als Monitor erkennbar wird, da nur noch eine kreisrunde Öffnung des Gehäuses einen kleinen Ausblick auf die Bildschirmoberfläche erlaubt. Dieses Verstecken der äußeren Form des Monitors steigert noch den Realitätscharakter des elektronischen Wassers. Wir werden dieses Prinzip bei seiner Installation *Flüssige Kristalle* im Café Florian in Venedig später wiederfinden.

Besides its reminiscence of Italian Arte Povera - because of the material applied, like the rusty ton - this work lives by the dialogue of opposites. The contrast between the impression of endless desert and the limited amount of water makes water the more valuable, while in Venice there is sometimes too much of the good thing - so much that Plessi invented and worked out projects, designs and proposals in the early seventies as, for example, the Sponge for a State of Emergency in case of Floods in Venice. *These plans and concepts have - because of their scientific-like exact details - realistic characteristics, and yet can only in rare cases be realised and shown. The sketching of an idea, however, that gives ample room to fantasy, in which the impossible becomes possible, is what Fabrizio Plessi enjoys, for: "The artist is an inventor of ideas that can be visually realised." (Günther Uecker).*

Interesting in his work Water Desert *is also that here, for the first time, a monitor is built into a casing in such a way that its form can hardly be recognised as such because only a small circular opening allows a glance at the screen. Hiding the outer shape of the monitor serves to heighten the realistic character of the electronic water. Later, we shall encounter this principle in his installation* Liquid Crystals *in the Cafe Florian in Venice.*

Accanto alle riminiscenze dell'Arte Povera italiana - poveri sono i materiali impiegati, come il bidone arrugginito - l'opera vive del dialoghi degli opposti. Il contrasto fra l'immagine dell'infinito deserto e la quantità limitata dell'acqua trasforma quest'ultima in una merce rara e la rende ancora più preziosa, a differenza della situazione di Venezia dove di acqua ve n'è addirittura fin troppa, così tanta che Plessi, all'inizio degli anni settanta, idea e elabora progetti e proposte a proposito, come ad esempio *Spugna per l'emergenza d'acqua alta*. Tali progetti acquistano, in virtù della loro precisione scientifica nei dettagli, carattere realistico senza essere, però, realizzabili nella maggior parte dei casi. Ma Fabrizio Plessi si sente attratto proprio dallo schizzo concettuale che lascia piena libertà alla sua fantasia nella quale l'impossibile diventa possibile e realizzabile in maniera figurativa, poichè »L'artista è un inventore di idee che si possono realizzare visualmente« (Günther Uecker).

Un altro aspetto interessante di *Water Desert* risiede nel fatto che, per la prima volta, un monitor viene inserito in una struttura in maniera tale da non essere più riconoscibile come tale in quanto nascosto dalla struttura stessa, ad eccezione di una piccola apertura circolare sullo schermo. Il mascheramento della forma esterna del monitor rafforza ancora di più il carattere realistico dell'acqua elettronica, un principio che incontreremo ancora più tardi nella sua installazione *Cristalli Liquidi* al Caffè Florian di Venezia.

WINNER

87001

FERRARA 1987
Museo Palazzo dei Diamanti
87001.1

PALMA DE MALLORCA 1989
Palau Solleric
87001.2

NAGOYA 1989
Biennale Nagoya
87001.3

PERUGIA 1995
Rocca Paolina
87001.4

SIEGER
Videoinstallation 1987
Schaufeln, Eisenplatten,
Eisengitter, Monitor,
Videorecorder, bespielte Kassette
700 x 700 cm

WINNER
Video installation 1987
Shovels, iron plates, iron lattice,
monitor, video recorder, recorded
video cassette,
700 x 700 cm

VINCITORE
Videoinstallazione 1987
Pale agricole, lastre di ferro
degradato, bamboo, grigliato
industriale, monitor, vhs, cassetta
registrata, 700 x 700 cm

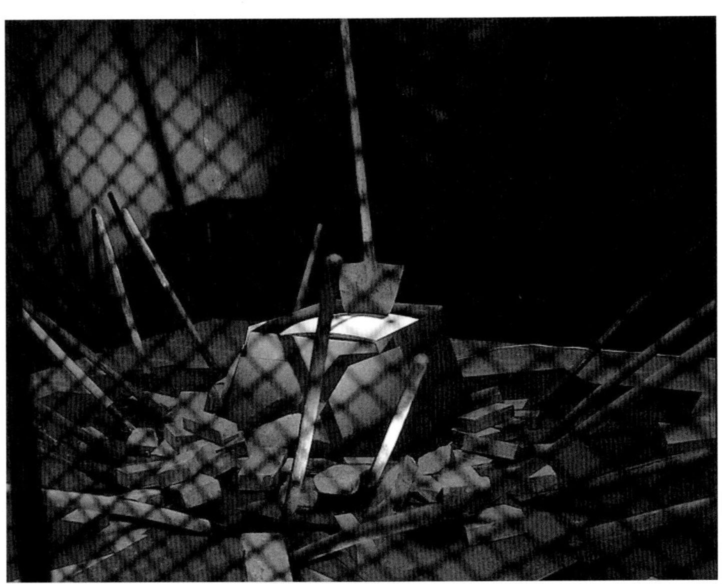

In der Videoskulptur *Winner* läßt sich ein deutlicher Bezug zu der Installation *Bronx* herstellen. Auch hier gibt es einen mit der Bildschirmfläche nach oben gerichteten Monitor, in dessen fließendem Wasser scheinbar eine Schaufel steckt. Doch hier ist das ganze Umfeld verändert. Anstelle einer unhierarchischen Struktur von Monitoren mit darin steckenden Schaufeln gibt es nur noch einen einzigen nach oben weisenden Schaufelstiel und einen einzigen Monitor, der von allen anderen Schaufeln angegriffen, bedrängt zu werden scheint. Doch ganz offensichtlich, wie schon der Titel bereits ankündigt, unterliegen die vielen anderen zugunsten des einen Siegers.

In his video sculpture Winner, *a clear reference to the installation* Bronx *can be seen. Here, too, is a monitor, its screen turned upwards, in the running water of which a shovel seems to be stuck, though the whole surrounding is changed. Instead of the in-hierarchical structure of monitors with inserted shovels there is only one shovel-shaft pointing upwards, and a single monitor that seems to be attakked by all the other shovels. Obviously though, as the title indicates, the many others lose to the one winner.*

Nella videoscultura *Winner* si intravede un forte riferimento alla installazione *Bronx*, anche qui un monitor con lo schermo rivolto verso l'alto e una pala conficcata nell'acqua che scorre. L'insieme è però mutato. La struttura non gerarchica dei monitors con le pale conficcate è sostituita da un solo manico di pala che tende verso l'alto e da un solo monitor, che appare attaccato, assediato da tutte le altre pale. Ma evidentemente, come già annunciato dal titolo, i molti soccombono in favore dell'unico vincitore.

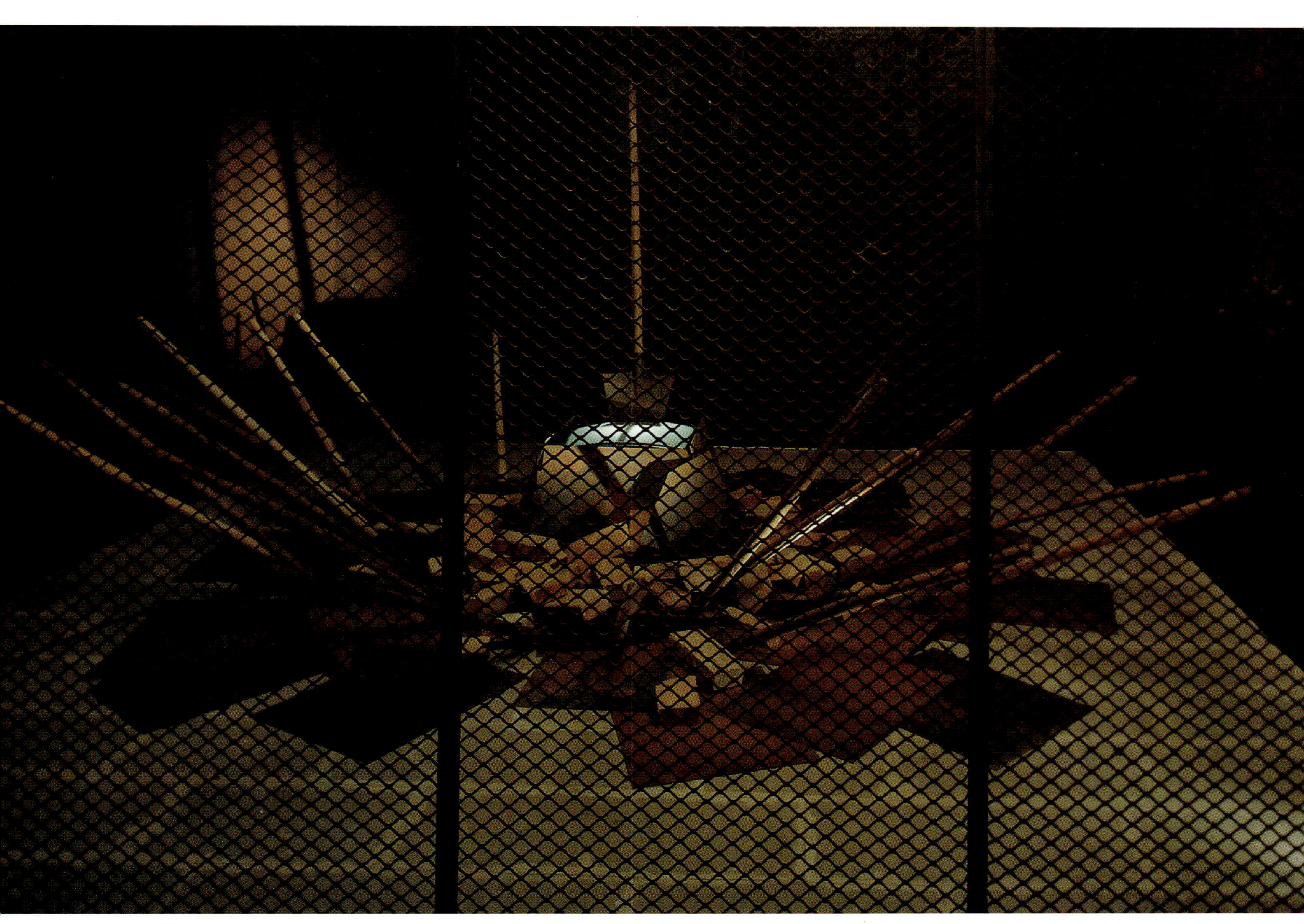

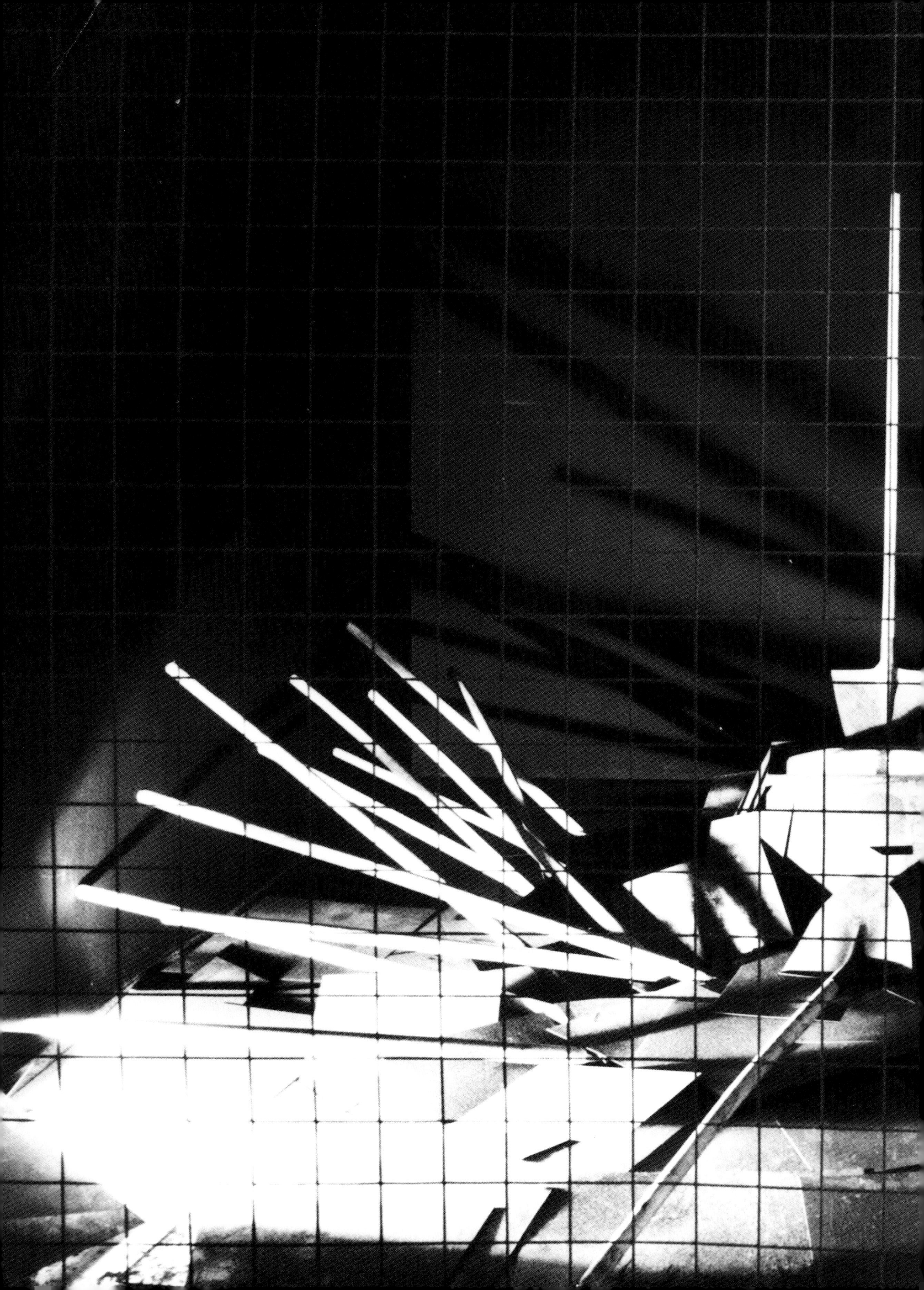

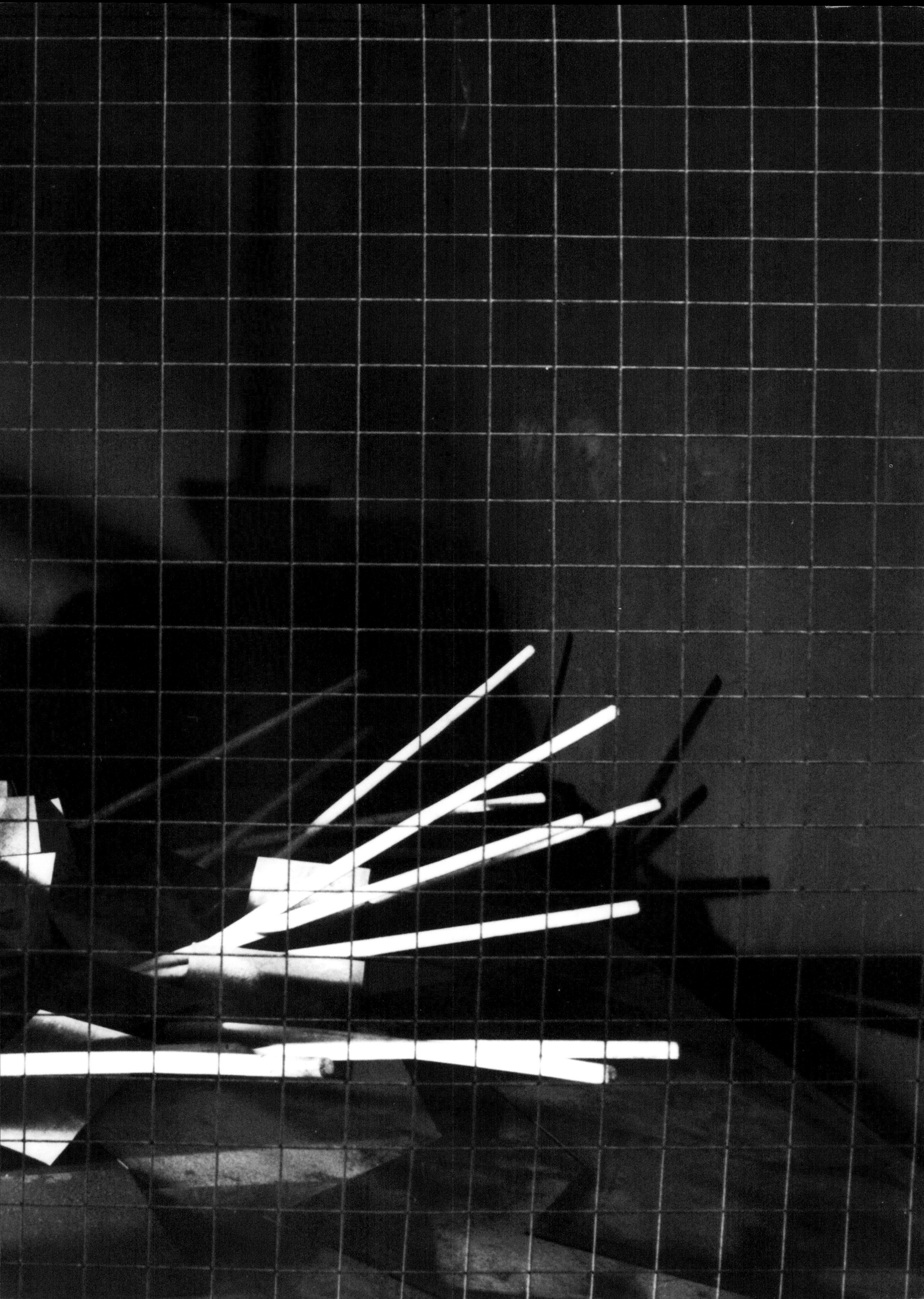

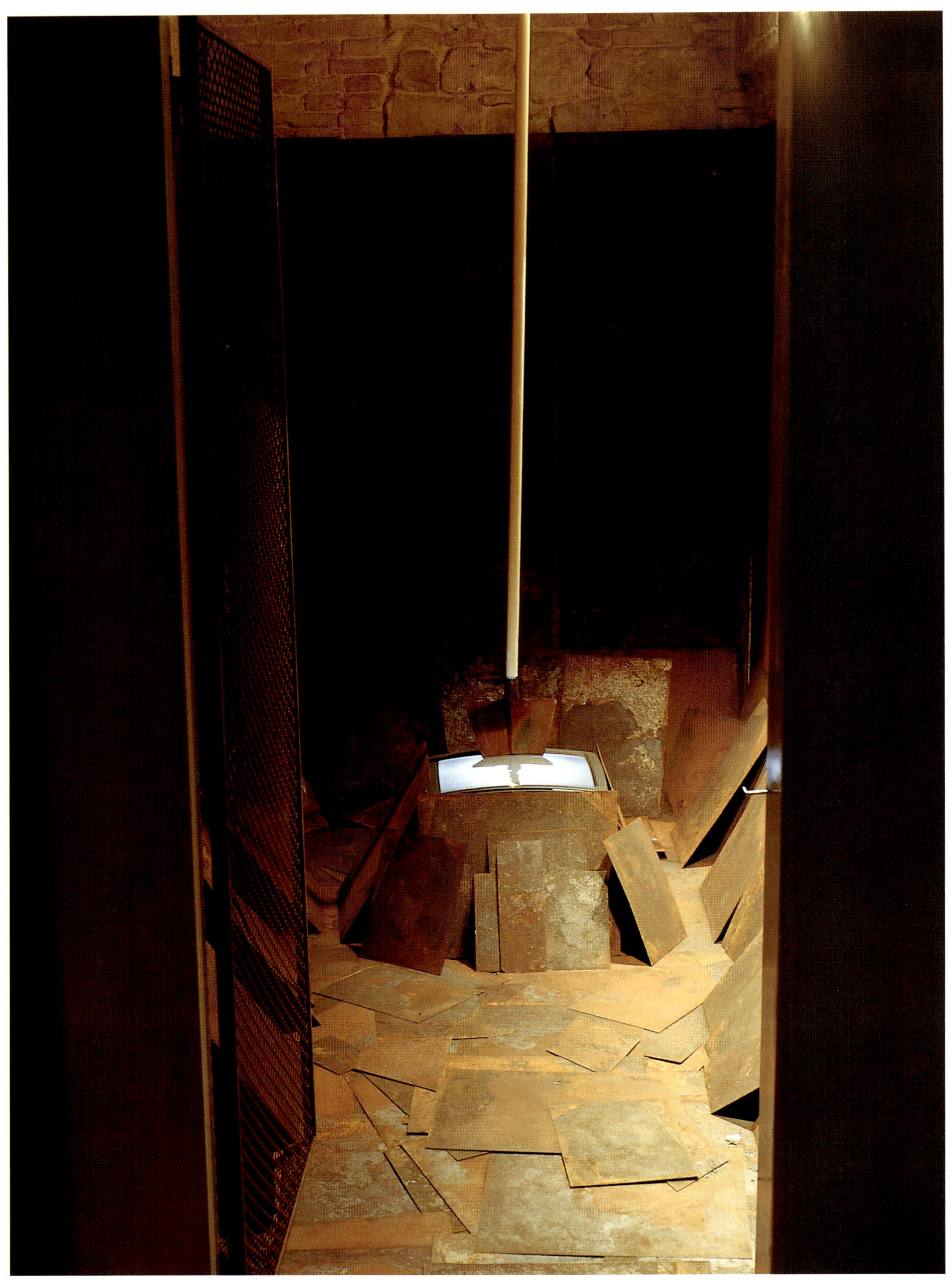

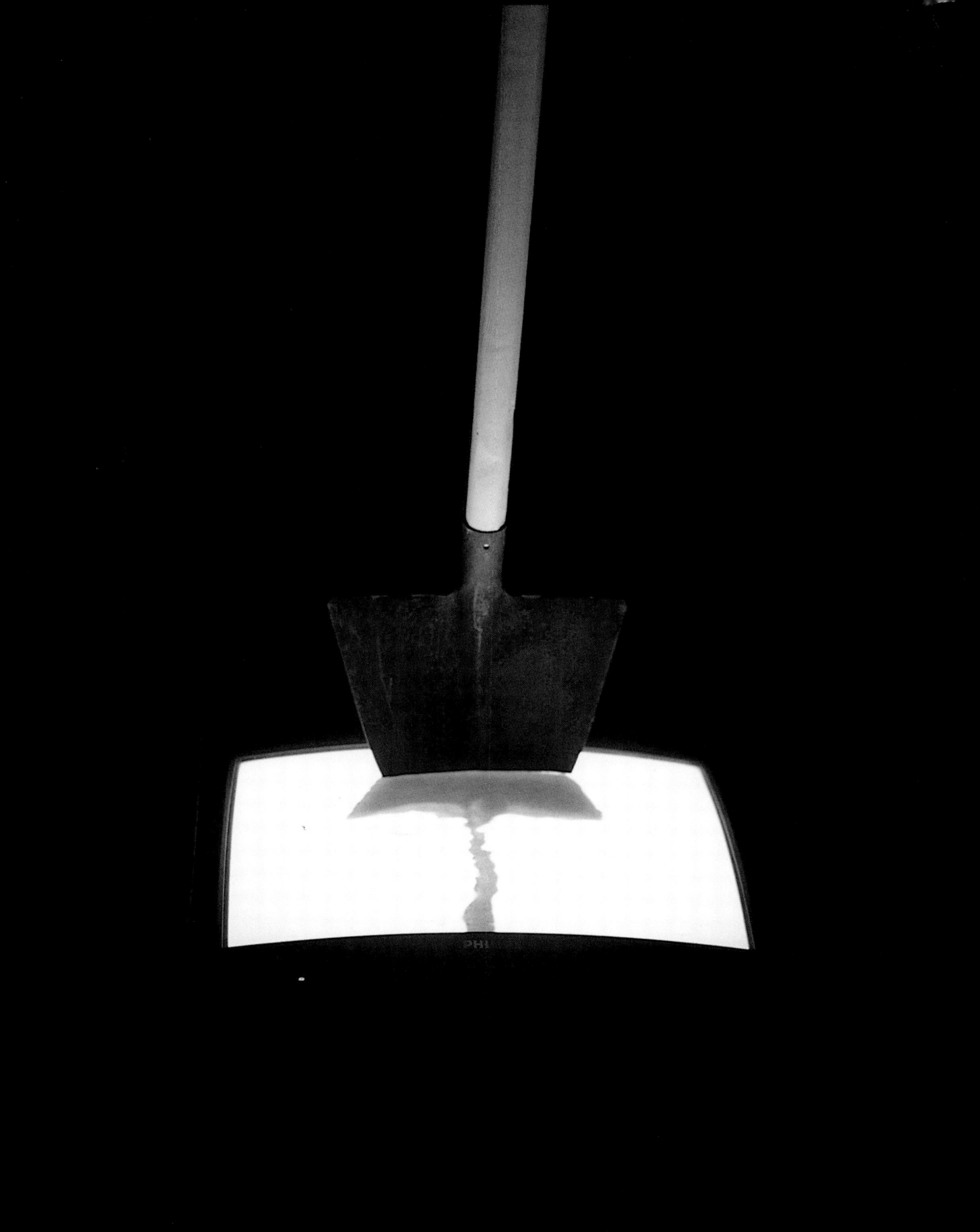

ROMA

87002

KASSEL 1987
Documenta 8
87002.1

MÜNCHEN 1987
Art Forum Raimund Thomas
87002.2

ROM
Videoinstallation 1987
Laufendes Förderband,
Travertinplatten, enkaustierte
Wände, Holzgehäuse, 36 Monitore,
2 Videorecorder, 2 bespielte
Kassetten, Tonaufzeichnung

ROME
Video installation 1987
Wooden structure, moving
conveyor belt, slabs of travertine
marble, encaustic walls,
36 monitors, 2 video recorders,
recorded video cassettes,
soundrecording

ROMA
Videoinstallazione 1987
Montacarichi in movimento,
struttura in legno, pareti
pompeiane ad incausto, lastre di
marmo travertino, 36 monitors,
vhs, cassette registrate, sonoro

Mit *Roma*, präsentiert auf der documenta 1987 in Kassel, hat Fabrizio Plessi vielleicht eine seiner eindrucksvollsten, raumgreifenden Videoinstallationen geschaffen, mit Sicherheit aber eine seiner bekanntesten und meist publizierten. Den Apollosaal der Orangerie verwandelt Plessi in ein Perpetuum mobile der Geschichte. Berninis Petersplatz in Rom nachzeichnend, ist eine kreisförmige Konstruktion geschaffen, bestehend aus auf dem Rücken liegenden Monitoren, die von Travertinplatten eingerahmt sind. Der ganze Raum ist in pompejanisches Rot getaucht. Überall an den Wänden und auch

With Roma, *presented at the documenta in Kassel in 1987, Fabrizio Plessi has perhaps created one of his most impressive spacious video installations, certainly one of his most popular and publicised ones. Plessi transforms the Apollo hall of the Orangerie into a perpetuum mobile of history. Following the example of Bernini's St. Peter's square in Rome, he creates a circular construction of monitors lying on their back, framed by plates of Travertine. The whole room is immersed in Pompejan red. On all walls as well as in the window niches more sheets of travertine are placed, like a*

Roma, presentata alla *documenta* di Kassel nel 1987, è probabilmente da considerarsi una delle più impressionanti videoinstallazioni di Fabrizio Plessi, sicuramente è la più conosciuta e pubblicata. L'artista trasforma la Sala di Apollo della Orangeria in un perpetuum mobile della storia. Ridisegnando la piazza di S. Pietro del Bernini, i monitors, adagiati sul pavimento e incorniciati da lastre di travertino, formano un cerchio quasi completo. Tutto l'ambiente è immerso in un rosso pompeiano. Lungo le pareti e vicino alle spallette delle finestre sono

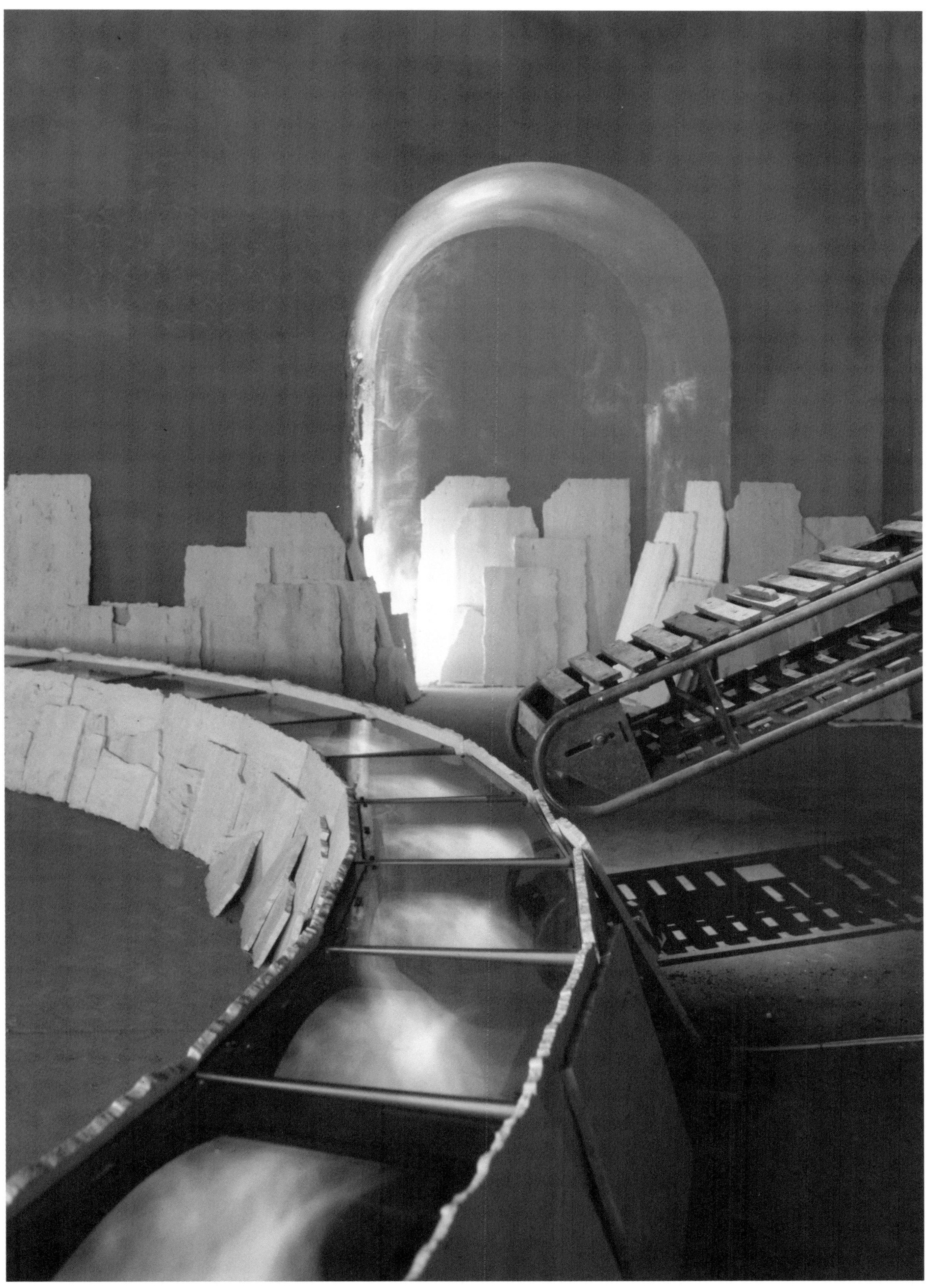

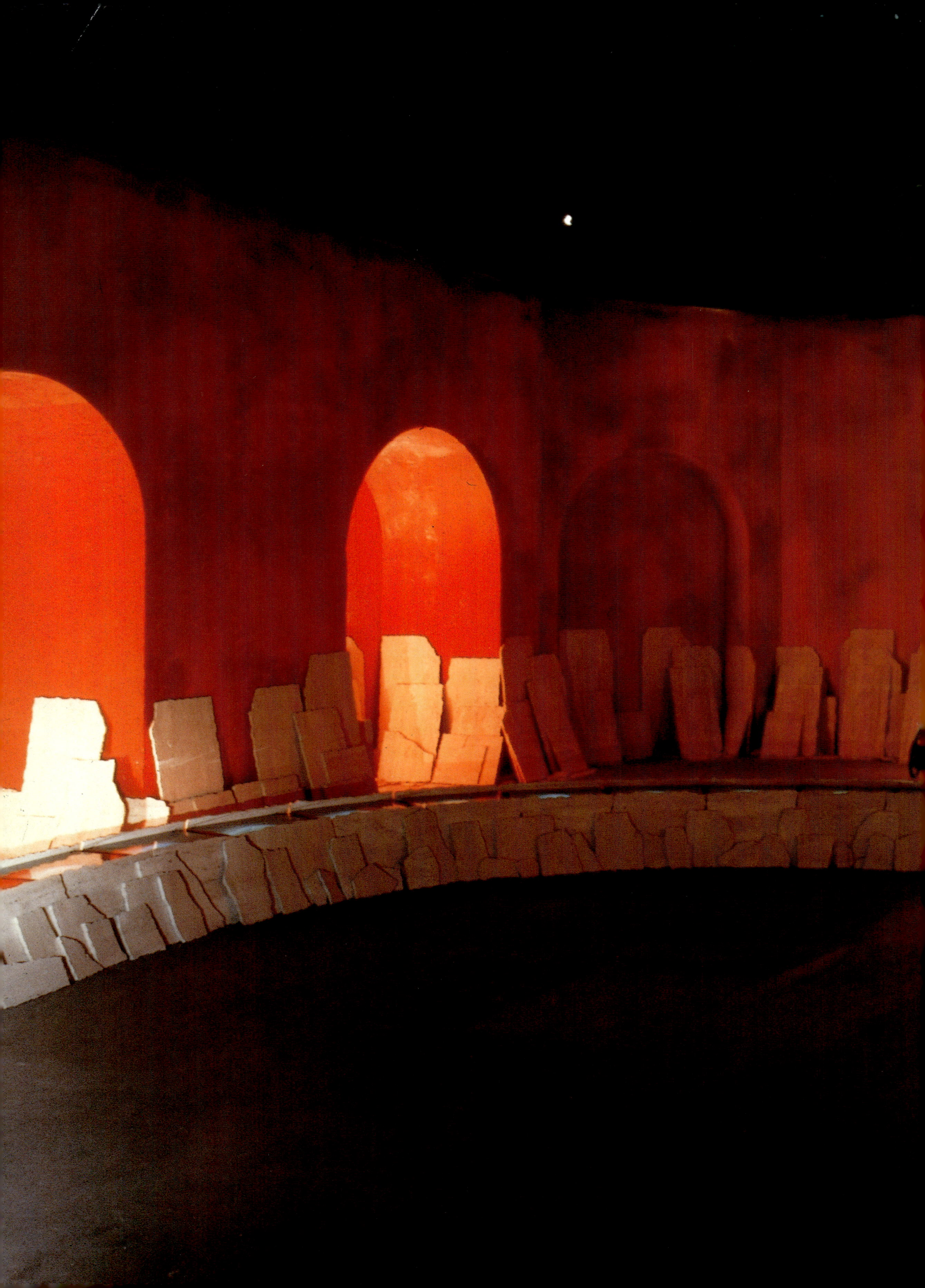

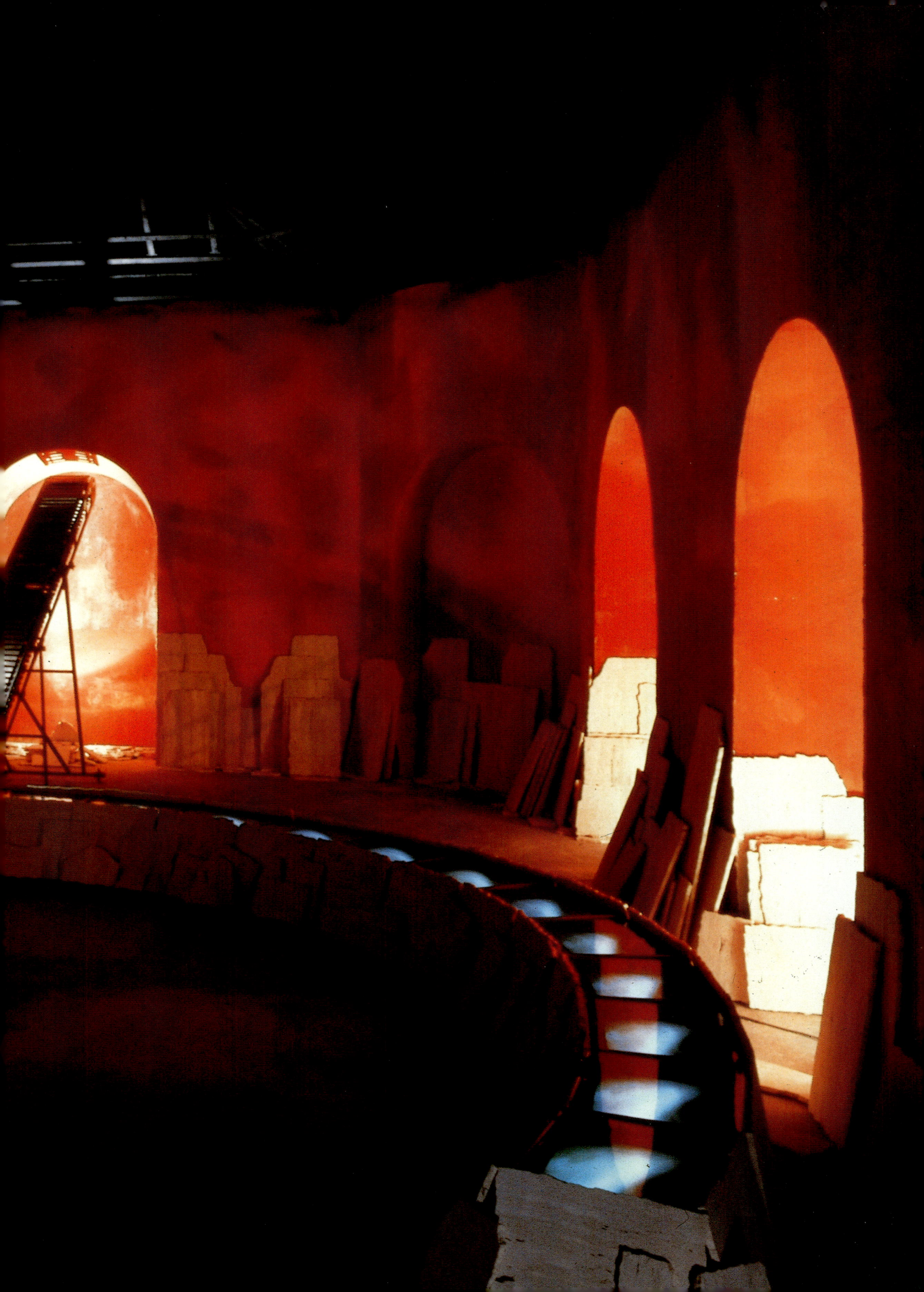

an den Fensterlaibungen stehen weitere Travertinplatten, wie als Momentaufnahme eines Augenblicks. An der Stirnseite des nahezu geschlossenen Kreises befindet sich ein Förderband, beladen mit imaginären Steinen, die in regelmäßigen zeitlichen Abständen in das elektronische Wasser fallen. Der Stein, dessen Aufprall auch hörbar ist, versinkt in der Tiefe des Wassers und wird unsichtbar. Das Wasser beruhigt sich nach einer kleinen Weile wieder und fließt in ruhiger Bewegung kreisförmig weiter. Es gibt einen deutlichen Verweis auf die Architektur und die Geschichte der Stadt Rom, eine Erinnerung an den römischen Niedergang, wo man antike Bauwerke als Steinbrüche für Neubauten verwendete. So verweisen der Stein, der ins Wasser fällt und die an den Wänden aufgestellten Travertinplatten auf die Vergänglichkeit der Architektur, auf den Verfall und damit auf Zeit. Daß nicht nur althergebrachte Kulturen im allgemeinen, sondern seine Wahlheimat Venedig im besonderen von einem Untergang der Architekturen, der Gemäuer, der Steine durch das Wasser bedroht ist, soll hier nur marginal erwähnt werden.

In dieser Videoinstallation ist zum ersten Mal ein signifikanter Städtebezug hergestellt, der im folgenden für zahlreiche weitere Arbeiten noch wichtig werden wird. Fabrizio Plessi hat vor allem in den 90er Jahren viele seiner größeren Environments mit Video direkt oder indirekt Städten oder Orten in der Welt gewidmet, wobei er jeweils ein allgemeines oder bekanntes Element zum Anlaß oder Ausgangspunkt seiner Arbeit nimmt, und dieses mit einem höchst spezifischen Plessi-Aspekt verbindet, mit einem Thema, das ihn persönlich angeht oder ihn persönlich interessiert.

momentary record of an instant in time. On the frontside of the almost closed circle a conveyorbelt is positioned, laden with imaginary stones that drop at regular intervals into the electronic water. The splash is audible, then the stone sinks into the water and becomes invisible. After a while, the water is calm again, and continues to circle in quiet movement. There is a clear reference to the architecture and history of Rome, a reminiscence to the fall of Rome, when antique buildings were used as quarries for new houses. In this way, the stone that drops into the water and the sheets of travertine on the walls refer to the transitoriness of architecture, to decay, and to time. That not only ancient cultures in general, but also his chosen hometown of Venice are threatened with destruction of architecture, walls, and stones through water needs to be mentioned here only marginally.

For the first time, this video installation creates a significant relation to cities, which consequently will be of importance for numerous other works. Fabrizio Plessi has - especially in the nineties - dedicated many of his larger environments with video directly or indirectly to cities or places all over the world, each time taking a general or known element as occasion or starting point for his work, combining it with a highly specific Plessi aspect, a subject interesting or involving himself.

posizionate altre lastre sempre di travertino, come se si trattasse di un'istantanea di un attimo. Nel punto frontale del cerchio un montacarichi trasporta pietre immaginarie che con ritmo costante cadono, in modo acusticamente percepibile, affondano e scompaiono nell'acqua elettronica. Dopo un breve lasso di tempo l'acqua si calma e continua il suo flusso nel cerchio. Non sfugge il riferimento all'architettura e alla storia della città di Roma, un ricordo della decadenza della storia romana, quando elementi costruttivi degli edifici storici furono impiegati per la costruzione di nuovi palazzi e chiese . Così il sasso e il travertino delle pareti alludono al carattere effimero dell'architettura, al declino e, di conseguenza, al tempo. Ma il declino non riguarda solo ed esclusivamente le antiche culture in generale ma, in particolare, anche la sua patria d'elezione Venezia, dove l'acqua minaccia di continuo gli edifici. Con tale videoinstallazione viene instaurato, per la prima volta, un rapporto significativo con la città che assumerà importanza in numerosi altri lavori successivi. Fabrizio Plessi dedica direttamente o indirettamente , soprattutto negli anni novanta, molti dei suoi environments a città o località del mondo selezionando un loro elemento rappresentativo come punto di partenza e combinandolo poi con una sua specifica tematica personale.

VIDEOLAND

87003

CAVAILLON 1987
CENTRE CULTUREL
87003.1

BOLOGNA 1987
GALLERIA D'ARTE MODERNA
87003.2

ROMA 1987
RAI UNO, ›IMMAGINA‹
87003.3

LINZ 1988
NEUE GALERIE DER STADT LINZ
87003.4

VIDEOLAND
Videoinstallation 1987
12 große eiserne Trichter, 12
hölzerne Leitern, Strohballen, 12
Monitore, Videorecorder, bespielte
Kassetten, Tonaufzeichnung. Linz:
blättrige Zweige; Cavaillon: Lavendel und Bruchsteine; Rom: Blumen

VIDEOLAND
Videoinstallazione 1987
12 coni in ferro, scale in legno,
balle di paglia, 12 monitors, vhs,
cassette registrate, sonoro
variazioni · Linz: in aggiunto
frasche fogliate; Cavaillon:
lavanda e pietre; Roma: fiori

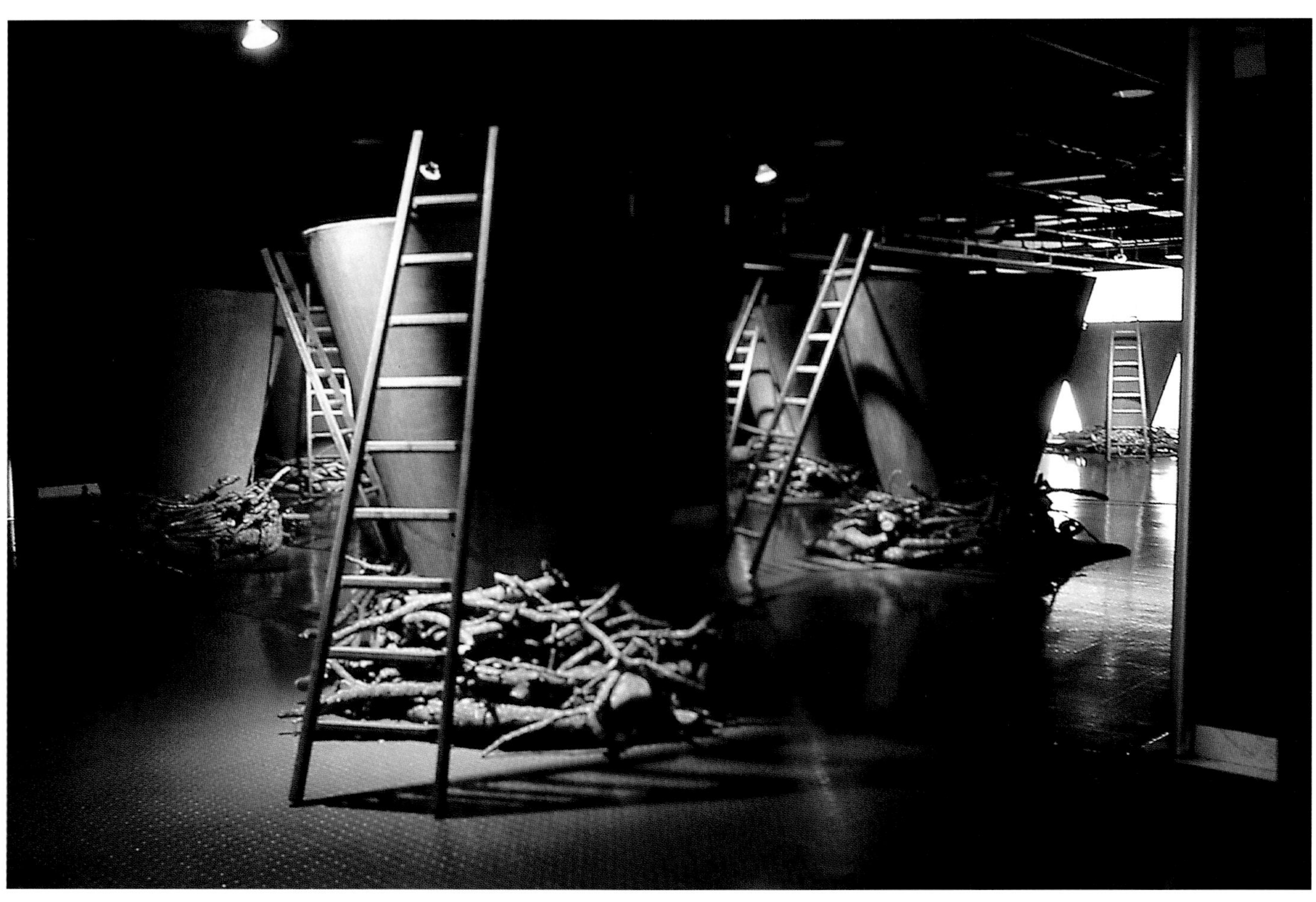

Bei der Installation *Videoland*
sind 12 riesige eiserne Trichter in
kreisförmige Strohbeete - bei
späteren Versionen auch Hölzer,
Lavendel, Äste oder ähnliches -
gestellt, in dessen elektronisches
Wasser am Grunde des Trichters
in unregelmäßigen Abständen ein
nur akustisch wahrnehmbarer
Stein fällt. Um auf den Grund
eines solchen Trichters schauen

In his video installation
Videoland, *12 huge iron funnels
are placed in circular beds of
straw - in later versions wood,
lavender, branches or the like. At
irregular intervals, a stone drops
into the electronic water at the
bottom of the funnel, but only the
sound can be perceived. To see
the bottom of such a funnel, one
has to climb a ladder, thus*

L'installazione *Videoland* è
composta di dodici giganti coni
metallici appoggiati su paglia
stesa per terra a forma di cerchio - più tardi saranno impiegati anche legno, lavanda, rami
o materiali simili - in cui affondano sassi nell'acqua elettronica, irregolarmente e solo
acusticamente percepibili. Per
poter vedere il fondo di uno

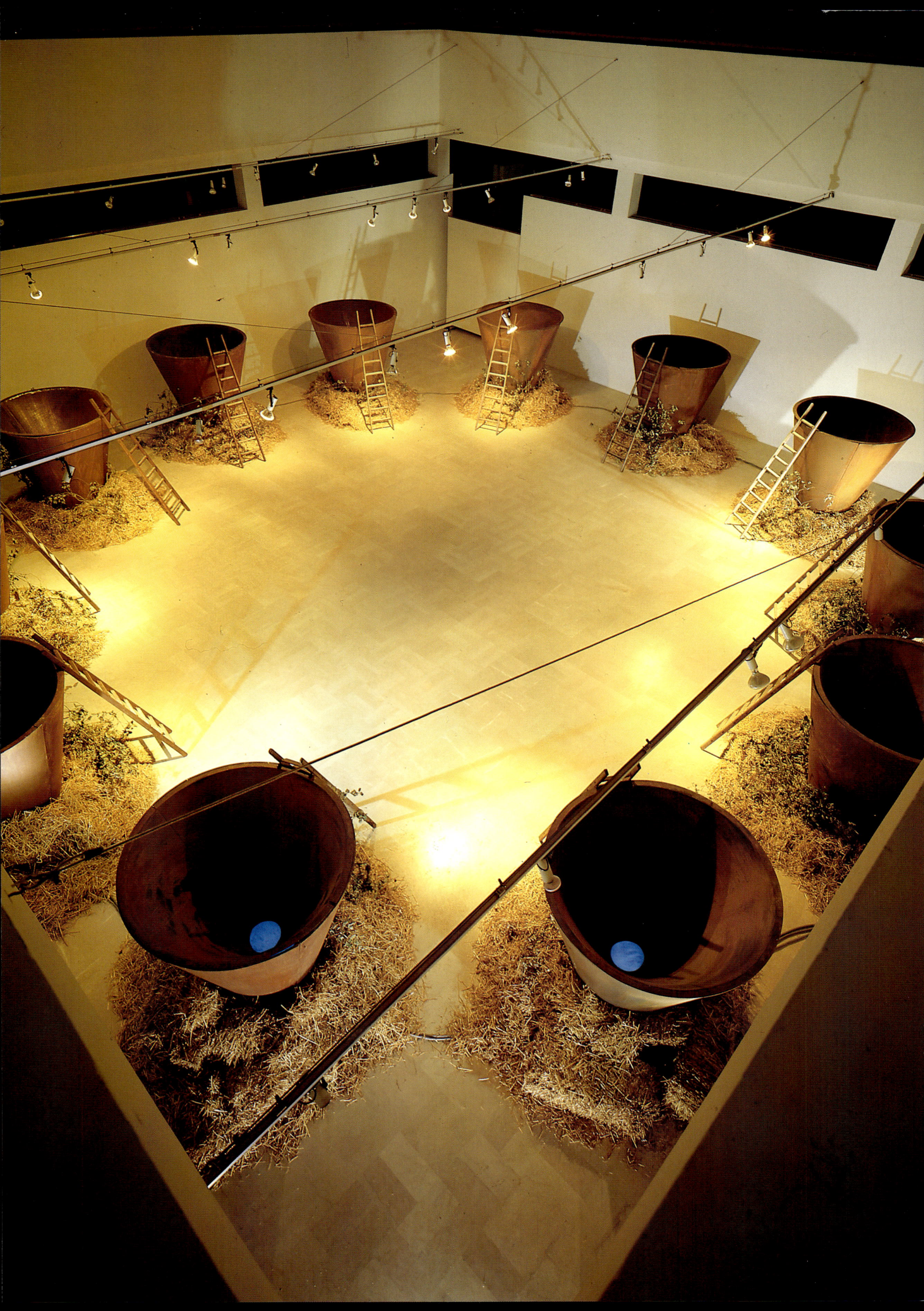

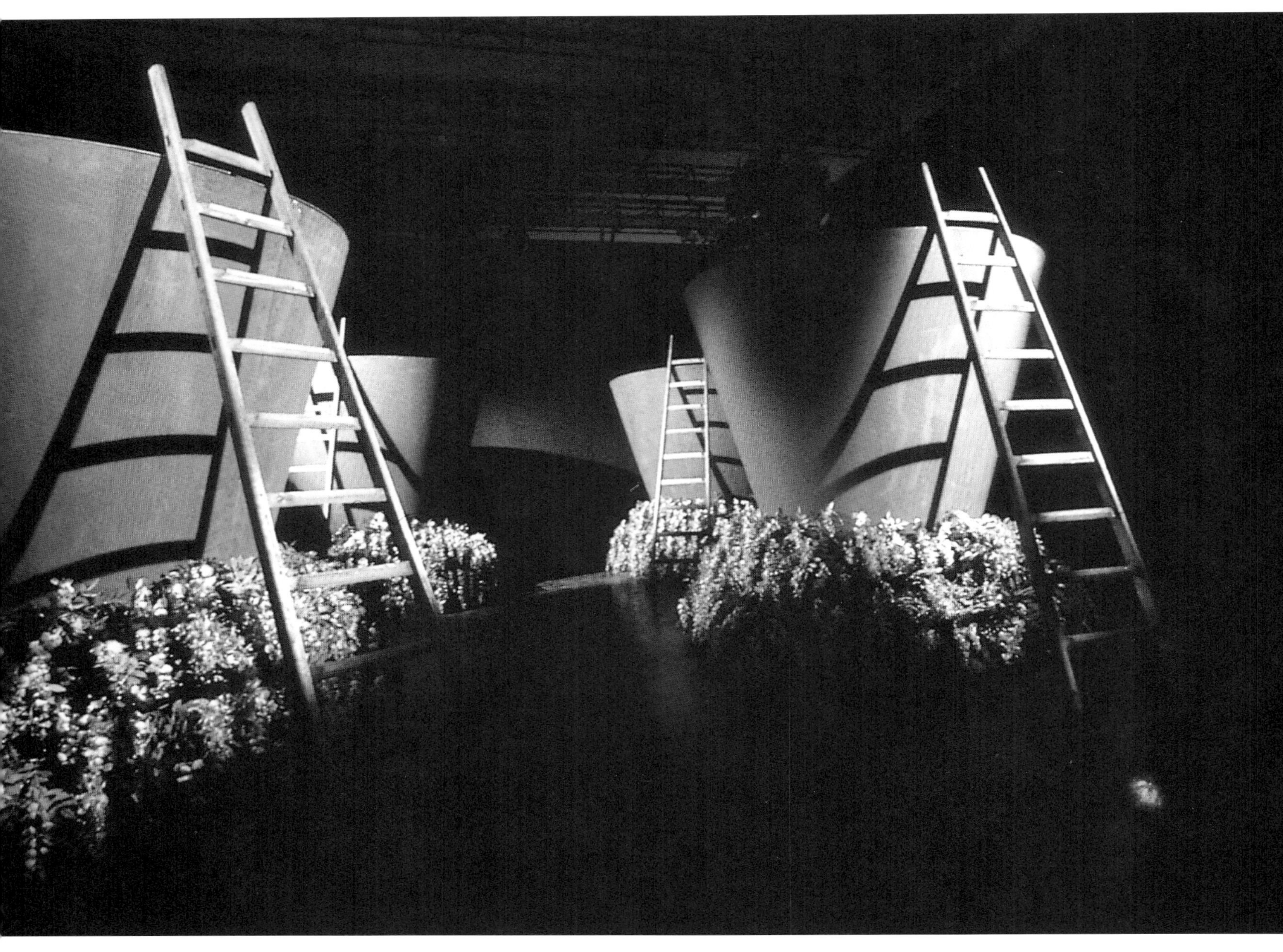

zu können, muß man eine Leiter
besteigen, so daß nur jeweils das
Innere eines Trichters sichtbar
wird. Auch bei dieser Installation,
ähnlich wie bei *Water Desert*, ist
die Erkennbarkeit des Monitors
auf ein Minimum reduziert. In
dem doppelwandigen riesigen
Trichter, der an seiner breiten
Oberseite einen Durchmesser von
nahezu 6 m erreicht, ist in der
Tiefe nur eine kreisförmige
Öffnung übriggeblieben.

*making only the inside of the
funnel visible. In this installation, too, like in* Water Desert, *the
visibility of the monitor is redu-
ced to a minimum. In the depth
of the double-walled funnel,
which, on its upper side has a
diameter of almost 6 metres, only
a small circular opening
remains.*

degli coni si deve salire una
scala. Anche in questa installazione, come in *Water Desert*, la
riconoscibilità del monitor è
ridotta al minimo. Nella profon-
dità del cono gigante a doppia
parete, di 6 metri di diametro
nel lato superiore, si intravede
solamente una piccola apertura
circolare.

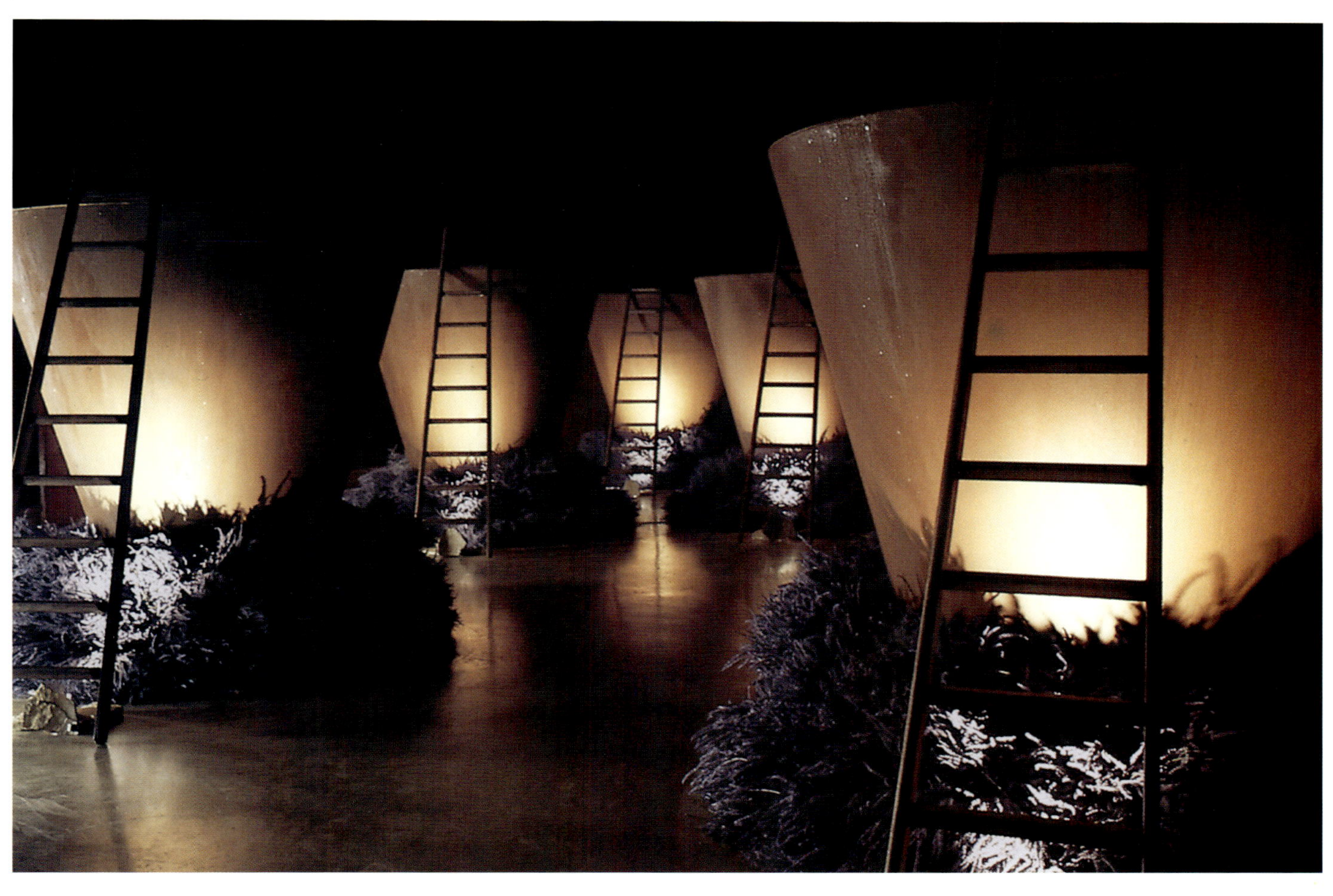

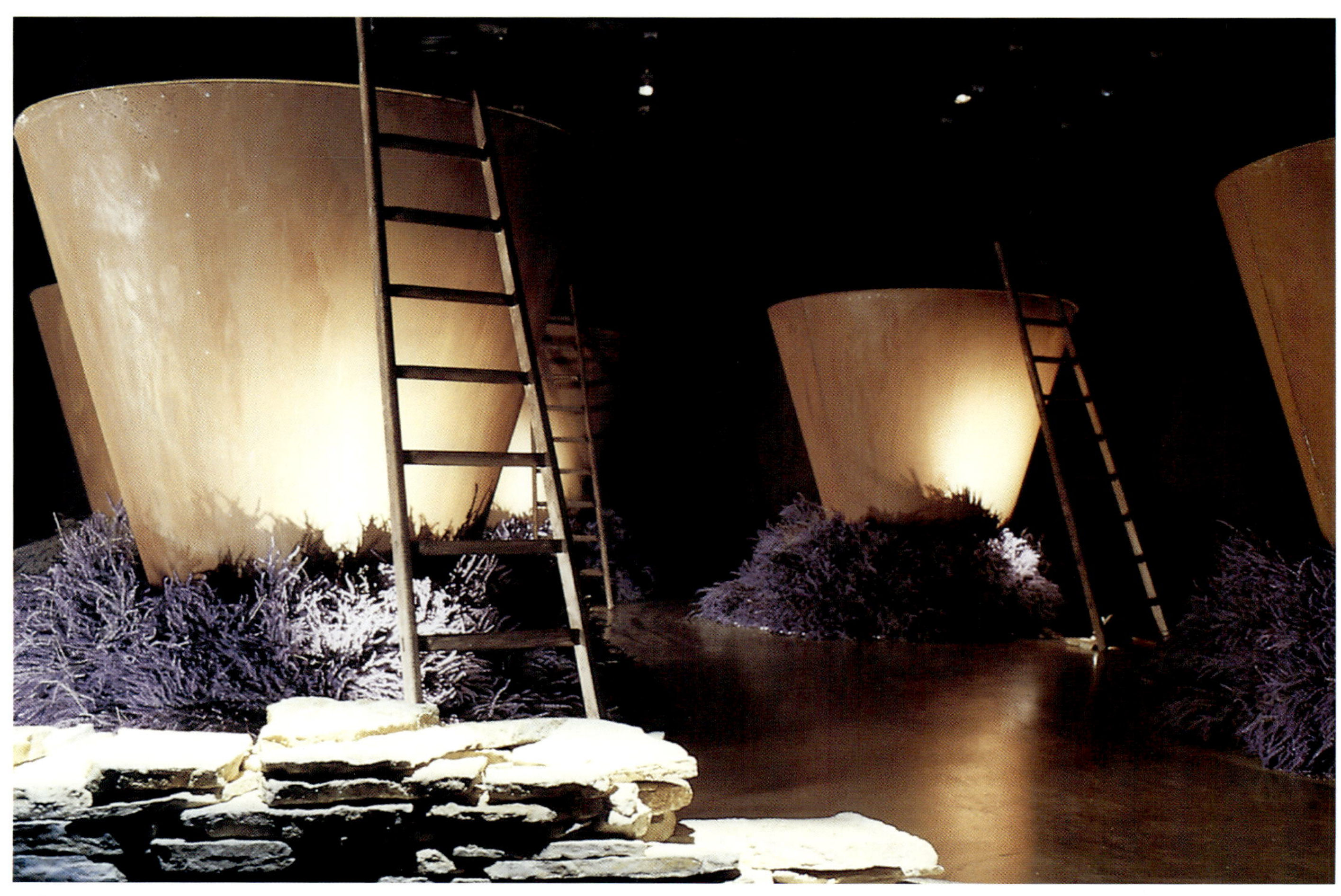

VIDEOCRUZ

88001

MADRID 1988
Museo Español de Arte Contemporaneo
88001.1

ROMA 1988
RAI uno, ›Immagina‹
88001.2

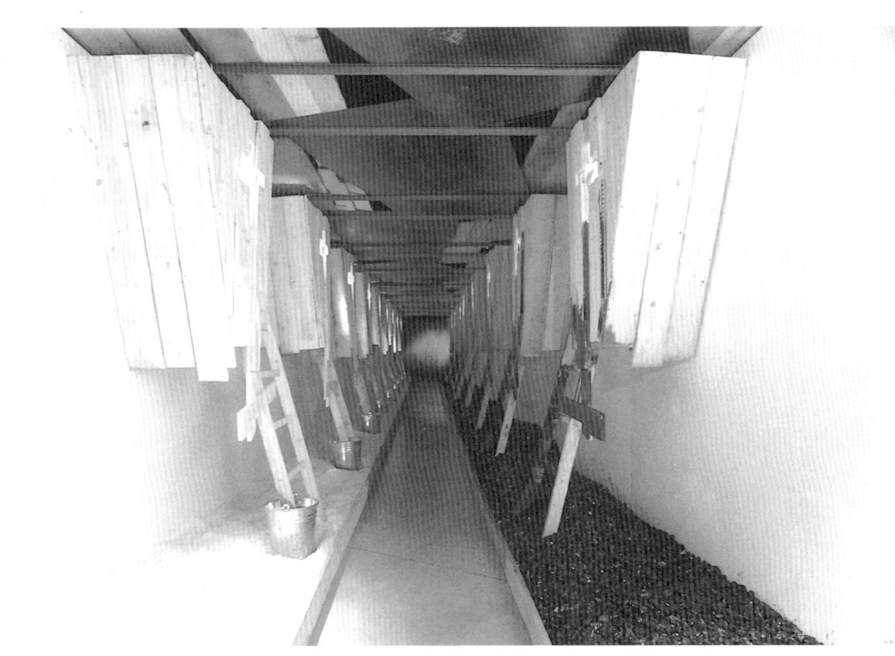

In der Installation *Videocruz*
von 1988 ist der dialektische
Gegensatz von Wasser und Feuer
zum Thema gemacht. In hölzerne
Dreieckskonstruktionen sind
kreuzförmige Ausschnitte geschaffen, die Durchblicke auf die
dahinter liegenden Monitore
erlauben. Eine Reihe von blau-
sprudelnden Wasser-Kreuzen
steht eine Reihe von rotleuchten-
den Feuer-Kreuzen gegenüber.
Leitern stellen die Verbindung
vom Boden zu den hölzernen
Konstruktionen her, die an der
Wand hängend angebracht sind.
Bereits das unterhalb der Kreuze
auf dem Boden liegende Material
verweist auf das, was weiter oben
zu sehen ist. Unter den blauen
Wasser-Kreuzen befindet sich
eine Salzschicht, unter den roten
Feuer-Kreuzen eine Kohleschicht.
In dieser Videoinstallation ist der
alte Gegensatz von Wasser und
Feuer enthalten, den bereits die
Vorsokratiker - jeder für sich auf
seine Weise - zum Thema gemacht haben.

Thales von Milet beantwortete
im 6. Jh. v.Chr. die Frage nach
dem Ursprung (αρχη) allen Seins,
die als Basis dafür gilt, wie das
Sein (φυσισ) des Seienden beschaffen ist, mit: »aus dem Wasser«. Thales sah im Meere und

The video installation Videocruz *of 1988 takes the dialectic
contrast of water and fire as its
subject. Sections in the form of a
cross are cut into wooden triangular constructions, allowing
views on the monitors positioned
behind them. A string of blue,
sparkling water-crosses is confronted by a row of shining red
fire-crosses. Ladders form the
connection from the ground to the
wooden structures that are placed
hanging on the walls. The material lying on the ground already
points to what can be seen further
up. Under the blue water-crosses
a layer of salt can be found, a
layer of coal below the red fire-
crosses. In this video installation
we find the old contrast between
water and fire, that has been
subject of the Pre-Socratics - each*

L'installazione *Videocruz* del
1988 tematizza il contrasto
dialettico fra acqua e fuoco.
Costruzioni lignee triangolari
presentano un'apertura a forma
di croce che permettono la
visione dei monitors al loro
interno. Una serie di croci di
acqua blu zampillante è con-
trapposta ad una serie di croci
di fuoco rosso. Delle scale
collegano il pavimento con le
costruzioni lignee appese alla
parete. Ma già il materiale sul
pavimento, al di sotto delle
croci, preannuncia ciò che si
vedrà in alto: uno strato di sale
al di sotto delle croci d'acqua e
uno strato di carbone al di sotto
delle croci di fuoco. La videoinstallazione interpreta l'eterno
contrasto fra acqua e fuoco, già
contemplato dai presocratici, e

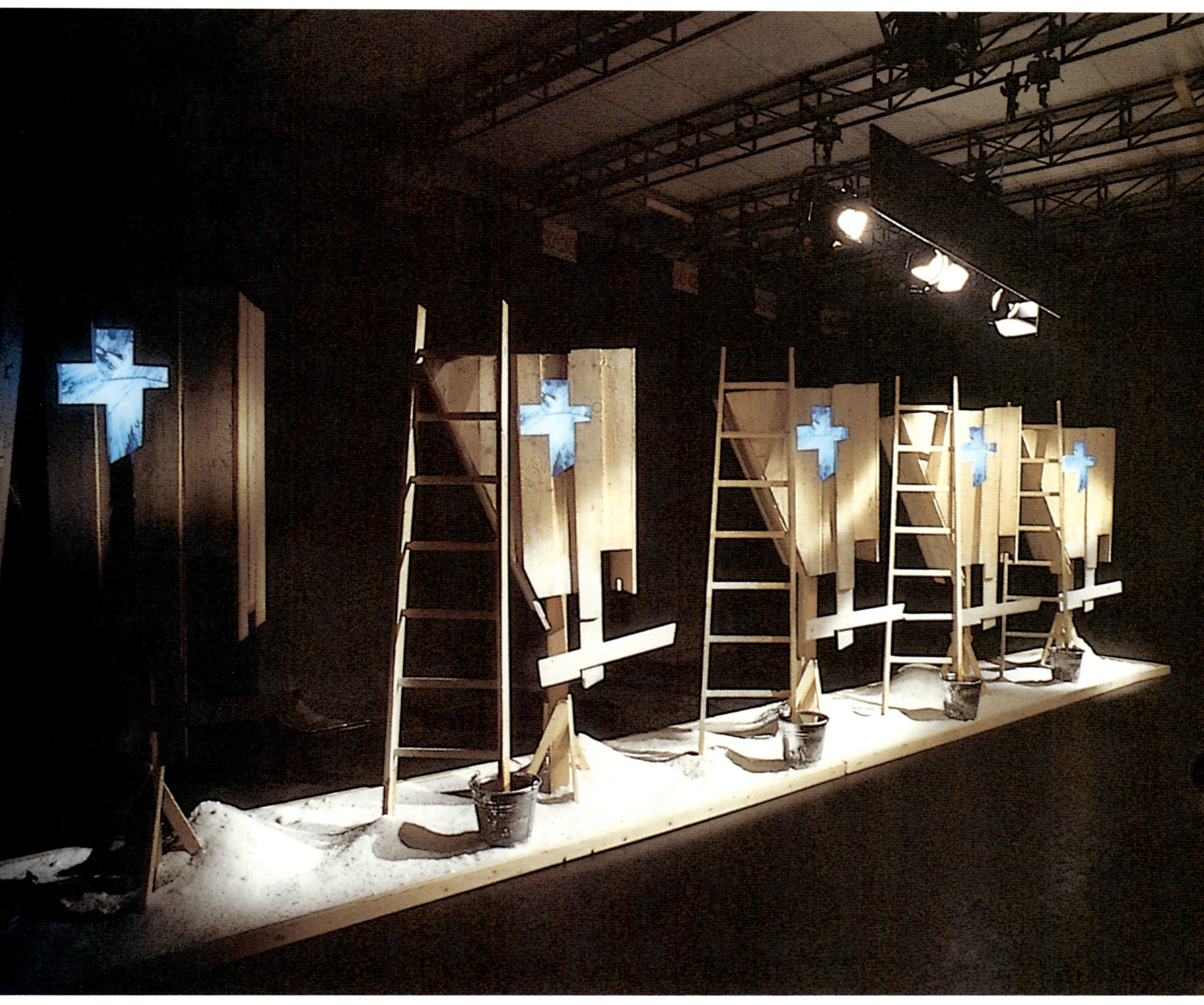

dem Wasser den alles umschlie-
ßenden Ozean, die bewegende
Kraft, das lebenspendende und
erhaltende Element, das auch in
der Luft in Form von Stürmen und
Regengüssen unentbehrlich für
jedes lebende, atmende Wesen
sei. Dagegen sah Herakleitos von
Ephesos - etwa eine Generation
jünger, um 500 v.Chr. - das Sein
als Fügung des Gegensätzlichen
durch den Verstand (λογοσ), in der
Verwandlung begriffen, im Wer-

in his own way - before.

In the sixth century B.C., Tha-
les of Milet answered the question
on the origin (αρχη) of all exist-
ence, that is considered the basis
of what existence (φυσισ) of the
existent is like: "From water."
Thales viewed the sea and water
as the all-encompassing ocean, the
moving force, life-giving and -
saving element which is also - in
the form of tempests and rainfalls
- indispensable for each living,

da ciascuno di essi in modo
proprio.

Tales da Mileto nel VI secolo
a. C. afferma che l'origine
(αρχη) dell'essere, cioè la base
della definizione dell'essenza
dell'essere (φυσισ), è l'acqua.
Egli riconosce nel mare e
nell'acqua, l'oceano che racchi-
ude tutto in sè, la forza spingen-
te, l'elemento che dona e con-
serva la vita, indispensabile,
anche nell'aria in forma di

141

den erfahrbar. Das Sein ist im Werden und in ständiger Veränderung begriffen, resultierend und sich nährend aus der Dialektik der Gegensätze. Einerseits basiert Heraklit in gewisser Weise auf Thales, andererseits fügt er dem Wasser noch das Feuer für den Ursprung (αρχη) der Dinge hinzu und sieht die Welt als ein Geschehen, einen Prozeß, ein ewiges Werden und Vergehen. Als Sinnbild ewigen Vergehens und Entstehens sieht er die Flamme, die den in sich zurücklaufenden Kreisprozeß, ähnlich wie bei der Arbeit *Roma*, erst in Gang setzt, an dessen Anfang und Ende das alles verzehrende und aus sich neugebärende Feuer steht. Das Werden ist im Fluß, die Welt ein fließendes Geschehen und alle Wahrnehmung des Beständigen, so Heraklit, ist Schein. Wie der Fluß, in den ich heute hineinsteige, nur scheinbar derselbe ist, wie der von gestern. »Τοισ ποταμοισ εμβεινομεν τε και ουκ εμβαινομεν«, »Es sind dieselben Flüsse und doch nicht dieselben Flüsse, in die wir hineinsteigen, oder vielleicht deutlicher: man kann nie zweimal in denselben Fluß hineinsteigen, weil sowohl der Fluß, als auch man Selbst, in der Zeit, die vergangen ist, ein anderer geworden ist.« »Παντα ρει« - »Alles fließt«, das Sein ist im Werden. Doch wenngleich Heraklit den Gegensatz als Vater aller Dinge ansieht, löst sich dieser Gegensatz am Ende in Einheit und Harmonie auf, denn im Kosmos waltet eine Vernunft (λογοσ).

Den Gegenpol zu der Heraklitschen Lehre vom Werden bildet die Eleatische Lehre vom einen unveränderlichen Sein, das sich im Denken ausdrückt. Parmenides von Elea, der Zeitgenosse Heraklits, formuliert diese Lehre und begründet damit die abendländische Ontologie.

breathing creature. Contrary to this, Herakleitos of Ephesos, about one generation later, that is around 500 B.C., saw existence as coincidence of opposites through reason (λογοσ), understood in change, experienced in its development. Being is in development, in permanent change, resulting and feeding on the dialectics of opposites. On the one hand, Herakleitos is based to a certain degree on Thales, on the other hand he adds fire to water as the origin (αρχη) of things and sees the world as a happening, a process, an eternal birth and death. He considers the flame as symbol of eternal death and growth that starts the circular, in itself revolving process - similar to the work Roma *- beginning and ending with the all-consuming and re-birthing fire. There is continuous development, the world is a flow of actions, and all conception of constancy, according to Herakleitos, is semblance, like the river, into which I go today, only appears to be the same as the one yesterday. "Τοισ ποταμοισ εμβεινομεν τε και ουκ εμβαινομεν", they are the same rivers, and yet not the same rivers, into which we step, or, even more specific: One can never step twice into the same river, because the river itself as well as oneself has altered during the time elapsed. "Παντα ρει" - everything flows, existence is in evolution. But even if Herakleitos considers antithesis as father of all things this contrast dissolves in the end in unity and harmony, for reason (λογοσ) rules in the universe.*

In contrast to Herakleitos' thesis of evolution there is the Eleatic doctrine of invariable existence that is expressed in thinking. Parmenides of Elea, contemporary of Herakleitos, formulates this theory, thus founding the occidental ontology.

pioggia o temporale, per ogni essere vivente. Eraclito di Efeso invece, una generazione più tardi, considera l'essere come i contrari uniti dalla ragione (λογοσ), in continua mutazione e percepibile nel divenire. L'essere risulta dalla dialettica degli opposti di cui si nutre. Se Eraclito in un certo modo si riallaccia alla teoria di Tales, aggiunge però il fuoco all'acqua quale origine (αρχη) delle cose e interpreta il mondo come un processo, un eterno divenire e svanire. L'immagine di tale eterno processo è la fiamma che avvia, simile alla installazione *Roma*, il ciclo, che ha come inizio e fine il fuoco che tutto consuma e tutto rigenera. Il divenire è un flusso, il mondo un processo fluido e la percezione della invariabilità, secondo Eraclito, apparenza. Così come il fiume che mi bagna oggi è solo apparentemente quello di ieri. »Τοισ ποταμοισ εμβεινομεν τε και ουκ εμβαινομεν«, »Sono gli stessi fiumi che ci bagnono e nello stesso tempo non lo sono« o, meglio, non ci si può mai bagnare nello stesso fiume poichè sia il fiume, sia la persona stessa sono cambiati nel tempo intercorso. »Παντα ρει« - »Tutto scorre«, l'essere diviene. Ma anche se Eraclito considera il contrasto il padre di tutte le cose, alla fine tale contrasto si scioglie nella unione e nell'armonia, perchè il cosmo è dominato dalla ragione (λογοσ).

La teoria di Eraclito è agli antipodi di quella eleatica, formulata da Parmenide di Elea, contemporaneo di Eraclito, e fondamento della ontologia occidentale, secondo la quale l'essere è assoluto e immutabile e si esprime nel pensiero.

CANAL D'ORO

88002

VENEZIA 1988
MUSEO CORRER
88002.1

GOLDENER KANAL
Videoinstallation 1988
Holzkonstruktion, Verkleidung mit
venezianischem Gold-Mosaik,
24 Monitore, 2 Videorecorder,
2 bespielte Kassetten
60 x 320 x 3000 cm

GOLDEN CANAL
Video installation 1988
Wooden structure, covered by
golden Venetian mosaics,
24 monitors, 2 video recorders,
recorded video cassettes
60 x 320 x 3000 cm

CANAL D'ORO
Videoinstallazione 1988
Struttura in legno rivestita di
mosaici d'oro veneziani,
24 monitors, 2 vhs, 2 cassette
registrate, sonoro
60 x 320 x 3000 cm

Canal d'Oro, entstanden für
und 1988 ausgestellt im Museum
Correr in Venedig ist im weitesten
Sinne seinen Städtearbeiten
zuzurechnen, denn sie ist zu
verstehen als eine Hymne an die
Stadt Venedig, die Stadt der
Wasserstraßen, die schon in
seiner Studentenzeit eine große
Faszination auf den Künstler
ausübte, und die ihn immer
wieder in ihren Bann zieht.
Vielleicht ist es sogar so, daß
sämtliche seiner Videoinstallationen, und auch schon seine früheren Aktionen und Performances,
die um das Thema Wasser krei-
sen, im übertragenen Sinn eine
Art Hymne an die Stadt bedeuten.

Canal d'Oro, *created for and*
exhibited in the Museum Correr
in Venice in 1988, is, in a broad
sense, to be counted among
Plessi's city-works, for it is to be
understood as a hymn to the city
of Venice, the city of waterways,
that has already highly fascina-
ted the artist during his years of
study, and which again and
again draws him into its spell.
Perhaps it is true that all of his
video installations, as well as his
early actions and performances
circling around the subject of
water, in a figurative sense are a
hymn to the city. Thus it is
remarkable that Fabrizio Plessi
builds artificial channels, in

Canal d'Oro, realizzata per il
Museo Correr a Venezia ed ivi
esposta nel 1988, è, in senso
lato, da annoverare fra le opere
dedicate alle città, in quanto da
intendere quale inno alla città
di Venezia, alla città dei canali
che già dai tempi
dell'Accademia esercita un forte
fascino sull'artista. Forse si può
affermare che tutte le videoinstallazioni, ma anche le prime
azioni e le performances dal
tema dell'acqua, rappresentano,
in un certo senso metaforico,
una sorta di inno alla città
lagunare. Così ad esempio salta
subito all'occhio che Fabrizio
Plessi in molte delle sue opere,

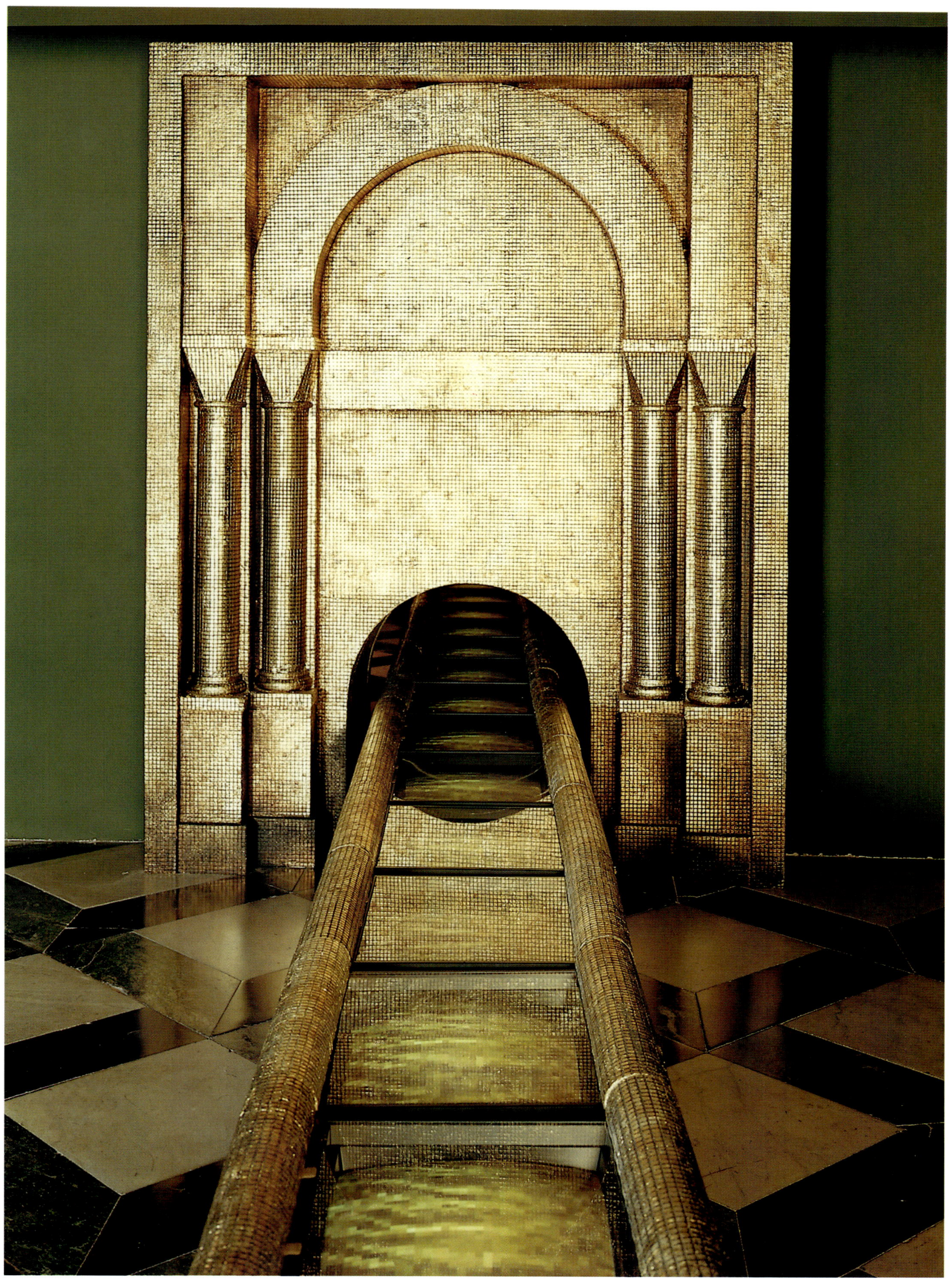

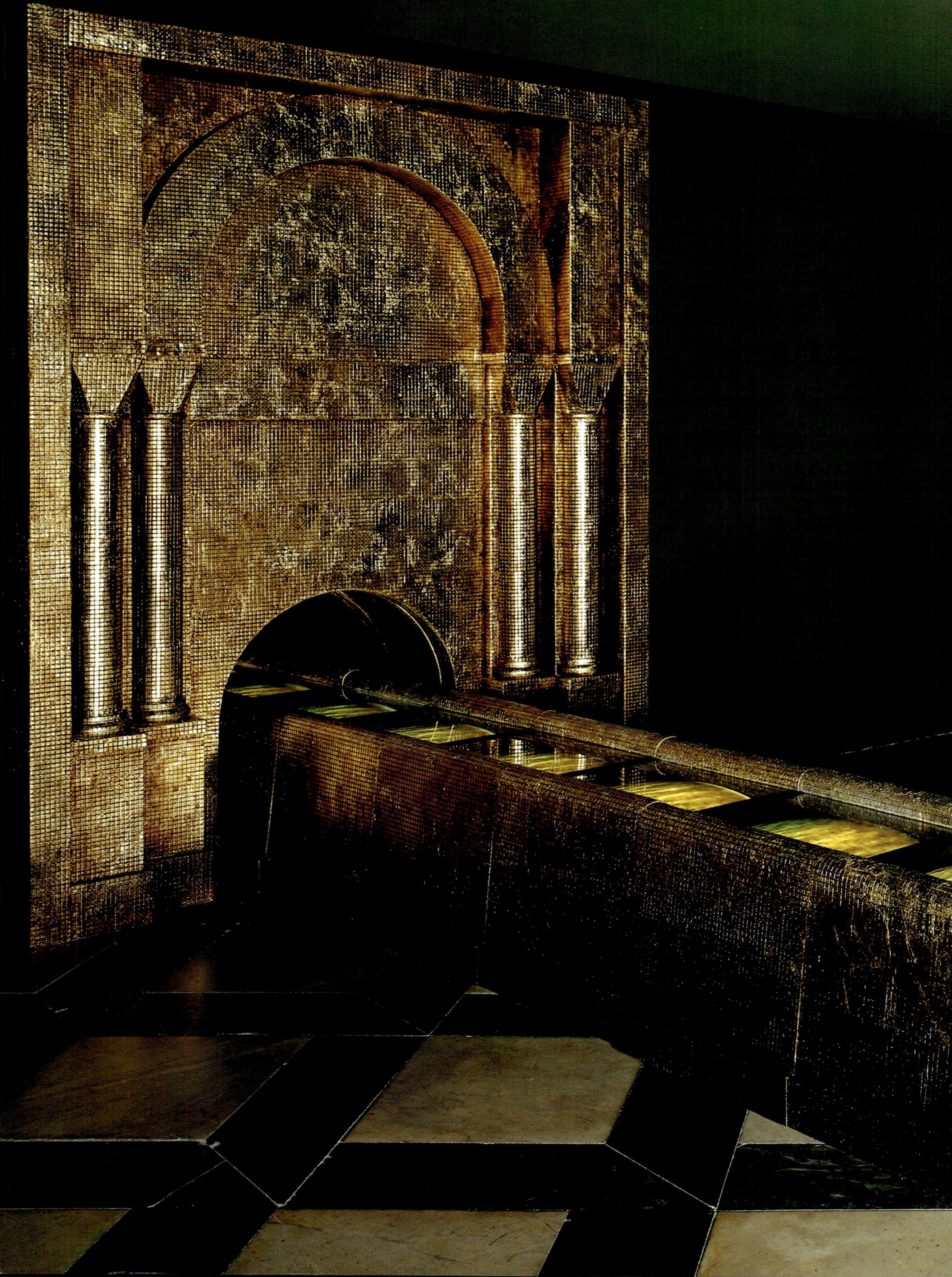

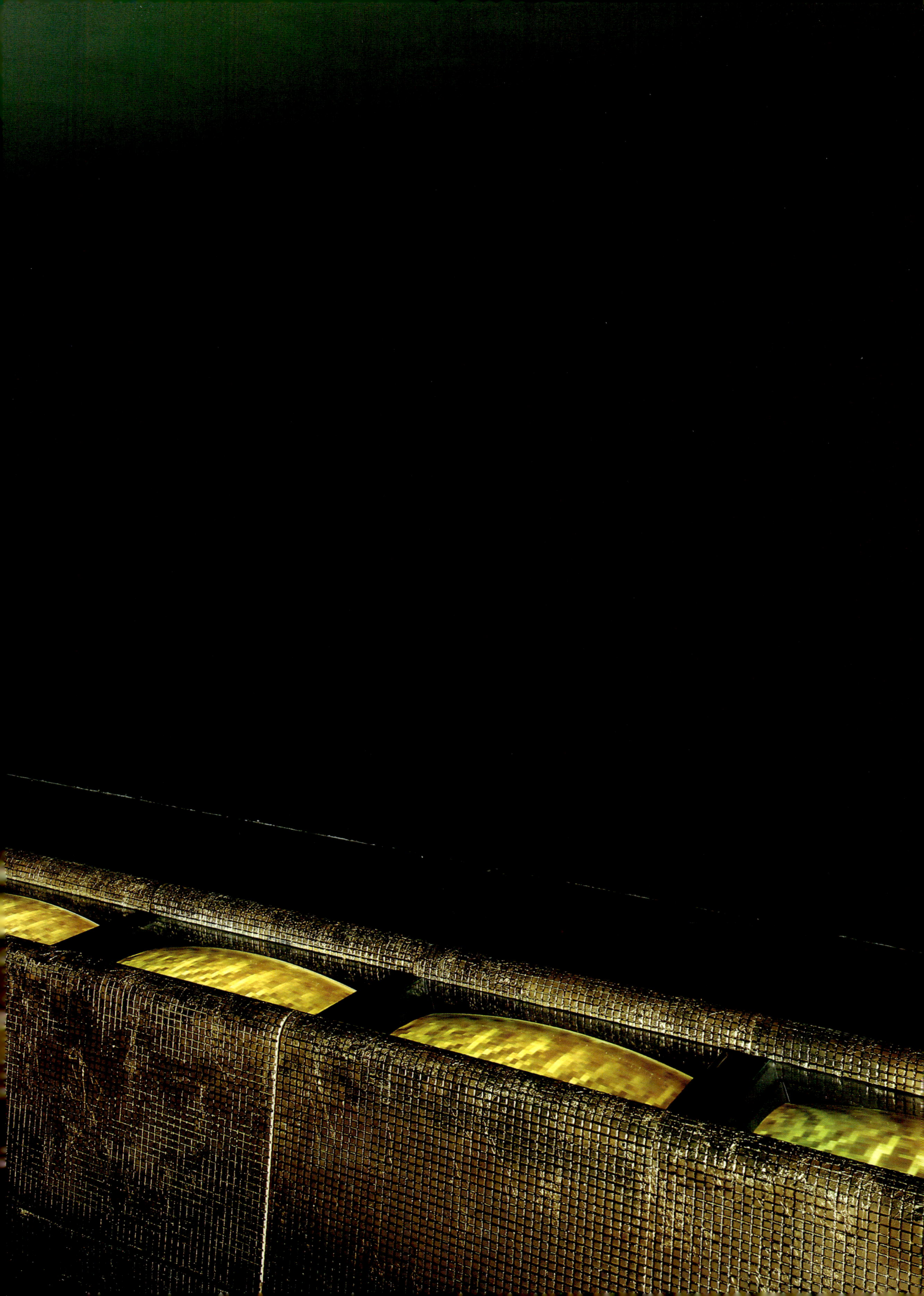

So fällt beispielsweise auf, das Fabrizio Plessi in vielen seiner Installation artifizielle Kanäle baut, in denen sein immaterielles, elektronisches Wasser fließt, wie auch hier, in dieser Installation. Es ist das Mysterium, das Geheimnis, die unheimliche Ausstrahlung dieser Stadt, die er erforschen will. *Ricerca sull'acqua* könnte man sein gesamtes Werk überschreiben, in dem seine Liebe zu Venedig immer wieder sichtbar wird.

Doch hinter dem Titel *Canal d'Oro* verbirgt sich nicht nur Fabrizio Plessis Faszination an dem Spiegeln der glänzenden und flirrenden Wasseroberflächen in den Kanälen Venedigs und den tanzenden Sonnenreflexen auf dem Mauerwerk der Brückenbögen, die er sich in seinen Videoinstallationen zurückzuholen oder vielleicht auf andere Weise neu zu erschaffen versucht, sondern es gibt darüber hinaus einen ganz konkreten Bezug zu Venedig. Bei dieser Installation strömt ein elektronisch in Wasser aufgelöstes Goldmosaik aus dem Markusdom in einem Kanal aus Bildschirmen, der von antik-anmutenden Triumphbögen überwölbt ist. Diese Triumphbögen sind als Holzkonstruktion mit einer golden schimmernden Oberflächenbearbeitung ausgeführt. Das Ganze wirkt, historisch auf das Werk Fabrizio Plessis bezogen, wie ein Vorweggriff auf die Mainzer Installation mit dem Titel *Der Fluß der Geschichte*, bei dem ein mosaikartiger elektronischer Fluß durch ein tatsächlich antikes Portal hindurchfließt. Eine zusätzliche venezianische Assoziation provoziert der Titel auch dadurch, daß er eine gedanklich-begriffliche Verbindung zwischen dem bekannten Bauwerk Ca' d'Oro (das Haus aus Gold oder der Palazzo aus Gold) und dem venezianischen Canale (Canale Grande) hervorruft.

which his immaterial electronic water flows, in many of his installations, just like in this installation. It is the mystery, the secret, the sinister aura of this city that he wants to explore. Ricerca sull'acqua *could be a possible headline for the totality of his work, in which his love of Venice becomes visible again and again.*

Yet under the title Canal d'Oro *can not only be found Fabrizio Plessi's fascination in the mirrors of glittering and flickering water surfaces in the channels of Venice, and the dancing reflections of the sun on the walls of arched bridges that he tries to remember or, by different means, attempts to recreate in his video installations, but there is, beyond this, a very concrete relation to Venice. In this installation, an electronic gold mosaic dissolved in water flows from St. Mark's cathedral through a channel of screens that is spanned by antique-like triumphal arches. These triumphal arches are executed as wooden structures with a surface treatment of shiny gold. The whole structure gives, historically seen in the context of Plessi's work, the impression of an early form of the installation in Mainz entitled* The River of History, *in which a mosaic-like electronic river flows through a real, antique portal. An additional association to Venice is provoked in the title by combining the famous Venetian building Ca' d'Oro (House or Palace of Gold) with the name of the Venetian channel (Canale Grande).*

così come in questa, fa uso di canali artificiali, nei quali scorre l'acqua immateriale ed elettronica. Egli esplora il mistero, il segreto e l'immenso fascino di questa città. *Ricerca sull'acqua* si potrebbe intitolare la sua opera omnia, che svela di continuo il suo amore per Venezia.

Dietro il titolo *Canal d'Oro* non si nasconde però solo il fascino che Fabrizio Plessi subisce per i riflessi dell'acqua lucida e tremolante dei canali veneziani e per gli effetti danzanti dei raggi solari sulla superficie degli archi dei ponti che egli cerca di recuperare o forse, in un certo modo, di ricreare. Esiste un nesso molto concreto con Venezia. In questa installazione un mosaico d'oro disciolto elettronicamente in acqua scorre, uscendo dal Duomo di San Marco, in un canale di monitors con al di sopra archi trionfali antichizzati e costruzioni lignee coperte con una patina dorata scintillante. Il tutto sembra, riferito all'evoluzione dell'opera di Fabrizio Plessi, un anticipo della installazione di Magonza dal titolo *Il Fiume della Storia* dove un fiume elettronico a forma di mosaico scorre sotto un portale realmente antico.Un'ulteriore associazione veneziana suggerisce il titolo creando un collegamento tra il famoso monumento Ca' d'Oro e il termine canale (Canale Grande).

ROMA II

88003

PRATO 1988
MUSEO D'ARTE CONTEMPORANEA ›LUIGI PECCI‹
88003.1

WIEN 1991
MUSEUM MODERNER KUNST, STIFTUNG LUDWIG
88003.2

DORTMUND 1993
MUSEUM AM OSTWALL
88003.3

PERUGIA 1995
ROCCA PAOLINA
88003.4

NEW YORK 1998
GUGGENHEIM MUSEUM SOHO
88003.5

SAN DIEGO 1998
MUSEUM OF CONTEMPORARY ART LA JOLLA
88003.6

ROM II
Videoinstallation 1988
Travertinplatten, 30 Monitore
(Wien: 50 Monitore),
2 Videorecorder, 2 bespielte
Kassetten

ROME II
Video installation 1988
Slabs of travertine marble,
30 monitors (Vienna: 50), 2 video
recorders, 2 recorded video
cassettes

ROMA II
Videoinstallazione 1988
Lastre di marmo travertino,
30 monitors (Vienna: 50), 2 vhs,
2 cassette registrate

Roma II ist in gewissem Sinne eine Modifikation der ursprünglichen Konzeption, wie sie auf der Kasseler documenta 1987 zu sehen war. Die Monitore sind nun zu einem geschlossenen Kreis zusammengestellt, so daß das Wasser im Kreis fließen kann und damit einen ewigen Kreislauf, den Kreislauf der Zeit, sichtbar macht. Die Travertinplatten, die in Kassel außerhalb des kreisförmigen Videokanals locker und lose an die Wand gestellt waren, bedecken nun den gesamten Boden der Kreisfläche. Die Installationen von *Roma II*, die auf diese Weise in Prato, Wien, Perugia und Dortmund präsentiert wurden, ist damit nach außen hin geschlossen.

In dieser Form der Präsentation spielen die Räumlichkeiten eine nicht geringe Rolle, denn Inszenierungen wie die in dem Kunsthistorischen Museum in Wien kommen dem barocken Elektroniker Fabrizio Plessi sehr entgegen. Das ganze Ambiente wirkt auf seine Weise mit, und man kann sehen, wie unterschiedlich dieselbe Konstruktion in unterschiedlichen Räumlichkeiten wirkt.

Roma II *is, in a certain sense, a modification of the original concept shown at the documenta in Kassel in 1987. The monitors are now put together in a closed circle, so that the water can flow in a circle, thus making visible the eternal circle of time. The sheets of travertine that were placed freely and without order on the walls outside the circular video channel in Kassel now cover all of the floor within the circle. The installation of* Roma II *presented in this way in Prato, Vienna, Perugia and Dortmund is thus completed.*

In this form of presentation, space plays a very important role, for stagings like the one in the Museum of the History of Art in Vienna are favoured by the baroque electronic artist Fabrizio Plessi. The ambience becomes - in its respective place - part of the whole, and one can see how different the same construction is received in different spaces.

Roma II modifica in un certo senso la concezione originaria della versione vista alla *documenta* di Kassel nel 1987. I monitors formano adesso un cerchio chiuso che permette all'acqua di ruotare creando così un circuito eterno, il cerchio del tempo. Le lastre di travertino, a Kassel esposte al di fuori del cerchio del canale e appoggiate alle pareti, coprono adesso l'intera superficie interna del cerchio. L'installazione di *Roma II*, esposta in forma identica anche a Prato, Vienna, Perugia e Dortmund, risulta quindi chiusa verso l'esterno.

Gli ambienti che ospitano le installazioni non ricoprono un ruolo secondario, scenografie come quella nel Kunsthistorisches Museum di Vienna accondiscendono molto alle intenzioni del tecnico elettronico barocco Fabrizio Plessi. Ogni ambiente dona a suo modo una caratteristica diversa all'opera e si può osservare come l'effetto della presentazione si modifichi secondo i differenti spazi.

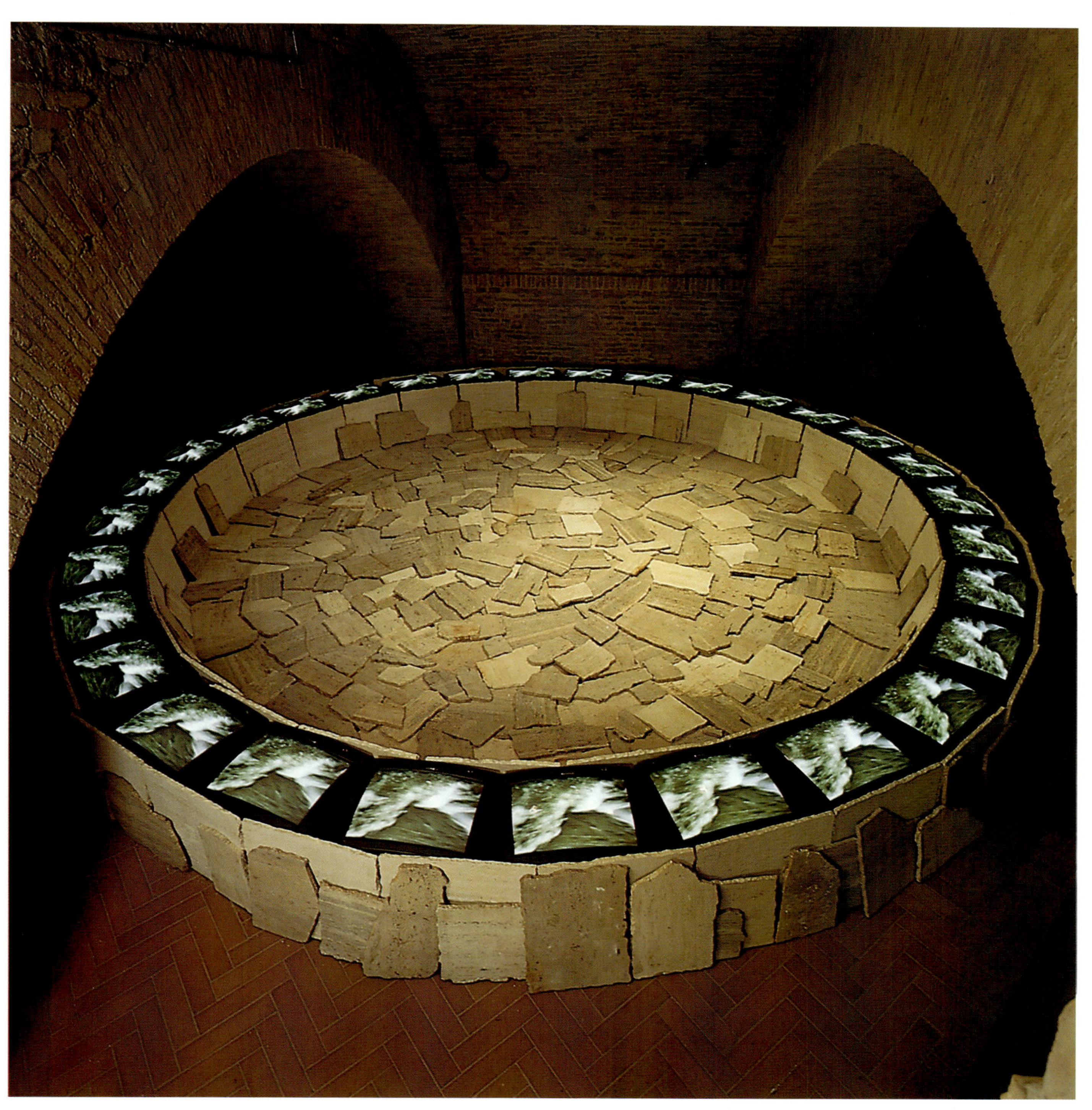

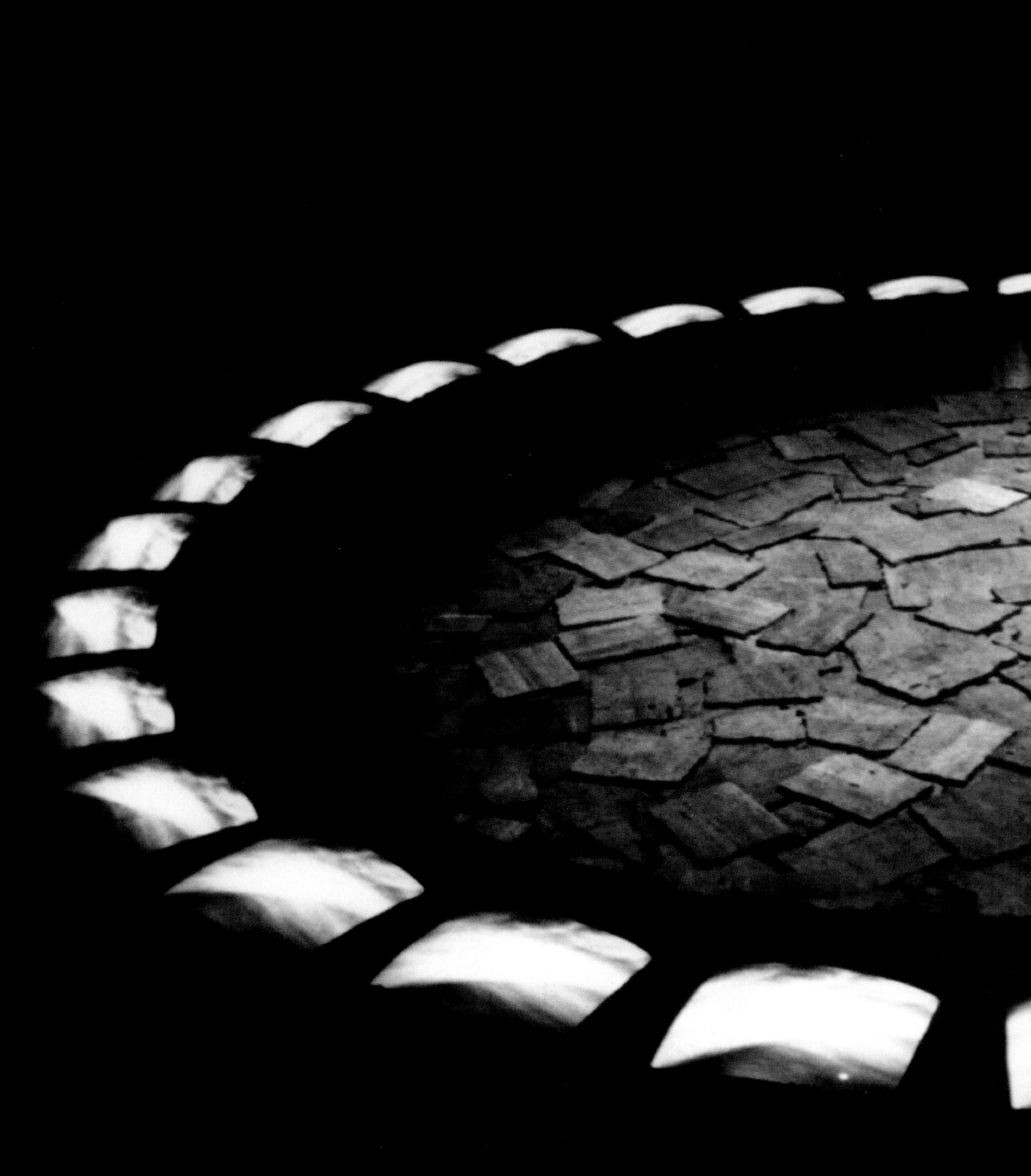

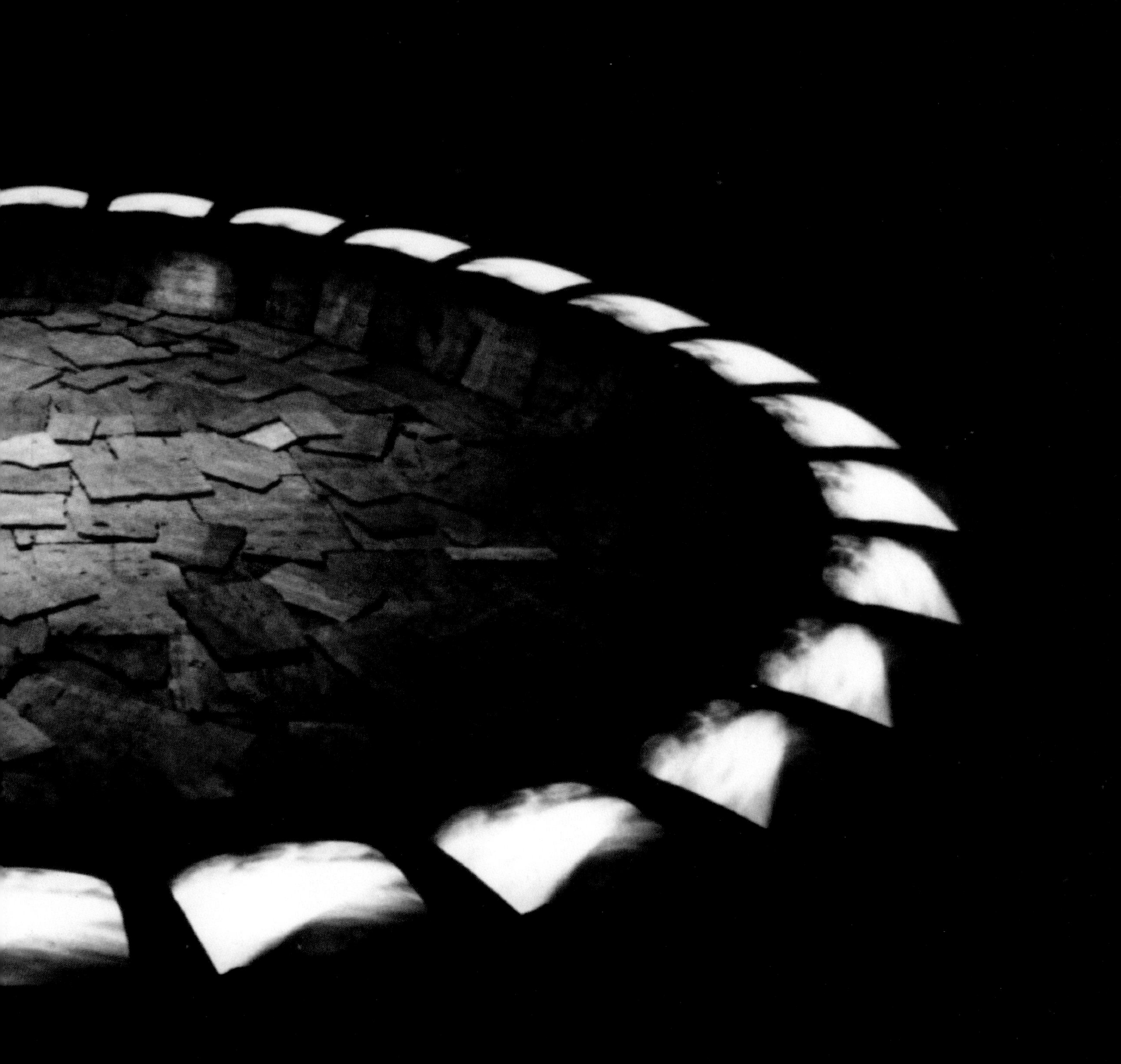

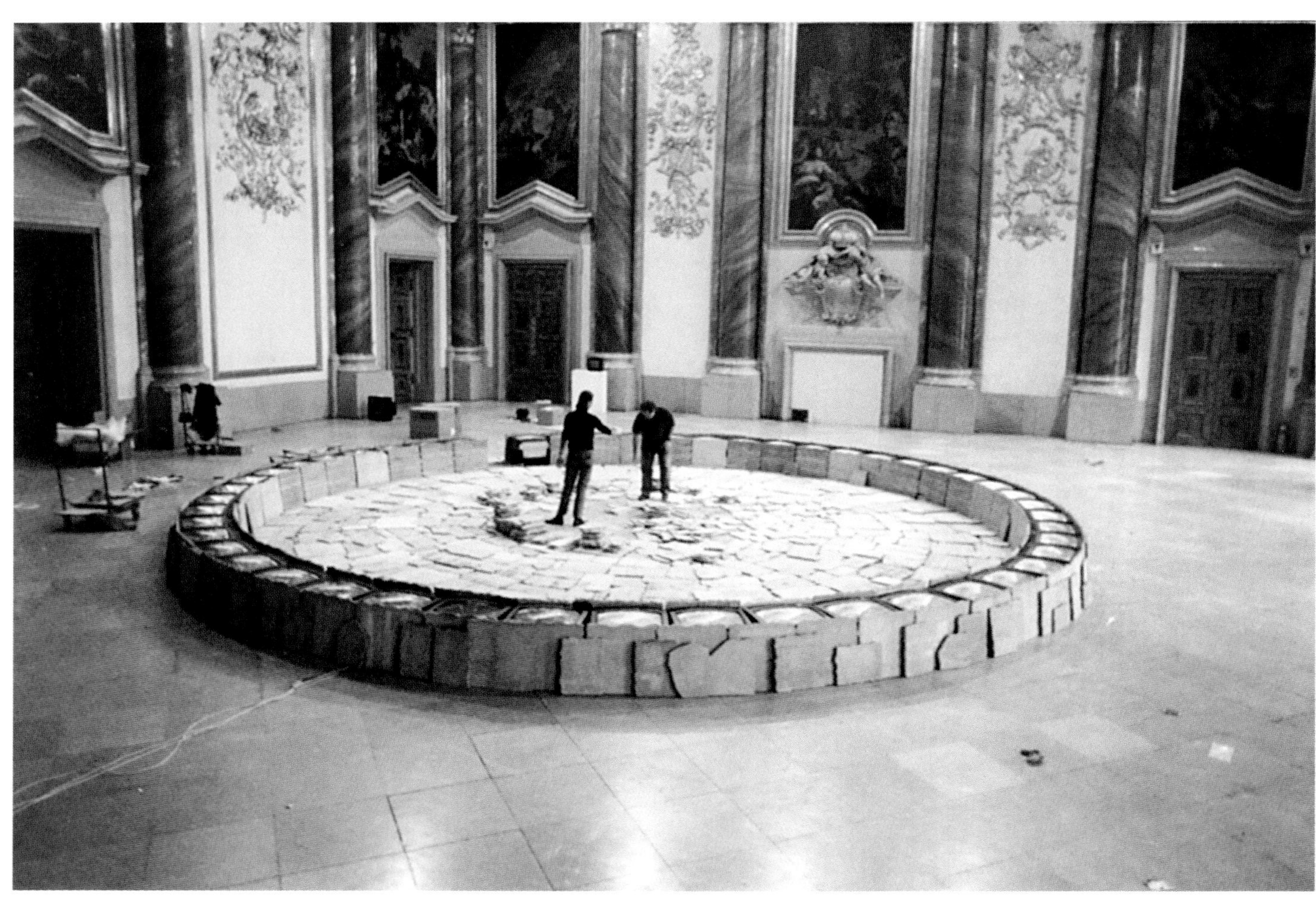

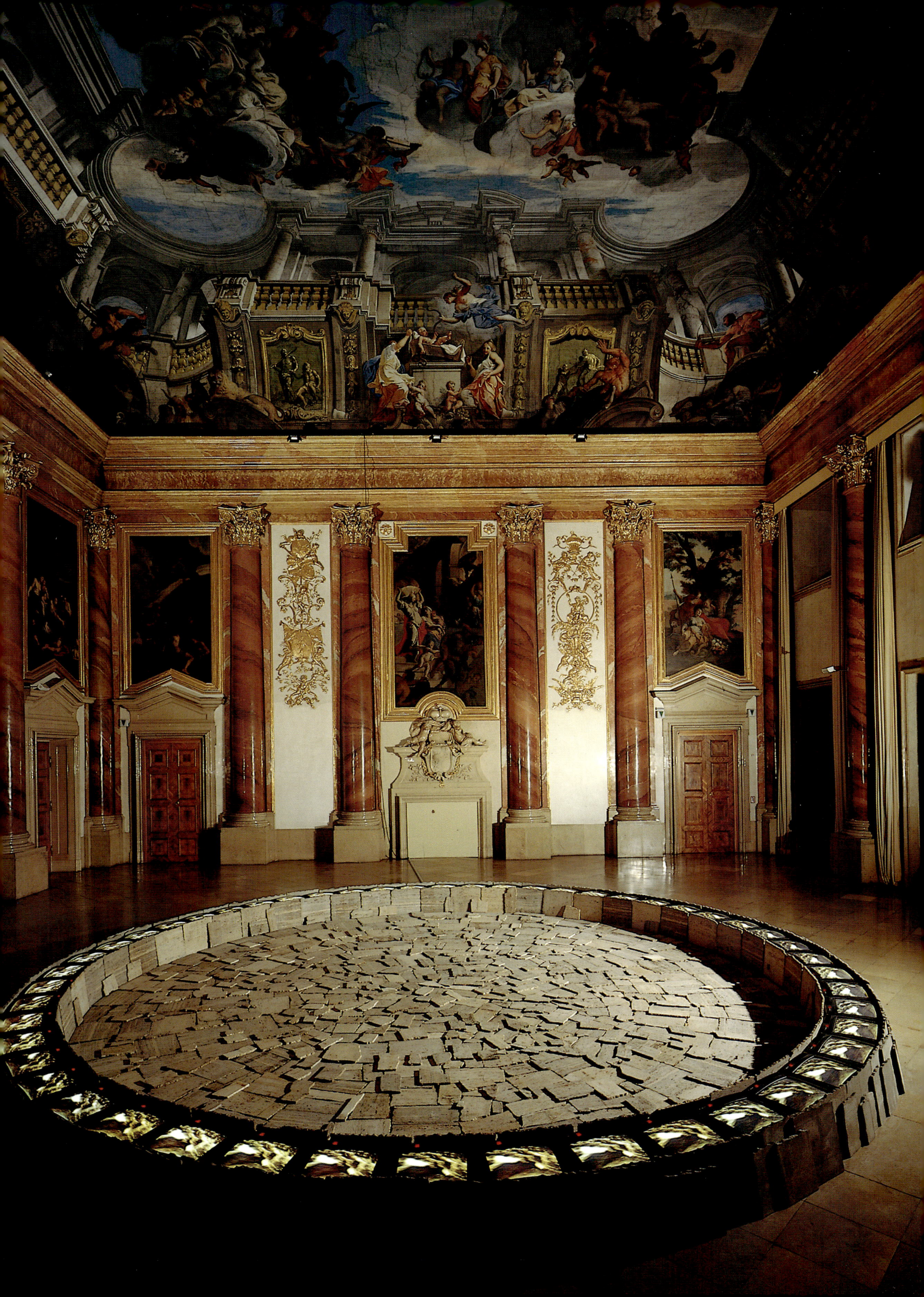

IL PESO DEL MONDO

88004

STIFT WILHERING 1988
NEUE GALERIE DER STADT LINZ
88004.1

DIE LAST DER WELT
Videoinstallation 1988
2 Gehäuse aus Holz, 8 Leitern,
Holzbretter, Kohle, Säcke, Salz,
Schnüre, Blecheimer, Wasser,
2 Monitore, Videorecorder,
bespielte Kassetten

THE BURDEN OF THE WORLD
Video installation 1988
2 wooden structures,8 ladders,
coal, sacks, salt, ropes, metal
buckets, water, 2 monitors, video
recorders, recorded video cassettes

IL PESO DEL MONDO
Videoinstallazione 1988
Due strutture in legno, 8 scale,
carbone, sacchi, sale, corde,
secchi di metallo, acqua,
2 monitors, vhs, cassette
registrate

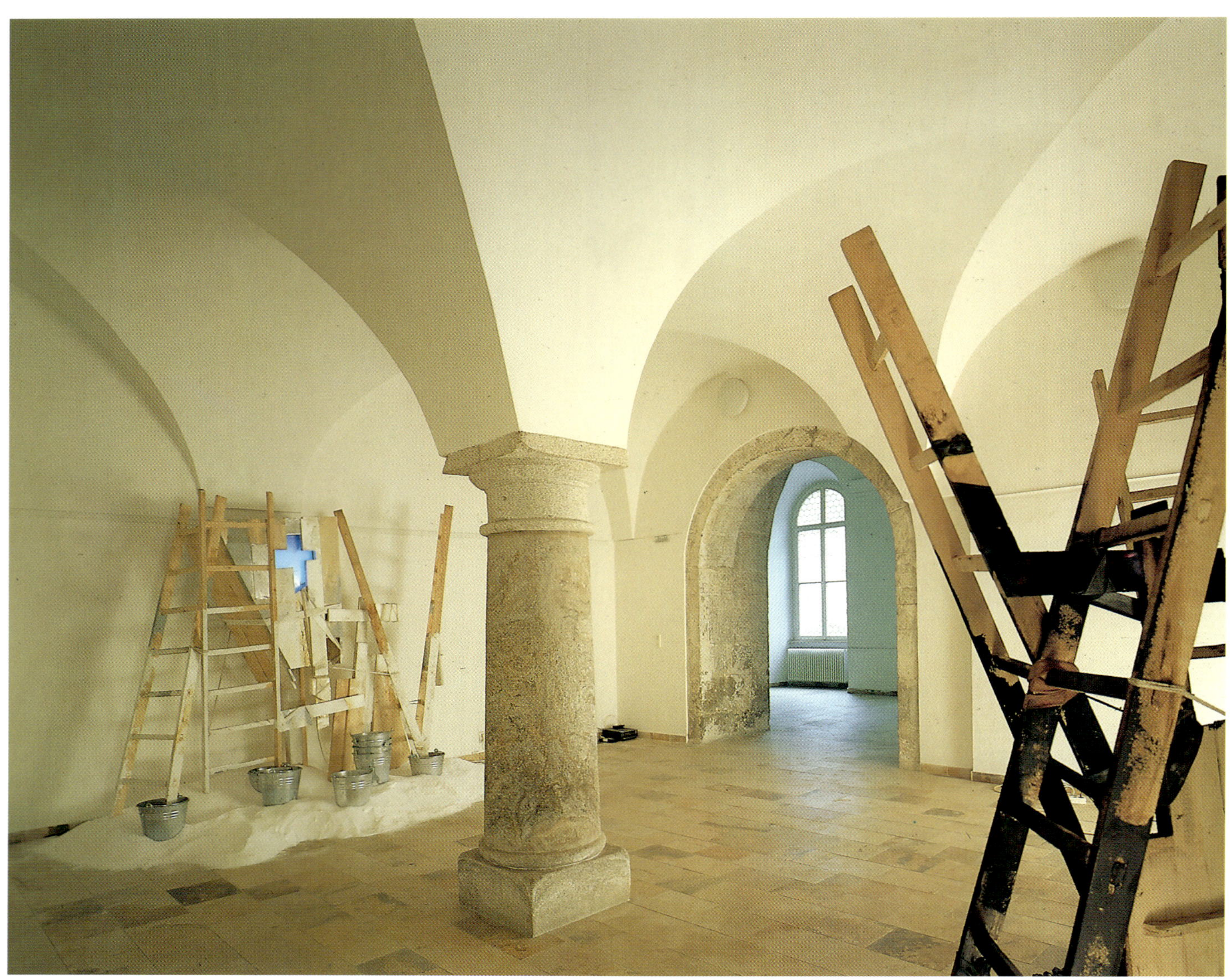

Die raumbezogene Arbeit *Il Peso del Mondo* (*Die Last der Welt*), die Fabrizio Plessi 1988 im Stift Wilhering (Nähe Linz an der Donau) realisiert hat, bezieht sich unmittelbar auf die im selben Jahr entstandene Videoinstallation

The space-related work Il Peso del Mondo (The Weight of the World) *that Fabrizio Plessi realises in Stift Wilhering (near Linz on the Danube) in 1988 directly refers to* Videocruz, *the video installation created in the*

Il lavoro *Il Peso del Mondo*, realizzato per il convento di Wilhering vicino Linz sul Danubio nel 1988 e che fortemente risente della sua ambientazione, si ricollega direttamente alla videoinstallazione Videocruz

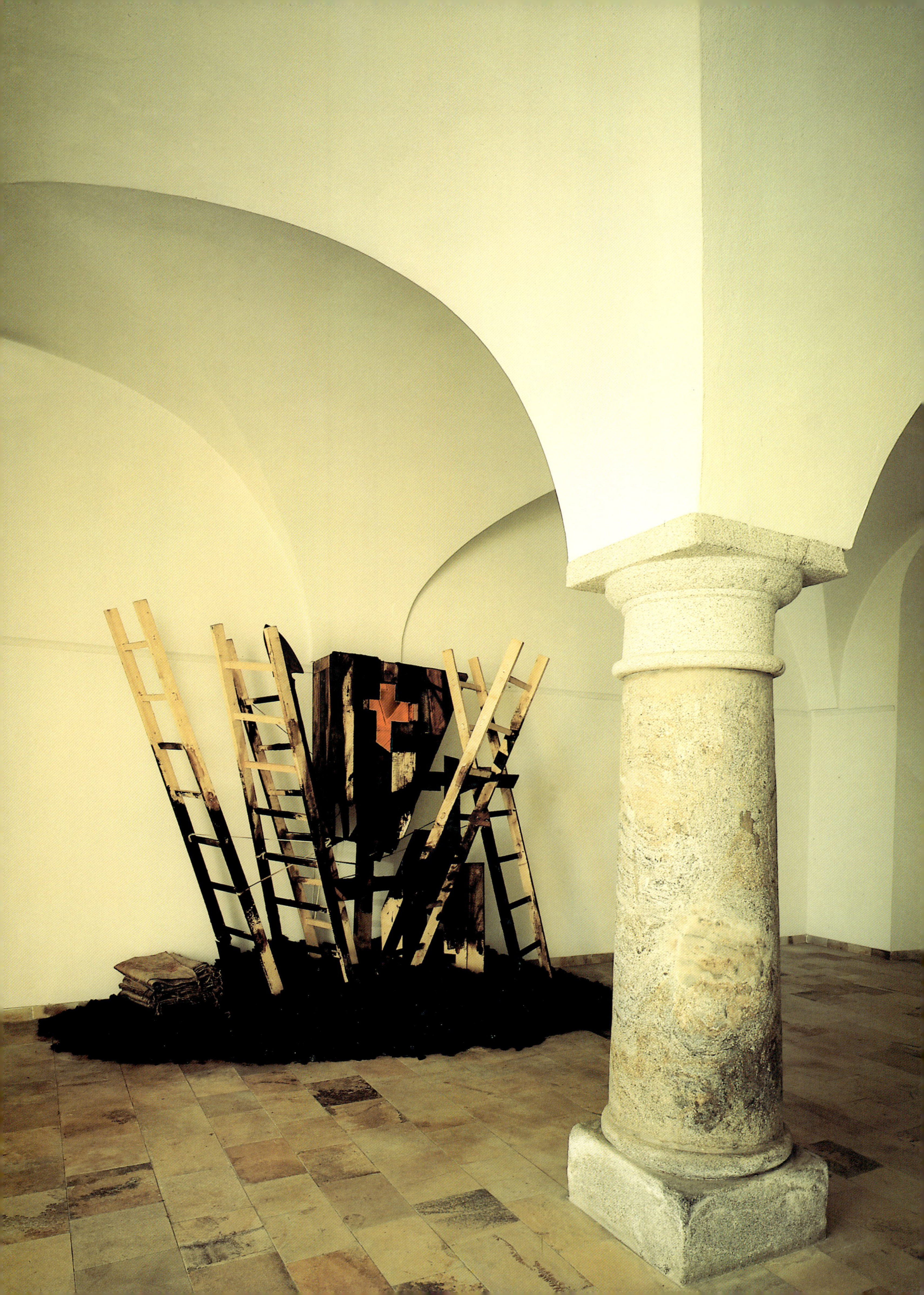

Videocruz. Der über einer zentralen Säule kreuzgratgewölbte Kapitelsaal des Klosters beherbergt gegenüberliegend, doch durch die Säule getrennt, zwei Holzkonstruktionen in der Art, wie wir sie bei *Videocruz* sahen, das heißt mit einer kreuzförmigen Öffnung und einem Monitor dahinter. Der eine Monitor zeigt elektronisches Feuer, der andere elektronisches Wasser. Der Kapitelsaal oder das Parlatorium eines Klosters ist gewissermaßen der Gesprächsraum. Der Raum, in dem Versammlungen stattfanden, in dem Meinungen ausgetauscht wurden und Beschlüsse gefaßt, im Gegensatz zu den anderen Räumlichkeiten, die entweder dem Beten oder dem Arbeiten (ora et labora) vorbehalten waren.

Mit dieser Videoskulptur im Raum eines Kapitelsaals verweist Fabrizio Plessi auf den Aspekt gedanklicher Freiheit und Toleranz dem anderen, vielleicht in Meinung und Haltung diametral Entgegengesetzten gegenüber, um in Harmonie zusammenleben zu können. Die Harmonie der Gegensätze, hier von Feuer und Wasser, ist in dieser Videoinstallation thematisiert und zu einem Kunstwerk geworden.

same year. The chapter-house of the monastery, cross-vaulted on a central pillar, accommodates two wooden constructions, opposed to each other and separated by the pillar, of a kind we have seen in Videocruz, *that is with an opening in the form of a cross and a monitor behind. The one monitor shows electronic fire, the other electronic water. The chapter-house or Parlatorium of a monastery is, in a way, the room for conversations, in which meetings are held, opinions exchanged, and decisions taken, different from other rooms which are reserved for prayer and work (ora et labora).*

With this video sculpture in the space of a chapter-house, Fabrizio Plessi points out the aspect of freedom of opinion, and tolerance towards others who might be of a diametrically different opinion and attitude, in order to be able to live in harmony. The harmony of opposites, here of fire and water, is subject of this video installation, and has become a piece of art.

dello stesso anno. La sala capitolare dalle volte a croce che poggiano su una colonna centrale ospita, separate da quest'ultima, due costruzioni lignee, posizionate una di fronte all'altra, simili a quelle di Videocruz, cioè con un'apertura a croce con dietro un monitor. Uno dei monitors rappresenta fuoco e l'altro acqua elettronica. La sala capitolare o anche parlatorium funge da sala di comunicazione di un convento, da spazio dove si svolgevano le riunioni, dove ci si scambiavano opinioni e dove si prendevano decisioni, al contrario degli altri ambienti riservati alla preghiera e al lavoro (ora et labora).

Con questa videoscultura, inserita in una sala capitolare, Fabrizio Plessi allude all'aspetto della libertà di pensiero e alla tolleranza verso l'altro, probabilmente di parere diametralmente contrario, per vivere insieme in armonia. L'armonia degli opposti, qui di acqua e fuoco uniti in un'opera d'arte, è il tema della installazione.

ROMA III

88005

ROMA 1988
RAI UNO, ›IMMAGINA‹
88005.1

REGGIO EMILIA 1990
MUSEO CIVICO D'ARTE MODERNA
88005.2

ROM III
Videoinstallation 1988
Travertinplatten, Förderband,
Lichtprojektionen, 26 Monitore,
Videorecorder, bespielte
Kassetten

ROME III
Video installation 1988
Slabs of travertine marble,
conveyor belt, light projection,
26 monitors, video recorders,
recorded video cassettes

ROMA III
Videoinstallazione 1988
Montacarichi, lastre di marmo
travertino, luce, 26 monitors, vhs,
cassette registrate

Bei *Roma III* handelt es sich in gewisser Weise um eine Kreuzung aus *Roma* und *Roma II*, denn ein kreisrunder elektronischer Fluß, dessen innere Freifläche mit Travertinplatten gefüllt ist, befindet sich in einem glutrot leuchtenden Raum. Die kreisrunde Form des elektronischen Flusses stammt von der Version *Roma II*. Doch das rote Ambiente und das Förderband, von dem bei *Roma* ein imaginärer Stein in den elektronischen Fluß fällt, sind hier hinzugefügt.

Roma III *is, in a way, a combination of* Roma *and* Roma II, *for here a circular electronic river, the inner area of which is covered with travertine plates, runs through a room steeped in ardent red. The circular form of the electronic river is taken from* Roma II, *while the red ambient and the conveyor-belt, from which - in* Roma - *an imaginary stone dropped into the electronic river, are added here.*

Roma III rappresenta in un certo modo un incrocio fra *Roma* e *Roma II*. Un fiume elettronico e circolare che delimita un cerchio colmo di lastre di travertino è immerso nel colore rosso fuoco di un ambiente. La forma del cerchio del fiume deriva dalla versione *Roma II*, ma sono stati aggiunti l'ambiente rosso e il montacarichi, dal quale in *Roma* precipita un sasso.

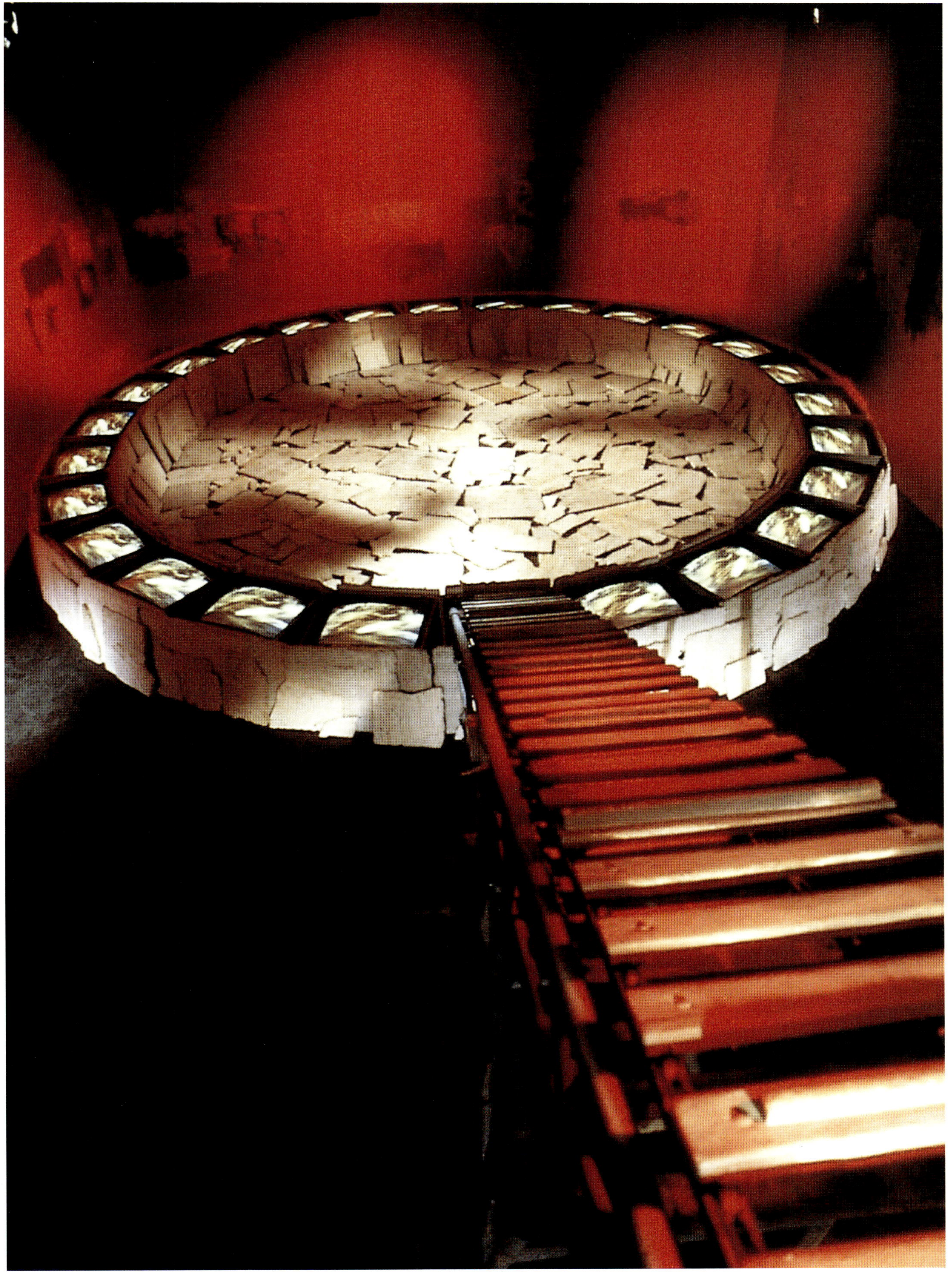

ROMA IV

88006

ZARAGOZA 1988
Palacio de Sástago
88006.1

ROM IV
Videoinstallation 1988
Travertinplatten, 44 Monitore,
2 Videorecorder, 2 bespielte
Kassetten

ROME IV
Video installation 1988
Slabs of travertine marble, 44
monitors, 2 video recorders,
2 recorded video cassettes

ROMA IV
Videoinstallazione 1988
Lastre di marmo travertino,
44 monitors, 2 vhs, 2 cassette
registrate

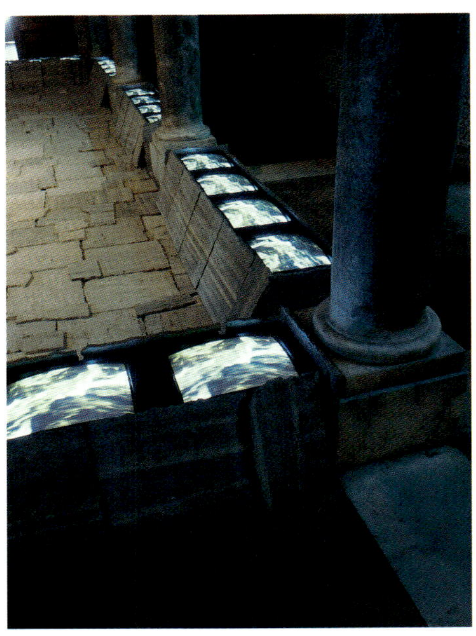

Viel deutlicher wird der Unterschied zwischen den ersten *Roma*-Versionen und *Roma IV* sichtbar. Die Präsentation in Zaragoza zeigt den elektronischen Fluß nun nicht mehr in rundem Verlauf, sondern in ein durch Säulen unterbrochenes Rechteck-Format. Das Innere des Rechtecks ist mit liegenden Travertinplatten belegt, wie in *Roma II* und *Roma III*. Doch hier kann man keinesfalls von einem Kreislauf der Geschichte sprechen. Im Gegenteil, vielmehr verweist diese Präsentation in einem historischen Palast in Spanien auf eine alte Neigung und nun wieder in den Blickpunkt des Künstlers rückenden Liebe zur Geometrie, die sich bald darauf in einer neuen Videoskulptur manifestieren wird. Doch auch die Säulen können den Kreislauf des elektronischen Wassers nur unterbrechen, aber nicht beenden.

The difference between the first versions of Roma *and* Roma IV *is more visible. The presentation in Zaragoza no longer shows the electronic river in circular, but in rectangular shape, interrupted by pillars. The inside of the rectangle is covered with travertine plates, as in* Roma II *and* Roma III, *yet here one can in no way talk of a circular course of history. On the contrary, this presentation in a historic palace in Spain reminds of the artist's old inclination - now again coming to the fore - and love for geometry that will soon after be manifested in a new video installation. The pillars can only interrupt but not stop the circulation of electronic water.*

Molto più evidente è la differenza fra la prima versione di *Roma* e *Roma IV*. La presentazione a Saragozza mostra un fiume elettronico non più circolare ma di forma rettangolare interrotta da colonne che, però, riescono solo ad interrompere il flusso dell'acqua elettronica, ma non a bloccarlo. All'interno del rettangolo si trovano, come in Roma II e Roma III, delle lastre di travertino. Questa versione, accolta in un palazzo storico della Spagna, certamente non allude più al cerchio della storia ma, al contrario, ad una propensione dell'artista e all'amore per la geometria, che qui balza al centro dell'attenzione e che ritornerà presto in un'altra videoscultura.

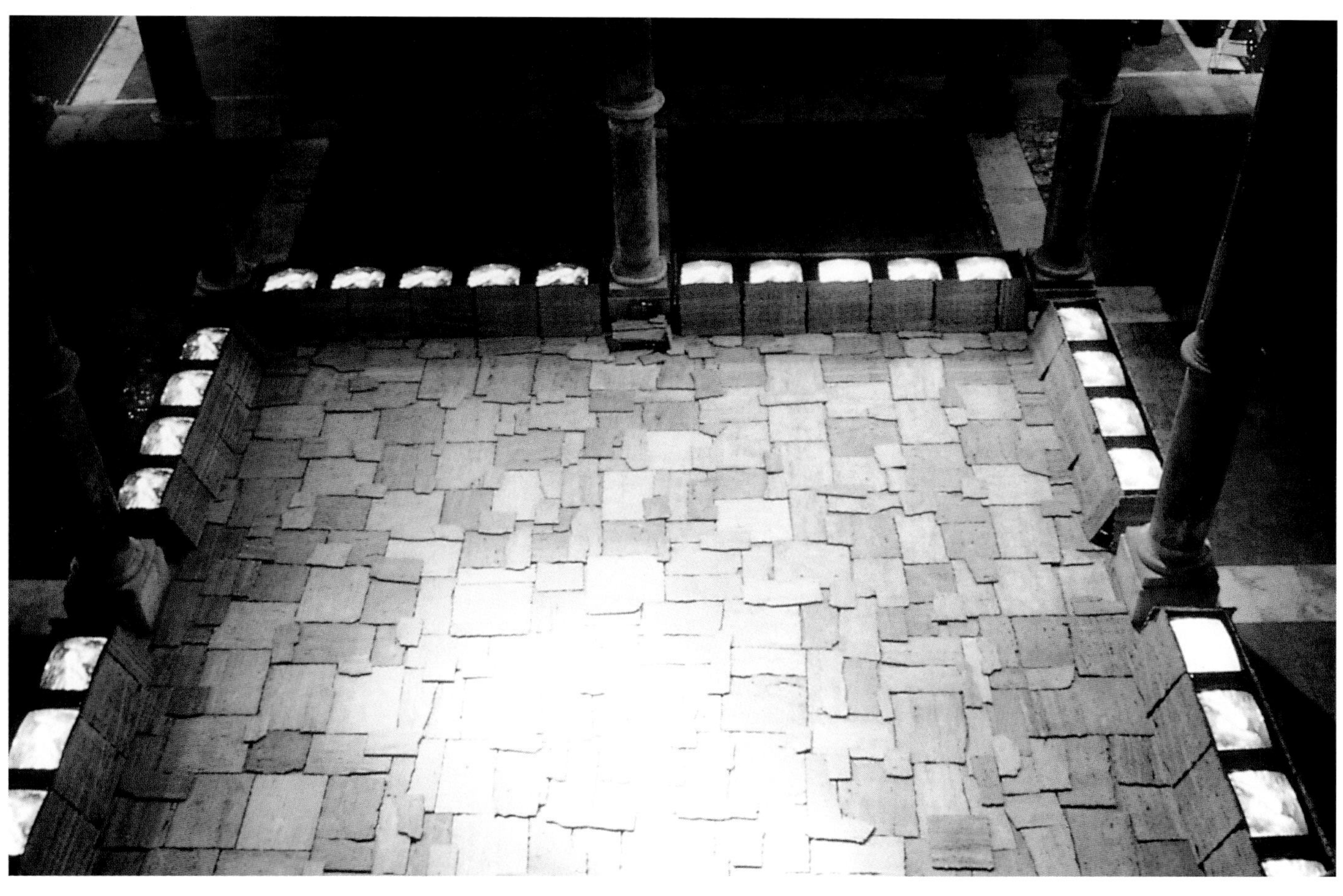

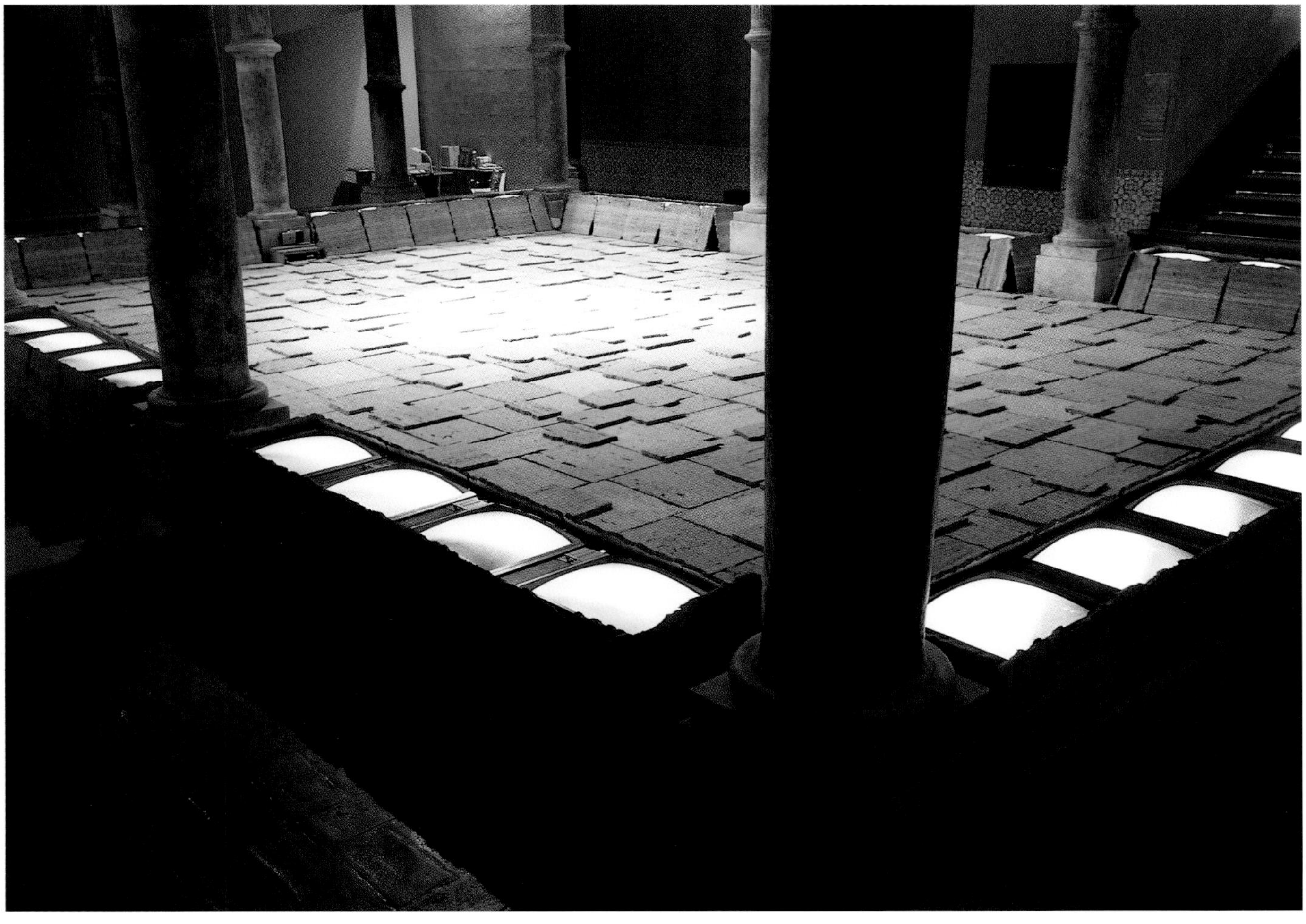

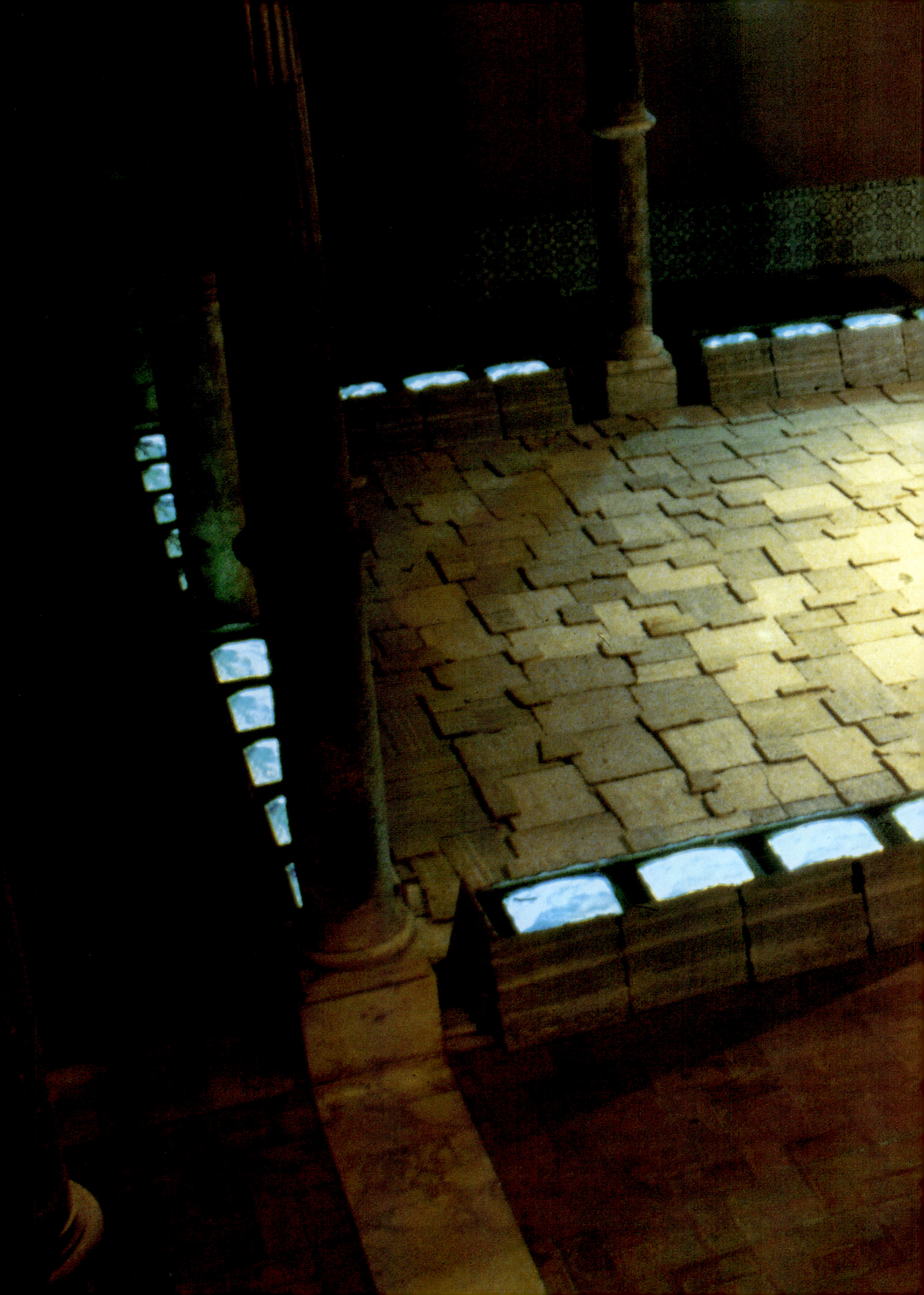

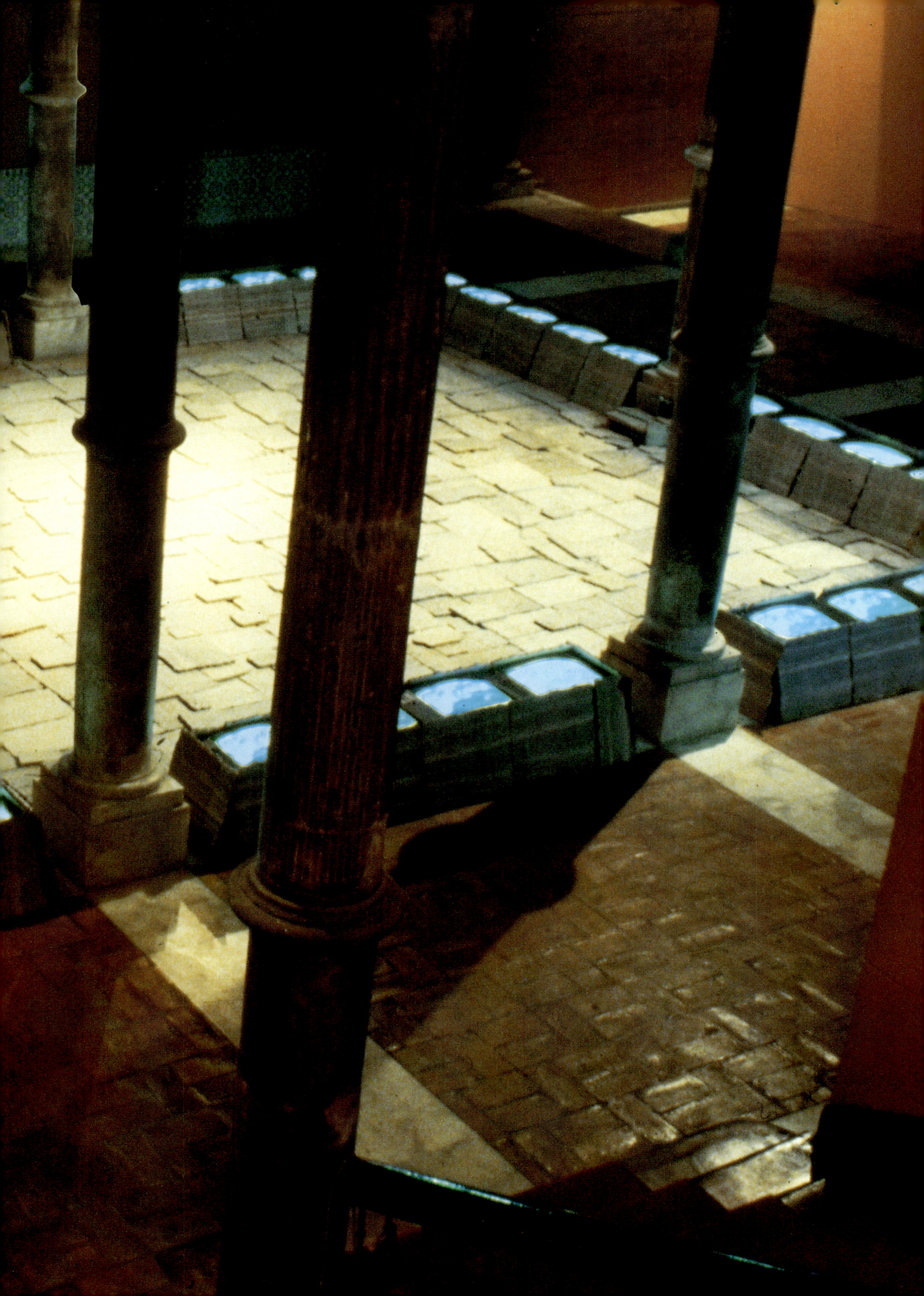

PALACIO ELECTRONICO

88007

ZARAGOZA 1988
PALACIO DE SÁSTAGO
88007.1

ELEKTRONISCHER PALAST
Videoinstallation 1988
Hohle Säulenabschnitte aus Gips,
je 1 Monitor, Videorecorder,
bespielte Kassetten

ELECTRONIC PALACE
Video installation 1988
Hollowed out plaster colums,
monitors, video recorders,
recorded video cassettes

PALAZZO ELETTRONICO
Videoinstallazione 1988
Colonne scavate di gesso,
monitors, vhs, cassette registrate

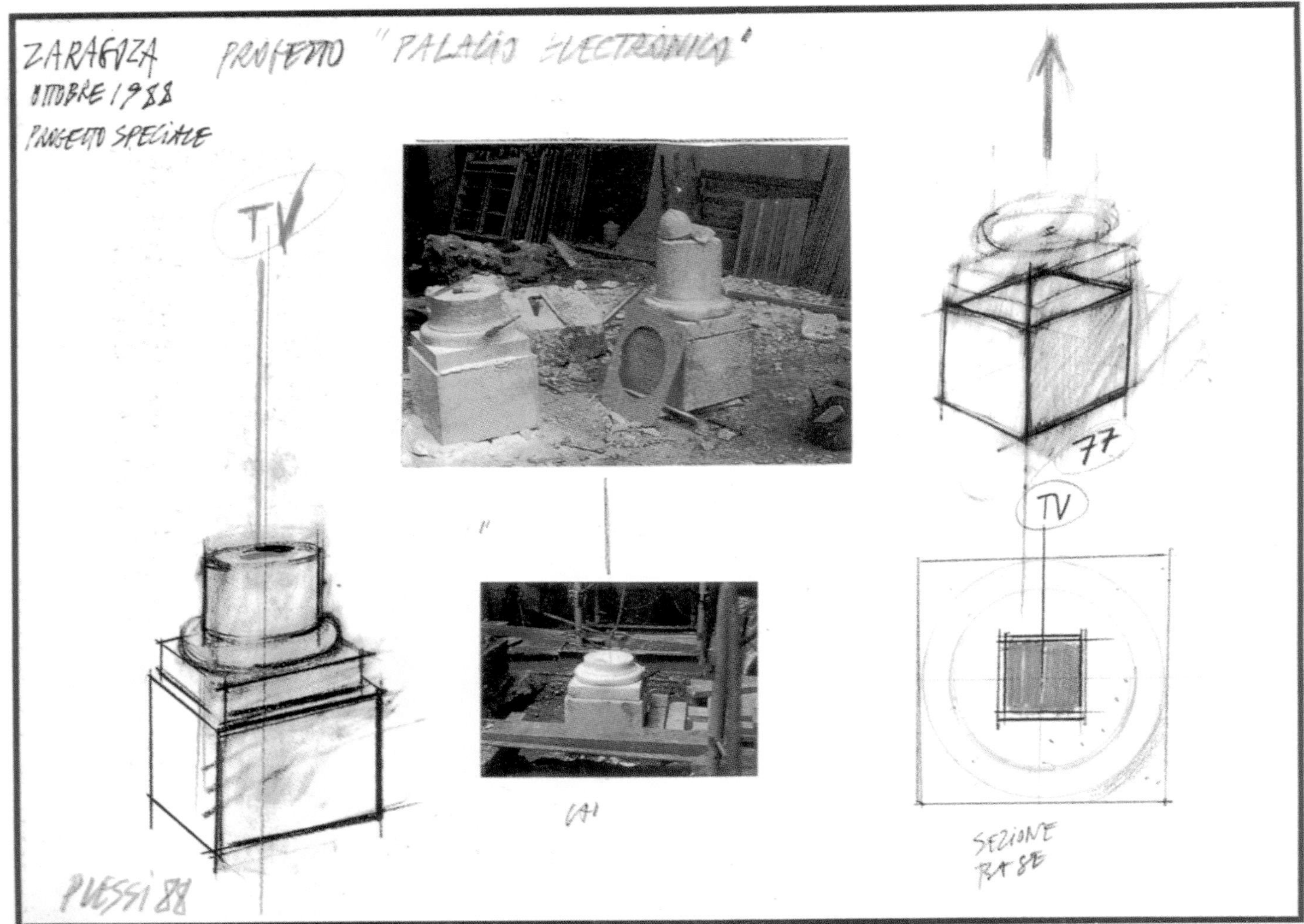

Auf dem Grund einer auf
halber Höhe zerteilten Alabaster-
Säule befindet sich ein Monitor,
der durch einen Kanal mit quadratischer Öffnung sichtbar wird. Der
Videofilm zeigt einen Stein, der
dem Betrachter von der Tiefe der
Säule entgegenzufliegen scheint,
wenn er durch die Öffnung des
Loches Einblick in die Seele der

At the base of an alabaster
pillar, cut halfway up, a monitor
is visible through a channel with
a square opening. The video film
shows a stone that appears to fly
from the depth of the pillar
towards the spectator when he
tries to have a look - through the
opening of the hole - at the soul
of the pillar. Altogether ten of

Sul fondo di una colonna di
alabastro divisa a metà si trova
un monitor visibile attraverso
un canale con un'apertura
quadrata. Il videofilm presenta
una pietra che, dal profondo
della colonna, sembra salire
verso lo spettatore quando egli
cerca di guardare all'interno,
nell'anima della colonna. Dieci

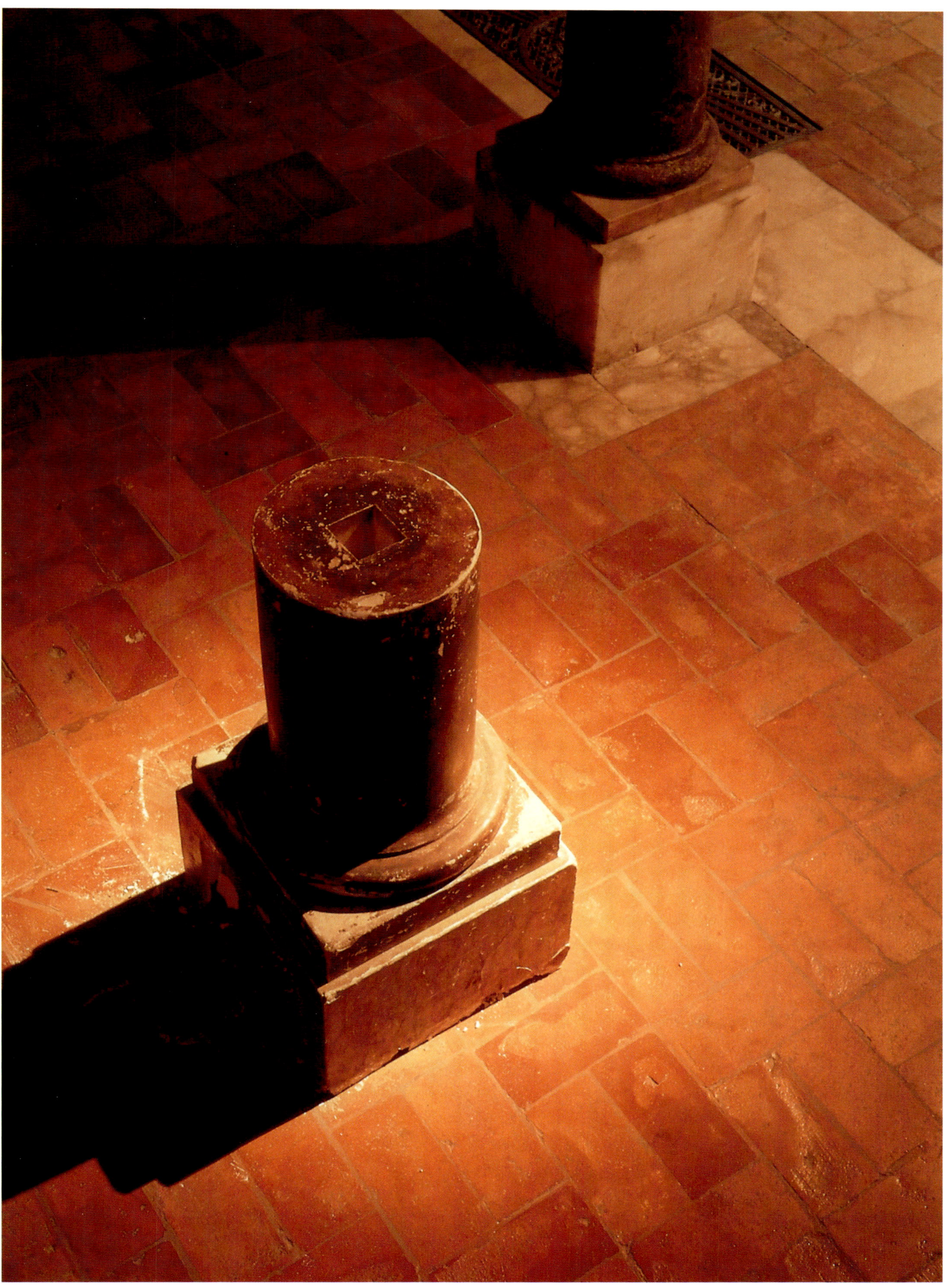

Insgesamt wurden von dieser Konstruktion 10 Exemplare aufgestellt, heute sind jedoch alle davon zerstört. Der Titel dieser Videoskulptur, *Palacio Electrónico*, war zugleich der Titel für die Ausstellung, in der auch *Roma IV* präsentiert wurde. Es ist ein Hinweis auf den Palast, in dem die Säulen, die Steine und auch das Fließen des Wassers elektronisch sind. Dieses Werk thematisiert Zeit und stellt eine Verbindung der Vergangenheit (durch den Palast), mit der Zukunft (durch die Elektronik) her, das Vergehen der Geschichte und das Entstehen der Vision.

these constructions were made, but all of them have been destroyed. The title of this video sculpture, Palacio Electrónico, *was at the same time the title of the exhibition in which* Roma IV *was shown. It is a hint to the palace in which the pillars, stones and the running water are electronic. The subject of this work is time, and it creates a connection between past (the palace) and future (electronics), the vanishing of history and the creation of vision.*

esemplari in tutto della costruzione furono esposti ma oggi sono purtroppo distrutti. Il titolo di questa videoscultura era identico a quello della mostra *Palacio Electrónico*, dove fu esposta anche *Roma IV*, e allude al palazzo in cui colonne, pietre e lo scorrere dell'acqua sono elettronici. L'opera tematizza il tempo e rappresenta il rapporto fra passato (il palazzo) e futuro (l'elettronica), il passare della storia e la nascita delle visioni.

COLATORAO

88008

ZARAGOZA 1988
Palacio de Sástago
88008.1

COLATORAO
Videoskulptur 1988
3 Gebilde aus schwarzem Stein, je
ein Trichter aus schwarzem Eisen
mit Monitor, Videorecorder,
bespielte Kassetten
je 400 x 300 x 100 cm

COLATORAO
Video sculpture 1988
3 structures of black stone, cones
of black iron, monitors, video
recorders, recorded video cassettes
400 x 300 x 100 cm (each)

COLATORAO
Videoscultura 1988
3 strutture di pietra nera, 3 coni
di ferro rovesciati, 3 monitors,
3 vhs, 3 cassette registrate
400 x 300 x 100 cm ognuno

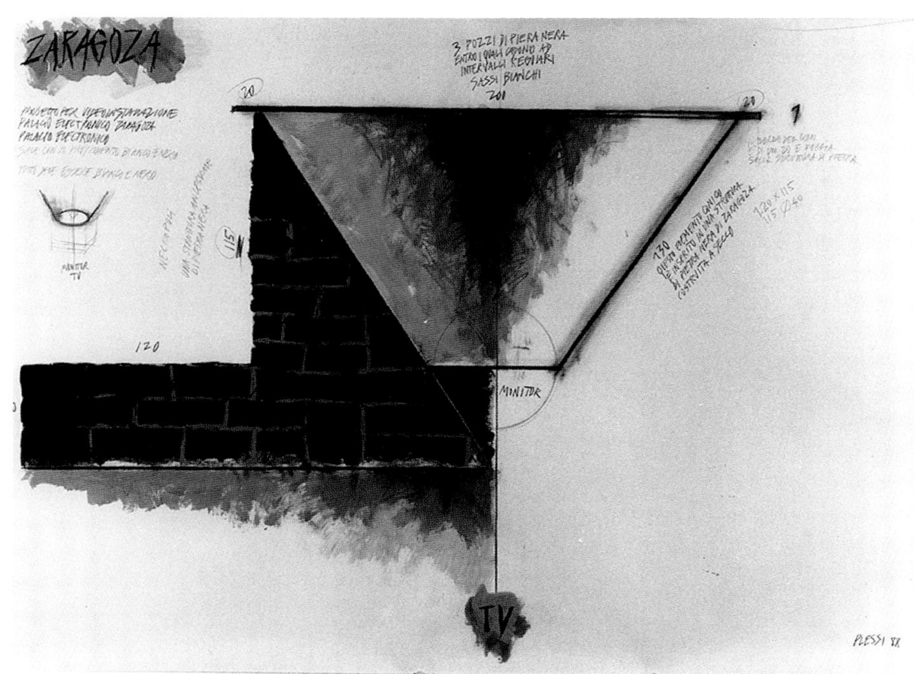

Immer wieder gibt es im Werk
Fabrizio Plessis Verbindungen
zwischen früheren und späteren
Arbeiten. Es sind Elemente und
Gegenstände, die aus dieser oder
jener Installation stammen und in
neuer Form in einer anderen
Installation wieder eingebaut
werden. Gelegentlich lassen sich
auch inhaltliche Verbindungen
oder Bezüge herstellen. Doch
vielfach entstehen eigene, neue
Installationen, die mit vorangegangenen nur materiell in Verbindung
stehen.

Bei der dreiteiligen Videoskulptur *Calatorao* gehen mehrere

Again and again Fabrizio
Plessi's œuvre shows connections
between earlier and later works.
Elements and objects stemming
from this or that installation are
included, in a new form, in other
installations. Sometimes, one can
also find thematic connections or
references. Yet most of the times
independent, new installations
are created that only have mate-
rial relations to former ones.

In the three-part video sculp-
ture Colatorao, *several known*
elements from earlier sculptures
enter a new relationship. In the
centre of the staging there is a

Di frequente si osserva un
diretto collegamento fra i primi
lavori di Fabrizio Plessi e quelli
più recenti. Elementi e oggetti
derivanti da questa o quella
installazione vengono inseriti,
sotto una nuova forma, in
un'altra opera. Di quando in
quando si creano anche rapporti
o riferimenti di contenuto ma
per lo più nascono nuove installazioni, che, al di là del materiale, non hanno niente in comune
con quelle precedenti.

Nella videoscultura *Colatorao* confluiscono vari elementi
di sculture precedenti. Il fulcro

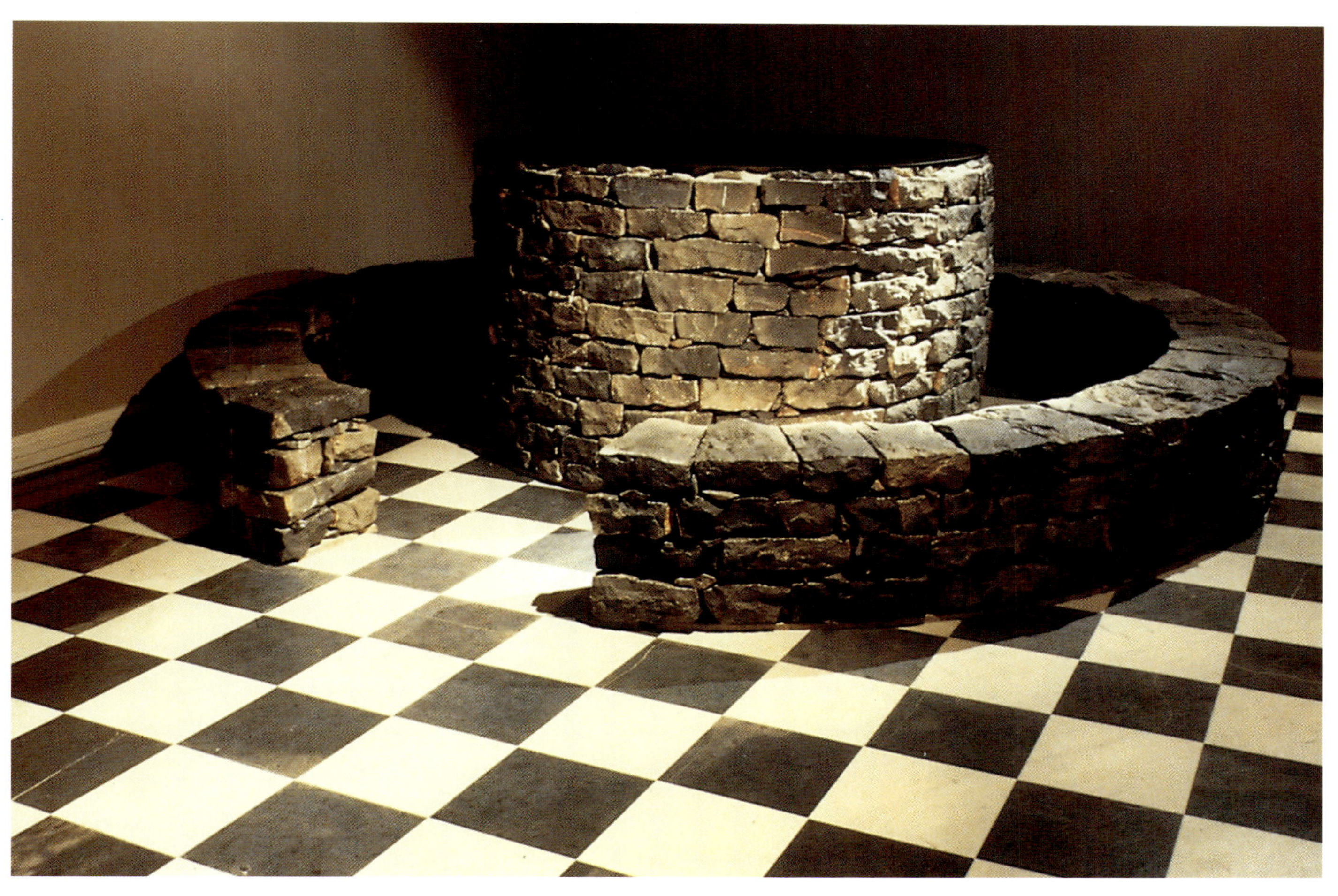

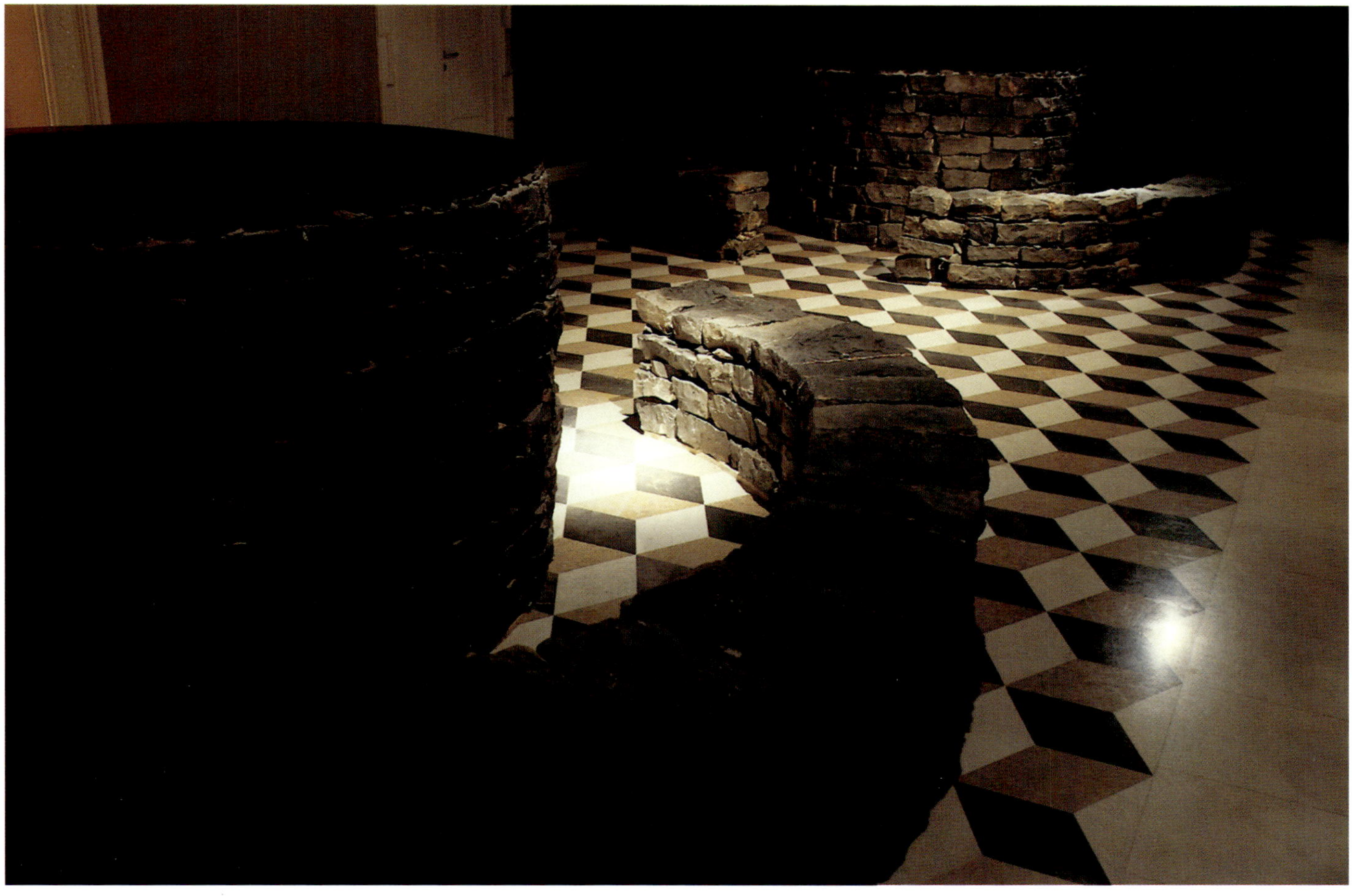

bekannte Elemente aus vorangegangenen Skulpturen eine neue
Beziehung ein. Im Mittelpunkt der
Inszenierung steht ein bestimmter
Steintyp aus Zaragoza, der auch
der Arbeit den Titel gibt *Calatorao*.
Mit diesem Stein, in handgehaue-
ner Quaderform, sind drei kreisförmige Brunnen gebaut, die von
einem niedrigeren, nahezu geschlossenen Kreis aus demselben
Material umringt sind. Das Äußere
dieser Brunnen erscheint wie ein
Zylinder. Im Inneren öffnet sich
die Konstruktion trichterförmig
nach unten zulaufend, an dessen
unterem Ende, auf dem Grund, ein
Monitor eingebaut ist. Der Film
zeigt einen weißen Stein, der in
unregelmäßigen Abständen, in das
schwarze Wasser dieser Brunnen
fällt und dabei ein natürliches
Geräusch, ein fast archaisch
anmutendes Konzert, erzeugt.
Neben dem Materialbezug sind hier
vor allem die konstruktiven Elemente und geometrischen Formen
interessant, da mit dieser Installation wieder einmal mehr das
Interesse Plessis an der Geometrie
sichtbar wird.

certain type of rock from Zara-
goza that gives the work its
title: Colatorao. *Three circular*
wells are built from hand-hewn
square blocks of this stone, and
are surrounded by a low,
almost closed circle of the same
material. The outside of the
wells looks like a cylinder. On
the inside, the construction
reminds of an open funnel
decreasing in size towards the
bottom, where, on the ground,
a monitor is placed. The film
on it shows a white stone
dropping at irregular intervals
into the well's dark water,
thereby creating a natural
sound, an almost archaic
concert. Beside the reference to
the material, here the construc-
tive elements and geometric
forms are interesting, since this
construction again reveals
Plessi's interest in geometry.

dell'allestimento è rappresenta-
to da un tipo specifico di pietra
proveniente dalla zona di Saragozza il cui nome costituisce
anche il titolo: *Colatorao*. Con
questa pietra, squadrata a mano,
sono stati costruiti tre pozzi a
base circolare, ciascuno circondato da un basso cerchio quasi
completo dello stesso materiale.
L'esterno dei pozzi appare come
un cilindro, l'interno si rastre-
ma verso il basso come un
imbuto dove, sul fondo è inserito un monitor. Il filmato fa
vedere una pietra bianca che
cade, ad intervalli irregolari,
nell'acqua nera del pozzo pro-
ducendo un suono naturale, un
concerto quasi arcaico. Oltre il
riferimento al materiale, risultano interessanti soprattutto gli
elementi costruttivi e le forme
pure che, ancora una volta,
sottolineano l'interesse di Plessi
per la geometria.

GEOMETRIA LIQUIDA

89001

FERRARA 1989
Museo Palazzo dei Diamanti
89001.1

BOLOGNA 1989
Arte Fiera
89001.2

DORTMUND 1993
Museum am Ostwall
89001.3

PERUGIA 1995
Rocca Paolina
89001.4

KÖLN 1997
Baukunst
89001.5

LEVERKUSEN 1997
Museum Schloss Morsbroich
89001.6

KÖLN 1998
Gerling Konzern
89001.7

FLÜSSIGE GEOMETRIE
Videoskulptur 1989
3 Elemente aus rostigem Eisen,
Eisengitter,8 Monitore,
Videorecorder, bespielte
Kassetten
300 x 600 x 60 cm

LIQUID GEOMETRY
Video sculpture 1989
3 iron elements (structure of rusted
iron), iron lattice, 8 monitors
each, video recorder, recorded
video cassettes
300 x 600 x 60 cm

GEOMETRIA LIQUIDA
Videoscultura 1989
3 elementi in ferro, grigliato
industriale, 8 monitors, vhs,
cassette registrate
300 x 600 x 60 cm

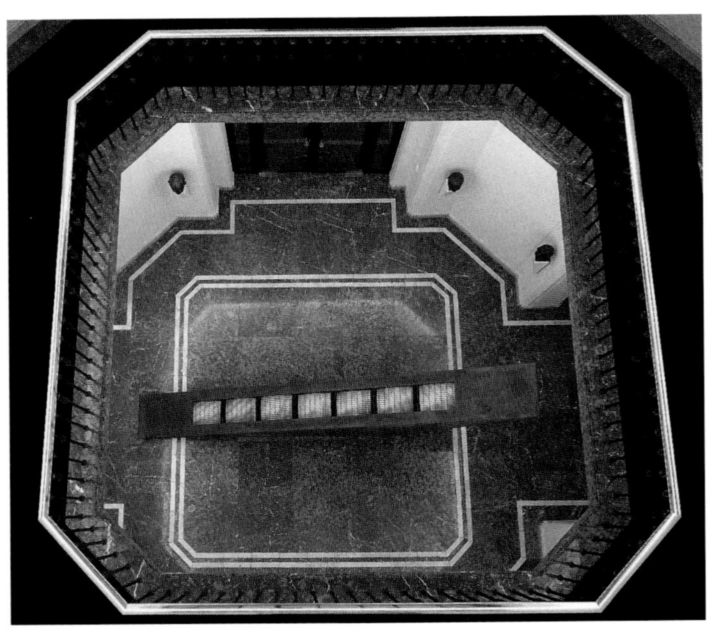

In vielen seiner Videoskulpturen greift Fabrizio Plessi Aspekte,
Themen oder Gedankenkonstruk-
tionen früherer Projekte, Aktionen
oder Performances auf. Dazu
gehört auch das Thema der *Flüssi-*
gen Geometrie. Bereits 1977 hat er
für seine Ausstellung in der
Kunsthalle Kiel ein Projekt entworfen, das er mit folgenden
Worten beschreibt: »Ich bezeichne
auf der Wasserfläche vor der
Kunsthalle drei große geometrische Formen: ein Quadrat, einen
Kreis, ein Dreieck. Ihre äußeren
Begrenzungen werden mit Tau
und Bojen fixiert. Von einem
Schlauchboot aus schneide, oder
besser gesagt, säge ich mit einer
einfachen Säge die genauen

In many of his video sculp-
tures, Fabrizio Plessi takes up
aspects, themes or ideas of
former projects, actions or
performances. Among these can
be counted the theme Liquid
Geometry. *Already in 1977 he*
designed a project for an exhibi-
tion in the Kunsthalle in Kiel
that he described with the follo-
wing words: "On the water of the
pool in front of the Kunsthalle I
define three large-sized forms: a
square, a circle, a triangle. Their
outer limits are fixed by ropes
and buoys. From a rubber-
dinghy, I cut - or rather saw - the
exact proportions of the formerly
fixed 'Sea-pieces' with a simple
saw. In three halls of the Kunst-

In molte delle sue videosculture Fabrizio Plessi riprende
aspetti, tematiche o concetti di
progetti, azioni e performances
precedenti, così anche il tema
della *Geometria Liquida.* Già nel
1977 delinea un progetto per la
Kunsthalle di Kiel che descrive
con queste parole: »Sulla superficie dell'acqua di fronte alla
Kunsthalle individuo tre grandi
forme geometriche: un quadrato, un cerchio e un triangolo
che saranno poi delimitate da
cime e da boe. Da un gommone
taglio, o meglio sego, con una
sega comune le esatte proporzioni dei ›pezzi di mare‹ prima
individuati. Nelle tre sale della
Kunsthalle proietto tre filmati a

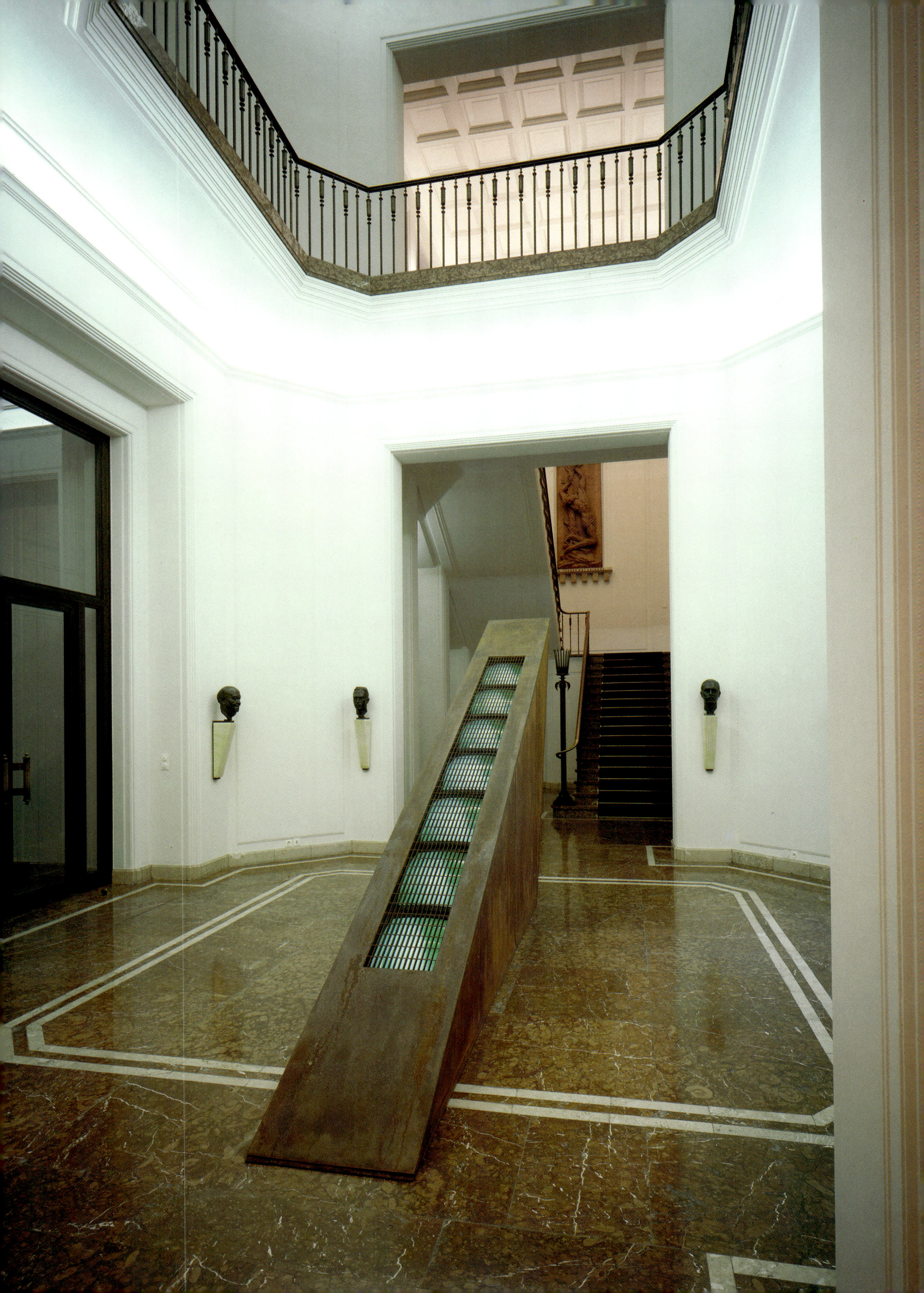

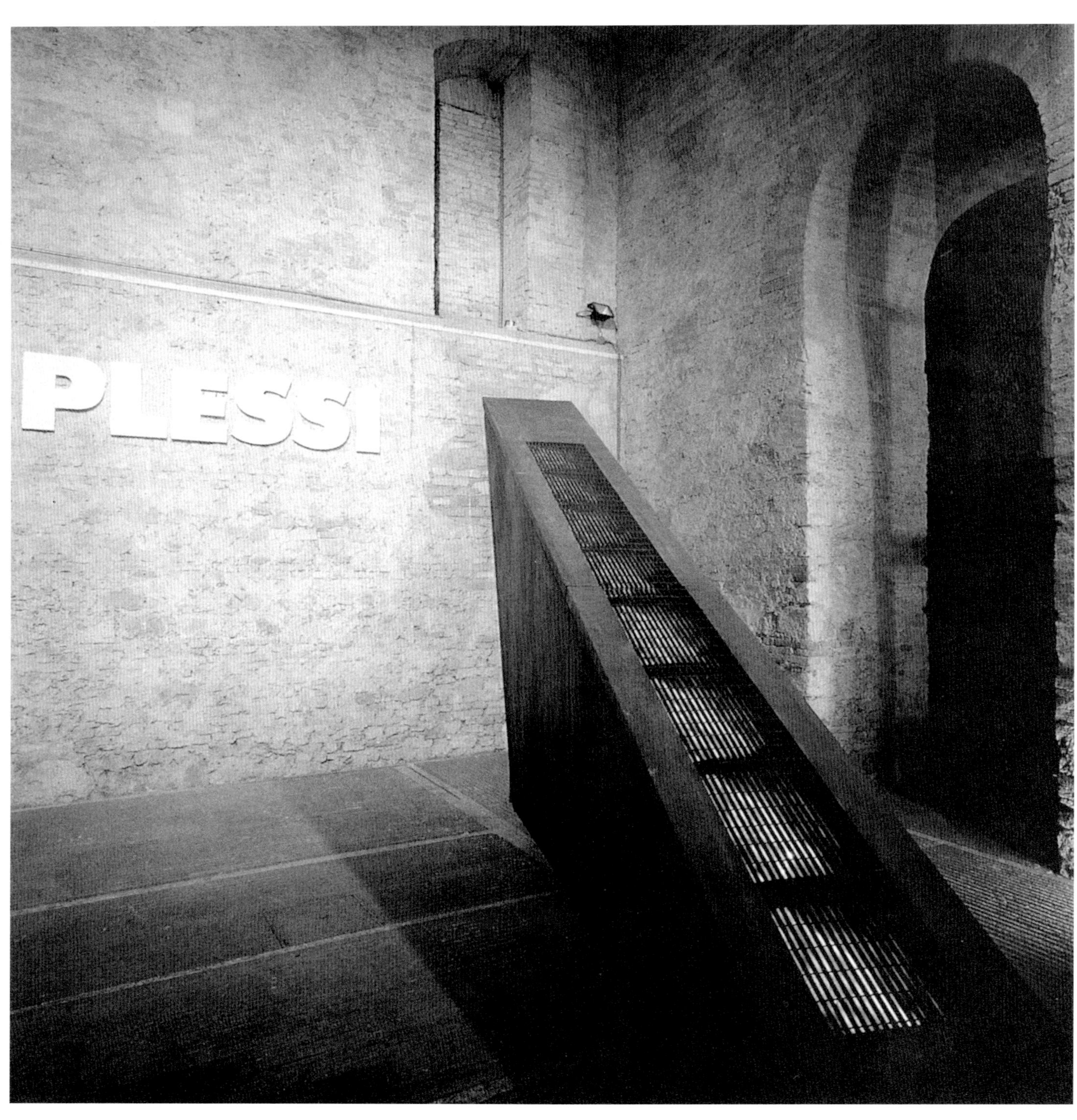
PLESSI

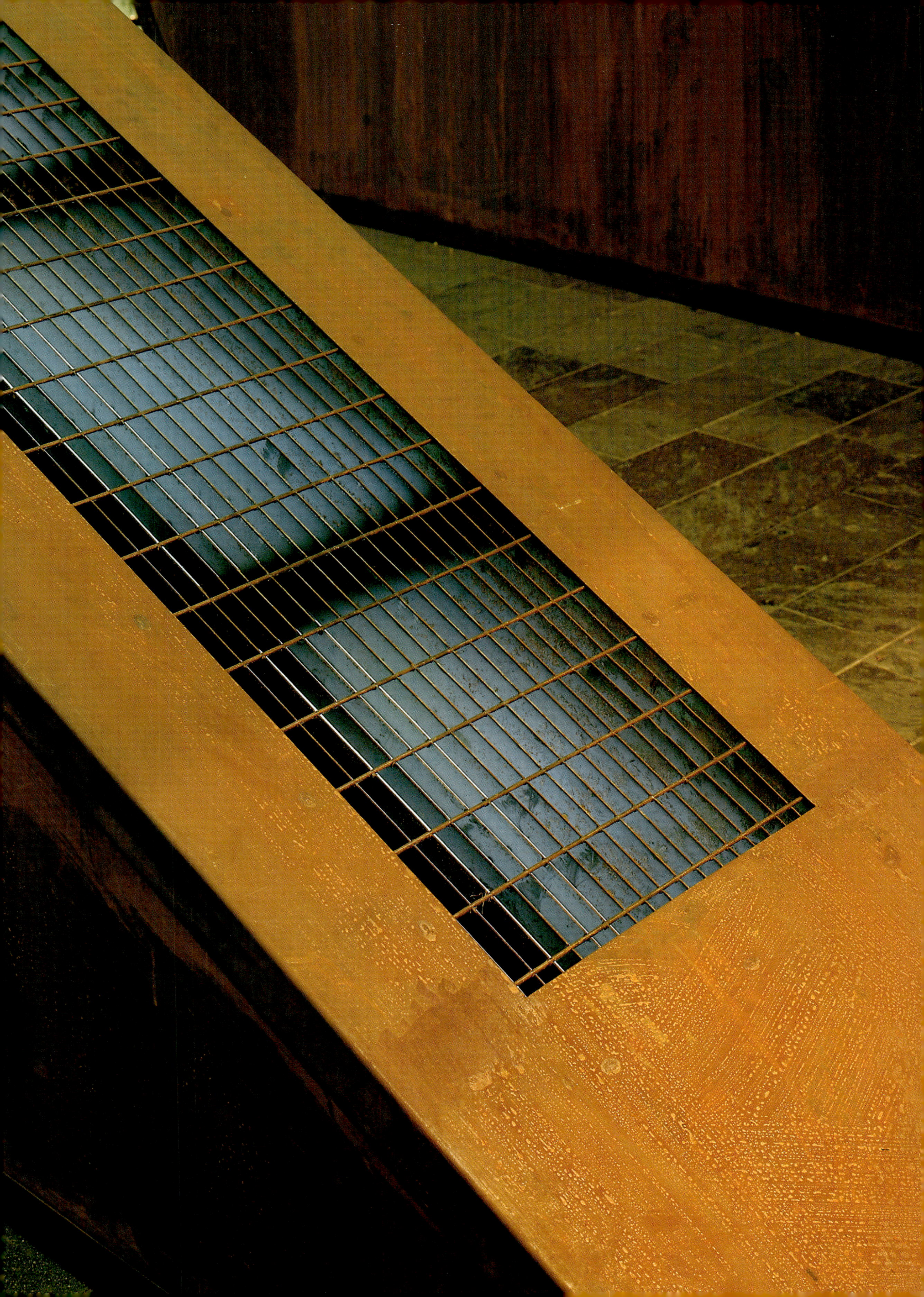

Proportionen der vorher bezeichneten ›Meeresstücke‹ aus. In drei Sälen der Kunsthalle projiziere ich drei Farbfilme, die diese Teile des Meeres wiedergeben, die so als *Flüssige Geometrie* ins Museum gekommen sind. Drei Tonbandgeräte geben das Geräusch des Meeres im Moment des Durchsägens wieder.« (Fabrizio Plessi, in: Katalog Kunsthalle zu Kiel, Kiel 1977)

Unter demselben Titel *Flüssige Geometrie* oder *Geometria Liquida* entsteht 1989 eine Videoskulptur, bei der eine geometrische Grundform, ein dynamisches Dreieck, einen Dialog mit dem informellen Lauf des elektronischen Wassers über mehrere Monitore hindurch eingeht. Es gibt mehrere Versionen dieser Konzeption in unterschiedlichen Proportionen und wechselnden Färbungen des elektronischen Wassers. Daß die Geometrie bei allem Sinn für Natur, natürliche Materialien und vielleicht auch Romantik schon früh im Werk Fabrizio Plessis eine Rolle spielte, konnte man bereits an der Kieler Aktion sehen. Doch wenn man die bis jetzt entstandenen Videoskulpturen und Videoinstallationen rückwirkend betrachtet, stellt man fest, daß informelle Strukturen und geometrische Formen sich stets in einem Wechselspiel befinden: einerseits Strukturen wie bei *Mare di Marmo* und *Bronx*, andererseits Kreise und Rechteck wie bei *Roma*, die Kreuzform oder auch Quadrat, Parallelen und Linien wie bei *Bombay-Bombay*, das man später sehen wird, und schließlich das Dreieck hier in der *Flüssigen Geometrie*.

Beobachtungen der Natur tragen dazu bei, anhand einzelner Erscheinungen, sinnliche Erfahrungen zu sammeln. Diese empirischen Wahrnehmungen sind nur Beispiele, als sinnliche Erfahrungen lassen sie keine Erkenntnis über das Wesen einer Sache (die Anima) zu. Dies

halle I project three colour films that show these sea-pieces that thus - as Liquid Geometry *- have entered into the museum. Three tape recorders reproduce the sound of the sea at the moment of sawing. (Plessi in: catalogue Kunsthalle zu Kiel, Kiel, 1977)*

Under the same title, Liquid Geometry *or* Geometria Liquida, *a video sculpture is realised in 1989, in which a basic geometric form, a dynamic triangle, enters into a dialogue with the informal course of the electronic water on several monitors. There are several versions of this concept in different proportions and varying colorations of the electronic water. That geometry, in spite of all interest in nature, natural materials and perhaps even romanticism, played a role in Fabrizio Plessi's early work, could be seen in the action in Kiel. Yet, if one looks back at the video sculptures and video installations realised up to now one can see that informal structures and geometric forms always show reciprocity: on the one hand there are structures, as in* Mare di Marmo *and* Bronx, *on the other hand circles and rectangles, as in* Roma, *the cross-form, square, parallels and lines, as in* Bombay-Bombay *that will be seen later, and finally the triangle here in* Liquid Geometry.

Observations of nature contribute to collect sensual experiences. These empirical observations are only examples, they do not - as sensual experiences - allow any knowledge of the nature of objects (anima). Descartes had recognised this in his Meditations (remember the wax-example), and therefore decided, as described in his Essay on the Method of Correct Use of Reason in Search of Truth in Sciences,

colori che riproducono quei pezzi del mare che così fanno il loro ingresso nel museo come Flüssige Geometrie. Tre registratori riproducono il rumore del mare mentre taglio l'acqua« (cfr. Fabrizio Plessi, in: catalogo Kunsthalle zu Kiel, Kiel 1977).

Con lo stesso titolo *Geometria Liquida* nasce nel 1989 una videoscultura nella quale una forma geometrica, un triangolo dinamico, entra in dialogo con il cammino informale dell'acqua elettronica dei diversi monitor. Esistono versioni differenti di questo assemblaggio con dimensioni diverse e varie colorazioni dell'acqua elettronica. Che la geometria occupasse presto un ruolo importante nell'opera di Fabrizio Plessi - natura, materiali naturali e forse anche un certo romantiscismo a parte - si poteva notare già nell'azione di Kiel. Ma passando in rassegna le videosculture e le videoinstallazioni finora realizzate si deduce che strutture informali e forme geometriche si influenzano reciprocamente: da un lato strutture come in *Mare di Marmo* e *Bronx*, dall'altro cerchi e rettangoli come in *Roma*, la forma della croce o anche il quadrato, parallele e linee come in *Bombay-Bombay*, realizzata più tardi, e infine il triangolo di *Geometria Liquida*.

L'osservazione dei singoli fenomeni naturali è un modo di raccogliere esperienze basate sui sensi. Tale percezione empirica ha carattere esemplificativo, ma come esperienza sensuale non ha nessun valore cognitivo rispetto alla natura delle cose (l'anima). Già Descartes lo riconosce nelle sue Meditazioni (si ricorda l'esempio della cera) e decide, come spiega nel suo Trattato sul metodo dell'uso corretto della

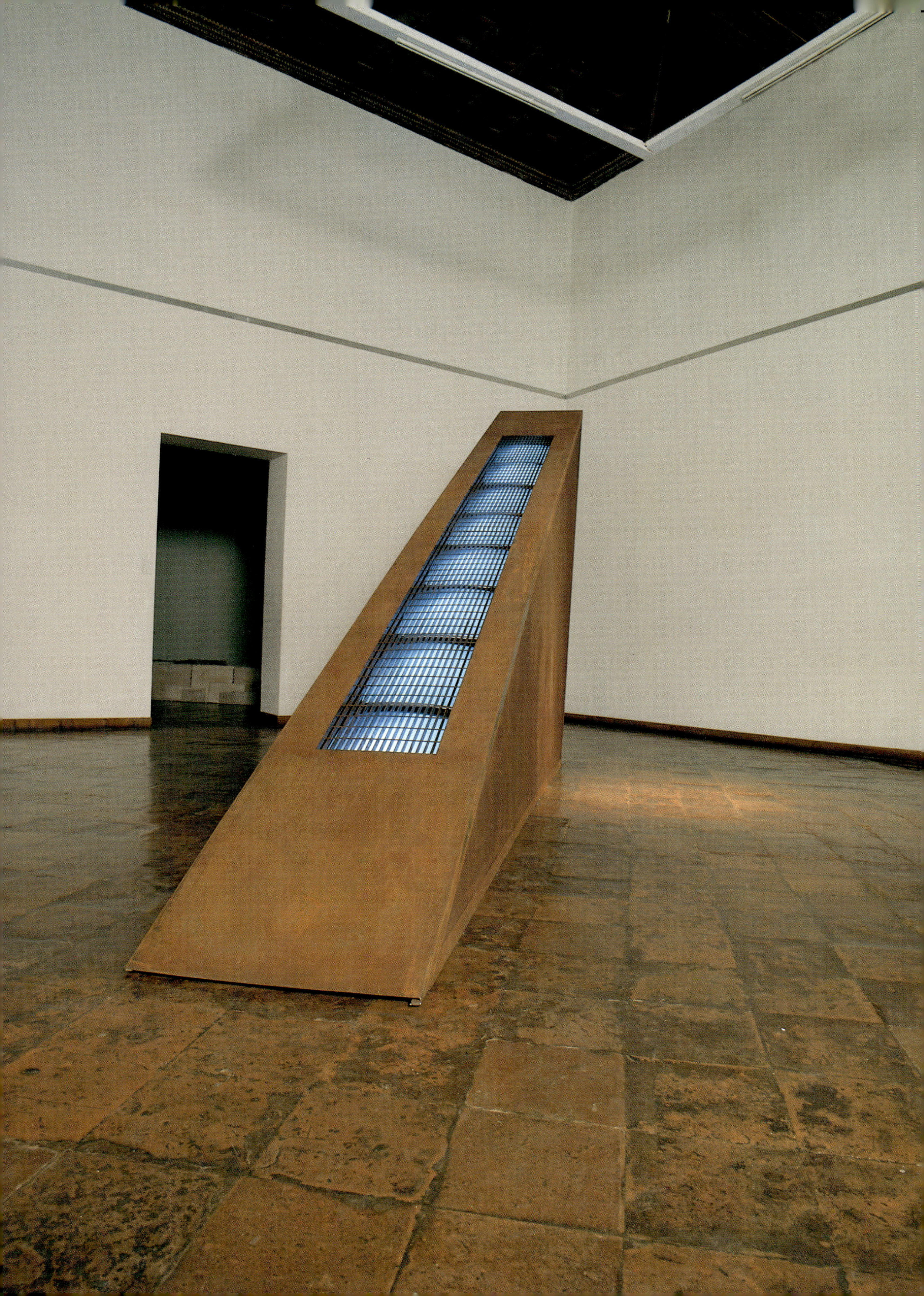

hatte schon Descartes in seinen *Meditationen* erkannt (ich erinnere an das Wachsbeispiel) und sich daher entschlossen, wie es in seiner *Abhandlung über die Methode des richtigen Vernunftgebrauchs auf der Suche nach der Wahrheit in den Wissenschaften* geschrieben steht, in seinen Überlegungen alles, was nicht gewiß ist, zu eliminieren, um schließlich zu wenigstens einer gültigen Gewißheit zu gelangen. Er gelangt auf seinem Weg »die wahre Methode zu suchen, um zu der Erkenntnis aller Dinge zu gelangen, die mein Geist fassen könnte« (Descartes: *Meditationen*) zur Mathematik, zur Logik, geometrischer Analysis und Algebra. Er wollte, wie es heißt, seinen Geist daran »gewöhnen, sich mit Wahrheiten zu nähren und nicht mit falschen Gründen zu begnügen« und wandte sich also den mathematischen Wissenschaften zu, die »bei aller Verschiedenheit ihrer Objekte doch darin sämtlich übereinstimmten, daß sie in ihren Objekten die verschiedenen Beziehungen oder Verhältnisse betrachteten«. Um der mathematischen Komplexität zu entgehen, entschloß Descartes sich »nur solcher Objekte anzunehmen, die mir die Erkenntnis derselben am meisten erleichtern würden« (ebd.) und »um sie besser im einzelnen zu betrachten, gerade Linien als Träger zu nehmen ... weil ich nichts einfacheres fand und meine Einbildung und mein Sinn nichts deutlicher vorstellen konnte«.(ebd.)

Die Geometrie ist also zur Erkenntnis wichtig, und Fabrizio Plessi liebt die Ordnung der Geometrie, aber zugleich fühlt er sich hingezogen zu der Freiheit der Phantasie und des Unbegrenzten.

to eliminate everything uncertain in order to finally reach one certain conclusion. On his way to "search for the true method of finding the cognition of all things my mind can grasp" (Descartes: Meditations) he arrives at mathematics, logic, geometric analysis and algebra. He wanted, as is said, to "accustom his mind to feed on truths, not to be content with false reasons", and therefore turned to mathematical sciences that "in all differences of their objects, all agree that they are observing the different relations and conditions in their objects." To avoid the complexity of mathematics, Descartes decided to "only accept those objects that alleviate their perception" and "to look at each one more closely, take straight lines as support...because I could not find anything more simple, and my imagination and mind could not imagine anything clearer." (ib.)

Thus, geometry is important for understanding, and Fabrizio Plessi loves the order inherent in geometry, feeling, however, simultaneously drawn to freedom of fantasy and limitlessness.

ragione, di eliminare dai suoi pensieri tutto ciò che non è certo, per giungere infine almeno ad una certezza valida. Nel suo cammino verso la ricerca del »metodo vero per giungere alla conoscenza delle cose che la mente può comprendere« (cfr. Descartes, Meditazioni) egli giunge alla matematica, alla logica, all'analisi geometrica ed all'algebra cercando di abituare la sua mente a »nutrirsi di verità e non accontentarsi di motivi falsi«. Alle scienze matematiche egli riconobbe che »con tutte le varietà degli oggetti esse concordavano di osservarne i rapporti e le relazioni differenti«. Per sfuggire alla complessità della matematica Descartes decise di »occuparsi solamente di quegli oggetti che mi avrebbero facilitato la loro comprensione« e di »scegliere forme lineari per poterle meglio osservare, perchè non trovai niente di più semplice e più immaginabile« (ibid.).

Senza geometria non si giunge alla conoscenza, e Fabrizio Plessi ama l'ordine della geometria essendo nello stesso momento attratto dalla libertà illimitata della fantasia.

TEMPO LIQUIDO

89002

PRATO 1989
Museo d'Arte Contemporanea ›Luigi Pecci‹
89002.1

PERUGIA 1995
Rocca Paolina
89002.2

FLÜSSIGE ZEIT
Videoskulptur 1989
Stahlkonstruktion mit Motorantrieb,
großes Rad in ständiger Drehung,
Eisengitter, Licht, Wasserpumpe,
fließendes Wasser, 21 Monitore,
Videorecorder, bespielte Kassette
(Perugia: Videopräsentation)

LIQUID TIME
Video sculpture 1989
Iron, iron lattice, motor drive,
light, constant movement, water
pump, running water, 21 monitors,
video recorder, recorded video
cassette
(Perugia: Video presentation)

TEMPO LIQUIDO
Videoscultura 1989
Ferro, grigliato industriale, moto
meccanico, luce, movimento
costante, pompa idraulica, acqua
corrente, 21 monitors, vhs,
cassetta registrata
(Perugia: presentazione video)

Auch zu der Videoskulptur *Tempo Liquido (Flüssige Zeit)* gibt es ein Performance-Projekt gleichen Titels von 1978. Auch hier handelt es sich im Grunde wieder um ein geometrisches Gebilde, bestehend aus einer Kreisform und einer Linie, und auch hier fließt, ähnlich wie bei der Installation *Roma*, Wasser im Kreis, zeigt den Kreislauf der Zeit an. Doch die Monitore liegen nicht mit der Rückseite auf dem Boden und ihren Bildschirmen nach oben gerichtet, sondern die Konstruktion steht frei im Raum wie eine elektronische Mühle, die sich um ihre Achse dreht. Die Monitore mit dem elektronischen Wasser sind nach außen gerichtet. Das Mühlrad scheint durch einen realen Wasserstrom angetrieben zu werden. Wie schon bei *Water Wind* bestimmt auch hier ein außenstehendes reales Element das elektronische Bild.

The video sculpture Tempo Liquido (Liquid Time) *is also based on a project for a performance from 1978. Here, too, we are looking at a geometrical structure, consisting of a circular form and a line, and here, too, similar to the installation* Roma, *water flows in a circle, indicating the circulation of time. The monitors are not, however, placed with their back to the ground, their screens pointing upwards, but the construction stands free in space like an electric mill that turns on its axle. The monitors with their electronic water show outwards, the mill wheel seems to be driven by a real stream of water. As already in* Water Wind *here, too, a real element from outside determines the electronic image.*

The title of the work indicates that this electronic mill points to

Anche la videoscultura *Tempo Liquido* è preceduta da un progetto per una performance omonima del 1978. Anche qui si tratta in fondo di una struttura geometrica costituita da una forma circolare e una linea, anche qui l'acqua scorre, simile alla installazione *Roma*, in un percorso circolare, in un cerchio del tempo. Ma questa volta i monitors non sono appoggiati per terra con gli schermi rivolti verso l'alto, ma fanno parte della ruota di un mulino elettronico che gira sul propria asse. I monitors con l'acqua elettronica sono rivolti verso l'esterno e la ruota sembra spinta da una corrente reale d'acqua. Come già avvenuto in *Water Wind*, anche qui un elemento esterno reale determina l'immagine elettronica.

Il titolo dell'opera fa supporre

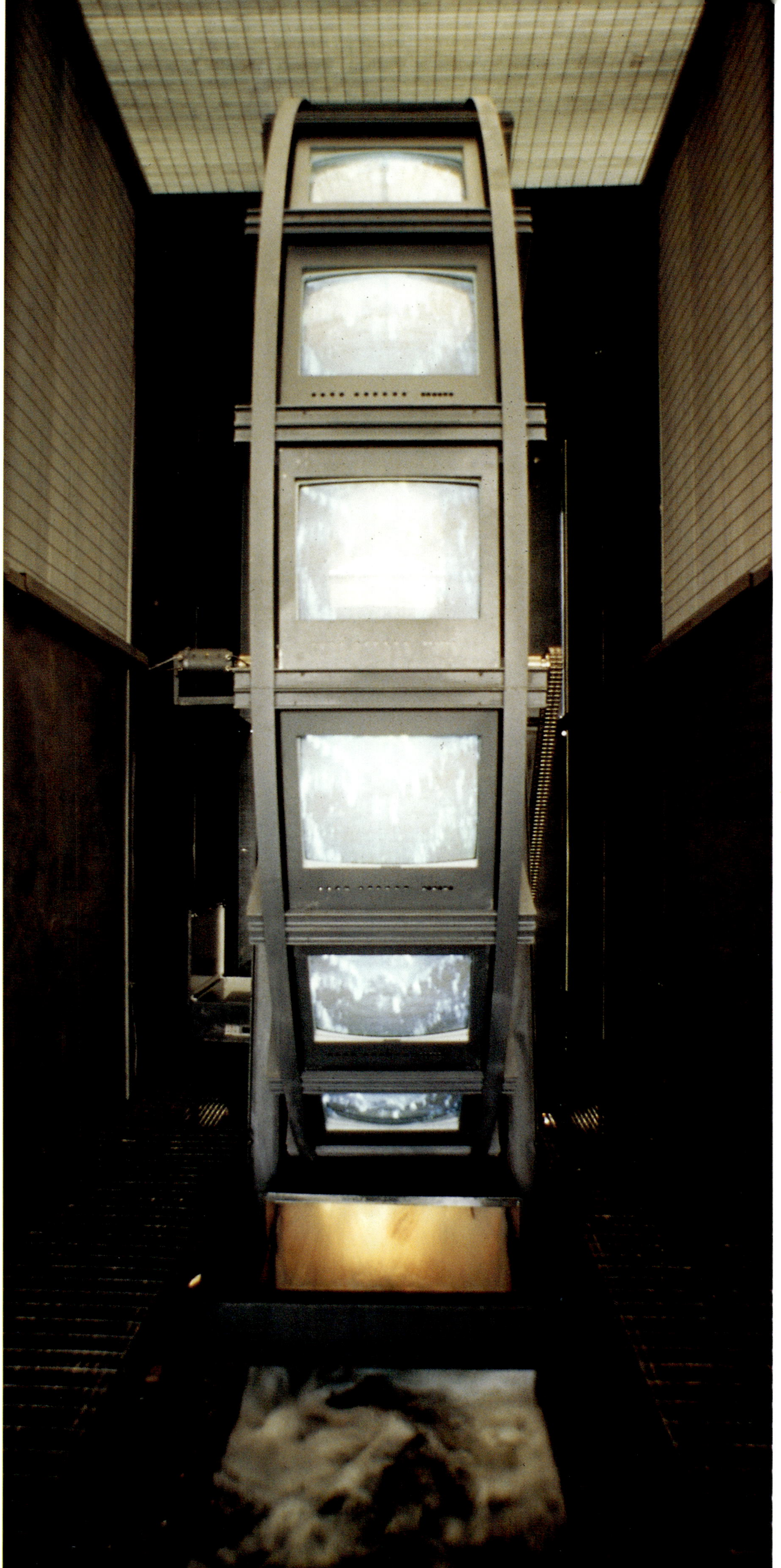

Der Titel der Arbeit läßt vermuten, daß diese elektronische Mühle auf mehr als nur einen mechanischen oder physikalischen Sachverhalt verweist. ›Zeit‹ und ›Raum‹ sind Begriffe, die uns der Verstand a priori, das heißt, ohne empirische Grundlagen gibt. Diese Begriffe sind dann selbst nicht anschaulich, liegen aber allen äußeren Anschauungen zugrunde (vgl. Immanuel Kant: *Kritik der reinen Vernunft*). Allein die Tatsache, daß man ein und denselben Gegenstand nacheinander in zwei verschiedenen Positionen sehen kann, macht deutlich, daß dieser Gegenstand sich von der einen Position in die andere Position bewegt haben muß, daraus folgt: Zeit ist vergangen. ›Zeit‹ ist selbst nicht sichtbar, sondern kann nur über Veränderung erkannt werden. Auch ›Raum‹ allgemein ist nicht sichtbar. Man kann sich nur einen bestimmten Raum vorstellen oder auch einen leeren Raum, aber man kann sich nicht vorstellen, daß es keinen Raum gibt. Raum und Zeit als Prinzipien der Erkenntnis a priori werden als die allgemeinen Bedingungen der Möglichkeit der Erscheinungen angesehen, auf welchen wiederum alle empirische Erkenntnis beruht (Kant). In diesem Zusammenhang weist Kant daraufhin, daß die Dinge nicht das an sich selbst sind, wofür wir sie anschauen, sondern nur in uns existieren. Daß alle unsere Anschauung also nichts als die Vorstellung von Erscheinung sei. Gerade in diesem Punkte werden die Möglichkeiten bildnerischen Schaffens deutlich, denn Farben, Linien, Flächen und Formen vom Künstler zueinandergebracht, suggerieren in der Vorstellungswelt des Betrachters Erscheinungen. Diese Erscheinungen orientieren sich an Phänomenen der Wirklichkeit. Der Betrachter sucht Orientierungspunkte, an denen er mit

more than one mechanical or physical context. 'Time' and 'Space' are terms that our mind gives us a priori, that is without empirical basis. These terms themselves are then not perceivable, but are the basis of all external perception (cf. Immanuel Kant: The Critique of Pure Reason*). The fact alone that one and the same object can be seen successively in two different positions is evidence that the object must have moved from one position to the next, from which follows: time has passed. 'Time' itself is invisible, but can only be recognised by change, and 'Space' in general cannot be seen. One can only imagine a certain space, or an empty room, but it is impossible to imagine that there is no space. Space and time as principles of perception a priori are considered as general conditions of the possibility of phenomena, on which all empirical cognition is based (Kant). In this context, Kant points out that the objects are not in themselves what we consider them to be, but only exist within us, that all our perception is nothing but the imagination of phenomenon. With this argument, the possibilities of creative design become evident, for colours, lines, planes and forms, united by the artist, suggest images in the mind of the spectator. These images orient themselves on phenomena of reality. The spectator looks for points of orientation which he can connect to his own experiences to approach the work, to recognise, to understand it. Thus a world can be created that goes far beyond the work, and manifests itself in a new realisation.*

Interestingly enough, the electronic mill offers numerous

che il mulino elettronico non alluda solamente ad uno stato meccanico o fisico delle cose. ›Tempo‹ e ›Spazio‹ sono due concetti che la ragione ci fornisce a priori, cioè senza fondamento empirico, due concetti non concreti che, però, costituiscono la base di ogni esperienza concreta (cfr. Immanuel Kant, Critica della ragione pura). Il solo fatto che si possa vedere lo stesso oggetto in due posizioni successive evidenzia che esso si è mosso da una posizione all'altra e, di conseguenza, che è passato del tempo. Il tempo in sè non è visibile ma riconoscibile solamente attraverso un cambiamento. Nello stesso modo non è visibile lo spazio in generale. È possibile immaginarsi un determinato spazio o uno spazio vuoto, ma non è possibile immaginarsi che non esiste lo spazio. Spazio e tempo come principì della conoscenza a priori sono considerati condizioni generali della possibilità delle forme; sulle quali a sua volta si fonda tutta la conoscenza empirica (Kant). In questo contesto Kant fa notare che le cose in sé non sono ciò che noi riteniamo che siano e che quindi esistono solamente nella nostra mente. Tutte le nostre esperienze concrete sono nient'altro che concetti di immagini. Ed è qui che si contraddistinguono le possibilità della creazione figurativa, in quanto i colori, le linee, le superfici e le forme ideate dall'artista suggeriscono immagini allo spettatore che si orientano ai fenomeni della realtà. Lo spettatore cerca nell'opera d'arte punti di riferimento ai quali applicare la propria esperienza per potersi avvicinare all'opera, per comprenderla e per interpretarla

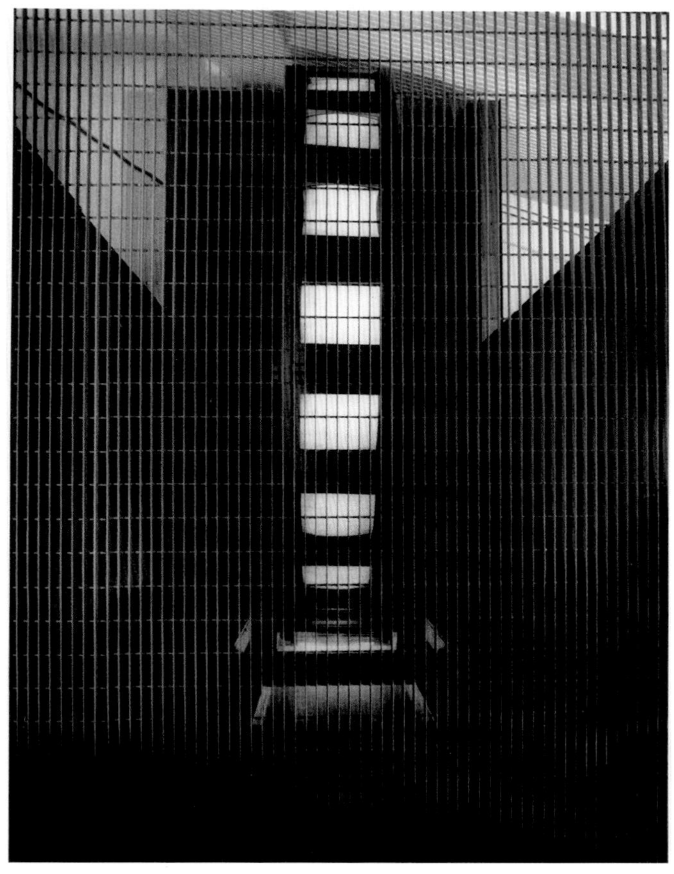 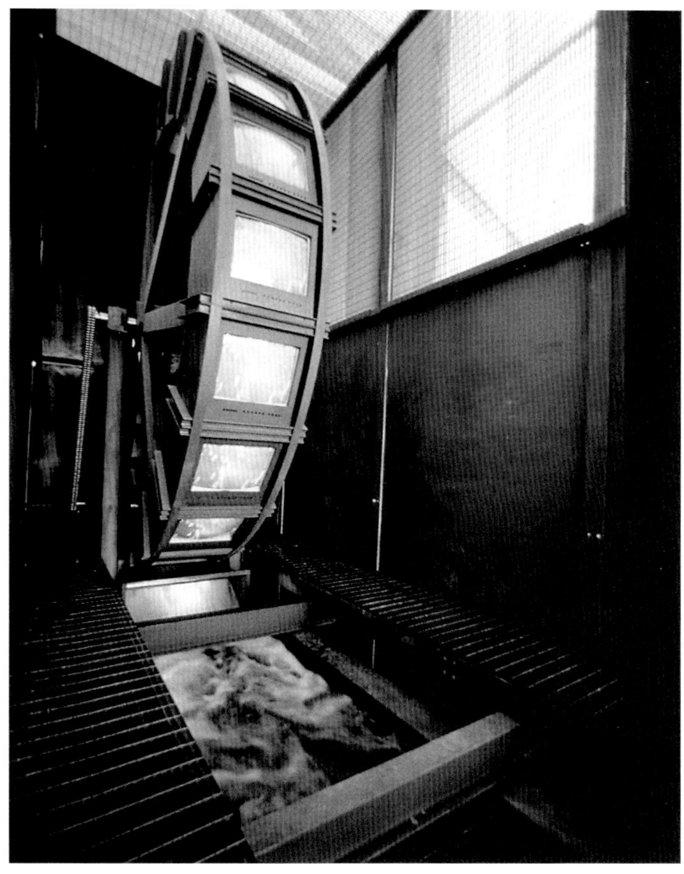

seinen Erfahrungen ansetzen kann, um sich dem Werk zu nähern, um es zu erkennen, zu entschlüsseln. Dabei kann eine Welt entstehen, die weit über das Werk hinausreicht und sich in einer neuen Erkenntnis manifestiert.

Interessanterweise bietet die elektronische Mühle noch zahlreiche weitere Assoziationsmöglichkeiten. Die Grundlage bildnerischen Schaffens bildet seit einigen Jahrhunderten in Europa das Papier, zumindest die Grundlage der Zeichnung. Gerade Fabrizio Plessi ist ein Künstler, der sämtliche seiner Projekte, Aktionen, ja selbst die Performances und schließlich die Videoskulpturen und Videoinstallationen zeichnerisch vorbereitet. Die Zeichnung ist für ihn ein ganz wichtiges Medium, sich selbst Klarheit über das geplante Vorhaben zu verschaffen. Zudem packt ihn die Lust am Zeichnen immer wieder, und am

other possibilities of association. Paper has, for some centuries now, been the basis of artistic creation, at least the basis of drawing. Fabrizio Plessi, especially, is an artist who prepares all of his projects, actions, performances, and even the video sculptures and video installations in drawing. For him, the drawing is a very important medium to clarify - for himself - the intended project. In addition, he again and again is affected by his love of drawing, and especially of drawing in Venice: "Drawing in Venice is very different from drawing in Berlin or Rome. The place itself alters your lines.

Water insinuates itself everywhere in Venice, it gets into every crack, even the most secret; this water wraps everything with its reflections,

creando con ciò un mondo possibile che supera ampiamente quello suggerito dall'opera e che si manifesta in una nuova conoscenza.

Ma il mulino elettronico offre numerose ulteriori possibilità di associazione. Da secoli la carta è, in Europa, alla base della creazione figurativa, la base del disegno. Fabrizio Plessi, in particolare, è un artista che per ogni progetto, ogni azione, performance, videoscultura e videoinstallazione realizza disegni preparatori. Il disegno rappresenta per lui un medium estremamente importante per potersi render conto di ciò che intende creare. Continuamente Plessi è preso dalla passione di disegnare, soprattutto di disegnare a Venezia: »Disegnare a Venezia è molto diverso che disegnare a Berlino o a Roma. Il lugo stesso ti altera il tracciato.

Zeichnen in Venedig im besonderen: »Das Zeichnen in Venedig ist gänzlich verschieden vom Zeichnen in Berlin oder Rom. Der Ort selbst verändert deine Linien. Wasser deutet sich in Venedig überall an. Es gelangt in jede Spalte, selbst in die geheimste. Dieses Wasser umhüllt alles mit seinen Reflexionen. Es breitet sich aus in den Zeichnungen, verwischt die Grenzen, verändert Zeichen des Stifts mit seiner Rückstrahlung wie eine unstete geschmeidige Wellenbewegung. Dieses leuchtende Schimmern, wenn es durch die großen Fenster einfällt, macht das Zeichnen flüssiger, unsteter, mobiler, flüchtiger, kaum faßbar. Ich könnte mir sogar vorstellen, daß der Stift über das Blatt Papier schwimmt.« (Plessi im Ausstellungskatalog des Museum Ludwigs, Köln 1993)

Interessanterweise hat der Weg des Papiers, das ja die Grundlage fürs Zeichnen ist, von Asien, wo es im 1. Jh. n. Chr. von einem chinesischen Staatsmann erfunden wurde, bis nach Europa unendlich lange gedauert. Schon bald nach seiner Erfindung kommt dem Papier in China eine vielseitige Verwendung zu, nicht nur in der Verwaltung, in Religion, Literatur und Wissenschaft. Bereits im 2. Jh. gibt es dort Papiertaschentücher, seit dem 7. Jh. Papiergeld, im 9. Jh. Toilettenpapier und am Ende des 9. Jh. Servietten und Kleider aus Papier. Im 10. Jh. schließlich sind in China bereits Spielkarten in Gebrauch, um nur einige Daten zu nennen. Erst etwa ein Jahrtausend nach seiner Erfindung gelangt das Papier über Arabien und Nahost nach Europa. In Italien beginnt die Papiermacherei ab der Mitte des 13. Jahrhunderts. Als eine der ältesten Papiermühlen Italiens gilt die 1276 in Fabriano bei Ancona gegründete Papiermühle. Erst gegen Ende des 14. Jahrhunderts entsteht die erste Papiermacherei in Deutschland. Ein

spreading out in the drawings, confusing the boundaries, modifying pencil signs with its reverberation, like an unstable, elastic undulation. This luminous shimmering, when it enters the large windows, makes drawing more fluid, unstable, mobile, evanescent, impalpable. I might even imagine that the pencil is floating across the sheet of paper." (Fabrizio Plessi, in: Catalogue Museum Ludwig, Köln 1993)

Interestingly, the arrival of paper, which is the basis of drawing, from Asia, where it was invented by a Chinese statesman in the first century A.D., to Europe has taken incredibly long. Soon after its invention, paper plays a multifaceted role in China, not only in administration, but in religion, literature, and science. As early as the second century there are tissue papers, in the seventh century paper money exists, toilet paper in the ninth century and, at the end of that century, napkins and paper clothes. In the tenth century playing cards are in use in China, to mention but a few dates. Only about a thousand years after its invention paper arrives - via Arabia and the Near East - in Europe. In Italy, the production of paper begins in the middle of the 13th century. The paper mill in Fabriano near Ancona, founded in 1276, is considered to be the oldest mill in Italy. Only at the end of the 14th century the first paper mill is established in Germany. Uhlmann Stromer, a businessman from Nuremberg, had, in 1389/90, one of his four grain mills, a water mill outside his hometown, converted into a paper mill by craftsmen from Lombardy. Fabrizio Plessi' s

L'acqua di Venezia si insinua ovunque, si infiltra in ogni anfratto, anche il più segreto; quest'acqua avvolge con i suoi riflessi ogni cosa, dilatandosi sui disegni, confondendone i confini e con il suo riverbero modifica i segni a matita come un elastico instabile ed ondulatorio. Questo tremolio luminoso, entrando dalle grandi finestre rende il disegno più fluido, instabile, mobile, evanescente, impalpabile. Potrei dire per assurdo che la matita galleggia a mia insaputa sul foglio.« (Fabrizio Plessi, in: catalogo Museum Ludwig, Colonia 1993).

Il percorso della carta, fondamentale per il disegno, dall'Asia, dove fu inventata nel I secolo d. C. da un uomo di stato cinese, in Europa curiosamente è durato un'eternità. Poco dopo la sua invenzione la carta trova già molteplici applicazioni in Cina, e non solo nell'amministrazione, nella religione, nella letteratura e nelle scienze. Nel II secolo esistono già fazzoletti di carta, dal VII secolo banconote di carta, nel IX secolo la carta igienica, tovaglioli e vestiti di carta e nel X secolo si fa uso di carte da gioco. Solo un millennio dopo la sua invenzione la carta approda, passando per l'Arabia e il Vicino Oriente, in Europa. In Italia la produzione di carta ha inizio nella metà del XIII secolo. Uno fra i più antichi mulini da carta italiani è quello di Fabriano presso Ancona, fondato nel 1276. Ancora più tardi, alla fine del XIII secolo, nasce la prima cartiera in Germania. Un imprenditore di Norimberga, di nome Uhlmann Stromer, nel 1389/90 fece trasformare da artigiani lombardi uno dei suoi quattro mulini ad acqua per il grano in un mulino da carta. Il mulino elettronico di

192

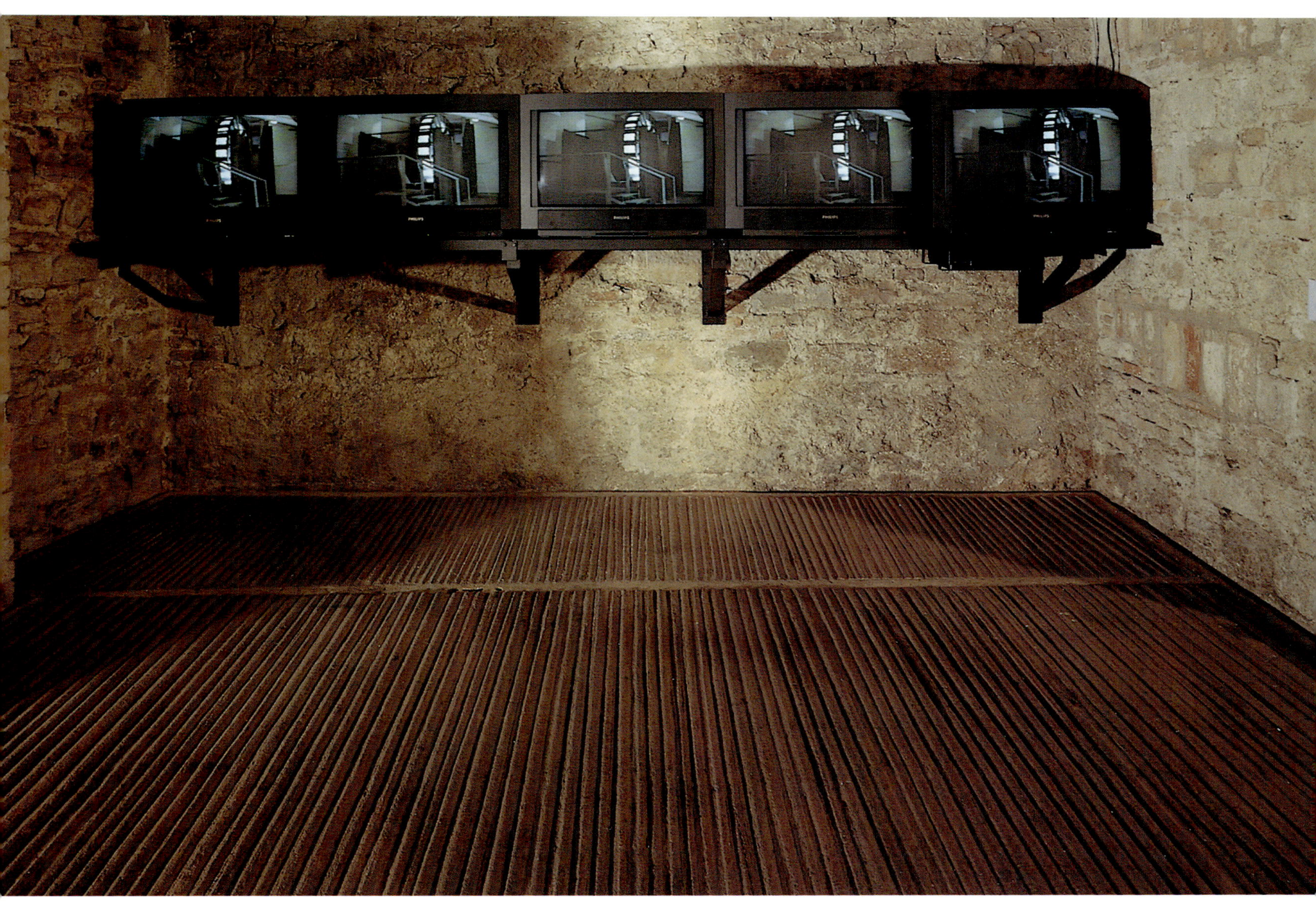

Nürnberger Unternehmer namens Uhlmann Stromer ließ 1389/90 eine seiner vier Getreidemühlen, eine Wassermühle, vor den Toren seiner Vaterstadt durch lombardische Handwerker in eine Papiermühle umbauen. Die elektronische Mühle Fabrizio Plessis, scheinbar durch reales Wasser angetrieben, könnte so gesehen auch als Papiermühle interpretiert werden, die die Grundlage für sein Zeichnen schafft, das Papier, als ›Conditio sine qua non‹.

Doch mehr als der Verweis auf die elektronische Wasser- oder Papiermühle liegt das Zentrum dieser Arbeit im Aspekt der Zeit. Pierre Restany schreibt dazu: »Die Zeit als flüssige Dimension zu begreifen entspricht dem Gefühl des universalen Flusses der Wahrnehmungstätigkeit und der Kommunikation zwischen Wesen, die fähig sind, die unbegrenzte Flexibilität der Existenz anzunehmen. Die Kunst Plessis präsentiert sich als eine Art von Gebet oder von ritueller Tätigkeit: Das Ritual unserer Modernität angesichts der undenkbaren Probleme des Seins und des Meeres. Das Meer als wahrnehmende Unendlichkeit, wie der Himmel es für viele andere Menschen sein kann. Die Luft des Himmels verwandelt sich in den Wind des Meeres und die Wolken bilden die Wellen.« (Aus: *Domus International*, 1986)

Eine Dokumentation der Videoskulptur *Tempo Liquido* wird später, 1995 in Prato, in fünf nebeneinander montierten Monitoren präsentiert, die während der Ausstellung in Perugia - stellvertretend für das Original - zu sehen ist.

electronic mill, apparently driven by real water, could thus be interpreted as paper mill, too, that creates the basis for his drawing, the paper, as 'conditio sine qua non'.

More than the hint to the electronic water or paper mill, the centre of this work is in the aspect of time. Pierre Restany comments: "To understand time as liquid dimension relates to the feeling of the universal flow of perception and communication between beings that are able to accept the unlimited flexibility of existence. Plessi's art presents itself as a sort of prayer, or ritual act: the ritual of our modernity in face of the unthinkable problems of being and of the sea: the sea as perceptive endlessness, as the sky is for many other people. The atmosphere of the sky is altered to the sea's wind, and the clouds form the waves." (in: Domus International, *1986)*

A documentation of the video sculpture Tempo Liquido *is later, in 1995 in Prato, presented on five monitors mounted side-by-side, and can be seen during the exhibition in Perugia - representing the original.*

Fabrizio Plessi, spinto apparentemente da acqua reale, potrebbe essere interpretato anche come mulino da carta che produce il materiale di base per il suo disegnare: la carta come ›conditio sine qua non‹.

Ma più che un'allusione ad un mulino ad acqua o da carta elettronico al centro dell'installazione sta l'aspetto del tempo. Scrive Pierre Restany: »Intendere il tempo come dimensione fluida corrisponde alla sensazione del flusso universale dell'attività percettiva e della comunicazione fra esseri capaci di accettare la flessibilità illimitata dell'esistenza. L'arte di Plessi si presenta come una forma di preghiera o rito: il rituale della nostra modernità di fronte ai problemi inconcepibili dell'essere e del mare, del mare infinito così come può essere per molte altre persone infinito il cielo. L'area del cielo muta in vento del mare« (da: Domus Internationale, 1986).

Una documentazione della videoscultura *Tempo Liquido* sarà presentata nel 1995 su cinque monitors, posizionati uno accanto all'altro ed esposti - in sostituzione dell'originale - alla mostra di Perugia.

CROSS

89003

FERRARA 1989
MUSEO PALAZZO DEI DIAMANTI
89003.1

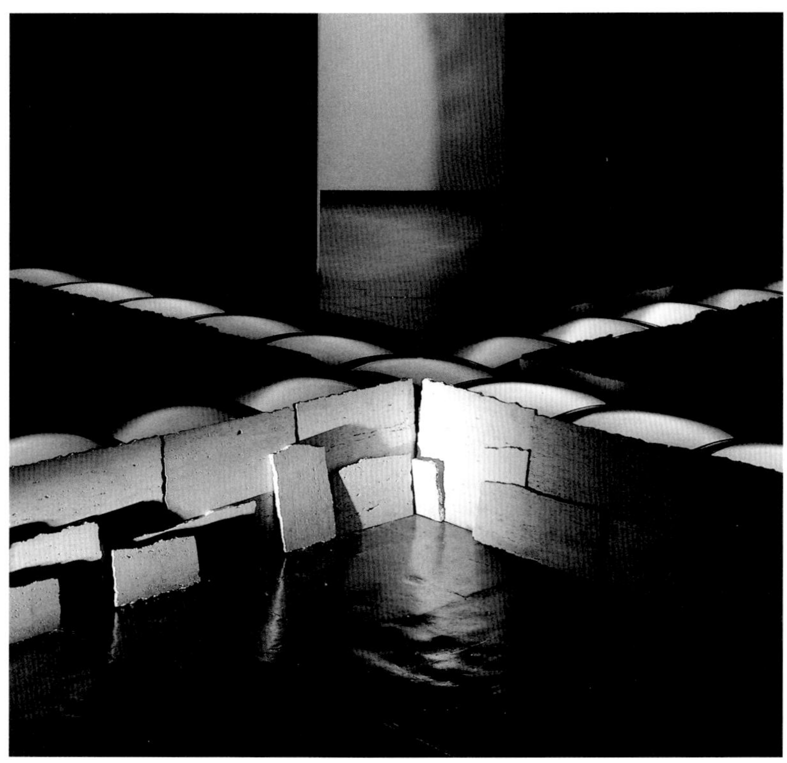

Diagonal in einen Raum gestellt sind zwei sich kreuzende Linien elektronischen Wassers, mit auf dem Rücken liegenden Monitoren, umstellt von Travertinplatten. Die Kreuzform *Cross* - wenn auch in anderer Art - ist aus den beiden Installationen *Videocruz* und *Il Peso del Mondo* bereits bekannt. Dort wie hier geht es um die Dialektik zweier entgegengesetzter Strömungen und die Frage, inwieweit ein harmonisches Miteinander dennoch möglich ist. Darüber hinaus kann die Kreuzform mathematisch oder religiös gedeutet werden.

Positioned diagonally in a room, two lines of electronic water, crossing each other, with monitors lying on their backs, surrounded by travertine slaps. Cross - in variation - is already known from the two installations Videocruz *and* Il Peso del Mondo. *There, as here, the subject is the dialectics of two opposing streams as well as the question of how harmonious coexistence is nevertheless possible. Beyond this, the form of the cross can be interpreted mathematically or religiously.*

Sull'asse diagonale del pavimento di un ambiente si incrociano due linee d'acqua elettronica dei monitors circondati da lastre di travertino. La forma a croce di *Cross* ricorda, anche se differente, quella delle due installazioni *Videocruz* e *Il Peso del Mondo* e rappresenta la dialettica fra due correnti opposte e il quesito di quanto sia tuttavia possibile una comune armonia. Inoltre, la forma della croce può avere un significato matematico o religioso.

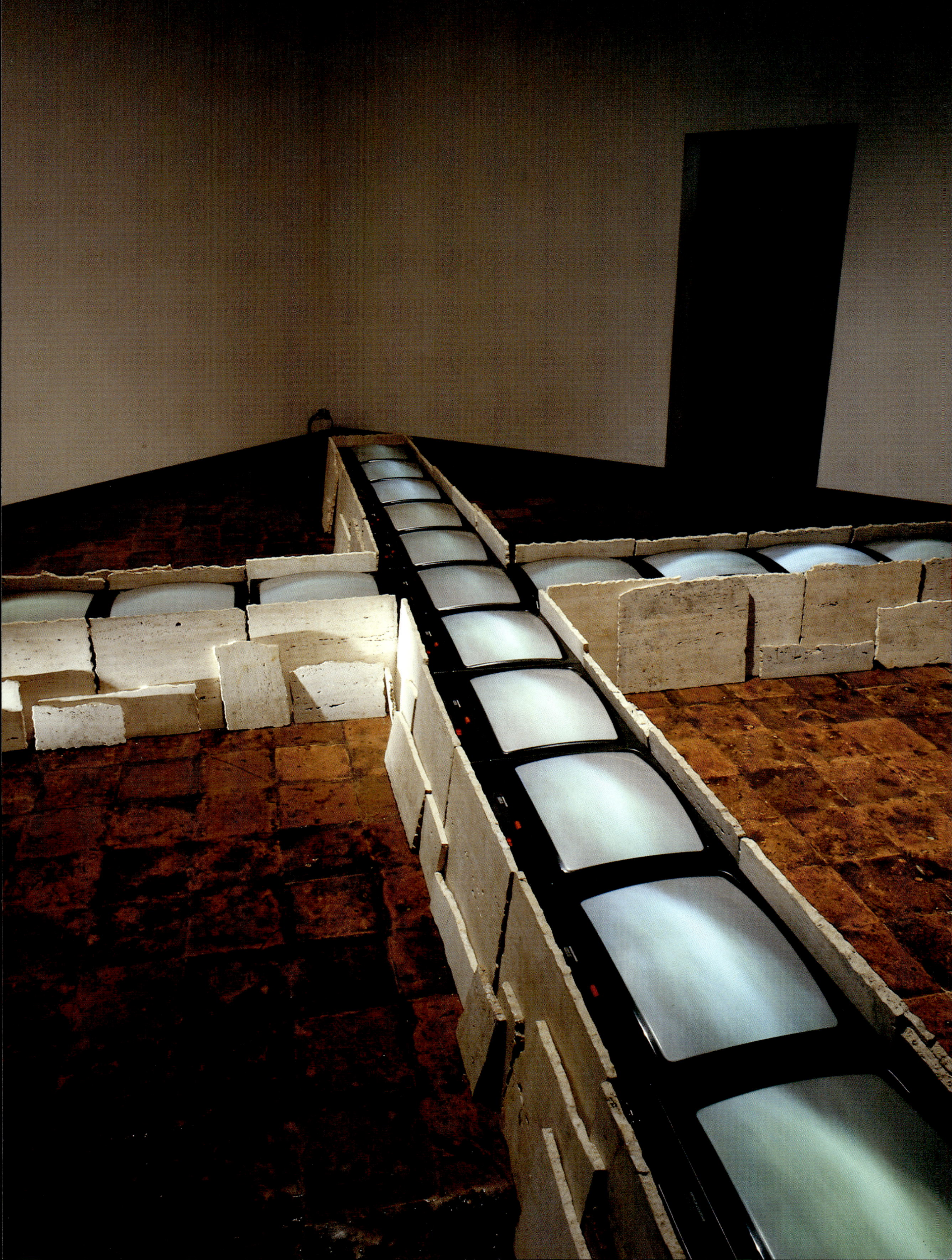

LA STANZA FRAGILE

89004

GENÈVE 1989
GALERIE BLANCPAIN STEPCZYNSKI
89004.1

ZERBRECHLICHER RAUM
Videoskulptur 1989
Eisenschränke mit Fächern,
Eisengitter, Glasplatten in
verschiedenen Größen,
4 Monitore, Videorecorder,
bespielte Kassetten
260 x 320 x 60 cm

FRAGIL CABINET
Video sculpture 1989
Iron construction with
compartments, iron lattice, glass
plates of various sizes an
thicknesses, 4 monitors, video
recorders, recorded video cassettes,
260 x 320 x 60 cm

LA STANZA FRAGILE
Videoscultura 1989
Struttura in ferro a scomparti,
grigliato industriale, lastre di
vetro di misure e spessori diverse,
4 monitors, vhs, cassette
registrate
260 x 320 x 60 cm

Mit der Arbeit *La Stanza Fragile* (*Zerbrechlicher Schrank*) beginnt die große Reihe der Arbeiten von Fabrizio Plessi, die mit Raum oder Gehäusen umgeht. Da mag der Begriff *La Stanza* ebenso auf die ›Stanzen‹ Raphaels im Vatikan in Rom anspielen und in gewisser Weise vielleicht eine Bindung dazu herstellen, wie auch der Begriff *Armadio* (Schrank) deutlich macht, daß diese Behältnisse etwas beinhalten; meistens sind es Materialien wie Äste, Steine, Stroh, Neonröhren u. ä.

Der Raum - das hatten wir oben gesehen - war nach Kant

The work La Stanza Fragile (Fragile Cabinet) *marks the beginning of the great series of Fabrizio Plessi's works dealing with spaces or casings. The term* Stanza *may as well point to Raphael's 'Stanzas' in the Vatican in Rome and, to a certain degree, form a connection to these, just as the term* Armadio (*Cabinet*) *indicates that these contain something; most of the times these are materials like branches, stones, straw, neon tubes and the like.*

Space - as we have seen before - was, according to Kant,

Con *La Stanza Fragile* ha inizio la lunga serie di lavori di Fabrizio Plessi che si occupa di spazio e contenitori. Così come il termine La Stanza fa venire in mente e forse, in un certo modo, crea un rapporto con le Stanze di Raffaello nel Vaticano, così la parola *Armadio* ricorda che questi contenitori contengono qualcosa, spesso materiali come rami, pietre, paglia, tubi al neon e così via.

Lo spazio - come si è visto sopra - è, secondo Kant, una delle due condizioni per la visibilità della cose.

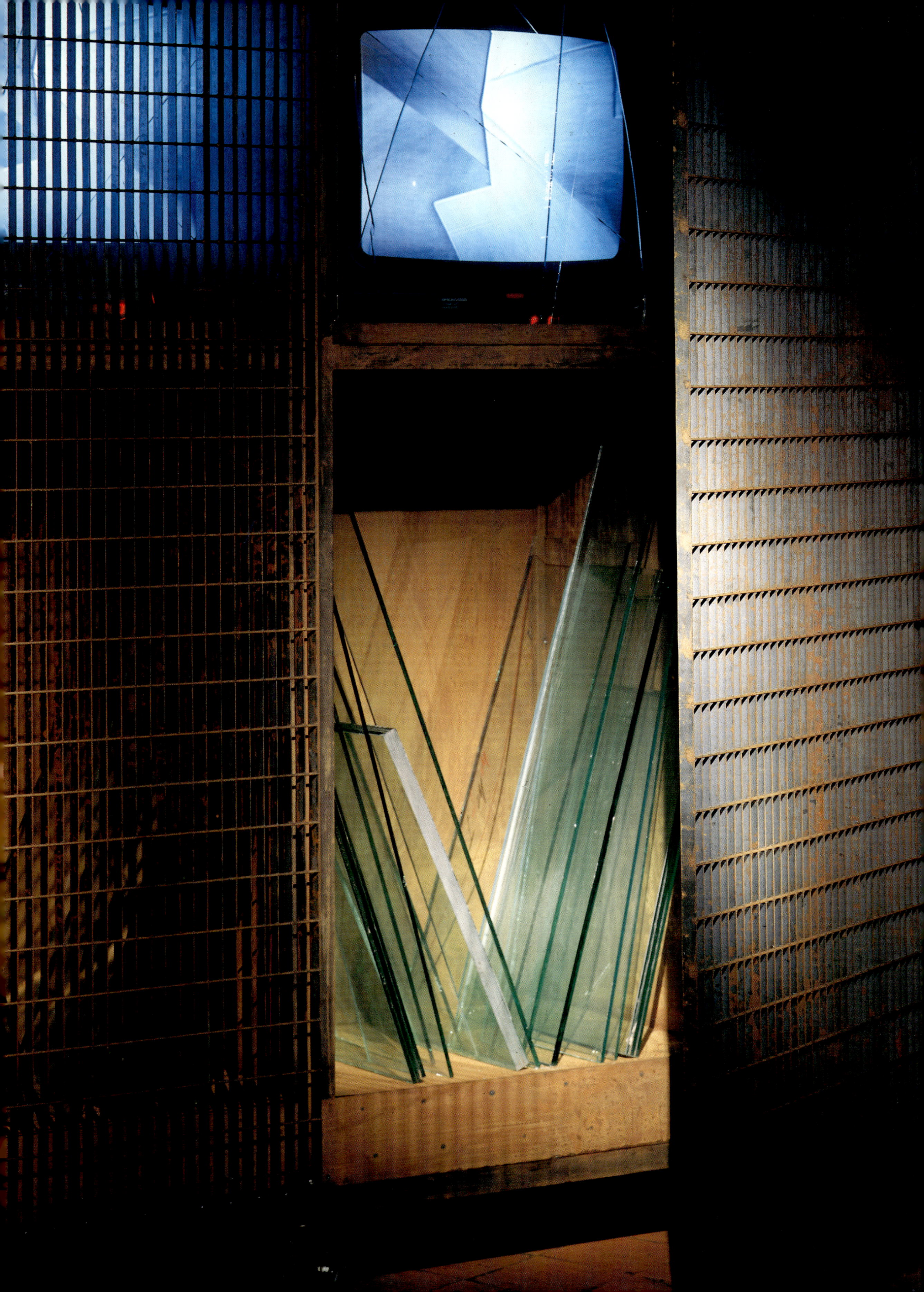

eine der beiden a priorischen
Bedingungen für Sichtbarkeit. Die
Vorstellung des ›Raumes‹ schafft
Raum für unsere Vorstellungen. In
dem Kapitel über die transzenden-
tale Ästhetik in Immanuel Kants
Kritik der reinen Vernunft von 1781
heißt es: »Daß alle unsere Anschauung nichts als die Vorstellung
von Erscheinung sei: daß die
Dinge, die wir anschauen nicht das
an sich selbst sind, wofür wir sie
anschauen, noch ihre Verhältnisse
als sich selbst beschaffen sind, als
sie uns erscheinen und, daß wenn
wir unser Subjekt oder auch nur
die subjektive Beschaffenheit der
Sinne überhaupt aufheben, alle die
Beschaffenheit, alle Verhältnisse
des Objekts im Raum und in der
Zeit, ja selbst Raum und Zeit
verschwinden würden und als
Erscheinungen nicht an sich selbst,
sondern nur in uns selbst existieren können. Was es für eine Be-
wandtnis mit den Gegenständen an
sich und abgesondert von aller
dieser Rezeptivität unserer Sinn-
lichkeit haben möge, bleibt uns
gänzlich unbekannt. Wir kennen
nichts als unsere Art, sie wahrzu-
nehmen, die uns eigentümlich ist.«
(Kant) Die Vorstellung wird also
geprägt von unserer persönlichen
Wahrnehmung oder Auffassung von
Realität. Eine objektive Realität in
diesem Sinne kann es nicht geben.
In dem unteren Teil des Schrankes
oder des Raumes, des Gehäuses,
sieht man verschieden große
Glasscheiben. Was dort als Realität
materiell präsentiert wird, setzt
sich oben im Monitor per Vorstellung immateriell fort. Die Präsentation der Glasscheiben im Video
ist futuristisch, konstruktivistisch,
kubistisch, ähnlich wie bei den
Monitoren der Installation *Video
Going* und erzeugt so die Vorstellung zerbrochenen Glases.

Eigentümlicherweise hat Fabrizio Plessi hier im Titel dieser
Arbeit *Zerbrechlicher Raum* nicht

*one of the two a priori conditi-
ons for visibility. The intuition
of 'space' creates room for our
perceptions. In the chapter on
transcendental aesthetics in
Immanuel Kant's* Critique of
Pure Reason *of 1781 he writes:
"... that all our intuition is
nothing but the representation
of phenomena; that the things
which we intuite, are not in
themselves the same as our
representations of them in
intuition, nor are their relations
in themselves so constituted as
they appear to us; and that if we
take away the subject, or even
only the subjective constitution
of our senses in general, then
not only the nature and relations of objects in space and time,
but even space and time themselves disappear; and that these,
as phenomena, cannot exist in
themselves, but only in us. What
may be the nature of objects
considered as things in themselves and without reference to the
receptivity of our sensibility is
quite unknown to us. We know
nothing more than our mode of
perceiving them, which is peculiar to us, ..." (translation by
J.M.D. Meiklejohn) Intuition
thus is defined by our personal
perception or understanding of
reality. In this sense, there
cannot be an objective reality.
In the lower part of the cabinet,
the room, or the casing one can
see glass panes of different size.
What is presented there materi-
ally as reality is continued
immaterially and imaginatively
on the monitor above. The
presentation of the panes of
glass is futuristic, constructivi-
stic, cubistic - similar to the
monitors of the installation*
Video Going *- and in this way
creates the impression of broken·
glass.*

Surprisingly, Fabrizio Plessi

Immaginarsi lo ›spazio‹ crea
spazio per le nostre immagina-
zioni. Nel capitolo sull'estetica
trascendentale della sua Critica
della ragion pura del 1781 Kant
afferma che »ogni nostra intui-
zione non è se non la rappresentazione di un fenomeno; che le
cose, che noi intuiamo, non
sono in se stesse quello per cui
noi le intuiamo, né i loro rapporti sono cosiffatti come ci
appaiono, e che, se sopprimessimo
il nostro soggetto, o anche
solo la natura subbiettiva dei
sensi in generale, tutta la natura, tutti i rapporti degli oggetti,
nello spazio e nel tempo, anzi lo
spazio stesso e il tempo spari-
rebbero, e come fenomeni non
possono esistere in sé, ma
soltanto in noi. Quel che ci
possa essere negli oggetti in sé
e separati dalla recettività dei
nostri sensi ci rimane interamente ignoto. Noi non conosciamo se non il nostro modo di
percepirli, che ci è peculiare ...«

L'immaginazione è quindi
determinata dalla nostra percezione o interpretazione personale della realtà e, quindi, non
può esistere, intesa in questo
senso, una realtà oggettiva.
Nella parte inferiore
dell'armadio, della stanza o del
contenitore si vedono lastre di
vetro di dimensioni diverse.
Questa presentazione della
realtà materiale si prolunga nel
monitor attraverso l'immaginazione immateriale. Le lastre
di vetro del videofilm hanno un
aspetto futuristico, costruttivi-
stico, cubistico - simile ai monitors della installazione di *Video
Going* - che suggerisce l'idea
del vetro rotto.

Stranamente il titolo *La
Stanza Fragile* non allude, come
altri lavori di questa serie, al
materiale inserito nel
contenitore ma ad una qualità

202

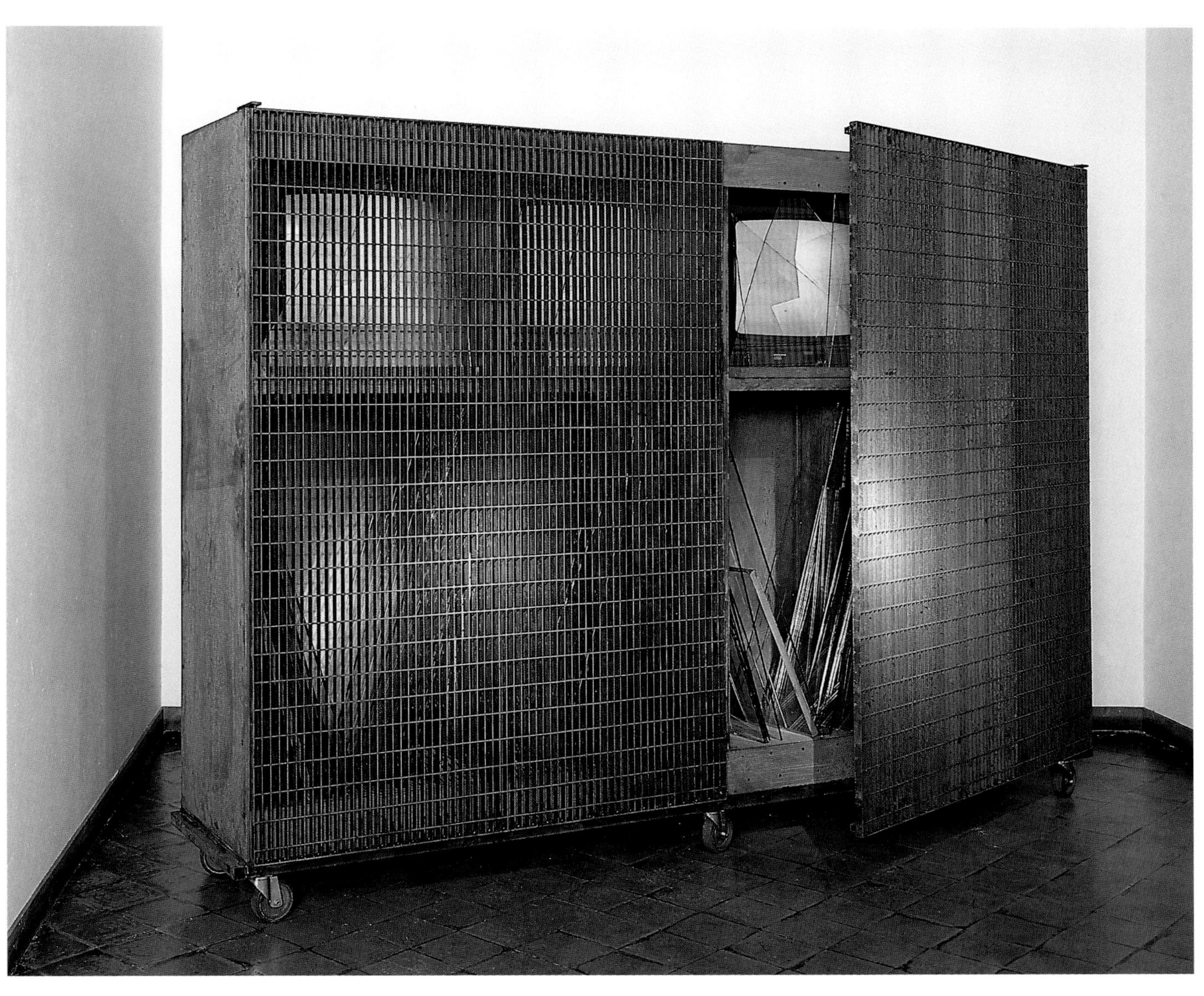

auf das Material verwiesen, das sich in dem Gehäuse befindet - wie bei anderen Arbeiten aus dieser Werkgruppe -, sondern auf eine Eigenschaft, die diesem Material Glas, zutiefst zu eigen ist: die Eigenschaft der ›Zerbrechlichkeit‹. Eigenschaften sind keine anschaulichen Gegenstände. Sie sind nur vorstellbar, wenn sie sich auf etwas, zum Beispiel einen Gegenstand, beziehen, ähnlich wie Dispositionen oder Kategorien. Zerbrechlichkeit ist eine Eigenschaft die nicht nur Glas zukommt, sondern auch vielen anderen Materialien. Nur wird das Glas hier zur Veranschaulichung der Idee verwendet. Daß der Begriff des Zerbrechlichen neben dem kategorialen Aspekt auch zahlreiche Assoziationsmöglichkeiten bietet, ist offensichtlich. Er könnte beispielsweise ein Hinweis auf Plessis Abkehr vom traditionellen Bild geben und zugleich auf die Gefährdung der Kunst verweisen, die Kunst, die man schützen und bewahren muß, wie man etwas in einen Schrank legt, um es aufzuheben.

has not, in the title of this work, pointed to the material placed inside the stanza - as in other works of this group of works - but to a characteristic that is profoundly peculiar to the material, glass: the characteristic of 'fragility'. Characteristics are, however, not perceivable objects. They can only be imagined if they refer to something, for example an object, similar to dispositions and categories. Fragility is not only a characteristic of glass, but of many other materials. Glass is here only taken to illustrate the idea. That the term of fragility offers, beside the categorical aspect, numerous possibilities of association is obvious. It could, for example, offer a hint to Plessi's departure from traditional image, as well as point to the jeopardy of art, art which has to be protected and preserved, as one stores something in a cabinet to keep it.

propria del materiale vetro: la fragilità. Le qualità non sono oggetti visibili. Esse sono, simili a disposizioni o categorie, immaginabili solo se riferite a qualcosa, per esempio ad un oggetto. La fragilità non è solo una qualità propria del vetro ma di tanti altri materiali, solo che qui esso funge da visualizzazione dell'idea. È ovvio che il concetto della fragilità offre, oltre all'aspetto categoriale, anche numerose possibilità di associazione. Per esempio potrebbe alludere all'allontanamento di Plessi dal quadro tradizionale e rimandare contemporaneamente al pericolo che incombe sull'arte che è da proteggere e da preservare, così come si depone un oggetto nell'armadio per conservarlo.

MATERIA PRIMA

89005

KÖLN 1989
KÖLNISCHER KUNSTVEREIN
89005.1

ROHSTOFF
Videoinstallation 1989
Hellgrauer Stein, graue Wände,
Schrift in Bronzebuchstaben,
Licht, 25 abgeschaltete Monitore

RAW MATERIAL
Video installation 1988
Light grey stone, grey walls,
bronze lettering, light,
25 switched-off monitors

MATERIA PRIMA
Videoinstallazione 1989
Pietra serena grigia, pareti grigie,
luce fortissima dall'alto, scritta in
rilievo in bronzo, 25 monitors
spenti

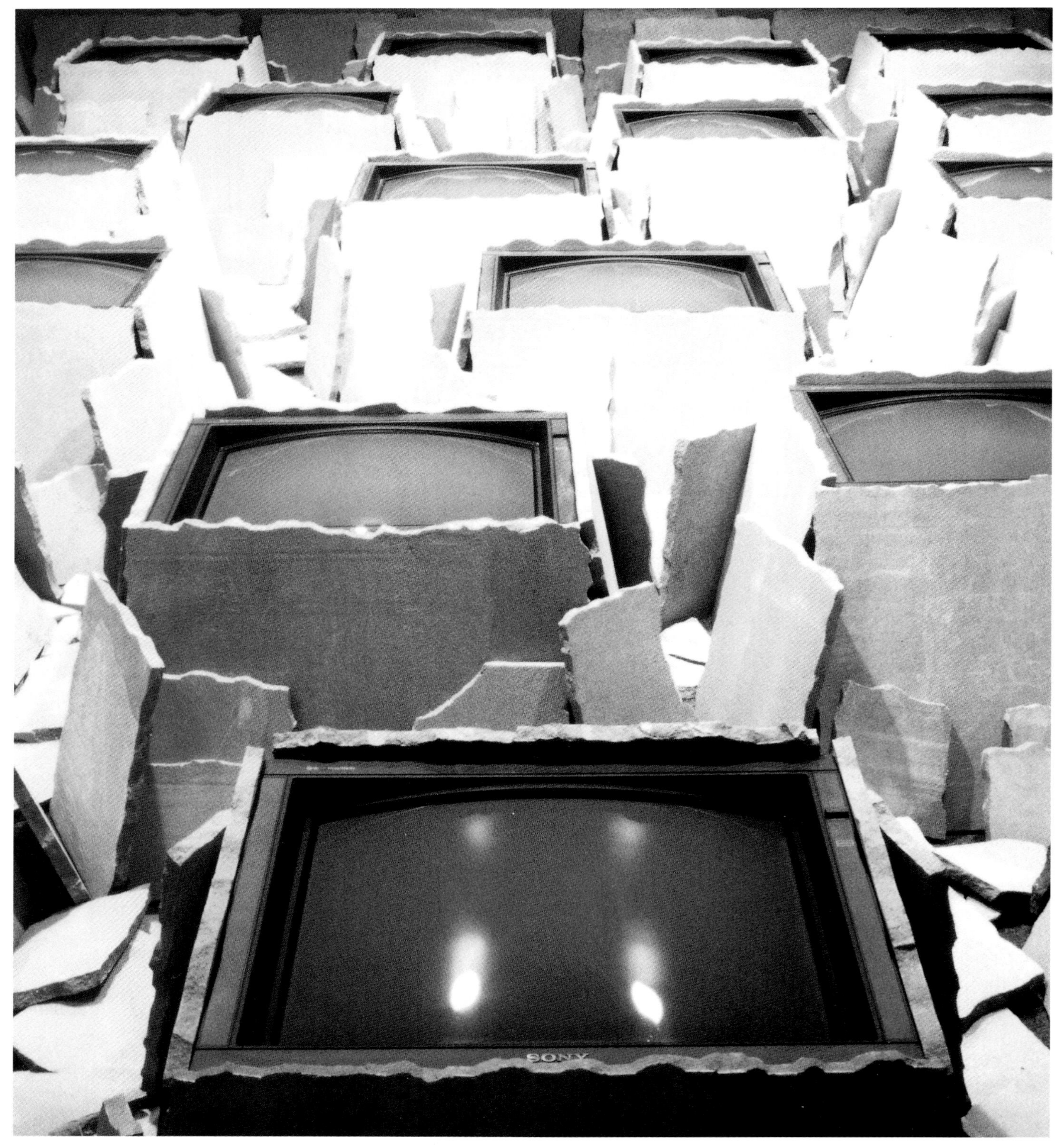

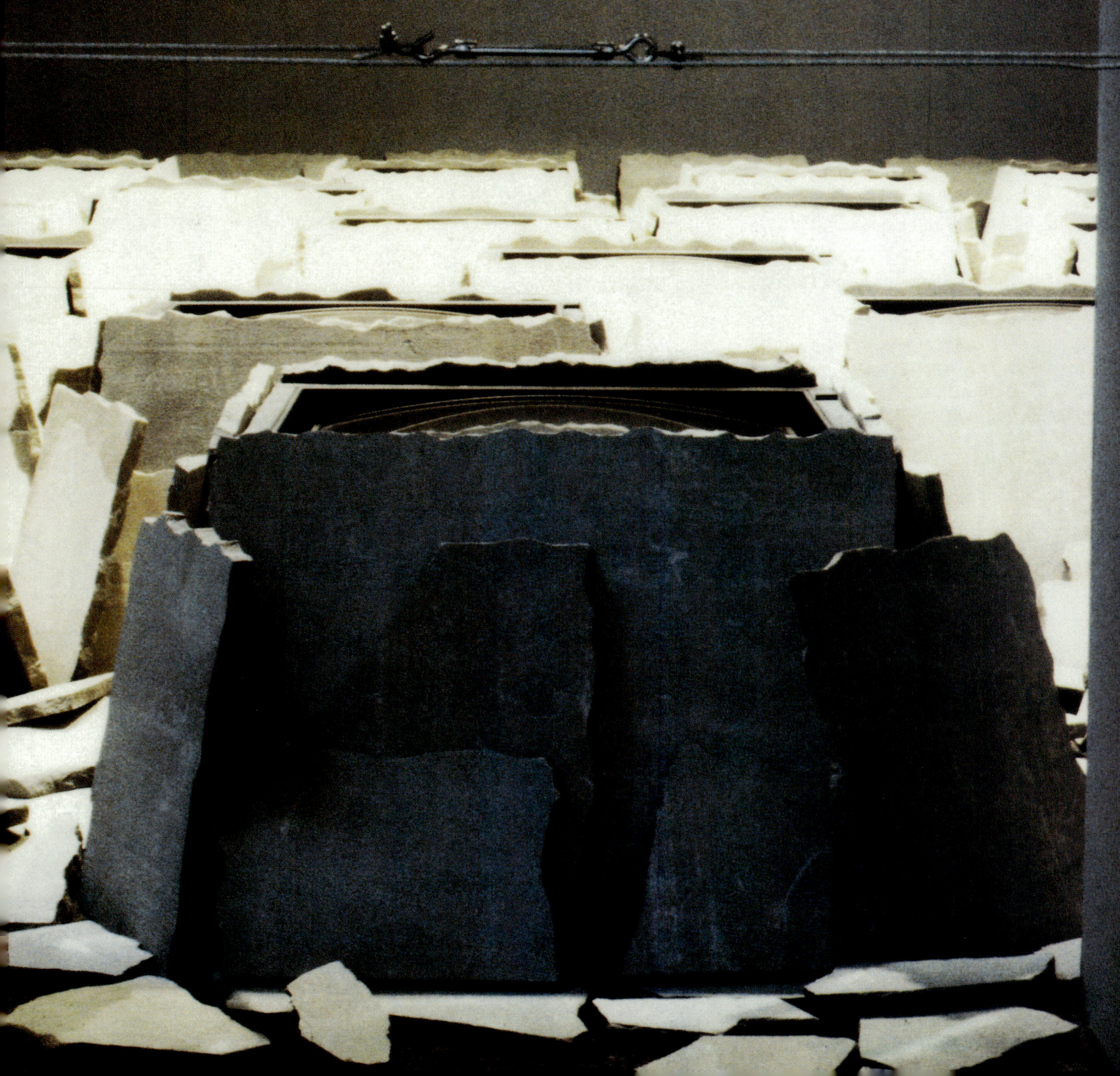
MATERIA PRIMA

Die Installation *Materia Prima (Rohstoff)* sieht auf den ersten Blick ganz ähnlich aus wie die Videoinstallation *Mare di Marmo*. Eine größere Anzahl von Monitoren wird mit dem Bildschirm nach oben unregelmäßig in einem Raum verteilt, umgeben von gestellten und gelegten Travertinplatten. Erst auf den zweiten Blick fällt auf, daß alle Monitore ausgeschaltet sind. »Der Künstler erschafft eine Archäologie der Zukunft«, schreibt Diana Conti im Katalog zur Dortmunder Ausstellung über *Materia Prima*. Die Radikalität des Vorgangs, mit dem Fabrizio Plessi in dieser Arbeit auf alles das verzichtet, was die vorangegangenen 20 Jahre das Wesen seines Werkes bestimmte, könnte auf einen Endpunkt der Thematik hinweisen. Doch der Titel belegt einmal mehr, daß für Plessi die Monitore nur Werkzeug und Ausdrucksmittel sind, wie für den Bildhauer Hammer und Meißel beispielsweise, nicht mehr und nicht weniger, eben ein *Rohstoff*, ein beliebiges Material. Doch die Magie, die selbst von den ausgeschalteten Monitoren ausgeht und die für Fabrizio Plessis Werk so signifikant ist, die gar in den Bereich der Metaphysik hineinreicht, beweist die Kraft die von seinem Werk ausgeht, selbst wenn es sich noch um mehr oder weniger ungeformtes und noch nicht zum Leben erwecktes ›Rohmaterial‹ handelt.

The installation Materia Prima (Raw Material) *looks - at first glance - very similar to the video installation* Mare di Marmo. *A larger number of monitors is - screens up - distributed irregularly in a room, surrounded by travertine plates, standing upright or placed on the ground. Only at second glance one realises that all monitors are switched off. "The artist creates an archaeology of the future", writes Diana Conti in the catalogue of the exhibition of* Materia Prima *in Dortmund. The radicality of procedure, in which Plessi here does away with everything that has defined the essence of his work during the past twenty years could indicate the end of this subject. Yet the title once more proves that the monitors are only tool and means of expression for Plessi, as, for example, hammer and chisel are not more or less than that for a sculptor, just any raw material. But the magic, emanating even from the switched-off monitors, which is so significant for Fabrizio Plessi's œuvre, and which even reaches into the metaphysical sphere, proves the power originating from his work, even if it is more or less unfinished raw material, not yet come to life.*

L'installazione *Materia Prima* assomiglia, a prima vista, a quella di *Mare di Marmo*: monitors distribuiti nella sala con lo schermo rivolto verso l'alto e circondati da lastre di travertino. Solo dopo ci si accorge che tutti i monitors sono spenti. »L'artista crea un'archeologia del futuro« dirà di *Materia Prima* Viana Conti nel catalogo della mostra di Dortmund. Il modo radicale con il quale Fabrizio Plessi in quest'opera fa a meno di tutto ciò che ha caratterizzato il suo lavoro dei vent'anni precedenti potrebbe indicare il punto finale della tematica. Il titolo, però, sottolinea ancora una volta che i monitors non rappresentano per Plessi nient'altro che uno strumento e mezzo d'espressione, così come martello e scarpello per lo scultore, ne più e ne meno, materia prima, un materiale qualsiasi. Ma la magia che irradia anche dai monitors spenti, che è così significativa per le opere di Fabrizio Plessi e che giunge, addirittura, nella sfera della metafisica, dimostra la forza che emana dalla sua opera, anche se si tratta ancora di una ›materia prima‹ piu o meno informe e senza vita.

L'ARMADIO DELL'ARTE

89006

PALMA DE MALLORCA 1989
Palau Solleric
89006.1

REGGIO EMILIA 1990
Museo Civico d'Arte Moderna
89006.2

DORTMUND 1993
Museum am Ostwall
89006.3

SCHRANK DER KUNST
Videoskulptur 1989
Eisenregal, Eisengitter, Neon,
Bilderrahmen verschiedener Maße
aus Holz, 3 Monitore,
3 Videorecorder, 3 bespielte
Kassetten, Tonaufzeichnung
240 x 240 x 60 cm

CABINET OF ART
Video sculpture 1989
Iron construction with
compartments, iron lattice, neon,
frames of various sizes, 3 monitors,
3 video recorders, 3 recorded video
cassettes, soundrecording
240 x 240 x 60 cm

L'ARMADIO DELL'ARTE
Videoscultura 1989
Struttura in ferro ad elementi,
grigliato industriale, scritte al
neon colorate, 32 telai in legno di
differenti misure, 3 monitors,
3 vhs, 3 cassette registrate, sonoro
240 x 240 x 60 cm

Der nächste Raum oder Schrank, der *Armadio dell'Arte* beinhaltet nicht nur Glasscheiben, sondern ganze Bilderrahmen. Hier wird wohl die ganze traditionelle Kunst selbst in den Schrank gepackt? Oder handelt es sich vielleicht um eine Hymne an dieselbe? In der ersten Version scheinen sich auf den Kopf gestellte Neonbuchstaben des Wortes ›ART‹ im elektronischen Wasser der Monitore zu spiegeln. Hier gibt es auch die Rückbindung an ein Filmprojekt aus der Serie *Underwater*, das 1982 vom Frigo in Lyon produziert wurde. Seinerzeit waren die Buchstaben ›ART‹ aus dem Neonwort ›WATER‹ herausmontiert und hatten sich schließlich im Bildschirm-Monitor gespiegelt. Die zweite Version zeigt die Verdoppelung der drei in Wasser

The next room or cabinet, Armadio dell'Arte, *not only contains glass panes but complete picture frames. Is all traditional art placed in the cabinet here? Or is this perhaps a hymn to art? In the first version, neon letters, placed upside down, forming the word 'ART', seem to mirror in the electronic water in the monitors. Here is, too, the connection to a film project from the series* Underwater, *that was produced by Frigo in Lyon in 1982. At that time, the letters 'ART' were taken from the neon word 'WATER' and mirrored in the TV monitor. The second version shows the reduplication of the three neon letters 'ART' reflected in water, while the origins of*

La stanza o l'armadio seguente, *L'Armadio dell'Arte*, contiene, oltre il vetro, anche delle cornici. Qui è stipata nell'armadio addirittura tutta l'arte tradizionale o si tratta di un inno ad essa? Nella prima versione le lettere al neon capovolte della parola ›ART‹ sembrano riflettersi nell'acqua elettronica dei monitors. Anche qui esiste un collegamento con un progetto filmato della serie *Underwater* prodotto da Frigo a Lione nel 1982, con la differenza che al posto della parola ›ART‹ si vede la parola ›WATER‹. La seconda versione mostra un raddoppiamento delle tre lettere della parola al neon ›ART‹ riflesse nell'acqua senza però impiegare le lettere al neon.

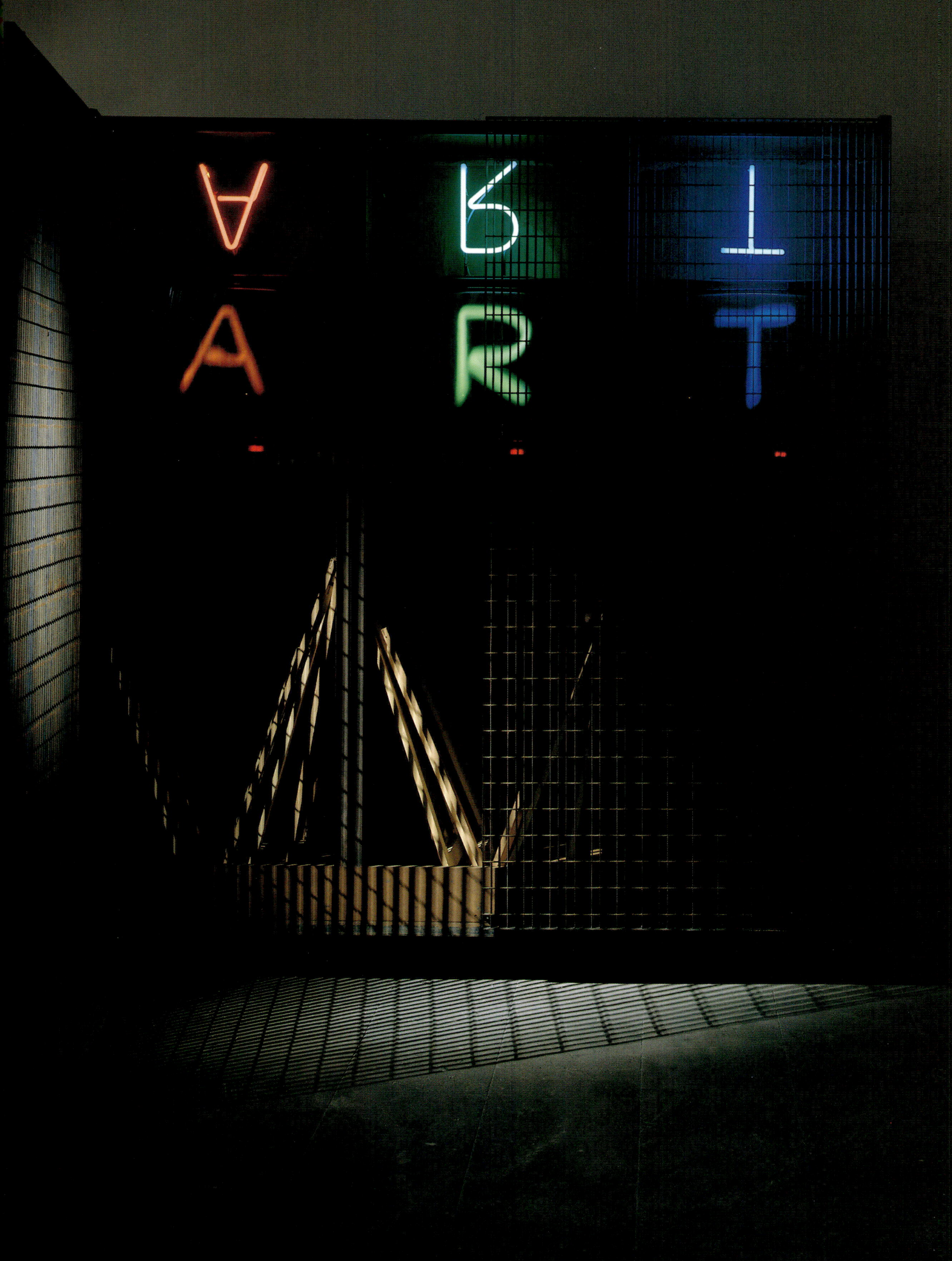
A
R
T

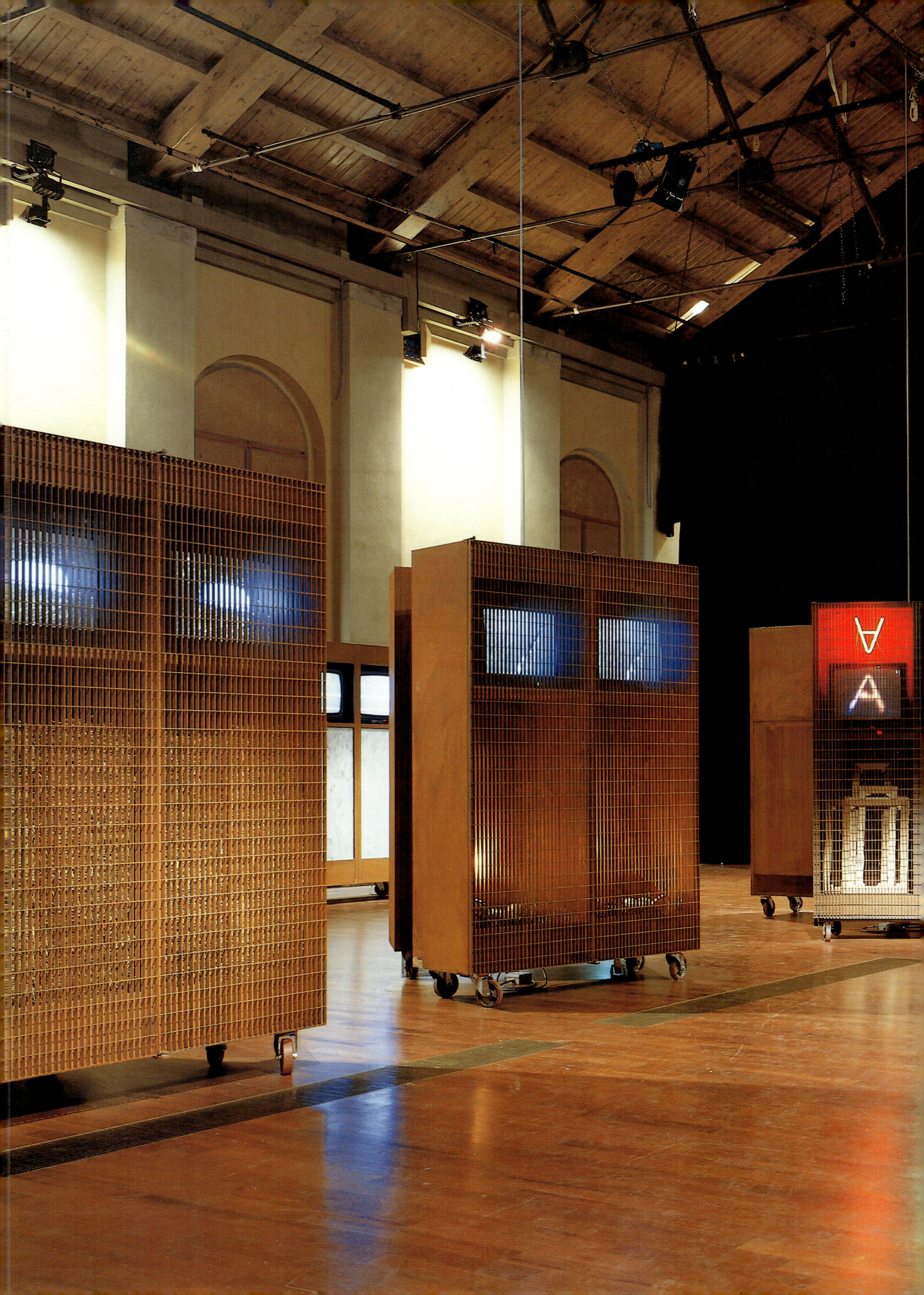

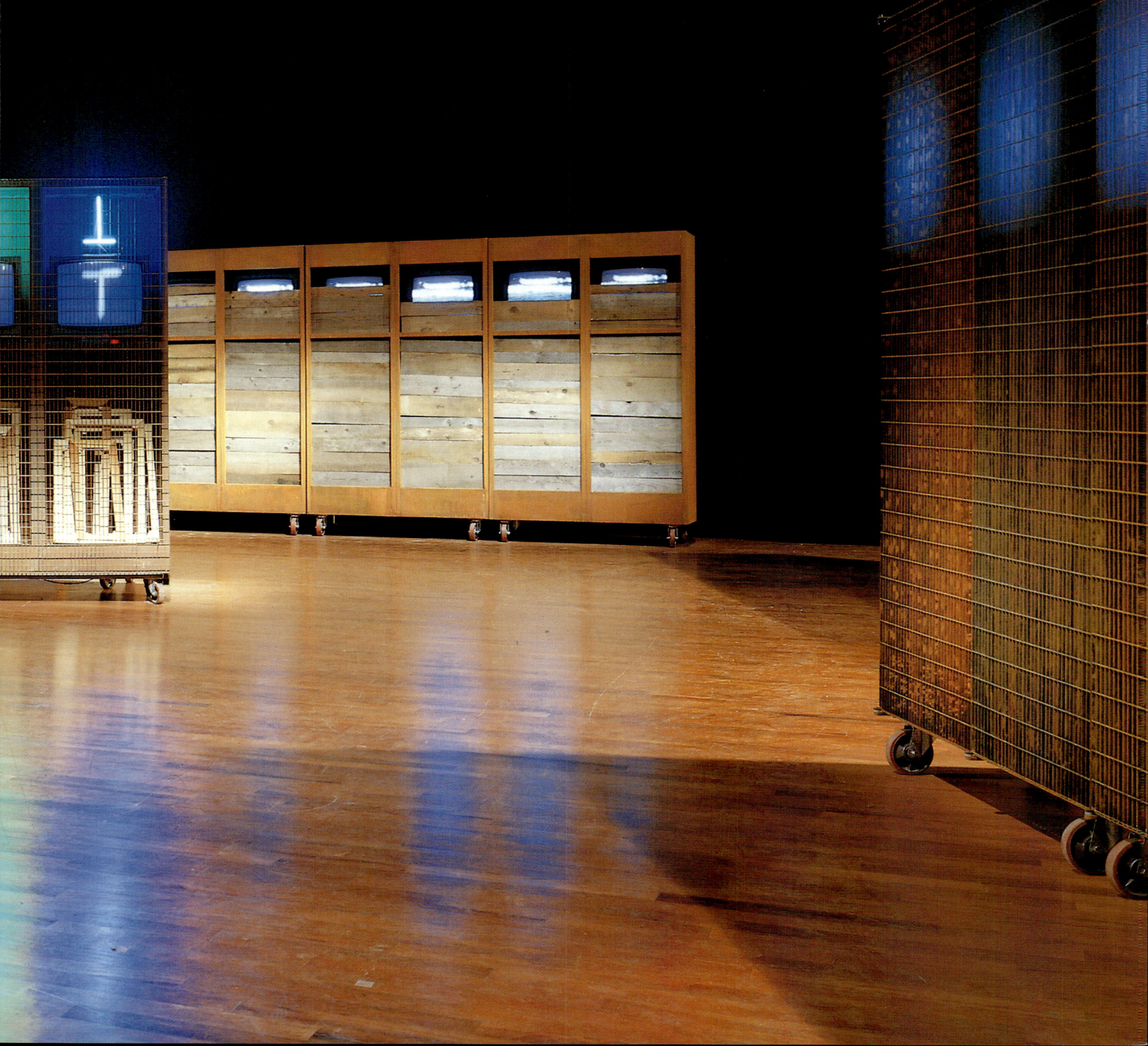

gespiegelten Neonbuchstaben
›ART‹. Auf die Erzeuger der Reflexion, nämlich die Neonbuchstaben
selbst, wurde bei der zweiten
Version von Präsentation verzichtet.

Alle einzelnen Elemente die
vorkommen, stammen aus dem
Bereich der Kunst und thematisieren sie: die Bilderrahmen, die
Videogeräte, Neonschrift und auch
das Stahlgehäuse selbst. Sie »cha-
rakterisieren in zitathafter Weise
das Arbeitsfeld des zeitgenössischen Künstlers. Die Neonschrift
stellt den heutigen Kunstbegriff
durch das Ausdrucksmedium und
durch die Umkehrung der Buchstaben demonstrativ in Frage und zur
Diskussion. Die im gefilmten
Wasser gespiegelte und sich permanent bewegende Leuchtschrift
verweist auf die Reflexion des
Künstlers über die Kunst, auf seine
Gedanken über ihre gestalterischen
Möglichkeiten und ihre Grenzen.
Die Geschehnisse aus den Video-
Monitoren machen darüber hinaus
deutlich, daß sich die Bereiche der
Kunst und des Lebens stets berüh-
ren, aber niemals zu einer Einheit
verschmelzen können ... Plessis
Versuch, die Kunst durch ihre
eigenen Medien zu definieren,
offenbart gleichzeitig die Unmög-
lichkeit, ihre Grenzen festlegen zu
wollen.« (Rolf Lauter, in: Katalog
Förderverein Schöneres Frankfurt,
Frankfurt 1990)

*the reflection, the neon letters
themselves, were left out in the
second presentation.*

*All elements involved here
originate in the sector of art,
and make art the theme of this
work: the frames, the video
sets, neon writing, and even the
steel casing itself. They !charac-
terise, quotation-like, the
sphere of work of the contemporary artist. The neon writing
demonstratively questions the
present definition of art through the medium of expression
and the reversal of the letters.
The neon writing, reflected in
the filmed, permanently moving
water indicates the artist's
reflection on art, his thoughts
and their creative possibilities
and limits. The actions on the
monitors moreover clarify that
the spheres of art and life
permanently interfere, yet can
never melt into one
unity...Plessi's attempt to define
art through its own media at
the same time shows the impos-
sibility to define its limits."
(Rolf Lauter, in: catalogue
Förderverein Schöneres Frankfurt, Frankfurt 1990)*

Tutti i singoli elementi
provengono dal mondo dell'arte
e lo tematizzano: le cornici, i
videoregistratori, la scritta al
neon e il contenitore di ferro
stesso. Essi »caratterizzano, in
modo di citazione, il campo
lavorativo dell'artista contemporaneo. La scritta al neon
mette in discussione dimostrati-
vamente, attraverso il medium
espressivo e il capovolgere delle
lettere, l'odierno concetto
dell'arte. La scritta luminosa
riflessa permanentemente
sull'acqua filmata e in continuo
movimento rinvia alla riflessione dell'artista sull'arte, ai suoi
pensieri sulle possibilità figurative e sui limiti dell'arte. Gli
avvenimenti dei videomonitors
evidenziano inoltre che le sfere
dell'arte e della vita sono in
continuo contatto fra di loro
senza mai assumere un'identità
... Il tentativo di Plessi di defini-
re l'arte attraverso i suoi mezzi
propri palesa contemporaneamente l'impossibilità di voler
fissare i suoi confini« (Rolf
Lauter, in: catalogo Förderverein Schöneres Frankfurt, Fran-
coforte 1990).

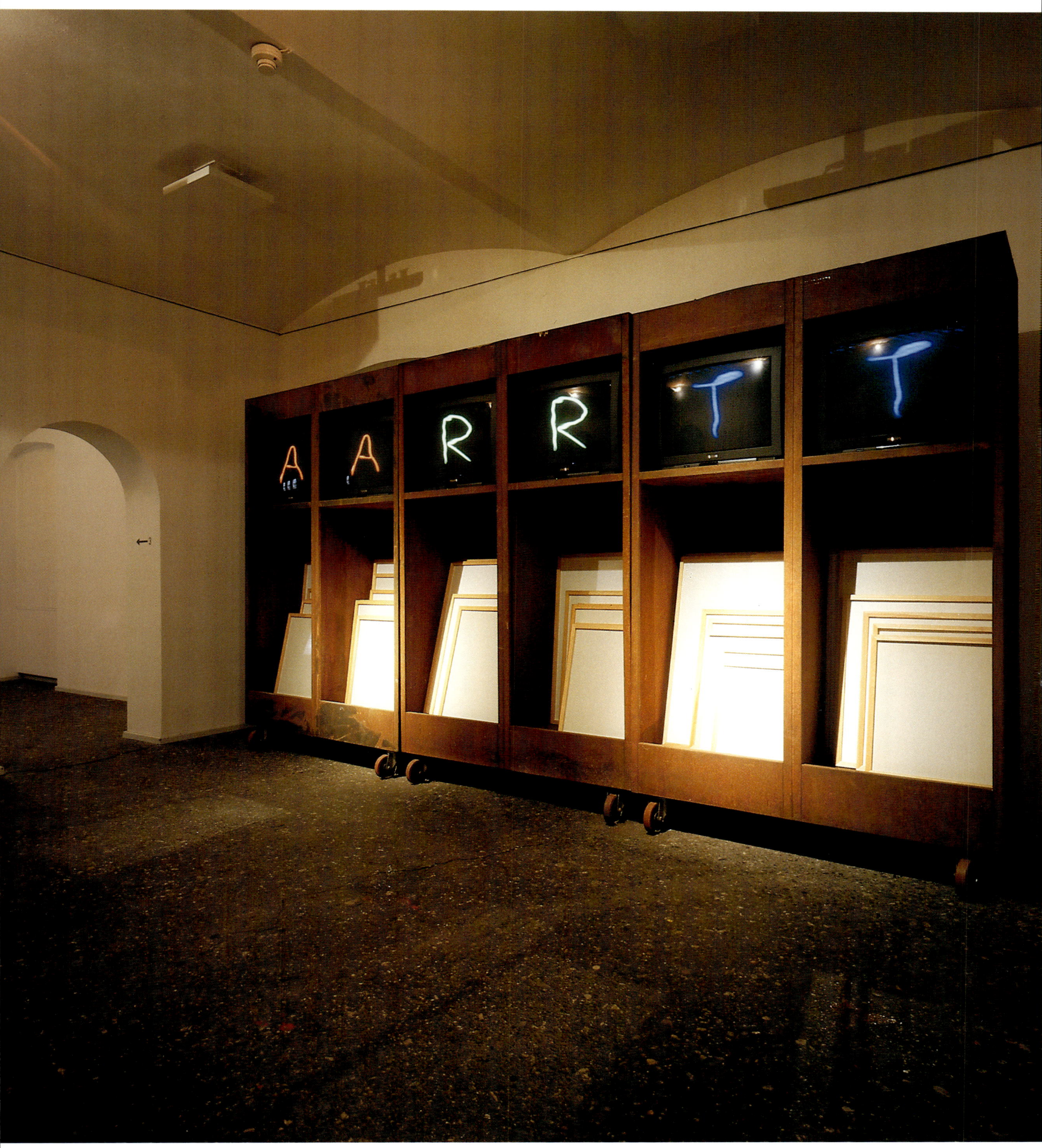

L'ARMADIO DI MARMO

89007

PALMA DE MALLORCA 1989
PALAU SOLLERIC
89007.1
REGGIO EMILIA 1990
MUSEO CIVICO D'ARTE MODERNA
89007.2

SCHRANK DES MARMORS
Videoskulptur 1989
Eisenschränke mit Fächern,
Eisengitter, Travertinplatten,
4 Monitore, Videorecorder,
bespielte Kassetten
260 x 320 x 60 cm

CABINET OF MARBLE
Video sculpture 1989
Iron construction with compart-
ments, iron lattice, slabs of tra-
vertine marble, 4 monitors, video
recorders, recorded video cassettes
260 x 320 x 60 cm

L'ARMADIO DI MARMO
Videoscultura 1989
Struttura a scomparti in ferro,
lastre di marmo travertino,
grigliato industriale, 4 monitors,
vhs, cassette registrate
260 x 320 x 60 cm

Armadio di Marmo (*Schrank des Marmors*) der dritte Schrank in dieser Reihe der *Armadi* oder *Stanzen* richtet sich nun an den Bildhauer, denn hier sind, ähnlich wie bei der *Stanza Fragile* die Glasscheiben, Marmorplatten in die Schränke eingestellt, und die vergitterten Schranktüren sind geschlossen. Fragmente dieser Marmorplatten verdecken auch große Teile der vier Bildschirm-Monitore, so daß ein Blick auf das dahinter liegende Video kaum noch möglich wird. Ob hier bei dieser Installation die traditionelle Kunst der Bildhauerei in ihre Schranken gewiesen oder in ihrem Schrank bewahrt werden soll, bleibt offen. Fließendes Wasser in den Bildschirm-Monitoren verweist auch hier auf die Vergänglichkeit des Augenblicks.

Armadio di Marmo (Cabinet of Marble), *the third cabinet in this series of* Armadi *or* Stanzas *now turns to the sculptor for here, similar to* Stanza Fragile, *the glass panes and marble slaps are placed inside the cabinets, and the grated doors are closed. Fragments of these marble slaps also cover most of the monitors, so that viewing of the video is almost impossible. Whether in this installation the traditional art of sculpture is to be barred or protected in its cabinet remains open. Flowing water on the TV monitors here, too, points to the transitoriness of the moment.*

L'Armadio di Marmo, il terzo della serie degli *Armadi* o delle *Stanze*, si rivolge allo scultore in quanto contiene, simile alle lastre di vetro di *Stanza Fragile*, lastre di marmo; le inferriate delle ante sono chiuse. Frammenti del marmo coprono gran parte degli schermi dei monitors ed impediscono quasi la visione dei filmati. La questione, se in questa installazione è posto un limite all'arte tradizionale della scultura o se essa dovrebbe essere conservata nel suo armadio, rimane aperta. L'acqua che scorre sugli schermi dei monitors allude anche qui alla fugacità dell'attimo.

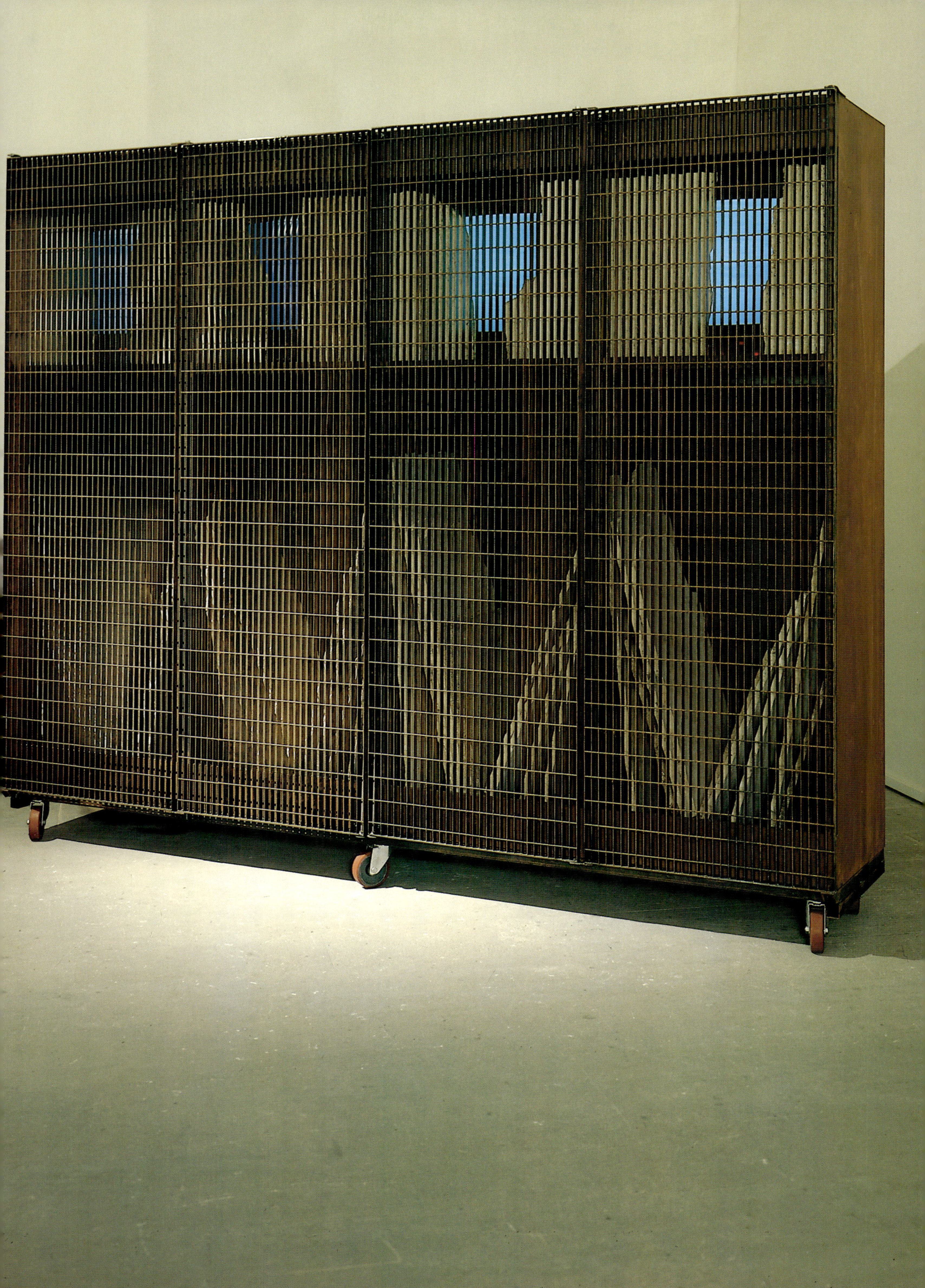

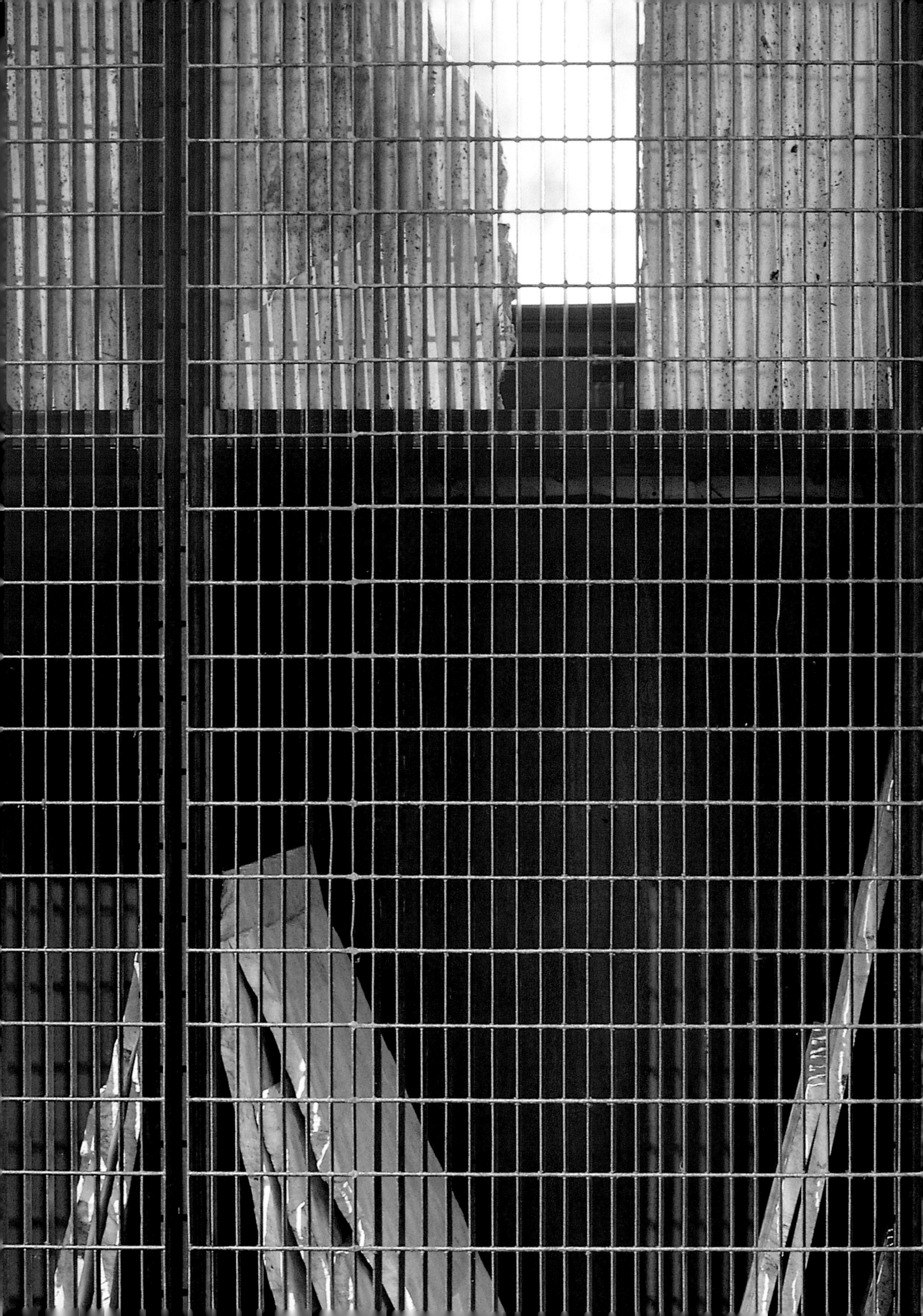

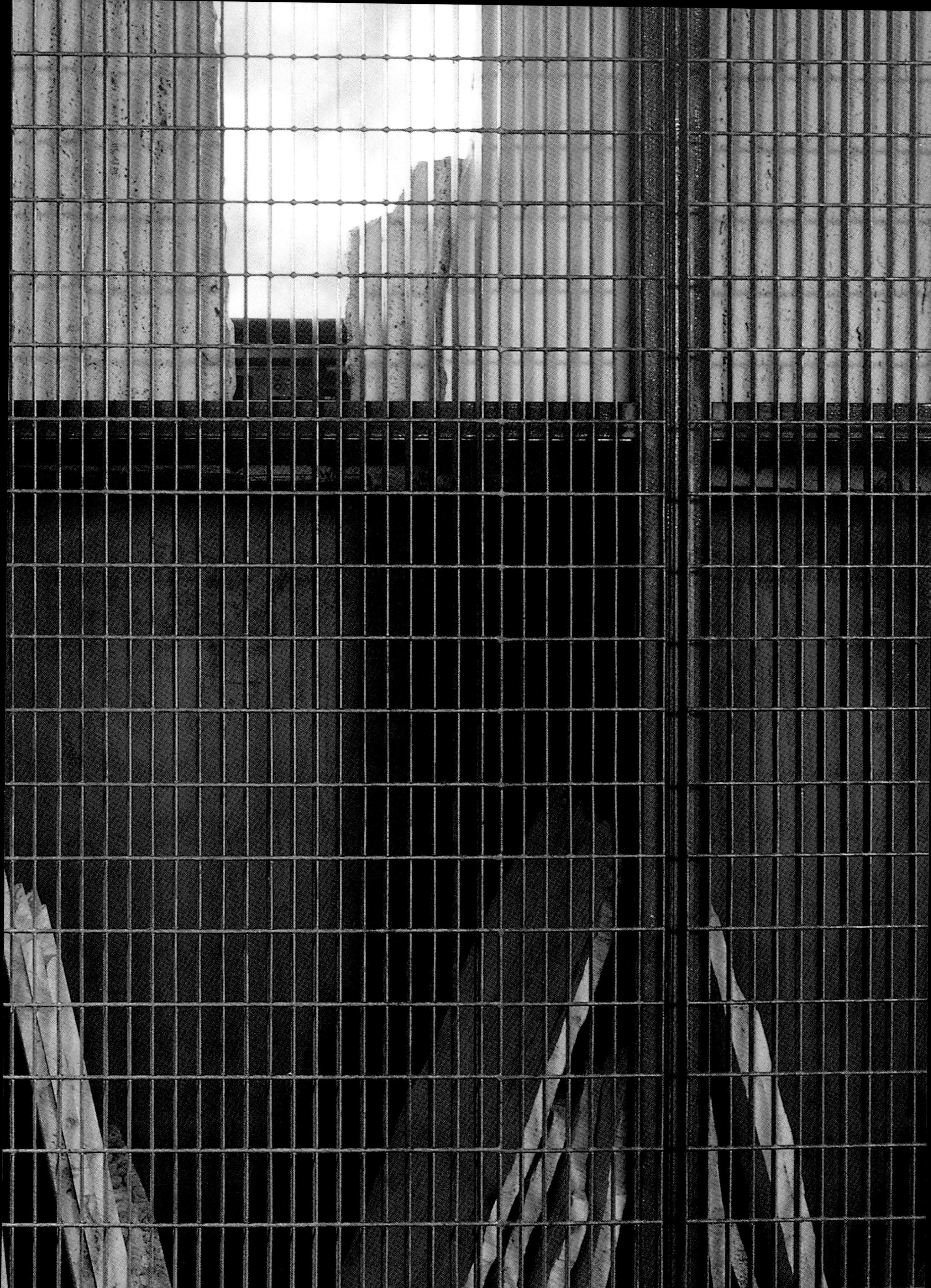

LA MÁQUINA SALADA

89008

PALMA DE MALLORCA 1989
PALAU SOLLERIC
89008.1

DORTMUND 1993
MUSEUM AM OSTWALL
89008.2

SALZMASCHINE
Videoinstallation 1989
3 große Eisenkegel, mit Kalk
geweißt, Holzleitern, mörtellos
aufgeschichtete Steine,
Blecheimer mit Salz, Wasser,
Salzsäcke, 3 Monitore, 3 Videorecorder, 3 bespielte Kassetten

SALT MACHINE
Video installation 1989
3 iron cones covered with plaster
mix, wooden ladders, architectural
structures of piled-up stones, metal
buckets filled with salt, water,
bags of salt, 3 monitors, video
recorders, video cassettes

LA MACCHINA SALATA
Videoinstallazione 1989
3 coni di ferro intonacati a calce,
scale agricole, muretti in pietra a
secco, secchi in metallo, sale,
acqua, sacchi di sale, 3 monitors,
vhs, cassette registrate

Drei große Strukturen aus
Metall trichterförmig zulaufend, in
der Form analog und nicht anders
als die üblichen Behältnisse, die
man zum Transport von Salz
benutzt, sind von außen weiß
gekalkt. Nur einige Roststellen
schimmern noch durch. Umgeben
sind sie von einer ringförmigen
Mauer aus Bruchstein, die ihrer-
seits wiederum umgestellt ist von
einfachen Zinkeimern, gefüllt mit
Salz aus den Salzwerken der
Umgebung. Im Inneren des Trichters befindet sich ein Monitor, der
einen aus der Höhe in Salzwasser
fallenden Stein im Video umkehrt.
Wenn man die einzelnen Grundele-
mente für sich betrachtet und
analysiert, den Stein, das Licht, das
Salz, das Weiß, das Wasser, der
Kalk, der Schatten, der Eimer, die
Leiter, der Monitor, so wird deutlich: Jedes Element ist wesentlich
für die gesamte Inszenierung der

Three large metal structures,
funnel-shaped, analogous in
form and not different from the
regular containers that are used
for the transport of salt, are
chalked white on the outside,
only a few rusty spots are visi-
ble. They are surrounded by a
circular wall of broken rocks
that again is encircled by simple
zinc buckets filled with salt from
the mines in the vicinity. Inside
the funnel there is a monitor that
reverses - on video - a stone
falling from the top into the salt
water. Considering the single
elements in themselves, and
analysing them : the stone, the
light, the salt, the white, the
water, the chalk, the shadow, the
bucket, the ladder, the monitor
clarifies that each element is
essential for the complete staging
of the Máquina Salada *in the*
Palau Solleric. They underline

Tre grandi strutture metalliche a forma di imbuto, non
diverse dai consueti contenitori
da trasporto del sale, sono
coperte esternamente da uno
strato di calce lasciando intravedere, qua e là, qualche mac-
chia di ruggine. Intorno alle
strutture è stato eretto un muro
circolare di pietra che, a sua
volta, è circondato da semplici
secchi zincati, riempiti di sale
delle saline vicine. All'interno
dell'imbuto si trova un monitor
che, nel filmato, inverte la
caduta di un sasso dall'alto in
acqua salata. Osservando ed
analizzando i singoli elementi in
sè, la pietra, la luce, il sale, il
bianco, l'acqua, la calce, il
secchio, la scala, il monitor, si
comprende che ogni elemento è
essenziale per l'intero allestimento de *La Máquina Salada*
nel Palau Solleric di Palma de

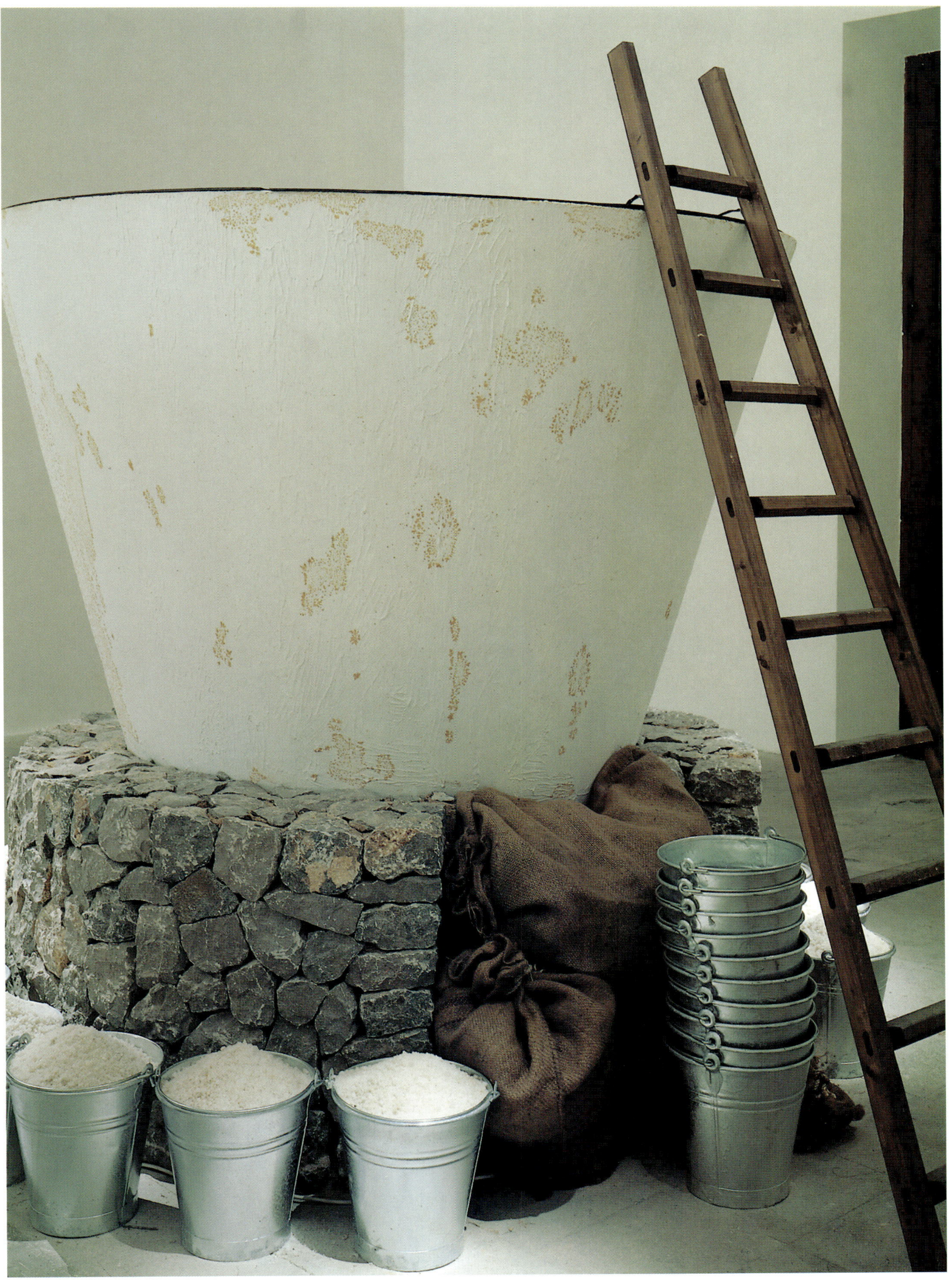

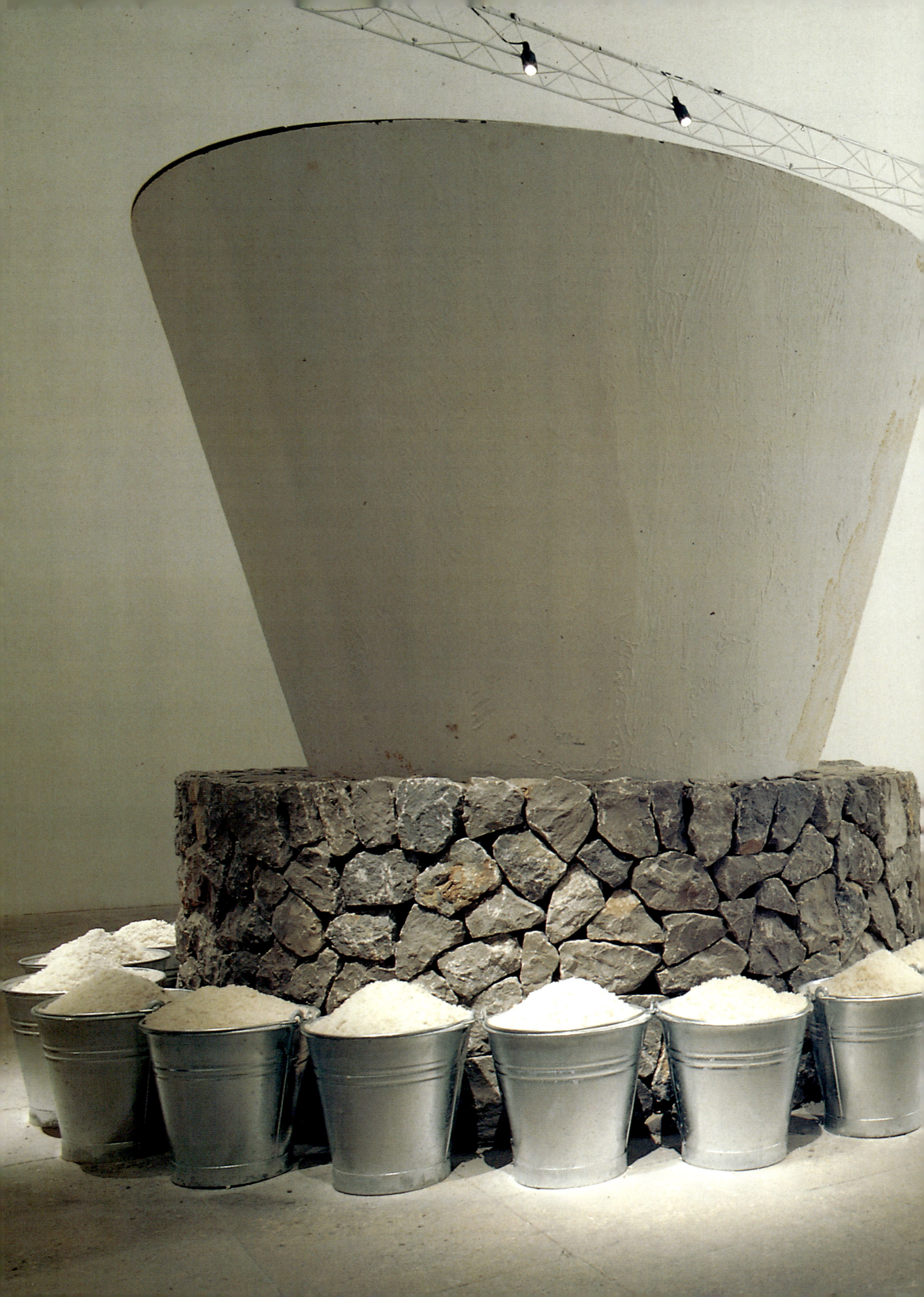

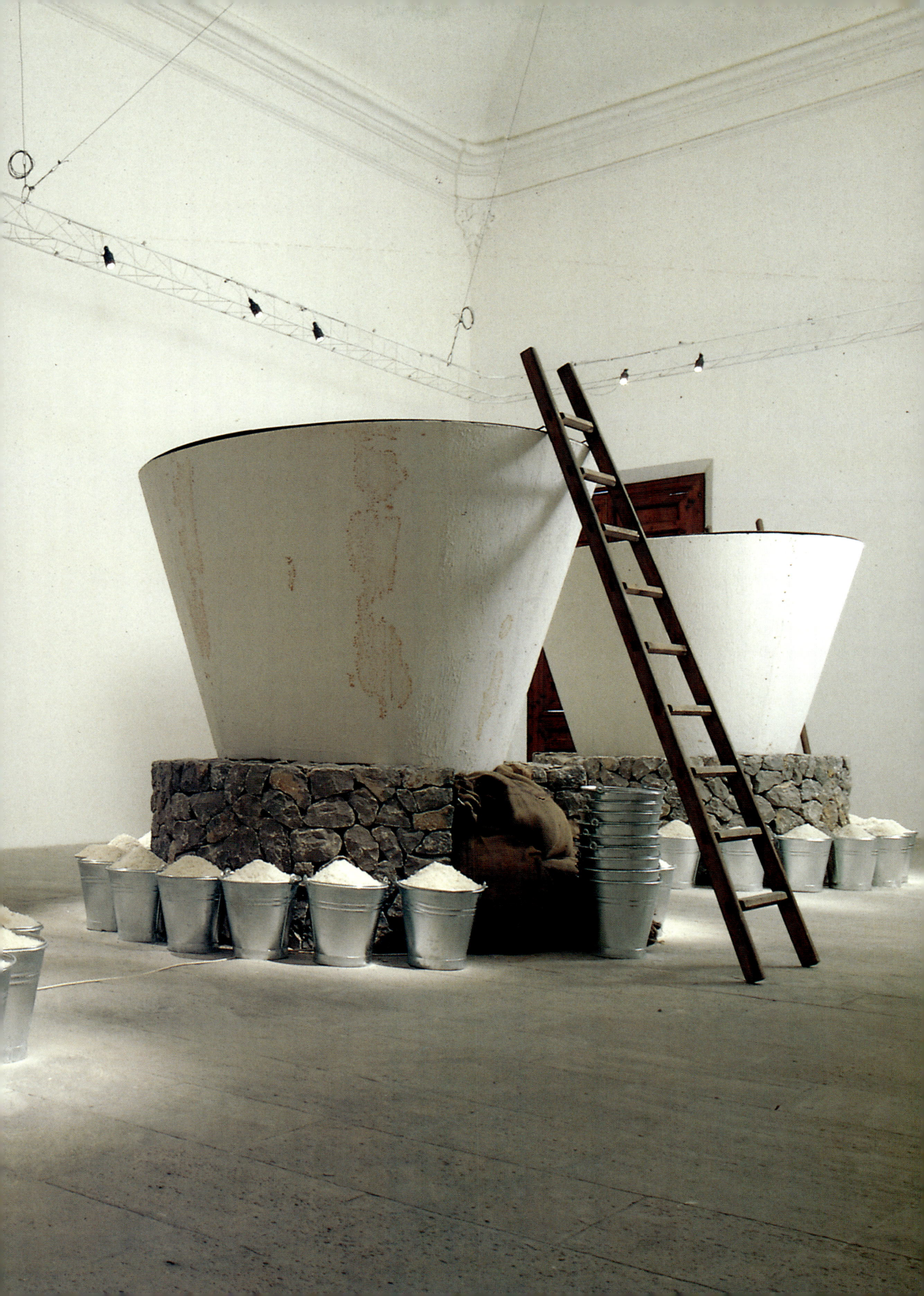

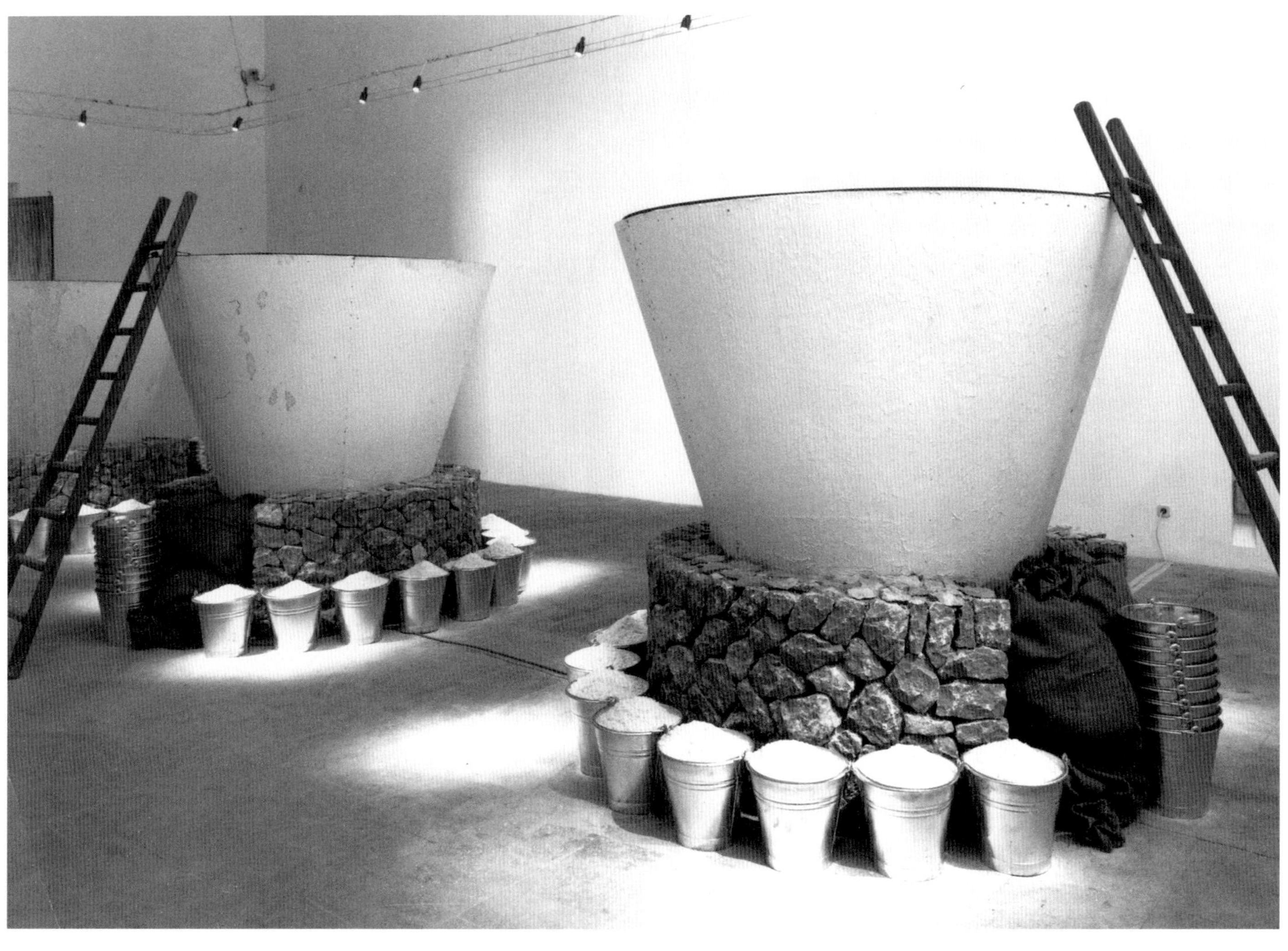

Máquina Salada im Palau Solleric. Sie unterstreichen den Realitätscharakter, haben eine sinn-
lich-taktische Präsenz und zugleich stehen die Formen und
Materialien klar für sich, deutlich
getrennt voneinander und ergeben in dem Gesamten einen
vergleichsweise abstrakten und
beinahe geometrisch konstruktiv
anmutenden Eindruck. Die von
außen hermetisch abgeschlosse-
nen Trichterformen, die ebener-
dig keinen Einblick in ihr Inneres
gewähren, erscheinen zunächst
als bloße Form und nur die Leiter,
die wie zufällig am Rande des
Trichters lehnt, erlaubt einen
Zugang, macht einen Einblick in
das Innere der Konstruktion
möglich, stellt Nähe her.

*the character of reality, have a
sensual, tactical presence, and at
the same time forms and material stand clearly on their own,
distinctly separate from each
other, thus giving - within the
complete ensemble - a compara-
tively abstract and almost geometric, constructive impression.
The funnel-shaped forms, completely closed, allowing no view
of their insides from the ground,
appear at first as mere forms,
and only the ladder that almost
accidentally leans at the side of
the funnel allows entrance,
makes insight into the construction possible, creates proximity.*

Mallorca. Essi sottolineano il
carattere della realtà, posseggono una presenza sensuale-
tattile. Nello stesso momento le
forme e i materiali si autorife-
riscono a sé stessi, ben separati
fra di loro, ed evocano
nell'insieme una relativa impressione astratta e quasi geo-
metrico-costruttiva. La forma ad
imbuto, vista dall'esterno,
ermeticamente chiusa non
permette la visione all'interno e
appare come forma nuda, solo la
scala, casualmente appoggiata
al bordo dell'imbuto, consente
l'accesso alla parte interna della
costruzione e crea vicinanza.

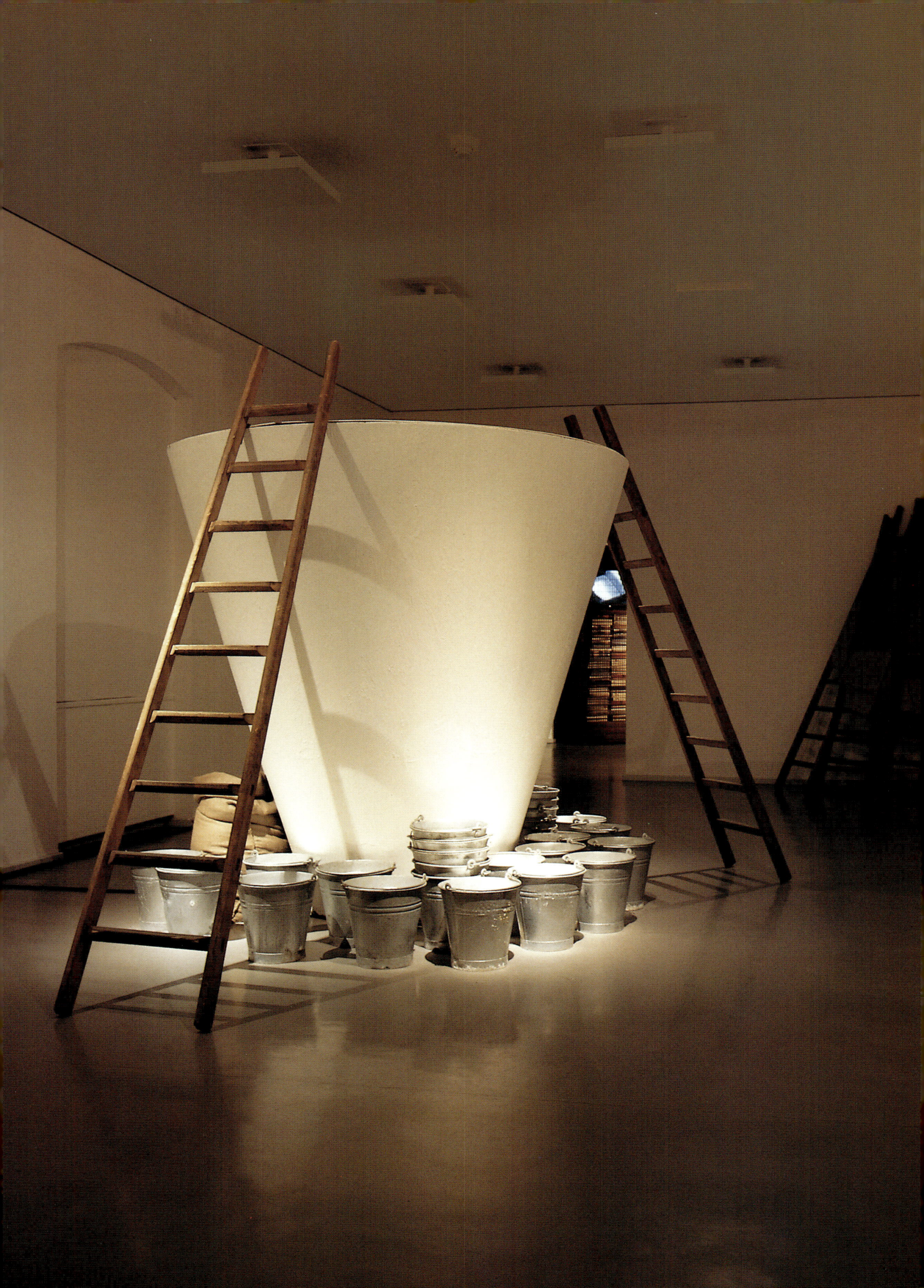

L'ARMADIO DEI SASSI

89009

VERONA 1989
STUDIO LA CITTÀ
89009.1

REGGIO EMILIA 1990
MUSEO CIVICO D'ARTE MODERNA
89009.2

ROMA 1990
GALLERIA L'ISOLA
89009.3

DORTMUND 1993
MUSEUM AM OSTWALL
89009.4

KÖLN 1995
GALERIE DOROTHEA VAN DER KOELEN, ART COLOGNE
89009.5

PADERBORN 1997
KAISERPFALZ
89009.6

SCHRANK DER STEINE
Videoskulptur 1989
Eisenschränke mit Fächern,
Eisengitter, Basaltsteine,
4 Monitore, 4 Videorecorder,
4 bespielte Kassetten,
Tonaufzeichnung
260 x 320 x 60 cm

CABINET OF STONES
Video sculpture 1989
Iron construction with compartments,
iron lattice, piled-up stones and rocks
of different heights, 4 monitors,
4 video recorders, 4 recorded video
cassettes, soundrecording
260 x 320 x 60 cm

L'ARMADIO DEI SASSI
Videoscultura 1990
Struttura in metallo arrugginito a
scomparti, grigliato industriale,
quattro cumuli a diverse altezze
di sassi e pietre, 4 monitors, 4
vhs, 4 cassette registrate, sonoro
260 x 320 x 60 cm

Wenn man versucht, die annähernd 20 *Armadi*, *Schränke* oder *Räume*, in irgendwelche Gruppen zusammenzufassen oder sie unter bestimmten Klassifizierungsstrukturen zu subsumieren, stellt man schnell fest, daß - abgesehen von dem Stahlgehäuse, das gelegentlich mittels verrosteter Gittertüren eine Barriere zwischen den Betrachter und das Material oder die Monitore setzt - sowohl das Material als auch das, worauf es verweist, gelegentlich sehr unterschiedlich ist. So gibt es beispielsweise Schränke, die mittels eines signifikanten Indizes auf etwas verweisen, das der Titel bereits zum Ausdruck bringt, wie beispielsweise die Bilderrahmen in dem *Schrank der Kunst* oder die Backsteine in dem *Schrank des Architekten*. Es gibt auch Räume, die auf die eigentümliche Beschaffenheit eines Materials verweisen, wie die *Stanza Fragile*, und es gibt darunter Räume, die Vorgänge beschreiben, wie *Work in Progress*. Es gibt Schränke, die auf frühere Videoskulpturen oder

In attempting to combine the almost 20 Armadi, *cabinets or spaces, in some sort of groups, or to submit them to certain categories of classification one soon discovers - apart from the steel construction that sometimes sets a barrier between spectator and material, or monitors with rusty grated doors - that the material as well as to what it points to sometimes is very different. Thus, there are cabinets that, with a significant hint, indicate something the title already expresses, as for example the frames in* Cabinet of Art *or the bricks in* Architect's cabinet. *There are also spaces that point to the characteristic of a material, like the* Stanza Fragile, *and among them are rooms that describe processes, like* Work in Progress. *There are cabinets that hint at earlier video sculptures and video installations, like the* Armadio di Wasserwagen *or* Armadio di Bronx. *There are, however, also cabinets that describe and analyse the essence*

Se si cerca di unire i circa venti *Armadi* in gruppi comuni o di classificarli in categorie, si scopre immediatamente che è - a parte il contenitore di ferro che in alcuni casi, attraverso le inferriate delle ante, pone una barriera fra spettatori e materiale o monitors - una fatica sprecata in quanto il materiale e ciò a cui esso allude sono spesso troppo divergenti. In tal senso esistono armadi che, attraverso indicazioni significative, si riferiscono a qualcosa già espressa dal titolo, come per esempio le cornici dell'*Armadio dell'Arte* o i mattoni dell'*Armadio dell'Architetto*. Come ci sono armadi che alludono alla natura stessa del materiale, come la *Stanza Fragile* o altri che descrivono processi, come *Work in Progress*. Altri ancora si riallacciano a videosculture o videoinstallazioni precedenti, come *Armadio di Wasserwagen* o *Armadio di Bronx*. Esistono però anche armadi che analizzano l'essenza

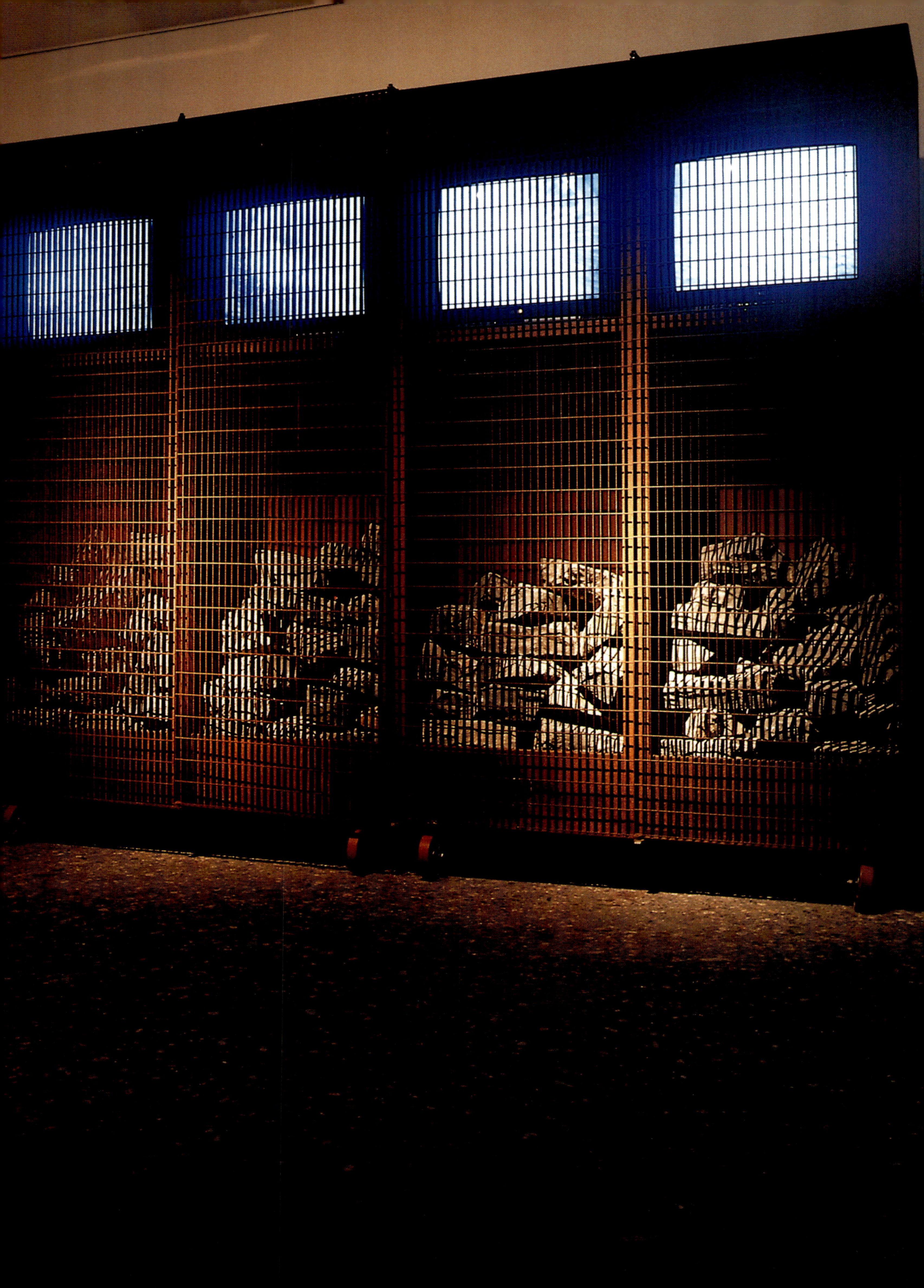

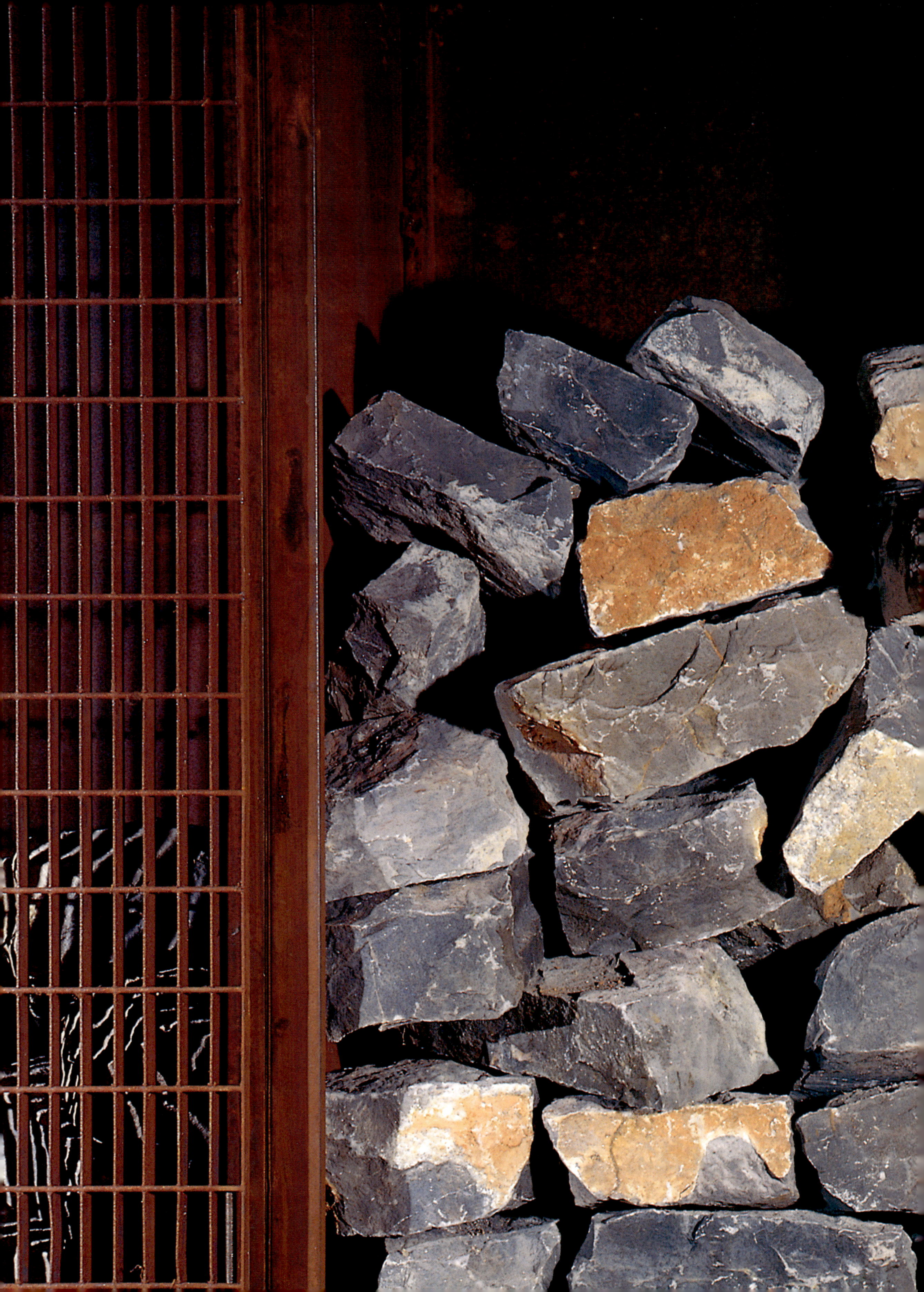

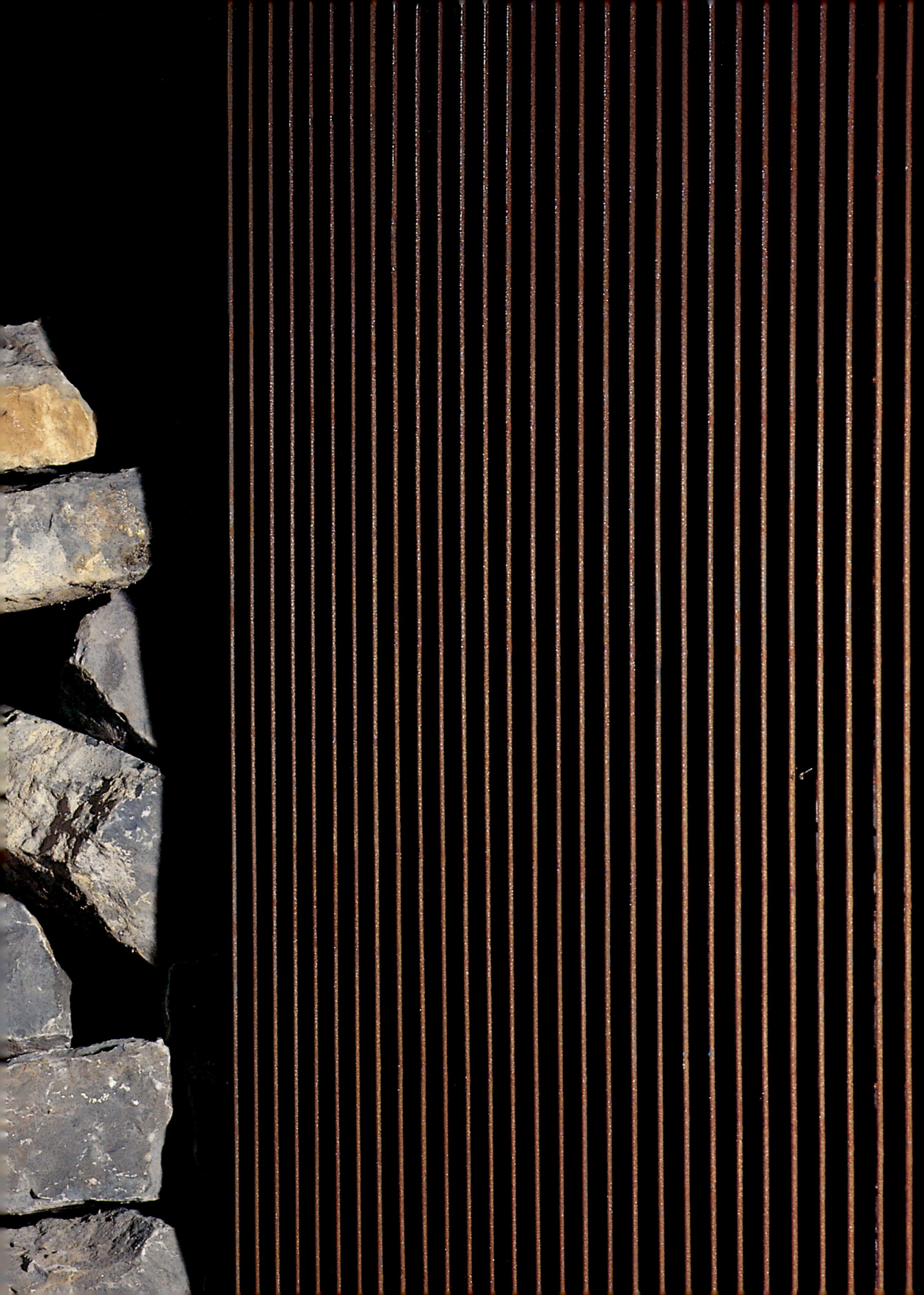

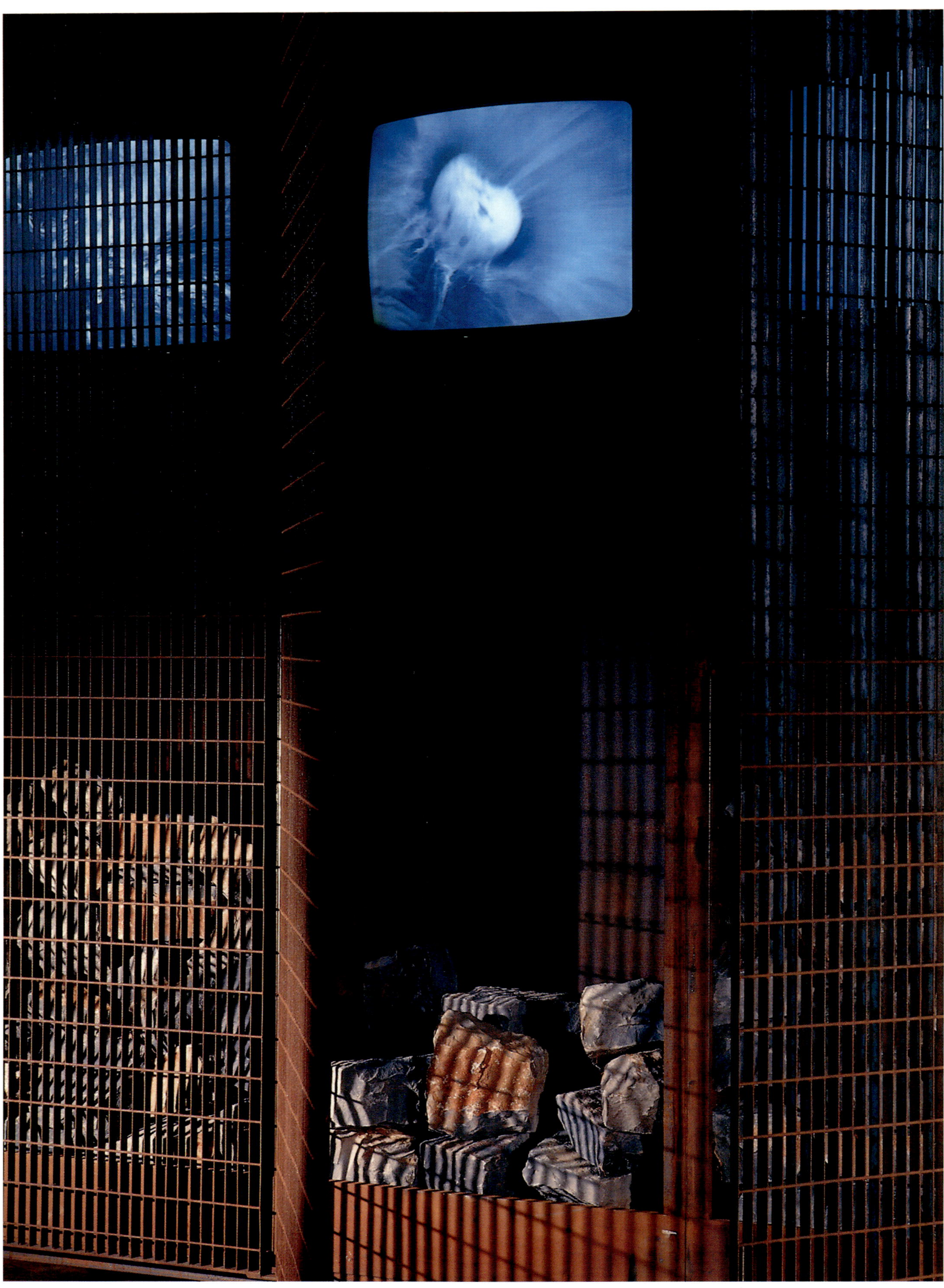

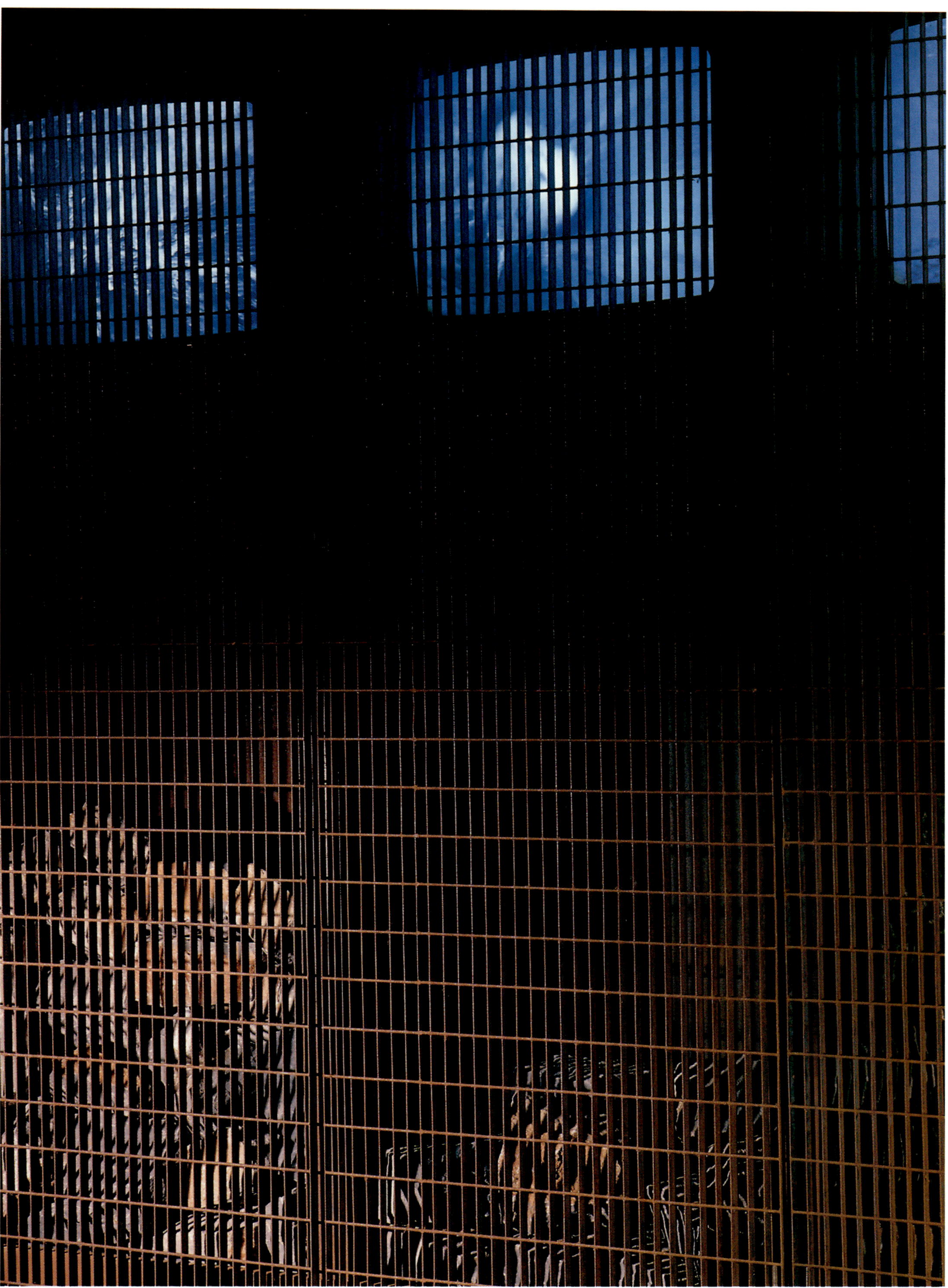

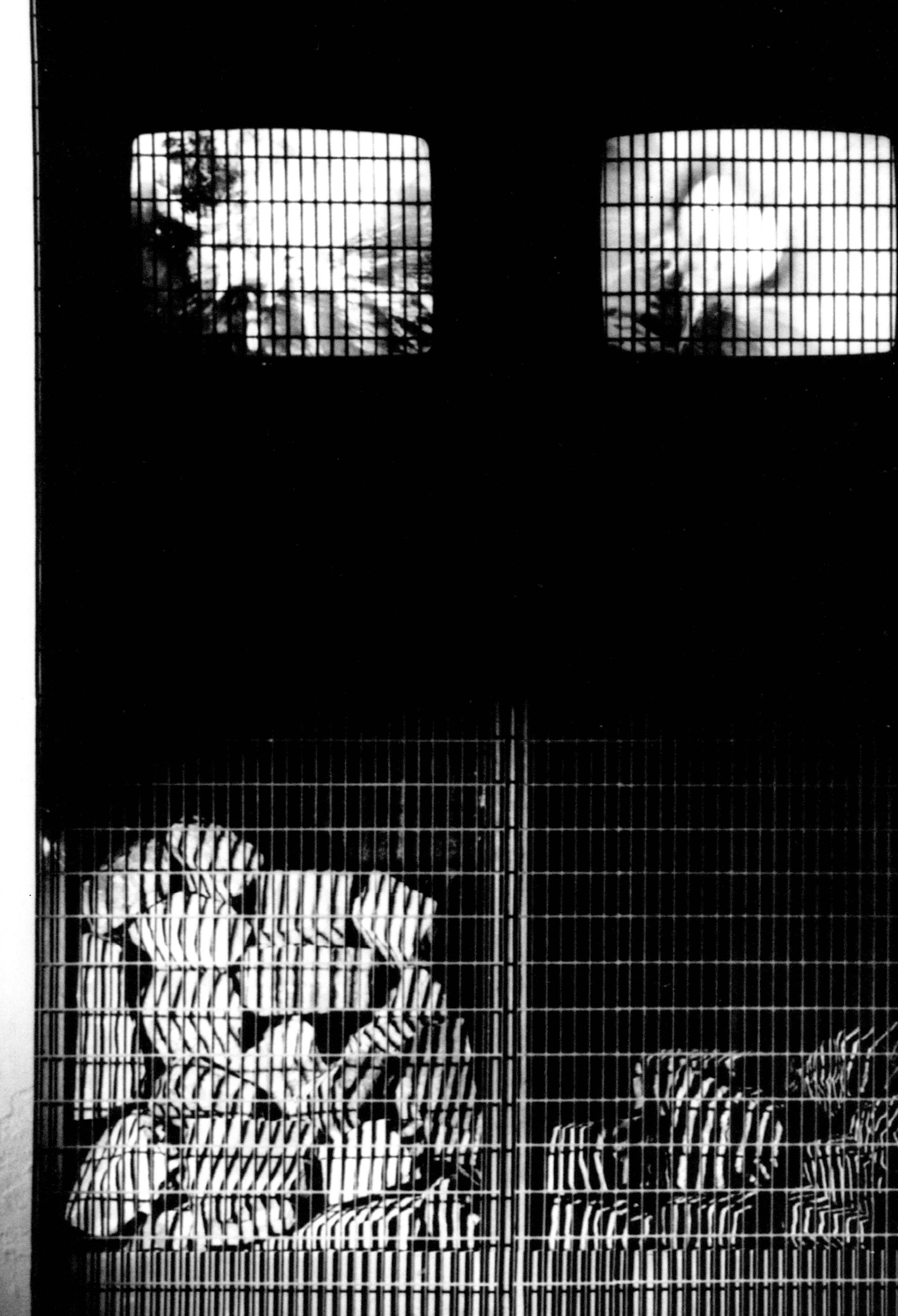

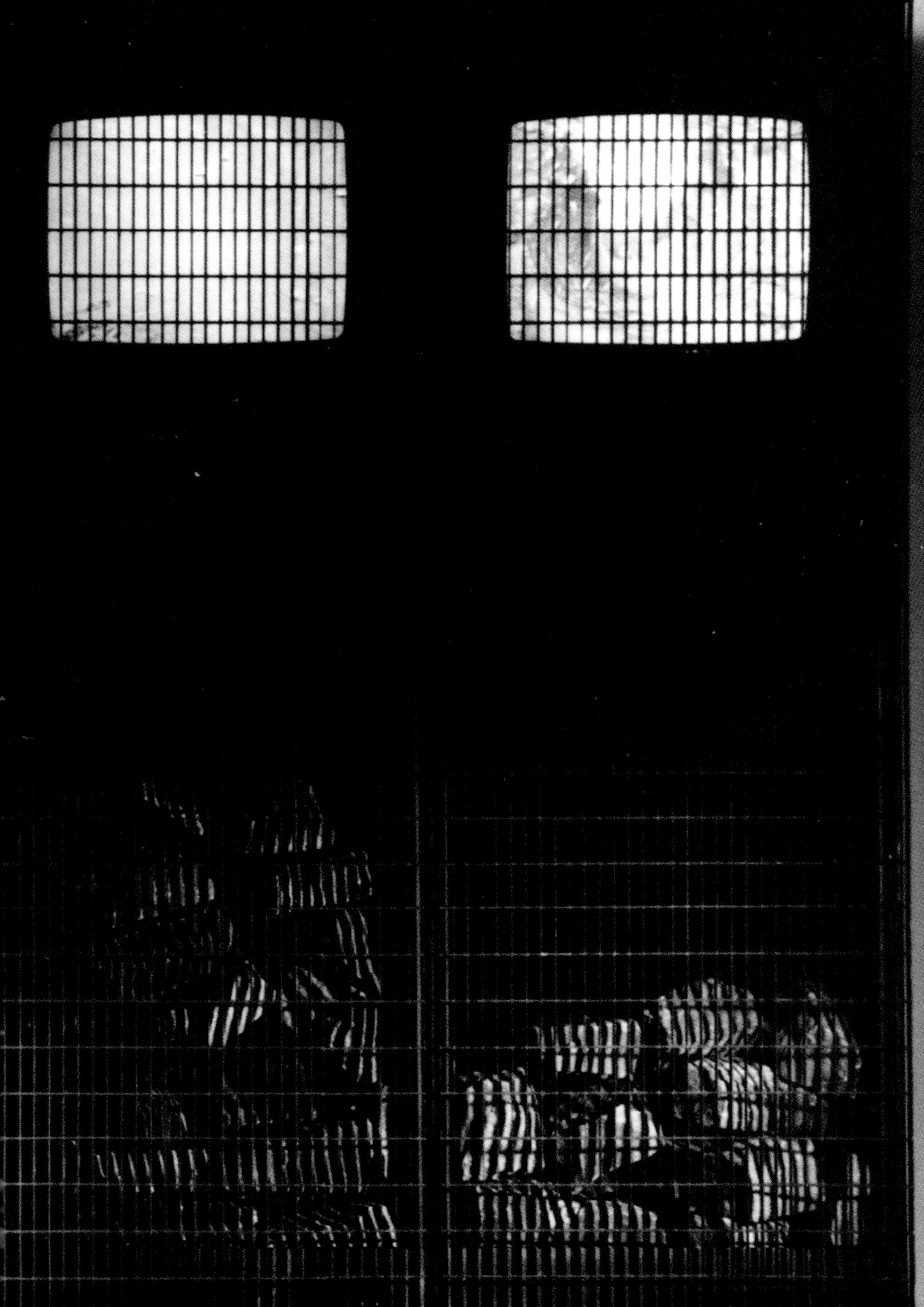

Videoinstallationen verweisen, wie
der *Armadio di Wasserwagen* oder
Armadio di Bronx. Es gibt aber auch
Schränke, die das Wesen oder die
Beschaffenheit eines Materials
beschreiben und analysieren, zum
Beispiel die von Holz oder Stroh, um
nur einige Beispiele zu nennen, und
es gibt Gehäuse wie hier den *Armadio dei Sassi*, den *Schrank der
Steine*, der scheinbar einen Hinweis
auf ein Material geben soll. In
Wirklichkeit aber werden, wie der
Videofilm zeigt, die Steine nur als
Material benutzt, um etwas außerhalb des Material Liegendes sichtbar zu machen, nämlich im Vorgang
des Fallens das Gesetz der Schwer-
kraft, der Gravitation, und damit
letztendlich Raum und zugleich in
dem Vorgang des Fließens den
Aspekt der Zeit. Im unteren Teil
dieses in vier Kammern aufgeteilten
Schrankes, liegen Bruchsteine aus
Basalt in verschiedener Größe und
verschieden hoch aufgetürmt. In
den Monitoren darüber ist Wasser
sichtbar, in das von Zeit zu Zeit in
unregelmäßigen Abständen und von
Monitor zu Monitor zeitversetzt ein
Stein fällt, Wellen erzeugt, das
Wasser in Dynamik versetzt und
schließlich in den Grund zu versinken scheint. Der ganze Vorgang
wirkt audiovisuell auf die Sinne,
denn man kann deutlich hören, wie
der Stein ins Wasser fällt.

Der Vorgang des ins fließende
Wasser Fallens eines Steines ist
nicht neu im Werk Fabrizio Plessis,
denn schon in seiner ersten *Roma*-
Installation, der Version, die in
Kassel zu sehen war, fällt bereits
ein Stein - wenn auch imaginär -
von dem Förderband in den elektronischen Kanal.

Zu einem regelrechten *Armadio
del Caos* wird der *Schrank der
Steine* schließlich in der Ausstellung
in Perugia 1995 mutieren.

*and condition of a certain
material, like those of wood or
straw, to mention but two
examples. And there are casings
like the* Armadio dei Sassi, *the
Cabinet of Stones, that seems to
hint at a material. In reality,
however, as the video film
shows, the stones are only used
as material to make something
outside it visible, that is - in the
process of falling - the law of
gravity, and thereby space, and
- in the process of flowing - the
aspect of time. In the lower part
of this cabinet, divided into
four chambers, pieces of basalt
in different size and piled up in
varying height are placed. On
the monitors above water can
be seen into which from time to
time - at irregular intervals
and at various times on each
monitor - a stone drops, creating waves, passing energy into
the water, and finally seeming
to sink to the ground. The
whole process works audio-
visually on the senses, for one
can clearly hear the stone drop
into the water. The process of a
stone falling into the water is
not new to Fabrizio Plessi's
work, for in his first installation of* Roma - the version shown
in Kassel - a stone drops -
though imaginary - from the
conveyor-belt into the electronic
channel.*

Finally, the Cabinet of
Stones *will mutate to a regular*
Armadio del Caos *in the exhibi-
tion in Perugia in 1995.*

o la consistenza di un materiale
come quella del legno o della
paglia. Altri contenitori, come
qui nell'*Armadio dei Sassi*, solo
apparentemente fanno riferimento ad un materiale, in verità
l'uso dei sassi serve, come
dimostra il videofilm, esclusivamente a far comprendere qualcosa che sta al di là del materiale stesso, cioè, attraverso l'atto
della caduta, la legge di gravità
e, attraverso il motivo dello
scorrere, l'aspetto del tempo.

Nella parte inferiore
dell'*Armadio dei Sassi*, suddiviso
in quattro sezioni, si trovano
frammenti di roccia di basalto di
grandezza e ad altezza diverse.
Nei monitors in alto si vede
l'acqua, nella quale cade, a
intervalli irregolari e non sincronizzati, un sasso che provoca
onde e le conferisce dinamicità
per poi scomparire nel fondo.
Tutto il processo appare audio-
visivo in quanto si sente acusticamente l'impatto del sasso con
l'acqua. Il concetto del sasso
che cade nell'acqua corrente
non è inedito nell'opera di
Fabrizio Plessi: già nella prima
versione di Roma, quella esposta a Kassel, un sasso precipita,
anche se a livello immaginario,
dal montacarichi nel canale
elettronico.

Nella mostra di Perugia nel
1995 infine *L'Armadio dei Sassi*
si trasformerà in un vero e
proprio *Armadio del Caos*.

FOR SALE

90001

REGGIO EMILIA 1990
Museo Civico d'Arte Moderna
90001.1

AUSVERKAUF
Videoskulptur 1990
Eisenschränke mit Fächern,
Glasscheiben, Neon, Packpapier,
4 Monitore, 1 Videorecorder, bespielte Kassette, Tonaufzeichnung
260 x 320 x 60 cm

FOR SALE
Video sculpture 1990
Iron construction with
compartments, panes of glass,
neon, wrapping paper, 4 monitors,
1 video recorder, recorded video
cassette, soundrecording
260 x 320 x 60 cm

VENDITA
Videoscultura 1990
Struttura a scomparti in ferro,
lastre in vetro, neon, carta da
imballagio, 4 monitors, vhs,
cassetta registrata, sonoro
260 x 320 x 60 cm

For Sale ist der Titel eines Gehäuses, das wie ein Schaufenster beim Umbau mit Papieren abgeklebt ist, Papieren, die ursprünglich vielleicht einmal als Packpapiere gedient haben mögen und nun keiner weiteren Verwendung bedürfen. Auch große Teile der Monitore im oberen Bereich des Schrankes sind mit verschieden großen Packpapierstücken und Klebestreifen partiell verdeckt. Der frühere Arbeitstitel auf einer Zeichnung von 1989, einer Skizze für die Skulptur, lautet *Schrank des Papiers*. Doch im endgültigen Titel *For Sale* wird nicht ein Material beschrieben, sondern eine Disposition zum Ausdruck gebracht. Die Monitore sind eingeschaltet, zeigen - wie selten in Videoinstallationen Plessis - jedoch kein Bild. Das diffuse Flimmern der Videos, wie auch der nahezu in Packpapier verpackte Schrank, deuten eine zeitliche Begrenztheit, eine Endlichkeit an, eine Aufhebung des aktuellen Zustands in eine Richtung, die ungewiß ist.

For Sale *is the title of a container that is - like a shop window during renovation - covered with paper, paper that originally may have been used to pack things and now is of no further use. A large portion of the monitors in the upper part of the cabinet is also partially covered with pieces of packing-sheets and adhesive tape. The title of an early drawing of 1989, a sketch for a sculpture, is* Cabinet of Paper. *The final title, however, does not refer to the material but expresses a disposition. The monitors are turned on, yet show - rare in one of Plessi's video installations - no picture. The diffuse flicker of the videos, as well as the almost completely covered cabinet, indicate a limit of time, finality, the end of a present state without knowledge of future directions.*

For Sale è il titolo di un contenitore con la parte anteriore incartata, forse una volta da imballaggio e adesso senza utilizzo, come una vetrina in allestimento. Anche i monitors della parte superiore dell'armadio sono parzialmente coperti da pezzi di carta e nastri da imballaggio. In un antecedente schizzo (del 1989) per la scultura il titolo era *Armadio della Carta*. Il titolo finale *For Sale* non descrive semplicemente un materiale ma esprime una predisposizione. I monitors sono accesi ma - come raramente accade nelle videoinstallazioni di Plessi - senza immagini. Il diffuso sfarfallio degli schermi, così come l'armadio con la facciata imballata, rinviano ad una limitatezza temporale, ad un finito e alla neutralizzazione dello stato attuale in una direzione incerta.

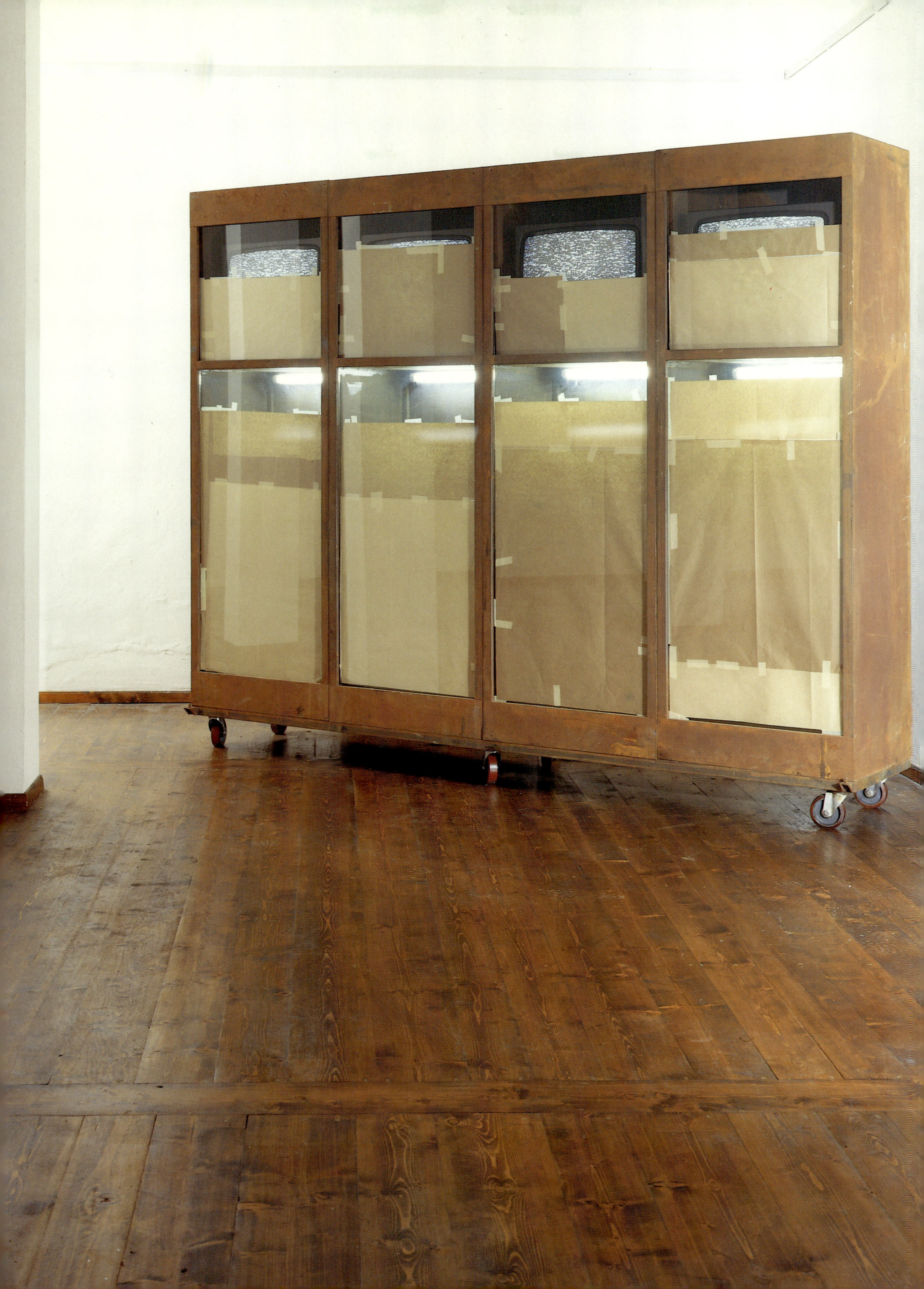

LA STANZA DEL MARE

90002

REGGIO EMILIA 1990
Museo Civico d'Arte Moderna
90002.1

TRENTO 1990
Galleria Civica di Arte Contemporanea
90002.2

HAMBURG 1991
Weisser Raum
90002.3

KØBENHAVN 1992
Charlottenburg
90002.4

KARLSRUHE 1997
Zentrum für Kunst und Medientechnologie
90002.5

MEERESRAUM
Videoskulptur 1990
Eisenschränke mit Fächern, rohe
Holzbretter, 12 Monitore, 2 Video-
recorder, 2 bespielte Kassetten
260 x 960 x 60 cm
Weitere Präsentation:
mit 20 Monitoren, Breite 1600 cm

SEA ROOM
Video sculpture 1990
Iron construction with compart-
ments, raw wooden boards,
12 monitors, 2 recorders, 2 video
cassettes, 260 x 960 x 60 cm
Subsequent presentation:
20 monitors, 1600 cm width

LA STANZA DEL MARE
Videoscultura 1990
Struttura in ferro e legno,
12 monitors, 2 vhs, 2 cassette
registrate, sonoro
260 x 960 x 60 cm
variazione:
20 monitors, 1600 cm larghezza

La Stanza del Mare, der *Mee-resraum*, zeigt eine lange Reihe dieser gleichartigen Schränke aneinander gestellt. Die Videos der Monitore im oberen Bereich der Schränke zeigen Meerwasser und die Wellen der Brandung. Anstelle der Türen sind zahlreiche Querlatten angebracht, die in der Höhe nach oben so weit reichen, daß sie die Monitore partiell verdecken. Die Hölzer sind unterschiedlich in Farbe und Qualität, Alter und Zustand, so daß eine poetische Struktur entsteht, beinahe wie ein impressionistisches Gemälde. Sie erinnern an Treibhölzer, die das Meer von Zeit zu Zeit an den Strand spült. Eben jene Hölzer sind es, die hier nun eine Barriere aufbauen, beinahe, als wollten sie das

La Stanza del Mare, the Space of the Sea, *shows a long row of similar stanzas next to each other. The monitors' videos in the upper parts of the cabinets show sea-water and breaking waves. Numerous horizontal laths replace the doors, partially covering the monitors. The pieces of wood are different in colour and quality, age and condition, so that a poetic structure is created, almost like an impressionistic painting. They remind of drift-wood, washed ashore from time to time by the sea. Now it is these pieces of wood that put up a barrier, almost as if they wanted to protect the sea from the spectators' eyes, from the visitors on the beach, the destroyers of the*

La Stanza del Mare è composta di una serie di armadi simili a quelli di *For Sale*. I monitors nella parte superiore presentano acqua di mare e onde che si infrangono. Al posto delle ante sono state applicate delle tavole di legno che in alto coprono in parte i monitors. Le tavole hanno colori, qualità, età e stato di condizioni diversi creando una struttura poetica, quasi come un dipinto impressionista. Esse ricordano il legname galleggiante che il mare di tanto in tanto getta sulla riva. Proprio questo legname costituisce una barriera, quasi come se volesse proteggere il mare dallo sguardo dello spettatore, dai visitatori delle spiagge o dai distruttori delle bellezze naturali. Questi

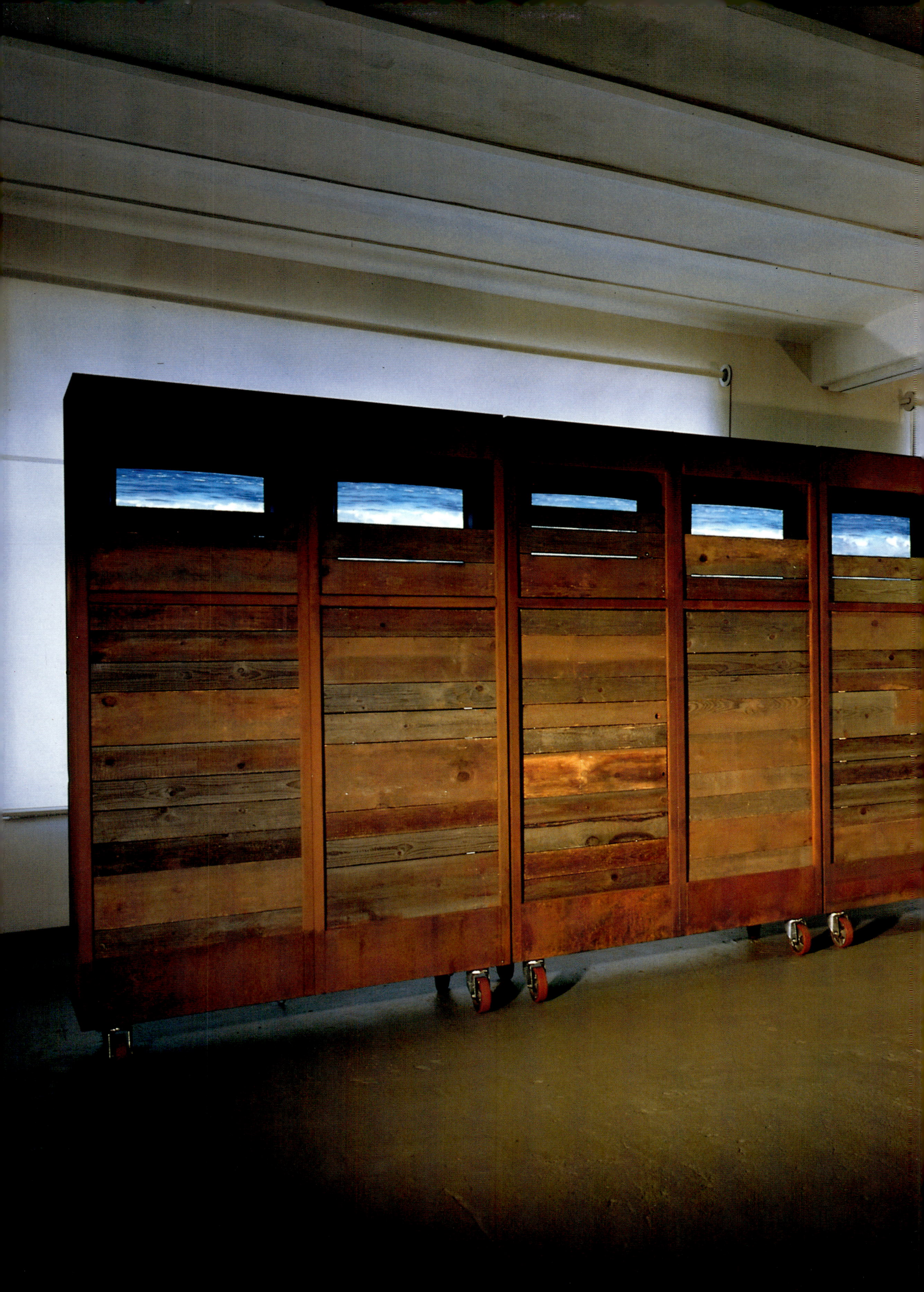

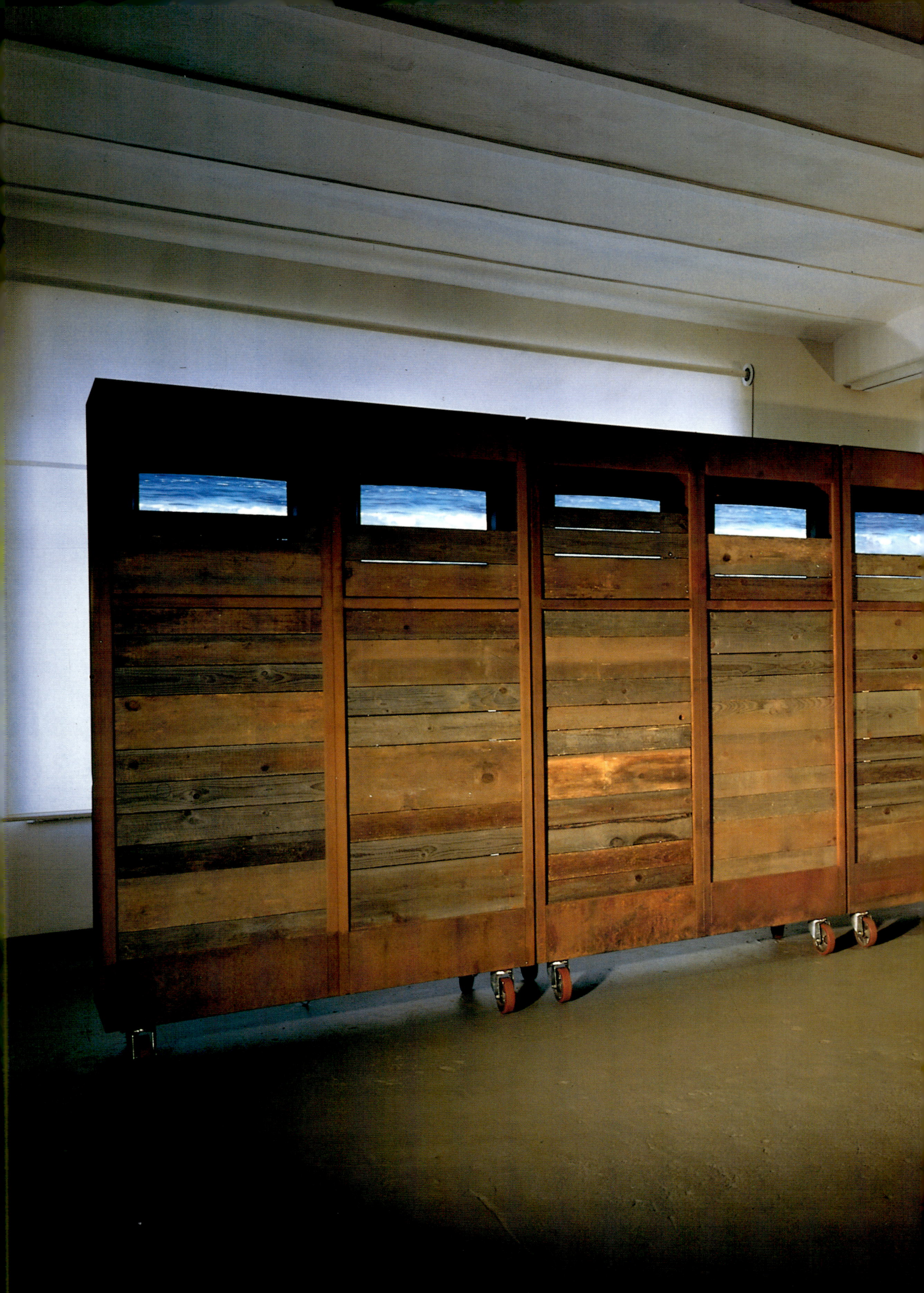

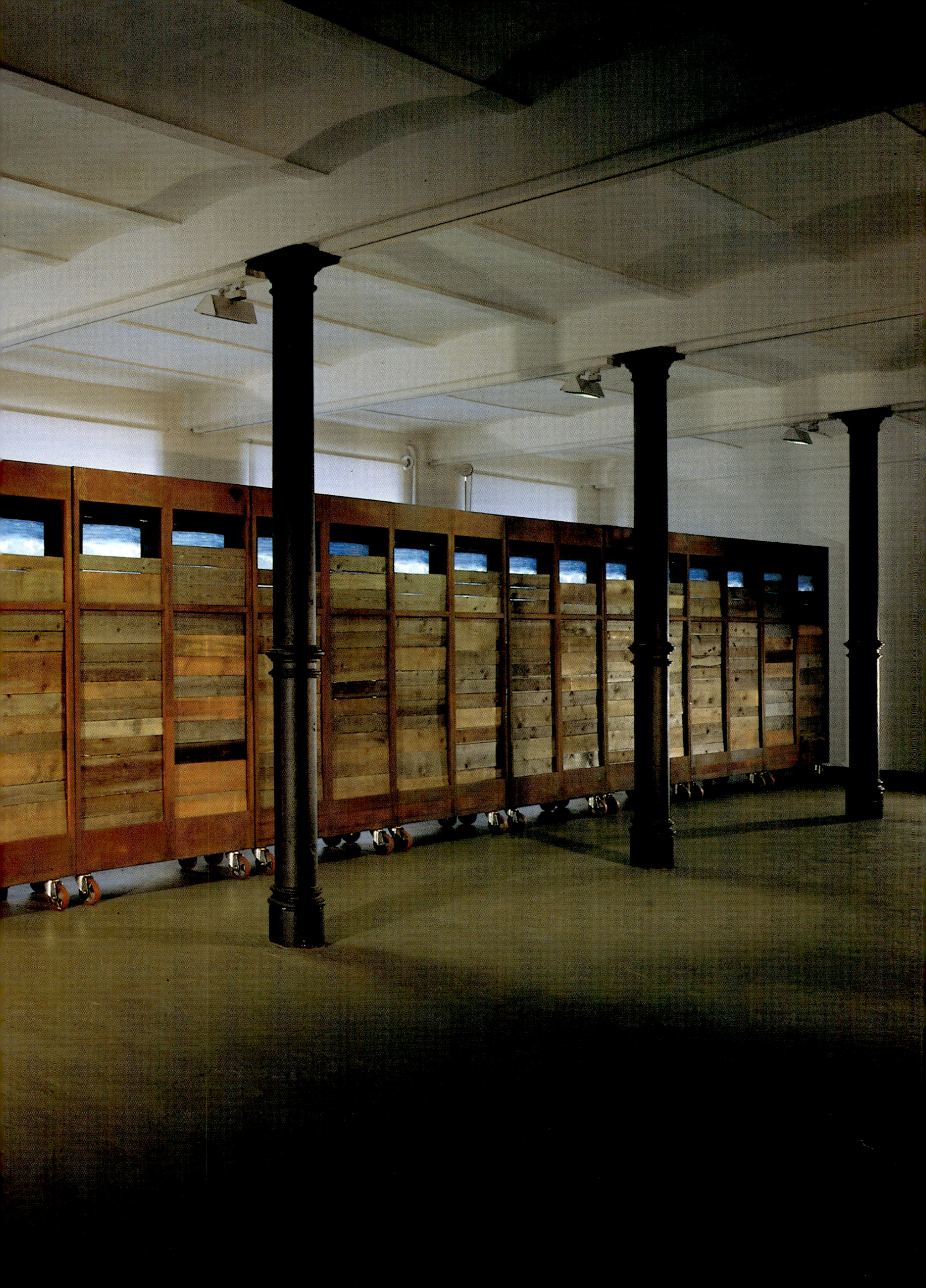

Meer beschützen vor den Augen der Betrachter, vor den Besuchern der Strände, vor den Zerstörern der Schönheit der Natur. Diese Schränke - hier als Raum bezeichnet - sind zu verstehen als eine Hymne an das Meer, eine Liebeserklärung an das Wasser.

Eine kleinere Version dieser Konzeption erscheint wenig später unter dem Titel *Proibito* (*Verboten*). Der Kontrast von Natur, hier durch die Hölzer zum Ausdruck gebracht, und Technologie, durch die Monitore und Videofilme, wird durch die Präsentation entschärft. Beide ihrem Wesen nach doch sehr verschiedene Elemente treten in ein symbiotisches Verhältnis.

beauty of nature. These cabinets, here called space, are to be understood as a hymn to the sea, a declaration of love to water.

A smaller version of this concept is shown soon after under the title Proibito *(Forbidden). The contrast between nature - expressed here through the pieces of wood - and technology - in monitors and video films - is lessened in this presentation. The two elements, different as they are in their essence, are now joined in a symbiotic relationship.*

armadi, qui chiamati stanza, sono da intendere come inno al mare, come una dichiarazione d'amore all'acqua.

Una versione più piccola appare poco più tardi sotto il titolo *Proibito* e appiana il contrasto fra natura, qui simboleggiata dal legno, e tecnologia, i monitors e i videofilms, unendo i due elementi in sè essenzialmente diversi in un rapporto di simbiosi.

L'ARMADIO DELL'ARCHITETTO

90003

REGGIO EMILIA 1990
MUSEO CIVICO D'ARTE MODERNA
90003.1

WIEN 1991
MUSEUM MODERNER KUNST, STIFTUNG LUDWIG
90003.2

MARBURG 1991
MARBURGER KUNSTVEREIN
90003.3

DORTMUND 1993
MUSEUM AM OSTWALL
90003.4

LUXEMBOURG 1997
CASINO LUXEMBOURG, FORUM D'ART CONTEMPORAIN
90003.5

SCHRANK DES ARCHITEKTEN
Videoskulptur 1990
Eisenschränke mit Fächern,
500 gebrannte Ziegel, 4 Monitore,
2 Videorecorder, 2 bespielte
Kassetten, 260 x 320 x 60 cm
Weitere Präsentation:
8 Monitore, 640 cm Breite

THE ARCHITECT'S CABINET
Video sculpture 1990
Iron construction with
compartments, 500 fired bricks,
4 monitors, 2 recorders, 2 video
cassettes, 260 x 320 x 60 cm
Subsequent presentation:
8 monitors, 640 cm width

L'ARMADIO DELL'ARCHITETTO
Videoscultura 1990
Struttura a scomparti in ferro
arrugginito, 500 mattoni di
fornace, 4 monitors, 2 vhs,
2 cassette registrate, sonoro,
260 x 320 x 60 cm
variazione: 8 monitors, 640 cm

Auch den *Schrank des Architekten* gibt es in einer kleineren und einer größeren Version. In dem unteren Teil der Schränke sind Ziegelsteine mauerartig, verschieden hoch, übereinander geschichtet, die Monitore darüber zeigen das Bild der Mauer. Interessant ist der Unterschied zu dem *Schrank der Steine*, denn auch hier handelt es sich materialiter um Steine, doch diese sind tektonisch gestaltet, konstruktiv zum synthetischen Herstellen eines Bauwerkes bestimmt. Der Architekt, dem dieser Schrank gewidmet ist, ist nirgendwo selbst zu sehen. Ähnlich wie bei dem *Schrank der Kunst* wird hier ein Verweis vorgenommen, eine Vorstellung erzeugt durch ein Material, das dem Architekten signifikant zugeordnet werden kann.

The Architect's Cabinet also exists in a smaller and larger version. In the lower part of the cabinets, bricks are piled up in different height, like a wall, the monitors above showing a picture of a wall. Here, the difference to the Cabinet of Stones is interesting to note, for, materialiter, we are looking at stones which, however, are formed tectonically, destined to construct a synthetic building. The architect, to whom the work is dedicated, is nowhere to be seen. Similar to the Cabinet of Art, *something is hinted at here, an idea is created through the material that can be clearly attributed to the architect.*

Apart from the title of the work and the video films,

Anche per *L'Armadio dell'Architetto* esistono una versione più piccola e una più grande. Nella parte inferiore degli armadi si trovano dei mattoni che formano muretti di altezze diverse, i monitors in alto riproducono l'immagine dei muretti. Risulta interessante la differenza con *L'Armadio dei Sassi*, solo che nella presente installazione i mattoni sono trattati in maniera tettonica e destinati costruttivamente all'edificazione sintetica di un monumento. L'architetto, al quale è dedicato l'armadio, non è presente. Simile all'*Armadio dell'Arte* ci troviamo di fronte ad un'allusione, ad un'immagine suggerita da un materiale che può essere attribuito, significativamente, all'architetto.

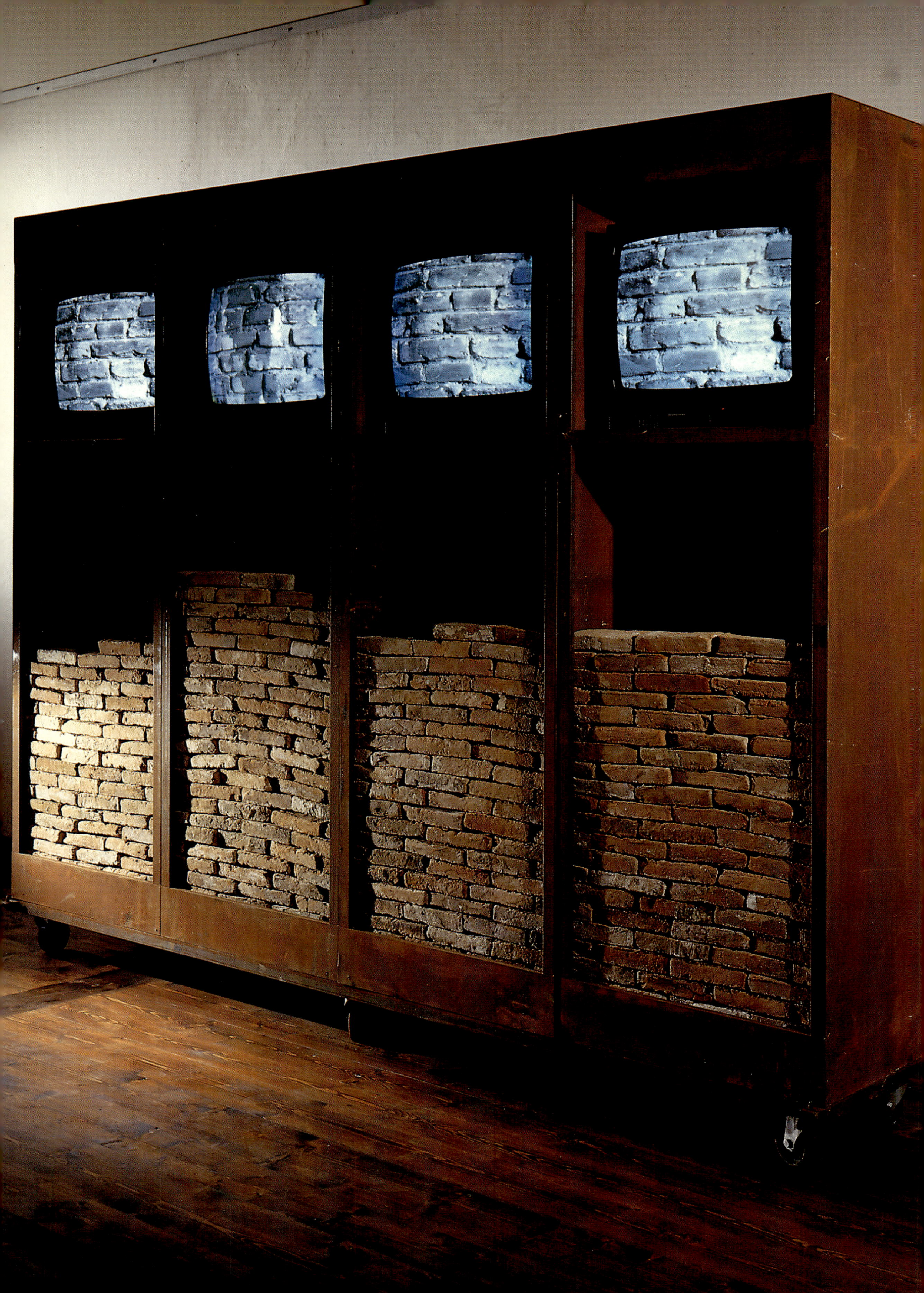

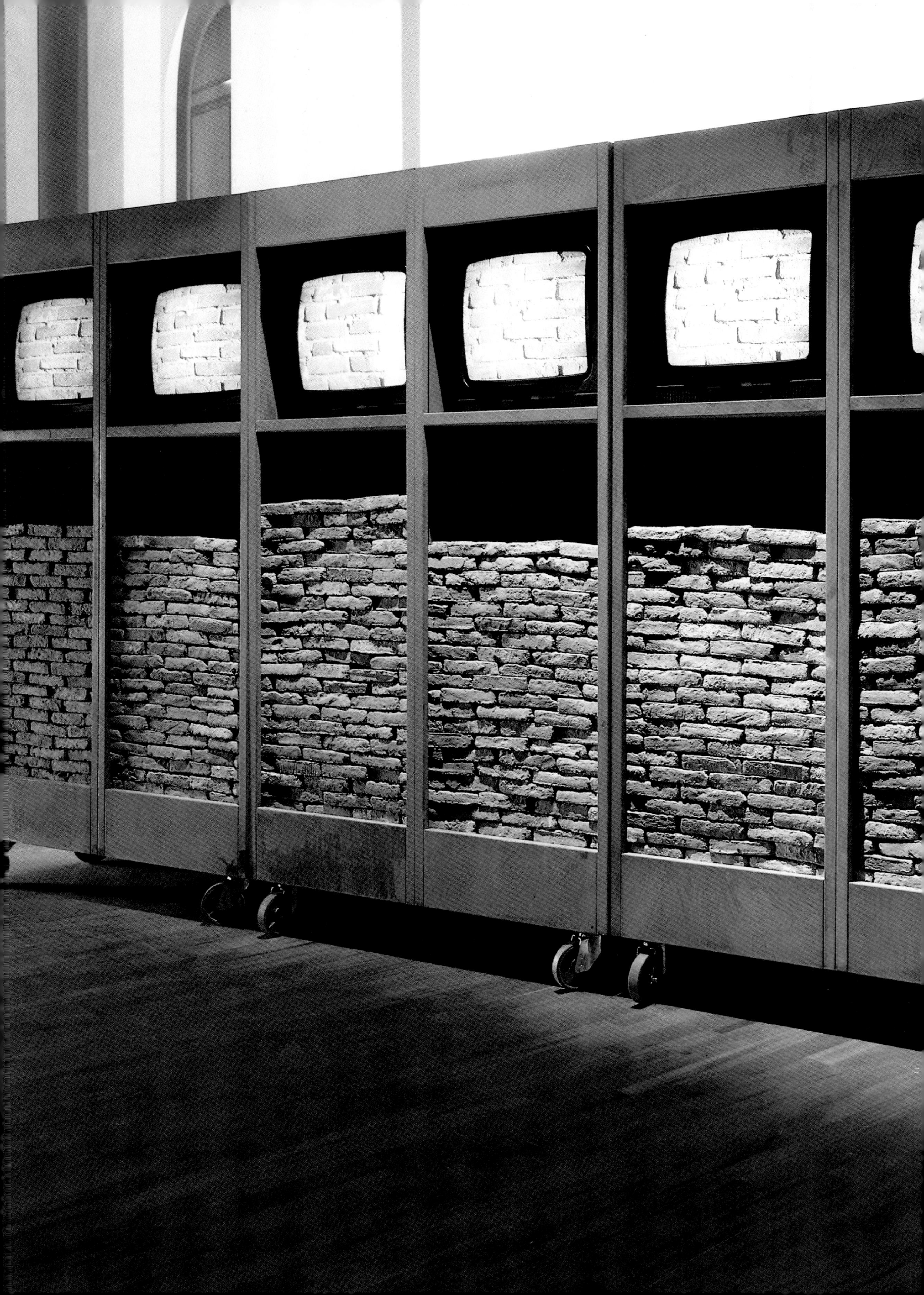

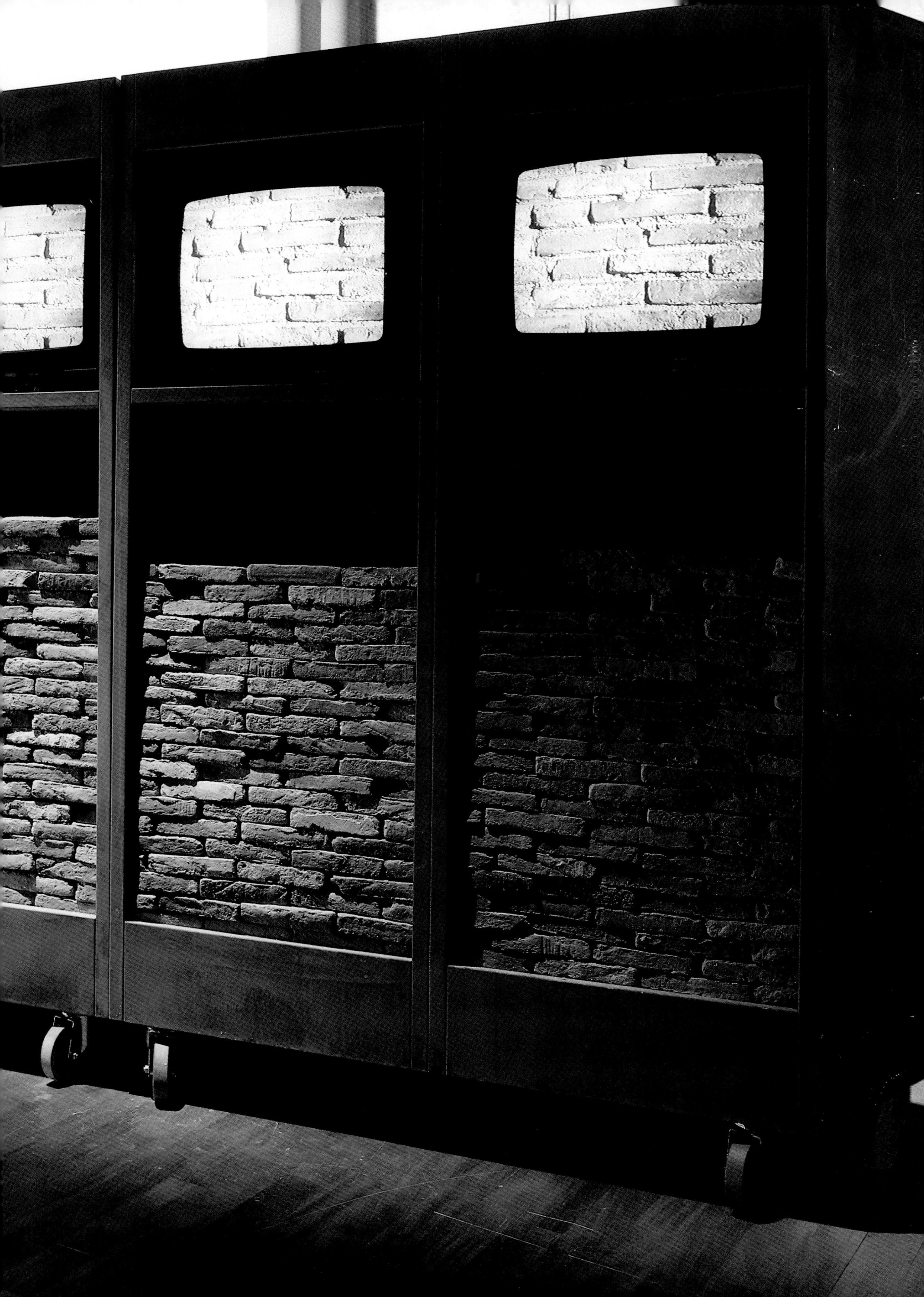

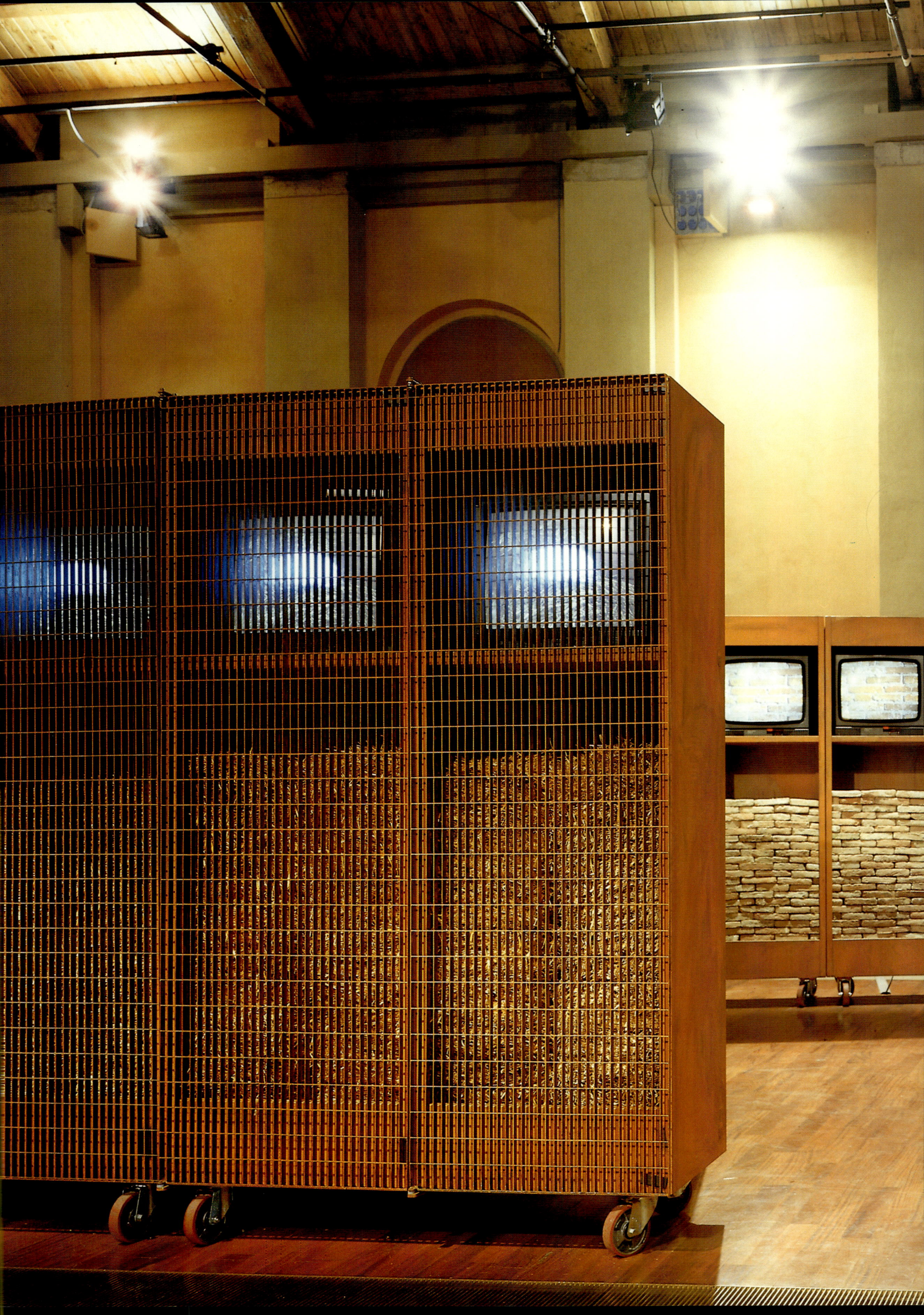

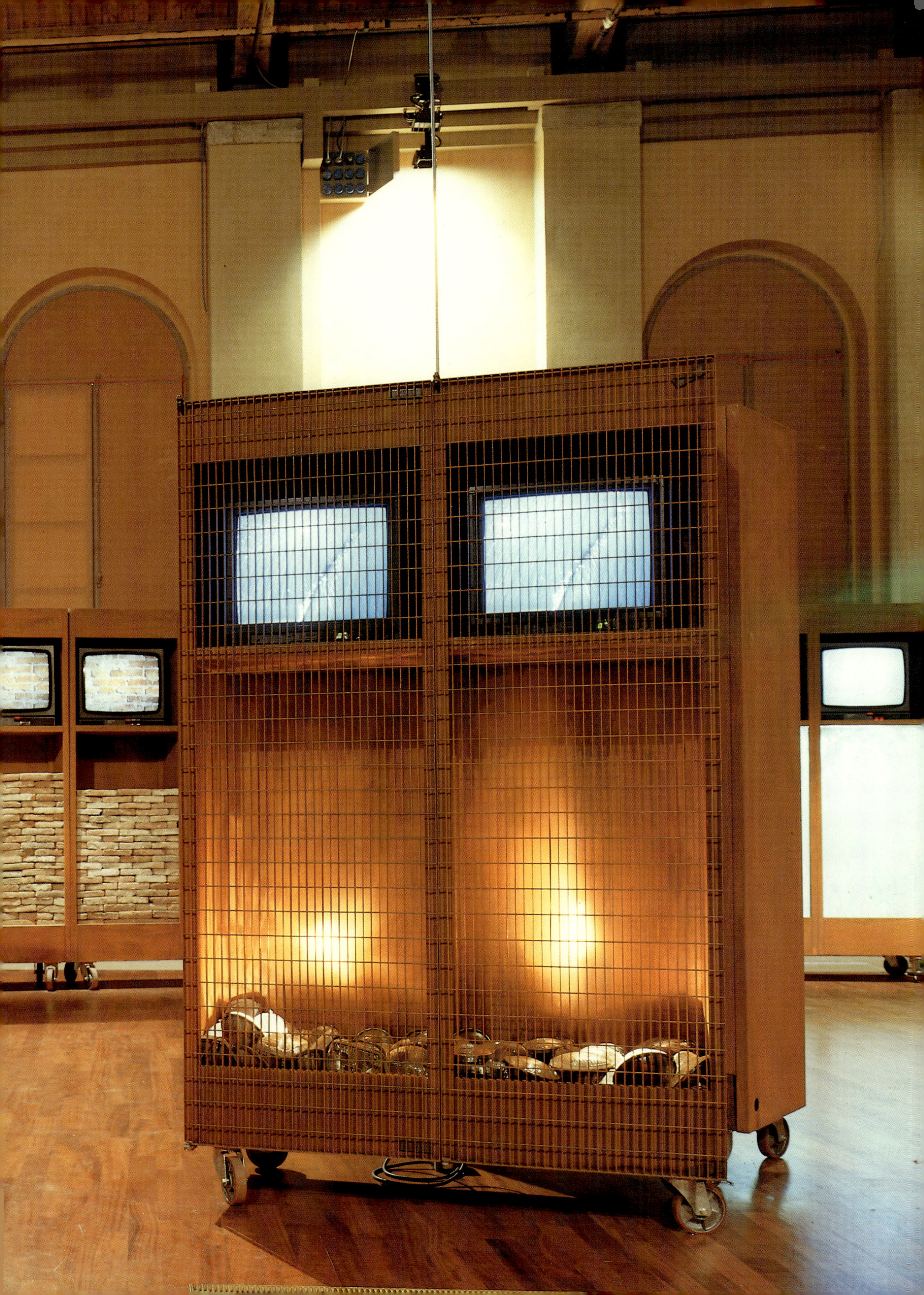

Abgesehen vom Titel der Arbeit und den Videofilmen liegt ein bemerkenswerter Unterschied zwischen diesem *Schrank des Architekten* und dem *Schrank der Steine* (s.o.), auch darin, daß die Steine selbst in gewisser Weise eine geometrische Form haben, als Backsteine geformt sind, zudem konstruktiv aufeinandergeschichtet und damit eine regelmäßige Struktur bilden, während die Steine von dem *Schrank der Steine* eher organisch wirken und eine informelle Struktur innerhalb der Schränke ausbilden.

another significant difference between this cabinet and the Cabinet of Stones (s.a.) is that the stones themselves have, to a certain degree, a geometric form, are moulded as bricks, constructively piled on one another, thus forming a regular structure, whereas the stones in the Cabinet of Stones give a rather organic impression, taking on an informal structure inside their container.

A parte il titolo e le immagini dei videofilms esiste un'altra differenza notevole fra *L'Armadio dei Sassi* e *L'Armadio dell'Architetto*: i mattoni in sè posseggono in un certo modo una forma geometrica e sono posati a strati formando una struttura regolare in contrasto con i sassi dell'*Armadio dei Sassi* che appaiono più organici conferendo agli armadi una struttura informale.

L'ARMADIO DELLA LUCE

90004

REGGIO EMILIA 1990
Museo Civico d'Arte Moderna
90004.1

SCHRANK DES LICHTS
Videoskulptur 1990
Eisenschränke mit Fächern,
Eisengitter, Neonröhren,
4 Monitore, Videorecorder,
bespielte Kassetten
260 x 320 x 60 cm

CABINET OF LIGHT
Video sculpture 1990
Iron construction with
compartments, iron lattice, neon
tubes, 4 monitors, video recorders,
recorded video cassettes
260 x 320 x 60 cm

L'ARMADIO DELLA LUCE
Videoscultura 1990
Struttura a scomparti in ferro,
grigliato industriale, neon,
4 monitors, vhs, cassette
registrate
260 x 320 x 60 cm

Der *Schrank des Lichtes* nimmt im Werk Fabrizio Plessis in gewisser Weise eine Sonderstellung ein, denn abgesehen davon, daß die Neonröhren und Neonstäbe, die hier im unteren Teil des Schrankes angebracht sind und sich in den Monitoren zu spiegeln scheinen, bereits in zahlreichen Projekten für Aktionen in den 70er Jahren eine Rolle spielten, als Video und Videofilme für Fabrizio Plessi sein Basismaterial bildeten, ist dieses Gehäuse sicher auch zu verstehen als eine Reminiszenz, eine Erinnerung an die frühen Neoninstallationen, die sich noch in realem Wasser spiegelten, wie das Wort ›WATER‹ in Duisburg oder ›EAU‹ in Lyon. Zugleich ist es eine Reminiszenz an frühe Videoskulpturen aus der ersten Hälfte der 80er Jahre, wie *Narziß* mit dem schwingenden Neonpendel oder *Arco Liquido* mit dem Neonbogen, der sich im Wasser spiegelt.

Auch hier ergibt sich wieder ein dialektischer Kontrast. Neon ist nie romantisch, weder als Material, noch in der Form oder in der Assoziation. Es gibt nur Linien und keine Flächen, manchmal bedeuten sie Schrift. Doch hier in dieser Videoskulptur wird sichtbar, wie sich plötzlich die Lichtlinie ins Immaterielle aufzulösen scheint und es wird deutlich: Licht ist nicht greifbar, nicht faßbar. Der Übergang zur Dunkelheit ist stufenlos.

Dieser *Schrank des Lichtes* gehört sicher zu Plessis konzeptu-

The Cabinet of Light *takes up a certain special position in Fabrizio Plessi's work, for, apart from the fact that the neon tubes and staffs that are fixed in the lower part and seem to mirror in the monitors played a role in numerous projects for events in the seventies, when video and video films were his main materials, this casing can certainly be understood as a reminiscence, a memory of earlier neon installations that still reflected in real water, like the words 'WATER' in Duisburg or 'EAU' in Lyon. At the same time it is a reminiscence of video sculptures from the first half of the eighties, like* Narcissus *with the swinging neon pendulum, or* Arco Liquido, *its neon arch mirroring in the water.*

Here, too, we find a dialectic contrast: neon is never romantic, neither as material nor in form or association. There are only lines, no planes; sometimes they represent writing. Yet in this video sculpture we see how all of a sudden the line of light seems to dissolve in immateriality, and it becomes clear: light is not tangible. The transition to darkness is not gradual.

This Cabinet of Light *certainly belongs to Plessi's most conceptual works, and is, at the same time, a symbol of the artist's relation to video. His relation to light, to neon light, results in his relation to video.*

L'Armadio della Luce occupa in certo qual modo una posizione particolare nell'opera di Fabrizio Plessi. Oltre il fatto che i tubi al neon, collocati in basso nell'armadio e che si riflettono nei monitors, sono già stati impiegati in numerosi progetti e azioni degli anni settanta costituendo quale videofilms il materiale di base, questa videoinstallazione è da considerare sicuramente anche una reminiscenza, un ricordo delle prime installazioni al neon che si riflettevano ancora nell'acqua reale, come la parola ›WATER‹ a Duisburg o ›EAU‹, a Lione. Nello stesso momento rappresenta una reminiscenza delle prime videoinstallazioni della prima metà degli anni ottanta, come *Narciso* con il pendolo al neon oscillante o *Arco Liquido* con l'arco al neon che si riflette nell'acqua.

Ancora una volta si crea un contrasto dialettico. Il neon non è mai romantico, nè come materiale nè nella forma o nelle associazioni. Esistono solo linee e piccole aree che di quando in quando significano scrittura. Ma qui, in questa videoscultura, si assiste al fenomeno che la linea al neon sembra sciogliersi all'improvviso e si apprende: la luce non è palpabile. Il passaggio all'oscurità è continuo, senza sbalzi.

L'Armadio della Luce è forse uno dei lavori più concettuali di

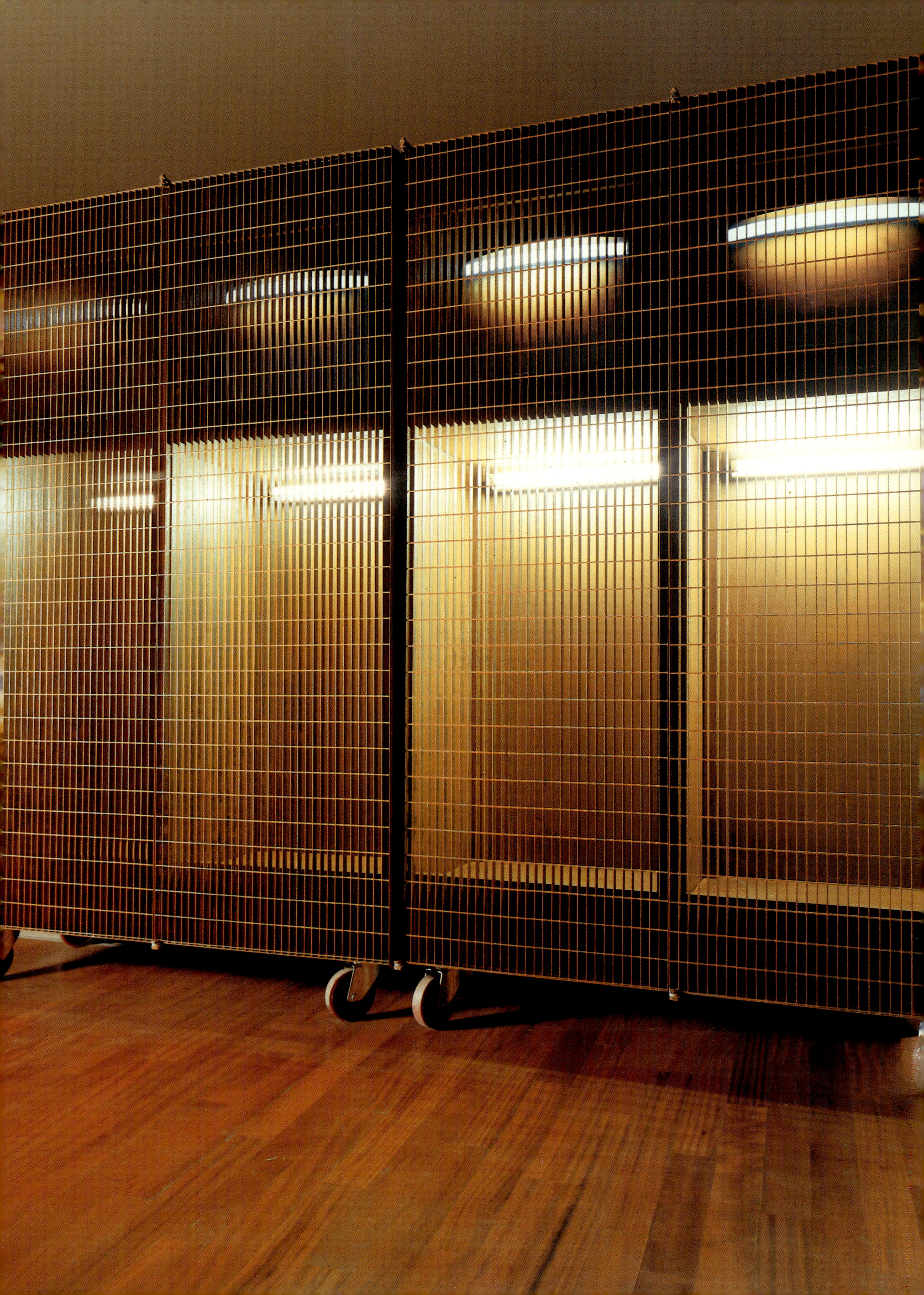

ellsten Arbeiten und ist doch
zugleich ein Sinnbild für des
Künstlers Verhältnis zum Video.
Aus seiner Beziehung zum Licht,
zum Neonlicht, resultiert letztendlich seine Beziehung zum Video.
»Von der Affinität zwischen Wasser
und Licht her kommt schließlich
auch die Verbindung Wasser und
Video zustande, die mehr ist als
lediglich der Einsatz eines weiteren anderen Mediums. Plessi
lapidar: »Beides bewegt sich!«
(Hans Gercke, in: Katalog Skulpturen-Museum Glaskasten, Marl
1984) Neon an sich ist unprätenti-
ös, eine starre, nicht besonders
schöne Röhre, die aber, und hier
liegt das Interesse Fabrizio Plessis,
sobald sie zu leuchten beginnt, die
Qualität einer nichtstofflichen
Erscheinung erhält und damit
zugleich die Grenzen ihrer fakti-
schen Gestalt auflöst.

Nicht nur das Entstehen und
Leben seiner gesamten Videoinstal-
lation und Videoskulpturen ver-
dankt Fabrizio Plessi dem Licht.
Schon in der alttestamentarischen
Schöpfungsgeschichte beginnt die
Erschaffung der Welt mit der
Erschaffung des Lichts. »Und Gott
sprach: Es werde Licht. Und es
ward Licht. Und Gott sah, daß das
Licht gut war. Und Gott schied das
Licht von der Finsternis. Und Gott
nannte das Licht Tag und die
Finsternis nannte er Nacht.«
(Genesis, 1,3 bis 5) Und an anderer
Stelle, im Johannes-Prolog, heißt
es: »Im Anfang war das Wort und
das Wort war bei Gott und das Wort
war Gott. Im Anfang war es bei
Gott. Alles ist durch das Wort
geworden und ohne das Wort
wurde nichts, was geworden ist. In
ihm war das Leben und das Leben
war das Licht der Menschen. Und
das Licht leuchtet in der Finsternis.« (Johannes, 1,1 bis 5) Auch bei
Plessi steht das Neonwort, das
Lichtwort, am Anfang seiner
Skulpturen mit Licht und Video.

*"The affinity of water and light
leads to the combination of
water and video that is more
than the mere use of an additional medium. Plessi remarks:
"Both move!" (Hans Gercke, in:
catalogue Sculpture-Museum
Glaskasten, Marl 1984) Neon is,
in itself, unpretentious, a stiff,
not especially pretty tube,
which, however, and that
causes Plessi's interest in it,
takes on the quality of an
immaterial apparition once it
starts to shine, at that time
dissolving the boundaries of its
factual form.*

*Fabrizio Plessi not only owes
creation and life of all of his
video installations and video
sculptures to light. In the Old
Testament, Genesis, the creation
of the world, begins with the
creation of light. "And God
said: Let there be light. And
there was light. And God saw
that the light was good. And
God divided light from darkness. And God called the light
day, and he called darkness
night." (Genesis, 1,3 - 5) And
elsewhere, in the prologue to
John, it is written: "At the
beginning there was the word,
and the word was God. At the
beginning it was with God. All
things were made through it,
and without it nothing was
made that was made. In it was
life, and the life was the light of
men. The light shines in the
darkness." (John, 1,1 - 5) In
Plessi's work, the neon word,
the light word, stands at the
beginning of his sculptures with
light and video.*

Plessi e nello stesso tempo il
simbolo dell'approccio
dell'artista al video; dal suo
rapporto con la luce, la luce al
neon, risulta alla fin fine quello
con il video. »Dall'affinità fra
acqua e luce nasce infine anche
il collegamento tra acqua e
video che è molto più del semplice impiego di un ulteriore
›medium‹ diverso. Plessi dice
concisamente: Ambedue si
muovono!« (Hans Gercke, in:
catalogo Skulpturen-Museum
Glaskasten, Marl 1984). Il neon
in sè non è pretenzioso, è un
tubo rigido e non particolar-
mente bello che però, e qui
l'interesse di Plessi, assume
appena si illumina un'apparenza
immateriale che immediatamente annulla i confini della sua
forma effettiva.

Non solo Fabrizio Plessi deve
la nascita e la vita di tutte le sue
videoinstallazioni e videosculture alla luce. Già nella Genesi
del Vecchio Testamento la
creazione del mondo inizia con
quella della luce. »E Dio disse:
›Sia la luce!‹. E la luce fu. Dio
vide che la luce era cosa buona
e separò la luce dalle tenebre e
chiamò la luce Giorno e le
tenebre Notte« (Genesi, 1,3-5). E
nel Vangelo secondo Giovanni si
legge: »In principio era il Verbo,
il Verbo era presso Dio e il
Verbo era Dio. Egli era in principio presso Dio: tutto è stato
fatto per mezzo di lui, e senza di
lui niente è stato fatto di tutto
ciò che esiste. In lui era la vita e
la vita era la luce degli uomini;
la luce splende nelle tenebre«
(Prologo, 1,1-5). Anche
nell'opera di Plessi la parola, la
parola al neon, è il principio
delle sue sculture di luce e
video.

L'ARMADIO DELLA PAGLIA

90005

REGGIO EMILIA 1990
MUSEO CIVICO D'ARTE MODERNA
90005.1

TRENTO 1990
GALLERIA CIVICA DI ARTE CONTEMPORANEA
90005.2

SCHRANK MIT STROH
Videoskulptur 1990
Eisenschränke mit Fächern,
Eisengitter,dicht gepreßtes Stroh,
4 Monitore, Videorecorder,
bespielte Kassetten
260 x 320 x 60 cm

CABINET OF STRAW
Video sculpture 1990
Iron construction with
compartments, iron lattice, straw,
4 monitors, video recorders,
recorded video cassettes
260 x 320 x 60 cm

L'ARMADIO DELLA PAGLIA
Videoscultura 1990
Struttura a scomparti in ferro,
grigliato industriale, paglia
imballata, 4 monitors, vhs,
cassette registrate
260 x 320 x 60 cm

Das *Gehäuse für Stroh* scheint wieder einmal das Material in den Blickpunkt zu rücken. Strohballen und ihre regelmäßig-unregelmäßige Struktur türmen sich auf unter den Monitoren, in denen Videos ein Licht im Stroh zeigen. So leuchtet das Stroh in den Filmen feuergefährlich, beinahe, als könnte es sich im nächsten Moment entzünden. Materie und Material interessieren Plessi sehr, weil grundsätzlich nahezu alles *Materia Prima*, also *Rohstoff*, zu einem Kunstwerk bei ihm sein kann: ob natürlich wie Holz, Stroh, Stein, Marmor, oder künstlich wie die Medientechnologie von heute.

The Container for Straw *again seems to place the material into the centre. Bales of straw and their regular-irregular structure pile up below the monitors, the videos on them showing a light in the straw. Thus the straw in the films shines dangerously, as if a fire could break out any moment. Plessi is very interested in matter and material, since almost all* Materia Prima *can become a work of art with him: natural, like wood, straw, or marble, and artificial, like today' media technology.*

L'Armadio della Paglia sembra porre ancora una volta la materia al centro dell'attenzione. Balle di paglia con la loro struttura al tempo stesso regolare e irregolare si innalzano al di sotto dei monitors: questi presentano videofilmati di luce che risplende nella paglia in maniera tale da fa temere da un momento all'altro un incendio. La materia e il materiale attirano molto l'interesse di Plessi in quanto fondamentalmente tutto può diventare *Materia Prima* per un'opera d'arte, sia essa naturale come legno, paglia, pietra o marmo sia artificiale come la odierna tecnologia mediale.

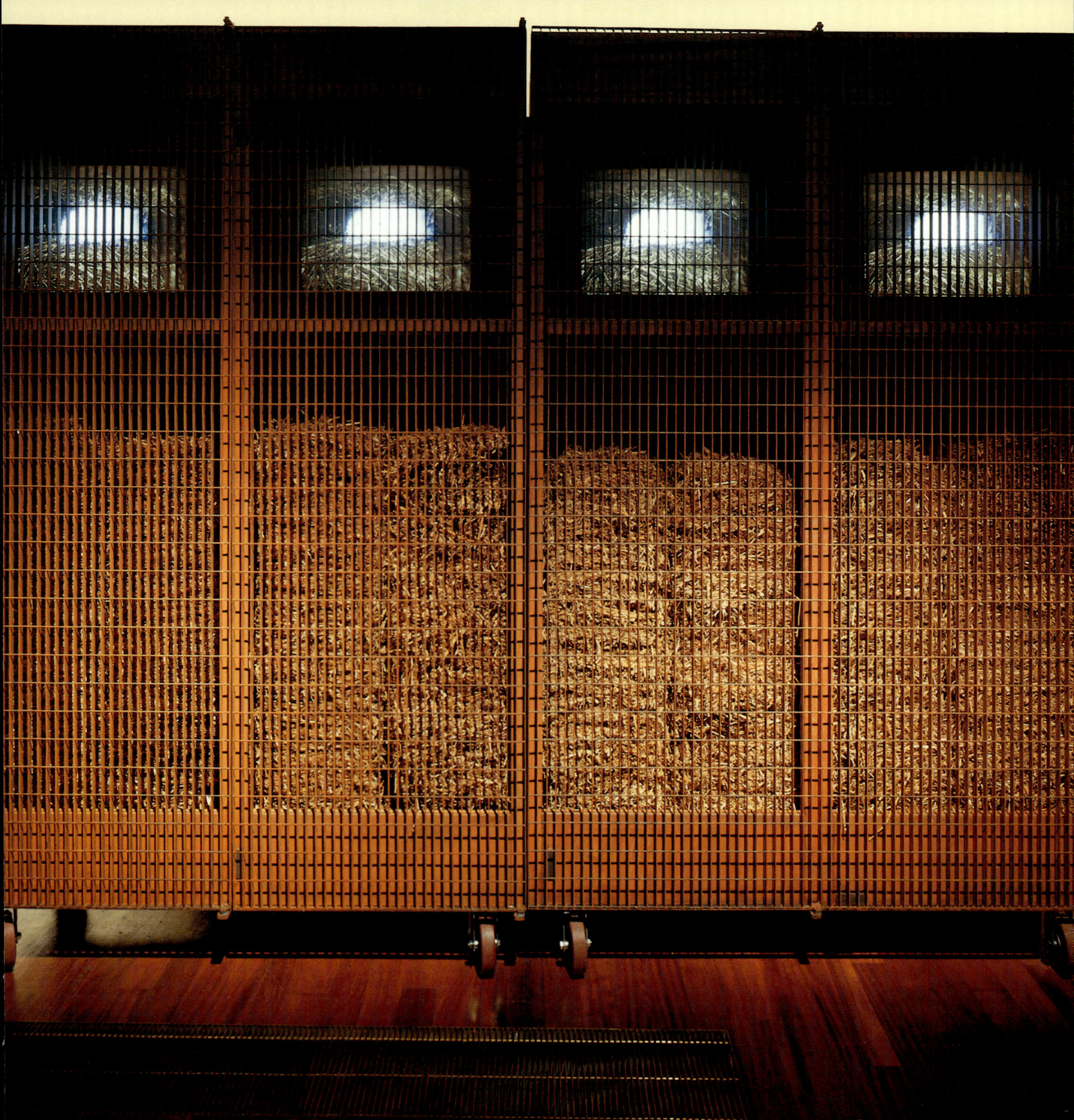

WORK IN PROGRESS

90006

REGGIO EMILIA 1990
Museo Civico d'Arte Moderna
90006.1

IN ARBEIT
Videoskulptur 1990
Eisenschränke mit Fächern, weiß
bemalte Doppelglasscheiben,
Neon, 4 Monitore,
4 Videorecorder, 4 bespielte
Kassetten
260 x 320 x 60 cm

WORK IN PROGRESS
Video sculpture 1990
Iron construction with
compartments, white painted
double glass panes, neon,
4 monitors, 4 video recorders,
4 recorded video cassettes
260 x 320 x 60 cm

LAVORO NEL PROGRESSO
Videoscultura 1990
Struttura in ferro a scomparti,
lastre dipinte di vetro doppio,
neon, 4 monitors, 4 vhs, 4 cassette
registrate
260 x 320 x 60 cm

Work in Progress zeigt einen Schrank, dessen Vorderseite aus Glasscheiben besteht, die mit weißer Farbe unregelmäßig bemalt sind. Auch die Monitore zeigen in ihrer malerischen Struktur eine Flüssigkeit in Bewegung, die synchron verläuft. Dieser Schrank versinnbildlicht einen Prozeß im Werden wie in einer Momentaufnahme, die den aktuellen Stand dokumentiert und zugleich auf das Unfertige verweist. Noch ist ungewiß, auf welches Resultat diese Handlung, die Aktion hinausläuft. Was wird das Ergebnis sein?

Dieser Schrank ist, wie in gewisser Weise auch die anderen Schränke - für den Betrachter, wie

Work in Progress *shows a cabinet the front of which is made of glass panes, painted irregularly with white paint. The monitors show - like a painting - synchronical movements of some liquid. This cabinet symbolises, as in a recording of a moment documenting the present state and hinting at the unfinished work, a process in growing. The aim is still uncertain. What will the result of this action be like?*

This cabinet is, as to a certain degree the others are, too, a sort of 'surprise-package' for spectator and artist that has to be unpacked or unveiled first to find the truth in it. For example,

Work in Progress è un armadio con il lato frontale di vetro coperto irregolarmente dal colore bianco. Anche i monitors presentano nella loro struttura pittorica un liquido in un moto sincronizzato. L'armadio rappresenta come in un'istantanea il processo del divenire, che documenta lo stato attuale indicando contemporaneamente l'incompiuto. Il risultato dell'azione ancora è incerto. Quale sarà?

L'armadio è, come in un certo modo anche gli altri, una sorta di ›scatola a sorpresa‹ sia per lo spettatore sia per l'artista che deve essere aperta per poter

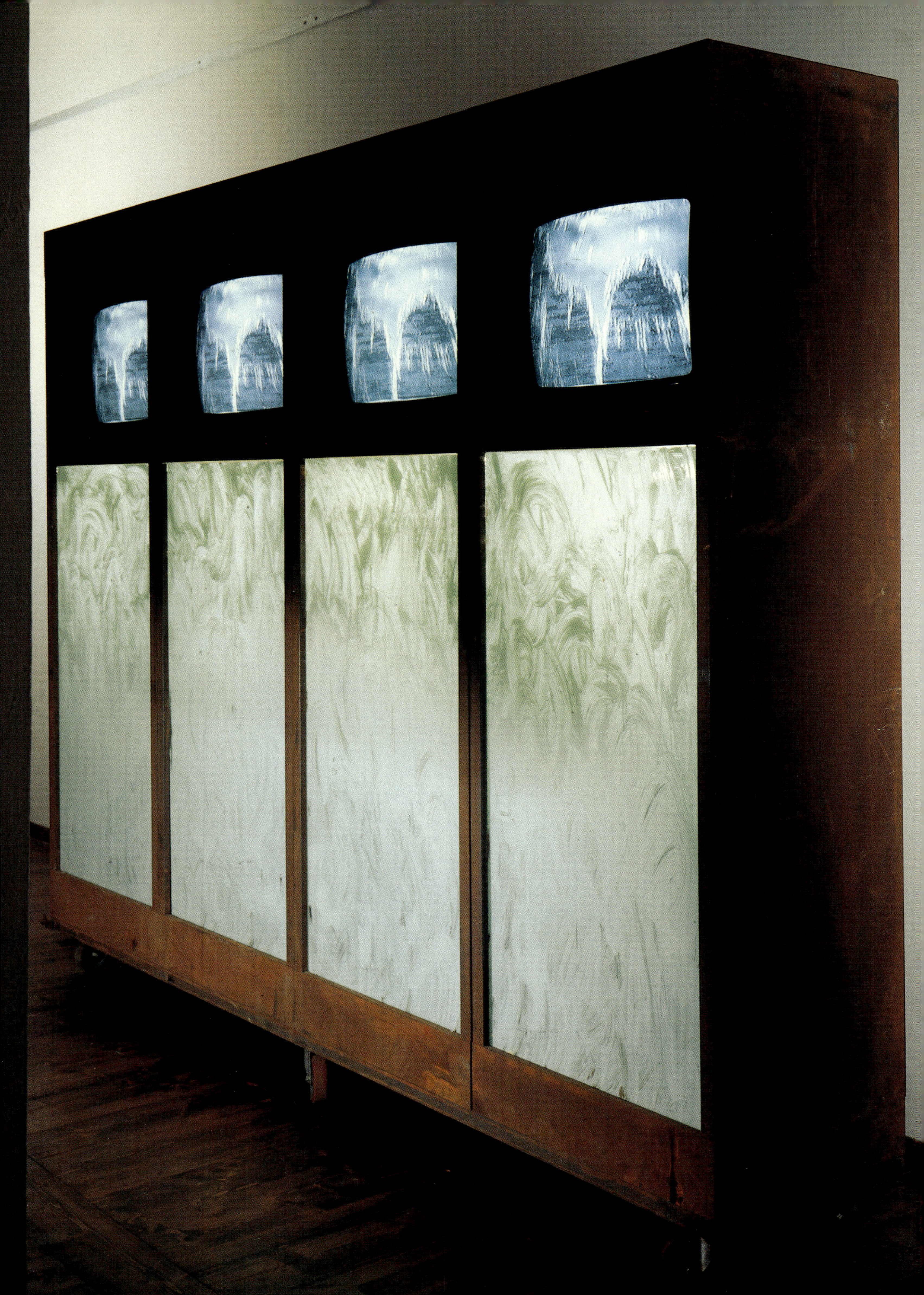

für den Künstler selbst - eine Art ›Überraschungspaket‹, das erst ausgepackt oder enthüllt werden muß, um der Wahrheit auf den Grund zu kommen. Viele der Monitore sind beispielsweise nur teilweise sichtbar, der andere Teil ist verbogen. Die Schränke leben aus der Koinzidenz der Gegensätze von Evidenz und Geheimnis. Das Wesen des Geheimnisses kann nicht aus einer wahrnehmbaren, vordergründigen Tatsache bestehen, die vielleicht in irgendeiner Weise deutbar ist, sondern das Geheimnis - oder die Faszination des Geheimnisses - entsteht dann, wenn etwas vertraut scheint, aber nicht bekannt ist. Dieses Phänomen macht auch die Faszination in der Kunst aus. Man wird durch ein Kunstwerk nur angesprochen, wenn irgend etwas in diesem Kunstwerk liegt, enthalten ist, was mit den Erfahrungen, den Erlebnissen, dem Wissen des Betrachters, seinen Wünschen und Hoffnungen zu tun hat. Etwas, das mit seinem Erfahrungsschatz in Einklang zu bringen ist, ihn daher berührt und ihm das Gefühl der Vertrautheit vermittelt. Doch zugleich muß etwas Geheimnisvolles in dem Kunstwerk stecken, etwas, das der Betrachter nicht auf den ersten Blick erkennen kann, also nicht kennt und das er zu erforschen, zu ergründen sucht. Also das Vertraute muß da sein, um die Bindung zum Kunstwerk herzustellen und das Geheimnis muß da sein, um die Bindung zu erhalten.

Das Video oder der Videofilm ist für Fabrizio Plessi nur ein Material wie jedes andere. Doch für seine Zwecke ist es ideal, weil es ein Stück der Realität vermittelt und zugleich einen irrealen, immateriellen Aspekt mit der Realität der Materie in Verbindung bringt.

many of the monitors are only partially visible, partly hidden. The cabinets live from the coincidence of the opposites of evidence and secret. The nature of a secret cannot consist of a visible, obvious fact that can be interpreted somehow, but the fascination of a secret is derived from the fact that something seems familiar, yet is not known. The same phenomenon also constitutes the fascination of art: one is only interested in a work of art if it contains something that has to do with the spectator's experiences, his knowledge, his desires and hopes, something that can be brought into the context of what he has lived through, therefore touching him and gives him the feeling of being familiar with it. Yet, at the same time the work of art has to have some secret, something the spectator cannot recognise at first glance, does not know, that he tries to discover and understand. Thus familiarity must be there to create a connection with the work of art, and a secret to uphold this connection.

For Plessi, video or video film are but material, like any other material. However, it is ideal for his purposes because it conveys some part of reality, at the same time creating a connection between an unreal, immaterial aspect and the reality of matter.

andare al fondo della verità. Alcuni monitors sono solo in parte visibili. Gli armadi si nutrono della coincidenza degli opposti, l'evidenza e il segreto. La natura del segreto non sta in un fatto percettibile a prima vista e in qualche modo interpretabile. Il segreto - o il fascino del segreto - nasce quando qualcosa sembra comune senza essere conosciuto. Lo stesso fenonemo costituisce il fascino dell'arte. Un rapporto con l'opera d'arte si instaura solo se esso contiene un elemento che ha a che fare con le esperienze, le conoscenze, i desideri e le speranze dello spettatore, qualcosa dunque che concorda con il suo bagaglio di esperienze, che lo tocca e che gli trasmette la sensazione di familiarità. Nello stesso tempo l'opera d'arte deve essere enigmatica, contenere qualcosa che per lo spettatore non è riconoscibile a prima vista, che è ignoto e lo invita ad indagare ed approfondire. In conclusione: l'opera d'arte deve incutere familiarità, confidenza per instaurare un rapporto con chi la guarda e deve essere enigmatica per mantenere tale rapporto.

Il video per Plessi non è altro che un materiale come tutti gli altri, ideale però per i suoi scopi in quanto trasmette un frammento della realtà e, contemporaneamente, mette in relazione un aspetto irreale, immateriale con la realtà della materia.

COME ERAVAMO
(OMAGGIO A PAIK)

90007

REGGIO EMILIA 1990
Museo Civico d'Arte Moderna
90007.1

WIE WIR GEWESEN SIND
(HOMMAGE À PAIK)
Videoskulptur 1990
Eisenschränke mit Fächern,
Eisengitter, 28 gebrauchte TV,
8 Monitore, 2 Videorecorder,
Kassetten, Tonaufzeichnung
260 x 640 x 60 cm

THE WAY WE WERE
(HOMAGE TO PAIK)
Video sculpture 1990
Iron construction with compart-
ments, iron lattice, 28 used TVs,
8 monitors, 2 video recorders,
video cassettes, soundrecording
260 x 640 x 60 cm

COME ERAVAMO
(OMAGGIO A PAIK)
Videoscultura 1990
Struttura a scomparti in ferro,
grigliato industriale, 28 televisori
vecchi, 8 monitors, 2 vhs, cassette
registrate, sonoro
260 x 640 x 60 cm

Eine große Reihe von Plessi-Schränken ist gefüllt mit horizontal und vertikal liegenden Fernsehern aus den 50er Jahren. In den darüberliegenden Monitoren erscheinen als Videofilm wiederum Monitore, hier jedoch schräg gestellt, die verzerrte Bilder zeigen. *Come eravamo (Wie wir gewesen sind)* ist der Titel dieser Arbeit, die unmittelbar den Bezug zur Nachkriegszeit herstellt, als die ersten Fernseher in Europa zunächst in die bürgerlichen Haushalte einzogen, um wenig später zu Kunstobjekten benutzt oder auch verwandelt zu werden. Mit der Entwicklung moderner Videotechnologie in den 60er und 70er Jahren konnte sich ein neues Kunstmedium durch das Fernsehen ausbilden, das in Form der

A long row of Plessi-cabinets is filled with TV sets from the fifties lying horizontally and vertically inside. On the monitors above them one can see films showing more monitors, standing askew, showing distorted pictures. Come eravamo (The Way we were) *is its title, referring directly to the post-war period when the first TV sets arrived in European middle-class households, to be soon after employed as or turned into objects of art. With the development of modern video technology in the sixties and seventies a new form of artistic medium could grow, and become more and more important in the form of video art and electronic art. The neo-dadaist action- and object*

Un grande numero di armadi è riempito di televisori degli anni cinquanta. Nella parte superiore altri monitors presentano un filmato con ancora altri monitors in posizione obliqua con immagini distorte. *Come eravamo*, così il titolo, crea un rapporto diretto con il dopoguerra quando i primi televisori entrarono innanzi tutto nelle case della borghesia per poi, poco più tardi, essere usati o trasformati in oggetti d'arte. Con l'evoluzione delle videotecnologie moderne si potè sviluppare, negli anni sessanta e settanta, un nuovo medium artistico che acquistò nella forma della Video-Art e della Electronic-Art una grande importanza. Fu soprattutto l'arte

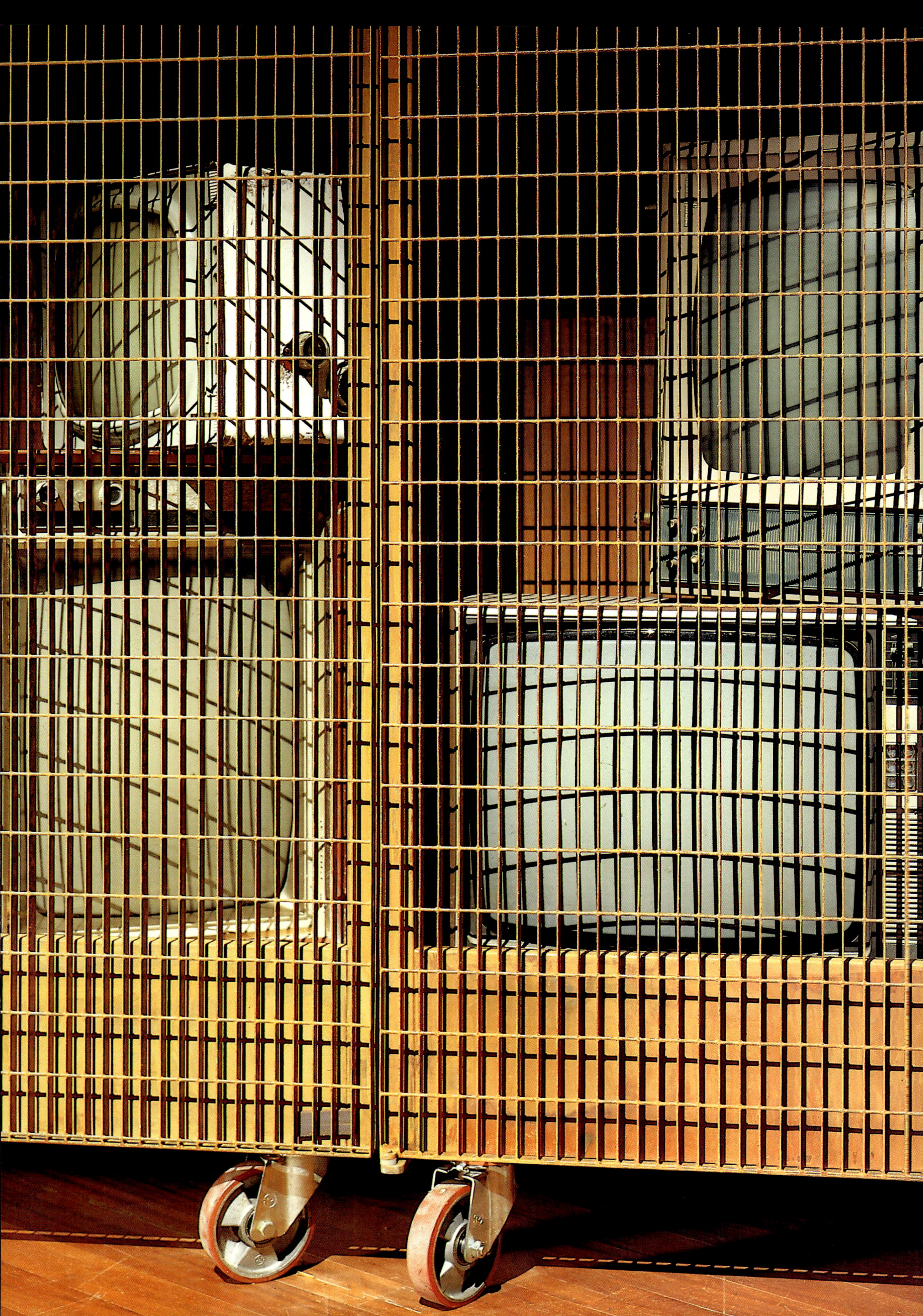

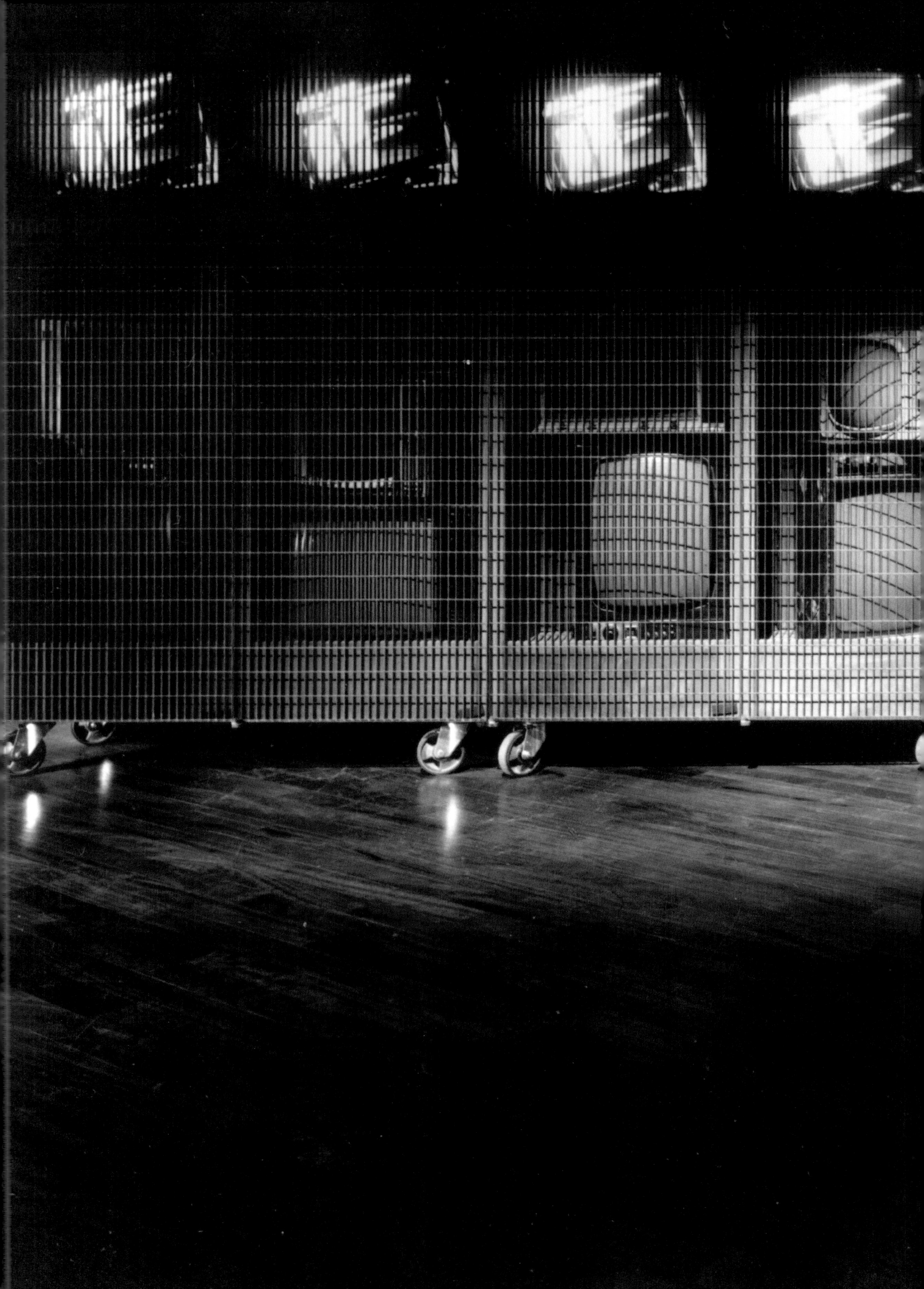

Video-Art und Electronic-Art eine
große Bedeutung erlangte. Vor
allem die neodadaistische Aktions-
und Objektkunst integrierte den
Fernsehapparat in ihre Produktio-
nen (Wolf Vostell und Edward
Kienholz). 1963 schließlich verwendeten Nam June Paik und Wolf
Vostell die technischen Mittel des
elektronischen Fernsehens als
bildnerisches Medium, indem sie
Fernsehbilder durch Manipulation
des elektromagnetischen Feldes
verzerrten und dadurch die normalen Bilder in abstrakte Sequenzen
überführten. Auf genau diese
künstlerische Handlung verweist
die Videodarstellung in dieser
Skulptur, und so ist es nicht ver-
wunderlich, daß der Untertitel
dieser Arbeit *Hommage a Paik*
lautet, denn durch diesen Künstler
erlebte die Videotechnik 1969 den
eigentlichen Durchbruch in die
Kunstszene, im selben Jahr, als
auch die erste, ausschließlich der
Video-Art gewidmete Ausstellung
mit dem Titel *TV is the creative
medium* in der New Yorker Howard
Wise Gallery stattfand. Zu Beginn
der 70er Jahre entwickelt Paik
dann die ersten TV-Skulpturen, und
so wurde im Laufe der 70er Jahre -
vor allem für die Künstler, die mit
Aktionen und Performances arbei-
teten - das Video ein wichtiges
Instrumentarium, um künstlerische
Intentionen zum Ausdruck zu
bringen, zu formulieren und zugleich zu dokumentieren. Eben
diesen Weg hat auch Plessi genom-
men: über die experimentellen
Filme, die zunächst in einem, dann
in mehreren übereinander gestellten Monitoren anläßlich einer
Ausstellung gezeigt wurden und
schließlich in Videoinstallationen
selbst Einzug nahmen.

*art, especially, integrated the
TV set in its productions (Wolf
Vostell and Edward Kienholz).
In 1963, Nam June Paik and
Wolf Vostell employed the
technical means of electronic
television as artistic medium by
distorting TV images through
manipulation of the electro-
magnetic fields, thus transfor-
ming the regular images into
abstract sequences. The video
picture in this sculpture points
to exactly this artistic action,
and it is therefore not surprising that the subtitle of this
work is* Homage to Paik, *for it
was this artist through whom
video technology broke into the
art scene in 1960, the same year
the first exhibition solely devoted to video art took place in
New York's Howard Wise Gallery under the title* TV is the
creative medium. *At the beginning of the seventies, Paik
develops the first video sculptures, and so video became -
especially for those artists who
worked with actions and performances - an important instru-
ment to express and formulate
artistic intentions, and to
document them at the same
time. Plessi has followed this
path, too: from experimental
films, at first shown on one,
then on several monitors placed
one upon another in an exhibition to complete, independent
video installations.*

oggettuale e delle azioni neoda-
daista che integrò il televisore
nelle sue produzioni (Wolf
Vostell e Edward Kienholz). Nel
1963 infine Nam June Paik e
Wolf Vostell impiegarono i
mezzi tecnici della televisione
elettronica come medium artistico distorcendo le immagini
televisive attraverso la manipo-
lazione del campo elettroma-
gnetico e trasformando immagini normali in sequenze astratte.
Il videofilmato di *Come eravamo*
allude proprio a quell'azione
artistica e non meraviglia il
fatto che l'opera è sottotitolata
Omaggio a Paik, perchè proprio
con tale artista la videotecnica
fa il suo ingresso nel mondo
dell'arte nel 1969, anno in cui
ebbe luogo presso la Howard
Wise Gallery di New York la
prima mostra interamente
dedicata alla videoarte: *TV is the
Creative Medium*. Poi, all'inizio
degli anni settanta, Paik ideò le
prime sculture TV e il video
divenne nel corso degli stessi
anni uno strumento di primaria
importanza - soprattutto per
quegli artisti che si espressero
con azioni e performances - per
trasportare, formulare e nello
stesso tempo documentare i
concetti artistici. Plessi ha
percorso la stessa strada: attraverso films sperimentali che
furono presentati inizialmente
in un solo monitor e, in occasione di una mostra, in più monitors per approdare infine alle
videoinstallazioni vere e
proprie.

L'ARMADIO DI WASSERWAGEN

90008

REGGIO EMILIA 1990
Museo Civico d'Arte Moderna
90008.1

HAMBURG 1995
Premiere, ›Studio Moore‹
90008.2

SCHRANK DES WASSERWAGENS
Videoskulptur 1990
Eisenschränke mit Fächern,
Eisengitter, alte VW Autoschein-
werfer, Scheinwerferlicht,
2 Monitore, Videorecorder,
bespielte Kassetten
260 x 160 x 60 cm

CABINET OF THE WATER CAR
Video sculpture 1990
Iron construction with
compartments, iron lattice, old
Volkswagen headlamps, spotlight,
2 monitors, video recorders,
recorded video cassettes
260 x 160 x 60 cm

L'ARMADIO DI WASSERWAGEN
Videoscultura 1990
Struttura a scomparti in ferro, fari
vecchi dei automobili, luce,
2 monitors, vhs, cassette
registrate
260 x 160 x 60 cm

Der *Armadio di Wasserwagen*
verweist nicht nur auf die etwa
10 Jahre zurückliegende Installation *Wasserwagen*, bei dem Video-
Scheibenwischer elektronisches
Wasser auf einer imaginären
Windschutzscheibe wegzuwischen
versuchen, sondern basiert im
wesentlichen auf dem Film *Wipers*
aus der Serie *Underwater*.

Zuerst gab es nur die elektronischen Scheibenwischer mit dem
elektronischen Wasser, dann
wurden diese per Monitor in
Volkswagen-Automobile (›Käfer‹)
eingebaut, und schließlich sind nur
noch die Videofilme von den im
Regen wischenden Scheibenwi-
schern in den Monitoren der
Schränke übriggeblieben. Ein
kleines wehmütiges Erinnerungs-
utensil, das den Realitätsbezug
dieser Arbeit wieder herstellt, sind
die Scheinwerfer der alten ›Käfer‹,
die sich in dem unteren Schrankteil befinden und wie Augen
manchmal zu leuchten scheinen.

Armadio di Wasserwagen *not*
only refers to the installation
Wasserwagen *dating back ten*
years, in which video windshield
wipers tried to wipe imaginary
water from an imaginary winds-
hield but is also based on the
film Wipers *from the series*
Underwater.

First there were only the
electronic windshield wipers and
the electronic water, then these
were built into Volkswagen cars
('Beetles') via monitor, and
finally only the video films of the
windshield wipers washing in
the rain are left on the monitors
in the cabinets. A small, melan-
cholic utensil of reminiscence,
recreating the reference to reality
of this work, are the headlights
of the old 'beetles' that are
placed at the bottom of the
cabinets, sometimes appearing to
glow.

L'Armadio di Wasserwagen
non rimanda solamente alla
videoinstallazione *Wasserwagen*
di dieci anni prima dove video-
tergicristalli liberano il parabrezza immaginario dall'acqua
elettronica, ma si basa innanzi
tutto sul film *Wipers* della serie
Underwater.

All'inizio c'erano solo i
tergicristalli elettronici con
l'acqua elettronica che poi sono
stati inseriti, con l'impiego dei
monitors, in un'automobile
(›Maggiolino‹) per ridursi infine
ai videofilms dei tergicristalli
azionati dei monitors degli
armadi. I fari dei vecchi ›Maggiolini‹ della parte inferiore
dell'armadio che, come occhi si
illuminano di tanto in tanto
costituiscono un ricordo malin-
conico che ristabilisce il rapporto dell'opera con la realtà.

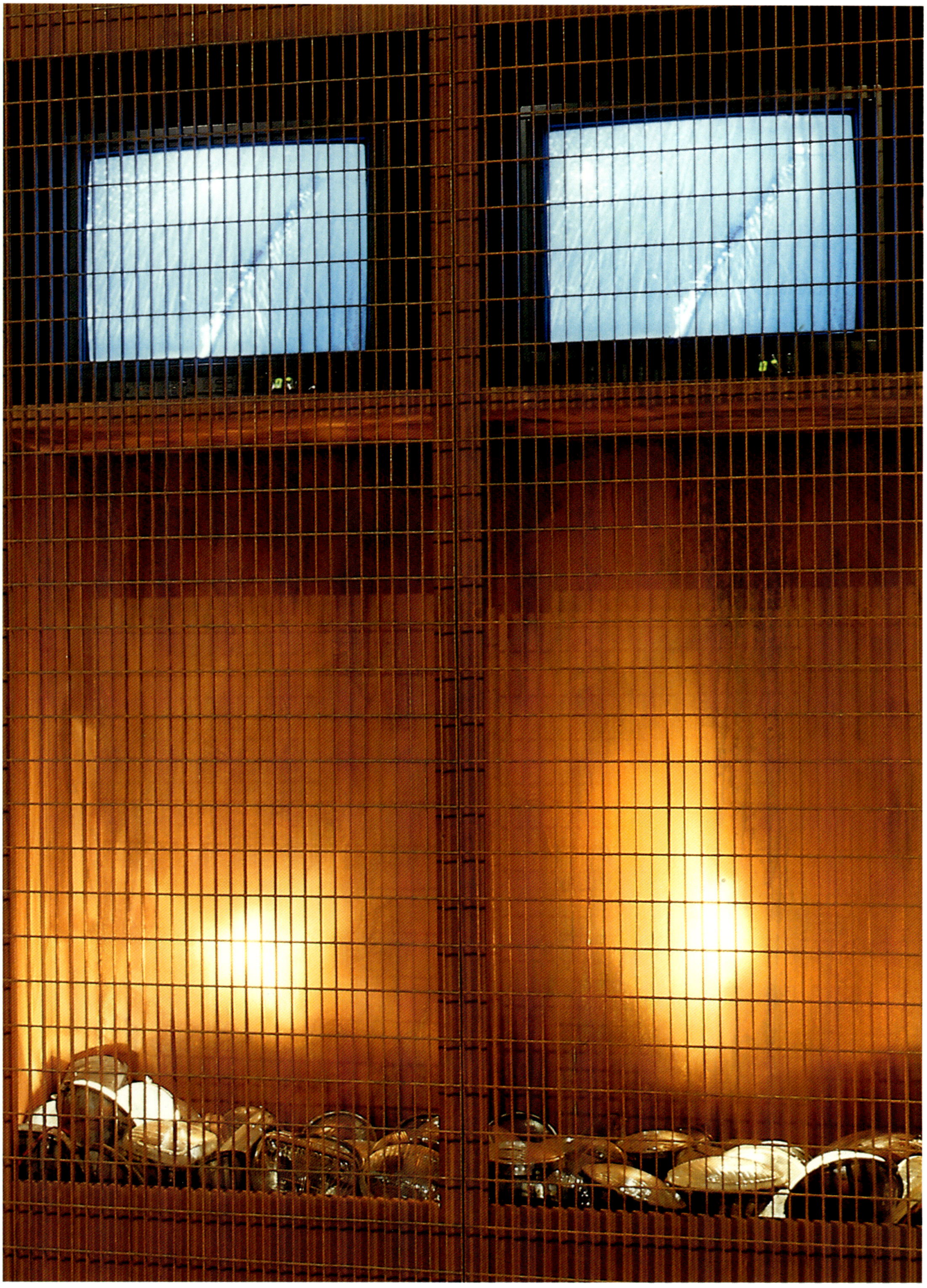

L'ARMADIO DELLE SCATOLE

90009

REGGIO EMILIA 1990
Museo Civico d'Arte Moderna
90009.1

SCHRANK DER SCHACHTELN
Videoskulptur 1990
Eisenschränke mit Fächern,
Eisengitter, 120 Schachteln aus
weißem Karton, 4 Monitore,
1 Videorecorder, bespielte
Kassetten
260 x 320 x 60 cm

CABINET OF BOXES
Video sculpture 1990
Iron construction with
compartments, iron lattice,
120 white cardboard boxes,
4 monitors, 1 video recorder,
recorded video cassettes
260 x 320 x 60 cm

L'ARMADIO DELLE SCATOLE
Videoscultura 1990
Struttura in ferro a scomparti,
grigliato industriale in ferro,
120 scatole di cartone bianche,
4 monitors, 1 vhs, cassette
registrate
260 x 320 x 60 cm

Der *Schrank der Schachteln*
(*Armadio delle Scatole*), der auf
den ersten Blick eine tautologische Assoziation hervorruft,
nämlich die Schachtel in der
Schachtel, hat bei genauerem
Hinsehen einen weitreichenden
kunsthistorischen Bezug. Im
ausgehenden 13. Jh. und begin-
nenden 14. Jh. hat der italienische
Maler und Baumeister Giotto die
gesamte Stilbewegung des 14. Jh.
beeinflußt und geprägt durch
seine Überwindung der unräumli-
chen Gestaltungsweise der älteren
Malerei des Mittelalters - wie
auch noch der seines Lehrers
Cimabue -, in dem er jeweils
einen Raum (eine ›Scatola Giottesca‹) in seine Bildgeschehen
einbaute und dadurch eine Bühne
mit Davor und Dahinter, also

Armadio delle Scatole, *the*
Cabinet of Boxes - *creating at
first a tautological association of
box in a box - has, at second
glance a far-reaching reference
to the history of art. At the end of
the 13th and beginning of the
14th century the Italian painter
and architect Giotto influenced
and changed the style of the 14th
century through his transgressi-
on of the two-dimensional mode
of middle-age painting - still
practised by his teacher Cimabue
- by including space ('Scatola
Giottesca') in each of his depic-
ted scenes, thus creating a stage
with in front and behind, that is
near and far, thus arriving at
the effect of perspective.*

*Fabrizio Plessi stands wholly
in this tradition. He, too, creates*

L'Armadio delle Scatole
richiama in un primo momento
un'associazione tautologica,
cioè la scatola nella scatola, in
un secondo momento svela però
un vasto retroscena storico-
artistico. Fra la fine del XIII e
l'inizio del XIV secolo il pittore
e architetto italiano Giotto
influenzò l'intero linguaggio
stilistico del XIV secolo con il
superamento della non-spazia-
lità della pittura medievale,
inclusa quella del suo maestro
Cimabue, inserendo nelle sue
scene uno spazio, la ›Scatola
Giottesca‹, e creando così un
palcoscenico con un davanti e
un dietro, cioè con vicinanza e
lontananza, che suggerisce un
effetto di prospettiva.

Fabrizio Plessi si inserisce in

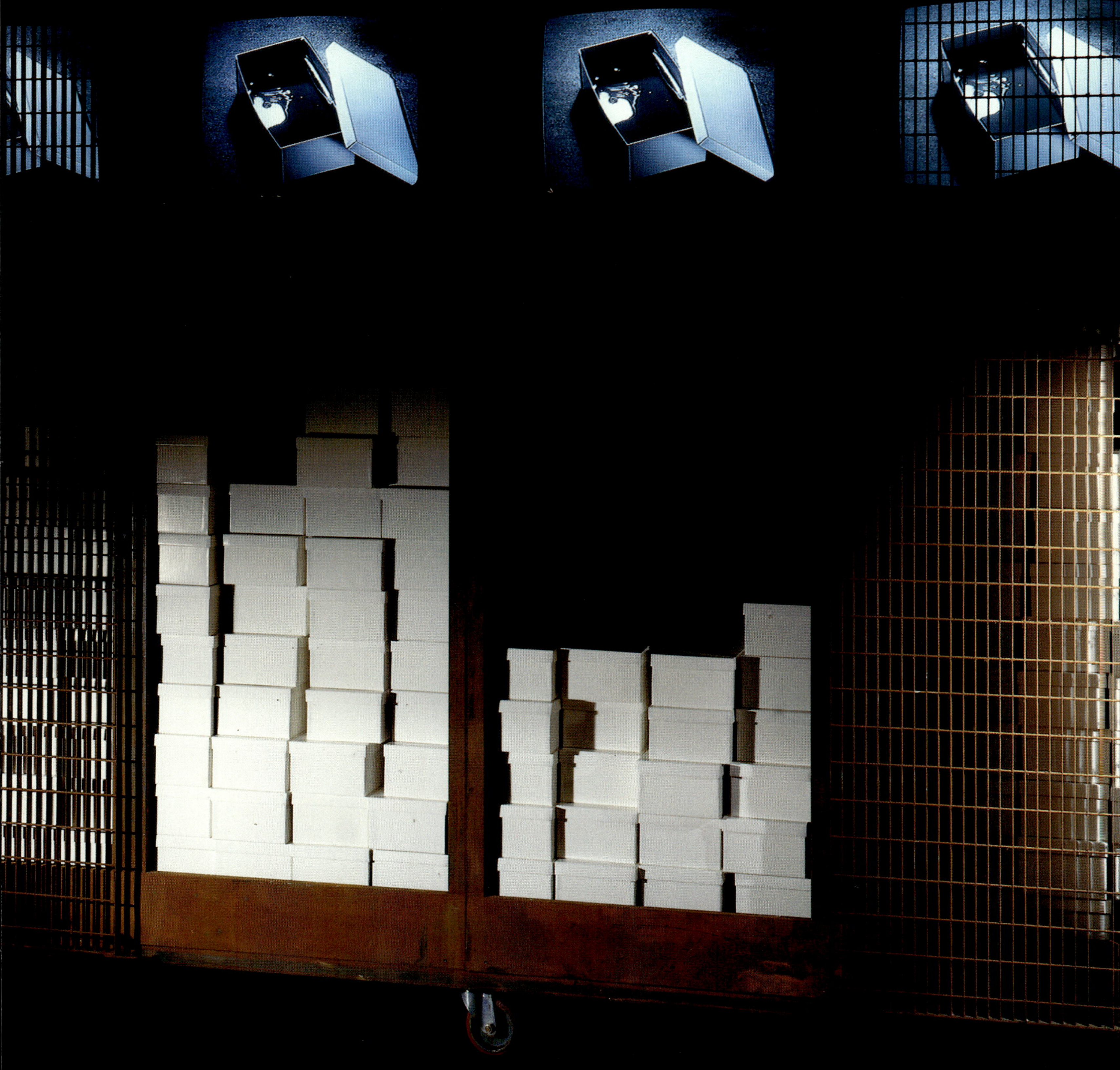

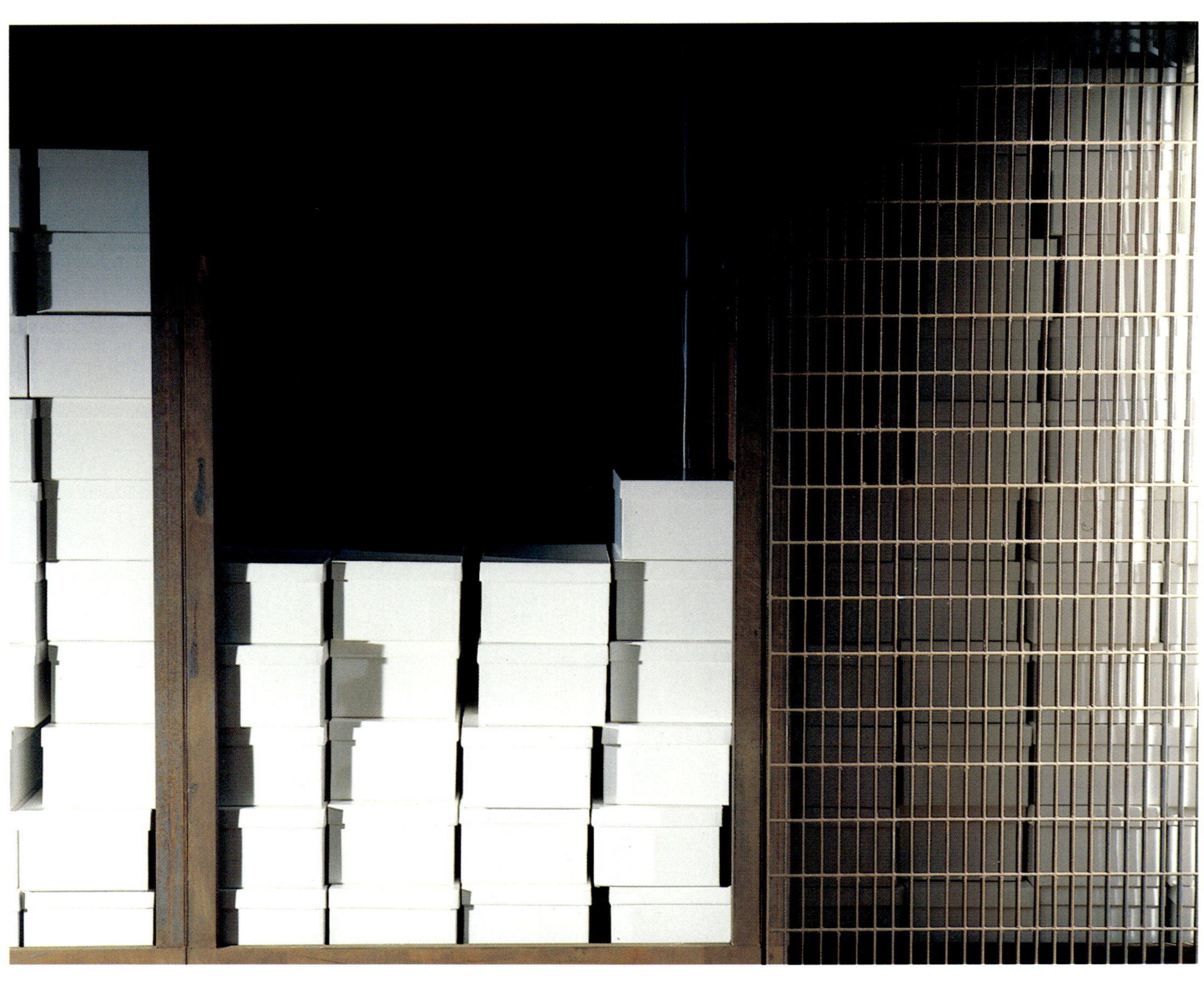

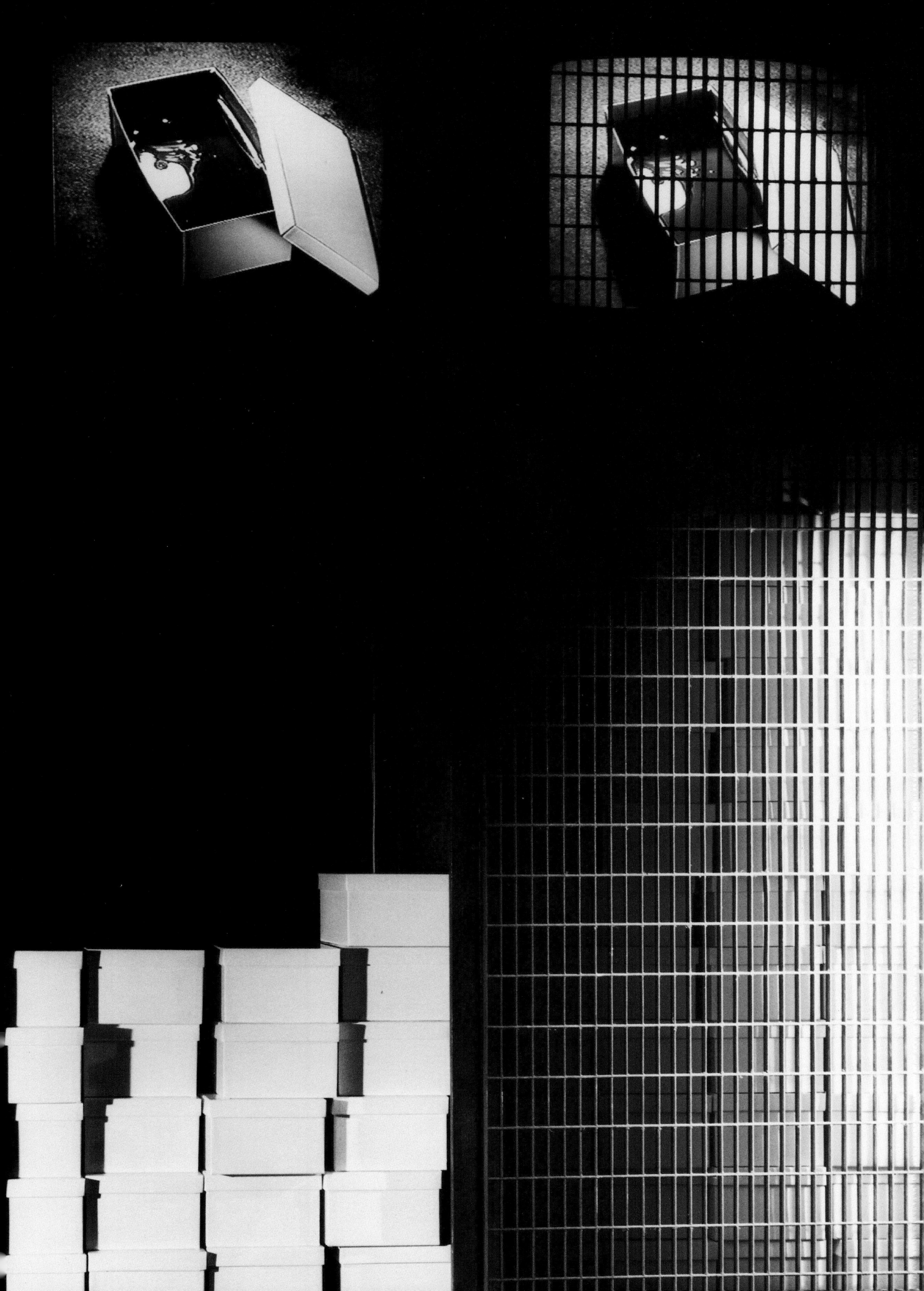

Nähe und Ferne, schaffte und so zur Wirkung der Perspektive gelangte.

Fabrizio Plessi steht ganz in dieser Tradition. Auch er schafft mit seinen Schränken eine Art Bühne, auf der sich alles abspielt. Doch darüber hinaus ist gerade diese Arbeit besonders geheimnisvoll und magisch, weil mehrere irreale Faktoren zur Wirkung kommen. Der untere Teil der Schränke ist mit geschlossenen Schachteln gefüllt, die leicht verschoben und unregelmäßig übereinander gestapelt sind. Die Schachteln erscheinen geheimnisvoll, weil sie geschlossen sind, und ihr Inhalt dem Betrachter verborgen ist. Doch das Geheimnis lüftet sich vielleicht in den oberen Monitoren. Dort, im Film, sind die Deckel der Schachteln leicht verrutscht, so daß der Inhalt sichtbar wird. Doch zum Erstaunen des Betrachters befindet sich in den papierenen Schachteln, die ja doch zumindest semipermeabel sind, Wasser. Wieviele Augenblicke es wohl dauern mag, bis das Wasser durch die Seitenwände der Schachteln nach außen gedrungen ist oder sich verflüchtigt hat? Und ob sich in den anderen Schachteln auch Wasser befindet? Diese Fragen bleiben geheimnisvoll, ungeklärt.

a sort of stage with his cabinets, on which everything happens. Beyond this, however, especially this work is highly secretive and magic by implying several unreal factors. The lower part of the cabinet is filled with closed boxes, piled irregularly and slightly shifted one upon another. The boxes appear to contain secrets, because they are closed, their contents hidden from the spectator. But perhaps the secret is unveiled on the monitors above. There, on film, the lids of the boxes are slightly moved aside, making the content visible. But to the spectator's surprise the paper boxes, that are at least semi-permeable, are filled with water. How long may it take the water to penetrate to the outside, or at least evaporate? And is there water in the other boxes, too? These questions remain secrets, unanswered.

questa tradizione. Anch'egli crea con i suoi armadi una specie di palcoscenico dove tutto si svolge. Ma oltre ciò quest'opera in particolare crea un effetto enigmatico e di magia, in quanto impiega più di un fattore irreale. La parte inferiore è riempita di scatole chiuse, una sopra l'altra e leggermente spostate. Le scatole sembrano misteriose perchè chiuse, nascondendo così il loro contenuto allo spettatore. Il segreto forse è presto svelato dai monitors della parte superiore. Qui, nel filmato, i coperchi delle scatole si sono leggermente spostati rendendo visibile il loro contenuto. Ma, a sorpresa dello spettatore, le scatole di carta che si presume siano almeno semimpermeabili contengono acqua. Quanti attimi potranno passare prima che l'acqua possa fuoriuscire dalle scatole o sparire? E le altre scatole, anche loro contengono acqua? Domande che rimangono senza risposta e irrisolte.

L'ARMADIO DELLA LEGNA

90010

REGGIO EMILIA 1990
Museo Civico d'Arte Moderna
90010.1

SCHRANK DES HOLZES
Videoskulptur 1990
Eisenschränke mit Fächern,
Eisengitter, 4 verschiedene Sorten
Brennholz, 4 Monitore,
4 Videorecorder, 4 bespielte
Kassetten
260 x 320 x 60 cm

CABINET OF WOOD
Video sculpture 1990
Iron construction with
compartments, iron lattice,
4 classes of fire-wood, 4 monitors,
4 video recorders, 4 recorded video
cassettes
260 x 320 x 60 cm

L'ARMADIO DELLA LEGNA
Videoscultura 1990
Struttura in ferro a scomparti,
grigliato industriale in ferro,
quattro tipologie di legname,
4 monitors, 4 vhs, 4 cassette
registrate
260 x 320 x 60 cm

Ganz anders als der *Schrank mit Stroh* präsentiert sich der *Schrank mit Holz (Armadio della Legna)* hier, obgleich es in beiden Fällen um eine Materialbeschaffenheit oder Materialanalyse geht. Doch während das Stroh sich in gleichartigen, gleichförmigen Strohballen in allen vier Schränken ähnlich präsentierte, sieht man bei dieser Videoskulptur in jedem Schrankteil eine andere Präsentation desselben Materials, nämlich Holz. Im ersten Schrank sieht man Holzscheite, wie sie für ein Kamin-Holzfeuer verwendet werden, in dem zweiten Schrank geraspeltes Holz, in dem dritten Schrank Holzäste, von Blättern befreit, und in dem vierten Teil, von ihrer Schnittfläche her betrachtet, runde Holzstämme. Dazu schwimmen in den Videos der oben zu sehenden Monitore einzelne Äste von Hölzern, zeit- und raumversetzt. Fast scheint es sich um eine Art Bestandsaufnahme oder akribische Analyse zu handeln, und man kommt in den Gedanken über das Material Holz zu dem Gedanken des Begriffs.

Interessanterweise würden wir diese vier sinnlich und optisch sehr unterschiedlichen Erscheinungsweisen eines Materials doch allesamt einheitlich mit dem Begriff ›Holz‹ beschreiben. Empirisch können also nur einzelne Gegenstände wahrgenommen werden oder ihreErscheinungsweisen, während Begriffe universell gültig sind, unabhängig von der temporären Erscheinungsweise des jeweili-

Totally different from the Cabinet of Straw *the* Cabinet of Wood (Armadio della Legna) *presents itself, although both have to do with the character or analysis of a material. Yet while the straw is presented in similar, equally shaped stacks in all four cabinets, this video sculpture shows - in each cabinet - a different presentation of the same material, wood. In the first cabinet one can see logs, as used for open fires, in the second woodchips, in the third, leafless branches, and in the fourth, looked at from their cutting-plane, round trunks of wood. In the videos of the monitors seen above single branches of trees are floating, at different times and space. It almost seems to represent a sort of inventory or very exact analysis, leading, from thoughts on the material wood to thoughts on the concept, the term wood.*

Interestingly enough, we would describe these four, mentally and optically very different states of one material uniformly with the term wood. Empirically, we can observe only single objects or single appearances of objects, while terms are universally valid, independent from the temporary shape of the respective material, as in this case. It can thus be stated that terms are ideas of objects or facts that refer to objects. The term is, however, not able to refer - different than the name - exactly to the object in

Del tutto diverso dall'*Armadio della Paglia* si presenta *L'Armadio della Legna* sebbene ambedue rappresentino un'analisi del materiale e della sua consistenza. Mentre le balle di paglia erano distribuite in maniera regolare nei quattro armadi si vede in questa videoscultura un tipo diverso di legno per ogni armadio. Nel primo si trova legna spaccata pronta per il camino, nel secondo legno raspato, nel terzo rami di legno liberati dalle foglie e nel quarto tronchi rotondi segati. Nei monitors superiori galleggiano inoltre singoli rami di legno a intervalli non sincronizzati. Sembra quasi di trovarsi di fronte ad un inventario specifico o ad un'analisi meticolosa e nella riflessione sul legno si arriva a quella sul concetto.

Curiosamente descriveremo le quattro forme di materiale così diverse fra di loro sia dal punto di vista sensuale sia da quello ottico con un solo e unico termine: legno. Empiricamente possono essere percepiti solo singoli oggetti e le loro singole forme mentre i termini acquistano una validità universale, indipendentemente, come in questo caso, dalla forma temporanea del rispettivo materiale. Fondamentalmente si può affermare che i termini corrispondono ai concetti di oggetti o di stati di cose che si riferiscono ad oggetti senza essere però in

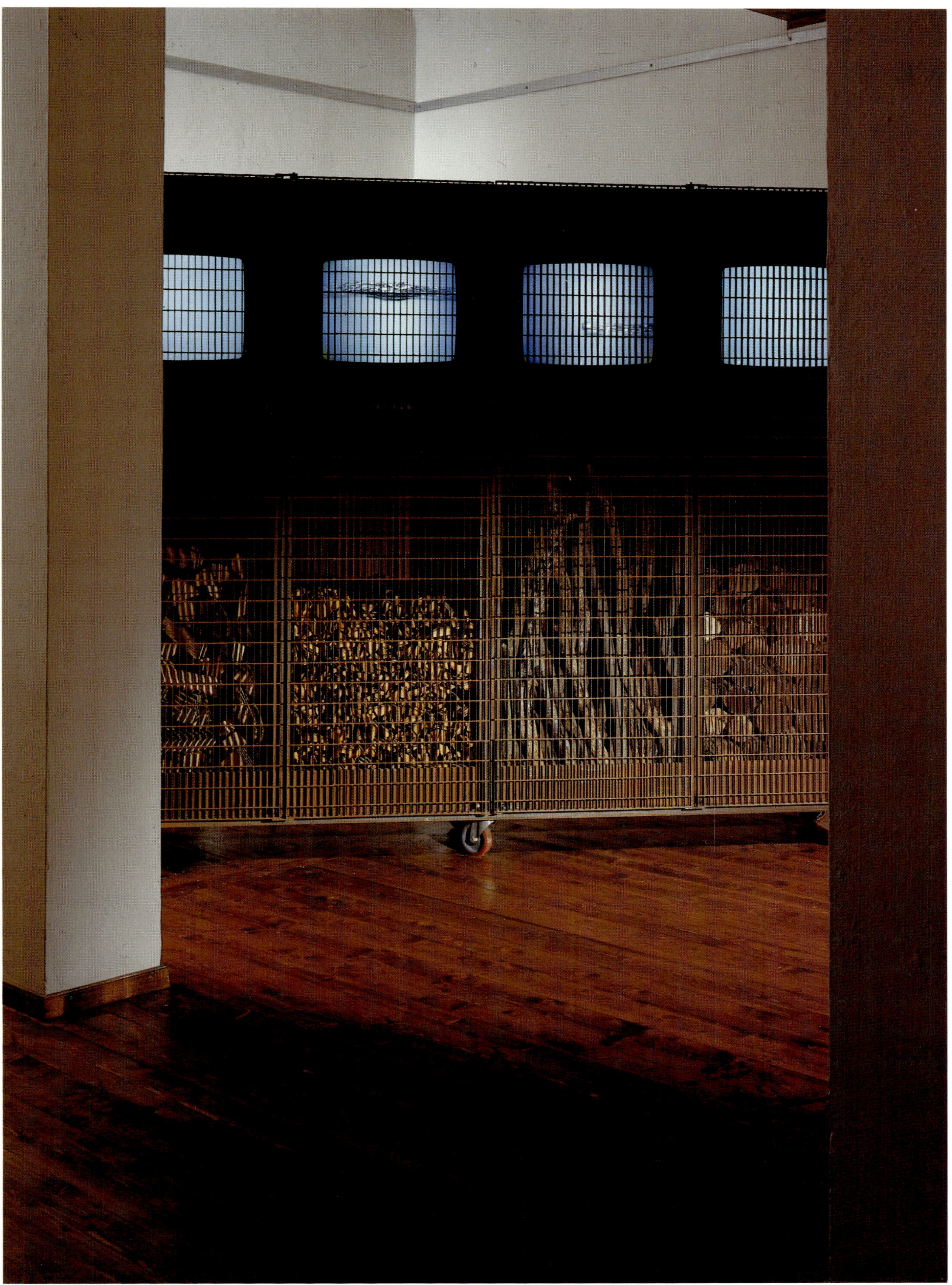

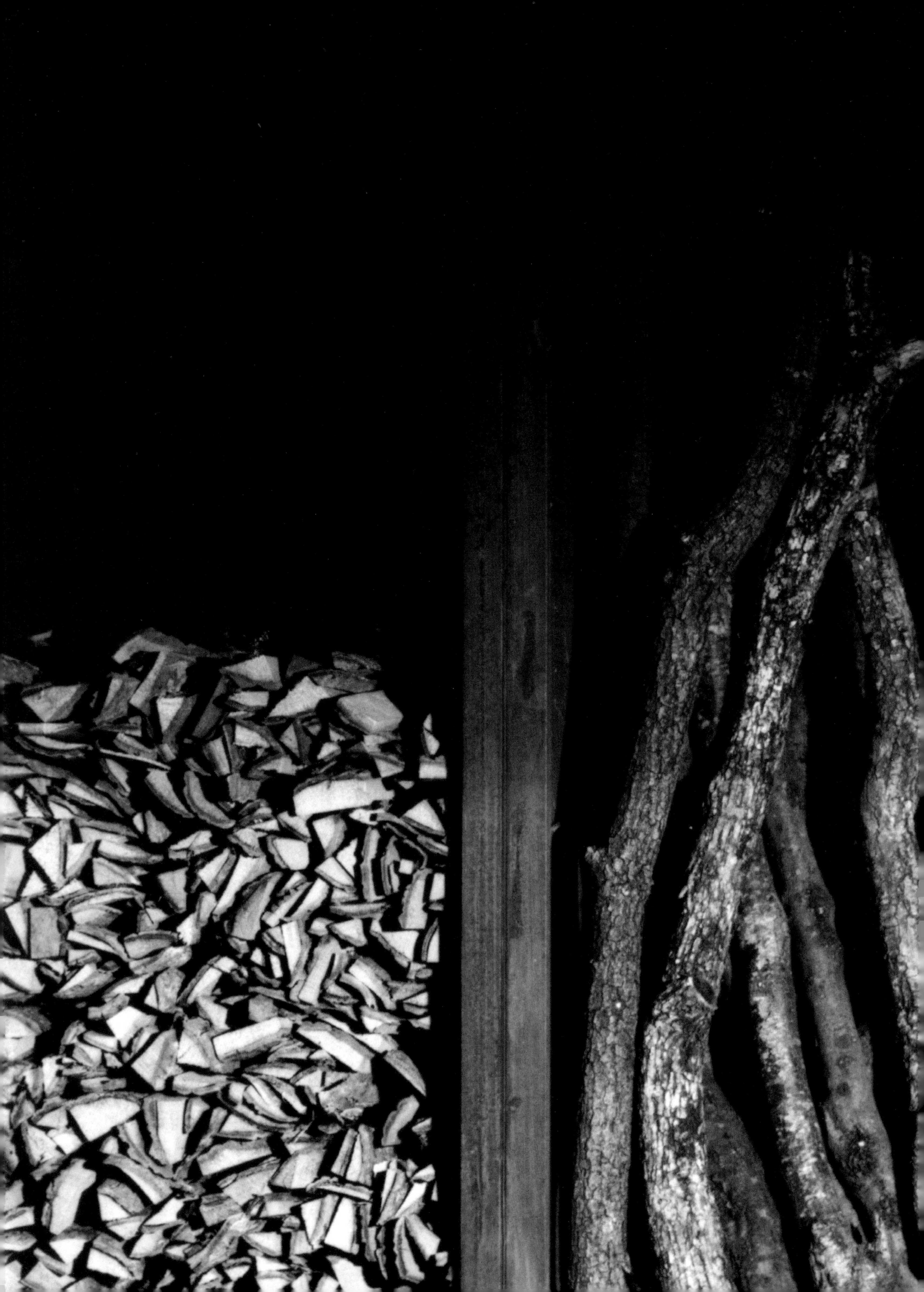

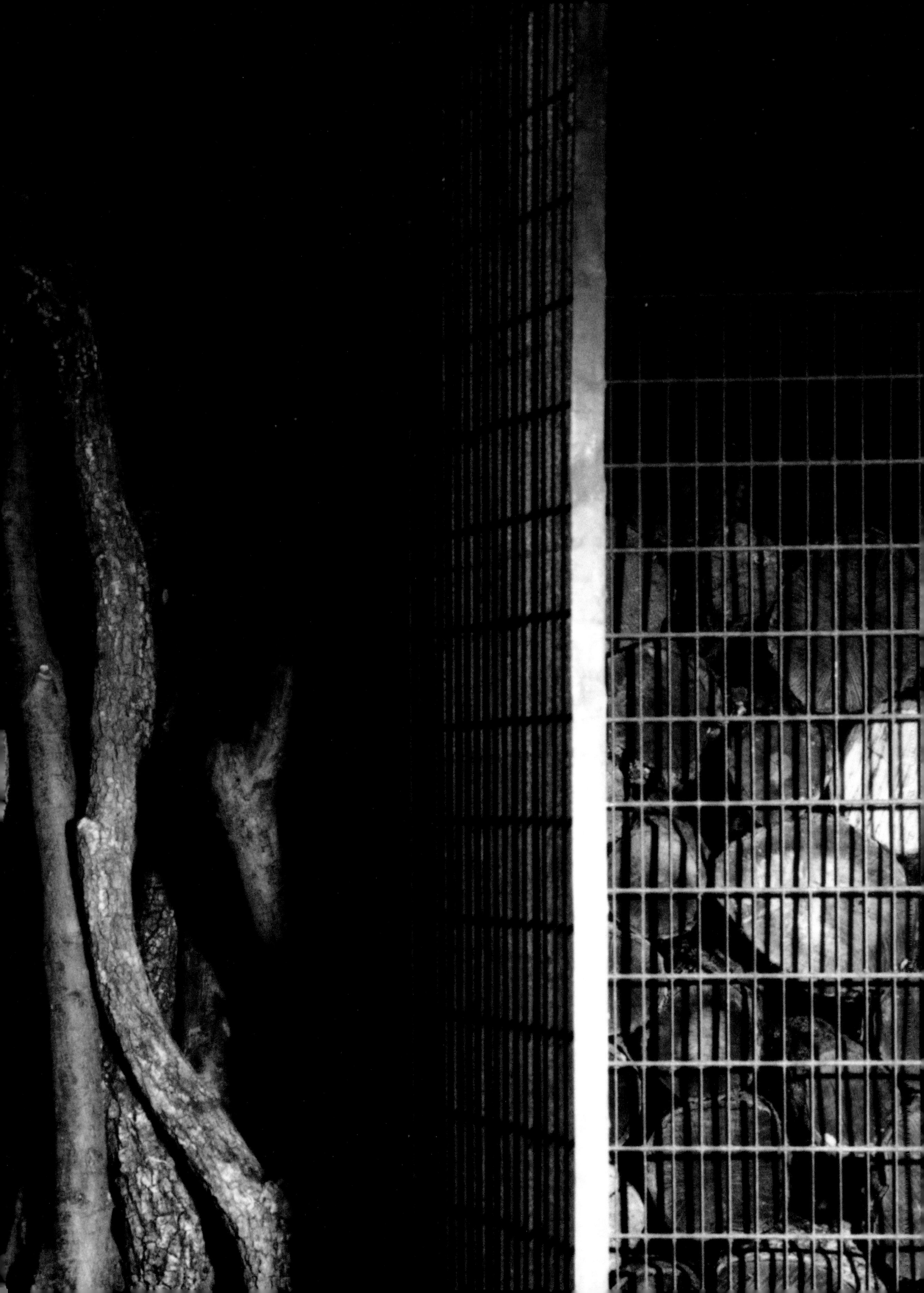

gen Materials, wie in diesem Falle. Grundsätzlich kann man sagen, daß Begriffe Vorstellungen sind von Gegenständen oder auch Sachverhalten, die sich auf Gegenstände beziehen. Dabei ist der Begriff nicht in der Lage - anders als der Name - sich völlig präzise auf den gemeinten Gegenstand zu beziehen, wie dieser in seiner eigenen Individualität in Zeit und Raum besteht. Der Begriff kann sich nur allgemein auf eine Gruppe von Gegenständen beziehen, die gewisse Gemeinsamkeiten haben. Notwendig ist nicht nur allgemeinen, sondern gelegentlich auch singulären Termini, eine gewisse Vagheit inhärent. »Ein singulärer Terminus, der einen physikalischen Gegenstand benennt, kann im Hinblick auf die raumzeitlichen Grenzen dieses Gegenstands vage sein, während ein allgemeiner Terminus im Hinblick auf das, was am Rande seiner Extension kreucht und fleucht vage sein kann.« (Williard van Orman Quine: *Word and Object*, Kap. 4 ›Vagaries of Reference‹, Cambridge Mass. 1960). Die Ungenauigkeit der Ausdehnung des gemeinten Begriffs erlaubt eine weitreichende Gültigkeit und ein universelles Bezugssystem. Der Begriff ›Holz‹ bezieht sich auf alle sichtbaren oder denkbaren Erscheinungen des Materials, während jede einzelne Darstellung von dem Holz, wie hier als Stamm, als Ast, als Kleinholz usw., nur jeweils einen Ausschnitt darstellt. Man muß sich darüber im klaren sein, daß nur aufgrund dieser Ungenauigkeit in bezug auf Ausdehnung und Abgrenzung eines Begriffes, die Möglichkeit zur Kommunikation unter den Menschen gegeben ist. Denn jeder einzelne verbindet unterschiedliche Gedanken, Erfahrungen, Empfindungen und daher Vorstellungen mit dem jeweiligen Begriff. Und der Begriff beinhaltet eine Vielfalt der Möglichkeiten von Erscheinungen und Vorstellungen.

mind, as it exists in its own individuality in time and space. The term can only refer in general to a group of objects that have certain similarities. Necessarily, a certain vagueness is inherent not only in general but sometimes in singular terms. "A singular term naming a physical object can be vague in point of the boundaries of that object in space-time, while a general term can be vague in point of the marginal hangers-on of its extension." (Williard van Orman Quine: Word and Object, *chap. 4 'Vagaries of Reference', Cambridge Mass. 1960) The lack of exactness in widening the term in mind allows for a far-reaching validity as well as a universal system of reference. The term 'wood' refers to all visible or thinkable forms of the material, while each single presentation of wood, as trunk, branch, chip etc. only represent one section. One has to understand that, only because of this inexactness in reference to expansion and limitation of a term, the possibility of communication between people exists. For everyone associates different thoughts, experiences, feelings and therefore perceptions with the respective term. And the term itself contains a variety of possible appearances and perceptions.*

grado - diversamente dai nomi - di relazionarsi precisamente con l'individualità temporale e spaziale dell'oggetto in questione. Il termine corrisponde solo in maniera generale ad un gruppo di oggetti che posseggono certe caratteristiche comuni. Necessariamente i termini non solo generali ma anche specifici, peccano di una qualche imprecisione. »Un termine specifico che indica un oggetto fisico può essere impreciso riguardo ai limiti spazio-temporali dell'oggetto stesso, così come un termine generale può essere impreciso rispetto a quello che si trova agli estremi della sua estensione« (Williard van Orman Quine, in: *Word and Object*, cap. 4 ›Vagaries of Reference‹, Cambridge Mass. 1960). L'imprecisione nell'estensione del termine in questione permette una validità ampia e costituisce un sistema relazionale universale. Il termine ›legno‹ indica tutte le forme visibili o immaginabili del materiale, mentre ogni singola rappresentazione del legno, come qui in forma di tronco, ramo o legnetto, riporta solo un parte frammentaria. Ci si deve render conto del fatto che solo grazie a questa imprecisione riguardo all'estensione e alla limitatezza di un termine esiste la possibilità di comunicazione fra gli uomini, perchè ogni singola persona associa pensieri, esperienze, sensazioni e quindi concetti diversi ad un determinato termine così come ogni singolo termine si riferisce ad una moltitudine di forme e concetti.

L'ARMADIO DI BRONX

90011

REGGIO EMILIA 1990
MUSEO CIVICO D'ARTE MODERNA
90011.1

KÖLN 1996
GALERIE DOROTHEA VAN DER KOELEN, ART COLOGNE
90011.2

LUXEMBOURG 1997
CASINO LUXEMBOURG, FORUM D'ART CONTEMPORAIN
90011.3

SCHRANK DER BRONX
Videoskulptur 1990
Eisenschränke mit Fächern,
Eisengitter, Schaufeln,
4 Monitore, Videorecorder,
bespielte Kassetten,
Tonaufzeichnung
260 x 320 x 60 cm

CABINET OF BRONX
Video sculpture 1990
Iron construction with
compartments, iron lattice,
shovels, 4 monitors, video
recorder, recorded video cassettes,
soundrecording
260 x 320 x 60 cm

L'ARMADIO DI BRONX
Videoscultura 1990
Struttura in ferro a scomparti,
grigliato industriale in ferro, pale,
4 monitors, vhs, cassette
registrate, sonoro
260 x 320 x 60 cm

Bei dem *Armadio di Bronx*, der sich - wie der Name bereits zum Ausdruck bringt - auf die große Videoinstallation von 1986 bezieht, die auf der Biennale in Venedig zu sehen war, ist nun inzwischen ein durchgreifend verändertes Bild der Präsentation entstanden. Keineswegs stammen die Videofilme in den Monitoren aus der ursprünglichen Installation, denn die Schaufeln stehen nicht senkrecht und aggressiv im Wasser. Im Gegenteil, sie lehnen im unteren Bereich des Schrankes, lässig an den Seitenwänden ihrer Kompartimente, so, als könne sie nichts und niemanden in Aufregung versetzen oder vielleicht auch, als warteten sie auf eine noch herzustellende Erfindung. Das elektronische Wasser in den Monitoren fließt leicht um sie herum, die Video-Schaufeln, die in analoger Haltung zu ihren realen Vorbildern, schräg im Wasser stehen und sich kaum noch darin zu spiegeln scheinen. Ein stabiles und ein mobiles Element werden miteinander in eine symbiotische Beziehung gebracht.

In Armadio di Bronx *that refers to - as the name indicates - the great video installation of 1986, shown at the Biennale in Venice, we now find a thoroughly changed form of presentation. The video films on the monitors are certainly not taken from the original installation, for the shovels do not stand upright and aggressive in the water. On the contrary, they now lean slack against the side walls in the lower part of their compartments, as if nothing and nobody could exite them, or perhaps as if they were waiting for a future invention. The electronic water on the monitors flows lightly around them, the video shovels stand in analogous posture to their real models obliquely in the water, barely mirroring in it. A stable and a mobile element are thus united in a symbiotic relationship.*

L'Armadio di Bronx come indica il titolo fa riferimento alla grande videoinstallazione del 1986 esposta alla Biennale di Venezia ma si presenta in una struttura del tutto cambiata. Le pale dei videofilms non sono più conficcate in maniera aggressiva nell'acqua ma, al contrario, si appoggiano in modo leggero alle pareti laterali dei loro scompartimenti come se nessuno o niente le potesse mettere in agitazione o come se fossero in attesa di una nuova invenzione ancora da venire. L'acqua elettronica dei monitors gira intorno alle pale dei filmati che, in posizione obliqua e analoga a quella delle pale reali, ci si riflettono appena. Un elemento stabile e uno mobile si uniscono in un rapporto di simbiosi.

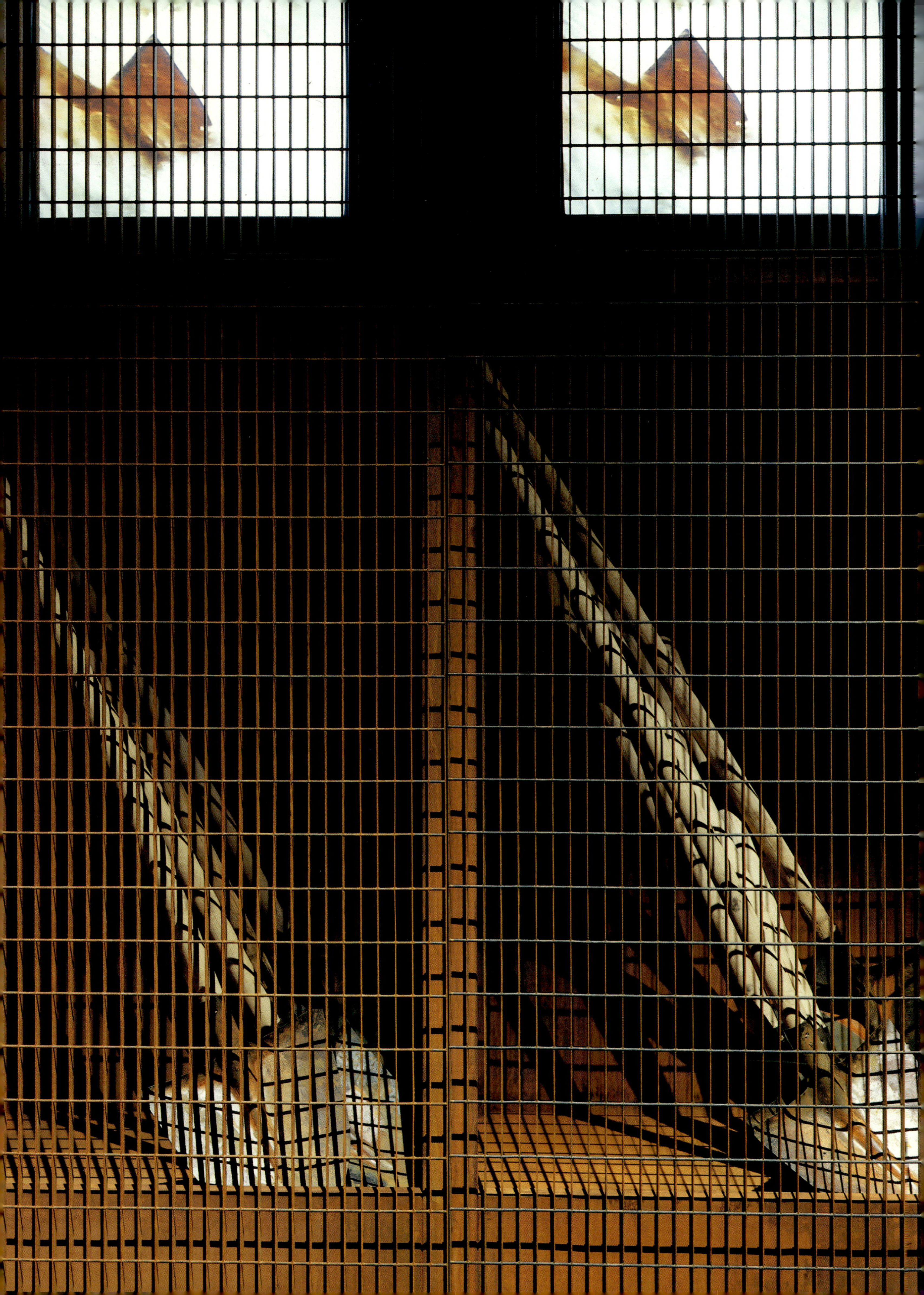

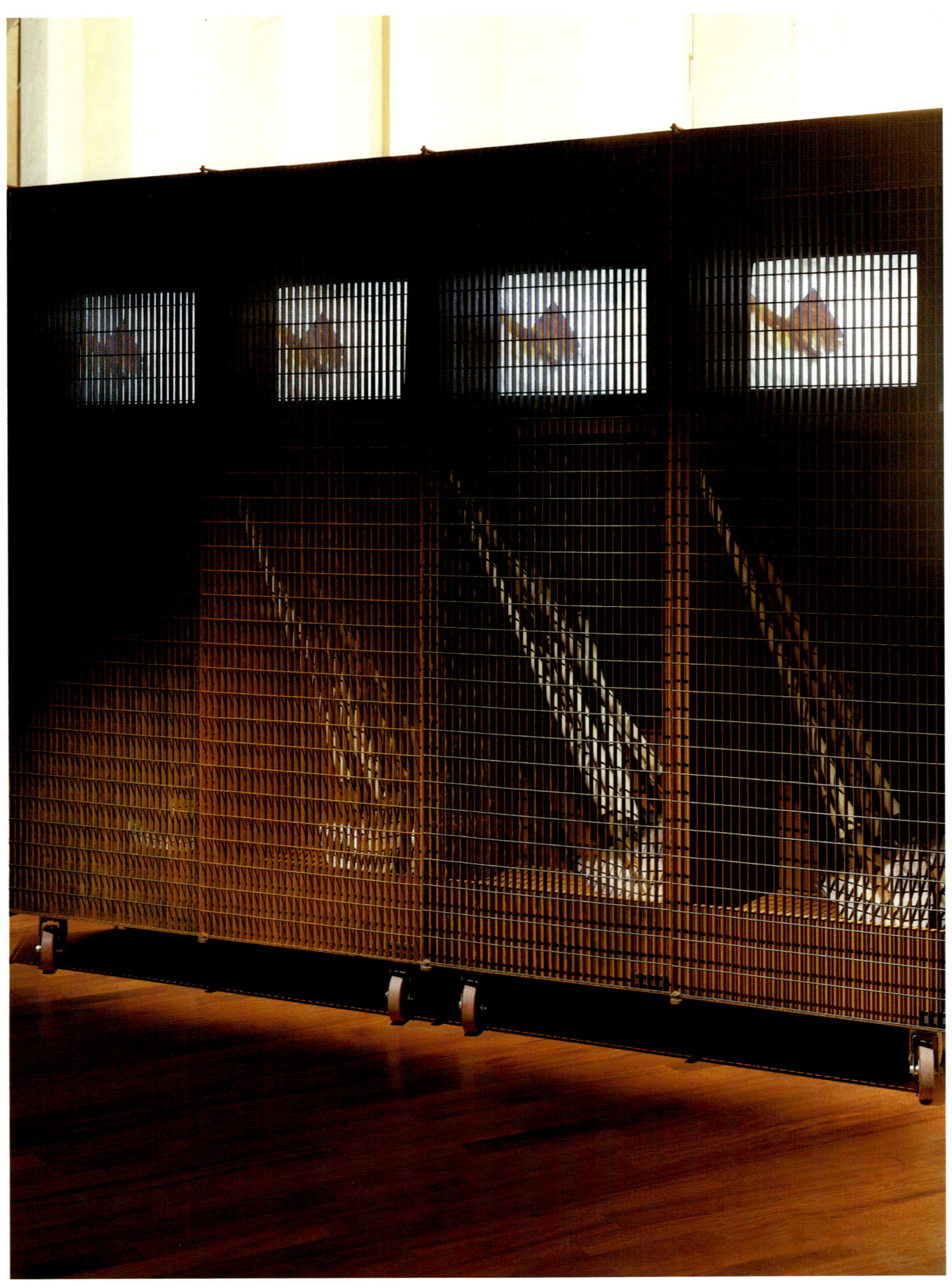

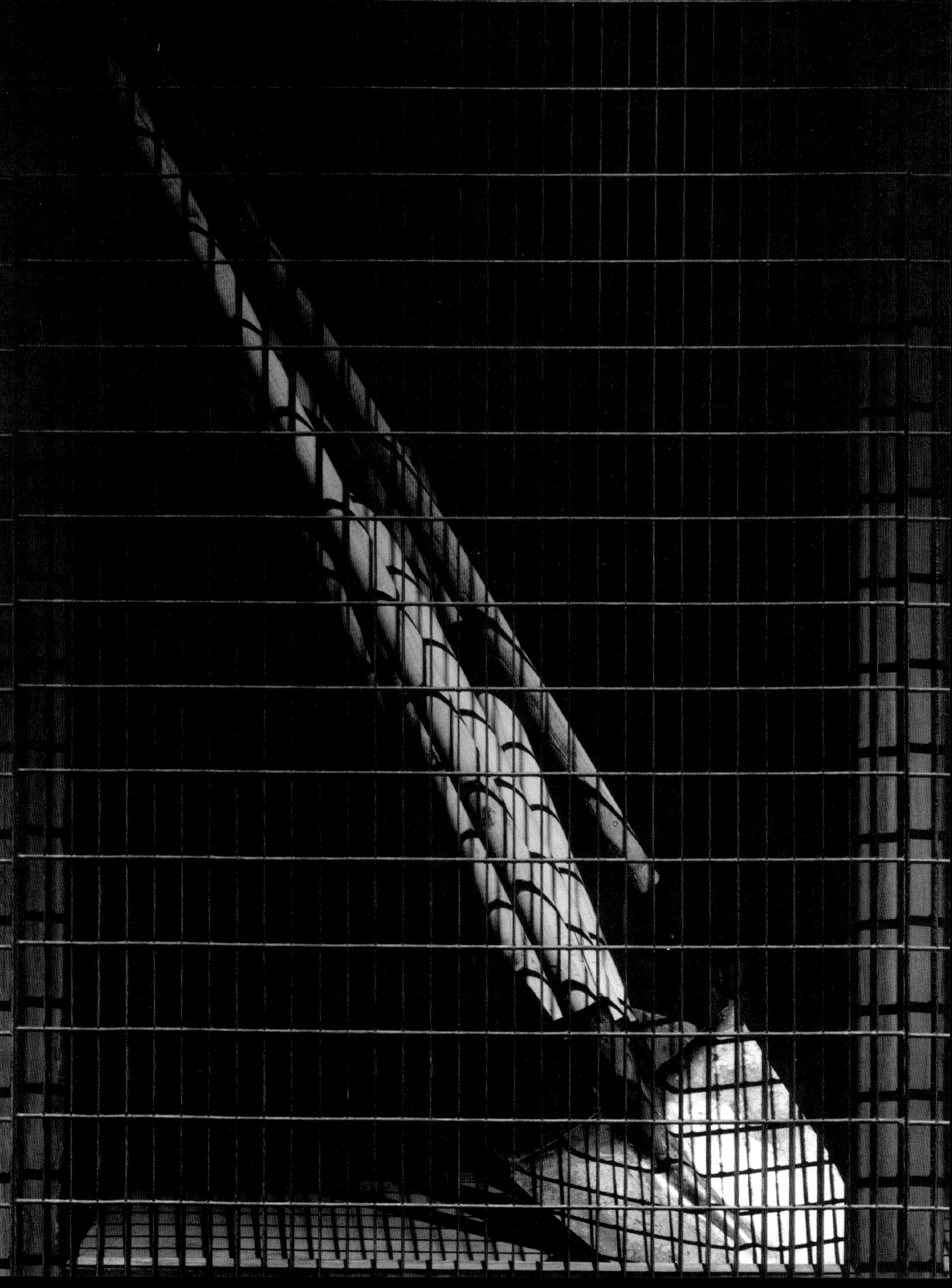

PROIBITO

90012

ROMA 1990
GALLERIA L'ISOLA
90012.1

DORTMUND 1993
MUSEUM AM OSTWALL
90012.2

VERBOTEN
Videoskulptur 1990
Eisenschränke mit Fächern, rohe
Holzbretter, 4 Monitore,
Videorecorder, bespielte Kassette
260 x 320 x 60 cm
Weitere Präsentation:
2 Monitore, 160 cm Breite

PROHIBITED
Video sculpture 1990
Iron construction with compart-
ments, raw wooden boards,
4 monitors, recorder, cassette
260 x 320 x 60 cm
Subsequent presentation:
2 monitors, 160 cm width

PROIBITO
Videoscultura 1990
Struttura in ferro a scomparti,
legno grezzo, 4 monitors,
1 vhs, cassetta registrata
260 x 320 x 60 cm
variazione:
2 monitors, 160 cm

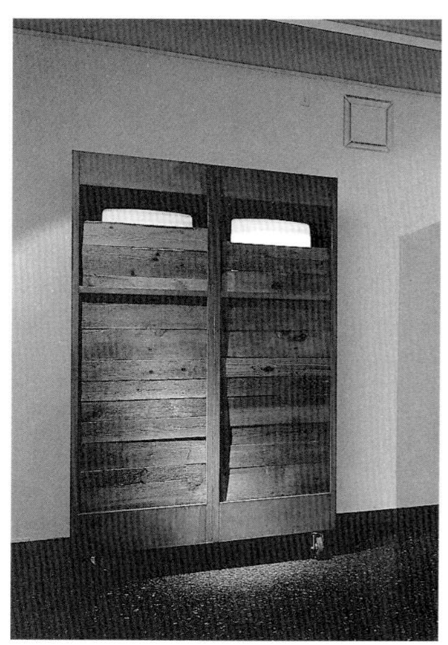

Proibito, oder in der deutschen
Übersetzung *Verboten*, stellt sich
als kleinere Version der *Stanza del
Mare* dar. Ein zwei- bis vierteiliger
Schrank ist von querliegenden
Holzbrettern in unterschiedlicher
Breite, Farbe und Alter verschlos-
sen bis hoch hinauf, so daß die
Monitore nur noch einen spaltbreit
sichtbar sind, zum Teil schon fast
verborgen. Dahinter sieht man das
bewegte Meer, das in Wellen auf
den Betrachter zuläuft. Der Titel
Verboten bringt deutlicher zum
Ausdruck, was sich in der größeren
Installation thematisch schon
ankündigt. Fabrizio Plessi will sein
Wasser - hier das Meer - vor Zu-
griffen schützen. Er baut eine
Barriere auf, er versteckt das Meer
in seinem Schrank wie in einem
Schatzkästchen, als wolle er es
behüten und zugleich bewahren.

Proibito, *or* Forbidden *is a
smaller version of* Stanza del
Mare. *A cabinet, divided in two
to four sections, is covered by
horizontal wooden boards of
different width, colour and age
all the way up, so that the monitors are only visible through a
small opening, almost concealed.
What can be seen is the motion of
the sea, approaching the spectator in waves. The title* Forbidden
*clearly indicates what is an-
nounced in the larger installation. Fabrizio Plessi wants to
protect his water - here, the sea -
from access. He erects a barrier,
hides the sea in his cabinet as in
a treasure box as if to protect
and keep it.*

Proibito è la versione più
piccola della *Stanza del Mare*. Il
lato frontale degli armadi è
chiuso da assi di legno orizzontali di larghezza, colore e età
diversi coprendo quasi interamente i monitors in alto. Dietro
di loro si vede il mare mosso
che viene in onde verso lo
spettatore. Il titolo *Proibito*
amplifica il messaggio della
installazione più grande. Fabrizio Plessi vuole salvaguardare la
sua acqua, il mare, costruendo
una barriera e nascondendolo
nel suo armadio come in uno
scrigno di tesori, quasi lo volesse nello stesso tempo custodire
e conservare.

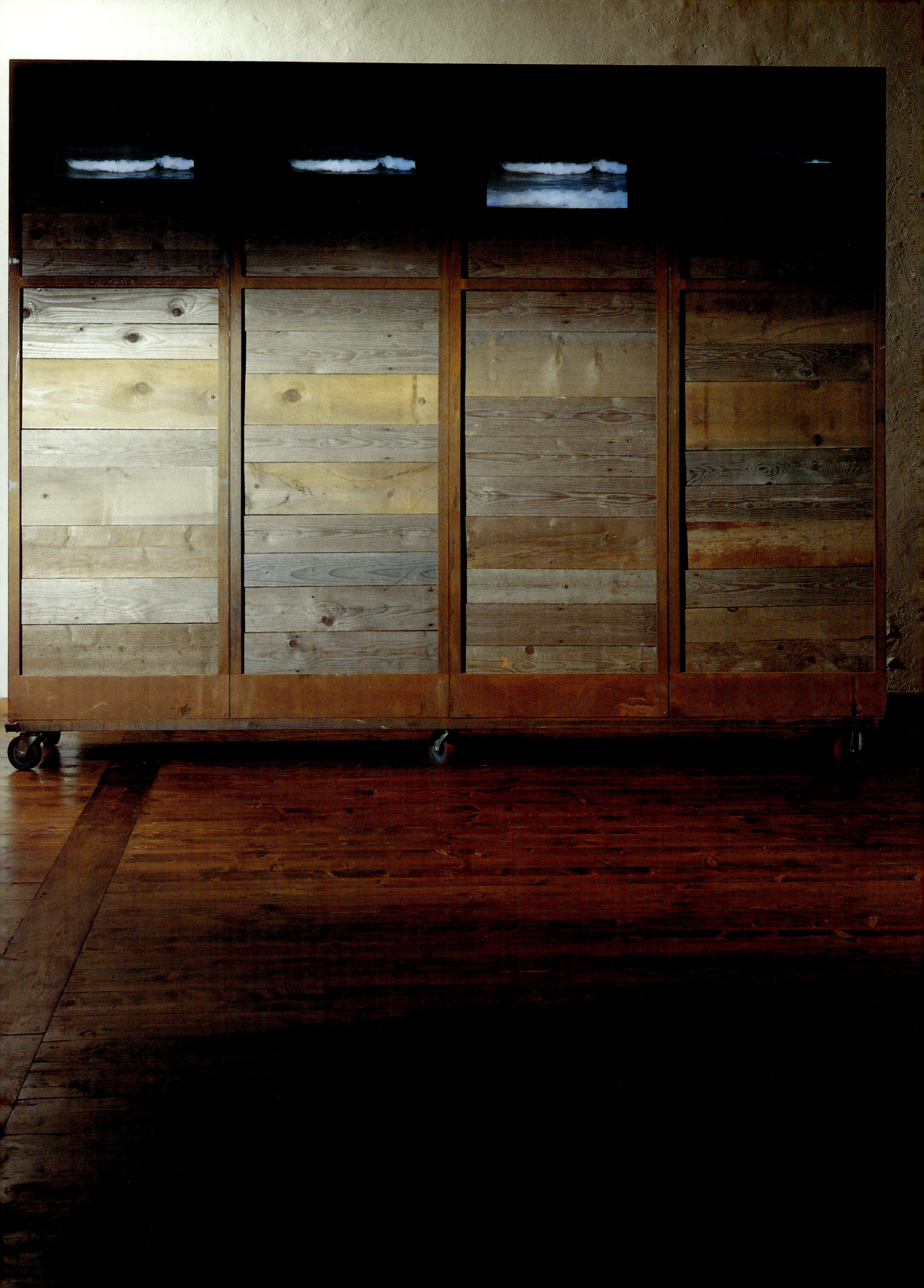

LA CARIATIDE DELL'ARCHITETTO

90013

VENEZIA 1990
GALLERIA TOTEM
90013.1

BARCELONA 1993
FUNDACIÓ JOAN MIRÓ
90013.2

KARLSRUHE 1997
ZENTRUM FÜR KUNST UND MEDIENTECHNOLOGIE
90013.3

DIE KARYATIDE DES
ARCHITEKTEN
Videoskulptur 1990
Eisengestell, 94 Ziegelsteine,
1 Monitor, Videorecorder,
bespielte Kassetten
260 x 50 x 50 cm

THE ARCHITECT'S CARYTID
Video sculpture 1990
Iron structure, 94 fired bricks,
1 monitor, video recorder, video
cassette
260 x 50 x 50 cm

LA CARIATIDE DELL'ARCHITETTO
Videoscultura 1990
Struttura in ferro, 94 mattoni,
1 monitor, 1 vhs, 1 cassetta
registrata
260 x 50 x 50 cm

Die erste *Karyatide* Fabrizio Plessis, ausgestellt in einer venezianischen Galerie, erinnert an seine Schränke; nur dieses Mal ist das Prinzip umgedreht: das Material ist oben und der Monitor unten im Gehäuse angebracht. Analog den Säulen in der Galerie ist die *Karyatide* zwischen Boden und Decke eingespannt. Wie bei dem *Schrank des Architekten* sind auch hier Backsteine ordentlich und systematisch übereinandergeschichtet als würden sie ein Bauwerk repräsentieren. Im Video des Monitors setzt sich die Struktur homogen fort. Das Ganze erscheint zunächst als stabile, durchgehende Säule, welche die Decke durchaus zu tragen imstande wäre. Im nächsten Moment jedoch wird der Betrachter gewahr, daß alles nur Illusion ist, denn die Basis der *Karyatide* ist immateriell, ein Bild, in virtuelles Erzeugnis, ein Abbild der Realität. Bei der Vorstellung, daß die schweren Steine und darüber hinaus vielleicht die Decke auf einer reinen Idee, also faktisch dem Nichts, lasten, wird die ganze so scheinbar stabile Konstruktion in einem Nu fragil.

Fabrizio Plessi's first Caryatid, exhibited in a gallery in Venice, reminds of his cabinets; only this time, the principle is reversed; the material is placed in the upper, the monitor in the lower part of the container. Analogous to the pillars in the gallery, the Caryatid is stretched between floor and ceiling. As in the Architect's Cabinet, here, too, bricks are piled orderly and systematically one upon another as if to represent a building. In the monitor's video the structure is continued homogeneously. The whole appears, at first glance, as stable, continuous pillar, able to carry the weight of the ceiling. The next moment, however, the spectator realises that this is an illusion, for the base of the Caryatid is immaterial, a virtual product, an image of reality. Considering that the heavy stones and perhaps the ceiling rest on a mere idea, that is in fact on nothing, the whole seemingly stable construction immediately turns fragile.

La prima *Cariatide* di Fabrizio Plessi, esposta in una galleria a Venezia, ricorda i suoi armadi con la differenza che l'assemblaggio adesso è stato invertito: il materiale si trova in alto e il monitor nella parte bassa del contenitore. In analogia con le colonne della galleria la Cariatide è bloccata fra pavimento e soffitto. Come nell'*Armadio dell'Architetto* anche qui i mattoni sono stati posati in maniera ordinata e sistematica come se rappresentassero un edificio, il monitor riproduce in maniera omogenea la struttura. L'insieme suggerisce in un primo momento una colonna stabile realmente in grado di sostenere il soffitto, poi però lo spettatore si accorge che è solo un'illusione, perchè la base della Cariatide è immateriale, un'immagine, un prodotto virtuale, una riproduzione della realtà. L'impressione che i mattoni pesanti e forse anche il soffitto stesso poggino su di una semplice idea, e quindi di fatto su nulla, trasforma in un attimo la costruzione apparentemente così stabile in una costruzione fragile.

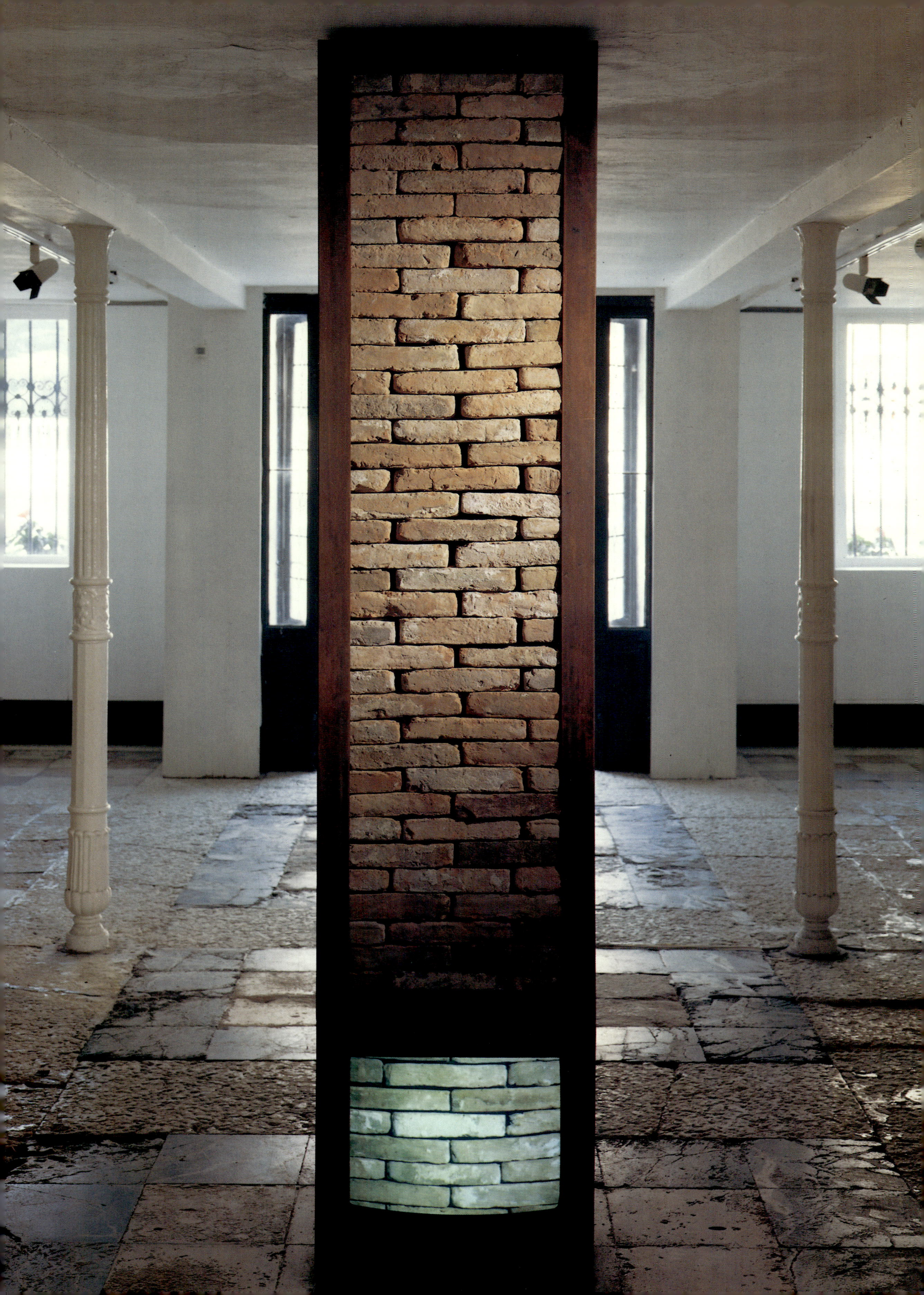

CAIRO-CAIRO

91001

TRENTO 1991
GALLERIA PAOLA STELZER
91001.1

KAIRO-KAIRO
Videoinstallation 1991
Eisenschränke mit Fächern,
Eisentische, verschiedene
Gewürze, Säcke, 2 Monitore,
2 Videorecorder, bespielte
Kassetten, Tonaufzeichnung
260 x 660 x 60 cm

CAIRO-CAIRO
Video Installation 1991
ron construction with
compartments, iron tables, spices,
sacks, 2 monitors, 2 video
recorders, recorded video cassettes,
soundrecording
260 x 660 x 60 cm

CAIRO-CAIRO
Videoinstallazione 1991
Struttura in ferro, 2 tavoli in ferro
e ruote, 6 cumuli di spezie,
2 sacchi di spezie africane,
2 monitors, 2 vhs, 2 cassette
registrate, sonoro
260 x 660 x 60 cm

Progetti del Mondo (*Projekte der Welt*) überschreibt Fabrizio Plessi eine Serie von Arbeiten, Videoinstallationen und Projekten, zeichnerisch festgehaltene Ideen-Notationen, die er vor Ort gemacht zu haben scheint, ähnlich wie in früherer Zeit reisende Künstler ihre Eindrücke und Erinnerungen in Aquarellskizzen tagebuchartig notierten. Wenn ein Künstler, ein bildender Künstler, in eine fremde Stadt oder in ein fremdes Land kommt, dann fallen ihm ganz eigenartige Phänomene auf. Er versucht, das Wesen dieser Stadt, die Ausstrahlung, mithin das, was die Stadt zu der Stadt macht, zu ergründen, herauszufinden und in seinen Notationen bildnerisch zu skizzieren oder in größere, visuell determinierte Präsentationsformen umzusetzen.

Bei Plessis Städteprojekten fällt auf, daß der Titel häufig verdoppelt auftritt - wie bei dieser Videoskulptur *Cairo-Cairo* oder in anderen Arbeiten *Paris-Paris, Bombay-Bombay* - beinahe, als wollte der Künstler mit Nachdruck auf die Örtlichkeit verweisen.

Kairo in Oberägypten, ganz anders als die Weite der Landschaft Unterägyptens, ist ein brodelnder

Progetti del Mondo (Projects of the World) *is the title Fabrizio Plessi gives to a series of works, video installations and projects, notations of ideas in drawing he seems to have done in situ, similar to the way travelling artists of earlier times took, diary-like, note of their impressions and memories in aquarelle sketches. An artist, especially a fine artist, coming to a foreign town or foreign country, remarks strange phenomena. He tries to fathom, find out and sketch images in his notes of the essence, the radiation, of all that makes it a town, and translate this into larger visual forms of presentation.*

In Plessi's city-projects we note that the title often appears reduplicated - as in this video sculpture, Cairo-Cairo, *or in other works like* Paris-Paris, Bombay-Bombay *- almost as if the artists wants to emphatically refer to the place.*

Cairo, in upper Egypt, totally different from the wide landscapes in lower Egypt, is a sort of boiling moloch, a conglomerate of totally different

Progetti del Mondo è il titolo di una serie di videoinstallazioni e progetti fissata da Fabrizio Plessi in annotazioni disegnate simili agli schizzi acquarellati che gli artisti di un tempo relizzarono per annotare, come in un diario, i loro ricordi e le loro impressioni. Un artista, un artista figurativo, che visita per la prima volta una città o un paese, viene subito colpito dai più singolari fenomeni, tenta di indagare e scoprire l'anima della città, il suo fascino, cioè quello che fa di una città quello che è e di tradurlo in annotazioni con la tecnica dello schizzo o in forme visive di presentazione più complesse.

Spesso si nota che il titolo dei progetti di Plessi dedicati alle città ripete il loro nome, come in questa videoscultura *Cairo-Cairo* o in altri lavori come *Paris-Paris, Bombay-Bombay,* quasi come se l'artista volesse rimandare con energia alla località.

Cairo nell'Alto Egitto, del tutto diverso dalla vastità dei paesaggi del Basso Egitto, è un Moloc gorgogliante, un conglomerato di elementi storici e

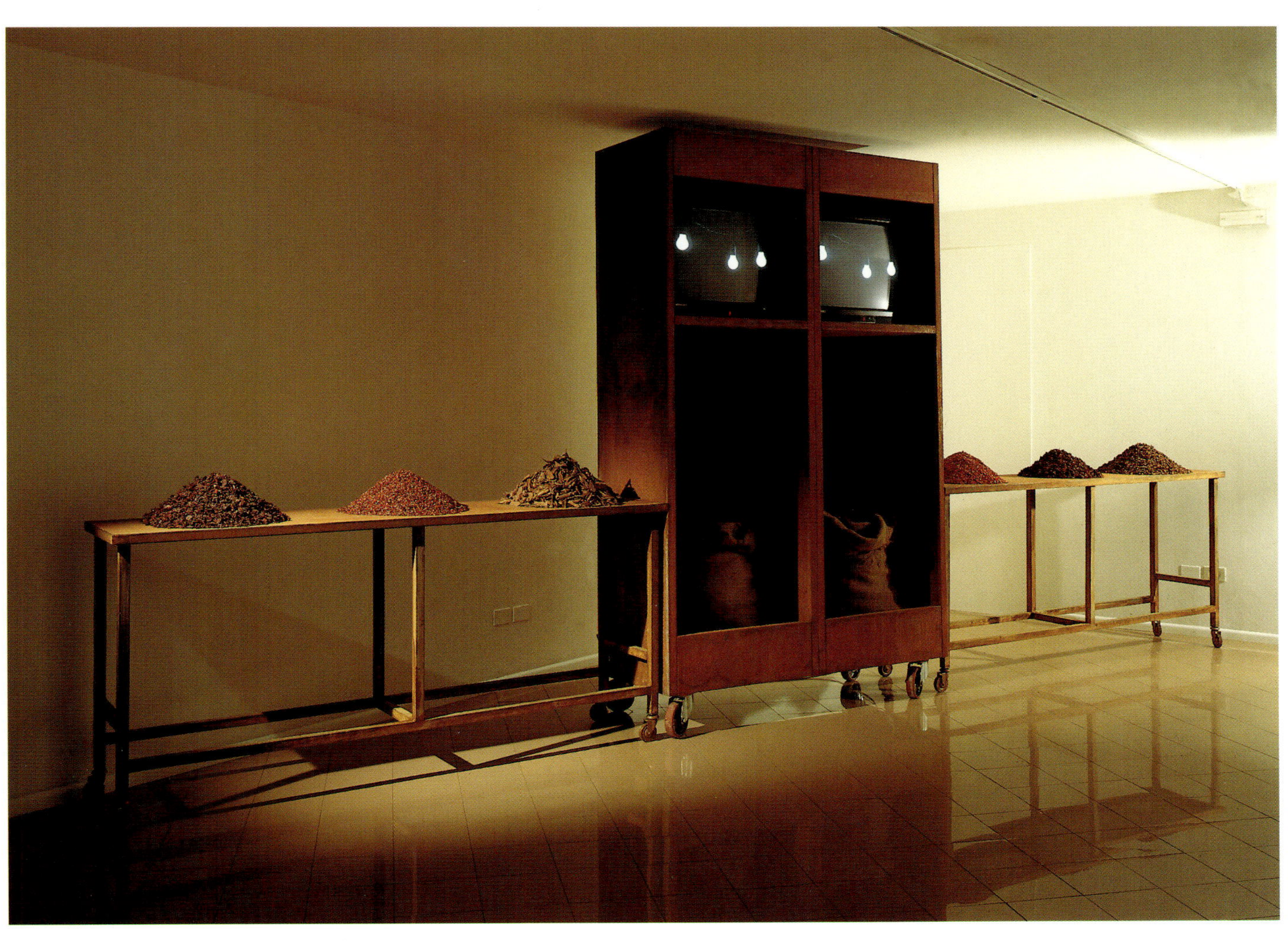

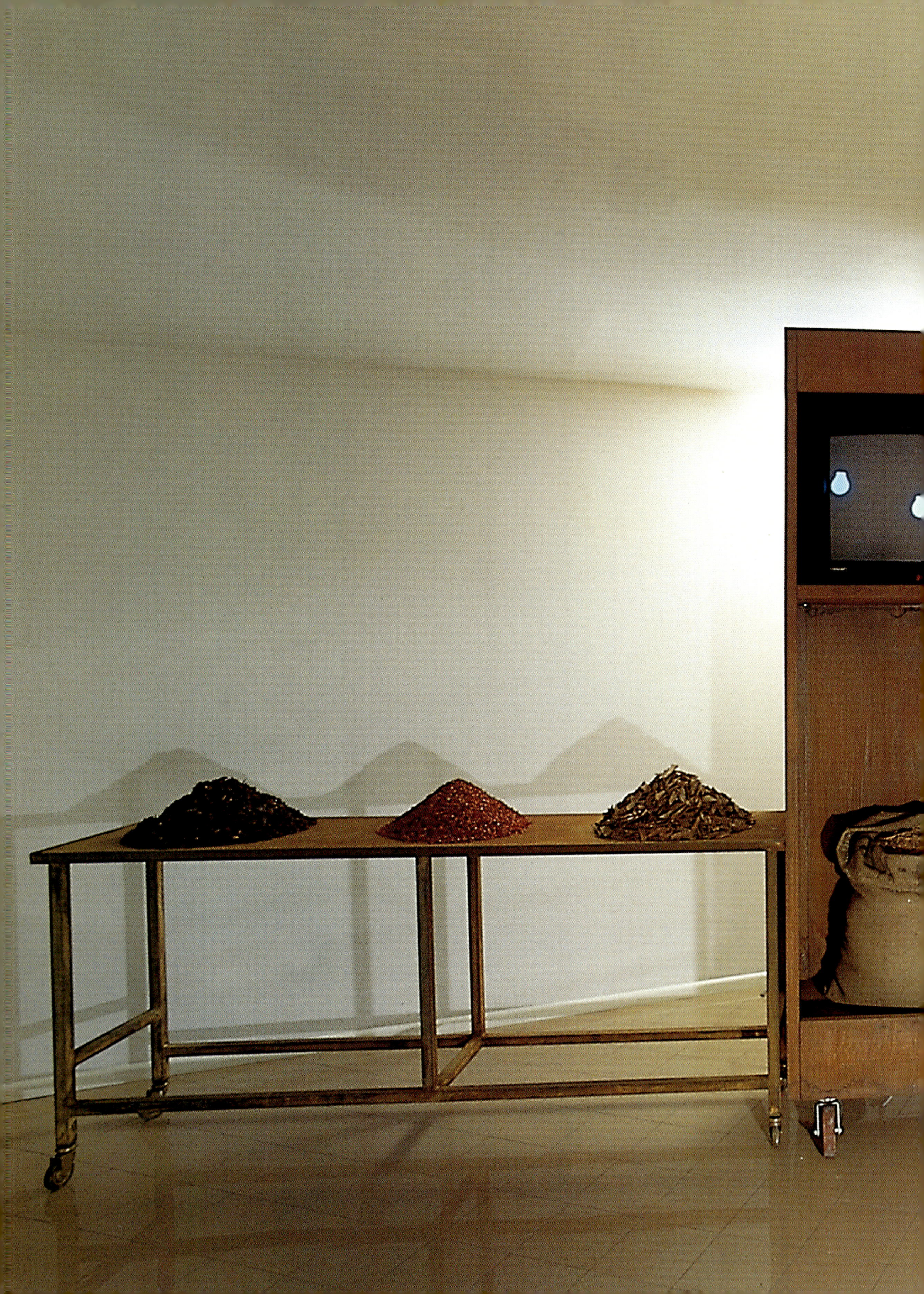

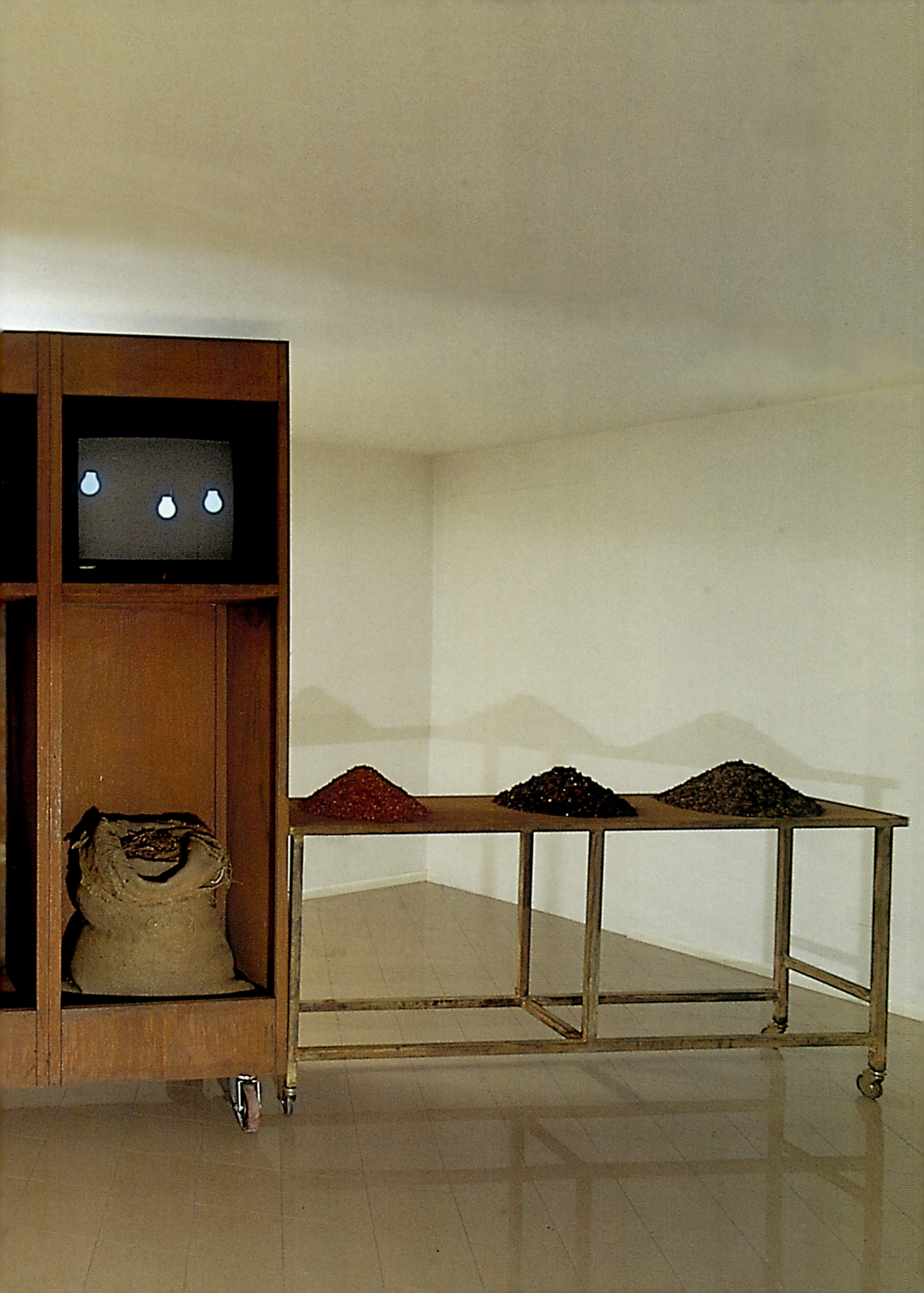

Moloch. Ein Konglomerat unterschiedlichster historischer und religiöser Entwicklungen. Eine Stadt, die aus ihren großen Kontrasten lebt. Die riesigen, jahrtausendealten Pyramiden, klar geformt, erhaben in der Ausstrahlung, dann die jahrhundertealten islamischen Bauwerke, die Moscheen und schließlich der Suk, der Markt in ›Old Cairo‹. Zahllose Händler in verwinkelten, kleinen, unübersehbaren Gassen haben auf engstem Raum in wenigen Quadratmetern ihre Firmen und Verkaufsstände eingerichtet. Stoffe, Gewürze, Kohle, Früchte, Gemüse, Duftstoffe, und immer wieder zwischendurch auch Kunsthandwerk - alles kann man kaufen, es wird für den Kunden persönlich abgewogen, ausgemessen, angefertigt. Ein wildes buntes Treiben findet dort statt. Die sogenannten ›Fabriken‹ in diesen alten Märkten, den Suks, sind eigentlich eher Manufakturen. Die meisten Konstruktionen der Präsentationsflächen sind improvisiert. Jedes Stück findet irgendwo wieder seine Verwendung. Jedes Material kann wieder einer neuen Funktion zugeführt werden, eines neuen Bedarfs.

Fabrizio Plessi hat in seiner Installation *Cairo-Cairo* die Stimmung auf diesen alten Märkten, den arabischen Suks, nachgebaut. Er hat Tische konstruiert, auf denen unterschiedliche Materialien, Gewürze etc. ordentlich getrennt voneinander zu kleinen Häuflein aufgeschüttet präsentiert werden. Zwischen den beiden Tischen steht einer seiner Schränke, eher dunkel gehalten, im unteren Bereich mit Kohlestücken gefüllte Säcke, in den Monitoren einfachste Glühbirnen, die nur ein düsteres Licht erzeugen. Ganz so, wie es auf diesen Märkten immer wieder vorkommt. Die Schönheit des Einfachen wird in dieser Videoskulptur poetisch transformiert.

historical and religious developments, a city living from its contrasts. The huge pyramids, thousands of years old, clearly shaped and exalted in their radiance, the Islamic buildings, the mosques, hundreds of years old, and finally the 'souk', the market in 'Old Cairo'. Numerous traders in small, crooked and immense lanes have erected their stands in narrow spaces of only a few metres each. Cloths, spices, coal, fruits, vegetables, incense, and, again and again in between, crafts - everything is on sale, is weighed, measured and produced for each customer individually. All is in tumultuous, colourful commotion. The so-called 'factories' in these old markets, the souks, are in reality manufactories. Most of the stand constructions are improvised. Everything is put to some use. Each material can take up a new function, fulfil new needs. Fabrizio Plessi has in his installation Cairo-Cairo reconstructed the mood of these old markets, the souks. He has built tables on which different materials, spices etc., clearly separated from each other, piled up in small heaps are presented. Between the two tables one of his cabinets is standing, looking rather dark, in its lower part bags filled with pieces of coal, simple bulbs on the monitors that only produce dim light, in a way that can be seen on these markets. The beauty of simplicity is poetically transformed in this video sculpture.

religiosi più diversi, una città che vive di forti contrasti: le gigantesche piramidi millenarie dalle forme pure e dal fascino sublime, i monumenti secolari islamici, le moschee ed infine il Suc, il mercato di ›Old Cairo‹. Innumerevoli commercianti con le loro bancarelle e imprese anguste, grandi poco più di qualche metro quadrato riempiono le numerossisime viuzze. Tutto di tutto è in vendita, viene pesato, misurato e prodotto secondo il desiderio di ogni singolo cliente: tessuti, spezie, carbone, frutta, verdure, profumi e dappertutto oggetti d'artigianato, un continuo andirivieni. Le cosiddette fabbriche di questi antichi mercati, i suc, sono in realtà piuttosto manifatture, la maggior parte degli allestimenti di presentazione è improvvisata, ogni cosa trova in qualche modo una sua utilizzazione, ogni materiale può essere riadattato alla funzione e alle necessità richieste.

Fabrizio Plessi nella sua installazione *Cairo-Cairo* ha rievocato l'atmosfera di questi antichi mercati, dei Suc arabi. Su due tavoli vengono presentati materiali diversi, spezie ecc., in piccoli mucchi accuratamente separati uno dall'altro. In mezzo ai tavoli è collocato uno dei suoi armadi con, nella parte inferiore, sacchi riempiti di pezzi di carbone, mentre i monitors mostrano comunissime lampadine che emanano una debole luce, proprio come in questi mercati. La videoscultura diviene la trasformazione poetica della bellezza, della semplicità.

MEDITERRANEA

91002

CAGLIARI 1991
GALLERIA D'ARTE MODERNA
91002.1

MITTELMEER
Videoskulptur 1991
Eisenschränke mit Fächern,
Eisengitter, 8 antike Amphoren,
8 Monitore, 1 Videorecorder,
bespielte Kassetten,
Tonaufzeichnung
260 x 640 x 60 cm

MEDITERRANEAN
Video sculpture 1991
Iron construction with
compartments, iron lattice,
8 antique amphoras, 8 monitors,
1 video recorder, recorded video
cassettes, soundrecording
260 x 640 x 60 cm

MEDITERRANEA
Videoscultura 1991
Struttura in ferro a scomparti,
8 anfore archeologiche di scavo,
8 monitors, 1 vhs, 2 cassette
registrate, sonoro
260 x 640 x 60 cm

Eine der späteren Schrankskulpturen, die noch nicht auf der großen Ausstellung 1990 in Reggio Emilia zuvor präsentiert werden konnte, heißt *Mediterranea (Mittelmeer)* und ist zu verstehen als eine weitere Hymne oder Hommage an das Wasser, hier spezifisch an das Meer, das Meer und die Geheimnisse, die es birgt. Denn in dem unteren Teil der Schränke sind antike Vasen plaziert, Amphoren und Gefäße, die als Fundstücke aus dem Meeresgrund herausgeholt wurden. Ihre Oberfläche ist noch bedeckt von Muscheln und kristallisiertem Leben im Wasser und weisen auf Zeit und Vergänglichkeit. Es sind Erinnerungsstücke vorangegangener Kulturen, die in diesem Schrank fast archäologisch archiviert zu werden scheinen. Eine Art von Spurensicherung wird hier betrieben und zugleich auf das Geheimnisvolle des Meeres, das immer wieder neue Schätze hervorbringt, verwiesen. In den oberen Monitoren laufen synchron Videofilme, die einen Ausschnitt eines solchen Gefäßes dem Betrachter halb zugewendet präsentieren, so daß er beinahe in das Innere zu schauen vermag. Doch das Geheimnis, was es letztendlich mit diesen Gefäßen und Amphoren auf sich hat, bleibt ungelüftet.

One of the later cabinet sculptures that had not been presented in the great exhibition in Reggio Emilia in 1990 is called Mediterranea (Mediterranean Sea), *and is to be understood as another hymn or homage to the water, here specifically to the sea and the secrets it hides. For, in the lower part of the cabinets antique vases are placed, amphoras and vessels that have been taken from the sea as objets trouvés. Their surface is still covered with mussels and crystallised aquatic life, and point to time and decay. They are reminiscences of former cultures, almost archeologically stored in this cabinet. A sort of securing of traces is practised here, at the same time pointing to the secrets of the sea producing ever new treasures. On the monitors above synchronised films are shown that present a section of one such vessel, halfway turned towards the spectator, so that he can almost look inside. But the secret of these vessels and amphoras remains veiled.*

Una delle sculture più tarde che impiega armadi e che non è stata esposta alla grande mostra di Reggio Emilia nel 1990 s'intitola *Mediterranea*: essa è da considerare un altro inno o omaggio all'acqua, qui specificatamente al mare con i suoi segreti nascosti. Nella parte inferiore degli armadi sono collocati vasi, anfore e contenitori ritrovati in fondo al mare. La loro superficie è ancora coperta da conchiglie e residui cristalizzati della vita nell'acqua che alludono al tempo e alla fugacità. Essi sono ricordi di culture passate e sembrano quasi reperti archeologici archiviati. Ci si trova di fronte ad una forma di indizio e contemporaneamente ad un'allusione all'enigma del mare che di continuo riporta in superficie nuovi tesori. I videofilms dei monitors presentano dettagli dei contenitori in modo tale che lo spettatore riesce quasi a intravedere l'interno senza svelare però il vero segreto dei vasi e delle anfore.

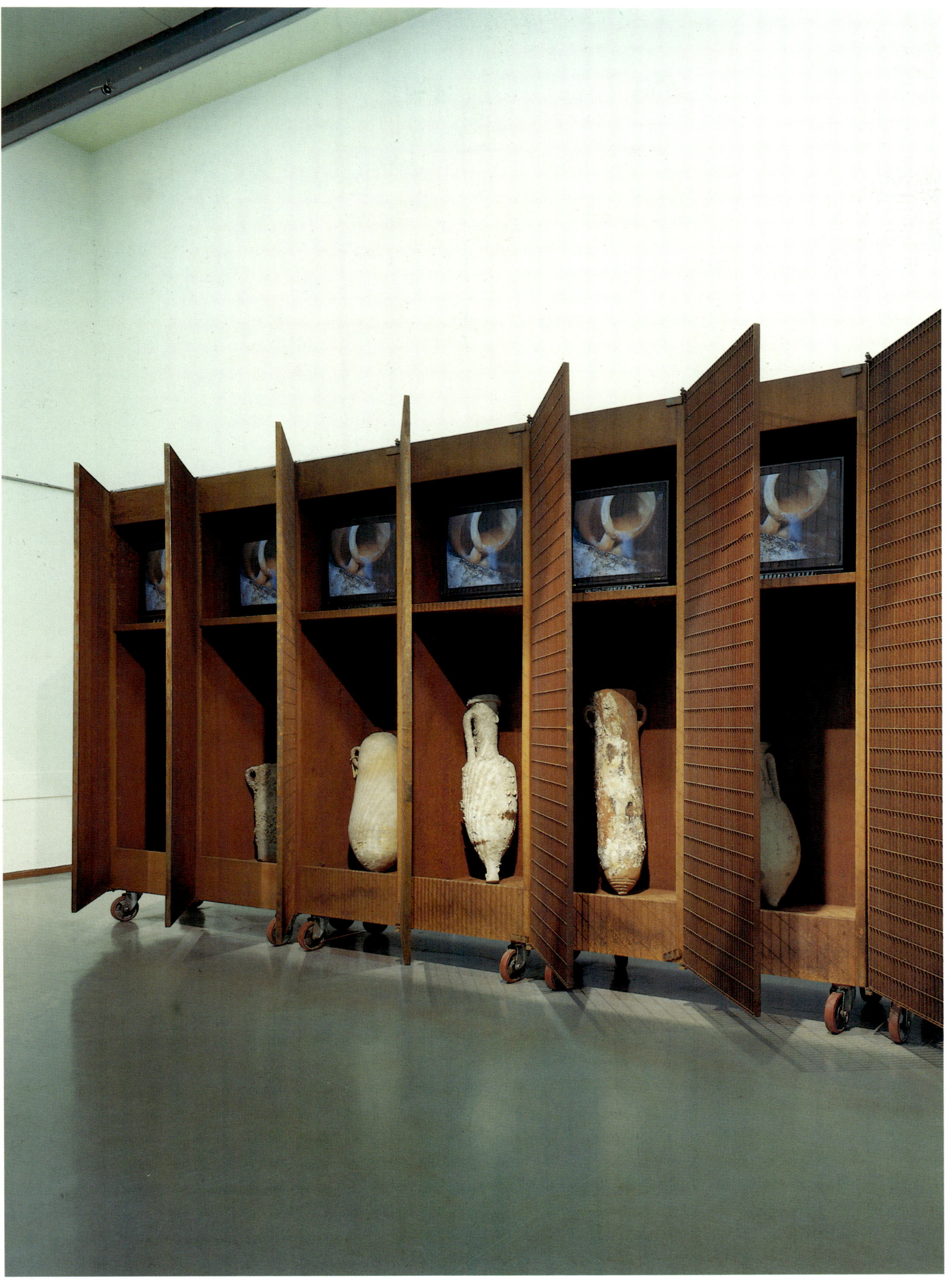

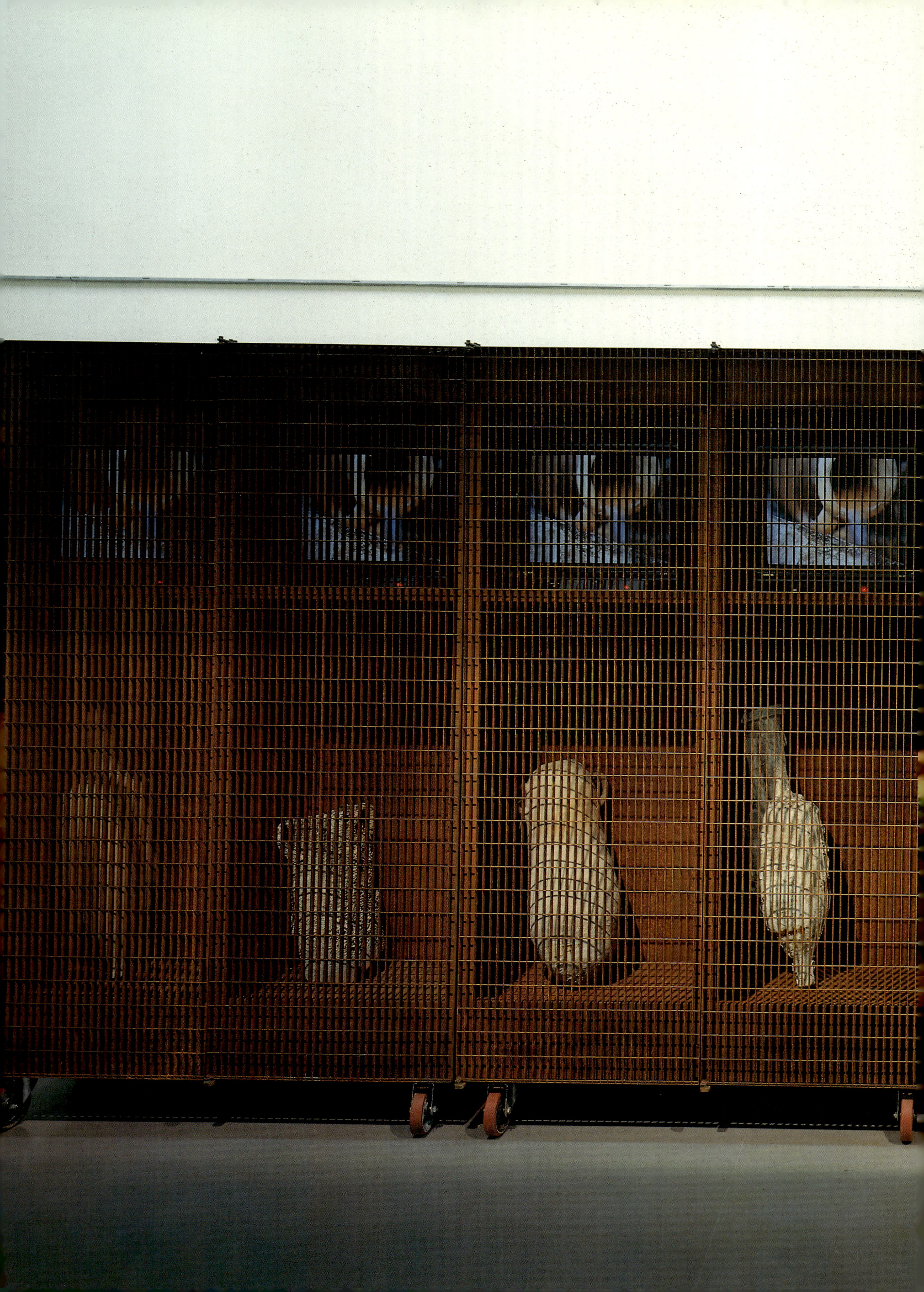

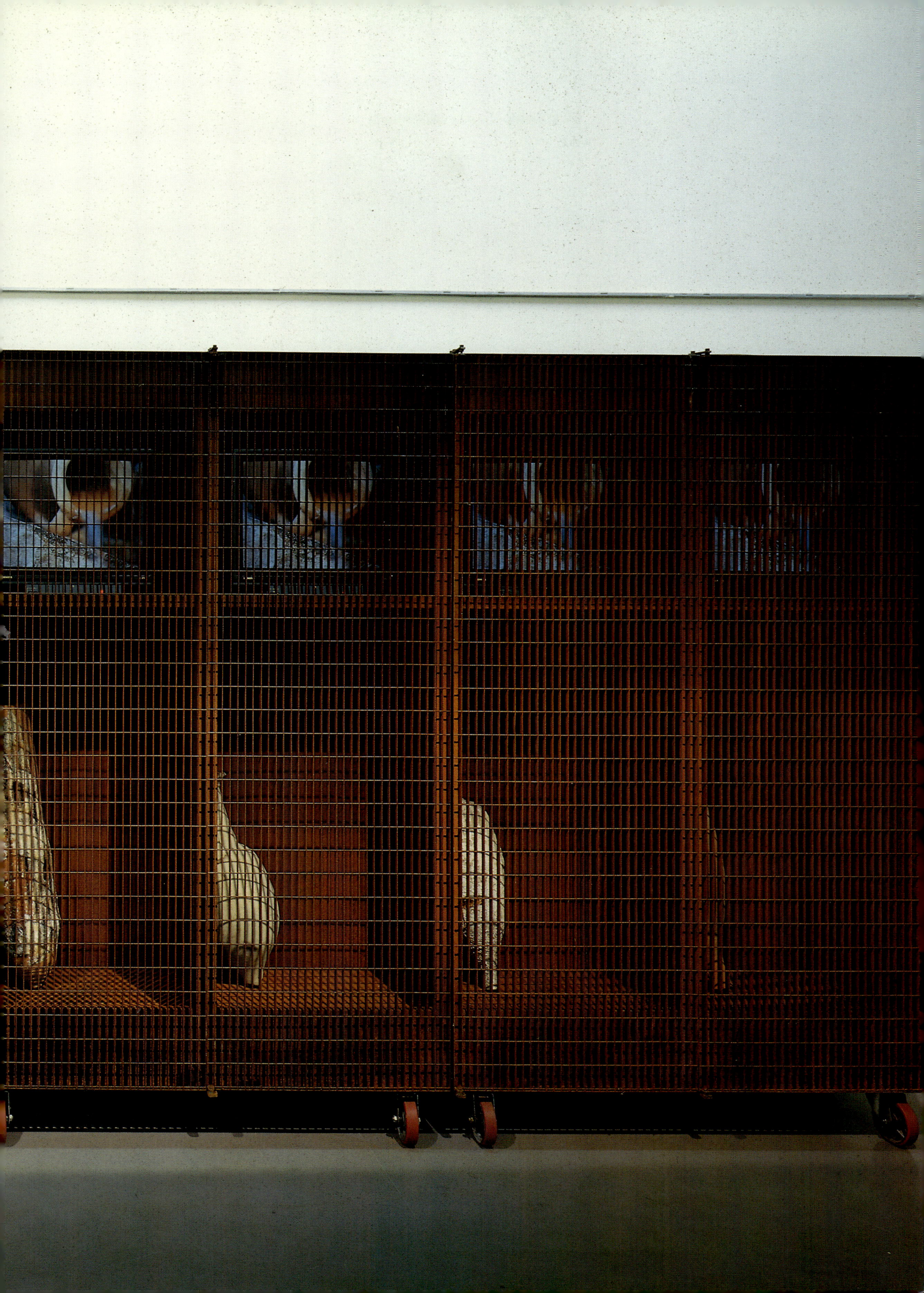

PORFIDO A PERGINE

91003

PERGINE 1991
CASTELLO DE PERGINE
91003.1

PORPHYR IN PERGINE
Videoinstallation 1991
Platten aus Porphyr, Stahlbänder,
14 Monitore, Videorecorder,
bespielte Kassette,
Tonaufzeichnung

PORPHYRY AT PERGINE
Video installation 1991
Porphyry slabs, iron belts,
14 monitors, video recorder,
recorded video cassette,
soundrecording

PORFIDO A PERGINE
Videoinstallazione 1991
Lastre di porfido di diverse
misure, cighie di metallo,
14 monitors, 1 vhs, cassetta
registrata, sonoro

Der zentrale, voluminöse achtekkige Pfeiler im Schloß von Pergine, der den Raum in vier kreuzgratgewölbte Joche unterteilt, ist mit Platten aus Porphyr ummantelt. Durch die Porphyrplatten, die Plessi in der Nähe eines Steinbruches bei Pergine gefunden hat, ziehen sich eisenhaltige Strukturen. Um den Pfeiler herum fließt ein kreisförmiger Ring aus elektronischem Wasser, ebenfalls eingefaßt in Porphyr. Die Ummantelung des Pfeilers, mit den Porphyrplatten in verschiedenen Grautönen, wird gehalten durch zwei Stahlbänder aus rostrotem Stahl. In dieser Farbigkeit leuchtet der elektronische Wasserring hell heraus. In den geschlossenen Eisenstrukturen, die im Steinbruch für den Transport der Platten dienen, hatte sich Wasser gesammelt und spiegelte die Umwelt. Das erinnerte Fabrizio Plessi unmittelbar an elektronisches Wasser wie in seinen Monitoren, und so versuchte er, dieses visuelle Erlebnis - das mit den örtlichen Gegebenheiten in Zusammenhang stand - in dem Saal des Schlosses von Pergine zu rekonstruieren.

The voluminous central octagonal pillar in Pergine castle that divides the room into four cross-arched sectors is mantled with sheets of Porphyry. These plates of porphyry, that Fabrizio Plessi has found near a quarry in Pergine contain iron ore structures. A circular ring of electronic water, also embedded in porphyry, flows around the pillar. The sheets of porphyry in different greys covering the pillar are held by two bands of rusty red steel. The electronic circle of water shines brightly in this field of colour. Water had collected in the closed iron structures that served to transport the plates in the quarry, reflecting their environment. That reminded Fabrizio Plessi directly of electronic water, as on his monitors, and so he tried to reconstruct this visual experience - that was connected with the local conditions - in the hall of Pergine castle.

Il pilastro centrale ottagonale del Castello di Pergine che divide la sala in quattro volte a croce è rivestito da lastre di porfido di diverse tonalità di grigio, trovate da Plessi vicino ad una cava presso Pergine. Le lastre sono attraversate da strutture metalliche. Nei monitors intorno al pilastro, a loro volta rivestiti di porfido, scorre in cerchio acqua elettronica. Il rivestimento del pilastro è tenuto da due fasce di ferro arrugginito. Dalle tonalità dei colori risalta chiaramente l'anello d'acqua elettronica. Le strutture chiuse metalliche, impiegate nella cava per il trasporto delle lastre e nelle quali si era accumulata l'acqua che rifletteva l'ambiente circostante, fecero ricordare a Fabrizio Plessi l'acqua elettronica dei suoi monitors e, di conseguenza, nella sala del castello egli cerca di ricostruire tale esperienza visiva, direttamente collegata con le caratteristiche locali.

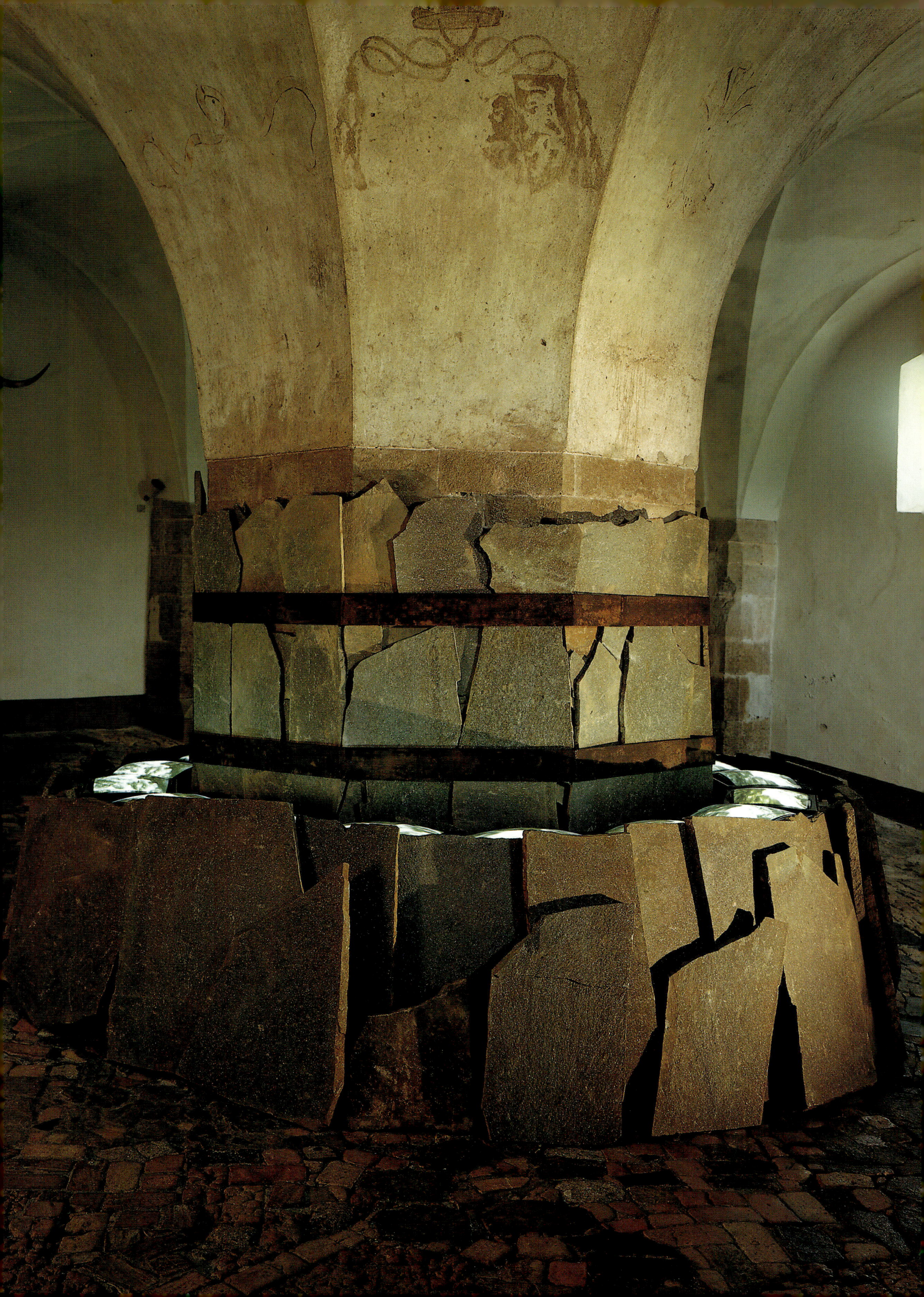

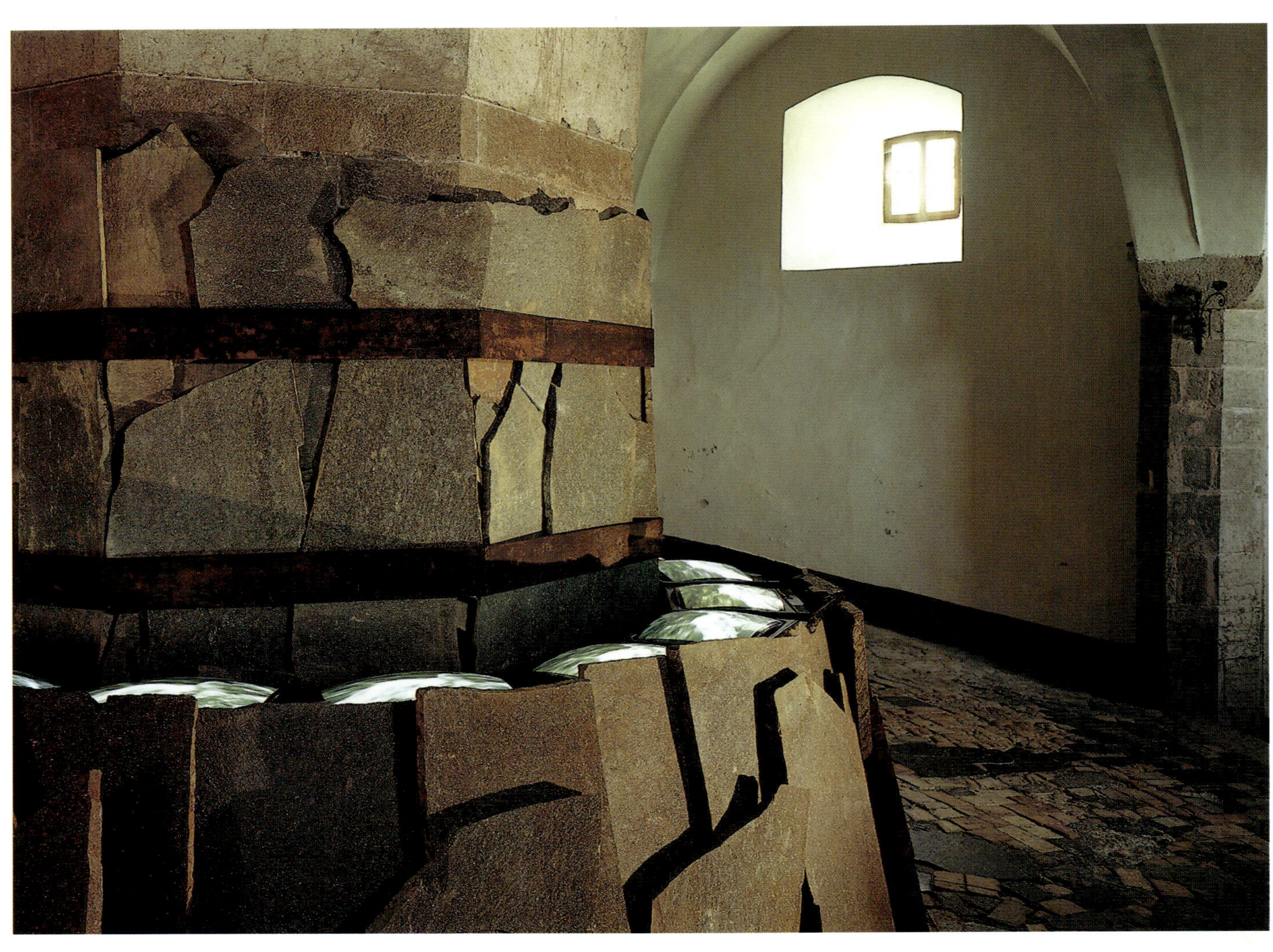

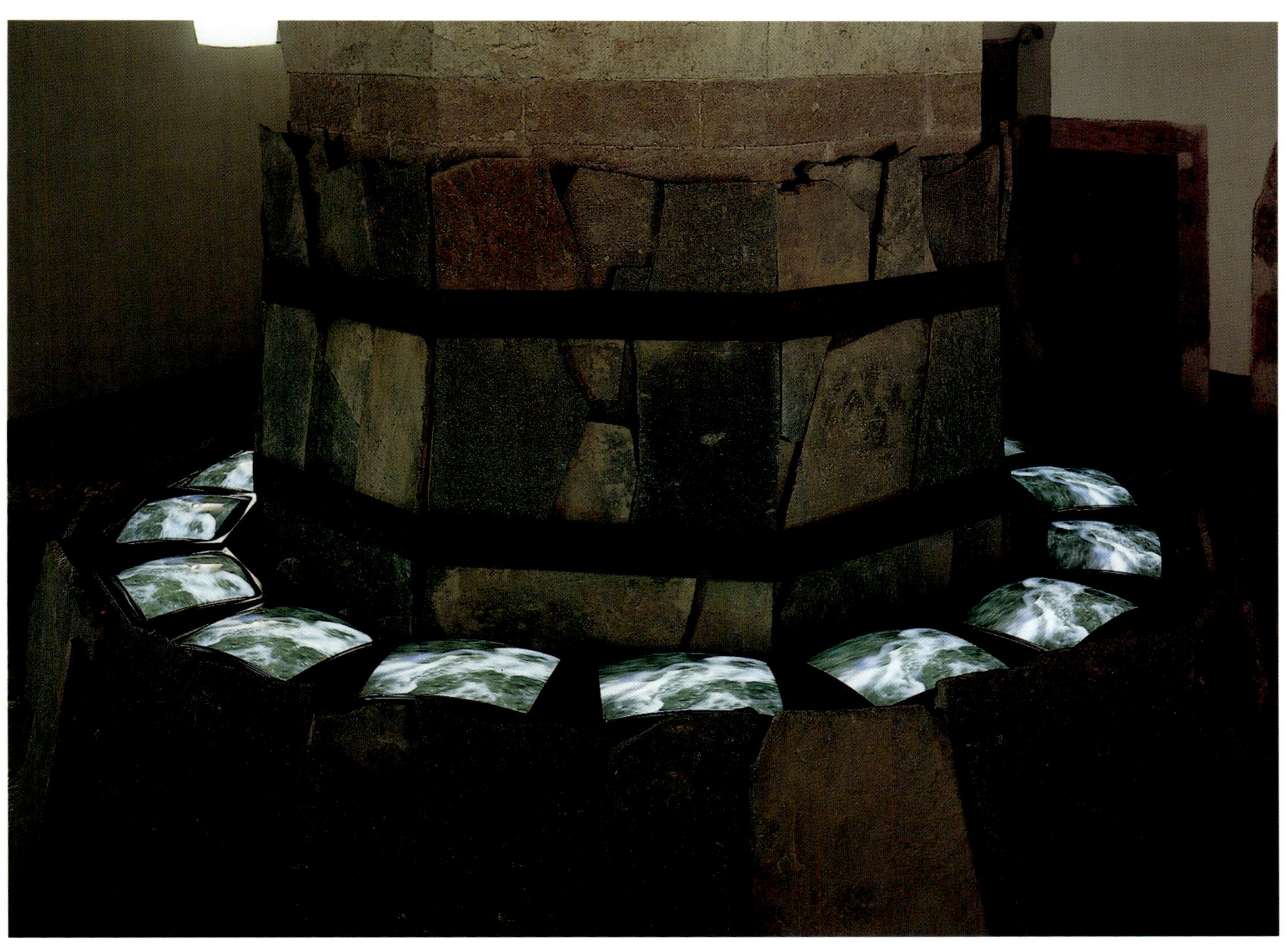

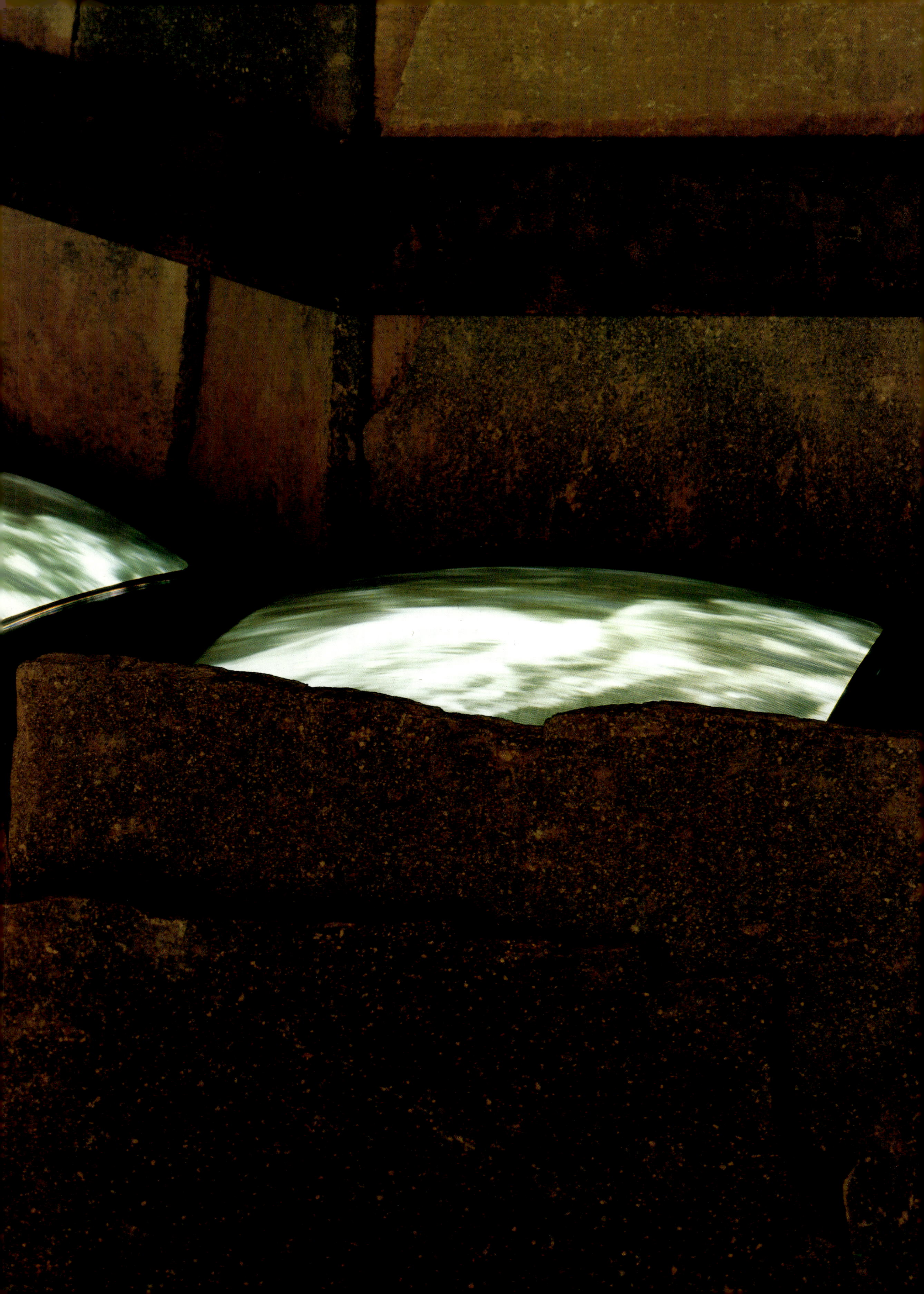

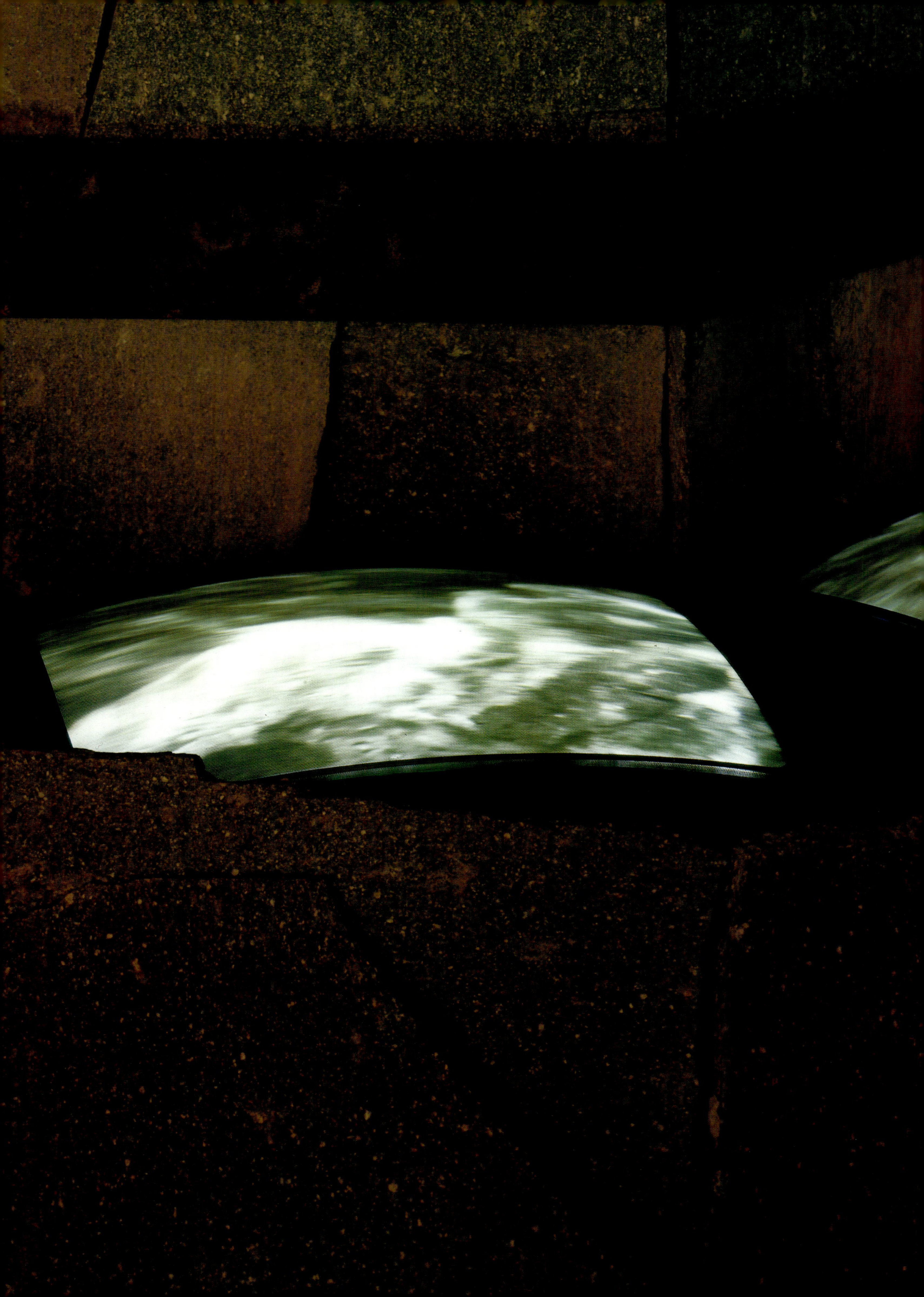

MATERIA PRIMA II

92001

MARIBOR 1992
UMETNOSTNA GALERIJA
92001.1

BOLOGNA 1997
GALLERIA D'ARTE MODERNA
92001.2

URMATERIE
Videoinstallation 1992
28 ausgeschaltete Monitore,
kreisförmige Zusammenstellung,
Travertinplatten und Platten aus
grauem Stein

PRIMEVAL MATTER
Video installation 1992
Slabs of Light grey stone and
travertine, 28 switched-off
monitors

MATERIA PRIMA II
Lastre di travertino e di pietra
serena grigia, 28 monitors spenti

Die zweite Version von *Materia Prima* ist im Gegensatz zur ersten, bei der die Monitore informell als Struktur über den Raum verteilt waren, nun zu einer Kreisform zusammengestellt. Die Monitore, mit der Bildfläche nach oben, sind nach wie vor ausgeschaltet. So, als warteten sie noch auf ihre Bestimmung.

Es gibt von Fabrizio Plessi ein schönes Gedicht dazu mit dem Titel *Urmaterie*:

Noch vor der Geburt des Lichts,
als alles noch regungslos lag,
Noch vor der Geburt des Feuers,
als Licht nur Sonnenlicht war,
Noch vor der Verfestigung der
Erde, als alles Sumpf war und
feuchter Schlamm,
Noch vor der Geburt des Wassers
aus dem Schlamm, als das Magma
aus Basalt und Quarz glühte,
Noch vor der Versteinerung der
Fossilien, als die grauen Steine
noch schwiegen,
Noch vor dem großen Erwachen,
als der Äther noch nicht von
verrückten Satelliten fremdartige
Alarmsignale in Codes übertrug,
Gab es jene Zeit - die Zeit der
›Urmaterie‹.

(Fabrizio Plessi, in: *Videoskulptur*, Köln 1989, S. 249)

The second version of Materia Prima, *other than the first in which the monitors were distributed informally as structure in space, now shows them in a circular form. The monitors, their screens upwards, are still switched off, as if waiting for their purpose.*

Fabrizio Plessi has written a beautiful poem, entitled Primeval matter, *about this:*

Even before the birth of light,
when everything rested
motionless, still,
Even before the birth of fire,
when light was sunlight alone,
Even before the Earth was solid,
when everything was swamp
and wet mud,
Even before the birth of water
from mud, when magma of
quartz and basalt glowed,
Even before the petrifaction of
fossils, when the grey stones
were silent still,
Even before the great awakening, when ether not yet transmitted alien codes of alarm from mad satellites,
There was that time - the time of
'primeval matter'.

Diversamente dalla prima versione di *Materia Prima* dove i monitors sono distribuiti in una struttura informale nell'ambiente, la seconda li presenta in forma di cerchio. Gli schermi rivolti verso l'alto sono, come prima, spenti come se aspettassero ancora la loro destinazione.

Per l'occasione Fabrizio Plessi ha composto una bella poesia dal titolo *Materia Prima*:

Prima ancora della nascita della luce,
quando tutto era cenere immobile ed
inerte,
Prima ancora del grande risveglio del
quarzo, quando il chiarore era solo
quello rituale del sole,
Prima ancora della fisicità opaca della
terra, quando tutto era fango e melma
umida,
Prima ancora dello scorrere gelido
dell'acqua, quando tutto era incandescente magma di basalto,
Prima ancora della solidità ostinata
del fossile, quando tutte le pietre
grigie della terra ancora dormivano,
Prima ancora che i grandi silenzi si
coprissero di lava, quando l'etere
ancora non trasmetteva sinistri
segnali d'allarme in codice, da lontani
terminali impazziti,
Quello! si, quello era il tempo della
›materia prima‹

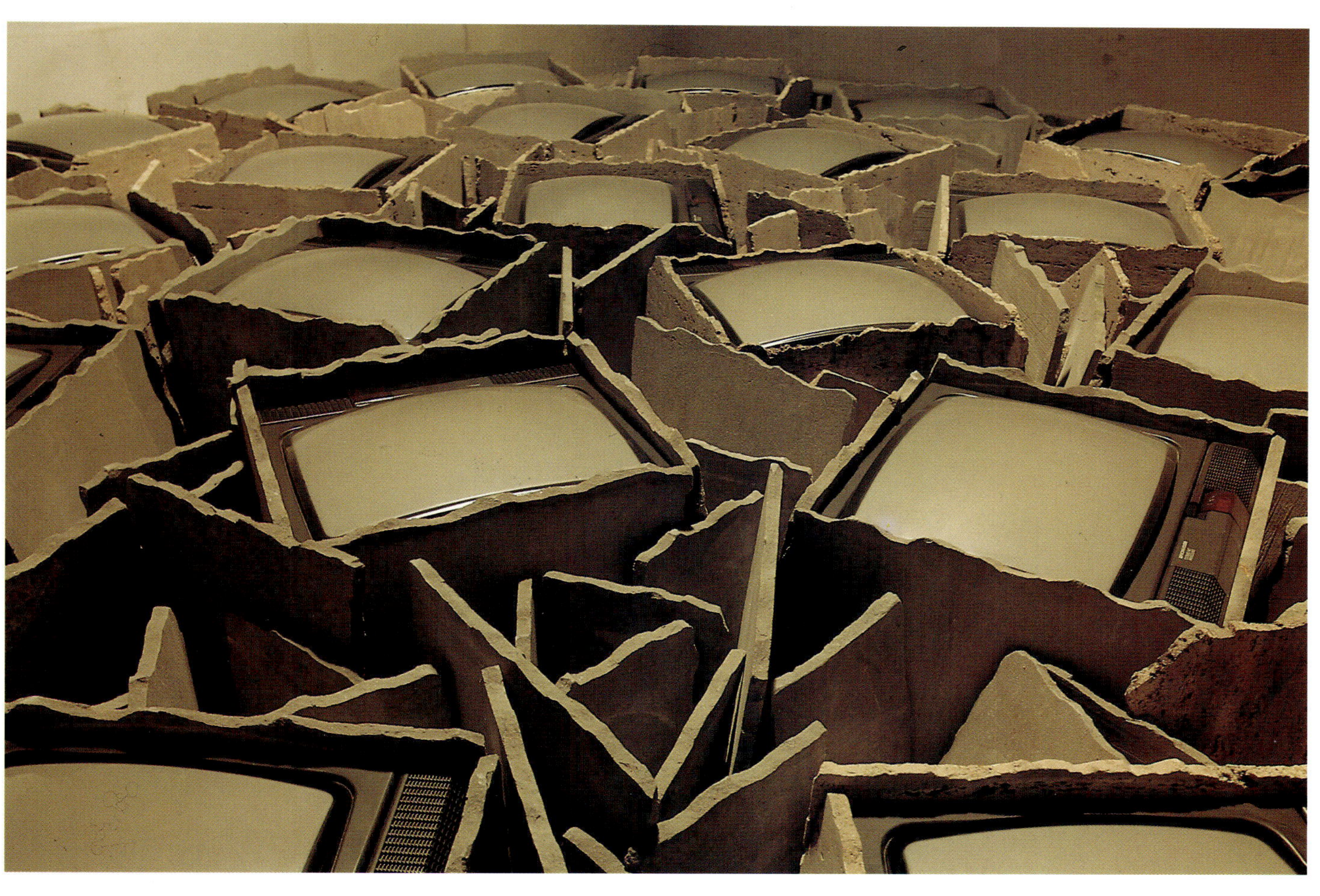

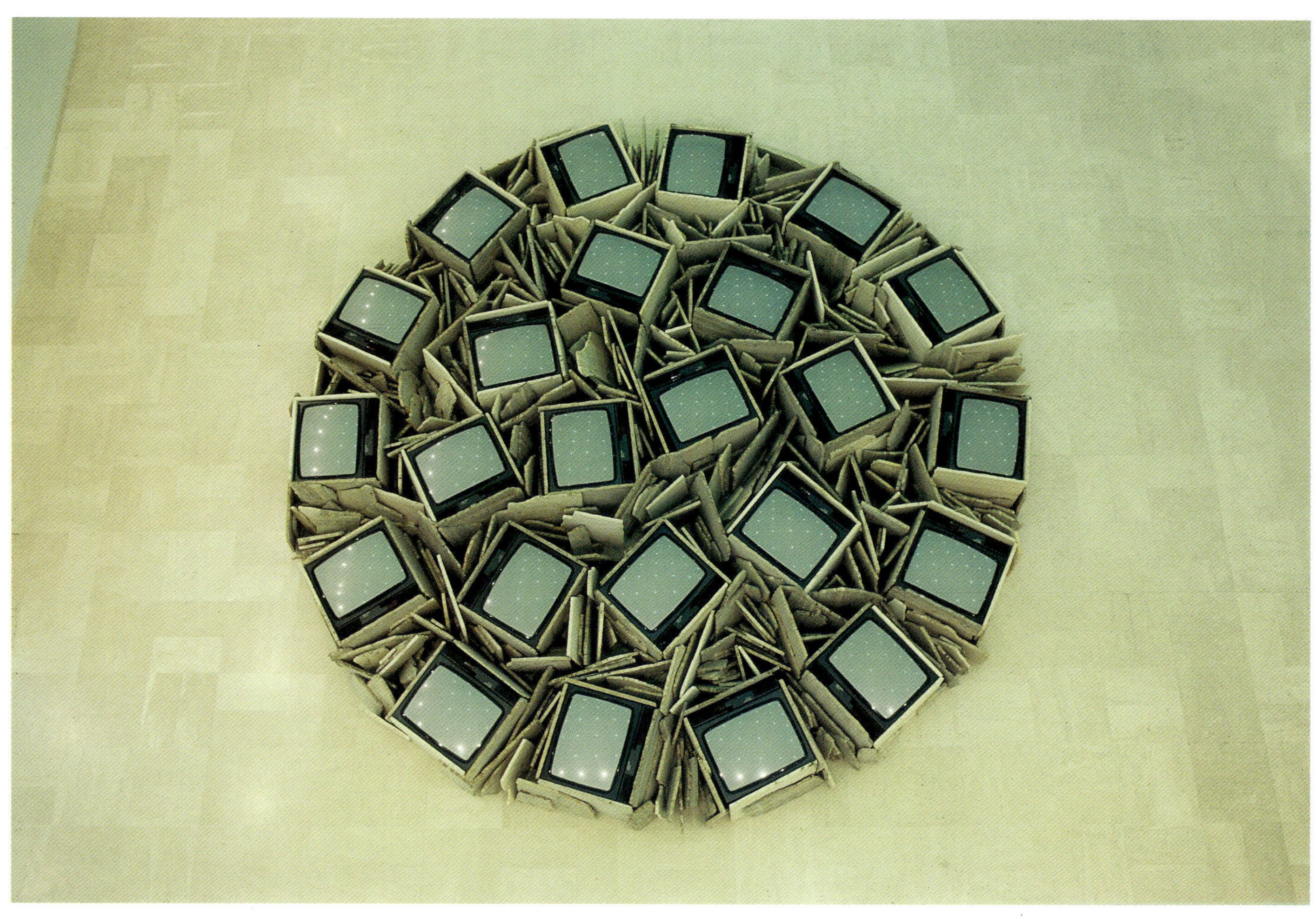

DIE KARYATIDEN DER ARMEN

92002

GRAZ 1992
HAUS DER ARCHITEKTUR
92002.1

DORTMUND 1993
MUSEUM AM OSTWALL
92002.2

MAINZ 1995
GALERIE DOROTHEA VAN DER KOELEN
92002.3

BASEL 1995
GALERIE DOROTHEA VAN DER KOELEN, ART BASEL
92002.4

PERUGIA 1995
ROCCA PAOLINA
92002.5

DIE KARYATIDEN DER ARMEN
Videoskulptur 1992
Gebrauchte Koffer, Schnüre,
elektrische Glühlampen,
4 Monitore, 4 Videorecorder,
bespielte Kassetten,
Tonaufzeichnung

THE CARYTIDS OF THE POOR
Video sculpture 1992
Used suitcases, electric bulbs,
ropes, 4 monitors, 4 video
recorder, video cassettes,
soundrecording

LE CARIATIDE DEI POVERI
Videoscultura 1992
Cumuli di vecchie valigie, corda,
lampadine, 4 monitors, 4 vhs,
cassette registrate, sonoro

»Im Unterschied zu früheren Arbeiten haben die *Karyatiden der Armen* einen aktuellen Realitätsbezug, der den Menschen in seiner Geschichte betrifft«, schreibt Claudia Posca zu der Videoinstallation im Dortmunder Katalog; und weiter heißt es dort: Zugleich sind auch die Karyatiden »Mittel zur Thematisierung der Historie. In freier Illustration und meidender Anspielung auf die gebälktragenden Gewandfiguren des Hellenismus und des Barock stapelt Fabrizio Plessi verschlossene Koffer bis zur Decke des verdunkelten Raumes zu vier Säulen auf je einem Monitor auf. Auf den Bildschirmen ist ein in Bezug zur jeweiligen Koffersäule stehendes Bild zu sehen, das von einem gleichmäßige sonoren

Suitcases are a symbol of travel, of change of space. "I travel by disposition, or rather as the result of a natural propensity for movement and the stimuli that I derive from it. I am a great observer, I believe, especially as far as the physicality of materials is concerned. Sometimes, as I lean an elbow on a table, I feel the material 'physically', or rather the marble, the stone, the ceramic communicate with me 'directly'." (Fabrizio Plessi in conversation with Evelyn Weiss, in: catalogue Museum Ludwig, Köln 1993).
Plessi very carefully deals with the inherent laws and inherent values of each individual material he uses, and creates dialogues between the sometimes

Valigie sono un simbolo per il viaggio, per cambiamenti spaziali. »Io viaggio per attitudine, anzi per una naturale attitudine allo spostamento e per gli stimoli che ne derivano. Sono un grande osservatore, credo, soprattutto della fisicità dei materiali. A volte sono appoggiato con un gomito ad un tavolo e fisicamente ›sento‹ il materiale, o meglio il marmo, la pietra, la ceramica comunicano con me ›direttamente‹.« (Fabrizio Plessi, in: Evelyn Weiss - *Un incontro con Fabrizio Plessi*, catalogo Museum Ludwig, Colonia 1993).
Plessi tratta l'autonomia e i valori propri di ogni suo materiale con molta delicatezza e crea dialoghi fra i materiali

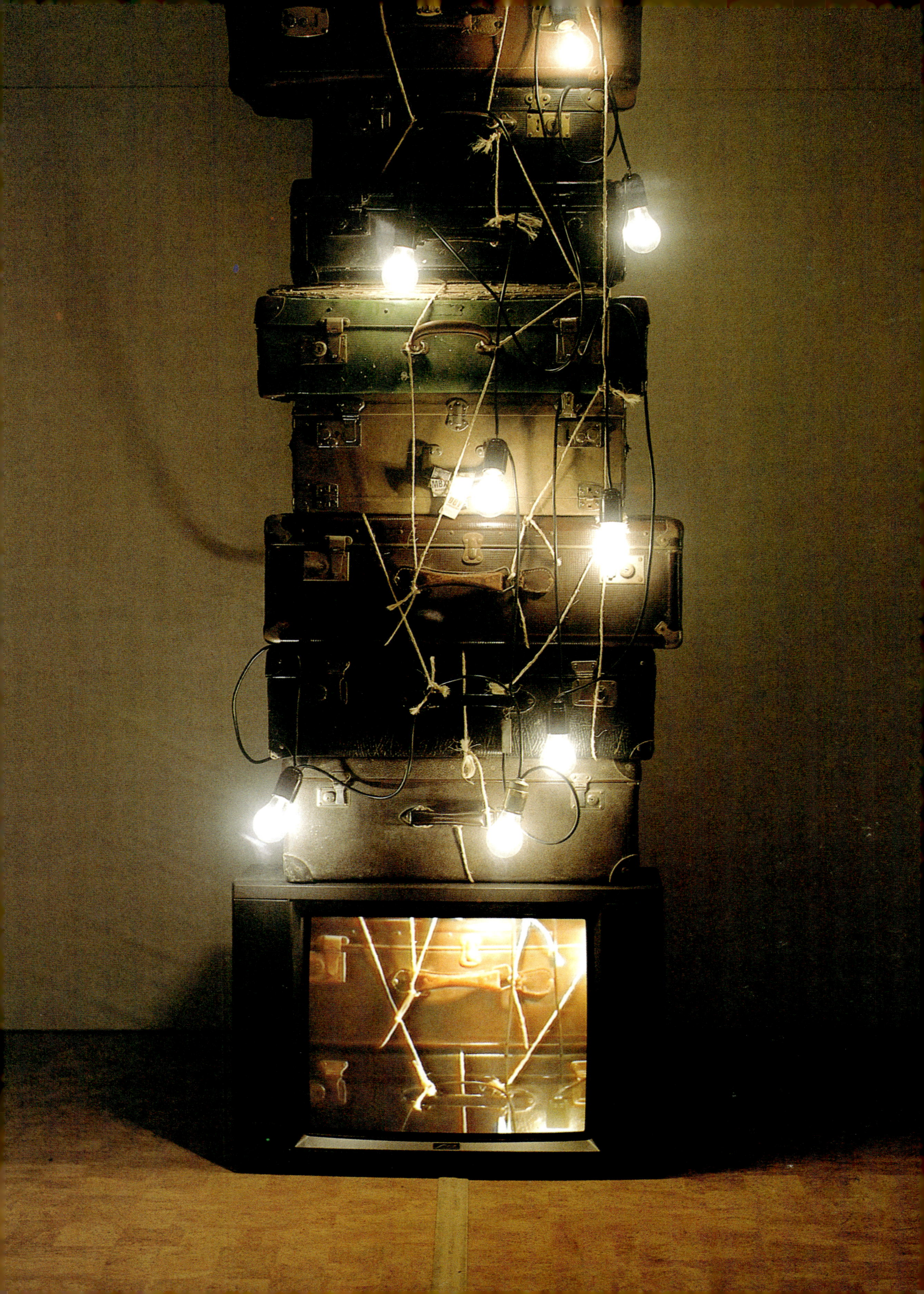

Summton begleitet wird«. Koffer
sind ein Symbol für Reisen, für
räumliche Veränderung. »Ich reise
aus einer Neigung heraus, besser
noch aufgrund einer natürlichen
Neigung zur Verlagerung und
wegen der Anreize, die sich hier-
aus ergeben. Ich glaube, ich bin
vor allem ein großer Beobachter
der Körperlichkeit der Materialien.
Manchmal stütze ich mich mit dem
Ellenbogen auf einen Tisch und
›fühle‹ körperlich das Material,
oder vielmehr kommunizieren der
Marmor, der Stein, die Keramik mit
mir unmittelbar.« (Fabrizio Plessi
im Gespräch mit Evelyn Weiss, in:
Katalog vom Museum Ludwig, Köln
1993).

Plessi geht mit der Eigengesetz-
lichkeit und Eigenwertigkeit jeden
einzelnen Materials, das er verwendet, sehr behutsam um, und er
stellt Dialoge der gelegentlich
recht heterogenen Materialien
untereinander her. »Von jeder
meiner Reisen kehre ich zurück,
wie man etwa im 18. Jh. von einer
großen Reise zurückgekehrt wäre:
mit einer unglaublichen Zahl
kleiner Zeichnungen, voller Noti-
zen über Materialien, Arten von
Erde, Farben, Wänden, Quellen
und Gegenständen, denen ich
begegnet bin. Die Arbeit des
Zusammenstellens und der Dokumentation geht immer der Entwicklung eines Projektes voraus, in
das diese Materialien später einge-
bracht werden sollen. Erst später
wird aus dieser Sammlung von
Beobachtungen wertvolles Material
für meine Arbeit.« (Fabrizio Plessi,
a.a.O.) Für Fabrizio Plessi ist, vor
allem mit Beginn der 90er Jahre,
das Reisen zum wichtigen Bestandteil seines Werkes geworden. So
hat er zahlreiche Projekte, Videoinstallationen und Zeichnungen
verschiedenen Städten, Orten,
Plätzen und Ländern, verteilt über
die ganze Welt, gewidmet und noch
längst sind nicht alle Zeichnungen

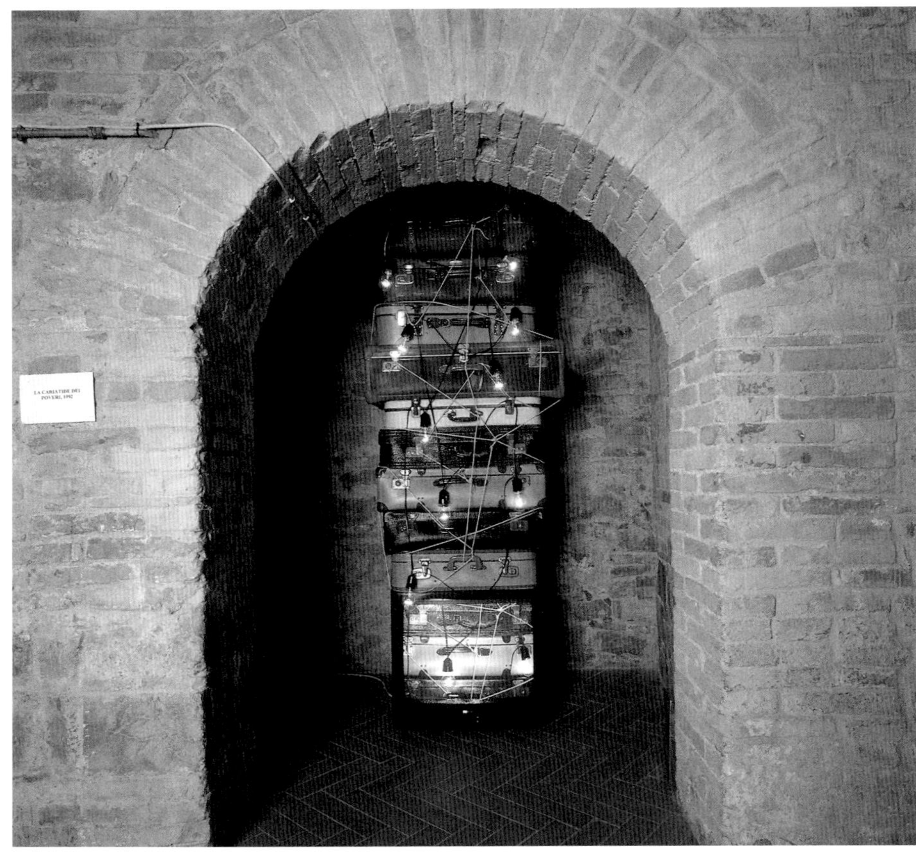

*rather heterogeneous materials.
"After each of my journeys, as if
returning from an 19th-century
Grand Tour, I come back with
an incredible number of small
drawings, full of notations of
materials, types of earth, colours, walls, fountains, grills,
utensils I have encountered. The
act of gathering and documenting always precedes the development of a project in which
to insert these materials. Only
later will this collection of
observations become precious
material for my work." (Fabrizio Plessi, loc.cit.) Travelling
has, especially since the beginning of the nineties, become an
important part of Fabrizio
Plessi's work. Thus he has
dedicated numerous projects,
video installations and drawings to different cities, towns,
places and countries all over the
world, and by far not all drawings and sketches have been*

spesso piuttosto eterogenei. »Da
ogni mio viaggio, come al ritorno da ogni peregrinare ottocen-
tesco, riporto uno sterminato
numero di piccoli disegni cari-
chi di annotazioni di materiali,
terre, colori, muri, fontane,
grigliati, utensili incontrati. Il
gesto del raccogliere e del
documentare precede sempre
l'esistenza di un progetto su cui
riversare questi materiali. Solo
più tardi questa natura collezio-
nata diventerà materia per il
mio lavoro.« (Fabrizio Plessi, op.
cit). Il viaggiare è diventato,
soprattutto dall'inizio degli anni
novanta, una parte importante
dell'opera di Fabrizio Plessi;
molti progetti, videoinstallazioni
e disegni sono dedicati alle
varie città, località e piazze e ai
paesi di tutto il mondo e ancora
molti disegni attendono la loro
conversione in videosculture e
installazioni. »Molti dei miei
lavori nascono dall'idea del

und Entwürfe in Videoskulpturen oder Installationen umgesetzt. »Viele meiner Arbeiten entstehen aus der Idee zu reisen. Im vergangenen Jahr zum Beispiel habe ich anläßlich der Ausstellung in Graz im *Haus der Architektur* eine Installation entworfen, die aus Karyatiden von Koffern besteht. Gerade bei dem Gedanken an diese Wanderungen, an diese Veränderungen, an diese traurige soziale und politische Instabilität jener Völker sind die *Karyatiden der Armen* entstanden. Das ehemalige Jugoslawien, der Balkan, Polen, Rußland, Ost-Europa sind nichts anders als riesige Container von Karyatiden. Diese Unbehagen, das für mich nicht nur literarisch oder ästhetisch ist, hat sich in ein wahres, fast körperliches Unbehagen verwandelt, das sich nur durch meine Arbeit ausdrücken läßt und darin sein kathartisches Moment findet.« (Plessi, a.a.O.)

Geschichts- oder Ortsbezug gibt es im Werk Plessis, in seinen Videoinstallationen und Zeichnungen eigentlich immer. Trotzdem überrascht und erschüttert diese deutliche Bezugnahme, vielleicht weil der historische Abstand fehlt, vielleicht weil alles dies aktuelle Wahrheit ist und weil Kunst, die in ihrer Zeit entsteht und Zeitbezüge sichtbar werden läßt, immer betroffen macht. Doch dieses Werk ist in mehrerlei Hinsicht interessant. Zum einen weist die Gegenwart der Videoskulptur auf eine Realität, die als wahr, für uns aber aus der Distanz kaum als wirklich empfunden wird. Zum anderen erscheint in dem Monitor verfilmt ein Ausschnitt der Installation selbst, Abbild, Vorstellung, Idee oder Kontinuum. Darüber hinaus stehen die Koffer als Sinnbild für örtliche Veränderung von Menschen schlechthin; die Vorstellung des Reisens und damit die Basis für zahlreiche Werke von Plessi ist impliziert.

realised in video sculptures or installations. "Many of my works are born from the idea of travel. Last year, for example, on the occasion of the exhibition in Graz at the Haus der Architektur *I had the idea of an installation composed of caryatids consisting of suitcases. The* Caryatids of the Poor *were born precisely from the thought of the migrations, the displacements, the painful political and social instability of those people. Former Yugoslavia, the Balkans, Poland, Russia, eastern Europe are nothing but enormous containers of caryatids. This feeling of unease, which for me is not merely literary or aesthetic, was traumatised into a real and almost physical uneasiness which is expressed and finds its cathartic moment only via my work." (Fabrizio Plessi, loc.cit.)*

There is almost always a reference to history and place in Plessi's work, in his video installations and drawings. Nevertheless, this clear reference surprises and irritates, perhaps because the historic distance is lacking, perhaps because all this is actual truth, and because art that refers to its present and makes these references visible always confounds. This work is interesting in many aspects: on the one hand the presence of the video sculpture points to a reality sensed as true, yet, from a distance, hardly considered as real by us. On the other hand, the monitor shows a film of a section of the installation itself, a copy, perception, idea or continuum. Beyond this, the suitcases are a symbol of people's change of locality in general, implying the idea of travelling and as such, the basis of numerous of Plessi's works.

viaggio. Lo scorso anno, per esempio, in occasione della mostra a Graz alla *Haus der Architektur* ho ideato un'istallazione composta da cariatidi di valige. Proprio pensando a queste migrazioni, a questi spostamenti, a questa dolorosa instabilità politica e sociale di quei popoli sono nate le *Cariatidi dei Poveri*. La ex-Yugoslavia, i Balcani, la Polonia, la Russia, l'est europeo non sono altro che enormi containers di cariatidi. Questo disagio, che per me non è soltanto letterario o estetico, si è tramutato in un vero disagio quasi fisico che, solo attraverso il mio lavoro, si esprime e trova il suo momento catartico.« (Fabrizio Plessi, op. cit.).

Riferimenti a località e alla storia sono una costante nell'opera di Plessi, nei suoi disegni e videoinstallazioni che tuttavia sorprendono e sconvolgono, forse perchè verità attuale e perchè l'arte che nasce dall'attualità del suo tempo coinvolge da sempre. Ma la *Cariatide dei Poveri* è interessante sotto molti aspetti. Da un lato la presenza della videoscultura rimanda ad una realtà che noi sentiamo vera ma dalla distanza non reale, dall'altro lato nel monitor appare filmato un dettaglio dell'installazione stessa: riproduzione, immaginazione, idea o continuità. Le valigie inoltre simboleggiano per antonomasia lo spostamento degli uomini nello spazio; l'idea del viaggiare, la base di numerose opere di Plessi, vi è implicitamente espressa.

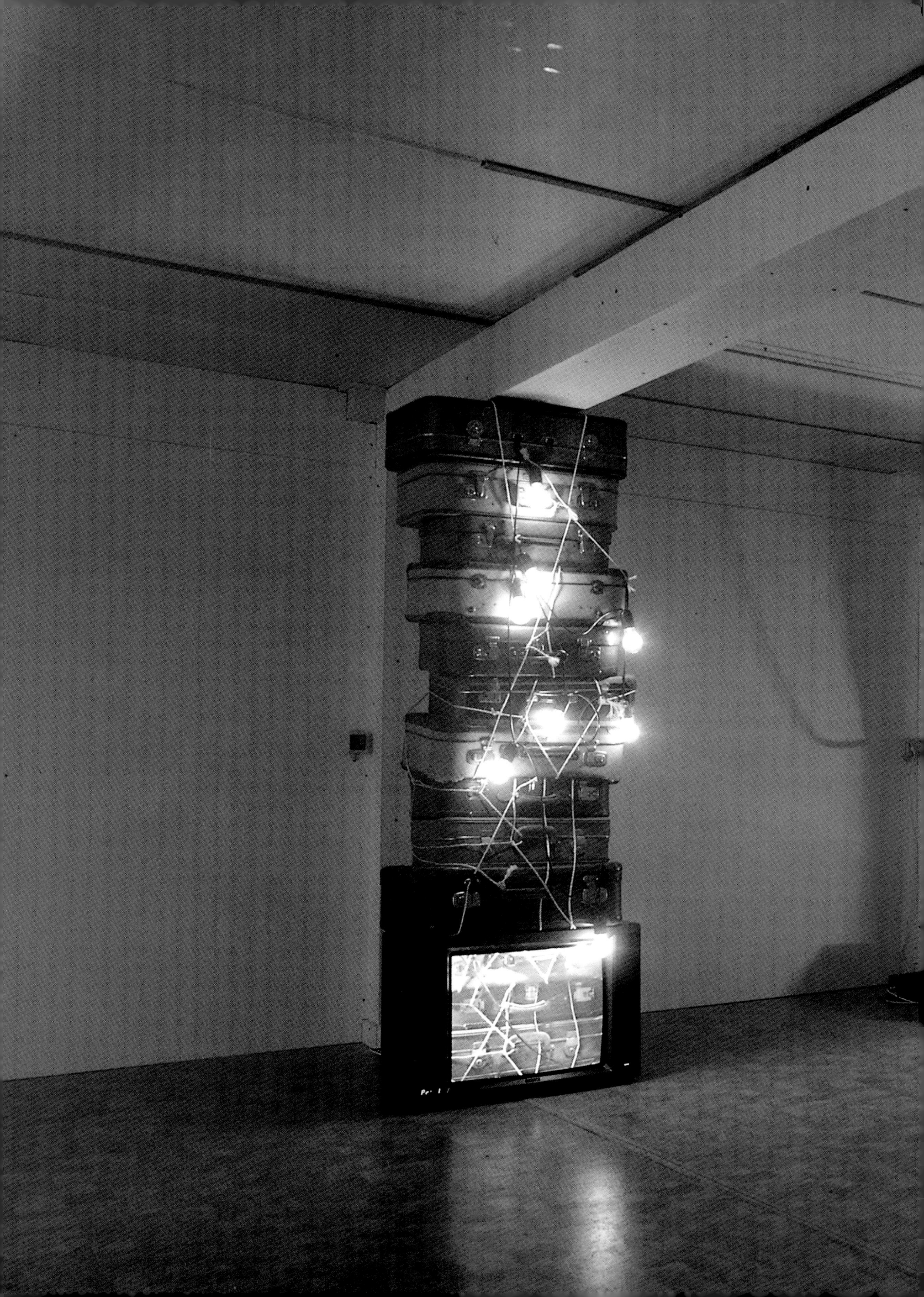

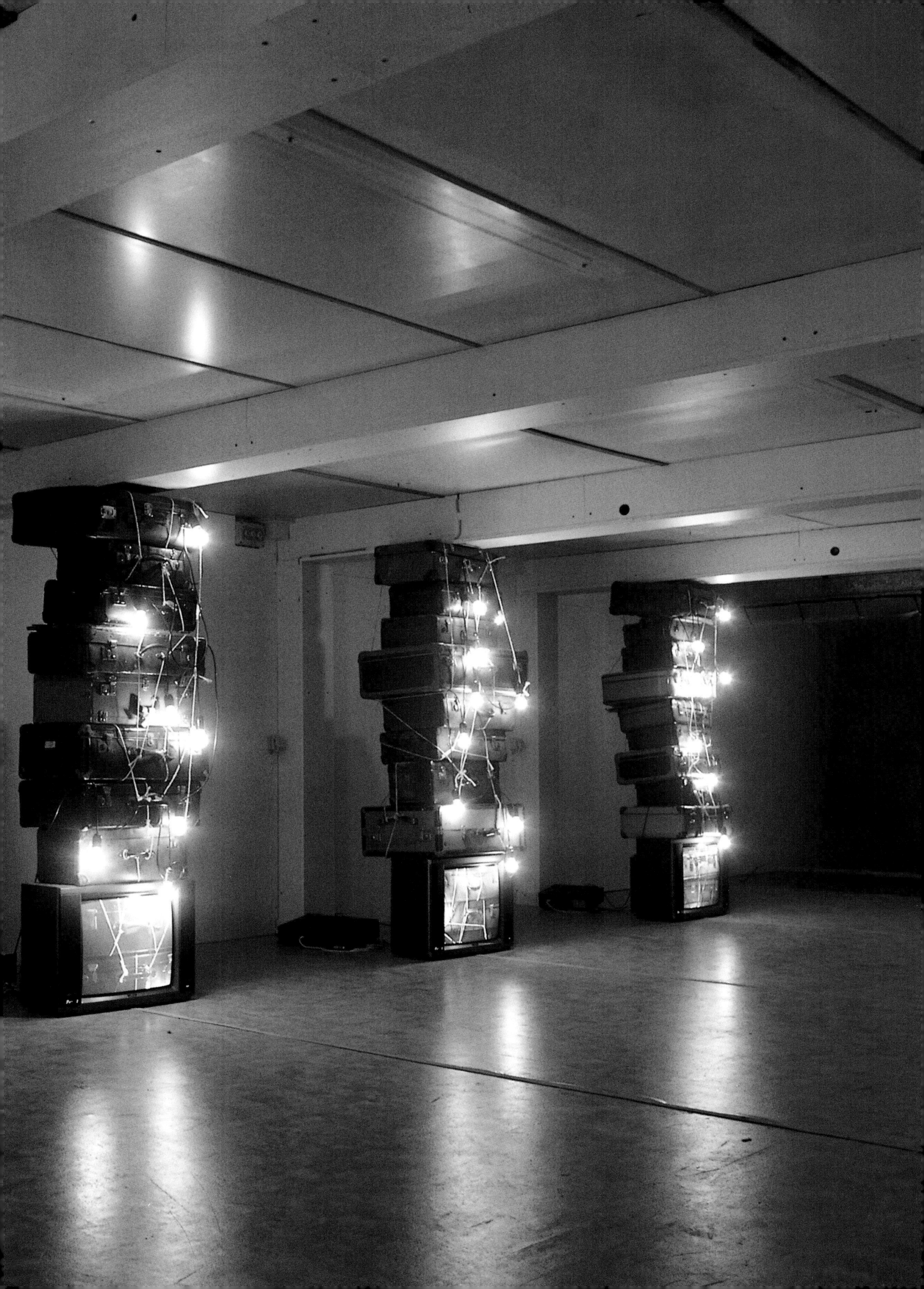

DER RAUM DER WÖRTER

92003

BERLIN 1992
Akademie der Künste
92003.1

DORTMUND 1993
Museum am Ostwall
92003.2

DER RAUM DER WÖRTER
Videoinstallation 1992
Eisenschränke mit Eisengittern,
2000 Bücher, Schraubzwinge,
Wasserhahn, Buch, 16 Monitore,
2 Videorecorder, bespielte
Kassetten, Tonaufzeichnung
260 x 1280 x 60 cm

ROOM OF WORDS
Video installation 1992
Iron construction with compart-
ments, iron lattice, 2000 books, screw
clamp, water-tap, book, 16 monitors,
2 video recorders, recorded video
cassettes, soundrecording
260 x 1280 x 60 cm

LA STANZA DELLE PAROLE
Videoinstallazione 1992
Struttura in ferro a scomparti,
grigliato industriale, 2000 libri,
sergente, rubinetto dell'acqua,
libro, 26 monitors, 2 vhs, cassette
registrate, sonoro
260 x 1280 x 60 cm

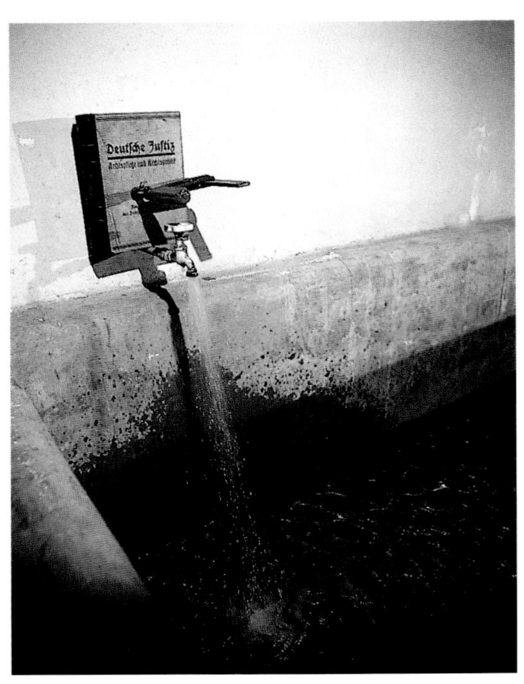

Mit dem *Raum der Wörter* in der Akademie der Künste in Berlin beginnt im Werk Fabrizio Plessis eine systematische Aufarbeitung der Geschichte. In eine lange Reihe der typischen Fabrizio-Plessi-Schränke sind 2.000 Gesetzbücher aus deutschen Archiven senkrecht, waagerecht und diagonal aufge-türmt. In den Monitoren darüber sieht man ein aufgeschlagenes Gesetzbuch, dessen Seiten ein elektronischer, unsichtbarer Wind umblättert. Über dem Wasserhahn am Eingang des Raumes ist mittels einer Schraubzwinge ein Buch befestigt; Titel *Deutsche Justiz, Rechtspflege und Rechtspolitik, Amtliches Blatt der Deutschen*

Beginning with the Room of words *at the Academy of Arts in Berlin, a systematic discourse of history is subject of Plessi's work. 2000 statute books from German archives are piled up vertically, horizontally and diagonally in a long row of typical Plessi cabinets. On the monitors above one can see an opened statute book the pages of which are turned by an invisible electronic wind. Above the water tab near the entrance to the room a book is fixed with vice grips; its title:* German justice, administration of justice, and legal policy, Official publication of German administration of

Con *Raum der Wörter* (La Stanza delle Parole) dell'Akademie der Künste di Berlin l'opera di Plessi dà inizio alla rielaborazione sistematica della storia. In una lunga fila di armadi tipici di Fabrizio Plessi sono accatastati in posizione orizzontale, verticale o diagona-le 2000 codici giuridici di archi-vi tedeschi; nei monitors supe-riori si vede un codice aperto con le pagine mosse da un vento elettronico invisibile. Al di sopra di un rubinetto all'ingresso della sala è fissato con un morsetto un libro dal titolo *Deutsche Justiz, Rechtspfle-ge und Rechtspolitik, Amtliches*

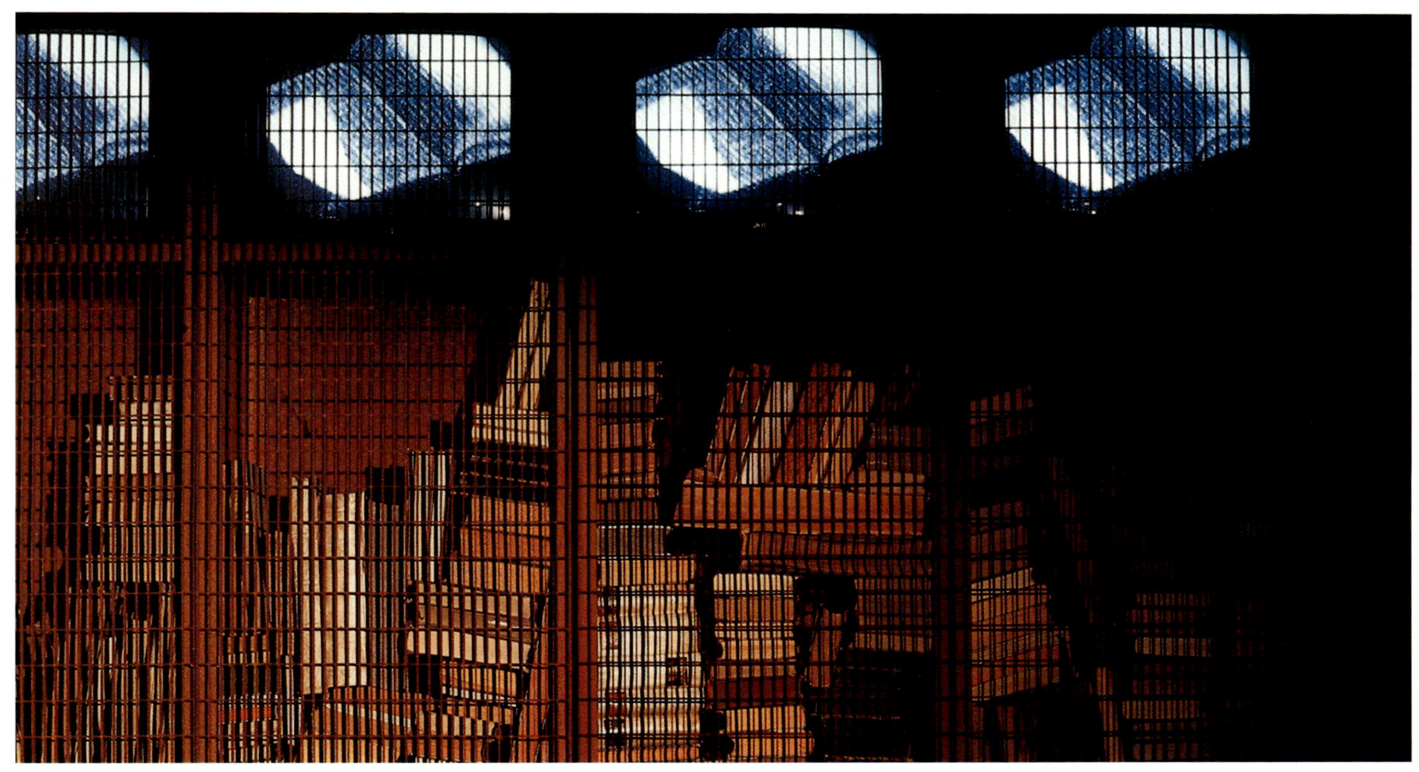

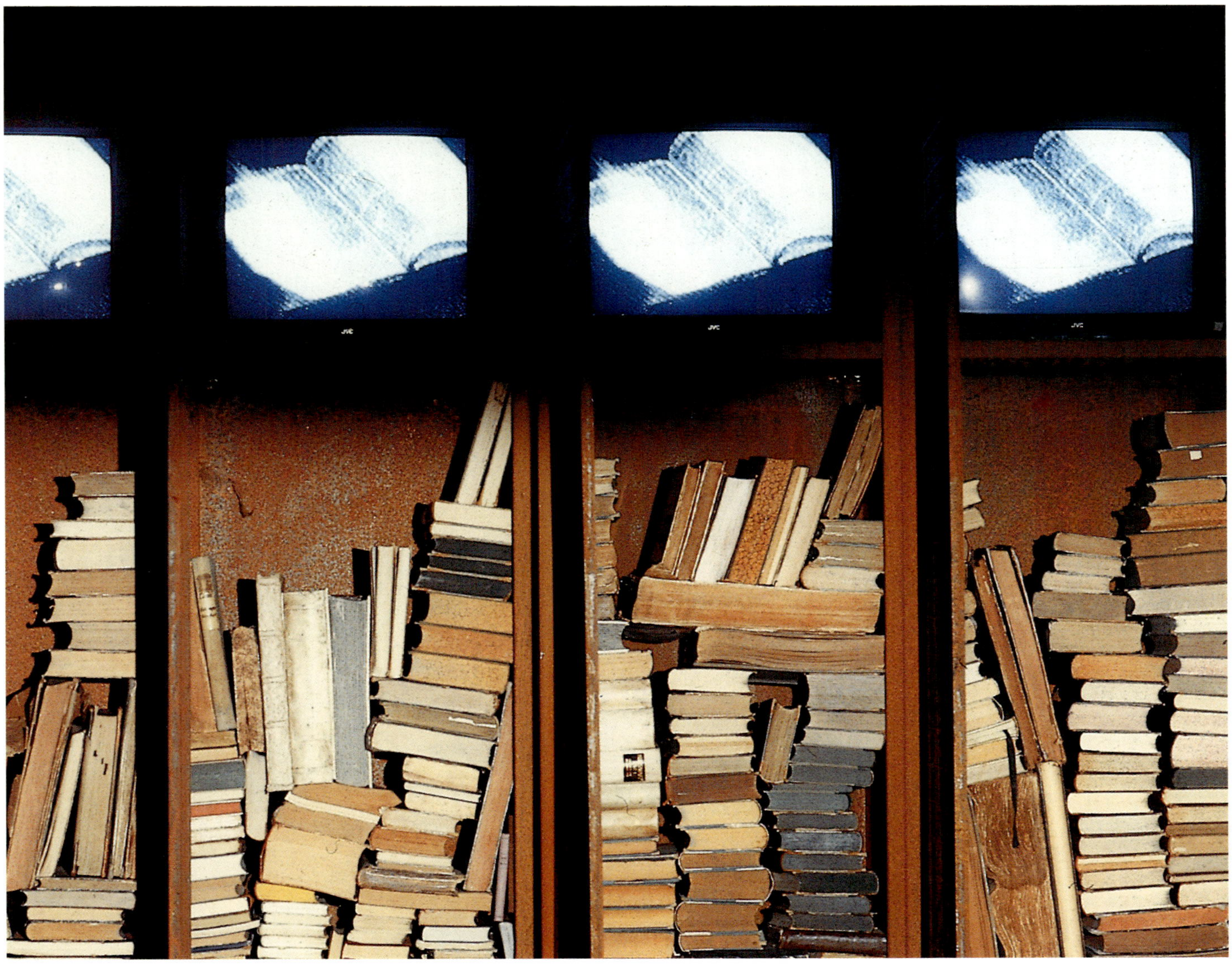

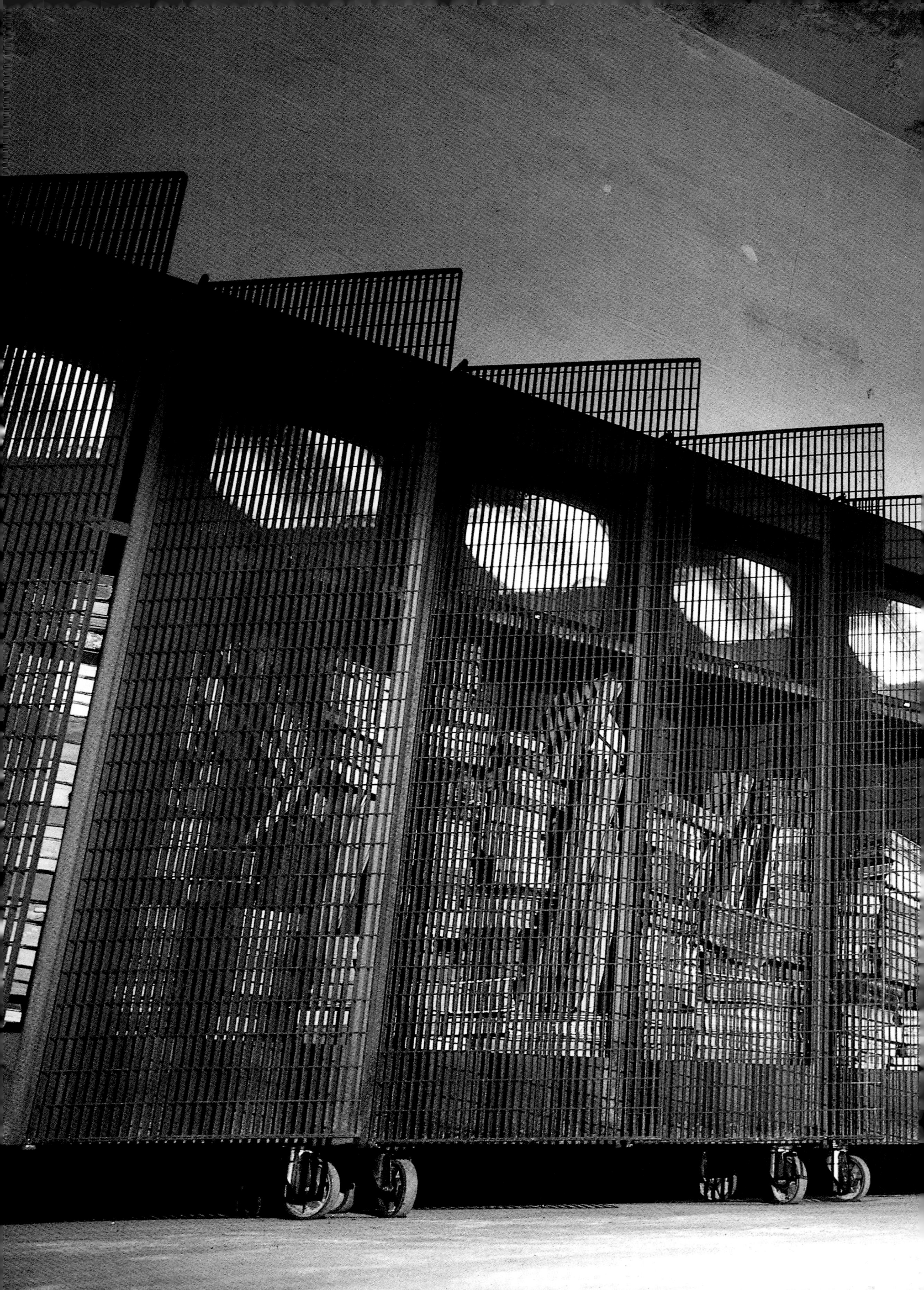

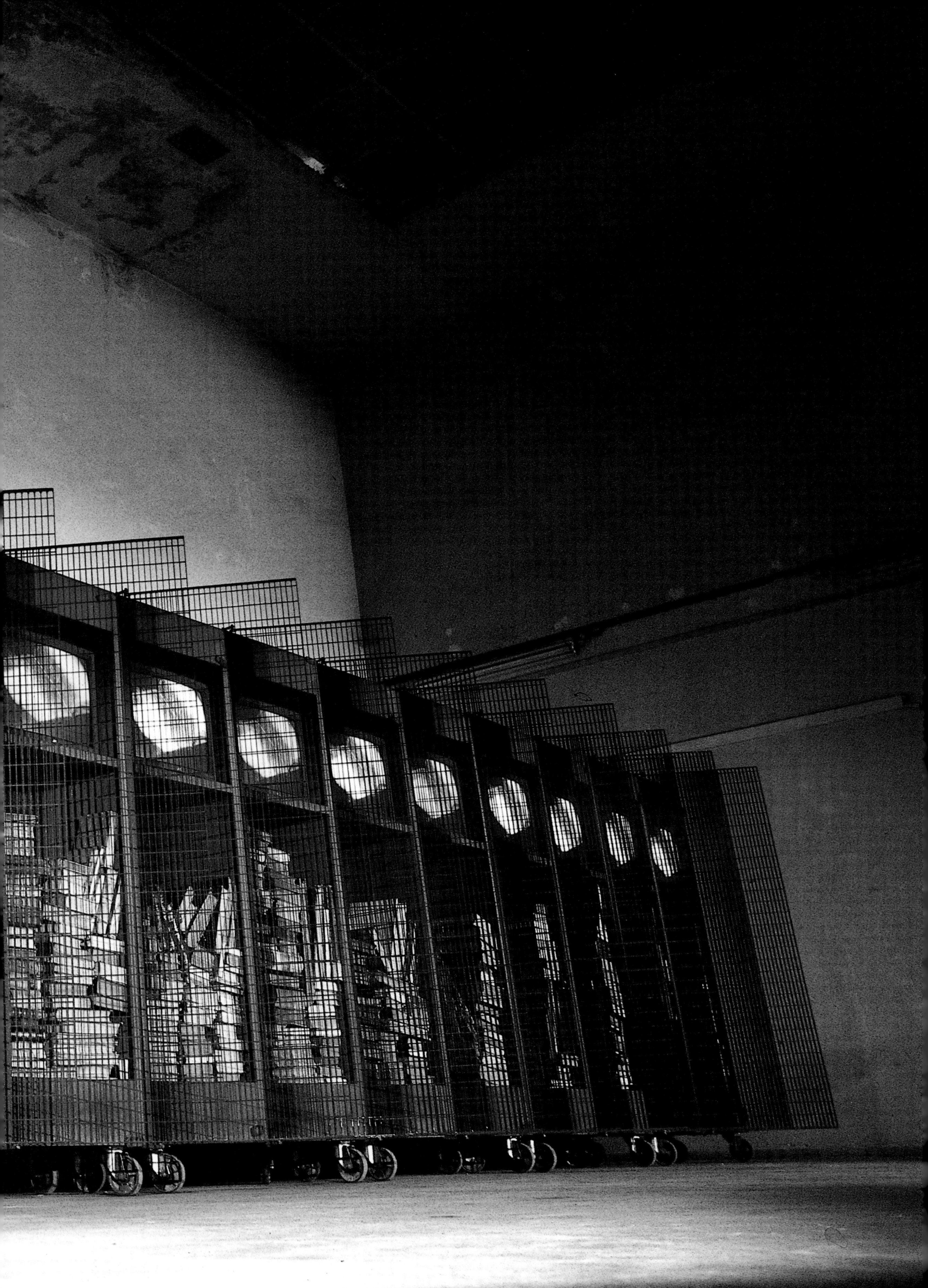

Rechtspflege. Es verweist darauf, daß alle diese 2.000 Bücher, die sich in den Schränken befinden, Gesetzesbücher sind. Das Deutsche Justizbuch scheint verschlossen; ein Buch, wie mit sieben Siegeln. Seine Auslegungen sind fließend, wie der geöffnete Wasserhahn, aus dem Wasser herausströmt, vermuten läßt. Nimmt man jedoch *Das deutsche Volksempfinden als Kunstmaßstab* - so der Titel einer Ausstellung, die Siegfried Salzmann 1979 im Wilhelm-Lehmbruck-Museum in Duisburg veranstaltete - wird deutlich, wie schnell ein Kunstwerk, mit ihm der Künstler und eine ganze Geisteshaltung abgeurteilt und verurteilt werden kann, wenngleich solche Werke nur wenige Jahrzehnte später die Meilensteine der Kunstgeschichte markieren.

justice. *It points to the fact that all the 2000 books in the cabinets are statute books. The book of German justice seems to be closed, a book with seven seals. Its interpretation is fluid, as suggested by the open tap from which water flows. However, if one looks at the* Perception of Art by the German People - *the title of an exhibition in the museum Wilhelm Lehmbruck in Duisburg, organised by Siegfried Salzmann in 1979 - it becomes clear how quickly a work of art and, with it, the artist as well as a whole mode of thought, can be judged and sentenced, although such works, only a few decades later, mark the milestones of the history of art.*

Blatt der Deutschen Rechtspflege (Giustizia tedesca, amministrazione e politica della giustizia, bollettino ufficiale dell'amministrazione giuridica tedesca) che indica che tutti i 2000 libri negli armadi sono codici giuridici. Il libro della giustizia tedesca sembra chiuso, un mistero. Le sue interpretazioni sono fluide come fa supporre l'acqua che scorre dal rubinetto. Se si prende però *Das deutsche Volksempfinden als Kunstmaßstab* (Il sentimento popolare tedesco come criterio dell'arte) - così il titolo di una mostra organizzata da Siegfried Salzmann al Wilhelm-Lehmbruck-Museum di Duisburg nel 1979 - si comprende come è facile che un'opera d'arte e con essa un artista e una mentalità intera possano essere processati e condannati anche se solo pochi decenni più tardi vengono considerati pietre miliari nella storia dell'arte.

BOMBAY-BOMBAY

93001

KÖLN 1993
MUSEUM LUDWIG
93001.1

BARCELONA 1993
FUNDACIÓ JOAN MIRÓ
93001.2

MÜNCHEN 1997
JUSTIZPALAST
93001.3

BOMBAY-BOMBAY
Videoskulptur 1993
In Doppelreihe liegende Eisen-
schränke, weiße, indische
Baumwolle, 36 Monitore, 2 Video-
recorder, bespielte Kassetten, Ton-
aufzeichnung, 60 x 1440 x 650 cm
(München: 24 Monitore, 960 cm)

BOMBAY-BOMBAY
Video sculpture 1993
Double row iron structure, clues of
white Indian cotton, 36 monitors,
2 video recorders, video cassettes,
soundrecording
60 x 1440 x 650 cm
(Munich: 24 monitors, 960 cm)

BOMBAY-BOMBAY
Videoscultura 1993
Struttura in ferro adagiata a terra,
cumuli di cotone bianco bagnato,
36 monitors, 2 vhs, 2 cassette
registrate, sonoro
60 x 1440 x 650 cm
(Monaco · 24 monitors, 960 cm)

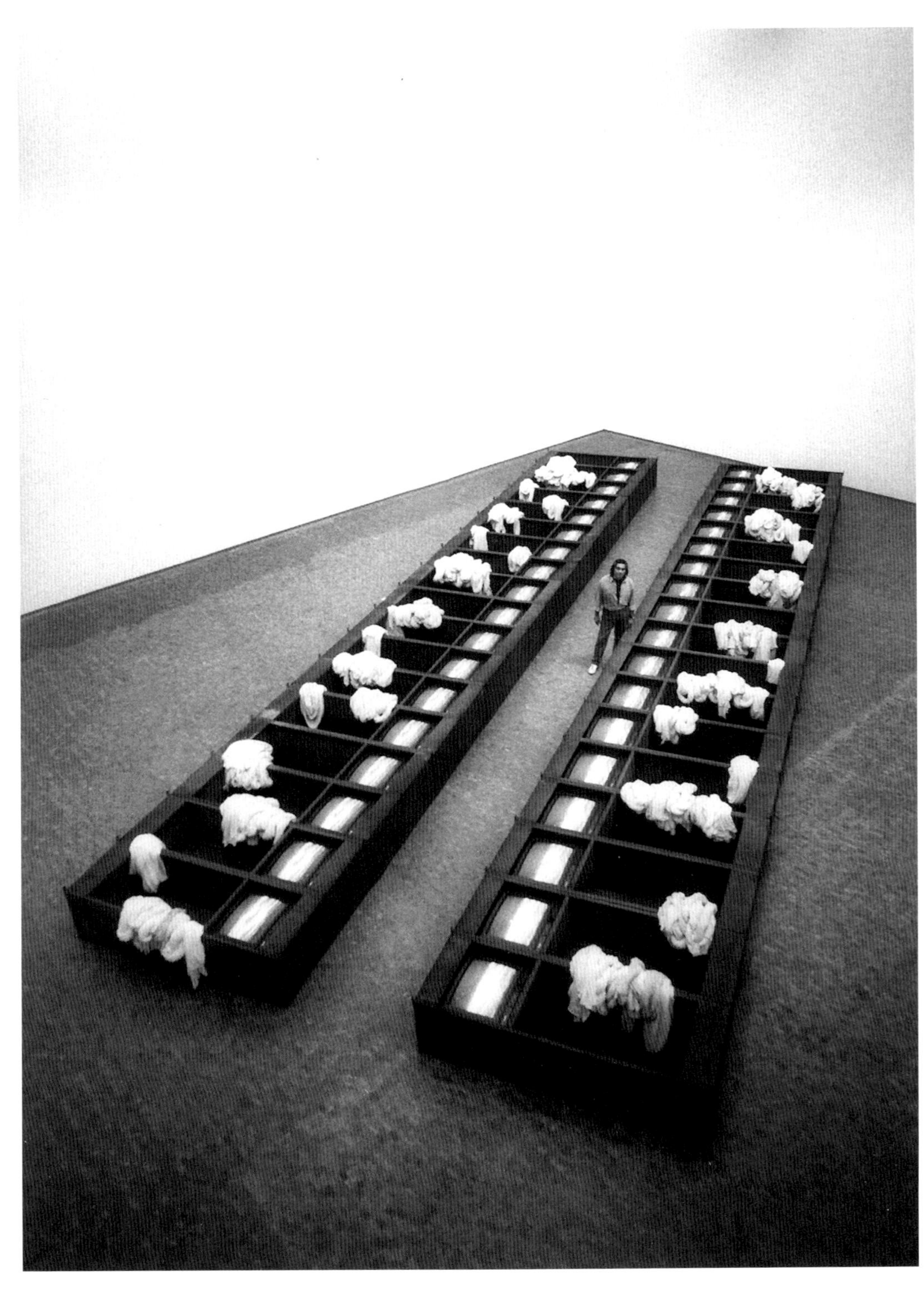

Bei der ersten Version von *Bombay-Bombay*, präsentiert im Kölner Museum Ludwig in zwei parallelen Linienanordnungen, läßt sich Plessis ursprüngliche visuelle Erfahrung bei seiner Reise nach Indien deutlich wiederfinden. Eine lineare Struktur von dachlos offenen Waschhäusern aus Stein wird exakt proportional transformiert in eine Struktur auf den Boden gelegten Eisenschränke Plessis. Die Übereinstimmung der Proportionen ist verblüffend. Die gewaschene oder noch zu waschende Wäsche, die in gebündelten Akkumulationen über den Seitenrändern der einzelnen Waschkompartimente liegt, wird in der Kölner Installation durch Haufen von feuchter Baumwolle repräsentiert. Dazu fließt elektronisches Waschwasser.

Indien, in unserer Illusion wie ein Märchen aus *Tausendundeiner Nacht* erschien dem Künstler bei seinem Besuch in der Realität ganz abgekehrt von seinem farbenprächtigen Glanz und »statt dessen in einem armen, grauen, ich würde fast sagen passolinischen Dasein in Lumpen und Staub ertrunken« (Plessi, in: Katalog Museum Ludwig, Köln 1993). Der Grund, diese Installation der indischen Waschhäuser als Merkmal seiner Erinnerung an Bombay zu fixieren, hat sicherlich mit der Proportionsidentität zwischen den Wascheinheiten und seinen Schränken zu tun. »Es war jene Abmessung folglich der Schlüssel zum Verständnis der Anziehungskraft, die mich seit dem ersten Augenblick an diesen Ort gefesselt hat. Tatsächlich entsprach die Struktur dieser Stein-Waschhäuser genau der Eisenstruktur meiner Schränke. Meine Skulpturen, an denen ich seit Jahren arbeite, Behälter meiner ganzen Phantasie. Eine Größe, die für mich mehr als eine Identität darstellt, mehr als eine Analogie und mehr als ein merkwürdiges Zusammentreffen. ...

Plessi's original visual experience on the occasion of his trip to India can be clearly felt in the first version of Bombay-Bombay, *presented in the Museum Ludwig in Cologne in two parallel linear structures. A linear structure of roofless, open laundry houses of stone is transformed in exact proportion into a structure of iron cabinets lying on the ground. The agreement of proportion is astonishing. The washed or still the be washed laundry, lying in bundles accumulated on the edges of the single laundry compartments is represented in the Cologne installation by piles of wet cotton. It is accompanied by the flow of electronic lye.*

On the occasion of his visit, India, in our imagination a tale from the Arabian Nights, left the artist with an impression totally different from its colourful glamour "... and was drowned instead in a sort of impoverished existential greyness, reminiscent almost of Pasolini, consisting of rags and dust." (Fabrizio Plessi, in: catalogue Museum Ludwig, Köln 1993). The reason for fixing this installation or reconstruction of Indian laundry houses as symbol of his remembrance of Bombay is certainly the identity of proportion between the laundry units and his cabinets. "It was this 'dimension', in fact, which was the key to my understanding the attraction which had bound me to that place from the very first; the structure of those stone wash-houses corresponded precisely with the iron structure of my cabinets, sculptures I've been working on for years, and which are the recipients of my entire imagination. A 'dimension' which represents for me something more than an identity, more than an analogy

Nella prima versione di *Bombay-Bombay*, presentata al Museum Ludwig di Colonia nell'allestimento a due linee parallele, si ritrova chiaramente l'esperienza visiva originaria fatta da Plessi durante il suo viaggio in India. Una struttura lineare di lavatoii di pietra senza tetto viene riportata in proporzioni esatte in una struttura di armadi di Plessi collocati per terra. La corrispondenza delle proporzioni è strabiliante. I panni lavati o ancora da lavare accumulati lungo i bordi delle singole vasche sono rappresentati a Colonia da mucchi di cotone bagnato, e in più scorre acqua elettronica.

L'India, per noi illusoriamente come una favola da *Mille e una notte*, in realtà appariva all'artista del tutto privata del suo magnifico splendore e »... invece annegava in un povero grigio esistenziale, direi quasi pasoliniano, di cenci e di polvere.« (Fabrizio Plessi, in: catalogo Museum Ludwig, Colonia 1993) La ragione della scelta di tale installazione o ricostruzione dei lavatoi indiani come segno del suo ricordo di Bombay sta certamente nell'identità delle loro proporzioni con quelle dei suoi armadi. »Era quella ›misura‹, dunque, la chiave per comprendere l'attrattiva che mi legava al luogo fin dal primo istante; infatti la struttura di questi lavatoi di pietra corrispondeva esattamente alla struttura di ferro dei miei *Armadi*, sculture a cui lavoro da anni, contenitori di tutto il mio immaginario. Una ›misura‹ che per me rappresenta più di un'identità, più di un'analogia e più di una curiosa coincidenza. ... Ed un'altra coincidenza: sia i lavatoi che la sala del museo si osservano dall'alto e ambedue

347

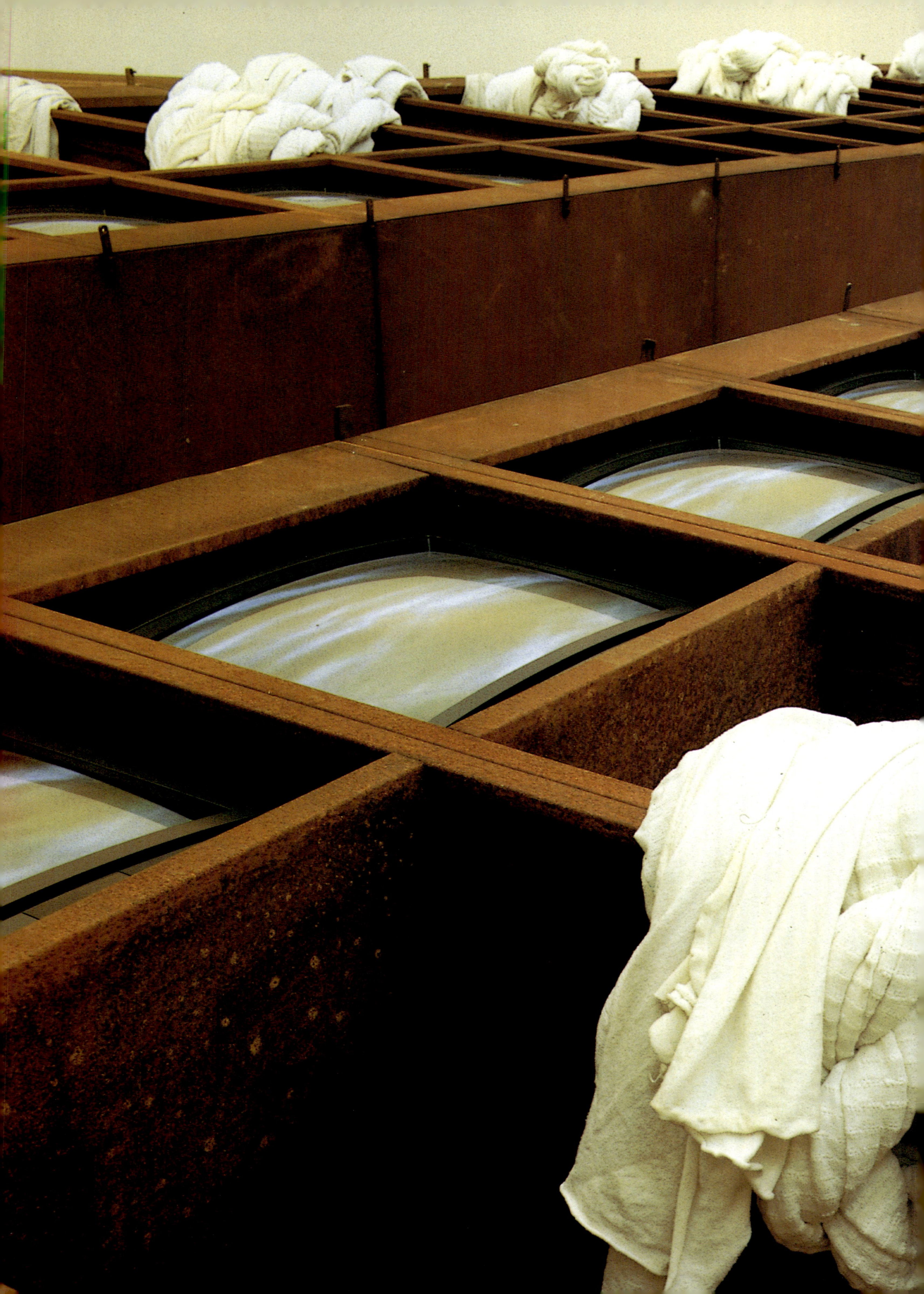

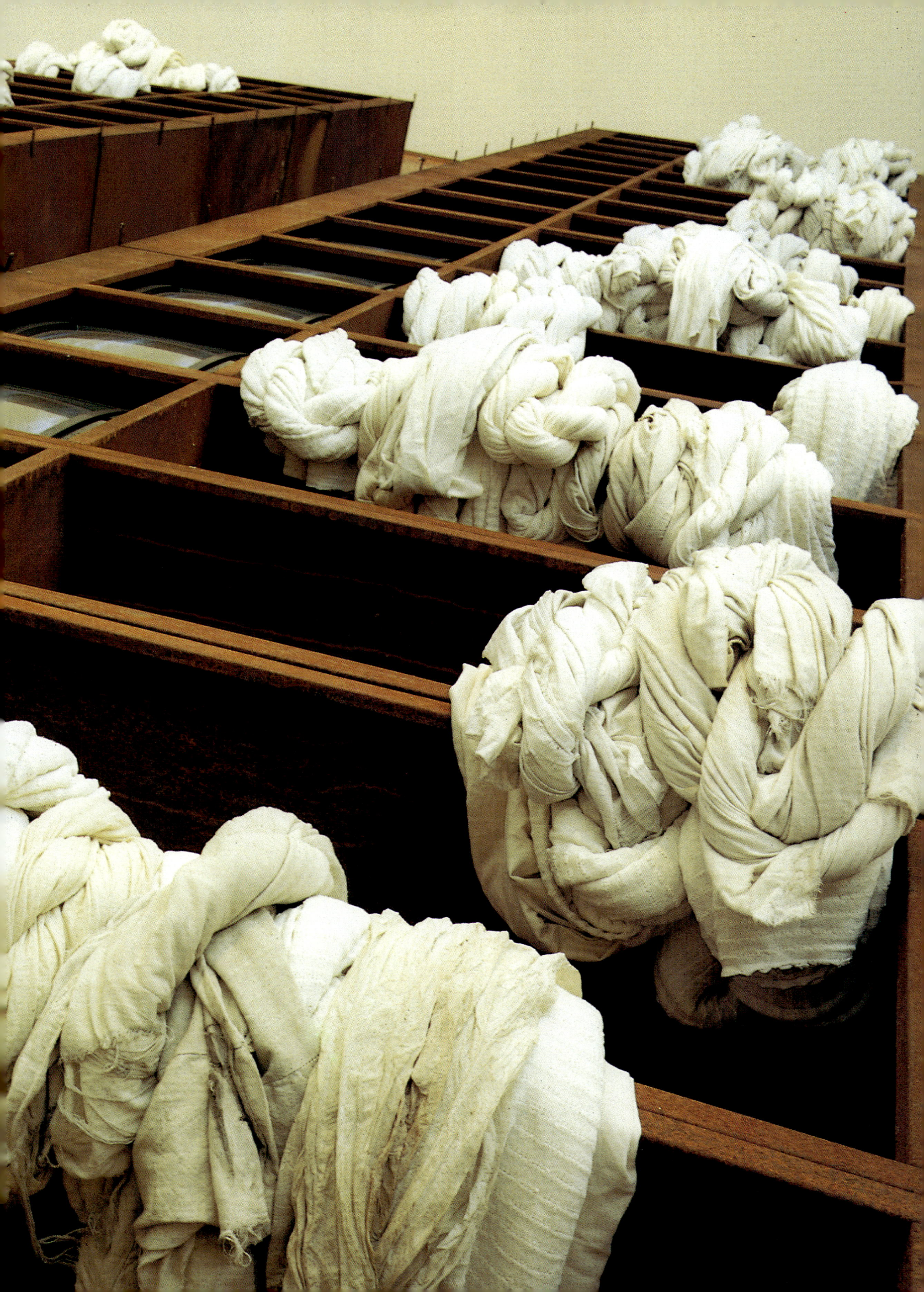

Noch ein Zufall: Sowohl die Waschhäuser als auch der Saal des Museums werden von oben betrachtet und beide gestatten den Zugang in das eigene Herz über Treppen. Die träumerische Ebene war ›geographisch‹ die gleiche. Das größte Problem bestand für mich darin, nun alles zu beseitigen, was rhetorisch und illustrativ war. ... Und diese minimalistisch geometrische Skulptur lebt nur von den Haufen feuchter Baumwolle als einziges taktiles Vorhandensein. Darüber hinaus der elektronische Fluß der zwei Wasserläufe und das evokatorische Schlagen der nassen Tücher, ..., nichts anderes.« (Plessi ebd.)

Die Waschung, wie das Baden im heiligen Fluß beispielsweise, hat in der hinduistischen Religion eine große Bedeutung. Ein Ritual, das weniger den Körper reinigt (vor allem, wenn man sich das schmutzige Wasser der heiligen Flüsse betrachtet), als vielmehr die Seele, die Waschung macht den Menschen im Inneren rein. In Paschupatinath in Nepal beispielsweise werden die Toten an den Ufern des Heiligen Flusses innerhalb der Tempelanlagen verbrannt, damit die Asche in den Fluß hineinwehen kann und so die Seelen der Toten auch im Nachhinein gereinigt. Auf diese Weise können die Menschen bei der Wiedergeburt, gereinigt von ihrem irdischen Dasein, in einer neuen, höheren Ebene ihr nächstes Leben leben. Sie wissen um ihre Bestimmung, und hadern nicht mit ihrem Schicksal, denn der Fluß der Zeit realisiert die Vorbestimmung.

and more than a curious coincidence. ... And another coincidence: both the wash-houses and the room in the museum are observed from above, and both allow access to the very centre via stairs. The level of vision was 'geographically' the same. The big problem for me was, then, to eliminate all that was rhetorical or illustrative. ... and this minimalist-geometric structure lives only from those piles of wet cotton which function as a unique tactile presence. Beyond that, the electronic flux of the two watercourses and the evocative beating of the wet washing which disappears in the air. Nothing else." (Fabrizio Plessi, loc.cit.)

Washing, like bathing in the holy river, is of great importance in Hinduism. It is a ritual that serves less for the cleansing of the body (especially if one considers the dirty waters of the Holy rivers) than that of the soul, cleansing the human being within. In Paschupatinath, Nepal, the dead are burned within the temples along the shores of the Holy rivers, so that the ashes can be blown into the river, and their souls thus cleansed. In this way, people can, cleansed of their wordly existence, when reincarnated, live their next life in a new, higher sphere. They know of their destination, and do not doubt fate, for the river of time verifies predestination.

consentono l'accesso nel proprio cuore attraverso scale. Il livello visionario era ›geograficamente‹ lo stesso. Il grande problema era per me, ora, di eliminare tutto ciò che vi era di retorico e di illustrativo. ... e questa struttura geometrica-minimalista vive soltanto di quei mucchi di cotone bagnato come unica presenza tattile. Oltre a ciò, il flusso elettronico dei due corsi d'acqua e il battito evocativo dei panni bagnati che si perdono nell'aria. Nient'altro.« (Fabrizio Plessi, op. cit)

L'abluzione riveste, come ad esempio il bagno nel Fiume Sacro, un'importanza significativa nella religione induista e fa parte di un rituale che più che il corpo purifica l'anima (soprattutto considerando l'acqua inquinata dei Fiumi Sacri). A Paschupatinath nel Nepal, per esempio, i morti vengono cremati nei templi vicini al Fiume Sacro per permettere alle loro ceneri di essere trasportate dal vento assicurando così la purificazione delle loro anime. In tal modo gli uomini purificati dalla loro esistenza terrena possono, con la loro rinascita, raggiungere un nuovo livello superiore nella vita successiva. Essi sono a conoscenza del loro destino e non si lamentano della propria sorte perchè il fiume del tempo compie la predestinazione.

CRISTALLI LIQUIDI

93002

VENEZIA 1993
CAFFÈ FLORIAN
93002.1

NEW YORK 1998
GUGGENHEIM MUSEUM SOHO
93002.2

SAN DIEGO 1998
MUSEUM OF CONTEMPORARY ART LA JOLLA
93002.3

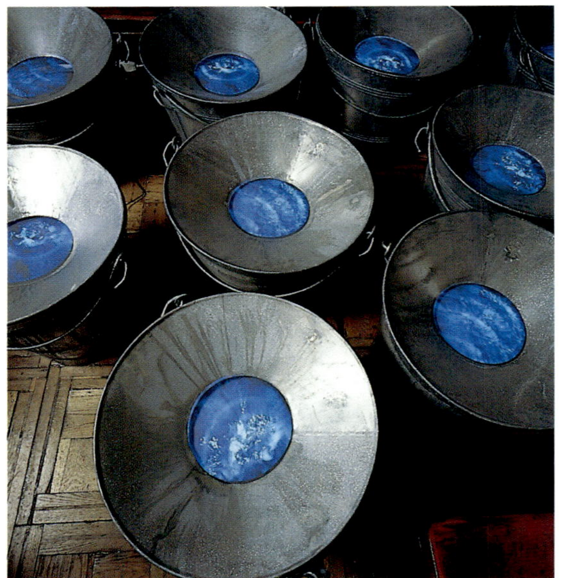

Eine seiner schönsten Installationen mit Video und Wasser konstruierte Fabrizio Plessi 1993 für das Café Florian in Venedig. An diesem historischen Ort waren 500 alte venezianische Gläser so an die Decke montiert, daß ihre Öffnungen nach unten wiesen. Unter den Gläsern standen 14 industrielle Zinkeimer, in welche Monitore eingelassen waren. Videokassetten simulierten in leuchtendblauem

Fabrizio Plessi built one of his most beautiful installations with video and water for the cafe Florian in Venice in 1993. In this historic place, 500 old Venetian glasses were fixed to the ceiling in such a way that their openings pointed downwards. Below the glasses, 14 industrial zinc buckets were placed, with monitors inside. Video cassettes simulated, in

Nel 1993 Fabrizio Plessi costruì una delle sue più belle installazioni con video e acqua per il Caffè Florian di Venezia. Sul soffitto di questo luogo storico furono montati cinquecento bicchieri veneziani antichi con le aperture rivolte verso il basso. Sul pavimento furono collocati quattordici secchi di zinco industriale con monitors inseriti al loro interno. Le

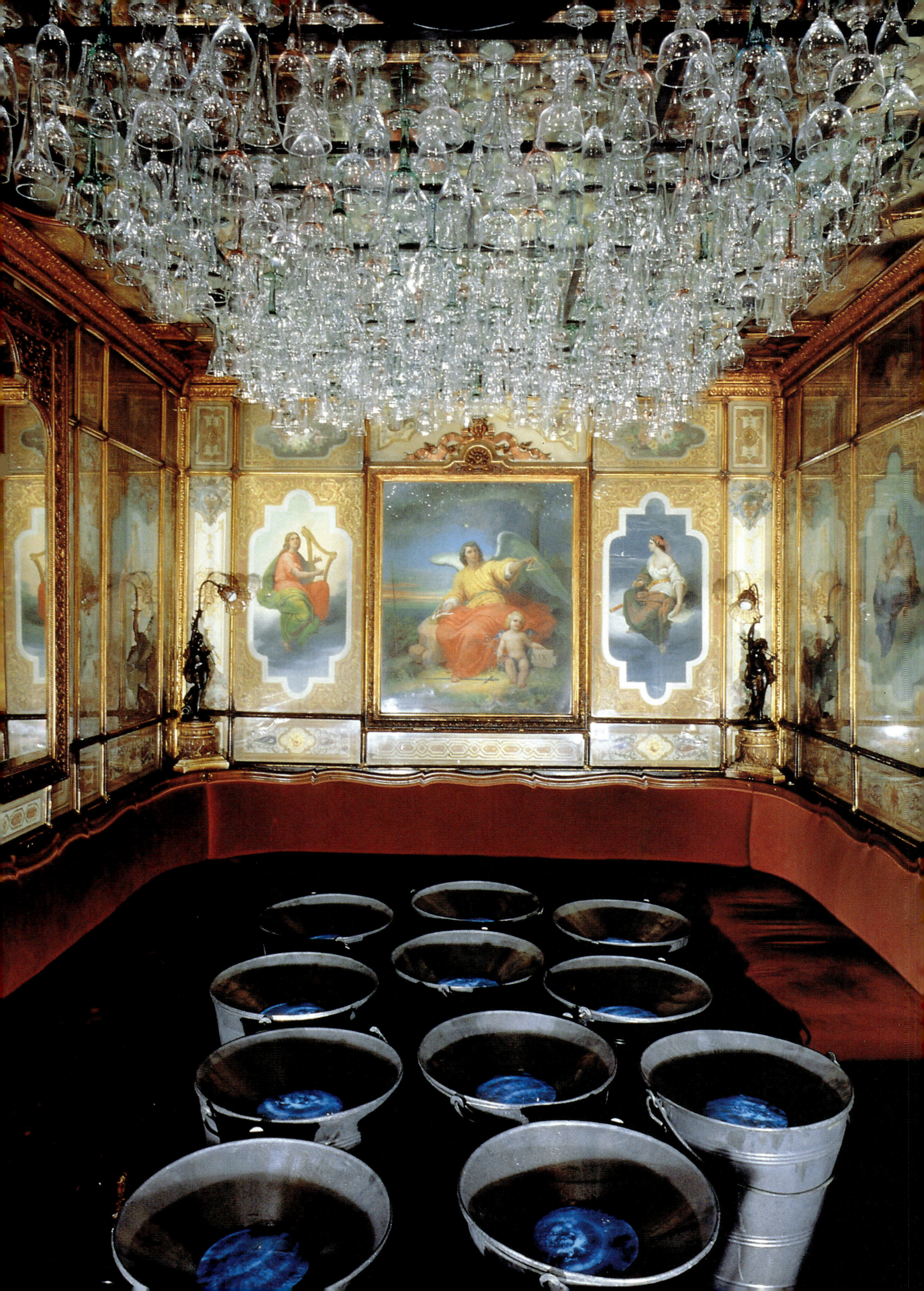

Wasser Tropfen, die aus den Gläsern in die Eimer fielen, begleitet von tropfendem Geräusch.

Das Café Florian war 1720 benannt nach dem Namen seines Besitzers Floriano Francesconi unter den Arkaden am Markusplatz in Venedig eröffnet worden und wurde schon bald darauf zum mondänen und kulturellen Herz der Lagunenstadt. Unendlich viele Persönlichkeiten haben das Café Florian in den vergangenen Jahrhunderten zu ihrem Treffpunkt gewählt. Doch die Installation Fabrizio Plessis verweist nicht nur auf jene bekannten Persönlichkeiten, von Chateaubriand bis Goethe, von Lord Byron bis Stendahl, von Wagner bis Dickens, von Ruskin bis Proust, bis hin zu D'Annunzio und Rubinstein, sondern auch auf jene zahlreichen Unbekannten, von denen nichts geblieben ist außer vielleicht dem Erinnerungstropfen, der virtuell von der Decke in die Behälter der Erinnerung fällt. Abgesehen von dem Geräusch könnten die Tropfen auch an eine Sanduhr erinnern und man würde erwarten, daß das Wasser in den Eimern steigt. Doch mit dem tropfenden Geräusch wird ewige Wiederkehr assoziiert. Vergangenheit oder ein Augenblick, der innehält, Geschichte eindrucksvoll präsent geworden, verbunden mit Schönheit und dem Gefühl des Fortdauerns als Kreislauf und ewigem Kontinuum.

Plessi konstruiert nicht nur ein Erinnerungsstück für die Vergangenheit, sondern vielmehr versucht er, die historische Vergangenheit mit der kulturellen Zukunft zu verbinden. Denn es ist nicht von ungefähr, daß vor genau 100 Jahren im Café Florian die Idee erwuchs, eine regelmäßig wiederkehrende Ausstellung zeitgenössischer Kunst in den Parkanlagen in Castello ins Leben zu rufen und so ist denn die Installation *Cristalli Liquidi*

shiny blue, drops of water that fell from the glasses into the buckets, accompanied by sounds of dripping.

The cafe Florian, named after its owner Floriano Francesconi, was opened under the arcades on St. Mark's square in Venice in 1729, and soon after became the mundane and cultural heart of the city on the lagoon. Innumerable personalities have chosen the cafe as a meeting-place during the past centuries. However, Fabrizio Plessi's installation does not only remind of those famous individuals, from Chateaubriand to Goethe, Lord Byron to Stendhal, Wagner to Dickens, Ruskin to Proust, D'Annunzio and Rubinstein, but of the numbers of unknown of whom nothing is left except perhaps the drop of memory that drops virtually from the ceiling into the vessel of memory. Apart from the sound, the drops could remind us of a sand-glass, and one would expect the water in the buckets to rise. Yet, we associate eternal rebirth with the sound of the drops, the past, or a still moment, history impressively become present, combined with beauty and the feeling of continuity as circle of eternal continuation.

Plessi not only constructs a piece of memory of the past, but rather tries to connect historic past to cultural future. For it is not by coincidence that. about 100 years ago, the idea was born in the cafe Florian to stage a regular exhibition of contemporary art in the park in Castello, and so the installation Liquid Crystals (Cristalli Liquidi) *was realised in the cafe Florian in Venice on the occasion of the 100th anniversary of the Biennale. Again, this*

videocasette simularono gocce che dal soffitto caddero, accompagnate dal rumore gocciolante dai bicchieri nell'acqua dal colore blu acceso dei secchi.

Il Caffè Florian sotto le arcate di piazza San Marco a Venezia fu inaugurato, prendendo il nome dal suo proprietario Floriano Francesconi, nel 1720 e divenne presto il cuore mondano e culturale della città lagunare. Un numero infinito di personalità ha eletto il Caffè Florian come luogo di incontro. Ma l'installazione di Fabrizio Plessi non ricorda solamente quei famosi personaggi, da Chateaubriand a Goethe, da Lord Byron a Stendhal, da Wagner a Dickens, da Ruskin e Proust fino a D'Annunzio e Rubinstein, ma anche quei numerosi sconosciuti di cui non è rimasto niente al di fuori di una goccia commemorativa. Rumore a parte le gocce potrebbero anche alludere ad una clessidra e ci si potrebbe attendere che il livello dell'acqua nei secchi si innalzi. Ma con il rumore delle gocce viene associato l'eterno ritorno, il passato, l'attimo che si arresta o la rappresentazione imponente della storia unita alla bellezza e alla sensazione del tempo come ciclo e continuità eterna.

Plessi non commemora semplicemente il passato ma tenta di collegare il passato storico con il futuro culturale. E non è un caso che esattamente cento anni fa nacque nel Caffè Florian l'idea di dare vita al progetto di una mostra periodica di arte contemporanea nei giardinetti a Castello; così l'installazione *Cristalli Liquidi* del Caffè Florian a Venezia fu realizzata in occasione del centenario della Biennale. Alla fin fine l'opera è un altro inno

(*Flüssige Kristalle*) im Café Florian in Venedig auch anläßlich des 100jährigen Jubiläums der Biennale entstanden. Letztendlich handelt es sich in dieser Installation wieder um eine Hymne an die Stadt, eine Hymne an Venedig. Der Raum ist aus Glas, die Decke ist aus Glas, die Gläser, ja selbst die Bildschirm-Monitore sind aus Glas, und alles glitzert und flirrt wie die gläsern scheinende Wasseroberfläche in den Kanälen Venedigs. Die ganze Inszenierung wird zu einer wunderbaren Verbindung zwischen Wasser, Geschichte und Venedig. Eine poetische Erinnerung, eine Manifestation des Augenblicks, eine schimmernde Hoffnung auf Zukunft.

installation is another hymn to the city, a hymn to Venice. The room is of glass, the ceiling is of glass, the glasses, even the TV monitors are of glass, and everything glitters and sparkles like the vitreous surface of the waters in Venice's channels. The whole scenario creates a wonderful unity of water, history, and Venice, a poetic reminiscence, a manifestation of a moment, a shimmering hope of future.

alla città di Venezia. La sala è di vetro, il soffitto e i bicchieri sono di vetro e gli stessi schermi dei monitors sono di vetro e tutto scintilla e brilla come l'aspetto vitreo della superficie dell'acqua dei canali di Venezia. L'intero assemblaggio diviene un'unione fra acqua, storia e Venezia, un ricordo poetico, una manifestazione dell'attimo, una speranza splendente di futuro.

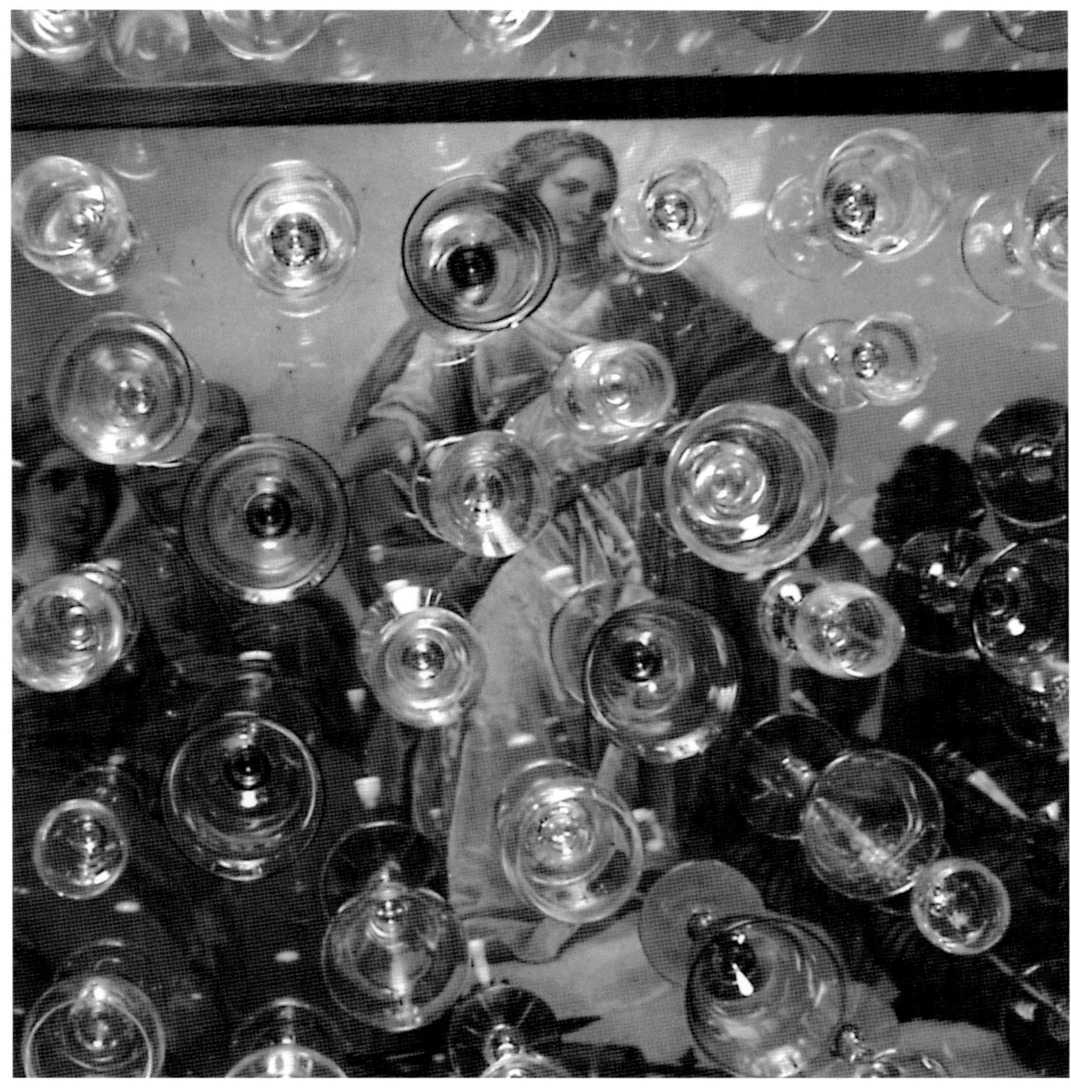

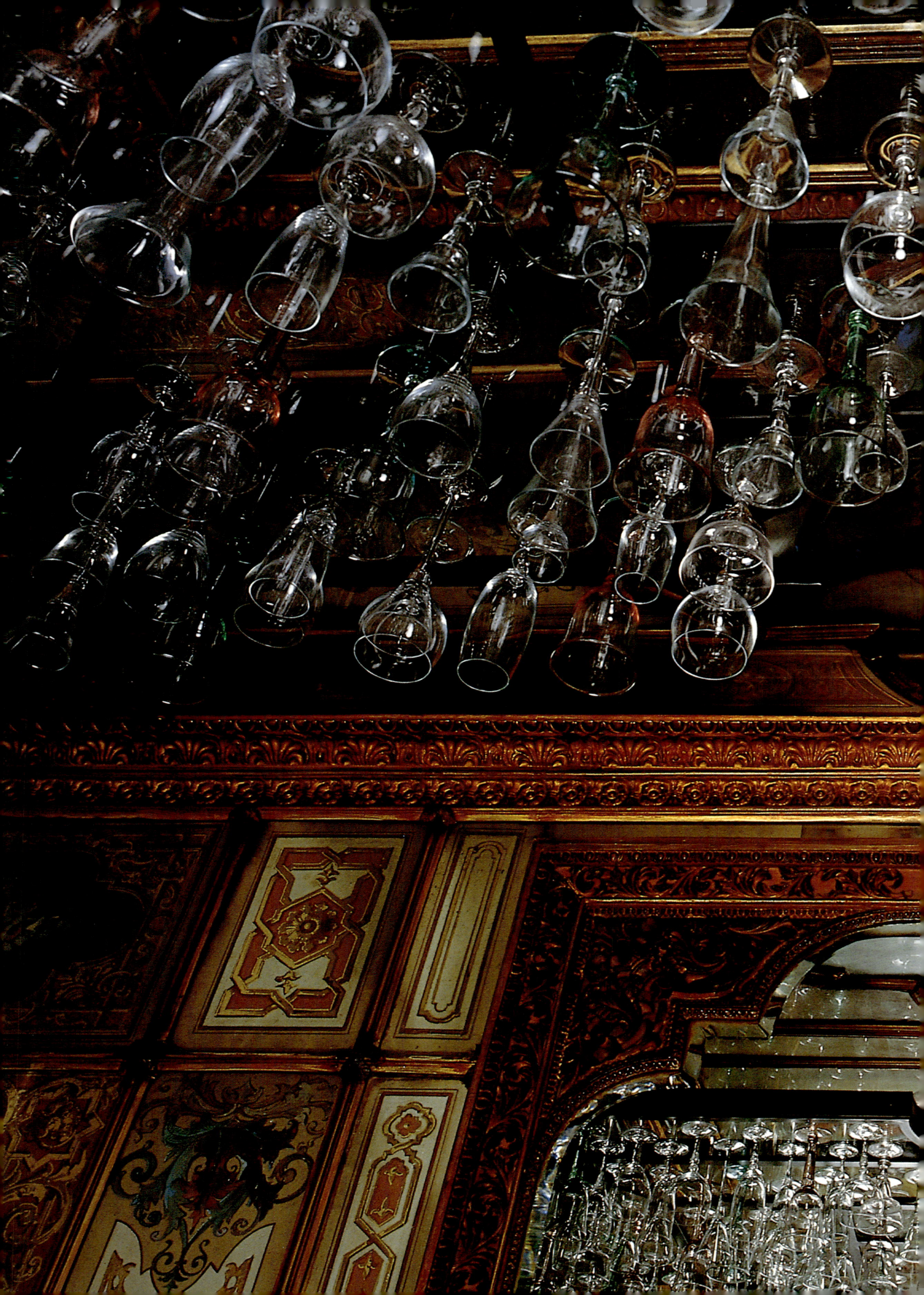

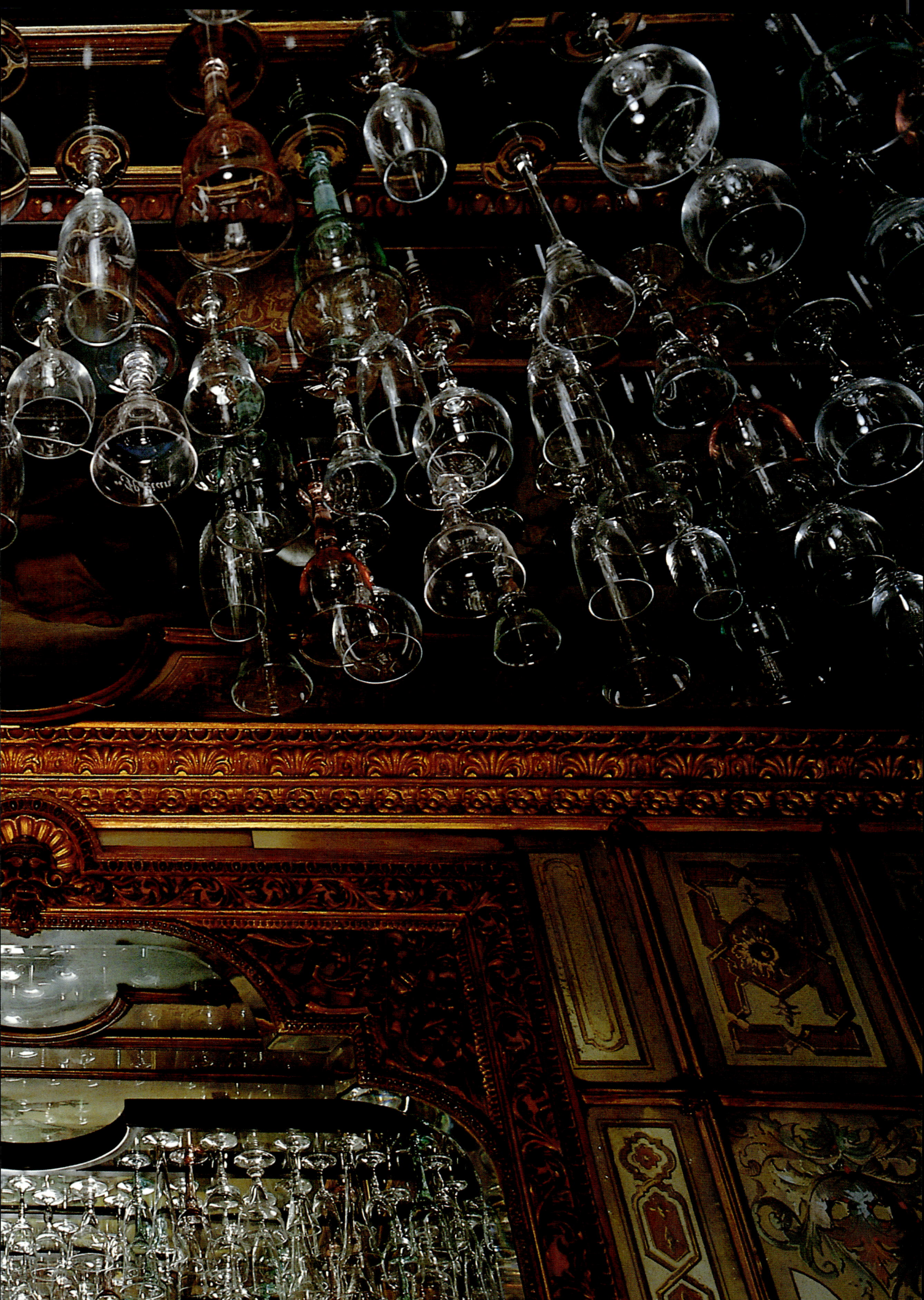

LIQUID TIME

93003

BERLIN 1993
PHILIPS
93003.1

KARSRUHE 1997
ZENTRUM FÜR KUNST UND MEDIENTECHNOLOGIE
93003.2

FLÜSSIGE ZEIT II
Videoskulptur 1993
Eisenkonstruktion mit Motor,
großes Rad in ständiger Drehung,
Eisengitter, Wasserpumpe,
fließendes Wasser, 21 Monitore,
2 Videorecorder, bespielte
Kassetten, Tonaufzeichnung

LIQUID TIME II
Video sculpture 1993
Iron, iron lattice, motor drive,
constant movement, water pump,
running water, 21 monitors,
2 video recorders, recorded video
cassettes, soundrecording

TEMPO LIQUIDO II
Videoscultura 1993
Struttura in ferro, grigliato
industriale, pompa idraulica,
parte elettrica in movimento,
acqua corrente, 21 monitors,
2 vhs, cassette registrate, sonoro

Die zweite Version von *Tempo Liquido (Flüssige Zeit)*, diejenige nämlich, die sich heute im ZKM, im Zentrum für Kunst und Medientechnologie in Karlsruhe befindet, ist aus rostendem Metall angefertigt, während die frühere Version in Prato (1989) aus graugestrichenem Stahl bestand und ein zu drei Vierteln geschlossenes Gehäuse um sich hatte. Mittels einer kleinen Metallbrücke konnte der Betrachter den realen Fluß überqueren, der das elektronische Mühlrad antreibt. Vorstellung und Realität verschwimmen hier miteinander, denn das Wasser, das man in den Monitoren sehen kann, das in seinem Rhythmus fließt, seine natürliche Farbe hat, ist zum Greifen nahe wie das andere Wasser, das real auf das

The second version of Tempo Liquido (Liquid Time), *the one that now is in the ZKM, the centre of art and media technology in Karlsruhe, is made of rusty metal, while the earlier version in Prato (1989) consisted of steel painted grey, and was enclosed by a casing, three-quarters of which were closed. On a small metal bridge the spectator could cross the real river that drives the electronic mill wheel. Imagination and reality here become indistinct, for the water visible on the monitors, flowing in its rhythm, has its natural colour is close at hand, like the other water that real, seems to influence the electronic water, yet is out of reach.*

The element of water in video

La seconda versione di *Tempo Liquido* del Zentrum für Kunst und Medientechnologie (ZKM) a Karlsruhe è stata realizzata con metallo arrugginito mentre quella di Prato del 1989 era fatta di accaio dipinto di grigio ed includeva una struttura chiusa simile ad un contenitore chiuso per tre quarti. Per mezzo di un ponte metallico lo spettatore poteva attraversare il fiume reale che spingeva la ruota del mulino elettronico. Immaginazione e realtà si confondono perchè l'acqua che si può vedere nei monitors con il suo colore naturale e che segue il suo percorso sembra a portata di mano come l'altra acqua che sembra agire realmente

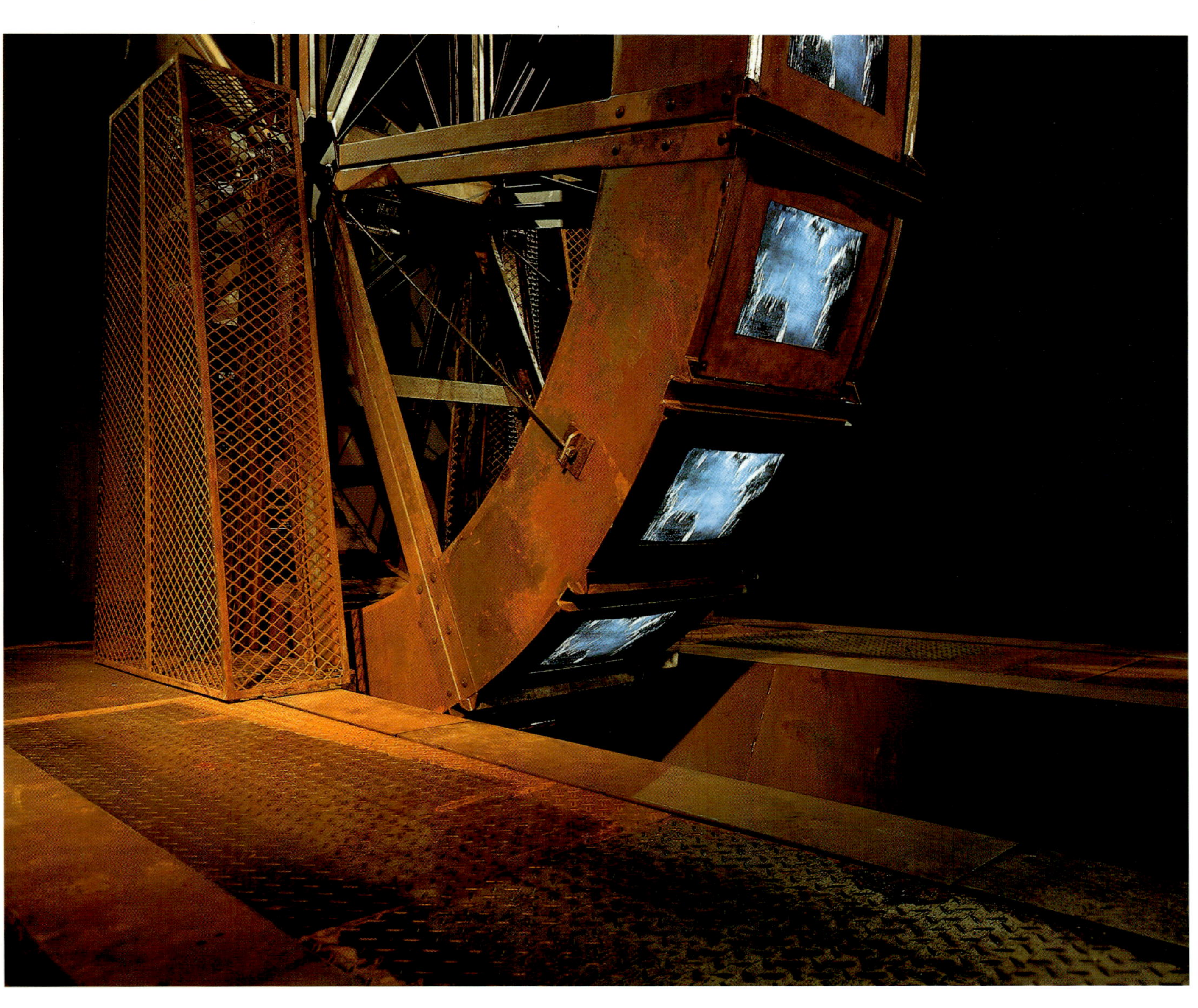

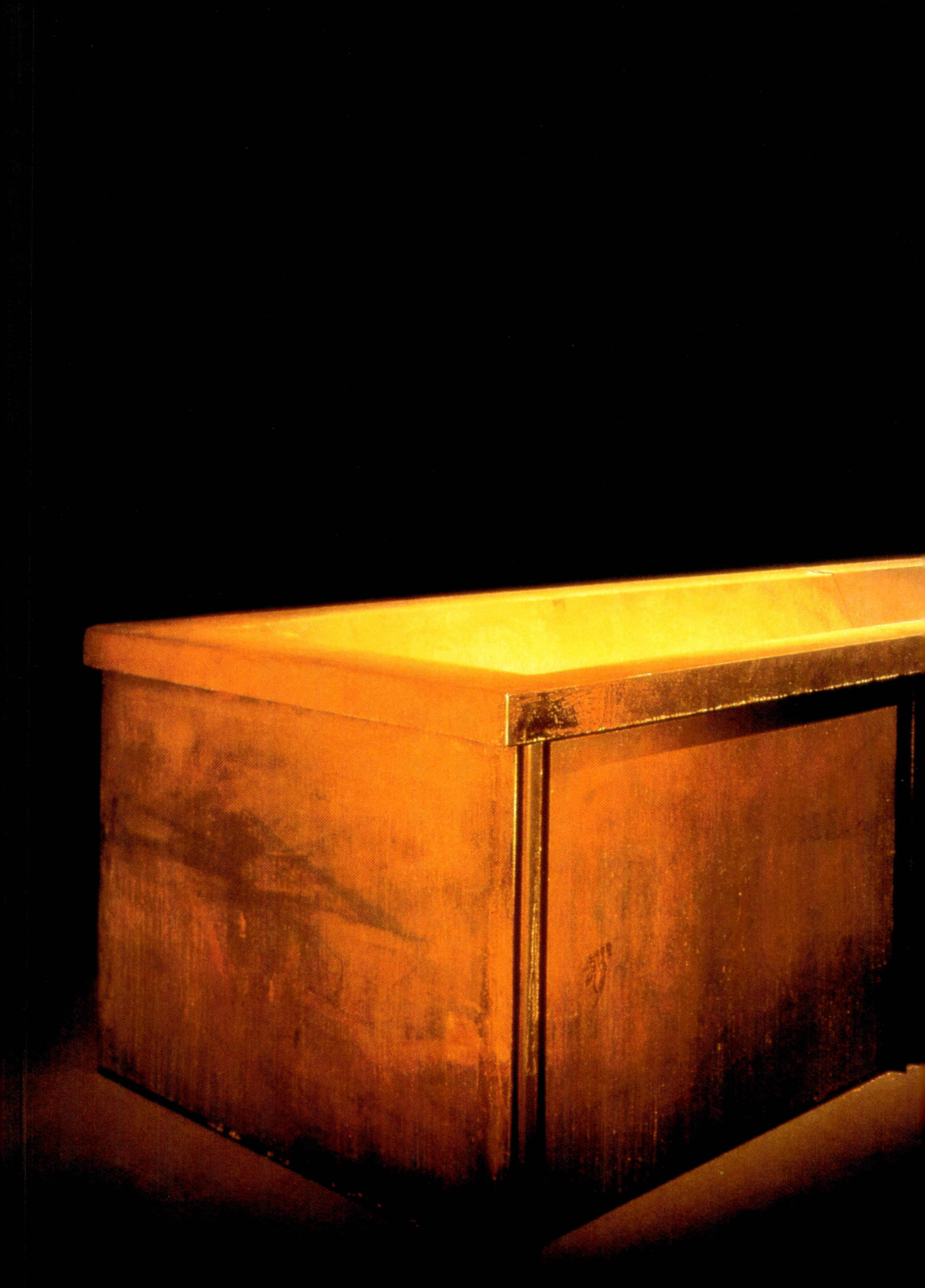

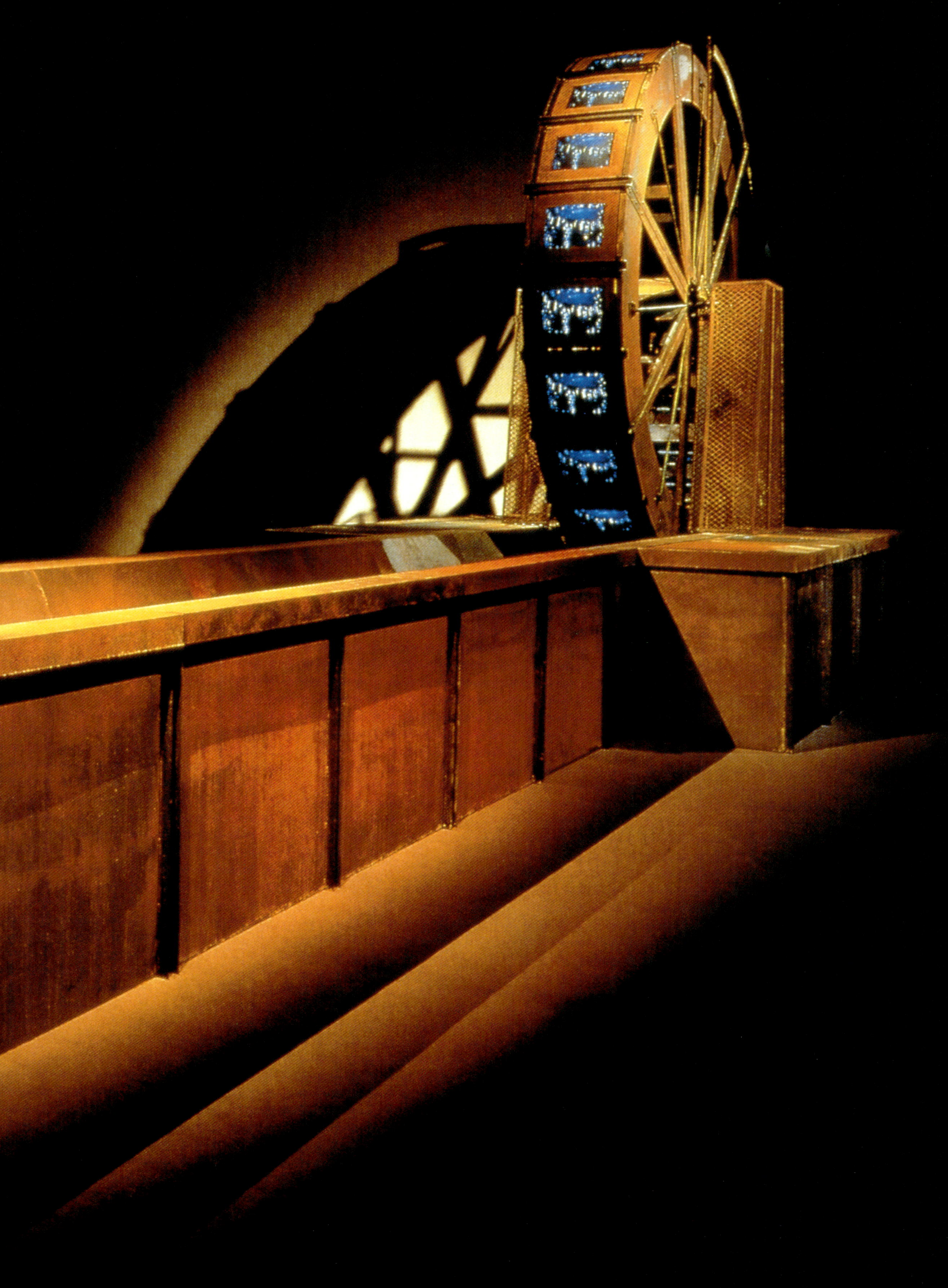

elektronische Wasser Einfluß zu nehmen scheint, aber nicht greifbar.

Das Element Wasser im Videofilm gehört zu den eigentümlichsten und damit signifikantesten Elementen seiner Arbeit. »Es gibt eine tiefgehende Übereinstimmung zwischen diesen beiden Elementen. Das Wasser ist das alte, ursprüngliche Element. Das Video ist ein Element der heutigen Zeit. Es ist mit unserem aufgeregten und telematischen Leben verbunden. Ich bin seit vielen Jahren der Auffassung, daß diese beiden Elemente, die nur dem Anschein nach so verschieden sind, praktisch eine Osmose untereinander bilden, oder besser gesagt, ein geheimes Leben leben, das voll von verborgenem Austausch ist. ... Aus diesem nur scheinbaren ›Aufeinandertreffen‹ und Zusammenfügen von so verschiedenen Elementen, aus dieser fortwährenden, ›unmöglichen Koexistenz‹ zwischen der Armut des Natürlichen und dem schillernden Reichtum der Technologie (...) wurden und werden noch sehr viele und vielseitige Entwürfe geboren ... Wasser und Video (...) waren die Konstanten einer ganzen Reihe von Vorgängen.« erklärt Plessi (Katalog Museum Ludwig, Köln 1993) den Zusammenhang der scheinbar heterogenen Elemente seiner Arbeit. Im Vergleich wird deutlich, wie wesensverwandt beide sind: immaterielle, bewegte, veränderliche, unendliche Bilder.

films belongs to the most peculiar, and therefore most significant elements of Plessi's work. "There is a profound analogy between the two elements: water is the ancient element, ancestral, original. Video is an element of today, linked to our exited and telematic lives. Nonetheless, you know that for many years now I have thought of these two only apparently different elements as being practically mutually osmotic, or better, as living a secret life full of undisclosed complicity. ... This merely apparent 'clash' between such different materials, this continuos, 'impossible cohabitation' between the poverty of the natural and the iridescent richness of the technological material have given birth to, and continue to give birth to, a host of various projects ... Water and video (...) have been the obsessive constants of a whole series of operations", Plessi explains (Fabrizio Plessi, in: catalogue Museum Ludwig, Köln 1993) the context of the apparently heterogeneous elements of his work. In comparison it becomes evident how close in spirit both are: immaterial, mobile, variable, indefinite images.

sull'acqua elettronica, solo che non è tangibile.

La caratteristica dell'accostamento dell'acqua al videofilm è uno dei più particolari e interessanti fattori dell'opera di Fabrizio Plessi. »C'è una profonda analogia fra i due elementi: l'acqua è l'elemento antico, ancestrale, originario. Il video è un elemento di oggi legato alla nostra vita concitata e telematica. Però tu sai come da molti anni io pensi che questi due elementi solo così apparemente diversi siano praticamente tra loro in osmosi, o meglio vivano una vita segreta carica di nascoste complicità ... Da questo scontro solo apparente di elementi così diversi, da questa continua ›convivenza impossibile‹ tra povertà del naturale e ricchezza cangiante del tecnologico, (...) sono nati e nascono ancora moltissimi e molteplici progetti ... L'acqua e il video (...) sono state le costanti ossessive di tutta una serie di operazioni«. Così spiega Plessi (in: catalogo Museum Ludwig, Colonia 1993) il legame fra gli elementi apparentemente eterogenei del suo lavoro che, al confronto, svelano la loro affinità: immagini in movimento, immateriali, mutevoli ed infinite.

PARIS-PARIS

94001

HAMBURG 1994
WEISSER RAUM
94001.1

PALMA DE MALLORCA 1996
LA LLONJA
94001.2

PARIS-PARIS 1994
Videoskulptur
Konstruktion aus schwarzem
Stahl, fließendes Wasser, 10
Monitore, 2 Videorecorder,
Kassetten, Tonaufzeichnung
300 x 300 x 1800 cm

PARIS-PARIS
Video sculpture 1994
Steel structure, running water,
10 monitors, 2 video recorders,
recorded video cassettes,
soundrecording
300 x 300 x 1800 cm

PARIS-PARIS
Videoinstallazione 1994
Struttura in ferro, acqua corrente,
10 monitors, 2 vhs, 2 cassette
registrate, sonoro
300 x 300 x 1800 cm

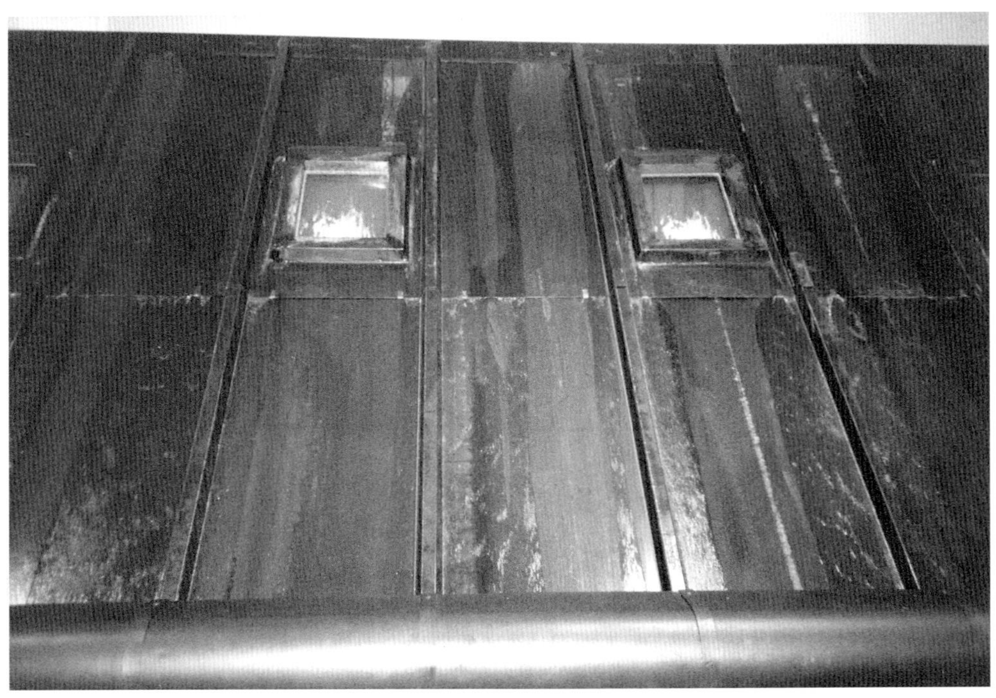

Auf die Dächer von Paris, geometrisch zu einem Halbrund gewölbt
oder einfach in metallener Schräge,
prasseln Regentropfen nieder. Das
Wasser gleitet an den längsstruktu-
rierten Bahnen aus Metall herab,
um sich in der Regenrinne zu
sammeln. Über den zeitweilig
engen, vollgestopften Gassen und
dann auch wieder monumental
großen, ausgedehnten Plätzen in
Paris, die Nuancen der Grautöne
aus dem Metall der Dächer, aus den
Steinen der Schornsteine, die
geometrischen Unterteilungen
durch Antennen, durch Vertikale,
Horizontale, Diagonale, die Kreisbö-
gen und Dreiecksgiebeln über den

Raindrops are falling on the
roofs of Paris, geometrically
arched in a semi-circle, or
simply in metallic sloping.
Water glides down the vertical-
ly structured metal sheets to be
collected in a gutter. Above the
sometimes narrow, crowded
lanes and monumental, large
and spacious squares of Paris
the nuances of grey on the metal
roofs and chimneys, geometric
divisions by aerials, horizontal,
vertical, diagonal, circular
arches and triangular gables
above the windows, the shimme-
ring light at the moment of rain
falling on the metal roofs, all

Sui tetti geometricamente
curvati e inclinati cade la
pioggia. L'acqua defluisce
lungo binari metallici verso il
basso e viene raccolta nella
grondaia. I vicoli stretti e
affollati, le piazze estese e
monumentali di Parigi, le
sfumature dei grigi dei tetti
metallici, i mattoni dei comi-
gnoli, le ripartizioni geometriche di antenne, verticali,
orizzontali e diagonali, gli
archi a tutto sesto, i timpani
triangolari delle finestre, lo
scintillio della luce dei tetti
bagnati dalla pioggia, tutto
questo affascinava Fabrizio

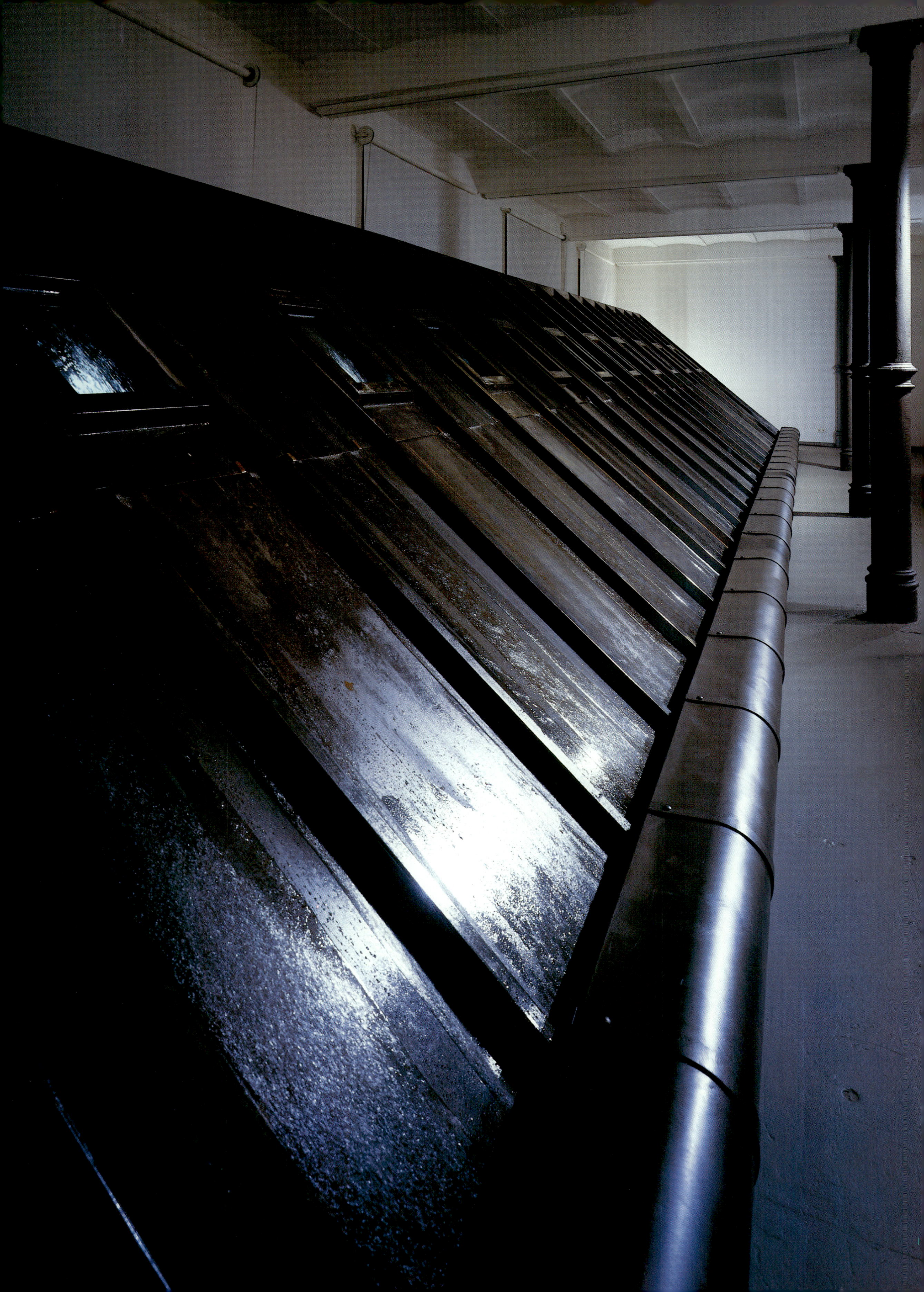

Fenstern, das Schimmern im Licht, gerade wenn Regen auf die metallenen Dächer fällt, alles das faszinierte Fabrizio Plessi und veranlaßte ihn zu dieser Videoinstallation *Paris-Paris*.

Von einer Metallkonstruktion, die dachähnlich schräg in einen Raum eingebaut ist, fließt unaufhörlich Wasser über die Schrägen gleitend in die untere Regenrinne. Es ist reales Wasser. Doch in den Monitoren, die wie Fenster in die Dachschrägen eingebaut sind, fließt zugleich elektronisches Wasser und man kann nicht einmal mit Bestimmtheit sagen, ob das elektronische Wasser aus den Fensteröffnungen der Monitore herauszufließen und dann über das Dach zu gleiten scheint oder etwa das reale Wasser von oberhalb der Dachfenster-Monitore kommend möglicherweise das elektronische Wasser erst in Gang setzt. Aus den Dachluken-Monitoren fällt Licht auf die rieselnde Konstruktion.

this fascinated Fabrizio Plessi, and motivated him to realise this video installation, Paris-Paris.

Incessantly, water flows over the slopes of a metal construction built inside the room like a roof, glides into the rain gutter below. It is real water. In the monitors, positioned like dormer windows in the sloping roof, electronic water flows, and it is impossible to say whether the electronic water from the window openings of the monitors seems to flow out and glide down the roof, or whether the real water, coming from above the window monitors, possibly sets the electronic water in motion. Light falls from the dormer windows onto the trickling construction.

Plessi e lo indusse a realizzare la videoinstallazione *Paris-Paris*.

Da una costruzione metallica, inclinata come un tetto, della sala d'esposizione scorre senza interruzione acqua reale verso una grondaia. Nei monitors, inseriti come abbaini nei piani in pendenza, scorre contemporaneamente acqua elettronica e non si può stabilire con certezza se essa fuoriesce dai monitors per defluire sul tetto o se l'acqua reale scende da sopra per agitare quella elettronica. Dagli abbaini-monitors cade luce sulla costruzione grondante.

ROVINA ELETTRONICA

95001

KRAICHTAL 1995
URSULA BLICKLE STIFTUNG
95001.1

KÖLN 1996
MUSEUM LUDWIG
95001.2

ELEKTRONISCHE RUINE
Videoskulptur 1995
Architektonischer Aufbau aus
Buntsandstein, 7 Monitore,
Videorecorder, bespielte
Kassetten, Tonaufzeichnung
300 x 110 x 800 cm

ELECTRONIC RUIN
Video sculpture 1995
Architectural structure of
sandstone walling, 7 monitors,
video recorder, recorded video
cassettes, soundrecording
300 x 110 x 800 cm

ROVINA ELETTRONICA
Videoscultura 1995
Struttura in pietra arenaria,
7 monitors, vhs, cassette
registrate, sonoro
300 x 110 x 800 cm

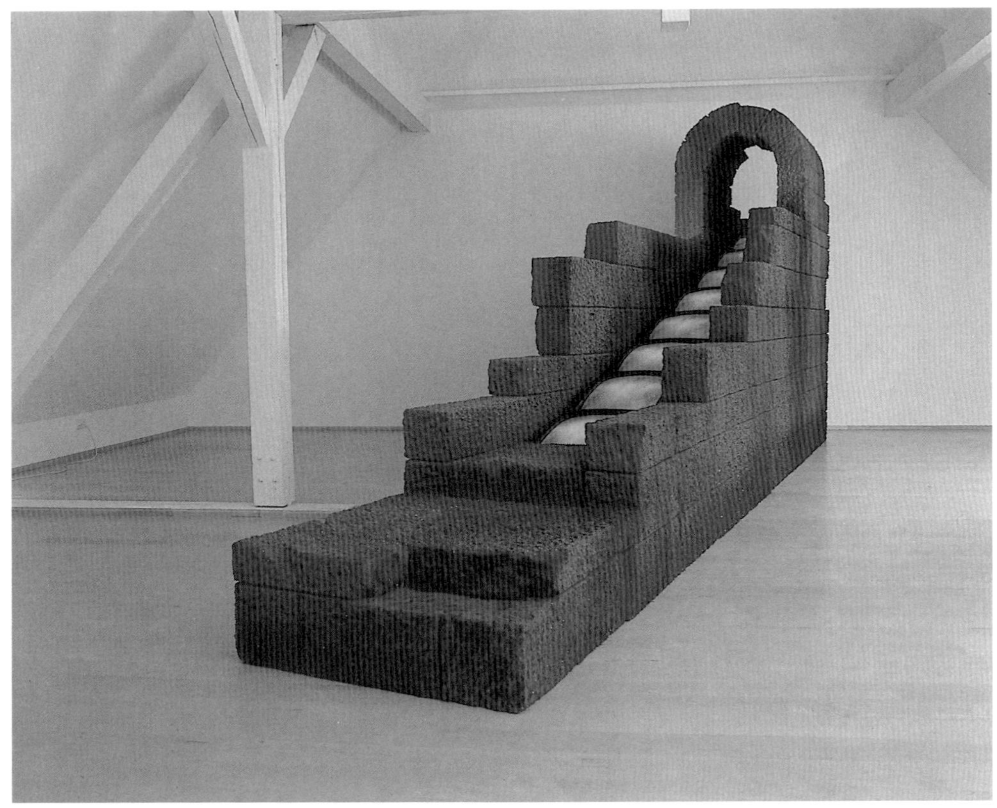

»Obwohl ihre Wirkung von der Wissenschaft der High Technology abhängt, ist Plessis Kunst mehr als alles andere von der romantischen Sehnsucht nach vergangenen Zeiten geprägt.« (Gérard A. Goodrow, in: Katalog Ursula Blickle-Stiftung, Kraichtal 1995) *Rovina Elettronica* (*Elektronische Ruine*) ist eine Videoskulptur, bei der ein elektronischer Wasserfall über eine Reihe von untereinander verbundenen Monitoren

"Although its result depends on the science of high technology, Plessi's art is, more than anything else, marked by a romantic desire for times past." (Gérard A. Goodrow, in: catalogue, Ursula-Blickle-Foundation, Kraichtal/Austria, 1995) Rovina Elettronica (Electronic Ruin) *is a video sculpture in which an electronic waterfall glides over a row of monitors connected to each other and*

»Sebbene l'effetto della videoscultura dipenda dalla scienza della High Technology, l'arte di Plessi è impressa più che da ogni altra cosa da nostalgia romantica per i tempi passati.« (Gérard A. Goodrow, in: catalogo Ursula Blickle-Stiftung, Heidelberg 1995). Nella *Rovina Elettronica* una cascata elettronica precipita nei monitors collegati fra di loro e inseriti fra blocchi di pietra arenaria rosa

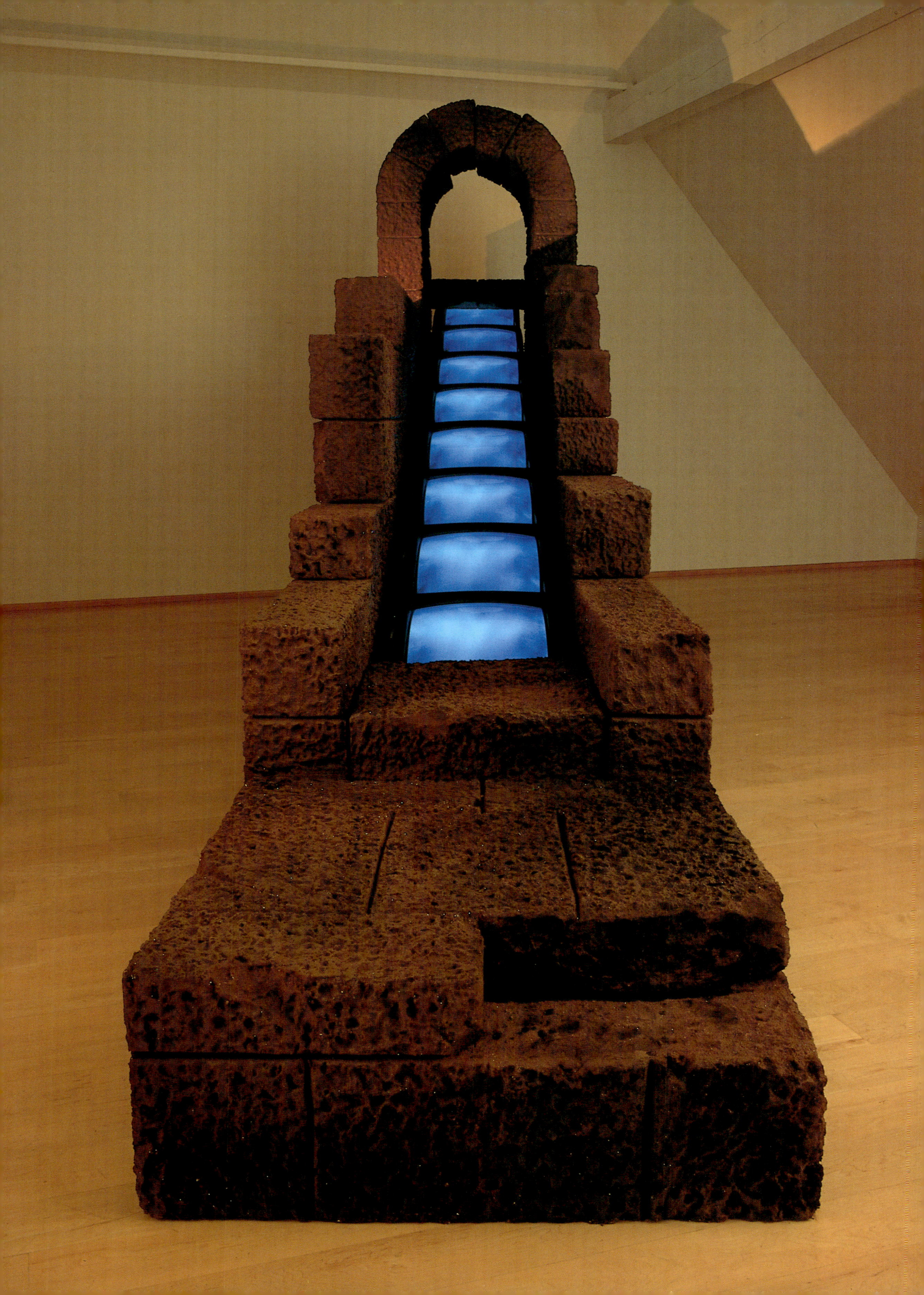

gleitet, die in rosafarbenen Buntsandstein eingebaut sind und eine
Ruine markieren. Die Steine stammen aus dem Steinbruch der
nahegelegenen Stadt Maulbronn
und sind dasselbe Material, aus
dem in vergangener Zeit Klöster,
Schlösser, Gefängnisse und Burgen
gebaut wurden. Schon insofern
wird die Ortsbezogenheit dieser
Videoskulptur deutlich. »Zutiefst
von seinen italienischen Vorgän-
gern inspiriert, vor allem von
Giovanni Batista Piranesi (1720 -
1778), dem römischen Künstler, der
insbesondere wegen seiner romantischen Faszination für die maje-
stätischen Ruinen der ewigen Stadt
bekannt ist, kann Plessi wirklich
nur in diesem Kontext verstanden
werden.« (Goodrow, a.a.O.)

Als Wahl-Venezianer hat Fabrizio Plessi natürlich eine starke
Bindung zu allem Vergänglichen,
zum Vergehenden, das ihn einerseits fasziniert und das er andererseits doch zu bewahren sucht. »Ich
bin Italiener, vom Temperament
her Angehöriger einer mediterra-
nen Kultur und ich finde das
Ruinenthema wieder in der italienischen Malerei, in der arkadi-
schen Landschaft, im Zerfall der
venezianischen Paläste, im Schwei-
gen der Lagune und natürlich in
den Resten der römischen Antike.«
(Fabrizio Plessi, a.a.O.) Ruinen
sind für ihn nicht nur Sinnbilder
oder Metaphern für Vergangenheit,
sondern auch für Gegenwart; eine
Gegenwart, die heute so schnelle-
big geworden ist, daß sie morgen
schon Vergangenheit sein kann.
(Wie der Fall der Berliner Mauer,
der von einem Tag auf den anderen
40 Jahre Geschichte zur Vergangenheit gemacht hat.)

*embedded in pink sandstone,
representing a ruin. The stones
come from the quarry of Maulbronn, a city close by, and are
the same material from which,
in former times, monasteries,
castles, prisons and manor
houses were built. By this alone,
the reference to place in this
video sculpture becomes evident. "Deeply inspired by his
Italian predecessors, especially
by Giovanni Batista Piranesi
(1720 - 1778), the Roman artist
who is known because of his
romantic fascination by the
majestic ruins of the Eternal
City, Plessi can only be understood in this context." (Goodrow, loc.cit.)*

*As Venetian-by-choice, Fabri-
zio Plessi of course has a strong
connection to everything transi-
tory and decaying that, on the
one hand, fascinates him, on the
other tries to preserve. "I am
Italian, in regard to temperament member of Mediterranean
culture, and I find the theme of
ruins in Italian painting, in
Arcadian landscapes, in the
decay of Venetian palaces, in
the silence of the lagoon, and,
of course, in the remains of
antique Rome." (Plessi, loc.cit.)*

*For him, ruins are not only
symbols or metaphors of the
past but of the present, a present that today is so fast-lived
that it can be past by tomorrow.
(As the fall of the Berlin wall,
that - from one day to the next -
turned 40 years of history into
past.)*

che simulano una rovina. Le
pietre, lo stesso materiale
impiegato nel passato nella
costruzioni di monasteri, castel-
li, prigioni e fortezze, provengono dalla cava della vicina città
di Maulbronn sottolineando
ancora una volta il diretto
collegamento con il luogo
geografico. »Profondamente
ispirato dalle faccende italiane,
innanzi tutto da Giovanni Batti-
sta Piranesi (1720 - 1778),
conosciuto principalmente per
la sua ammirazione romantica
delle rovine maestose della
Città Eterna, Plessi può essere
compreso esclusivamente in tale
contesto.« (ibid.)

Fabrizio Plessi è, in quanto
veneziano d'elezione, ovviamen-
te legato fortemente a tutto ciò
che è fugace ed evanescente,
che lo affascina e che egli al
tempo stesso cerca di conservare. »Io sono italiano, per il mio
temperamento appartengo a una
cultura mediterranea ed io
ritrovo il tema delle rovine nella
pittura italiana, nel paesaggio
arcadico, nei palazzi veneziani
che stanno cadendo a pezzi, nel
silenzio della laguna e natu-
ralmente, nei resti dell'antichità
romana.« (Plessi, op. cit.). Le
rovine sono per Plessi non
solamente simboli o metafore
del passato ma anche del presente, un presente dalla vita
così febbrile che già domani può
sembrare passato (così come la
caduta del muro di Berlino che
da un giorno all'altro ha trasfor-
mato quarant'anni di storia in
passato).

IN VINO VERITAS

95002

KREMS 1995
KUNSTHALLE KREMS
95002.1

IN VINO VERITAS
Videoinstallation 1995
Weinranken, 8 Holzfässer,
8 Monitore, Videorecorder,
bespielte Kassetten

IN VINO VERITAS
Videoinstallazione 1995
Viticci, 8 botte di legno,
8 monitors, vhs, cassette
registrate

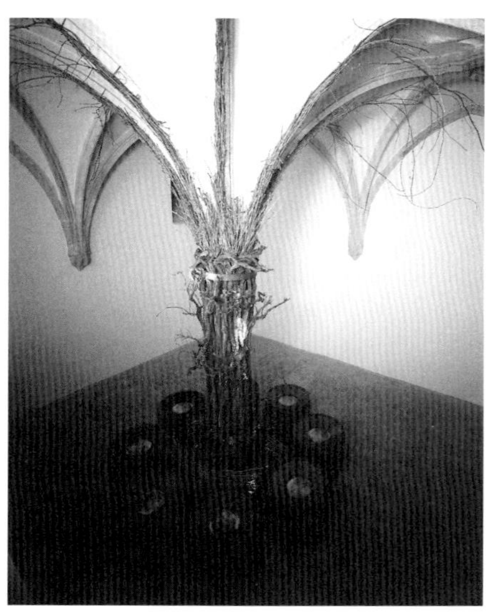

In den Videoinstallationen von Fabrizio Plessi fließt nicht nur Wasser, wie die Videoskulptur in Krems mit dem Titel *In Vino Veritas* deutlich zeigt. Um den zentralen Pfeiler eines Sterngewölbes ranken sich bis ins Gewölbe hinein Äste von Weinstöcken. Rundherum um diese Konstruktion sind acht Weinfässer kreisförmig plaziert, in deren Rundöffnung elektronischer Wein sprudelt. Wein, der unsere Sinne nur visuell betört, so daß der Geist wach bleibt. ›In vino veritas‹ (Im Wein liegt die Wahrheit) steht bereits geschrieben über einem der Fässer in dem mittelalterlichen Zisterzinser-Kloster Eberbach im Rheingau. Schon die Zisterzinser-Mönche haben Wein hergestellt und dieses nicht nur für die Liturgie des Gottesdienstes.

In Fabrizio Plessi's video installation not only water flows, as the video sculpture In Vino Veritas *in Krems clearly shows. Branches of vines climb the central pillar of a star-shaped vault, up to the ceiling. All around this construction, eight wine-barrels are placed in a circle, electronic wine sparkling in their round openings, wine that only visually infatuates our senses, keeping the mind clear. 'In vino veritas' (There is truth in wine) is written above one of the barrels in the medieval Zisterziensan monastery of Eberbach in the province of Rheingau. These monks already made wine, and not only for the liturgy of mass.*

Nelle videoinstallazioni di Fabrizio Plessi non scorre solo acqua, come dimostra la videoscultura *In Vino Veritas* esposta a Krems. Intorno ad un pilastro si arrampicano rami di una vite, attorno sono disposte in cerchio otto botti, nel cui interno sgorga vino elettronico. Vino che solo visualmente inganna i nostri sensi, mentre la mente si mantiene sveglia. Il motto ›In vino veritas‹ si ritrova già scritto su una botte nel monastero cistercense medievale Eberbach nel Rheingau. Già i monaci cistercensi producevano vino e non solo per il rito liturgico.

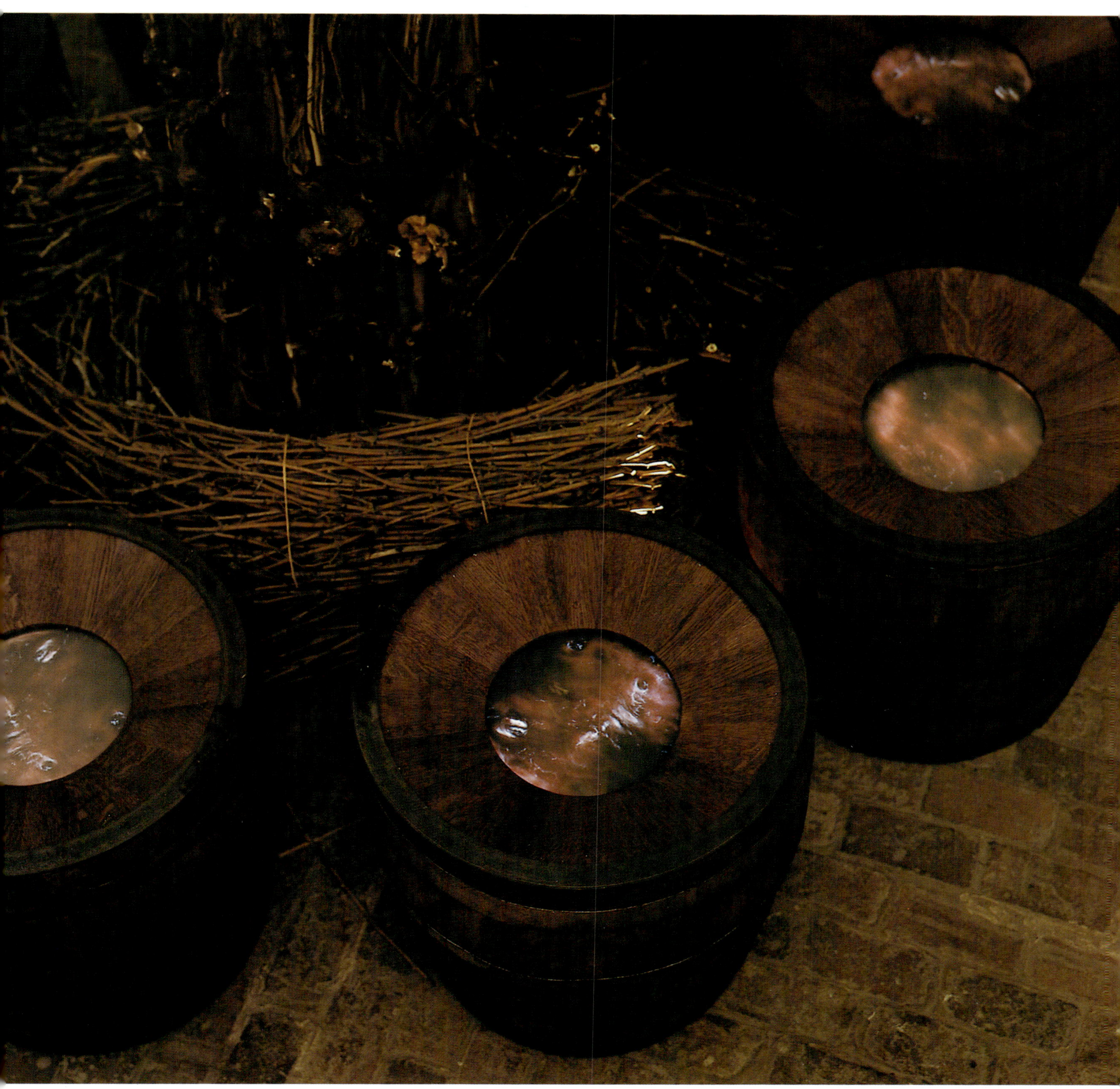

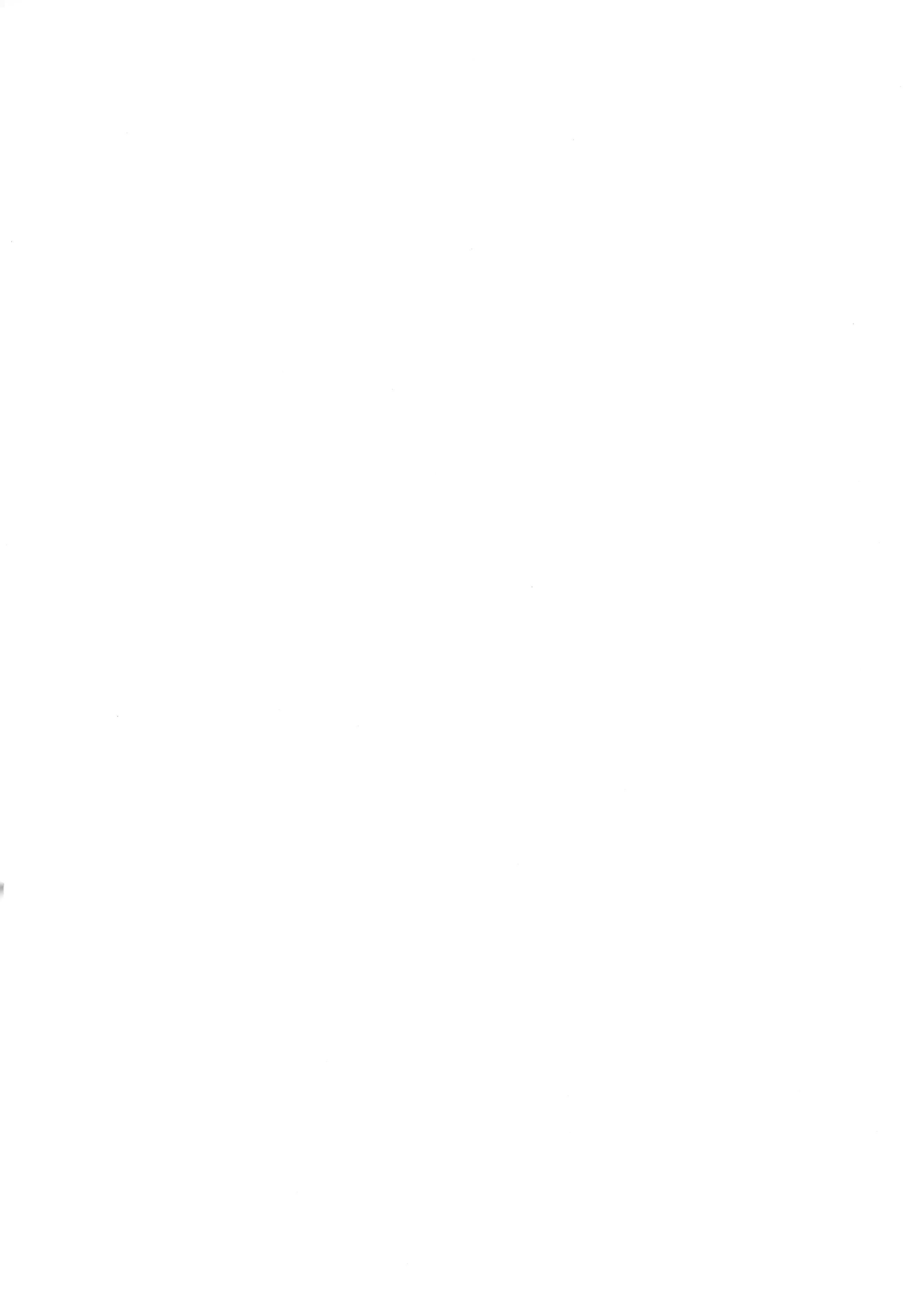

RHEIN-RAUM

95003

BONN 1995
RHEINISCHES LANDESMUSEUM
95003.1

STRASBOURG 1995
MUSÉE D'ART MODERNE ET CONTEMPORAIN
95003.2

NIJMEGEN 1996
MUSEUM COMMANDERIE VAN SINT JAN
95003.3

RHEIN-RAUM
Videoskulptur 1995
Eisenschränke mit Fächern,
aufgestapelte Holzstämme,
6 Monitore, Videorecorder,
bespielte Kassetten,
Tonaufzeichnung
260 x 480 x 60 cm

RHINE ROOM
Video sculpture 1995
*Iron construction with
compartments, piled-up wooden
trunks, 6 monitors, video
recorders, recorded video cassettes,
soundrecording*
260 x 480 x 60 cm

LA STANZA DEL RENO
Videoscultura 1995
Struttura in ferro a scomparti,
castate di tronchi di legno,
6 monitors, vhs, cassette
registrate, sonoro
260 x 480 x 60 cm

Eine der späteren Videoskulpturen Plessis ist der *Rhein-Raum,*
entstanden anläßlich der Ausstellung *Der Rhein - ein Europäischer
Strom in Kunst und Kultur des
20. Jh.* In die inzwischen bekannte
Struktur aus Eisen, sind querlie-
gend gleichlang geschnittene
Rundholzstämme übereinander
aufgestapelt. Im Video der darüber
präsentierten Monitore scheint -
sichtbar in der Bewegung des
Wassers - ein Stamm im Rhein zu
schwimmen und durch die Dynamik
und Richtung des Flusses angetrieben zu werden. Neben den bekannten Aspekten von Zeit und Bewegung rückt in dieser Videoskulptur
eine weitere Dimension des Wassers in den Blickpunkt, nämlich
seine Aufgabe als Transportweg.

Der Rhein ist ein internationales

*One of the later video sculp-
tures is the* Rhine Room, *created
on occasion of the exhibition*
The Rhine - a European Stream
in Art and Culture of the 20th
Century. *Round logs of equal
length are placed inside the by
now well-known iron structure,
on top of another. In the video
on the monitors placed above, a
log - visible in the movement of
the water - seems to float in the
river, driven by the dynamic
and direction of the Rhine river.
Beside the known aspects of time
and motion this video sculpture
centres on another dimension of
water, its function as means of
transport. The Rhine is an
international water touching
four different countries: Switzer-
land, Germany, France and the*

Una delle videosculture
recenti di Fabrizio Plessi è
Rhein-Raum realizzata in occasione della mostra *Der Rhein -
ein Europäischer Strom in Kunst
und Kultur des 20. Jahrhunderts*
(Il Reno - un fiume europeo
nell'arte e nella cultura del XX
secolo). Nella ormai consueta
struttura metallica sono accatastati traversalmente pezzi tondi
di legna della stessa lunghezza.
Nei monitors posti superior-
mente, un tronco - visibile nel
movimento dell'acqua - sembra
galleggiare nel Reno spinto
dalla dinamica e dalla direzione
del fiume. Agli aspetti noti del
tempo e del movimento si aggiunge un'altra dimensione
dell'acqua: la sua funzione di
via di trasporto.

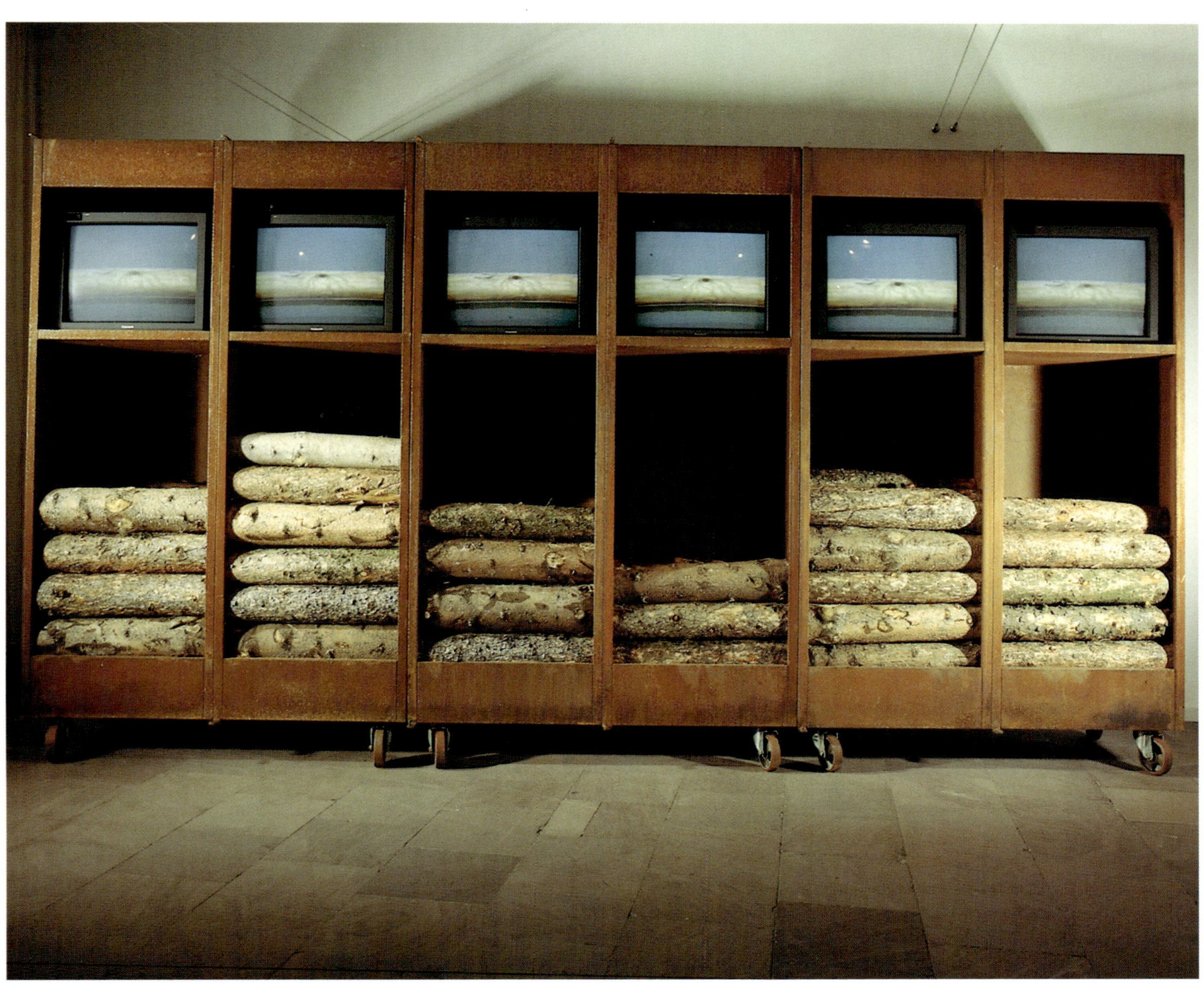

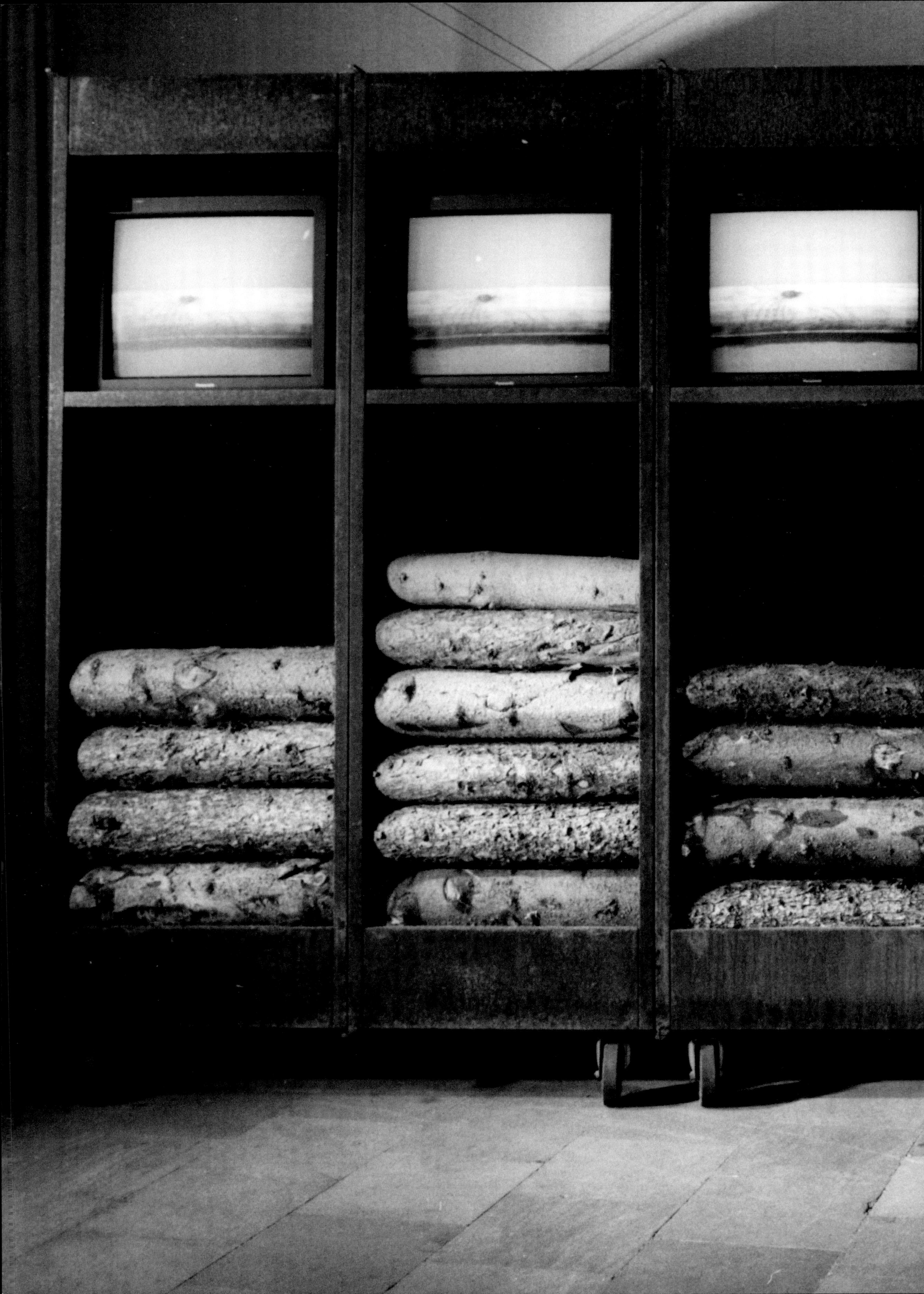

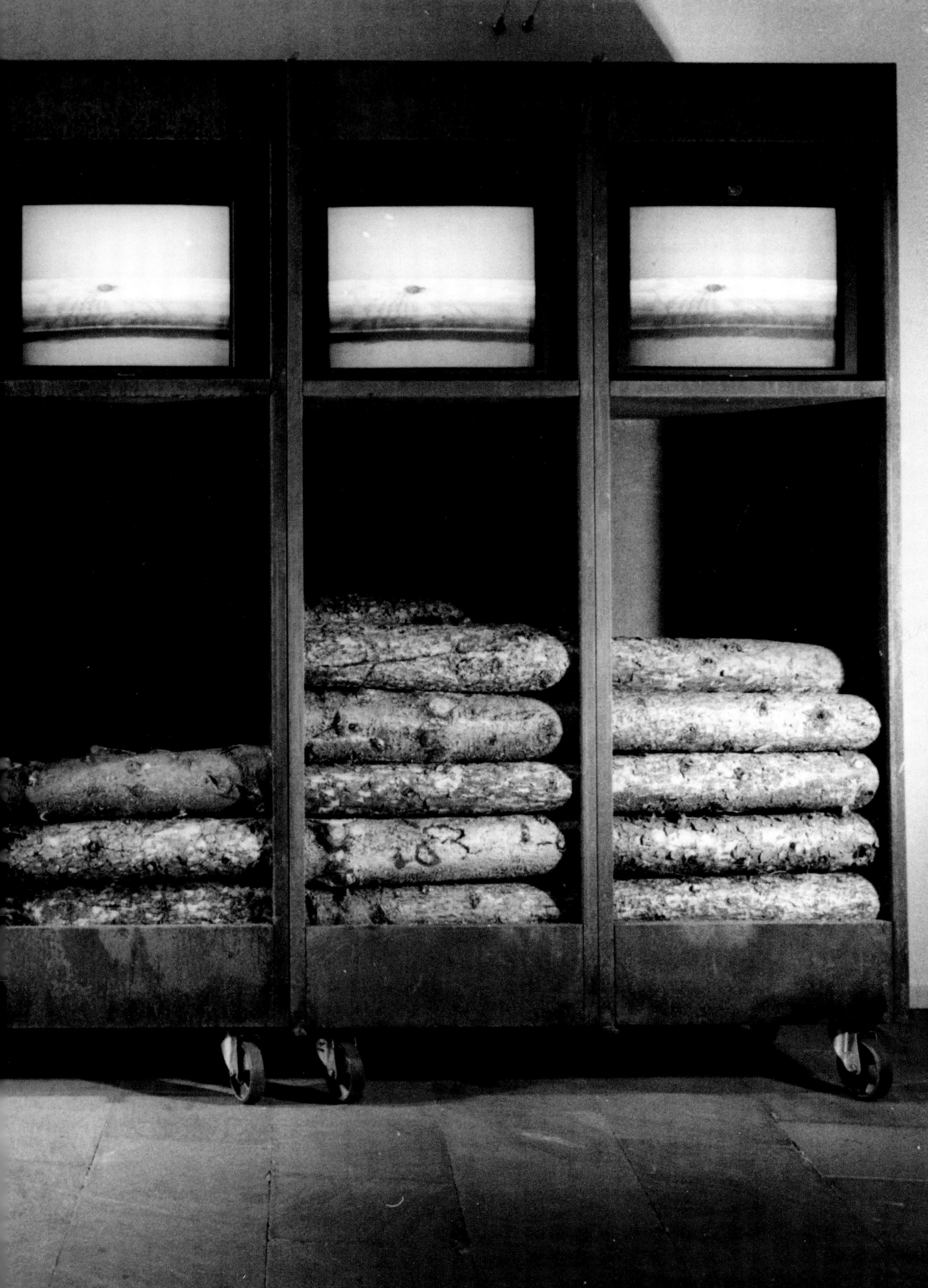

Gewässer, das vier verschiedene Länder berührt: die Schweiz, Deutschland, Frankreich und die Niederlande. Über Jahrhunderte hinweg bis hin zu heutiger Zeit wurden und werden auf dem Rhein mit Selbstfahrern und Schubschiffen Materialien, Güter und Waren transportiert, und es ist faszinierend zu beobachten, wie schnell ein solches Transportschiff sich mit der Strömung bewegt und wie hart es gegen die Strömung ankämpfen muß, wenn der Transportweg rheinauf geht. Die Strömung des Rheines ist schneller als die Fortbewegungszeit eines normalen Fußgängers. Also etwa sechs Kilometer pro Stunde. Die Internationalität gerade diesen besonderen Wassers dieses Flusses Rheines hat die Kuratoren veranlaßt, die Ausstellung über den *Rhein in Kunst und Kultur des 20. Jh.* als Wanderausstellung zu konzipieren und neben Bonn auch in Straßburg und Nimwegen zu zeigen.

Netherlands. Over centuries, and up to today, materials, goods, and wares were and are transported by ship on the Rhine, and it is fascinating to observe how fast such a unit moves with the current, and how hard it has to fight the current when the transport is upstream. The current's speed of the Rhine is faster than that of a pedestrian, about six kilometres per hour. The international and particular character of the water of the river Rhine were reason enough for the curators of the exhibition on the Rhine in Art and Culture of the 20th Century *to conceive it as a travelling show, and exhibit, beside Bonn, in Strasbourg and Nijmegen, too.*

Il Reno è un fiume internazionale che attraversa quattro paesi diversi: la Svizzera, la Germania, la Francia e i Paesi Bassi. Da secoli barche e navi trasportano materiali e merci sul Reno ed è affascinante osservare con quale facilità una nave da trasporto si muova con la corrente e con quali sforzi invece contro la corrente. La velocità della corrente del Reno è superiore a quella normale di un pedone, cioè circa sei chilometri all'ora. L'internazionalità proprio di questa particolare acqua del fiume Reno ha spinto i curatori a concepire la mostra come itinerante e a presentarla a Strasburgo nonchè a Nijmegen.

FUOCO FATUO

95004

PALMA DE MALLORCA 1995
Fundació Pilar i Joan Miró
95004.1

IRRLICHT
Videoskulptur 1995
Kinderschaukel,
Drehmechanismus, Baumstamm,
1 Monitor, Videorecorder,
bespielte Kassette

IGNIS FATUUS
Video sculpture 1995
Swing, rotating suspension, trunk,
1 monitor, video recorder,
recorded video cassette

FUOCO FATUO
Videoinstallazione 1995
Altalena, tronco di legno,
1 monitor, vhs, cassetta registrata

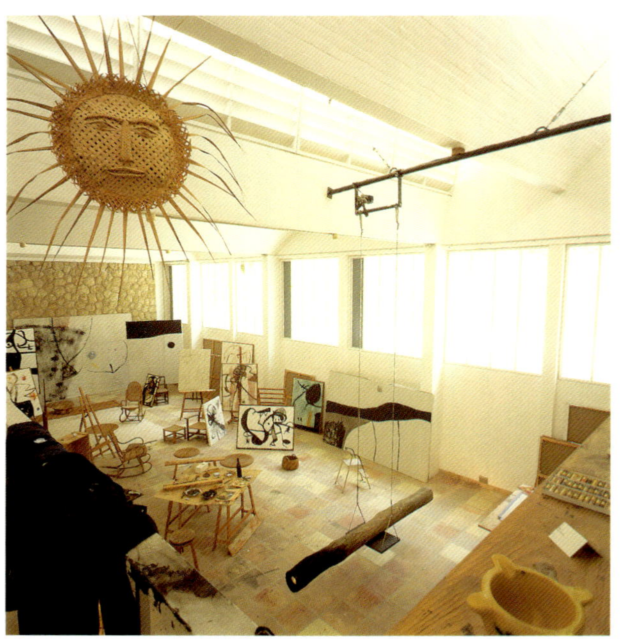

Der Titel *Fuoco Fatuo*, was in
der deutschen Übersetzung soviel
wie *Irrlicht* bedeutet, bezieht sich
auf eine Videoskulptur, die Fabrizio Plessi in dem ehemaligen
Atelier Mirós in Palma de Mallorca inszenierte, und er selbst
schreibt dazu: »In dem unzugäng-
lichen Atelier-Heiligtum Mirós
trägt eine sich unaufhörlich
bewegende Schaukel einen Baumstamm. Seine Seele aus elektronischem Feuer spiegelt und ent-
flammt erneut die tiefe und
quälende Leidenschaft, die in
jenen Jahren und genau an diesem Ort im Inneren des Künstlers
brannte.« (Fabrizio Plessi, in:

The title Fuoco Fatuo, *me-*
aning will-o'-the-wisp, refers to a
video sculpture Fabrizio Plessi
staged in Miró's former studio in
Palma de Mallorca, and he
writes: "In the inaccessible
studio-sanctuary of Miró, a
perpetually moving swing sup-
ports a tree trunk. Its soul of
electronic fire mirrors and
enflames anew the deep and
tormenting passion which bur-
ned in the heart of the artist in
those years and exactly in this
place." (Fabrizio Plessi, in:
Gérard A. Goodrow ed., Fabrizio
Plessi - Progetti del Mondo,
Dumont, Köln 1997, p. 46)

Il titolo *Fuoco Fatuo* si riferisce ad una videoscultura che
Fabrizio Plessi ha allestito
nell'ex-atelier di Mirò a Palma
de Mallorca. Scrive Plessi:
»Nell'inaccessibile sacrario-
studio di Miró un'instancabile
altalena in movimento sostiene
un tronco d'albero. La sua
anima di fuoco elettronico
rimanda e riaccende la profonda
e lacerante passione che brucia-
va dentro all'artista in quegli
anni e in quel preciso luogo.«
(Fabrizio Plessi, in: Gérard A.
Goodrow, *Fabrizio Plessi -
Progetti del Mondo*, Dumont,
Colonia 1997, p. 46) L'estremità

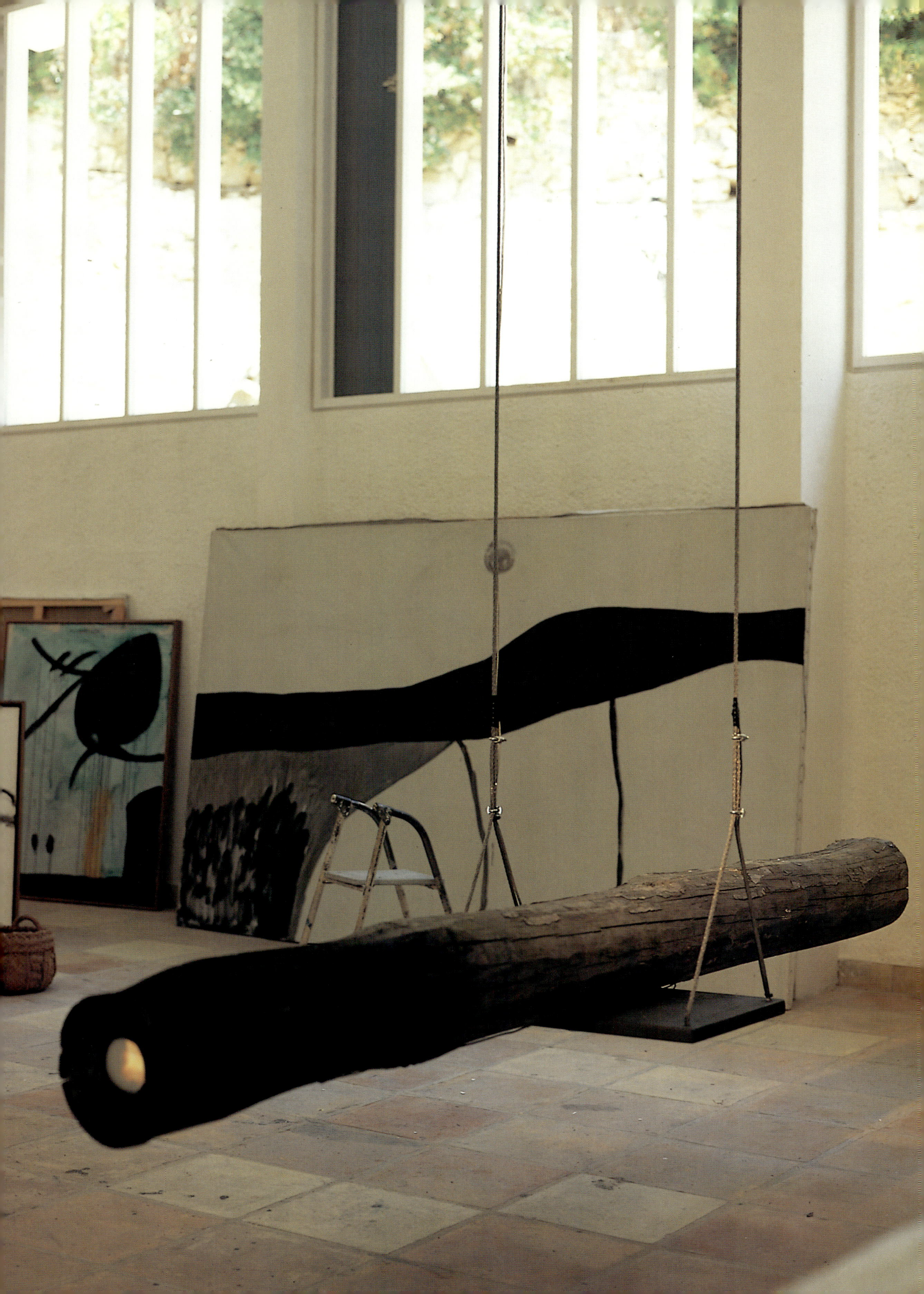

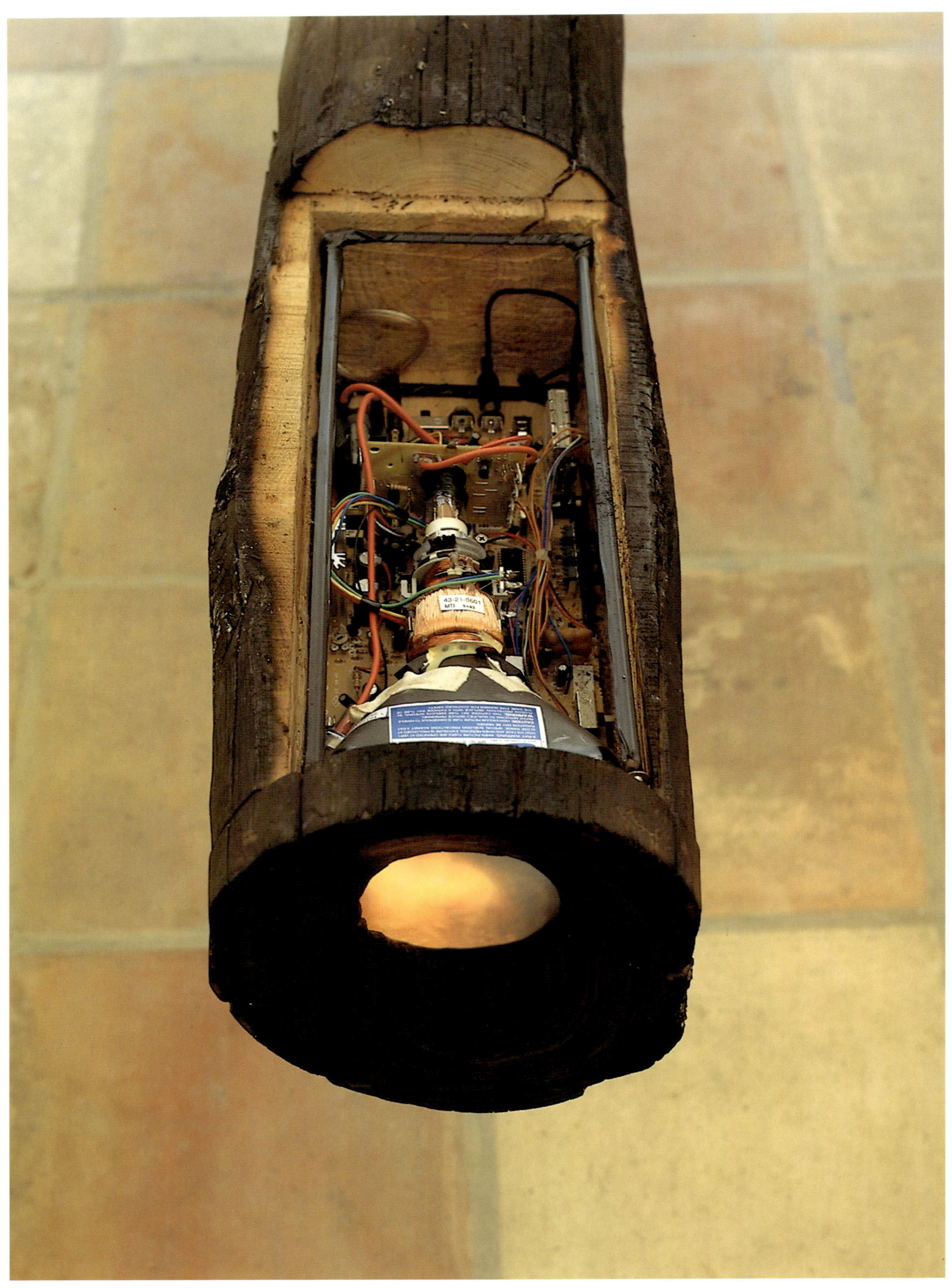

43-21-0601
MTI

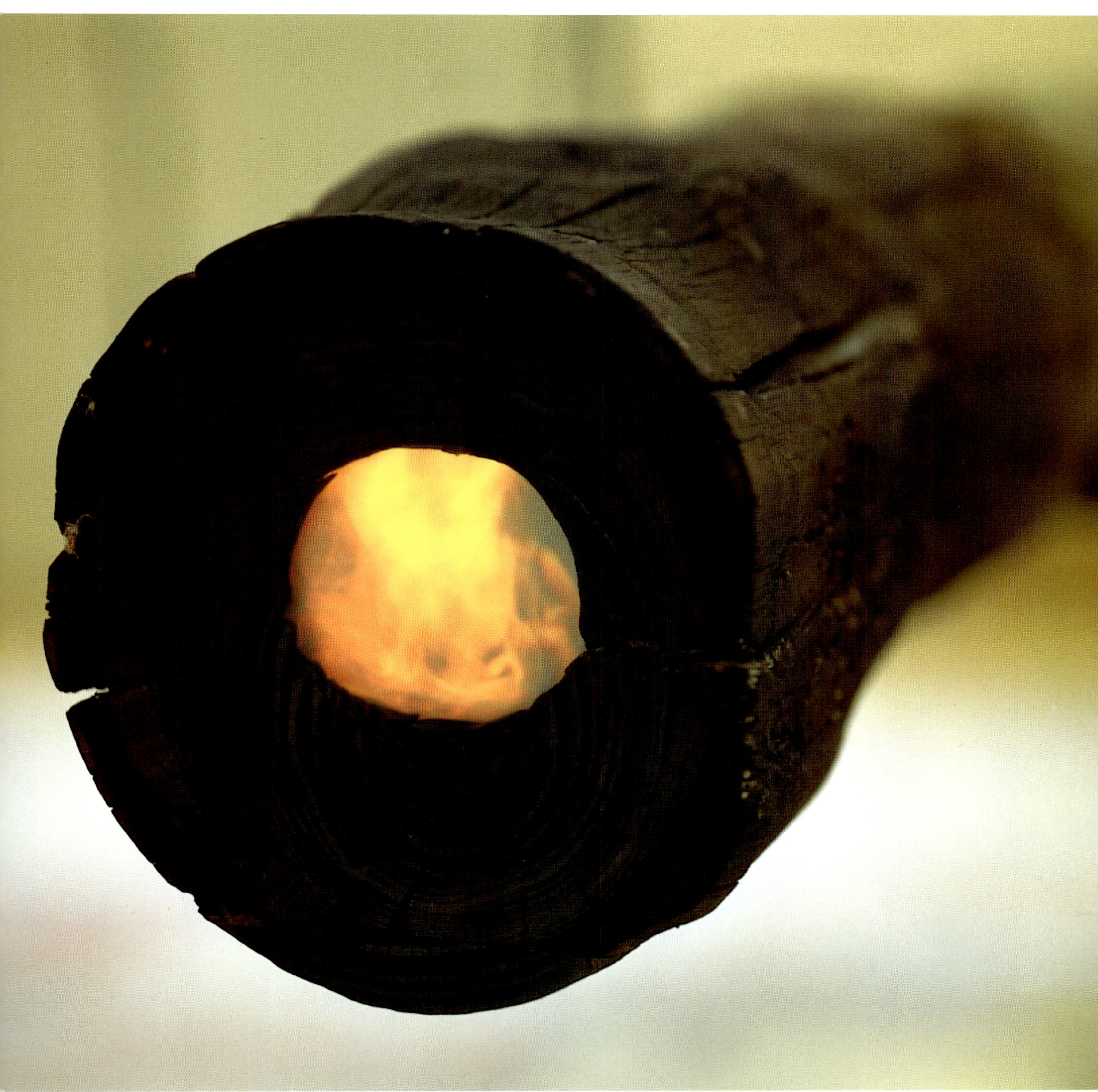

Gérard A. Goodrow hrsg., *Fabrizio Plessi - Progetti del Mondo*, Dumont, Köln 1997, S. 46) Das Ende des Baumstamms, in welches das elektronische Feuer per Monitor eingebaut ist, weist in seinem Äußeren deutliche Brandspuren auf, so als hätte das Feuer auch heute noch lodernde Kraft. Und in dem zunehmenden Maße wie Fabrizio Plessi sich heute mit der ›Seele der Materie‹ befaßt, wird diese Arbeit aus späterer Sicht als Vorstudie für die Videoskulptur *Le Due Anime della Materia (Die zwei Seelen der Materie)* verstanden werden können.

The end of the log, into which the electronic fire is built via a monitor, shows on its outside clear traces of burning, as if the fire still had blazing strength. And in the growing measure in which Fabrizio Plessi is interested in the soul of matter this work - looking back later - will be understood as pre-study for the video sculpture Le Due Anime della Materia (The Two Souls of Matter).

del tronco dove è collocato il monitor con il fuoco elettronico evidenzia vistose tracce di bruciato come se il fuoco avesse ancora una forza divampante. Considerando l'interesse crescente con cui oggi Fabrizio Plessi si occupa ›dell'anima della materia‹ si può intendere l'opera quale progetto che anticipa la videoscultura *Le Due Anime della Materia.*

FUOCHI FATUI

95005

PALMA DE MALLORCA 1995
FUNDACIÓ PILAR I JOAN MIRÓ
95005.1

IRRLICHTER
Videoinstallation 1995
3 Beichtstühle, aufgehängt in
konstanter Drehbewegung, 6 Monitore, Videorecorder, bespielte
Kassetten, Tonaufzeichnung
je 280 x 100 x 200 cm

IGNES FATUI
Video installation 1995
3 confessionals, constantly
rotating suspension, 6 monitors,
video recorders, recorded video
cassettes, soundrecording
280 x 100 x 200 cm (each)

FUOCHI FATUI
Videoinstallazione 1995
3 strutture in legno, macchine
rotanti in movimento, 6 monitors,
vhs, cassette registrate, sonoro
280 x 100 x 200 cm (caduna)

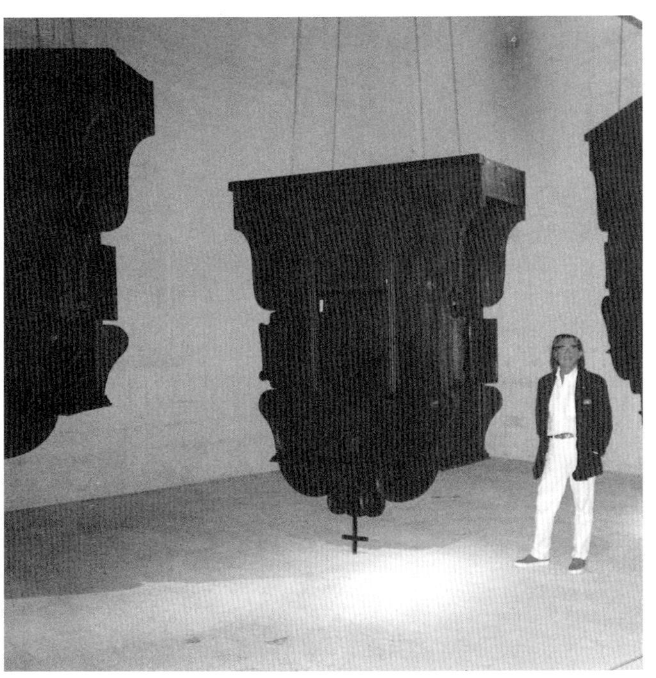

Zeitgleich findet in der Fundació Miró in Palma de Mallorca eine weitere Videoinstallation Plessis statt. In dem großen Ausstellungsraum sind drei Beichtstühle, schwebend mit dem Kopf nach unten aufgehängt, die seitlichen kleinen Fensteröffnungen, durch die normalerweise die Kommunikation des Beichtenden mit dem Priester möglich wird, sind geöffnet und zeigen in einem Monitor elektronisch loderndes Feuer. Auch hier verwendet Fabrizio Plessi den Titel *Fuochi Fatui (Irrlichter)*, diesmal im Plural. Eine magische Inszenierung, die etwas von der Dante'schen Vorhölle, dem ›Inferno‹ oder vielleicht dem ›Purgatorio‹, dem Fegefeuer, an sich hat, so, als müsse man durch dieses Stadium erst hindurch, wolle man ins Paradies gelangen.

At the same time, another video installation by Plessi is shown in the Fundació Miró in Palma de Mallorca. Three confessionals are suspended, upside down, in the great exhibition hall. The small window openings on he side, through which normally the conversation of the confessor with the priest takes places are opened and show, on a monitor, blazing electronic fire. Here, too, Fabrizio Plessi employs the title Fuochi Fatui *(wills-o'-the-wisp), this time in plural form. A magic scenario, owning characteristics similar to Dante's Inferno, or perhaps his Purgatorio, the purgatory, as if one had to pass this stage in order to enter paradise.*

Un'altra videoinstallazione nella Fundació Miró a Palma de Mallorca presenta tre confessionali capovolti appesi al soffitto. Le piccole finestre laterali, attraverso le quali si stabilisce per solito la comunicazione fra il credente e il sacerdote, sono aperte e mostrano in un monitor il fuoco fiammeggiante. Il titolo è simile a quello dell'altra opera, qui al plurale: *Fuochi Fatui*. La magica messa in scena ricorda in certo qual modo l'Inferno dantesco o forse il Purgatorio, che devono essere attraversati se si vuole entrare in Paradiso.

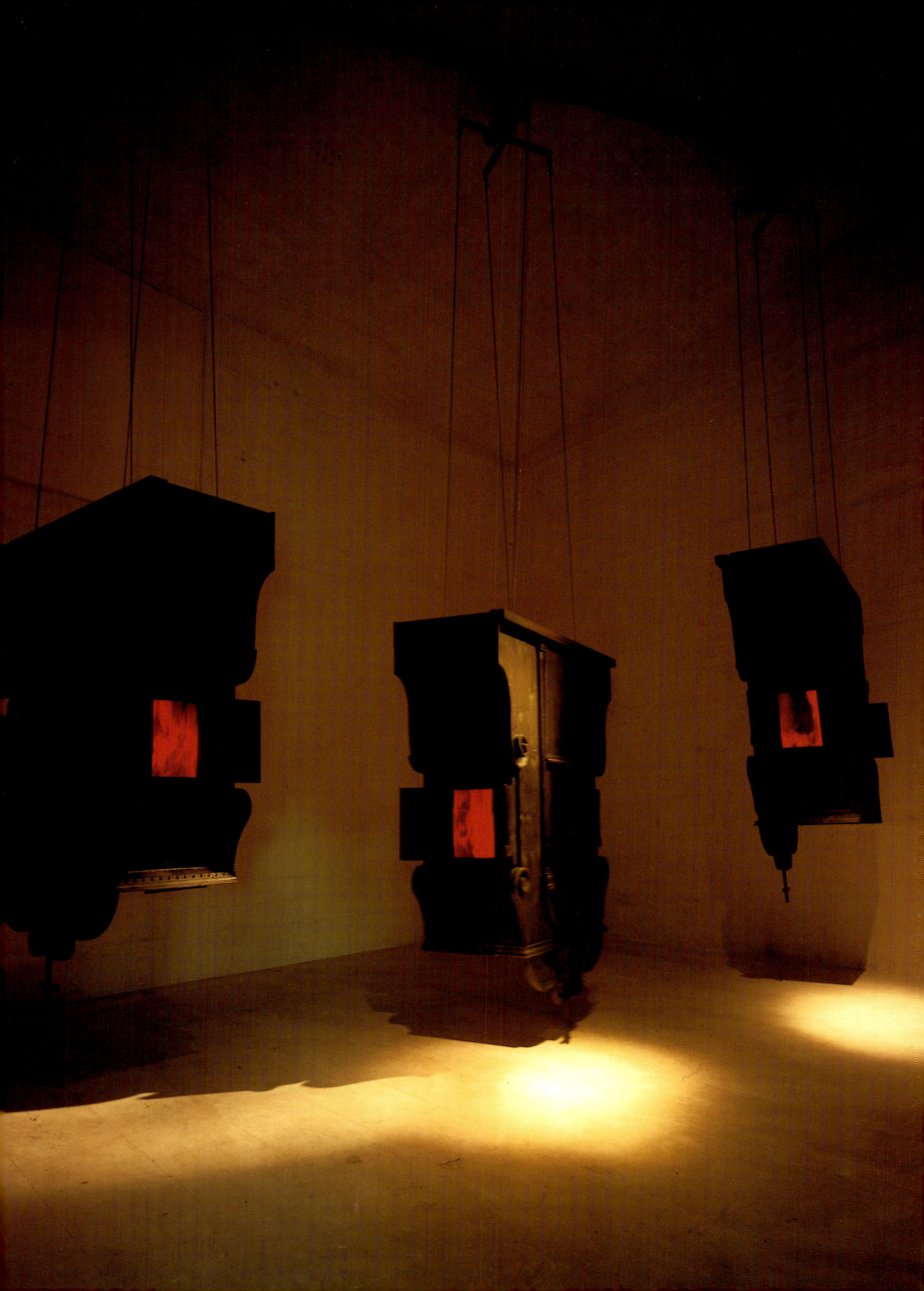

DEPOSITO DELL'ARTE

95006

PERUGIA 1995
Rocca Paolina
95006.1

SÃO PAULO 1998
Fundação SECS, Pompeia
95006.2

KUNST-DEPOT
Videoinstallation 1995
Eisenschränke mit Fächern,
60 leere Keilrahmen
verschiedener Größen,
3 Monitore, 3 Videorecorder,
3 bespielte Kassetten

Im Gegensatz zu dem *Armadio dell'Arte*, dem *Kunstschrank*, ist bei dem *Deposito dell'Arte* die Präsentation auf den gesamten Raum ausgedehnt. In der Rocca Paolina, dem Ausstellungsinstitut in Perugia, fehlen die Neonbuchstaben, die das Wort ›ART‹ als Reflexion im elektronischen Wasser erzeugen. Anstelle der Bilderrahmen gibt es nur noch Keilrahmen, wie jene, auf die der Maler normalerweise seine Leinwand erst aufspannt, bevor er zu malen beginnt. Diese Keilrahmen sind in verschiedenen Größen in die Schränke hineingestellt, lehnen aber auch von außen daran und rechts und links zu Seiten des Raumes an der Wand. Sie stehen stellvertretend für potentielle Bilder, die der Betrachter sich nun selbst vorstellen mag. Es findet hier eine Gegenüberstellung traditioneller Formulierungen bildnerischer Ideen mit der modernen, zeitgenössischen, medientechnisch orientierten Formulierung durch das Video statt.

Den Dialog zwischen Tradition und Moderne, zwischen Überlieferung und Erneuerung, zwischen Bindung an die Geschichte und Loslösung hat Fabrizio Plessi immer wieder provoziert und dies macht auch seine Sonderstellung unter den ›Videokünstlern‹ aus. Er selbst sieht sich weniger als Videokünstler denn vielmehr als ein

ART DEPOSIT
Video installation 1995
Iron construction with compartments, 60 empty frames of different sizes, 3 monitors, 3 video recorders, 3 recorded video cassettes

Contrary to Armadio dell'Arte, *the cabinet of art, the presentation of* Deposito dell'Arte *encompasses the entire room. In the Rocca Paolina, the exhibition centre in Perugia, the neon letters that create the term 'ART' as a reflection in electronic water are absent. Instead of the regular frames, there are only wedge frames like those on which the painter usually fixes his canvas before beginning to paint. These wedge-frames, of different size, are placed inside the cabinets, but also lean on the outside, as well as left and right on the walls of the room. They are representatives of potential paintings the spectator can imagine for himself. We here encounter a confrontation of traditional ways of artistic expression with one that is modern, contemporary, and orientated by media-technology in form of a video.*

Fabrizio Plessi has again and again provoked a dialogue between tradition and modernity, tradition and renewal, bonds to and separation from history, and this constitutes his special position among 'video artists'. He regards himself less as a video artist but rather as an artist whose artistic means of expression contain - among

DEPOSITO DELL'ARTE
Videoinstallazione 1995
Struttura in ferro, 60 telai di legno di diverse misure, 3 monitors, 3 vhs, 3 cassette registrate

Contrariamente all'*Armadio dell'Arte* la presentazione di *Deposito dell'Arte* si estende su tutta una sala della Rocca Paolina. Nel centro espositivo di Perugia mancano le lettere al neon che danno origine alla parola ART come riflesso nell'acqua elettronica. Le cornici sono state sostituite da telai di grandezze diverse, come quelli sui quali il pittore tende normalmente la tela prima di iniziare a dipingere. Essi sono appoggiati all'interno ed anche all'esterno degli armadi, così come alle pareti laterali della sala e fanno le veci di dipinti potenziali, che lo spettatore deve immaginarsi autonomamente. Si assiste al confronto fra forme tradizionali di idee figurative e forme moderne, contemporanee e orientate alla tecnica mediale attraverso il video.

Il dialogo fra tradizione e moderno, fra memoria e rinnovamento, fra vincolo storico e distacco dalla storia, da tempo provoca Fabrizio Plessi e caratterizza la sua posizione particolare fra i ›videoartisti‹. Egli stesso non si considera tanto un videoartista quanto un artista che, accanto ad altri materiali, impiega il video come forma d'espressione; le sue opere

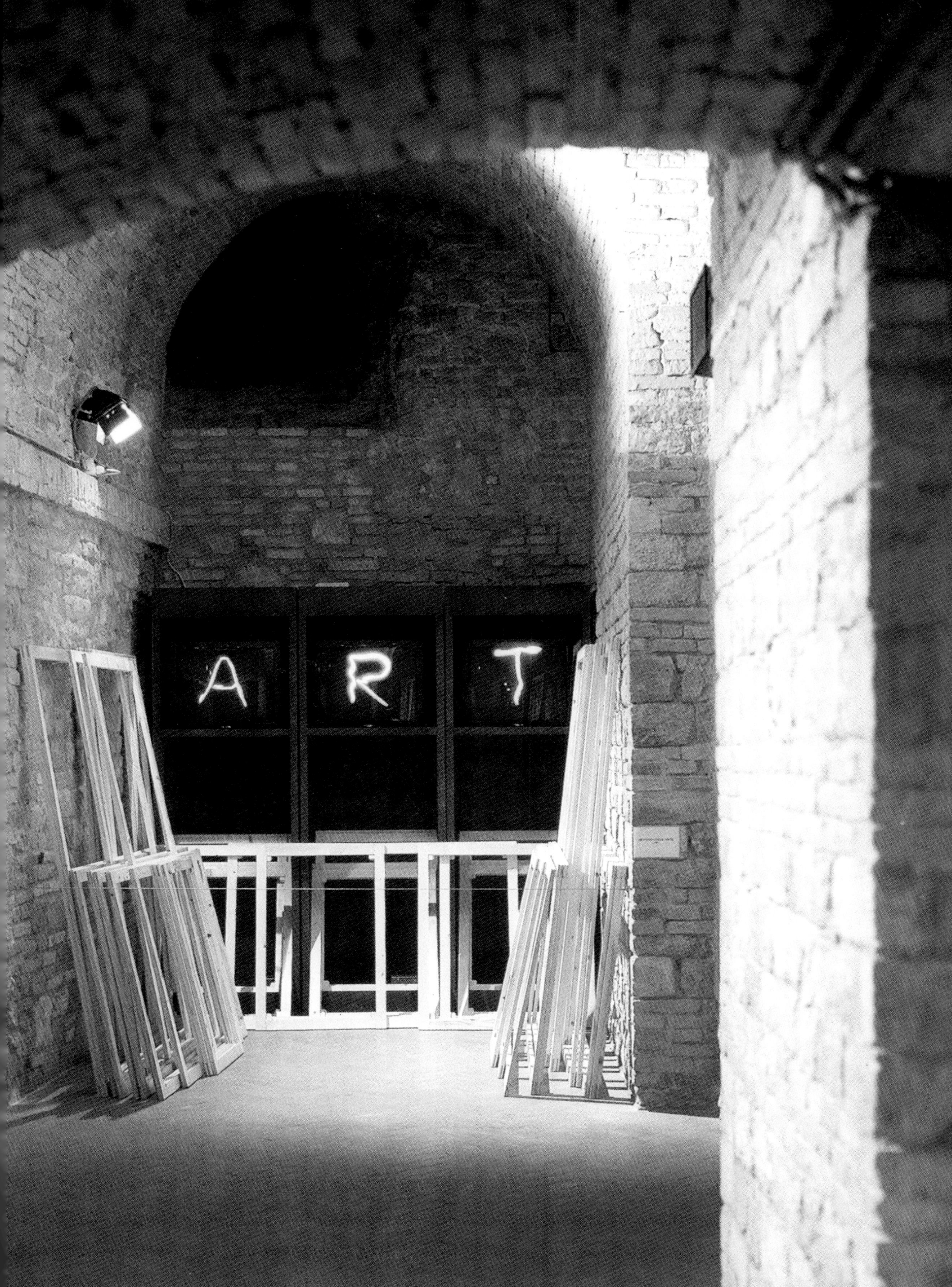
ART

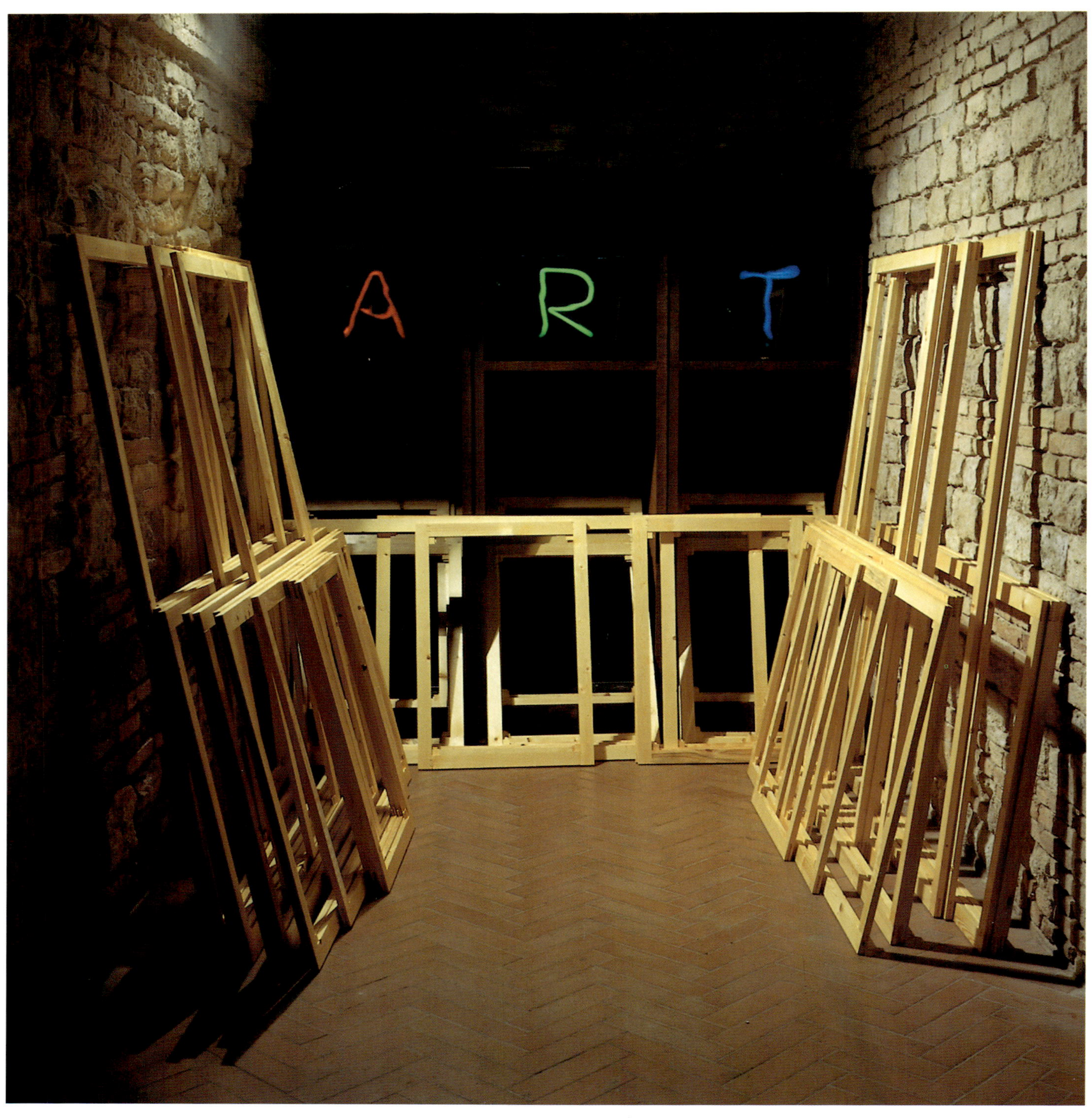

Künstler, dessen bildnerisches Ausdrucksmittel, neben anderen Materialien, Video beinhaltet. So zeigen seine Arbeiten trotz des Einsatzes komplexer Technologien immer eine Handschrift. Ein wesentlicher Bereich seiner Arbeit ist die unermeßliche Anzahl von Zeichnungen, die zwar größtenteils in Bezug zu Videoinstallationen oder Projekten stehen, doch nicht

others - video. In this way, his work always shows, in spite of employing complex technologies, the same 'handwriting'. An essential part of his work is the immeasurable number of drawings, most of which are related to video installations or projects, but are not only sketches of ideas or portraits of his video sculptures to be regarded

rivelano malgrado l'uso di tecnologie complesse una calligrafia personale. Un ruolo essenziale occupano i suoi innumerevoli disegni che, anche se per la maggior parte si riferiscono alle videoinstallazioni o ai progetti, non sono da considerare semplicemente annotazioni di idee o ritratti delle sue videoinstallazioni - quasi fossero supplementari -

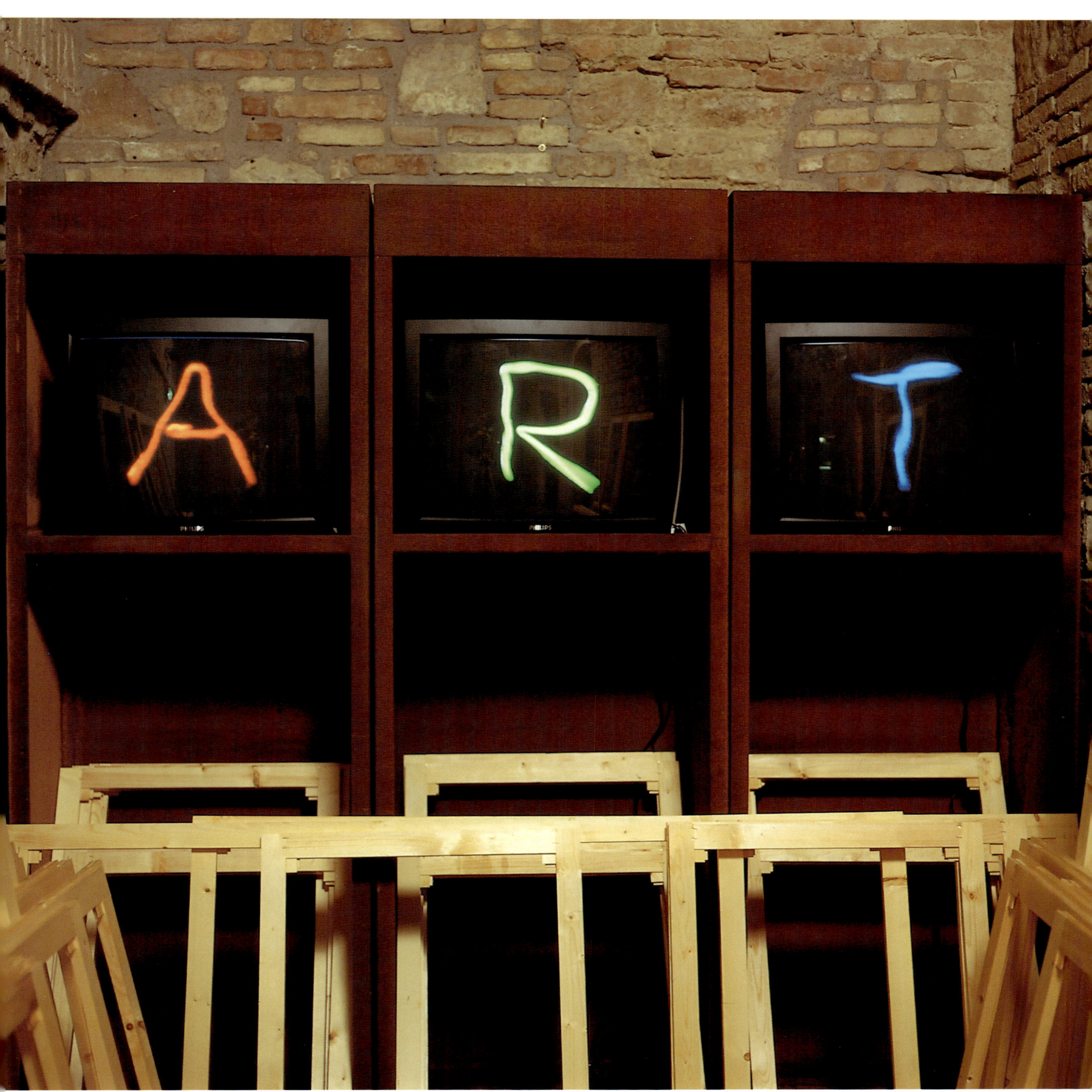

nur als Ideen-Notationen oder
vielleicht Portraits seiner Videoskulpturen - als Supplements gewissermaßen - zu sehen sind, sondern

as supplement, but mark an
independent, large and valuable
sector of his work. Beside the
transformation of his ideas in

ma costituiscono una parte
pregiata autonoma della sua
arte. Accanto alla concretizzazione tecnologico-mediale delle

397

die einen eigenen großen wertigen Bereich innerhalb seiner Kunst markieren. Neben den medientechnologischen Umsetzungen seiner Ideen und dem damit verbundenen Zeitbezug zu hier und heute, tritt Fabrizio Plessi immerwährend in den Dialog mit der Geschichte, der Geschichte nicht nur europäischer Kultur.

Es ist die Kultur, die letztlich auch ihn als Künstler hervorgebracht hat, und vielleicht kann in Europa in besonderem Maße ein Italiener den *Arco Liquido*, einen *Fließenden Bogen* von der Vergangenheit zur Gegenwart und von der Gegenwart zur Zukunft herstellen. »Kosmos, Materie, persönlicher Umraum und seelische Befindlichkeit bilden für Plessi die Angelpunkte elementarer, sinnlich vital erfahrbarer Gestaltung. Bei aller Expressivität und direkten Anschaulichkeit sind seine Objekte und Installationen immer auch denkerischer, philosophischer Anlaß einer Beschäftigung, die über die inszenierte Metapher des Einzelfalles hinaus allgemeine Gültigkeit beansprucht« schreibt Peter Baum im Katalog zur Ausstellung im Museum Moderner Kunst in Wien, 1991. Diese eigenartige Mischung aus Tradition und Moderne machen Fabrizio Plessi - obgleich er alle seine Videoskulpturen und Installationen in Zeichnungen und Konzepten vorbereitet - dennoch nicht zu einem Konzeptkünstler oder Minimalisten. Denn die Bindung zur Geschichte, die Metaphorik der verwendeten Utensilien und nicht zuletzt sein traditionelles Studium der Malerei an der Kunstakademie in Venedig lassen sein Werk nur schwer kunstgeschichtlich einordnen, räumen dem Künstler eine Sonderstellung ein, die - weil so vielseitig und ohne Vorbilder im eigentlichen Sinne - schwer in Worte zu fassen und zu klassifizieren ist.

technological media, and the reference to the present time connected with this, Fabrizio Plessi enters permanently into a dialogue with history, not only the history of European culture.

It is culture that has produced artists like him, and perhaps an Italian is predestined to create the Arco Liquido *in Europe, a liquid arch from the past to the present, and from present to future. "The cosmos, matter, his personal environment and spiritual situation constitute for Plessi the key points of his elemental art, which can represent a sensuously vital experience for the beholder." writes Peter Baum (in: catalogue Museum Moderner Kunst in Vienna, 1991). This singular mixture of tradition and modernity make Fabrizio Plessi - although he prepares all his video sculptures in drawings and concepts - nevertheless not a conceptual artist or minimalist. For the bond to history, the metaphors of the utensils applied, and, last but not least his traditional studies of painting at the Academy of Art in Venice, make it difficult to classify his work in the history of art, give the artist a special position that - because so versatile, and without real model - is difficult to describe and classify.*

sue idee e al conseguente rapporto con l'attualità Fabrizio Plessi non cessa mai di cercare il dialogo con la storia e non solo quella della cultura europea.

È la cultura che ha informato anche lui quale artista, e forse riesce proprio ad un italiano tendere in Europa un *Arco Liquido* fra passato e presente e fra presente e futuro. »Cosmo, materia, ambiente personale e stato d'animo rappresentano per Plessi i cardini della creazione elementare e vitale, sensualmente percepibile. Con l'espressività e l'immediatezza dei suoi oggetti e delle sue installazioni essi costituiscono motivo di riflessione, che va oltre la metafora inscenata del singolo caso e reclama validità assoluta« afferma Peter Baum nel catalogo della mostra nel Museum Moderner Kunst di Vienna del 1991. Tale curiosa mescolanza fra tradizione e modernità non fanno di Fabrizio Plessi un artista concettuale o minimalista, anche se le sue videoinstallazioni e sculture vengono precedute da disegni preparatori e concettuali. Il rapporto con la storia, il carattere metaforico degli utensili impiegati e, non da ultimo, i suoi studi tradizionali della pittura presso l'Accademia delle Belle Arti a Venezia rendono arduo un inquadramento storico-artistico di Fabrizio Plessi e gli conferisce una posizione particolare complessa che, in quanto senza precedenti, difficilmente è definibile e classificabile.

GLI ARMADI DEL CAOS

95007

PERUGIA 1995
ROCCA PAOLINA
95007.1

DIE SCHRÄNKE DES CHAOS
Videoinstallation 1995
Eisenschränke mit Fächern,
160 Steine, 6 Monitore,
3 Videorecorder, 3 bespielte
Kassetten, Tonaufzeichnung

CABINETS OF THE CHAOS
Video installation 1995
Iron construction with
compartments, 160 stones,
6 monitors, 3 video recorders,
3 recorded video cassettes,
soundrecording

GLI ARMADI DEL CAOS
Videoinstallazione 1995
3 strutture di ferro,
160 pietre, 6 monitors, 3 vhs,
3 cassette registrate, sonoro

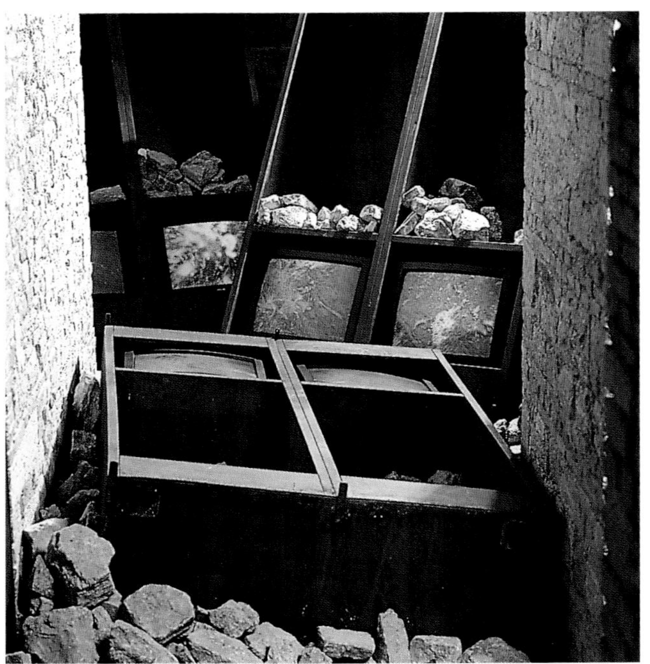

In den Räumen der Rocca Paolina in Perugia sind die Schränke Fabrizio Plessis in einem wilden Durcheinander liegend, stürzend, auf den Kopf gestellt, wie nach einem Erdbeben. Steine wie Geröll befinden sich in den türlosen Schrankgehäusen, scheinen in das elektronische Wasser der Video-Monitore zu fallen, geschleudert zu werden, beinahe so, als wollten sie darauf hinweisen, daß trotz des Chaos die Zeit nicht still steht. Ungehindert der chaotischen Anordnung und des Durcheinanders von Geröll nehmen sich die Stahlgehäuse und Monitore innerhalb des Mauerwerks recht konstruktiv aus. Sie erscheinen beinahe wie

Within the rooms of the Rocca Paolina in Perugia Fabrizio Plessi's cabinets are lying, falling, upside down in wild chaos, as if after an earthquake. The doorless casing are filled with stones, like rubble, seem to fall into the electronic waters of the video monitors, thrust in a way as if trying to point out that, in spite of the chaos, time does not stand still. Notwithstanding the chaotic arrangement and the muddle of stones the steel casings and monitors within the walls look rather constructive. They almost appear like a section from a cubist or futuristic painting in which the simultaneity of different moments in time is

Gli armadi di Fabrizio Plessi sono distribuiti in maniera disordinata negli ambienti della Rocca Paolina a Perugia, capovolti, come caduti dopo un terremoto. All'interno degli armadi, privi di porte, si trovano a mo' di detriti pietre che sembrano cadere o essere scagliate nell'acqua elettronica dei monitors, quasi volessero indicare che il tempo non si ferma mai, neanche nel caos. A dispetto della disposizione caotica e della confusione dei detriti i monitors e i contenitori metallici fra i muri assumono un aspetto alquanto costruttivo. Essi appaiono quasi come il particolare di un dipinto cubista

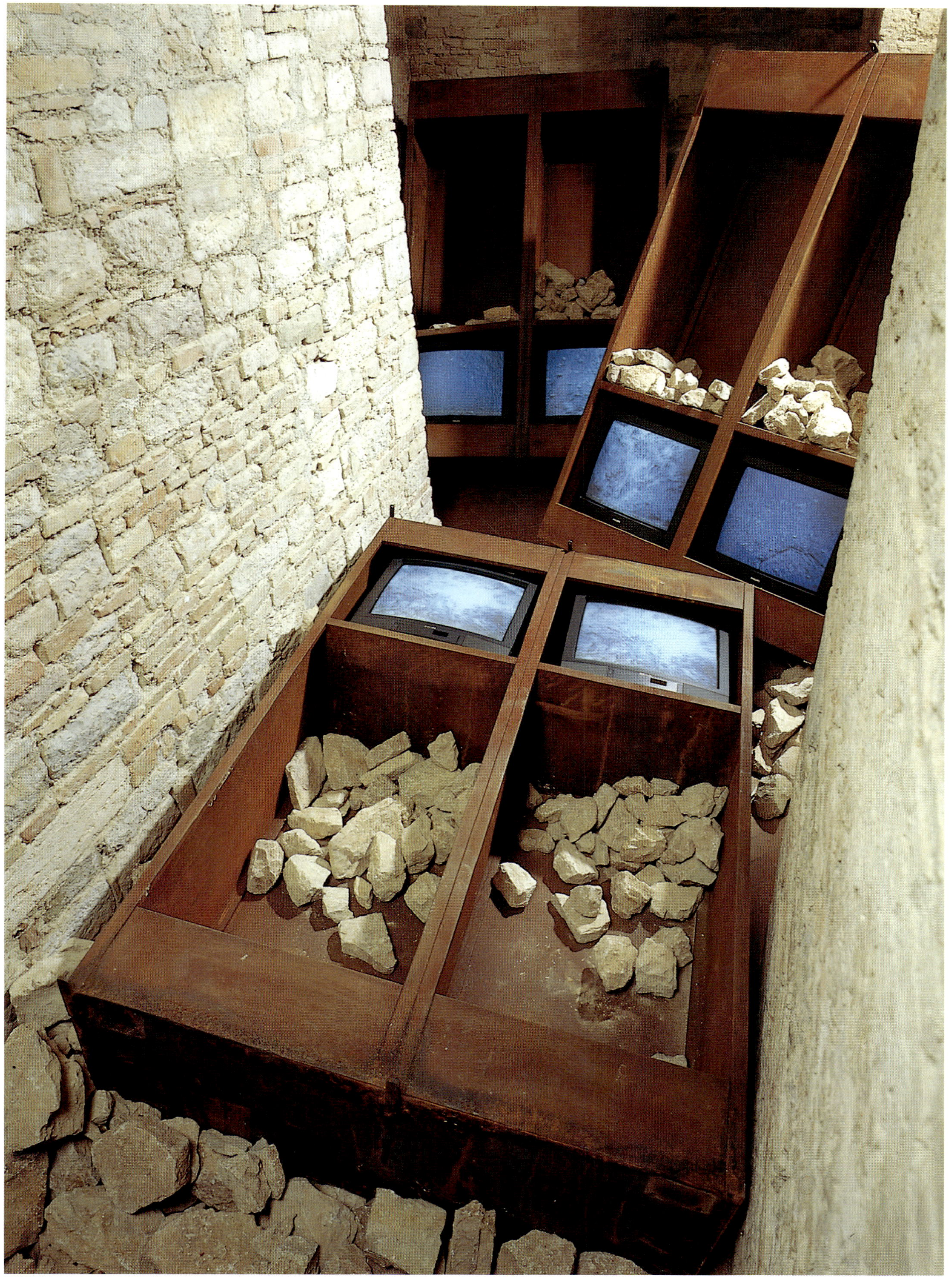

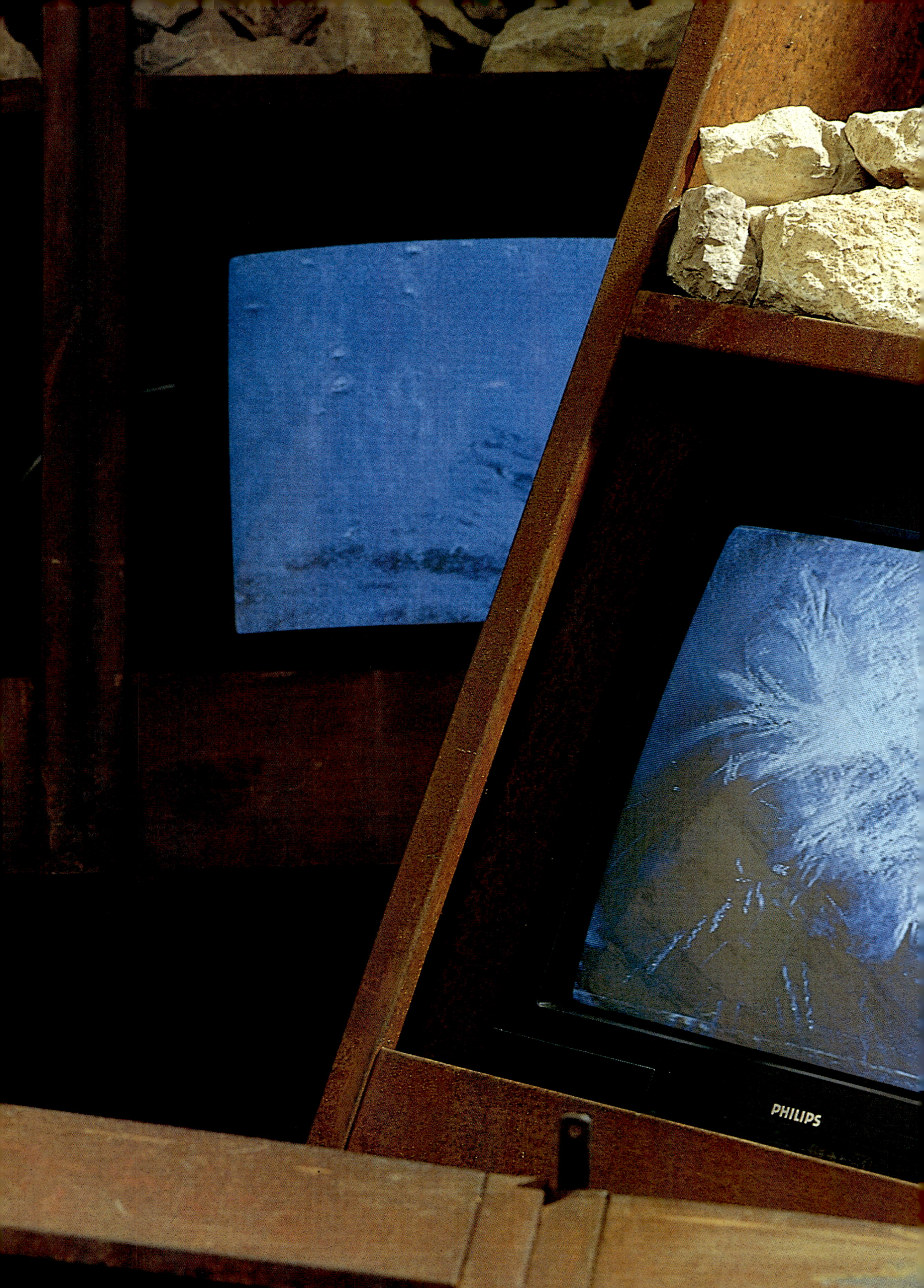
PHILIPS

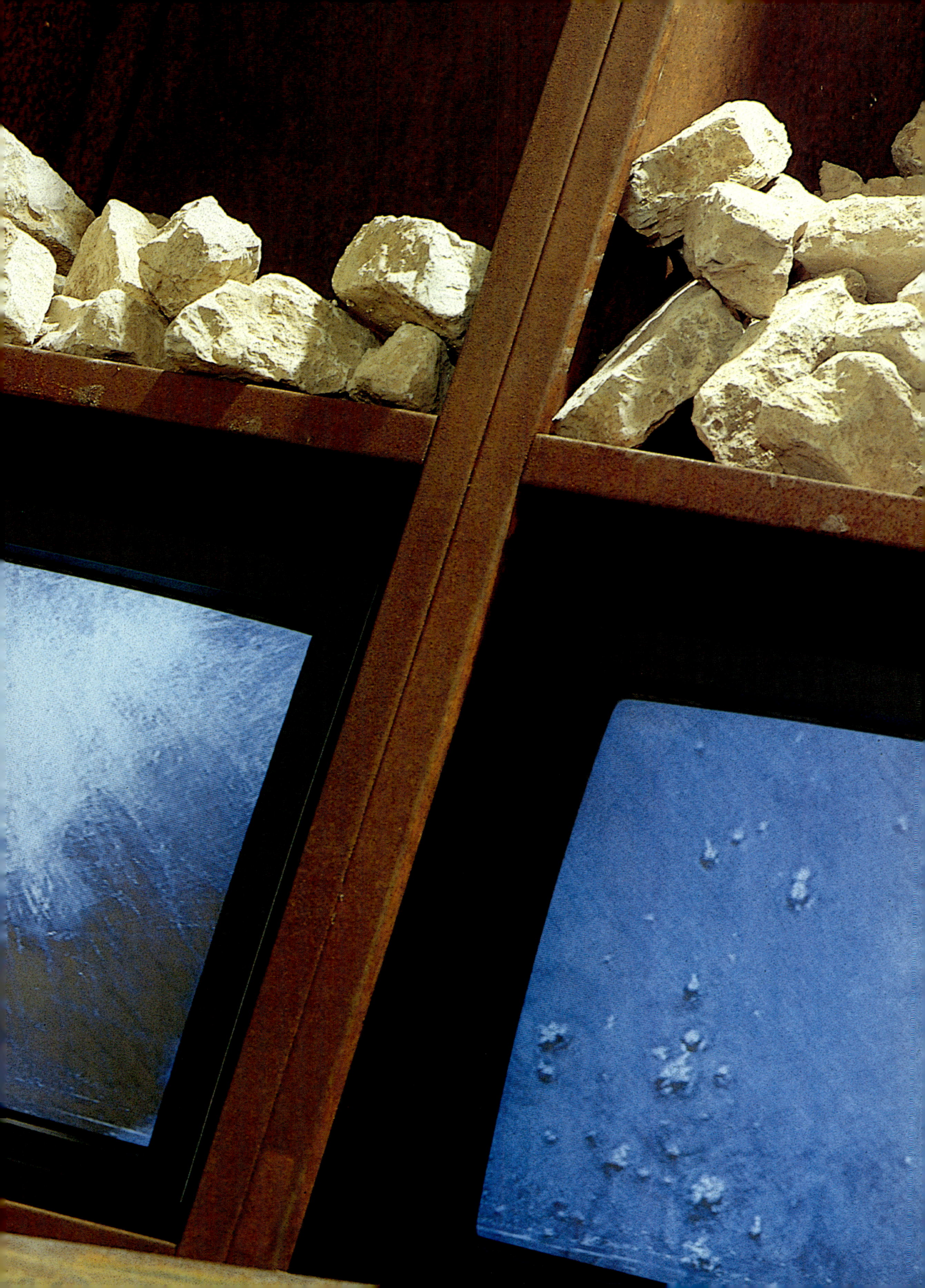

ein Ausschnitt aus einem kubistischen oder futuristischen Bild, bei dem die Simultaneität verschiedener zeitlicher Momente zeitgleich präsentiert werden, und somit schließt sich wieder der Kreis der Zeit. Ein Verweis auf die frühere Videoskulptur *Video Going* wird sichtbar und damit erneut das Pendeln zwischen Vergangenheit, Gegenwart und Zukunft. »Das Vorwärts als Zurück ohne über den Weg zu plaudern. Das Recht des Unbesprochenen« schrieb einmal der deutsche Dichter Hanns-Josef Ortheil. Rückgriff auf den Ursprung der futuristischen Tendenzen oder Weltuntergang einer Fin-de-siècle-Stimmung? Auflösung des Bestehenden und Bestimmten, des Determinierten; um irgendwo anzukommen, muß man auch irgendwo weggehen.

presented, closing the circle of time. 'Visible' is a hint to the earlier video sculpture Video Going, *and thereby, the oscillation between past, present and future. "The forward move as way back, without chatting about the way. The right of the undiscussed" the German poet Hanns-Josef Ortheil once wrote. Recourse to the origin of futuristic tendencies, or apocalypse of a fin-de-siècle mood? Dissolving of existence and destiny, of determination; to arrive somewhere, one has to leave.*

o futurista che rappresenta la simultaneità di momenti temporanei differenti, chiudendosi così di nuovo il ciclo del tempo. È evidente l'allusione alla videoscultura *Video Going* e, di conseguenza, ancora una volta all'oscillazione fra passato, presente e futuro. »Il procedere come il retrocedere senza discorrere sul percorso. Il diritto del non espresso ...« scrisse una volta il poeta tedesco Hanns-Josef Ortheil. Regresso verso l'origine delle tendenze futuriste o la fine dell'atmosfera da Fin-de-siècle? Annullamento dell'esistenza e del determinato; forse si deve partire per arrivare da qualche parte.

CRISTALLO LIQUIDO

95008

PERUGIA 1995
ROCCA PAOLINA
95008.1
WIEN 1996
95008.2

FLÜSSIGES KRISTALL
Videoinstallation 1995
Eisentisch, Trinkglas, Zinkeimer,
1 Monitor, Videorecorder,
bespielte Kassette,
Tonaufzeichnung

In den Gewölben der Rocca Paolina in Perugia ist eine verkleinerte Version der Konzeption aus dem Café Florian in Venedig realisiert, nicht flüssige Kristalle sondern ein *Cristallo Liquido*. Ein einzelner Blecheimer steht in der Mitte eines Raumes. Über ihm hängt ein Tisch an der Decke, die Tischplatte schräg nach unten gerichtet; auf dieser ist ein Glas befestigt, gleichfalls mit der Öffnung nach unten weisend. Aus dem Glas tropft ein imaginärer Tropfen in das elektronische Wasser im Video, das als Monitor in den Blecheimer eingebaut ist. Hatten im Café Florian die 500 venezianischen Gläser, die an der Decke des Cafés montiert waren, noch auf die Vielzahl der Persönlichkeiten und Personen, die jemals das Café besucht und dort Kaffee getrunken hatten, verwiesen, so macht sich bei dieser Installation eher eine Stimmung von Einsamkeit breit. Ein einzelner Gast kann nicht kommunizieren, wenn kein anderer da ist. So ist diese ästhetisch schöne Installation auf Kommunikation und den Dialog mit dem Betrachter aus, während die schillernde Erscheinung im Café Florian sich in gewisser Weise selbst genügt.

LIQUID CRYSTAL
Video installation 1995
Iron table, drinking-glass, metall bucket, 1 monitor, video recorder, recorded video cassette, soundrecording

In the vaults of the Rocca Paolina in Perugia a smaller version of the concept for the cafe Florian in Venice is realised, not liquid crystals but one Cristallo Liquido. *A single metal bucket stands in the middle of the room, hanging above it a table on the ceiling, the table top pointed askew, downwards; on it, a glass is fixed, its opening also towards the floor. An imaginary drop falls into the electronic water on the monitor's video that is built into the bucket. While the 500 Venetian glasses, fixed to the ceiling of the cafe Florian, had hinted at the multitude of personalities and persons that ever visited the cafe and had their coffee there, this installation rather leads to a feeling of loneliness. A single guest cannot communicate if nobody else is present. In this way this aesthetically beautiful installation is intended for communication and dialogue with the observer, while the iridescent apparition in the cafe Florian in a way suffices itself.*

CRISTALLO LIQUIDO
Videoinstallazione 1995
1 tavolo di ferro, 1 bicchiere,
1 recipiente di zinco, 1 monitor,
1 vhs, 1 cassetta registrata, sonoro

Nella Rocca Paolina è stata realizzata una versione ridotta rispetto a quella del Caffè Florian a Venezia, non più cristalli liquidi ma un solo *Cristallo Liquido*. Un singolo secchio zincato è posto al centro dell'ambiente. Dal soffitto pende in maniera obliqua un tavolo con il piano rivolto verso il basso al quale è fissato un bicchiere da cui cade una goccia immaginaria nell'acqua elettronica del monitor inserito nel secchio. Se i cinquecento bicchieri del soffitto del Caffè Florian alludevano alla pluralità delle personalità e delle persone che hanno visitato il Caffè e che lì hanno bevuto un caffè, quest'installazione diffonde un'atmosfera di solitudine. Un singolo ospite non può comunicare senza la presenza di un altro. Così l'installazione esteticamente bella cerca la comunicazione e il dialogo con lo spettatore, mentre la forma cangiante nel Caffè Florian si dimostra in un certo modo autosufficiente.

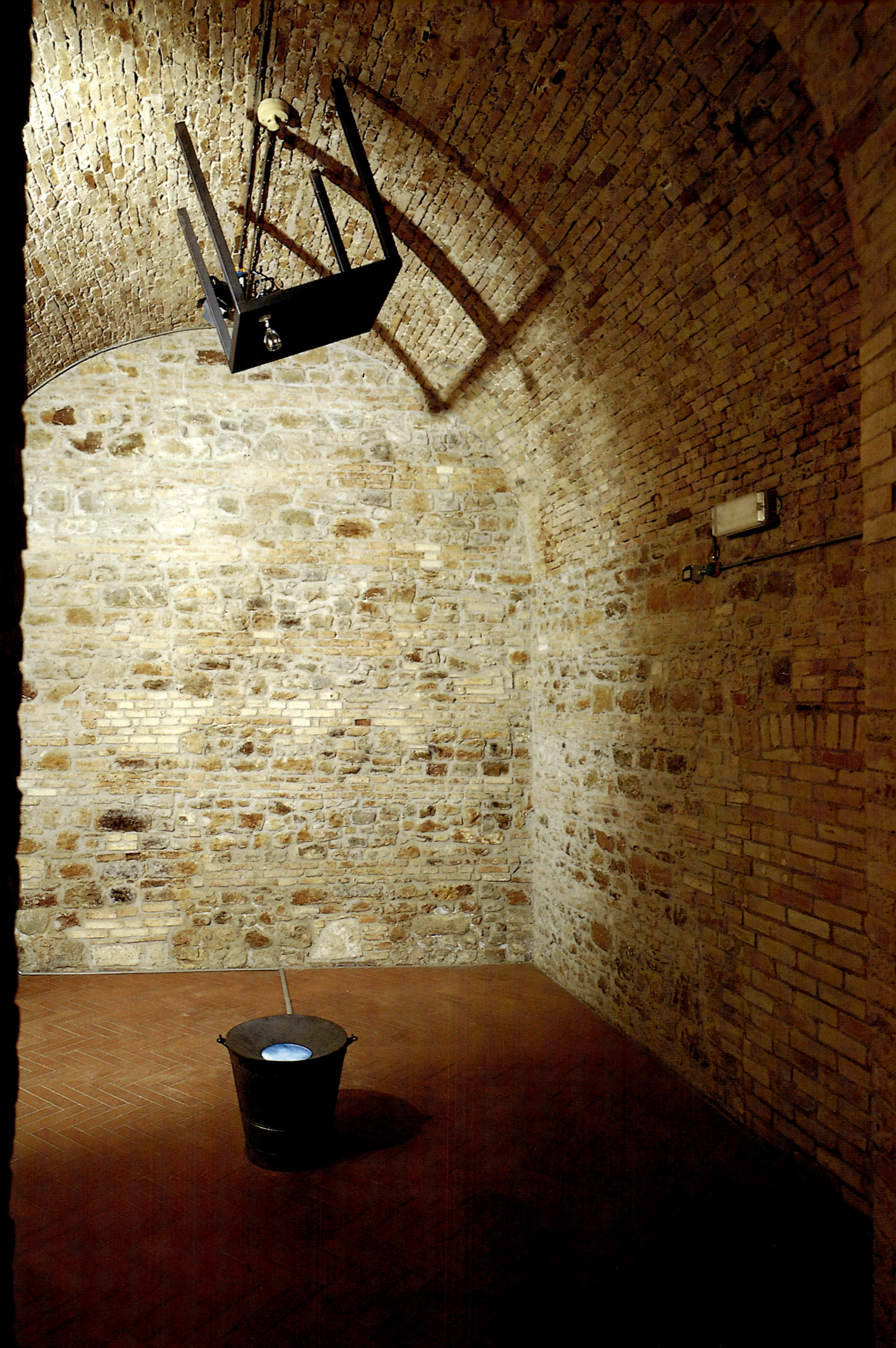

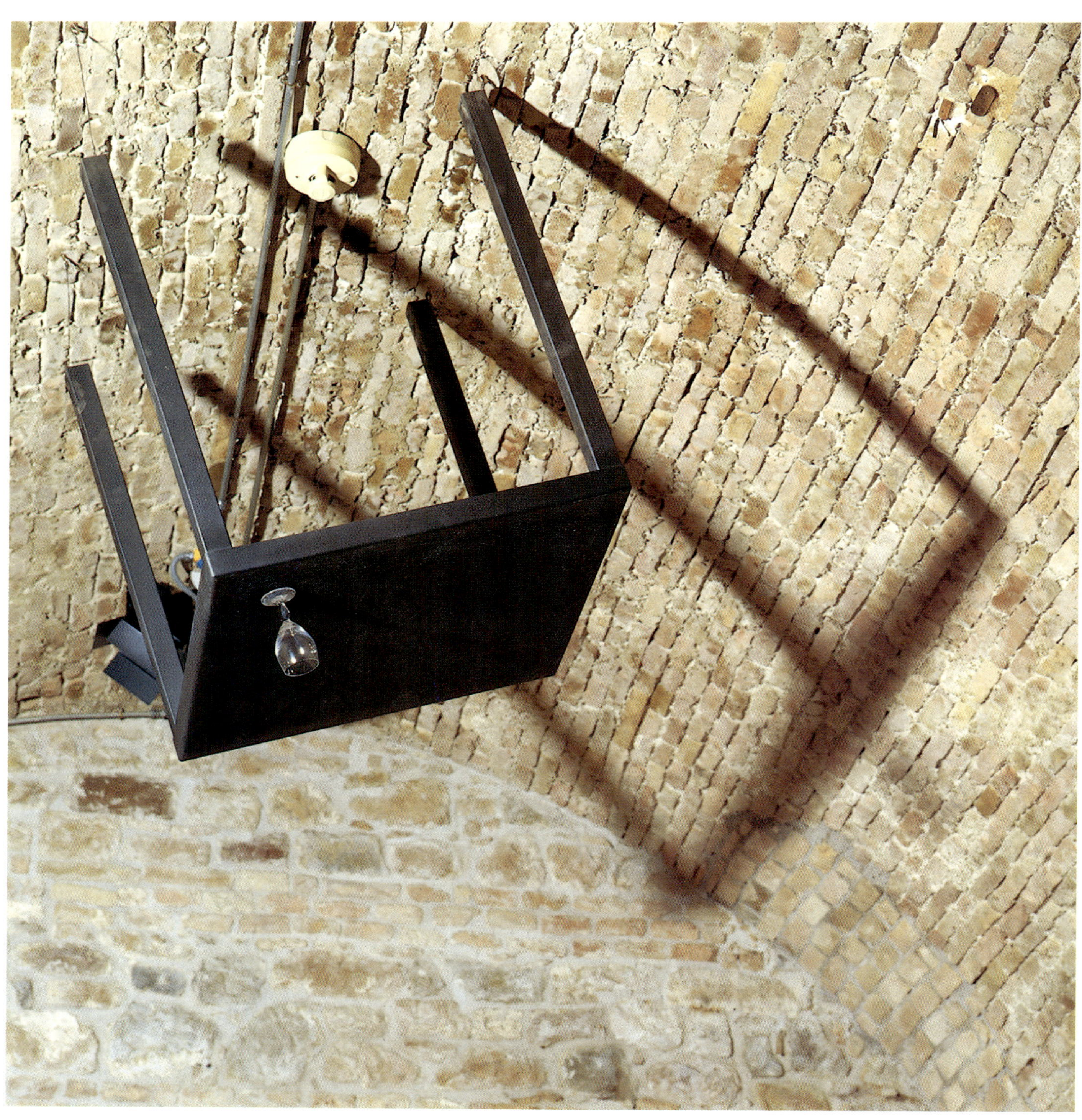

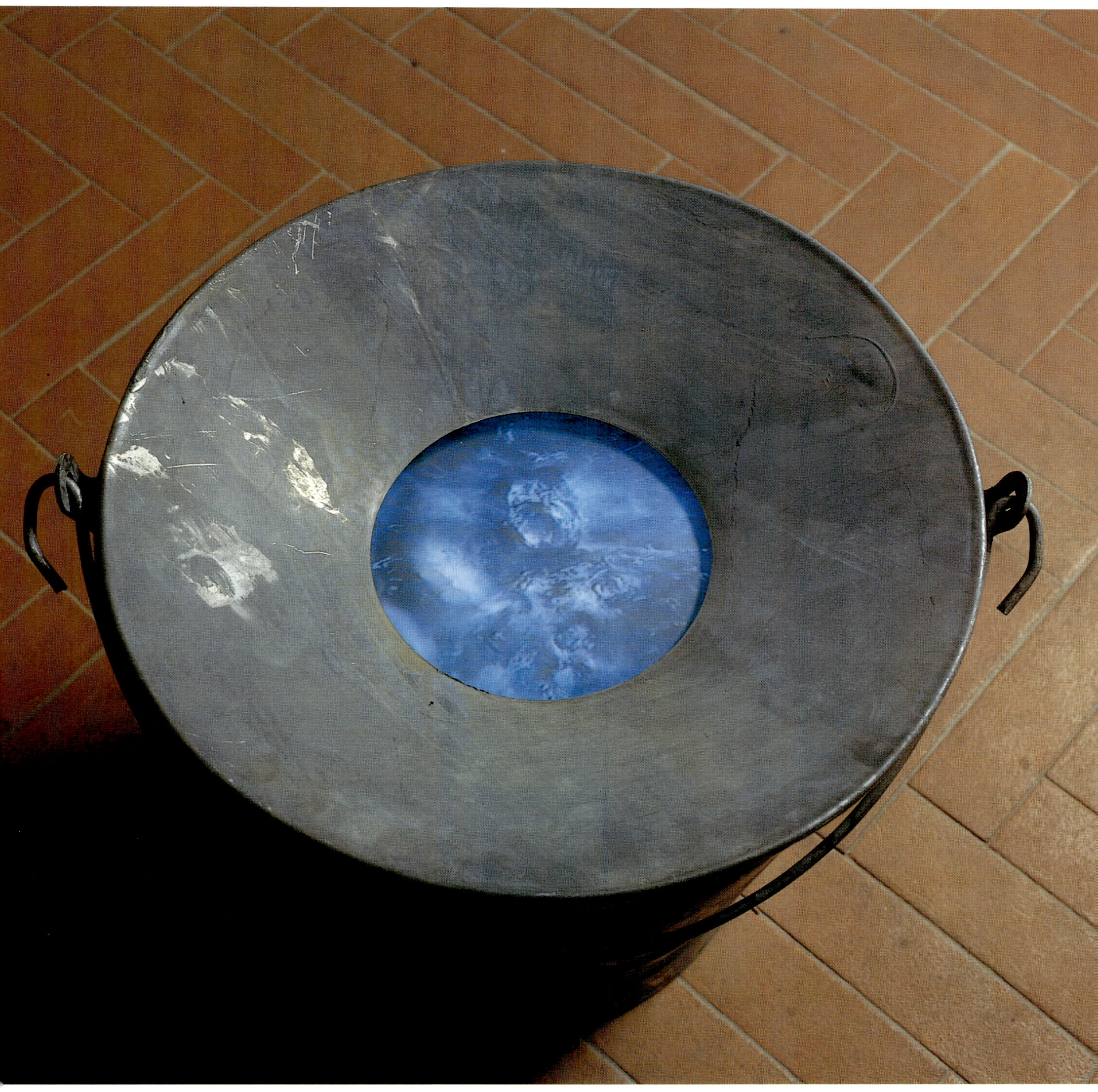

BOMBAY-BOMBAY II

95009

PERUGIA 1995
ROCCA PAOLINA
95009.1

BOMBAY-BOMBAY II
Videoskulptur 1995
Einreihig angeordnete waagrecht
liegende Eisenschränke, weiße,
indische Baumwolle, 12 Monitore,
Videorecorder, bespielte
Kassetten, Tonaufzeichnung
60 x 960 x 260 cm

BOMBAY-BOMBAY II
Video sculpture 1995
Iron structure, clues of white
Indian cotton, 12 monitors, video
recorders, recorded video cassettes,
soundrecording
60 x 960 x 260 cm

BOMBAY-BOMBAY II
Videoscultura 1995
Struttura in ferro adagiata a terra,
cumuli di cotone bianco bagnato,
12 monitors, vhs, cassette
registrate, sonoro
60 x 960 260 cm

Gleichfalls in Perugia findet
sich auch eine Präsentation der
Bombay-Bombay-Installation. Nur
dieses Mal sind die am Boden
liegenden Schränke mit der
nassen Baumwolle und den elektronisches Wasser spiegelnden
Monitoren linear angeordnet. Der
architektonische Rundbogen, der
sich wie eine Brücke über die
Konstruktion herüberwölbt, stellt
wieder eine Beziehung zu Venedig
her, macht das in Kanälen fließende Wasser mit seinen Brücken
assoziierbar. Mit dieser Art der
Präsentation hat Fabrizio Plessi
eine Bindung zwischen Venedig
und Bombay hergestellt, einen
Bogen über die Welt geschlagen.

A presentation of the installa-
tion Bombay-Bombay *can also be*
seen in Perugia. Only this time
the cabinets, lying on the
ground, filled with wet cotton
and monitors reflecting electro-
nic water are in linear order.
The architectural arch spanning
the construction like a bridge
again creates a relation to
Venice, enables associations to
the water flowing in its channels
and under its bridges. With this
kind of presentation Fabrizio
Plessi has created a connection
between Venice and Bombay, has
spanned an arch over the world.

BOMBAY-BOMBAY II
Video sculpture 1995

A Perugia è presente anche
l'installazione *Bombay-Bombay*,
solo che questa volta gli armadi
con il cotone bagnato e i monitors che riflettono acqua elettronica sono sdraiati per terra in
maniera lineare. L'arco a tutto
sesto che si inarca come un
ponte sopra la costruzione crea
di nuovo un collegamento con
Venezia e richiama alla memoria i suoi ponti e l'acqua che
scorre nei suoi canali. Con tale
presentazione Fabrizio Plessi ha
creato un legame fra Venezia e
Bombay, ha teso un arco sopra il
mondo.

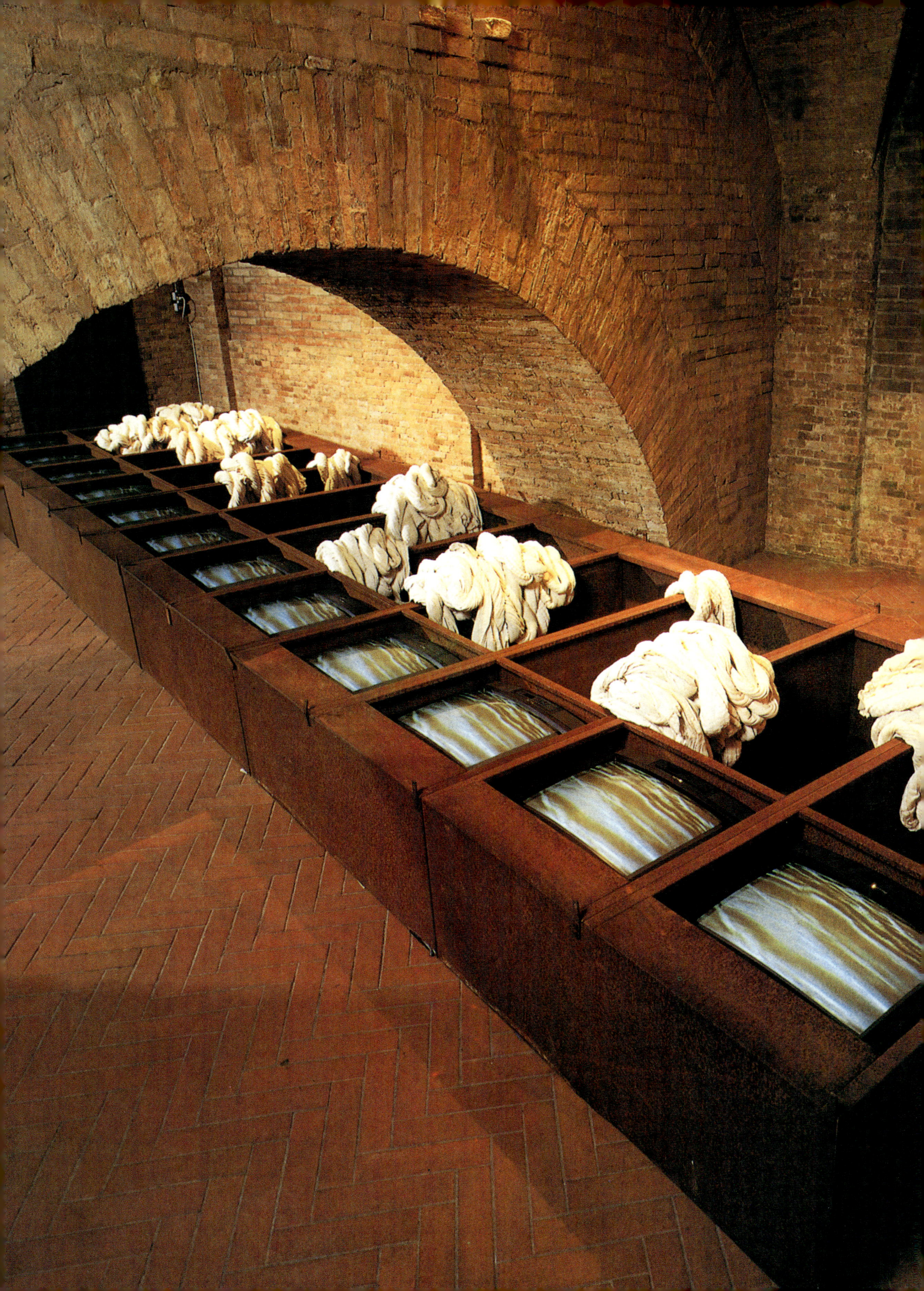

L'ANIMA DELLA PIETRA

95010

PERUGIA 1995
ROCCA PAOLINA
95010.1

DEN HAAG 1996
CITY-HALL
95010.2

DIE SEELE DES STEINS
Videoinstallation 1995
21 Gestelle aus Stahl, 21
Steinblöcke, 21 Monitore,
21 Videorecorder,
21 bespielte Kassetten

Anläßlich der Ausstellung in
der Rocca Paolina entsteht eine
vielteilige Videoinstallation, die
nicht nur ortsbezogen ist, also auf
die Räumlichkeiten eingeht,
sondern auch geschichtsbezogen.
Im äußeren Mauerwerk der Rocca
Paolina läßt sich, bei genauerem
Hinsehen eine ehemalige Tür
erkennen, die nun zugemauert ist.
Oberhalb des Torbogens sind
Überreste von Steinskulpturen
erhalten, unter anderem der
fragmentarische Kopf eines
Königs. Dieser Königskopf, das
Überbleibsel einer ehemaligen
Skulptur aus Stein, wird zum
Anlaß und Gegenstand einer

SOUL OF THE STONE
Video installation 1995
21 racks of steel, 21 stone blocks,
21 monitors, 21 video recorders,
21 recorded video cassettes

On the occasion of the exhibit
in the Rocca Paolina a multi-
sectoral video installation is
realised that is not only referring
to place, that is considers the
space, but also to history. In the
outer wall of the Rocca Paolina
a former door can, at close
glance, be seen, now filled with
bricks. Above the arched gate,
remains of stone sculptures are
visible, among others the frag-
mented head of a King. This
royal head becomes cause and
subject of an almost archaeologi-
cal research and analysis of the
essence and soul of stone,
L'Anima della Pietra.

L'ANIMA DELLA PIETRA
Videoinstallazione 1995
21 strutture in ferro, 21 blocchi di
pietra, 21 monitors, 21 vhs,
21 cassette registrate

In occasione della mostra
alla Rocca Paolina nasce
un'opera complessa con riferimenti non solo geografici,
riferiti cioè alla località specifica, ma anche storici. Osservando attentamente le mura esterne
della Rocca Paolina si riconosce
un'antica porta adesso murata.
Sopra l'arco della porta sono
conservati resti di sculture, fra
l'altro la testa frammentaria di
un re. Tale testa reale, residuo
di un'antica scultura di pietra,
diviene motivo e oggetto di una
ricerca quasi archeologica e di
un'analisi della natura de
L'Anima della Pietra.

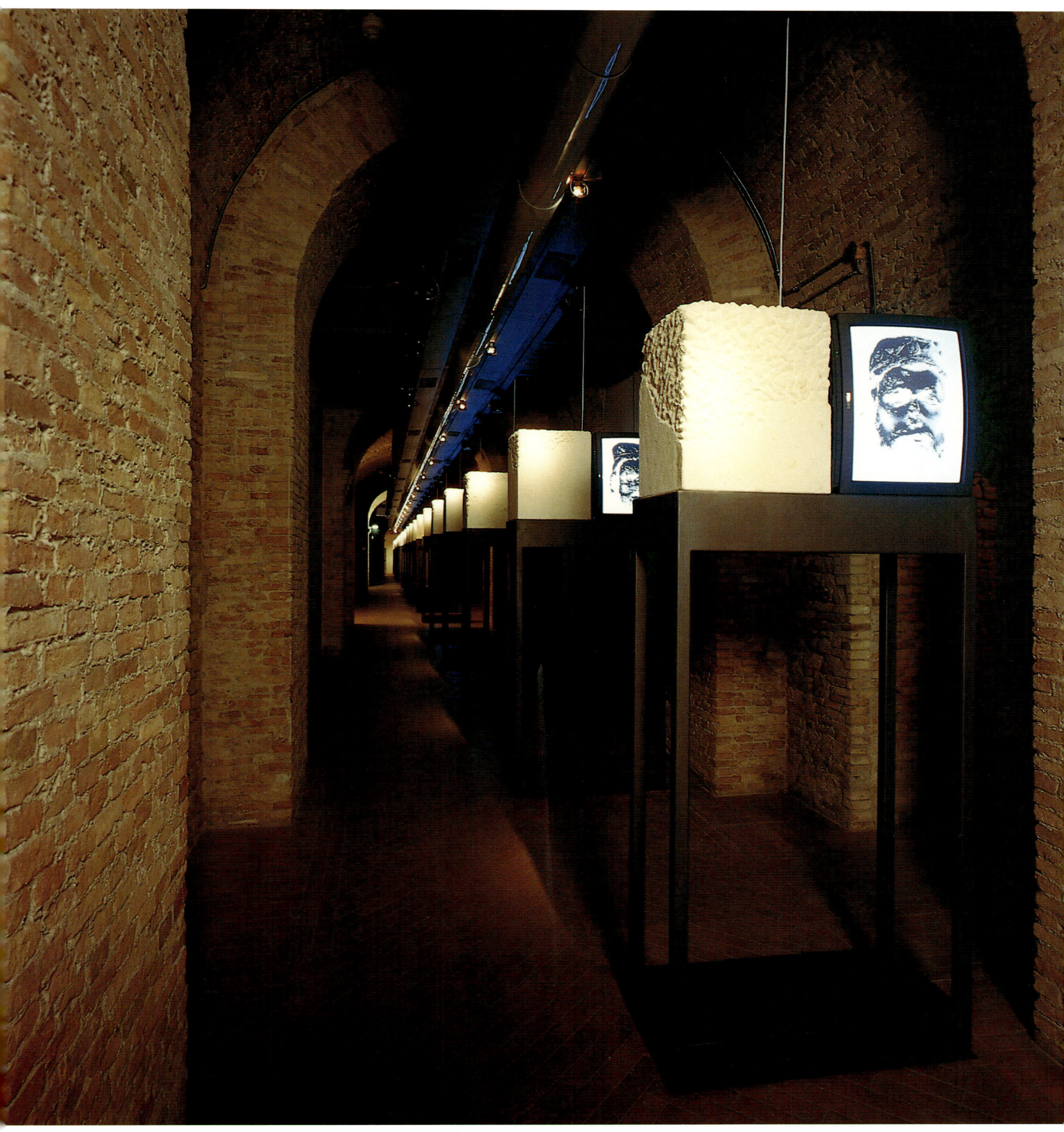

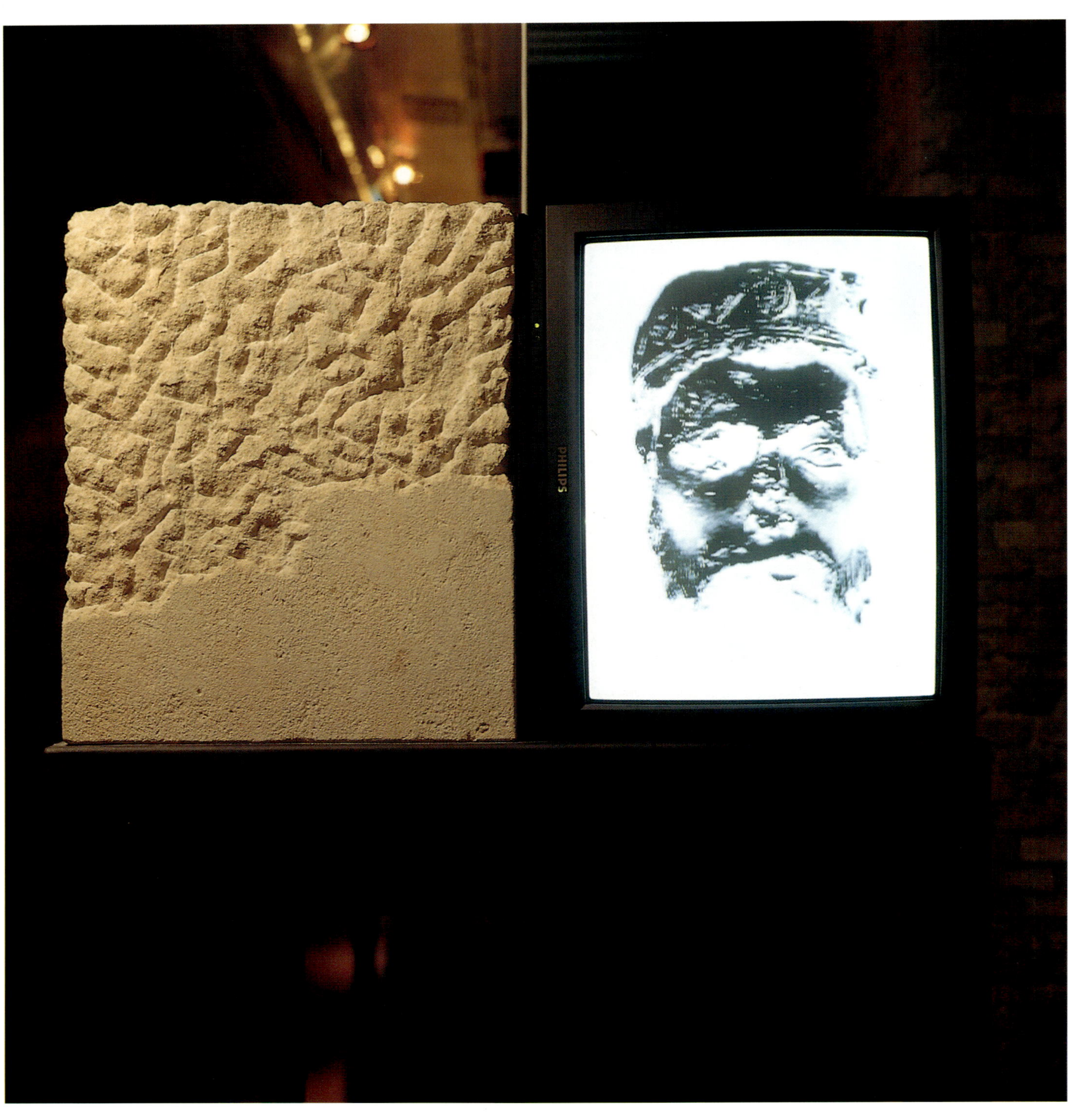

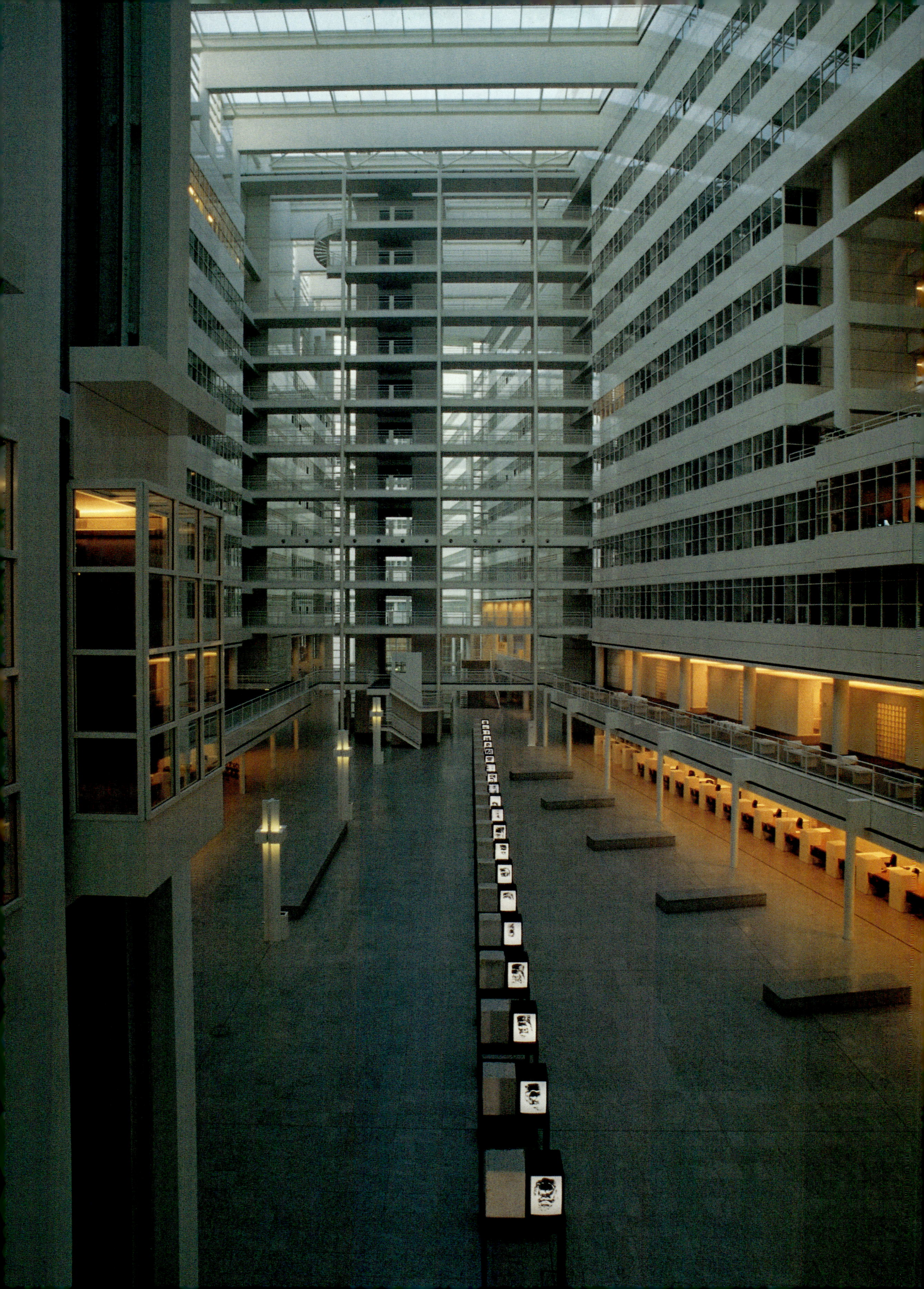

beinahe archäologischen Recherche und Analyse über das Wesen und die Seele des Steins, *L'Anima della Pietra.*

Auf zwei Meter hohen Metallsockeln ohne Seitenwände befinden sich - 21x vervielfacht - jeweils ein vertikal gestellter Monitor und daneben in gleicher Größe ein Stein, der Arbeitsspuren von Bildhauerei zeigt. Der Stein ist in gleicher Größe wie der Monitor - gewissermaßen als Gegenstück - konzipiert. In dem Monitor erscheint geisterhaft mysteriös der Königskopf, als hätte man eine Röntgenaufnahme von ihm gemacht, wie das Foto eines Negatives von dem Stein oder eine Aufnahme mit dem Metalldetektor. Eine unheimliche Kraft geht aus dem virtuellen Königskopf hervor.

Fabrizio Plessi versucht mit dieser Installation und Präsentation der Wesenhaftigkeit eines Steines auf den Grund zu kommen. Um eine Gleichwertigkeit zwischen der imaginären Steinskulptur und der virtuellen Steinskulptur im Monitor herzustellen, ist ein Lichtstrahler auf den Stein gerichtet, so daß er die gleiche Helligkeit wie der Monitor neben ihm erhält und ebenso leuchtet. *L'Anima della Pietra* ist der Titel dieser Arbeit, *Die Seele des Steins.* Schon Michelangelo Buonarroti hatte gesagt, daß die Skulptur, die der Bildhauer herstellt, im Stein bereits enthalten sei und es nur noch die Aufgabe des Bildhauers ist, diese Skulptur aus dem Stein herauszuschlagen, sie gewissermaßen aus der Materie zu befreien. So ist diese Videoinstallationen von Fabrizio Plessi auch zu verstehen, als Aufforderung zur Rücksichtnahme der Seele gegenüber, die nicht nur in jedem Menschen, sondern auch in jeder Materie und in jedem Sein enthalten ist.

On metal pedestals of two metre height, and without side walls - copied 21 times - one vertically positioned monitor each can be seen, beside it one done in stone that shows traces of a sculptor's work. The stone is, in equal size as the monitor, conceived as sort of counterpiece to the monitor. On the monitor, the head of the King appears, ghost-like, mysterious, as if an x-ray had been taken of it, like a photo of a negative of the stone, or a recording with a metal detector. A sinister force emanates from the head.

In this installation and presentation, Fabrizio Plessi tries to fathom the essence of stone. To create equality between the imaginary stone sculpture and the virtual one on the monitor, a light beam is pointed at the stone, giving it the same brightness as the monitor beside it, shining like this. L'Anima della Pietra *is the title of this work,* The Soul of Stone. *Michelangelo Buonarroti had already stated that the sculpture the sculptor creates is already contained in the stone, and it is the task of the sculptor to cut this sculpture from the stone, to free it from the matter. This is how Fabrizio Plessi's video installation are to be understood, too: as invitation to consideration of the soul that is not only inherent in every human, but in every matter and being.*

Sovra basi metalliche lateralmente aperte e alte due metri sono collocati, moltiplicati per ventuno volte, rispettivamente un monitor verticale con accanto una blocco di pietra che evidenzia tracce di lavoro di uno scultore. La pietra ha le stesse dimensioni - quasi come un pendant - del monitor nel quale appare misteriosamente la testa spettrale del re, come se fosse una sua radiografia, una foto della pietra al negativo o un'immagine di un metaldetector. La virtuale testa regale emana una forza inquietante.

Con questa installazione e presentazione Fabrizio Plessi cerca di indagare la specificità di una pietra. Per assicurare equivalenza fra la scultura di pietra immaginaria e quella virtuale del monitor un faro illumina il blocco di pietra in modo tale che acquisti la stessa luminosità del monitor. Il titolo dell'opera è *L'Anima della Pietra.* Già Michelangelo Buonarroti affermò che l'opera dello scultore è a priori contenuta nella pietra e che è compito dell'artista ricavare tale scultura dalla pietra, liberarla praticamente dalla materia. Questa videoinstallazione è da intendere così, come un invito al rispetto verso l'anima, che non è propria solo di ogni singolo uomo, ma anche di ogni singola materia e di ogni singola pietra.

BOMBAY-BOMBAY III

95011

BOLOGNA 1995
Museo La Salara
95011.1

BOMBAY-BOMBAY III
Videoinstallation 1995
Viereckig angeordnete Struktur
von liegenden Eisenschränken,
aufgehäufte weiße, indische
Baumwolle, 32 Monitore,
Videorecorder, bespielte
Kassetten, Tonaufzeichnung

BOMBAY-BOMBAY III
Video installation 1995
Iron structures in rectangular
arrangement, clues of white Indian
cotton, 32 monitors, video
recorders, recorded video cassettes,
soundrecording

BOMBAY-BOMBAY III
Videoinstallazione 1995
Struttura in ferro adagiata a terra,
in forma rettangolare, cumuli di
cotone bianco bagnato,
32 monitors, vhs, cassette
registrate, sonoro

Die Präsentation der dritten Version von *Bombay-Bombay* im Museo la Salara in Bologna steht wieder in Beziehung zu den räumlichen Gegebenheiten. Dieses Mal ist die Präsentation der liegenden Schränke mit der nassen Baumwolle und dem fließenden Wasser nicht linear oder parallel wie bei den ersten beiden Versionen, sondern um die vier Säulen des Raumes herum im Viereck organisiert, so daß in der Mitte ein quadratischer Platz frei bleibt. Die magische Höhe der Räume erzeugt eine beinahe sakrale Stimmung, und man sieht wieder einmal mehr, wie sehr die räumliche Präsentation Einfluß auf Wirkung und Ausstrahlung der Videoinstallationen Fabrizio Plessis nimmt. Wären auch die vier Eckpunkte der Installation miteinander verbunden, so könnte man sich vorstellen, das ganze Wasser fließt im (viereckigen) Kreis. Doch so ist die Konstruktion an den jeweiligen vier Eckpunkten unterbrochen, und die Präsentation gliedert sich in vier einzelne Abteilungen; in der Anordnung vergleichbar mit Bänken in der Kirche, die alle in Richtung des Altarraumes gedreht sind.

The presentation of the third version of Bombay-Bombay *in the Museo la Salara in Bologna again relates to the conditions of space. This time the presentation of the lying cabinets with the wet cotton and the flowing water is not linear or parallel as in the first two versions, but arranged in a rectangle around the four pillars of the room, leaving a square place in the centre open. The magic height of the rooms creates an almost sacral mood, and once again it can be seen how the spatial presentation influences result and impression of Plessi's video installations. If the four corners of the installation were connected to each other one could imagine the water flowing in a "rectangular" circle. Yet here the construction is interrupted at the four corner points respectively, and the presentation is divided into four separate sections, in their positions comparable to benches in a church that are all turned towards the altar.*

Anche la terza versione di Bombay-Bombay del Museo la Salara a Bologna si riferisce direttamente alle circostanze ambientali del luogo. Questa volta gli armadi con il cotone bagnato e con l'acqua che scorre non sono più organizzati in una struttura lineare o di parallele come nelle prime due versioni, ma in forma quadrata intorno alle quattro colonne dello sala espositiva. L'altezza magica dello spazio irradia un'atmosfera quasi sacrale e ancora una volta si comprende quanto la presentazione spaziale dell'opera modifichi l'effetto delle videoinstallazioni di Fabrizio Plessi. Se i quattro punti angolari dell'installazione fossero collegati fra di loro si potrebbe immaginare che l'acqua scorre in un cerchio (quadrato). Ma la composizione è interrotta ai rispettivi angoli e presenta quattro singole sezioni nella loro disposizione paragonabili ai banchi di una chiesa tutti rivolti in direzione dell'altare.

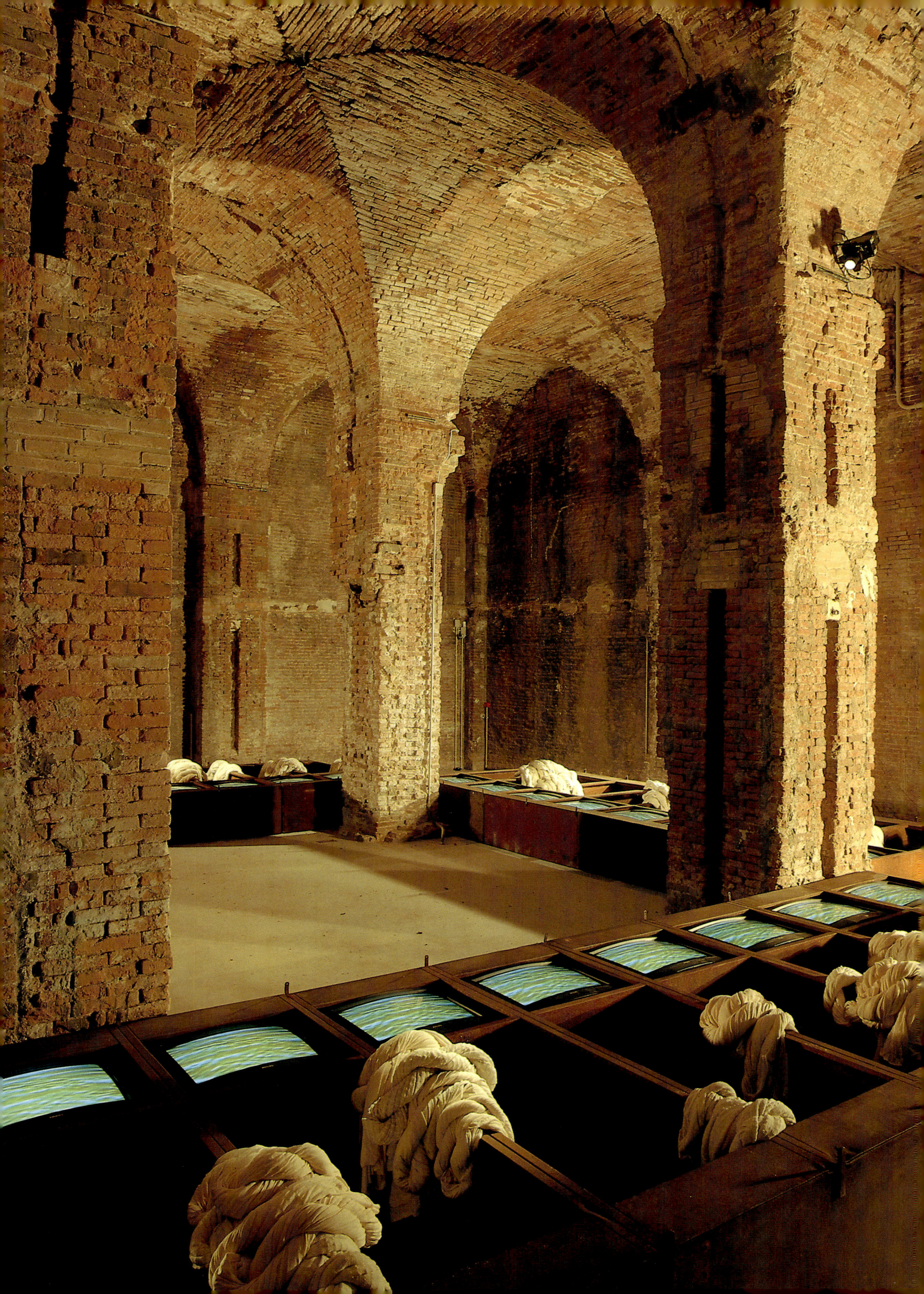

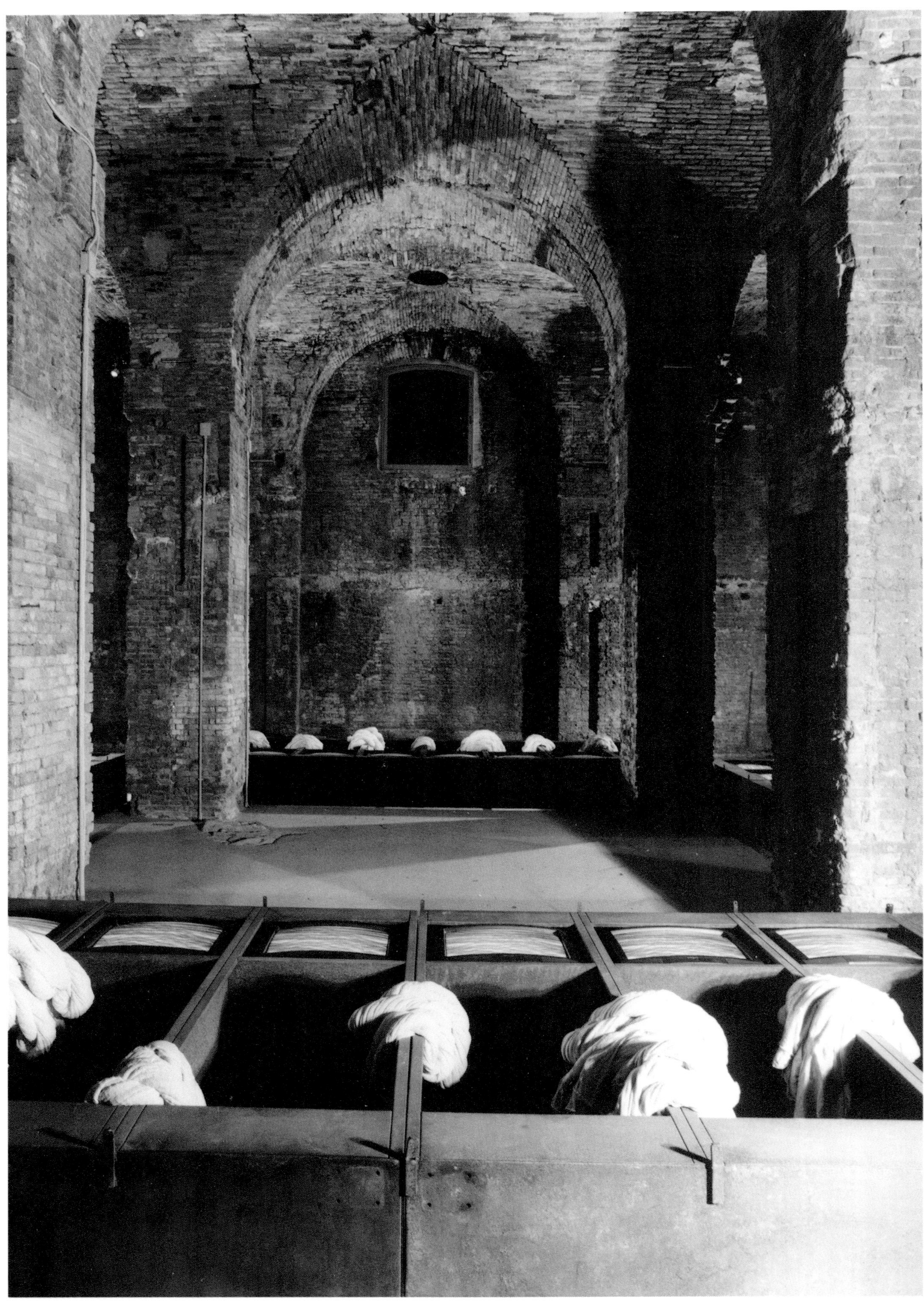

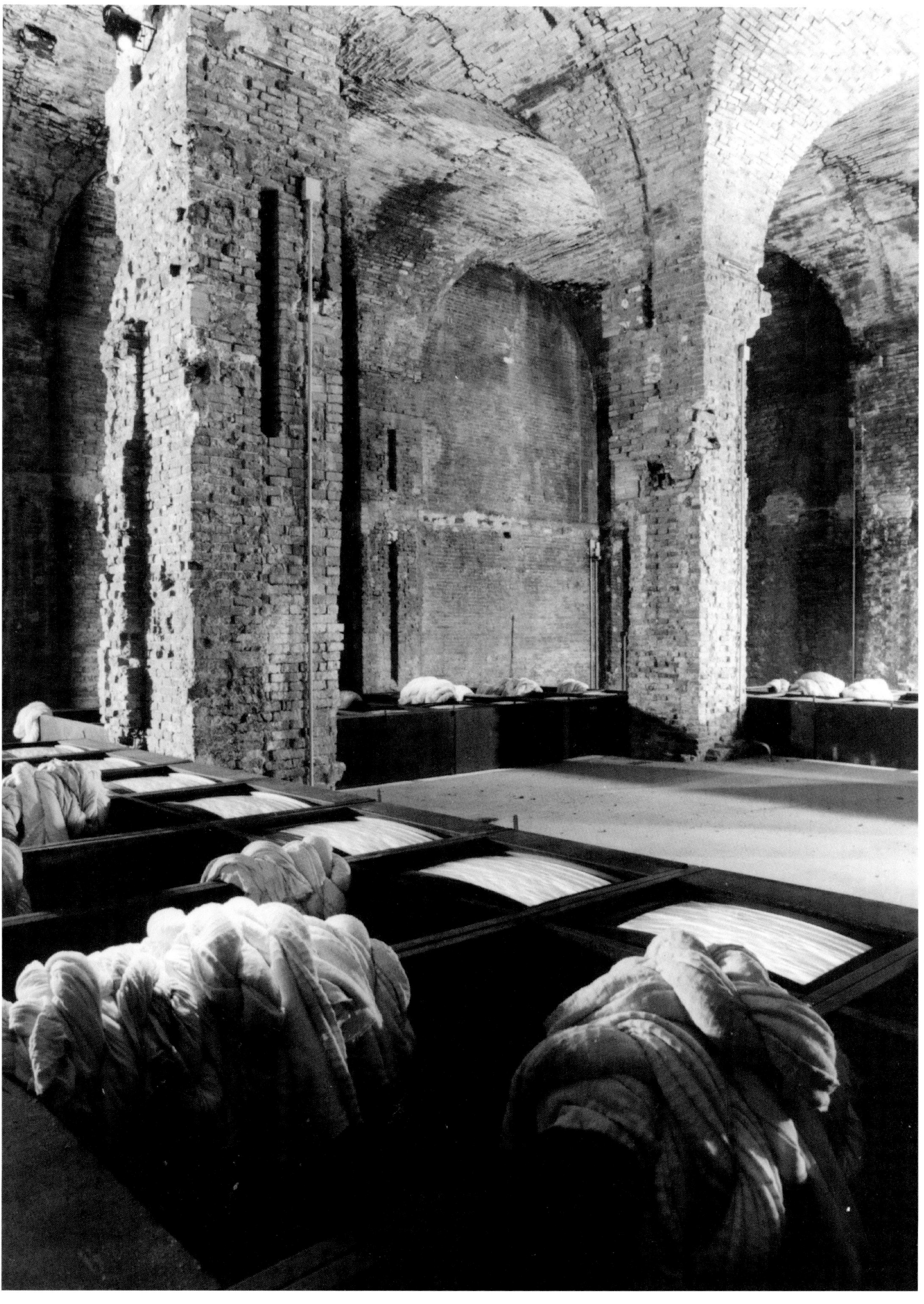

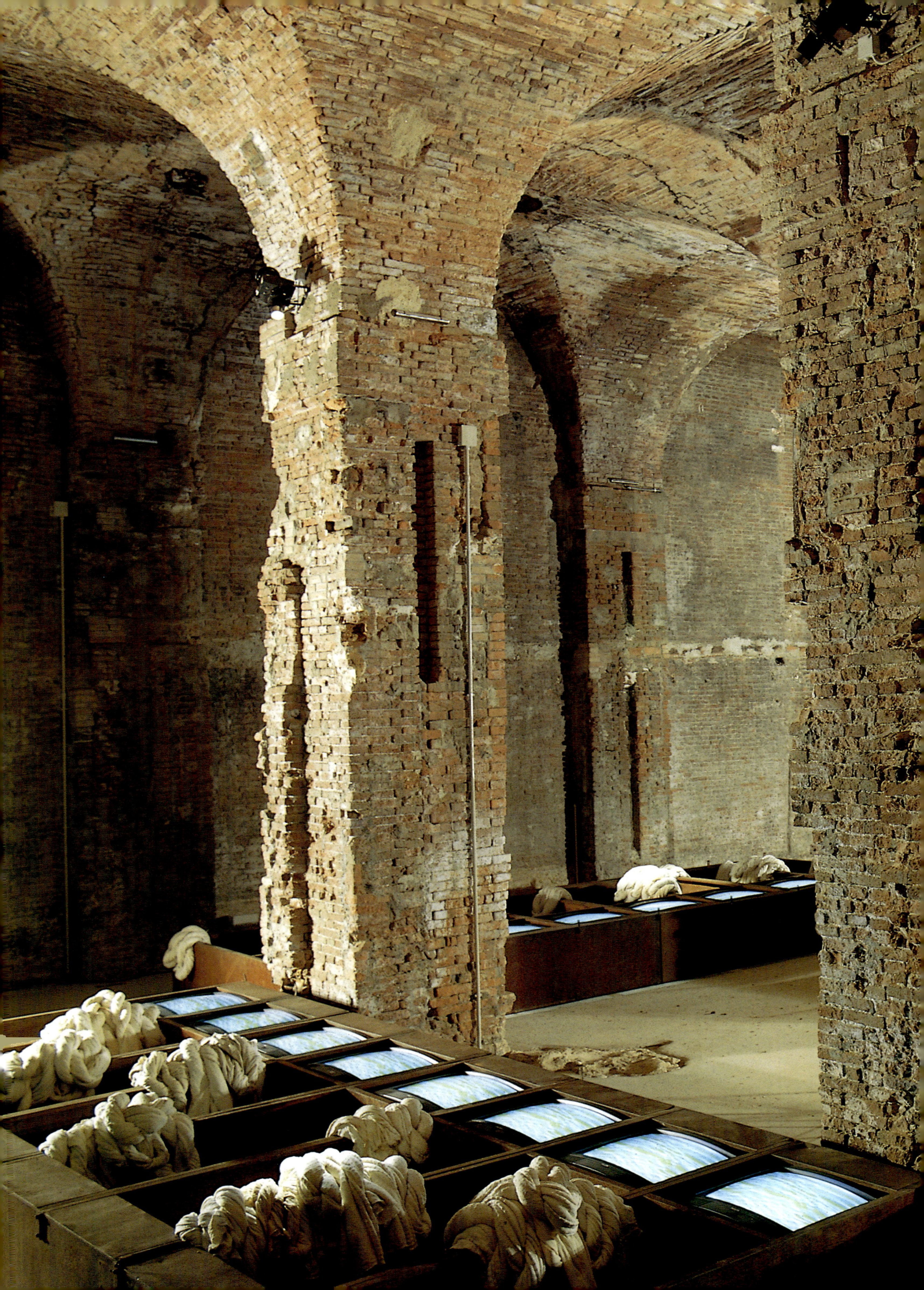

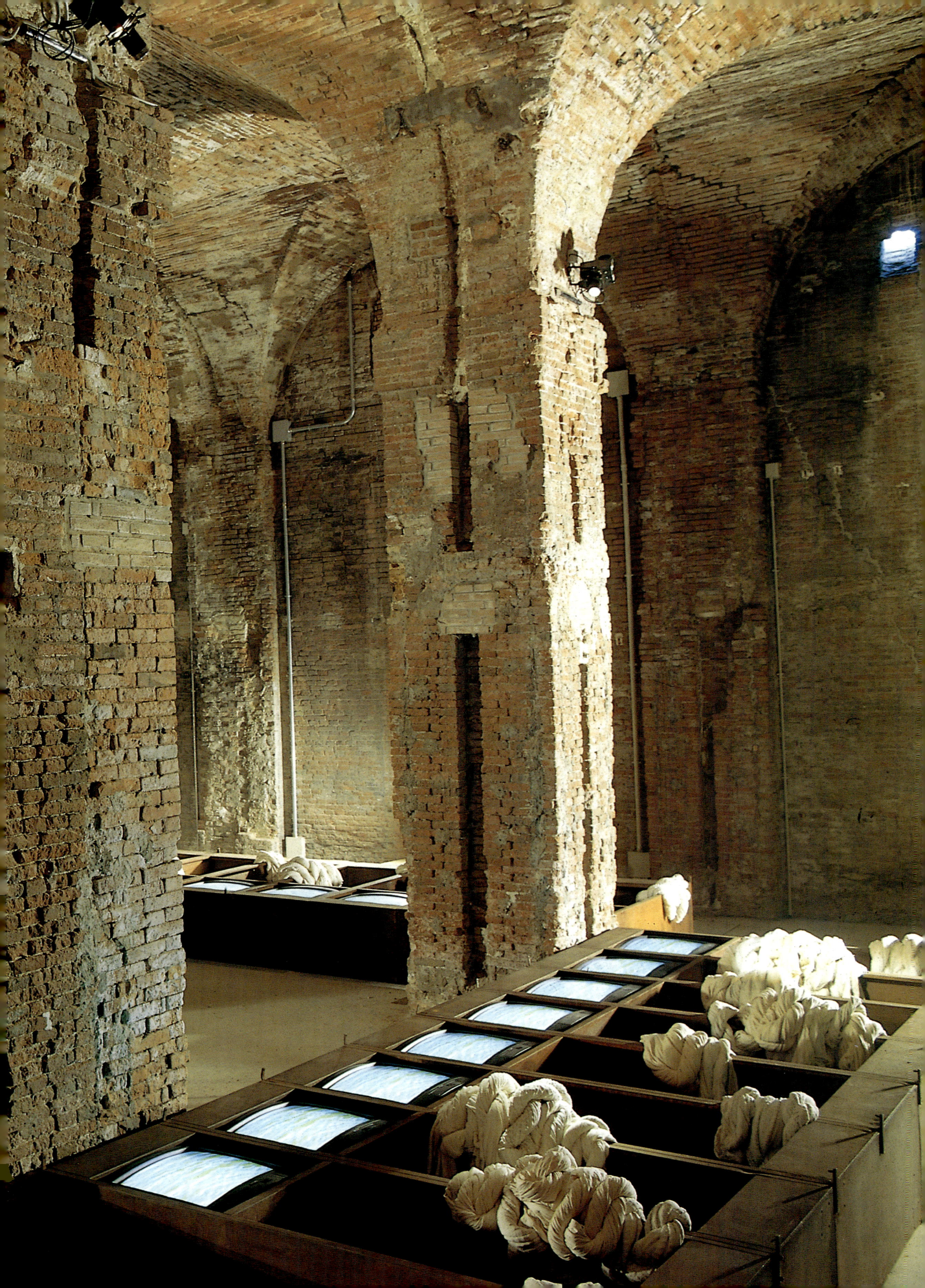

LE DUE ANIME DELLA MATERIA

95012

PARIS 1995
GALERIE PIECE UNIQUE
95012.1

DIE ZWEI SEELEN DER MATERIE
Videoskulptur 1995
Hängevorrichtung,
Drehmechanismus, Baumstamm,
2 Monitore, 2 Videorecorder,
bespielte Kassetten

THE TWO SOULS OF MATTER
Video sculpture 1995
Swing, rotating suspension, trunk,
2 monitors, 2 video recorder,
recorded video cassettes

LE DUE ANIME DELLA MATERIA
Videoscultura 1995
Congegno di sospensione,
macchina rotante, tronco di legno,
2 monitors, 2 vhs, cassette
registrate

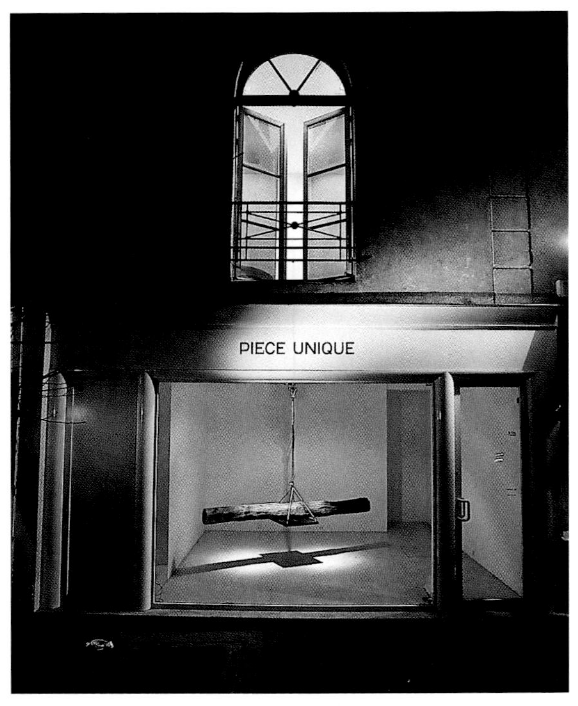

Fabrizio Plessi befaßt sich in zunehmendem Maße mit dem Wesen oder der Seele von Materie, dies macht auch folgende Arbeit deutlich. Die von der Grundkonzeption her auf der Videoskulptur *Fuoco Fatuo* im Atelier basiert. Zu sehen ist ein quer über einer Schaukel liegender Baumstamm, der an jeder seiner beiden Stirnseiten eine Öffnung aufweist. Hinter diesen Öffnungen verbergen sich Monitore, die auf *Die zwei Seelen der Materie* hinweisen. In dem einen Monitor sieht man sprudelndes, leuchtendes, helles, blaues Wasser; dieses Ende des Baumstammes ist feucht und dadurch in

More and more, Fabrizio Plessi looks at the essence or soul of matter; the following work indicates this, too, the concept of which is based on the video sculpture Fuoco Fatuo *in his studio. It shows a tree trunk, lying across a swing, with an opening on both front sides. Behind these openings monitors are hidden, pointing to* The Two Souls of the Matter. *On the one monitor, sparkling, shining, bright blue water is seen; this end of the trunk is wet, therefore of darker colour. The other side of the trunk is slightly burnt, the monitor in it*

Fabrizio Plessi si occupa sempre di più della natura o dell'anima della materia come si evince anche dal presente lavoro che dal punto di vista concettuale si basa sulla videoscultura *Fuoco Fatuo* dell'atelier Miró. Un tronco d'albero giace traversalmente su un'altalena e presenta alle sue estremità un'apertura dietro alla quale si nascondono i monitors che rimandano alle *Due Anime della Materia*. In uno di loro si vede acqua chiara, di colore blu, zampillante e luminosa; l'estremità del tronco è umida e di conseguenza di colore piú

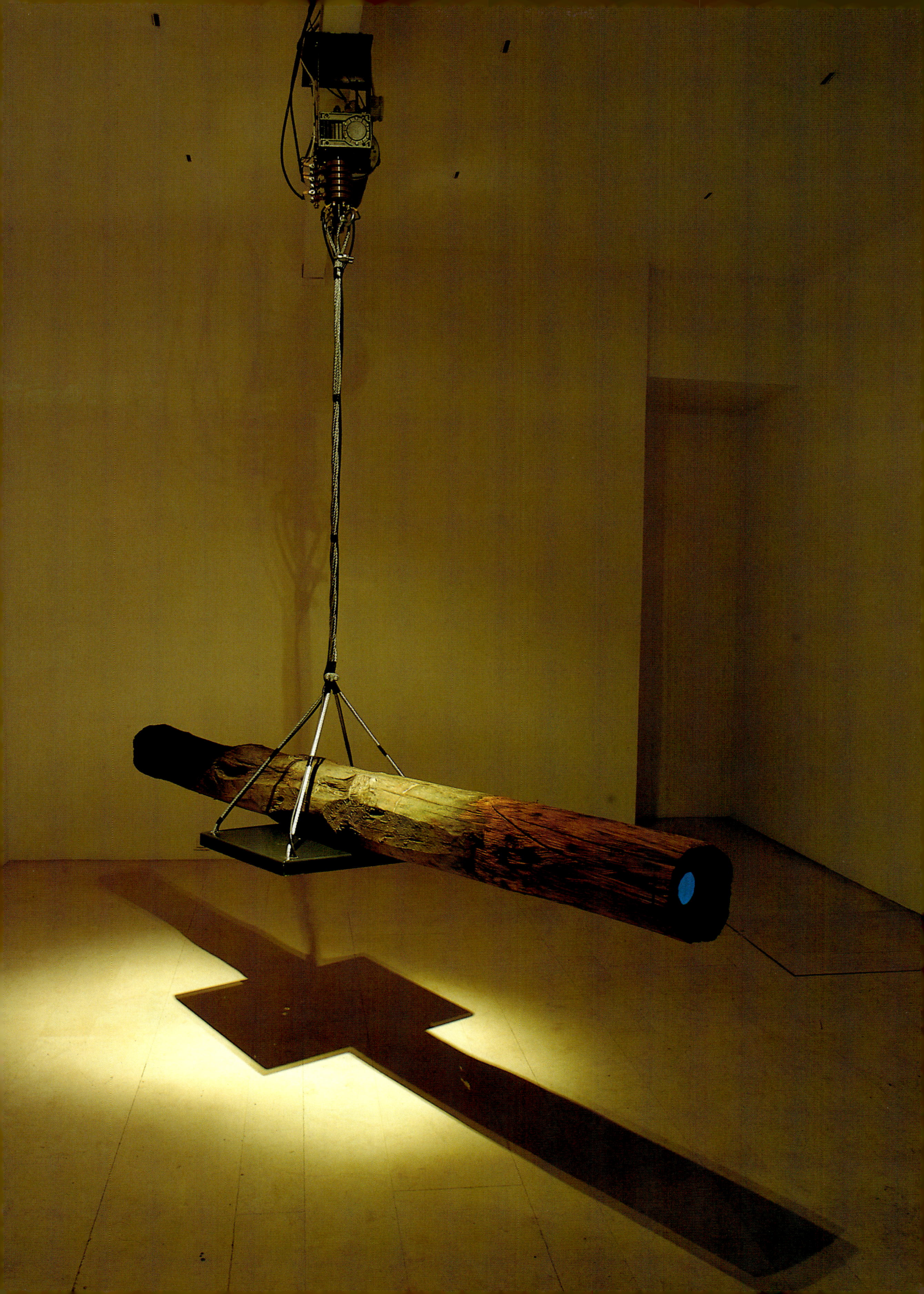

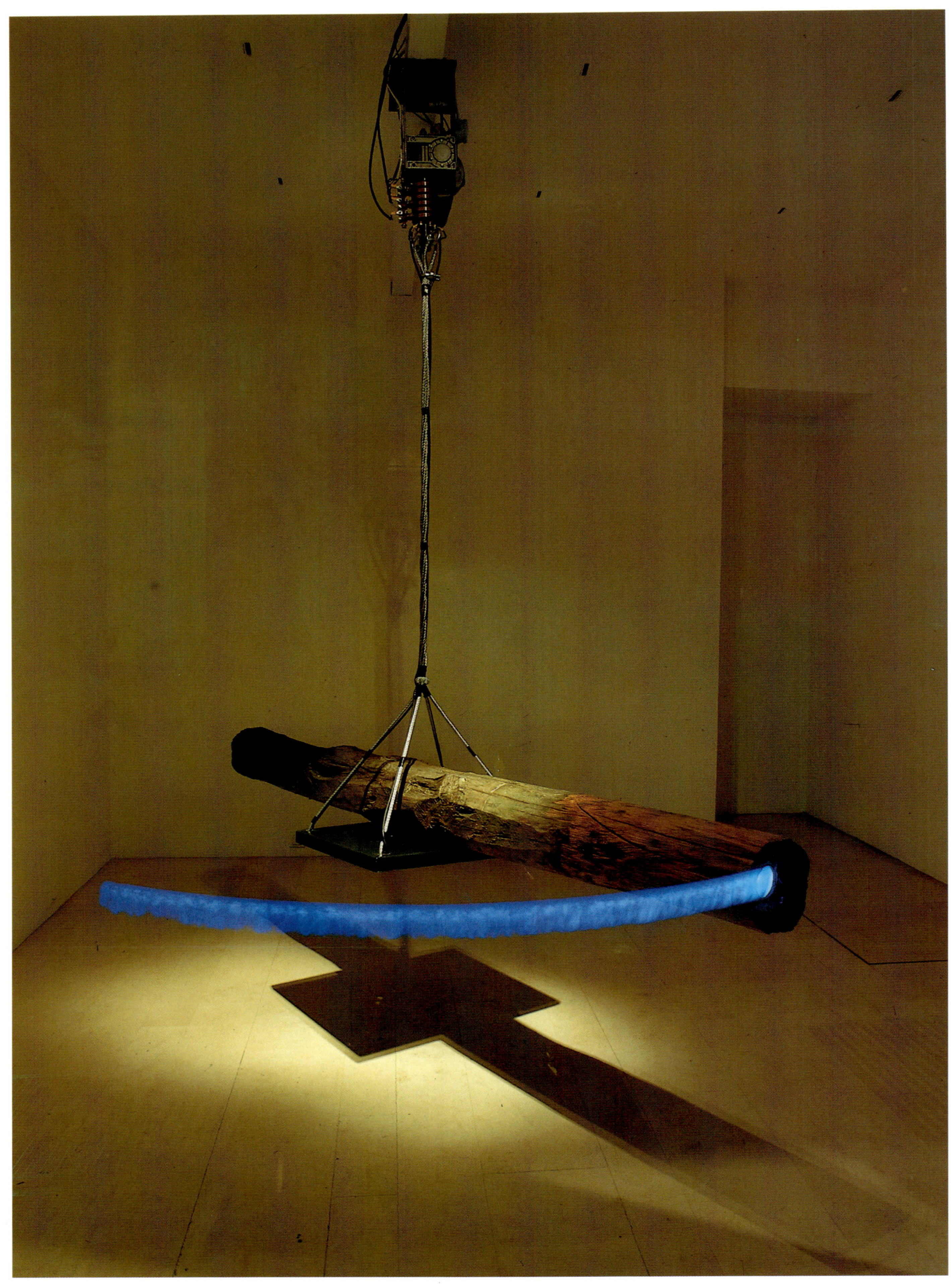

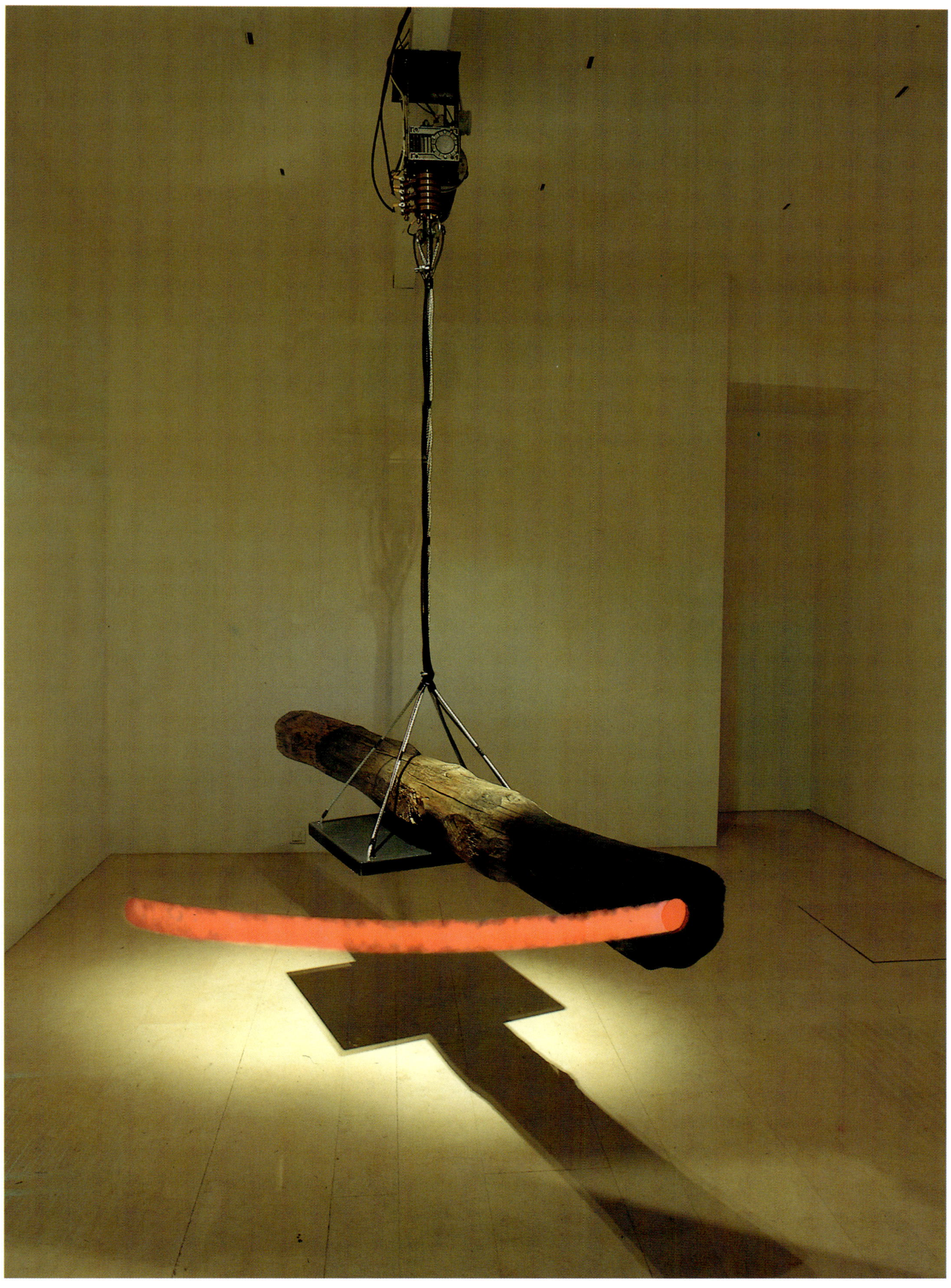

der Färbung dunkler. Das andere Ende des Baumstammes ist leicht verbrannt; der Monitor darin zeigt loderndes Feuer. Wasser und Feuer, das dialektische Gegensatzpaar, wird hier in einem Kunstwerk vereint, weist hin auf die zwei Seelen, die in der Brust des Künstlers wohnen. Seine Liebe zu Wasser, seine Lust am Feuer und die Faszination am Wechsel der beiden, die ja laut Heraklit erst die Welt erzeugen. Um die Dynamik der Präsentation noch zu unterstreichen, ist die Schaukel an einer Hängevorrichtung angebracht, die sich langsam aber unaufhörlich im Kreise dreht, so daß für den Betrachter abwechselnd die eine, wasserblaue, und die andere, feuerrote Seele der Materie (Baumstamm) sichtbar wird.

showing blazing fire. Water and fire, the dialectic contrasts, are here united in a piece of art, point to the two souls in the artist's heart: His love of water, his pleasure in fire, and the fascination in exchanging both that, according to Herakleitos, create the world. To increase the dynamics of the presentation, the swing is mounted on a structure that slowly but permanently circles, in turns offering the observer a view of the one, water-blue, and the other, burning-red soul of matter (of the tree trunk).

scuro. L'altra estremità è leggermente bruciata e il monitor mostra al suo interno fuoco fiammeggiante. Acqua e fuoco, gli opposti dialettici, sono uniti in un'opera d'arte e alludono alle due anime che stanno a cuore all'artista: il suo amore per l'acqua, la sua passione per il fuoco e il fascino del loro scambio reciproco, che secondo Eraclito sono all'origine del mondo. Per sottolineare ancor più la dinamica della presentazione l'altalena é fissata ad una struttura che rotea lentamente senza mai interrompersi, in modo tale che allo spettatore traspare alternativamente l'una, blu acqua, e l'altra, rosso fuoco, anima della materia (tronco d'albero).

MYSTERIUM WEIN

96001

SPEYER 1996
HISTORISCHES MUSEUM DER PFALZ
96001.1

MYSTERIUM WEIN
Videoskulptur 1996
Stahlkonstruktion, Stahlbecken,
1000 Liter Rotwein, 40 Monitore,
Videorecorder, bespielte
Kassetten, Tonaufzeichnung
480 x 480 x 480 cm

WINE MYSTERY
Video sculpture 1996
Steel construction, steel basin,
1000 litres of red wine, 40 moni-
tors, video recorders, recorded
video cassettes, soundrecording
480 x 480 x 480 cm

MISTERIO VINO
Videoscultura 1996
Struttura di ferro, vasca in ferro,
1000 litri di vino rosso,
40 monitors, vhs, cassette
registrate
480 x 480 x 480 cm

Neben der zunehmend historischen Determination seiner Videoskulpturen macht sich zugleich eine immer häufiger erscheinende religiöse Tendenz bemerkbar. In der Videoskulptur *Mysterium Wein*, die zur gleichnamigen Ausstellung in Speyer konzipiert und realisiert wurde, ist innerhalb einer Stahlkonstruktion eine nach vorne geneigte Kreuzform ausgeprägt, die mit 40 Monitoren gefüllt ist. Nicht allein Wasser, sondern auch Wein, gelegentlich sogar Rotwein, kann in den Monitoren als virtuelles elektronisches Gebilde fließen, das ist spätestens seit der Kremser Videoskulptur im Werk Fabrizio Plessis bekannt. Daß aber virtueller Wein realem Wein gegenübergestellt wird und sich

Beside the increasingly historic determination of his video sculptures a growing tendency to religious subjects becomes evident. In the video sculpture Mystery Wine, *conceived and realised for the exhibition of the same name in Speyer, the form of a cross, leaning forward, is executed within a steel construction, filled with 40 monitors. Not only water, but wine, sometimes even red wine, can flow on the monitors as virtual electronic form, as known in his work from the video sculpture in Krems. That virtual wine is, however, confronted real wine, in addition even mirrors in it, as is the case in the installation in Speyer, in which a square basin filled with red wine is placed in front of the*

Oltre la crescente determinazione storica delle videosculture si percepisce al tempo stesso sempre di più una tendenza religiosa. Nella videoscultura *Mysterium Wein* concepita e realizzata per l'omonima mostra a Spira, si sviluppa all'interno di una costruzione di ferro una forma a croce riempita di quaranta monitors. Che nei monitors delle opere di Plessi possa scorrere in forma di massa elettronica virtuale non solo acqua, ma anche vino, a volte persino vino rosso, lo si è già visto nella videoscultura di Krems. Ma contrapporre vino virtuale e farlo riflettere in vino reale come nell'installazione di Spira, dove una vasca quadrata riempita di vino rosso è antepo-

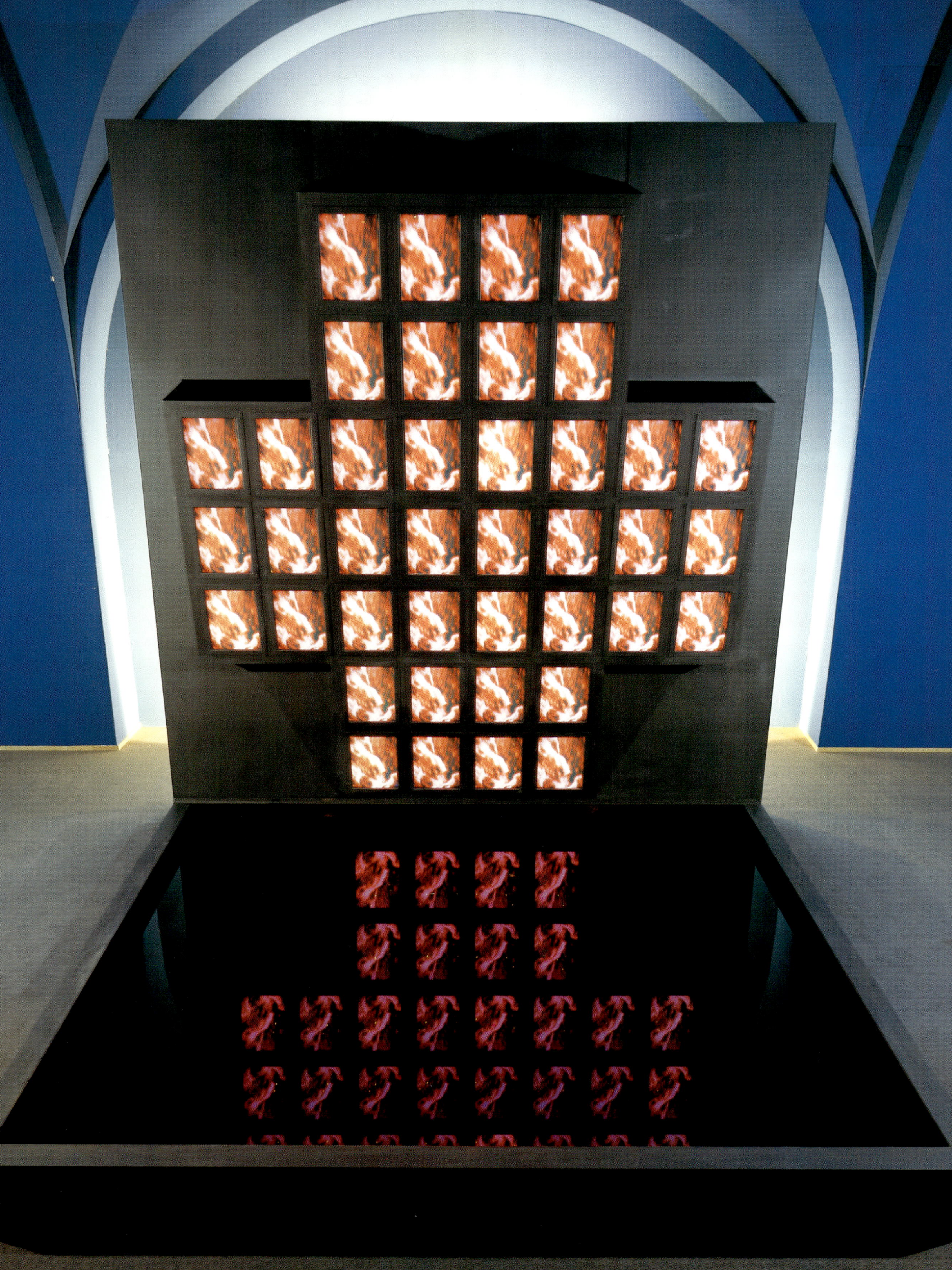

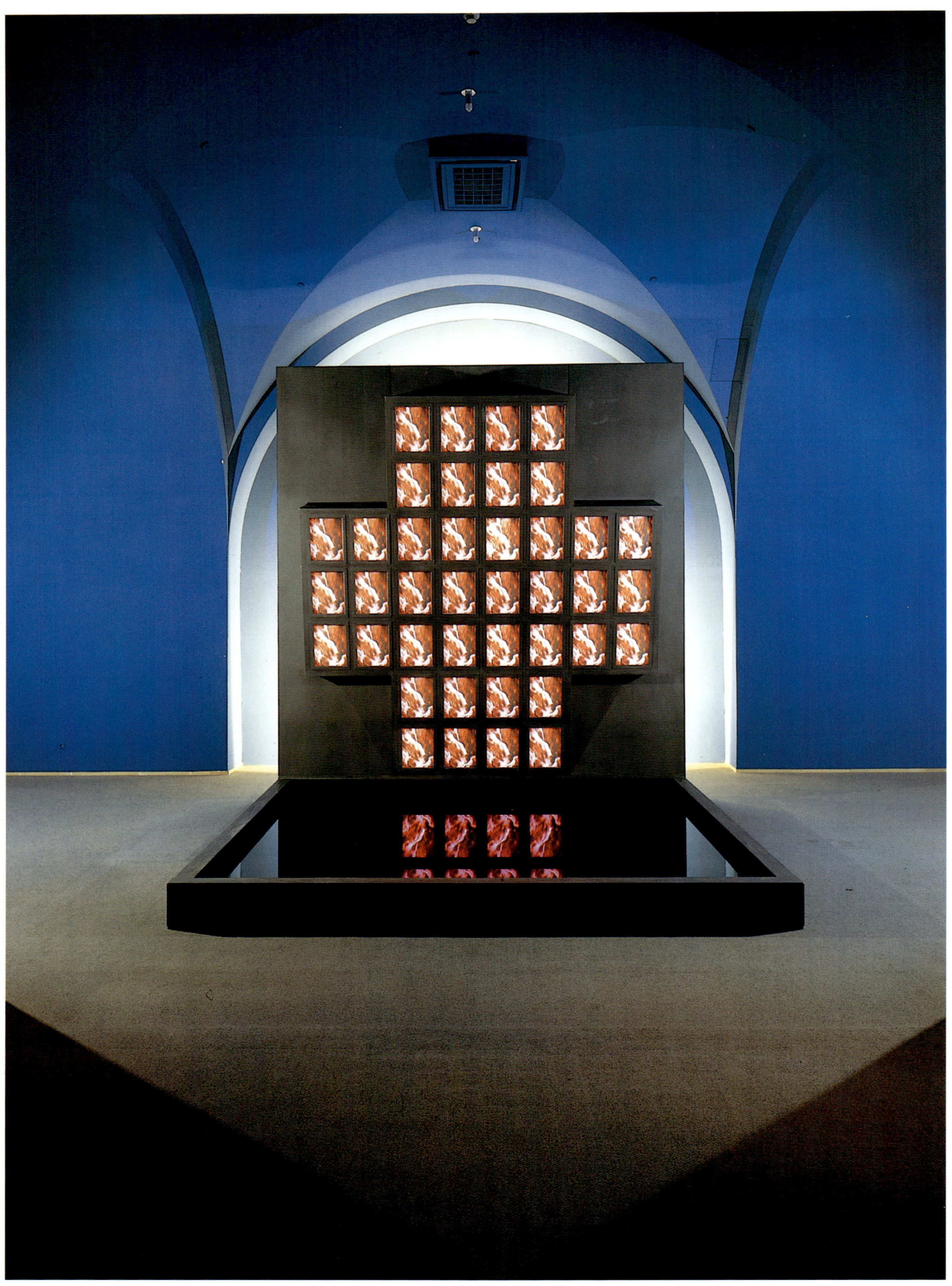

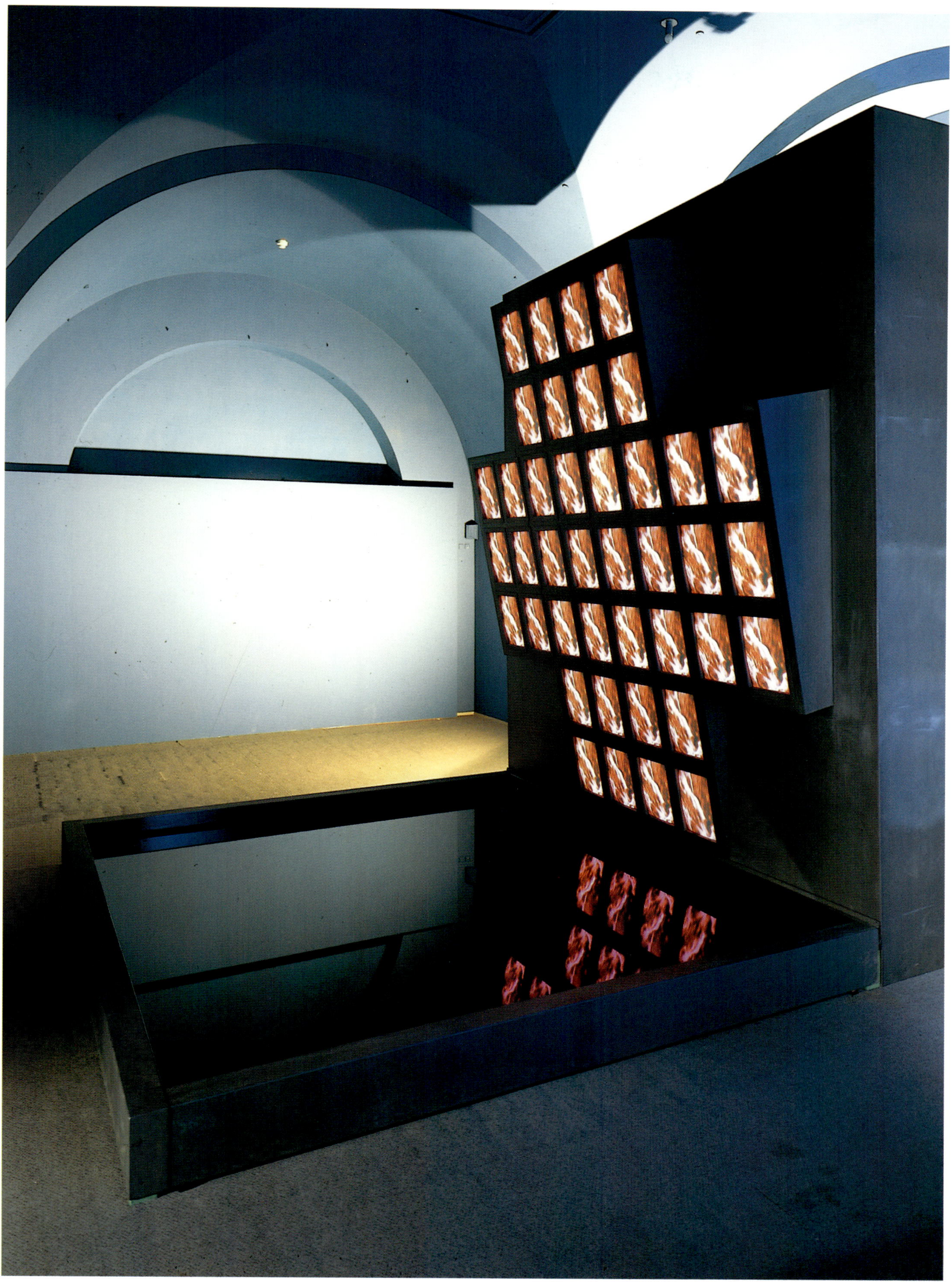

in diesem zudem spiegelt, wie in der Speyrer Installation, in der ein quadratisches Becken, gefüllt mit Rotwein, vor dem schwebenden bzw. hängenden Videokreuz angebracht wurde, bringt das ganze Gefüge in ein verwirrendes und beinahe tautologisches Verhältnis zueinander und erinnert doch zugleich an den *Narziß*, der fasziniert von seinem eigenen Spiegelbild sich diesem entgegen neigt.

Aus der Sicht des Ausstellungskurators beschreibt Meinrad Maria Grewenig den Beitrag Plessis zu seiner Ausstellung *Mysterium Wein* folgendermaßen: »Mächtig steht die monumentale Wand mit den kreuzförmig angeordneten Monitoren dem Betrachter gegenüber. Der permanent unter großen Getöse herabrauschende Weinfall spiegelt sich in dem quadratischen Bassin mit über 1.000 Litern Rotwein. Das Rauschen, der übermächtige bewegte Eindruck der Monitorbilder und der intensive Weingeruch verbinden sich zu einem umfassenden sinnlichen Erlebnis. Die Form des quadratischen Kreuzes erinnert an mittelalterliche Vorbilder. Der rote Wein assoziiert das Blut Christi und wird zum Hinweis auf die Transsubstantiation. Das beeindruckende Erlebnis der virtuellen Medienwelt spiegelt sich im realen Wein und scheint in ihm zu versinken. Die Videoinstallation ist im umfassenden Sinn Ausdruck des Mysteriums Wein. Sinnlich, ein umfassendes Erlebnis, verknüpfen sich die Eindrücke und Hinweise mit Assoziationen der abendländischen Geschichte.« (Meinrad Maria Grewenig in: Katalog *Mysterium Wein*, Historisches Museum der Pfalz, Speyer 1996, S. 308)

suspended, or rather hanging, video cross puts the whole structure into a confusing, almost tautological relationship to one another, and, at the same time, reminds of Narcissus who, fascinated by his own reflection, leans towards it.

From the point of view of the exhibition curator, Meinrad Maria Grewenig describes Plessi's contribution to his exhibition as follows: "The monumental wall with its monitors in the shape of a cross stands mighty before the observer. The winefall, permanently and loudly rushing down, is mirrored in the square basin filed with more than 1000 litres of red wine. The rushing sound, the overwhelming impression of moving images on the monitors and the intense smell of wine combine to an encompassing sensual experience. The shape of the square cross reminds of medieval models. The red wine associates Christ's blood, and indicates transubstantiation. The impressive experience of a virtual medial world is reflected in the real wine, and seems to drown in it. The video installation is, in an encompassing sense, expression of the mystery wine. An encompassing sensual experience, the impressions and suggestions combine with associations to occidental history." (Meinrad Maria Grewenig in: catalogue Mysterium Wein (Mystery Wine), *Historisches Museum der Pfalz, Speyer 1996, p. 308)*

sta ad una croce sospesa o appesa, crea un rapporto sconcertante, quasi tautologico ricordando allo stesso tempo Narciso che si china verso la sua immagine riflessa di cui rimane affascinato.

Dal suo punto di vista di curatore della mostra Meinrad Maria Grewenig descrive il contributo di Plessi alla mostra *Mysterium Wein* come segue: »Lo spettatore sta di fronte alla imponente parete con i monitors disposti a croce. Mormorando ininterrottamente e con gran frastuono, la cascata di vino si riflette nei mille litri di vino rosso del bacino quadrato. Il mormorio, la potentissima e mossa impressione delle immagini dei monitors e l'intenso odore del vino si uniscono in un'avvolgente esperienza sensuale. La forma della croce quadrata rievoca modelli medievali, il vino rosso richiama il sangue di Cristo e allude così alla transustanziazione. L'esperienza sconvolgente del virtuale mondo mediale si riflette nel vino reale e sembra sprofondarvi. La videoinstallazione è in tutti i sensi l'espressione del mistero vino. Sensualmente, esperienza avvolgente, le impressioni e le allusioni si collegano con le associazioni della storia occidentale.« (Meinrad Maria Grewenig in: catalogo *Mysterium Wein*, Historisches Museum der Pfalz, Spira 1996, p. 308)

IL FIUME DELLA STORIA

96002

MAINZ 1996
LANDESMUSEUM MAINZ
96002.1

FLUSS DER GESCHICHTE
Videoskulptur 1996
Stahlkonstruktion, antikes Portal,
22 Monitore, Videorecorder,
bespielte Kassetten,
Tonaufzeichnung

RIVER OF HISTORY
Video sculpture 1996
Steel construction, Roman portal,
22 monitors, video recorders,
recorded video cassettes,
soundrecording

IL FIUME DELLA STORIA
Videoscultura 1996
Struttura in ferro, portale romano,
22 monitors, vhs, cassette
registrate, sonoro

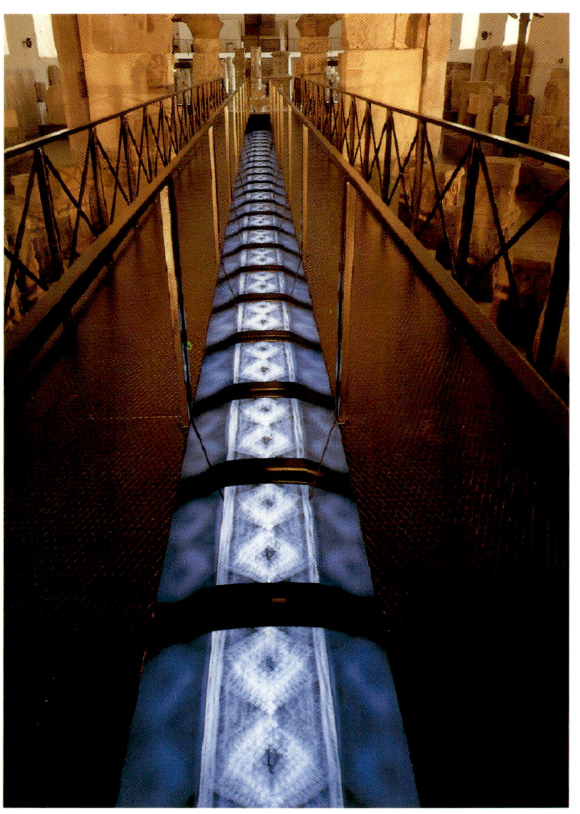

Il Fiume della Storia (Der Fluß der Geschichte) in der Steinhalle des Mainzer Landesmuseums zeigt ein mosaikartiges, elektronisches Gewässer, das durch einen römischen Portalbogen fließt. Ein begehbares Geländer rechts und links zu Seiten des elektronischen Mosaikflusses erlaubt dem Betrachter, den Fluß der Geschichte, auf seinem Weg durch das Portal zu begleiten oder ihm entgegen zu gehen. Ähnlich einem Kaleidoskop, verändert sich die mosaikartige Erscheinungsweise des

Il Fiume della Storia (The River of History) *in the Steinhalle of the Landesmuseum (provincial museum) in Mainz shows a mosaic-like electronic river flowing through a Roman portal. The spectator can, on a balustrade on both sides of the electronic mosaic river, accompany the river of history on its way through the portal - or walk towards it. Similar to a kaleidoscope, the mosaic-like appearance of the river changes, thus reminding directly of*

Il Fiume della Storia nella Steinhalle del Landesmuseum di Magonza presenta un'acqua elettronica a mo' di mosaico che scorre sotto un arco di un portale romano. Una struttura percorribile ai lati del fiume a mosaico elettronico permette allo spettatore di accompagnare o di venire incontro al flusso della storia lungo il suo percorso attraverso il portale. Simile ad un caleidoscopio l'aspetto a mosaico del fiume muta rimandando immediatamente al suo

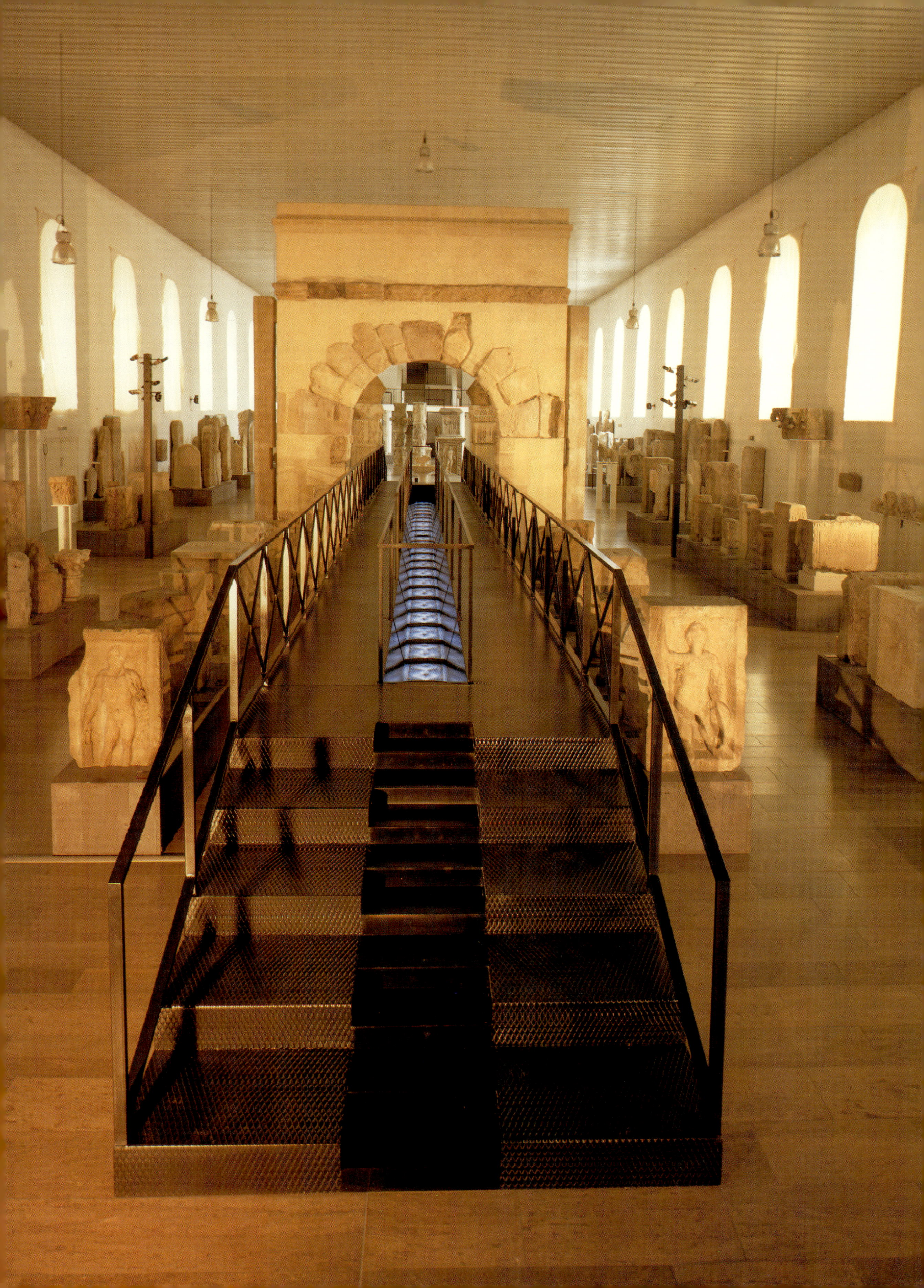

Flusses und erinnert so ganz unmittelbar an seinen Vorgänger und venezianisches Gegenstück, den *Canal d'Oro*, der nahezu 10 Jahre zuvor im Museum Correr in Venedig präsentiert worden war. Doch während das antikisierende Portal bei der Installation in Venedig nur eine nachgebaute mit Gold überzogene Holzkonstruktion war, handelt es sich hier in der Mainzer Steinhalle um ein reales Altertumsstück.

Hier ist Fabrizio Plessi wieder auf die örtliche Begebenheit, die Mainzer Steinhalle, und zugleich auf die römische Stadtgeschichte von Mainz, eingegangen. Die 2.000 Jahre alte römische Geschichte wird den Künstler auch weiterhin beschäftigen, wie die im selben Jahr nur wenig später entstandene die Installation eines *Elektronischen Aquäduktes* im Heidelberger Kunstverein zeigt. Auch in Mainz hat es seinerzeit ein solches Aquädukt, eine römische Wasserleitung gegeben, die ein Tal überbrückte, um in einem höhergelegenen Castell, einem Lager, die Wasserversorgung zu sichern.

its Venetian predecessor and counterpart, the Canal d'Oro *that, almost ten years before, had been shown in the Museum Correr in Venice. Yet while the portal imitating antiquity had only been a replica, a gold-plated wooden construction the one in Mainz is a real antique portal.*

Here, Fabrizio Plessi again takes the local conditions of the stone hall in Mainz into consideration, as well as, at the same time, the city's Roman history. The 2000 year old history of the city will continue to occupy the artist, as the installation of the same year, realised shortly after, of an Electronic Aqueduct *in the Kunstverein in Heidelberg shows. In Mainz, too, there used to be such an aqueduct, a Roman water-pipe, that bridged over a valley in order to supply a castello, a camp, with water.*

predecessore e pendant veneziano *Canal d'Oro* presentato circa dieci anni prima al Museo Correr di Venezia. Ma mentre il portale antichizzato dell'installazione di Venezia era semplicemente una ricostruzione di legno dorato, nella Steinhalle di Magonza ci troviamo di fronte ad un autentico elemento antico.

Di nuovo Fabrizio Plessi si interessa della specificità locale, cioè della Steinhalle di Magonza, e contemporaneamente della storia romana della città di Magonza. E la storia romana di 2000 anni sarà ancora al centro dell'attenzione dell'artista come dimostra l'installazione *Acquedotto Elettronico* del Kunstverein di Heidelberg realizzata poco più tardi nello stesso anno. Anche a Magonza esistette a suo tempo un acquedotto romano che attraversava una valle per assicurare l'approvviggionamento di acqua in un accampamento di un castello situato in alto.

FEZ-FEZ

96003

GRAZ 1996
KIRCHE ›MAUSOLEUM‹
96003.1

KAUFBEUREN 1997
KUNSTHAUS KAUFBEUREN
96003.2

LINZ 1998
NEUE GALERIE DER STADT LINZ
96003.3

ROTTENBURG AM NECKAR 1998
KULTURVEREIN ZEHNTSCHEUER
96003.4

MAINZ 1998
GALERIE DOROTHEA VAN DER KOELEN
96003.5

FEZ-FEZ
Videoskulptur 1996
Struktur aus einzelnen Eisenele-
menten mit trichterförmigen
Öffnungen, eiserne Trittstufen,
rote Wolle, 16 Monitore,
Videorecorder, bespielte
Kassetten, Tonaufzeichnung

FEZ-FEZ
Video sculpture 1996
Iron structure of individual
elements, conical openings, iron
steps, red wool, 16 monitors, video
recorders, recorded video cassettes,
soundrecording

FEZ-FEZ
Videoscultura 1996
Struttura in ferro arrugginito,
aperture coniche, gradini in ferro,
lana rossa, 16 monitors, vhs,
cassette registrate, sonoro

Die Videoinstallation *Fez-Fez*,
die zum ersten Mal im Mausoleum
einer Kirche in Graz präsentiert
wurde und inzwischen auch an
zahlreichen anderen Ausstellungsorten zu sehen war, bezieht
sich auf eine örtliche Begebenheit
in Nordafrika und beschreibt den
›Souk des teinturiers‹, den Markt
der Wollfärber in Nordafrika.
Plessi war sofort fasziniert von
den Eindrücken, den Formen, den
Farben und den Gerüchen dieser
Wollfärberei, und er beschreibt
seine Eindrücke: »Von warmem
Exotismus gesättigte Schatten,
Kreisförmigkeit der Wannen und
repetitive Modulgeometrie. Der
Safran, der Indigo, die Minze, das
Antimon, der Mohn. Das Rot des
Mohns färbt die Wolle, die sich an
den Rändern häuft. Ein atavisti-
sches Handwerk, das hier in den
alten Gesten sein ursprüngliches
Flair wiederfindet.« (Fabrizio
Plessi, in: *Progetti del Mondo*, S.
48) Plessi versucht, seiner Faszi-
nation in der Grazer Installation

The video installation Fez-
Fez, *shown for the first time in*
the mausoleum of a church in
Graz and exhibited later in
several other places refers to a
local event in Northern Africa
and describes the 'Souk des
teinturiers', the market of wool-
dyers. Plessi was at once fasci-
nated by the impressions,
shapes, colours and smells of
this place, and he describes his
impressions: "Shadows bathed
in warm exoticism. The circula-
rity of troughs and the repetiti-
ve modular geometry. The
saffron, the indigo, the mint,
the antimony, the poppy. The
red of the poppy dyes the wool
which piles up on the edges. An
atavistic craft which, here, in
the ancient gestures, finds its
original flair again." (Fabrizio
Plessi, in: Progetti del Mondo,
p. 48) Plessi tries to express his
fascination in the installation
in Graz. The ambience is of a
different kind, yet not less

La videoinstallazione *Fez-
Fez*, esposta per la prima volta
nel mausoleo di una chiesa a
Graz e nel frattempo in molte
altre cittá, si riferisce ad una
località nell'Africa del Nord e
descrive il ›Souk des teinturiers‹, il mercato dei tintori di
lana. Plessi fu immediatamente
colpito dalle impressioni, dalle
forme, dai colori e dagli odori
di tale attività e descrive le sue
sensazioni: »Ombre cariche di
caldo esotismo. Circolarità
delle vasche e geometria
modulare ripetitiva. Lo zaffer-
ano, l'indaco, la menta,
l'antimonio, il papavero. Il
rosso del papavero tinge le
lane ammucchiate ai bordi. Un
artigianato atavico che qui
ritrova, nei gesti antichi, il suo
primitivo sapore.« (Fabrizio
Plessi, in: *Progetti del Mondo*,
p. 48) Plessi cerca di esprimere
tutto il suo entusiasmo
nell'installazione *Fez-Fez* di
Graz. L'ambiente è diverso ma

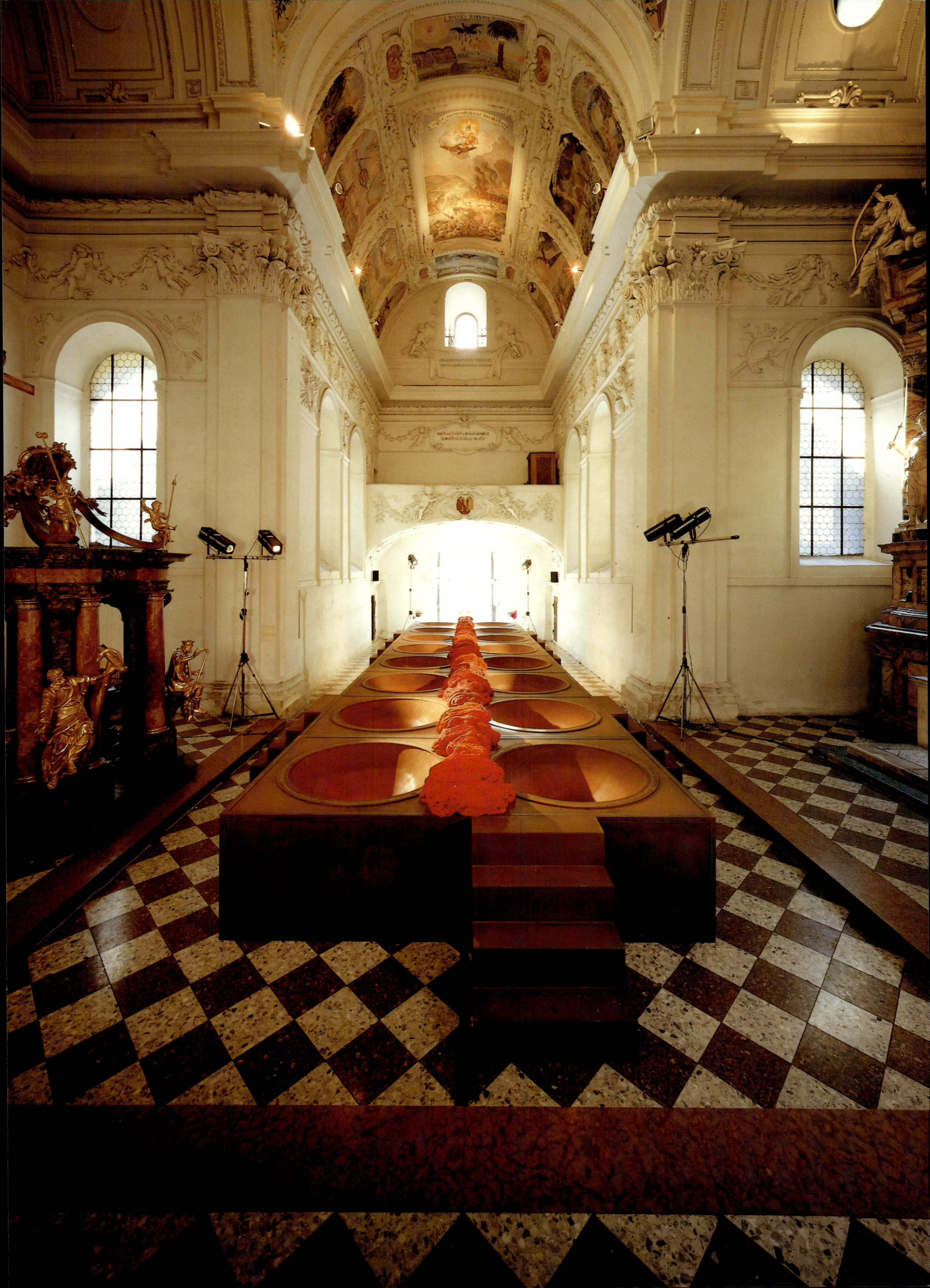

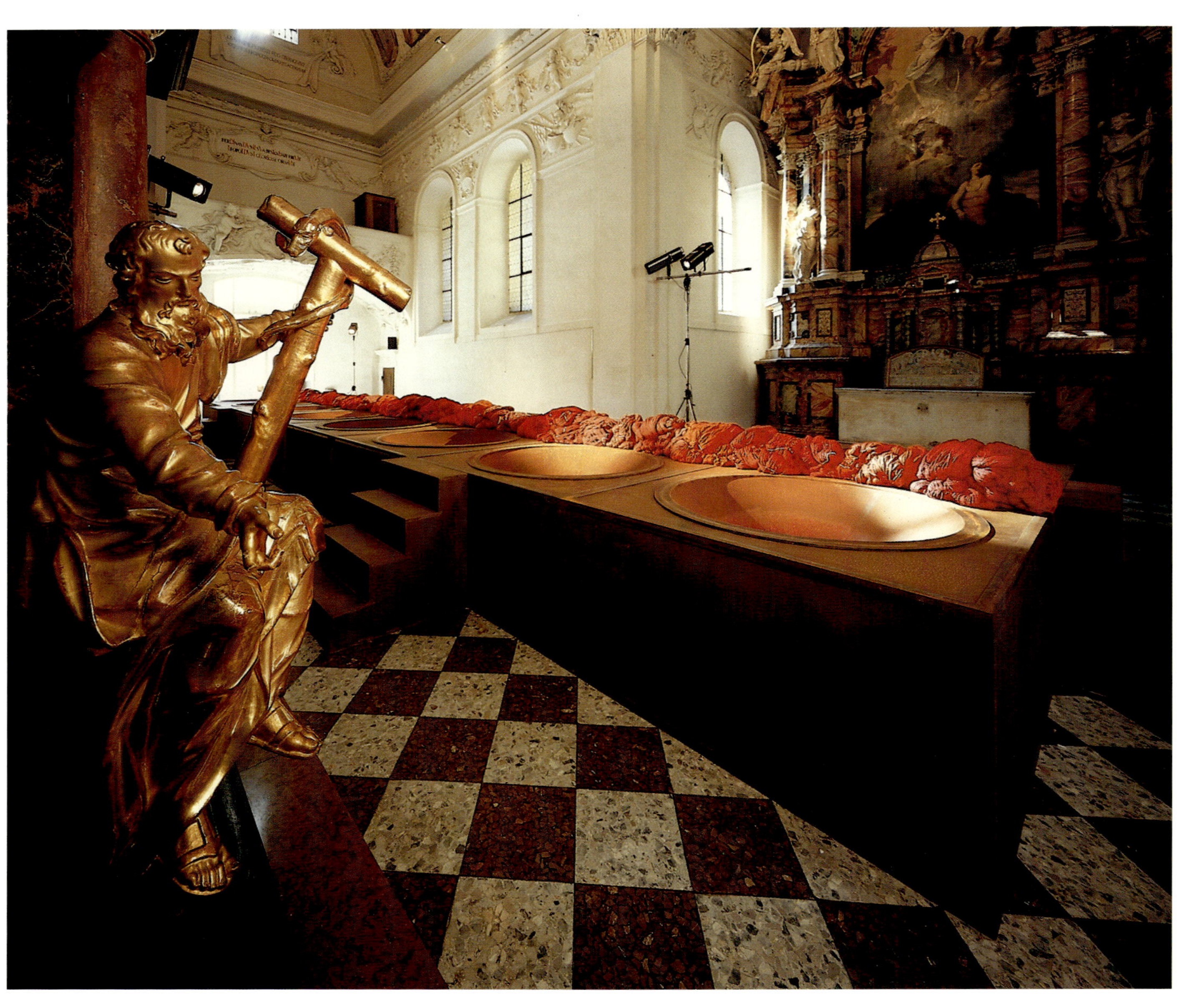

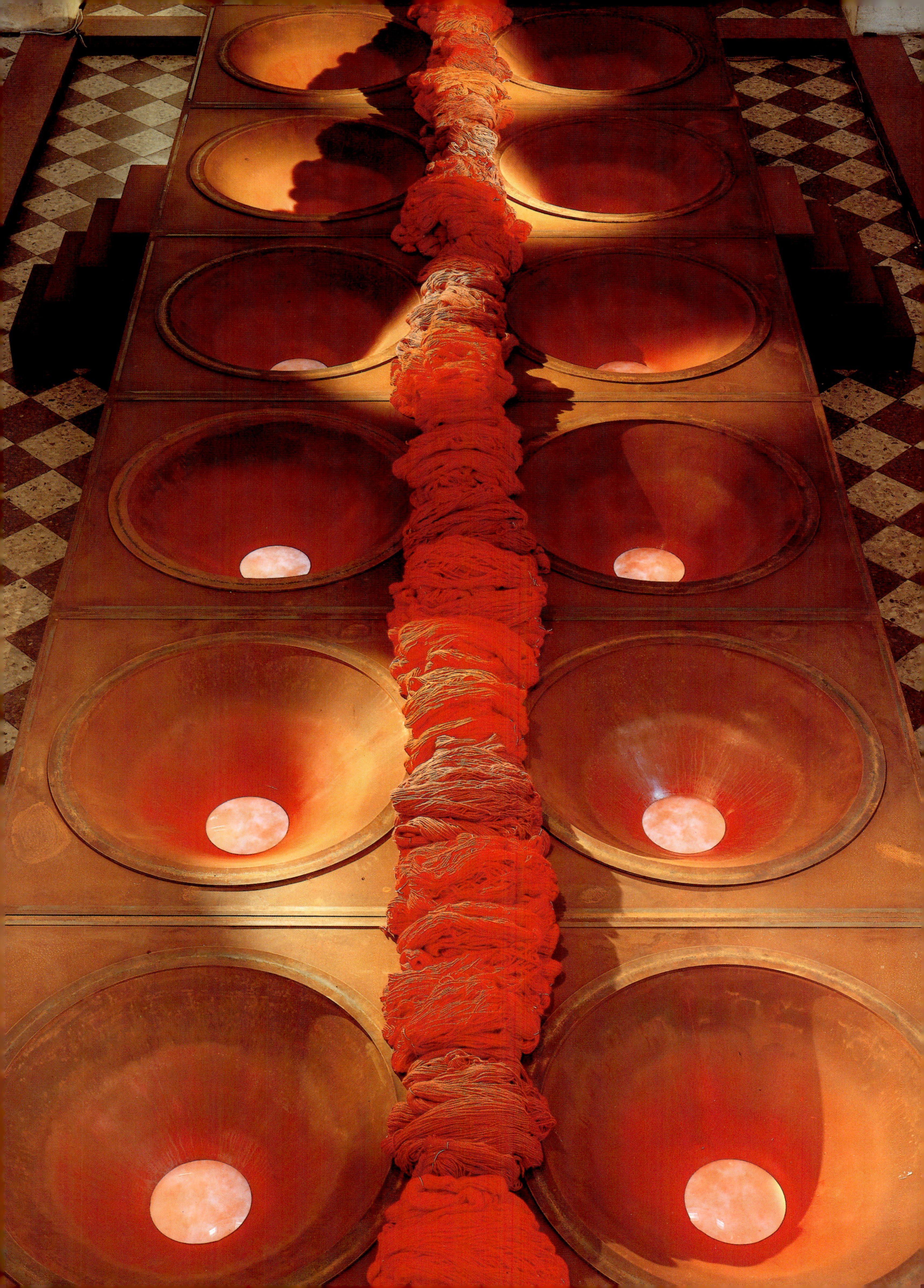

Fez-Fez Ausdruck zu verleihen. Das Ambiente ist von anderer Art, doch nicht weniger stark in der Ausstrahlung.

Im Mittelschiff der Barockkirche sind 16 quadratische Blöcke paarweise aneinandergestellt. Trichterförmige Vertiefungen weisen in ihrer Unterseite ein kreisrundes Loch auf und lassen den Blick auf die versteckten, darunter liegenden Monitore zu. In der Mittelachse sind rotgefärbte Wollbündel aufgebahrt. Von mehreren Seiten führen jeweils vier Stufen auf die Ebene der lagernden Wolle und erlauben einen Einblick in die schalenartigen Ausbuchtungen, in deren Tiefe virtuelles rotes Wasser sprudelt und in Bewegung ist. Die streng geometrische Anordnung steht im Kontrast zu der reichen Barockkirche, doch die in warmen Tönen gehaltene Farbigkeit harmoniert mit ihr. Die Faszination, die diese Wollfärbereien auf den Künstler ausgeübt haben müssen, ist einleuchtend und nachvollziehbar. Angesichts der geometrisch klaren, kreisrunden Öffnungen, in denen große Mengen rotleuchtender Farbe fließt, muß dem Maler und Zeichner Fabrizio Plessi das ganze Ambiente im Markt von Fez wie ein überdimensionierter Aquarellkasten vorgekommen sein, aus dem man sich nach Herzenslust bedienen könne: riesige Bilder malen, oder vielleicht die ganze Welt rot anstreichen. Die Präsentation der jeweils 2 x 2 Meter großen quadratischen Konstruktionen, in deren Rundöffnungen sich die Monitore befinden, ist nicht nur linear denkbar, sondern - je nach Räumlichkeit - auch in quadratischer Anordnung oder U- und S-förmig. Es ist eine Videoinstallation von mitreißender Ausstrahlung, intensiver Dynamik trotz klarer Strenge und unendlicher Schönheit.

strong in its radiance.

In the centre aisle of the baroque church 16 square blocks are - in pairs - placed together. Funnel-like indentions have, on the bottom, a circular hole, allowing a glimpse on the hidden monitors below. In the middle axis, bundles of wool dyed red are placed. Four steps lead on several sides up to the level of wool, permitting insight into the bowl-like holes, in the depth of which virtual red water sparkles and moves. The strictly geometric arrangement is in contrast to the rich baroque church, but the warm red coloration is in harmony with it. The fascination these places of wool-dying must have had on the artist is evident and intelligible. In face of the geometrically clear, circular openings containing large amounts of red shining colour one can imagine that the ambience of the market in Fez must have appeared to the painter and draughtsman Plessi like a huge colour box to which one can help oneself at will: to paint immense pictures, or perhaps to paint the whole world red. The presentation of the square constructions of two by two metres, with the monitors inside, is not only possible in a linear, but also - depending on the space - in rectangular arrangement, as well as U- or S-shaped. It is a video installation of exciting radiation, intense dynamics, and, in spite of its clear austerity, of boundless beauty.

non meno efficace nell'atmosfera.

Nella navata centrale della chiesa barocca sono disposti a coppia sedici blocchi quadrati. Cavità semicircolari mostrano nel lato inferiore un foro e permettono la visione dei monitors nascosti e posizionati in basso. Lungo l'asse centrale si trovano mucchi di lana tinta di rosso. Rispettivamente quattro gradini conducono dai vari lati al livello dove si trova la lana e consentono di guardare all'interno delle cavità dove in basso sgorga e si muove acqua virtuale rossa. La disposizione rigorosamente geometrica è in contrasto con la lussuosa chiesa barocca ma la tonalità dei colori caldi crea un'armonia reciproca. Il fascino che le tintorie di lana avranno evocato nell'artista diviene evidente e comprensibile. Di fronte alle aperture tonde e geometricamente chiare nelle quali scorre in grandi quantità il colore rosso intenso, l'intero ambiente del mercato di Fez sarà apparso al pittore e disegnatore Fabrizio Plessi come una tavolozza di acquerelli sovradimensionata da cui attingere a piacere: dipingere quadri grandi o, forse, colorare di rosso il mondo intero. L'allestimento delle costruzioni quadrate che misurano due metri per due e dove sono inseriti i monitors è immaginabile non solo in forma lineare ma anche - secondo gli spazi espositivi - a forma di U o S. *Fez-Fez* è un'installazione dall'atmosfera entusiasmante, dalla dinamica intensa nonostante la severità pura, e di una bellezza infinita.

ACQUEDOTTO ELETTRONICO

96004

HEIDELBERG 1996
HEIDELBERGER KUNSTVEREIN
96004.1

ELEKTRONISCHES AQUÄDUKT
Videoskulptur 1996
Holzkonstruktion, 20 Monitore,
Videorecorder, bespielte
Kassetten, Tonaufzeichnung

ELECTRONIC AQUEDUCT
Video sculpture 1996
Wooden construction, 20 monitors,
video recorders, recorded video
cassettes, soundrecording

ACQUEDOTTO ELETTRONICO
Videoscultura 1996
Struttura in legno dipinto,
20 monitors, vhs, cassette
registrate, sonoro

Das *Elektronische Aquädukt* im Heidelberger Kunstverein ist unmittelbar entstanden in der Auseinandersetzung Fabrizio Plessis mit der römischen Geschichte durch die Mainzer Installation. In riesiger Dimension, den Raum sprengend, in den es diagonal hineingestellt ist, birgt das nachgebaute Fragment eines römischen Aquäduktes einen elektronischen Wasserlauf. Im 1. Jh. nach Christus ist das römische Aquädukt in Mainz entstanden, von dem heute nur noch einige der Pfeilerreste in situ vorhanden sind. Das einst gequaderte Äußere der römischen Pfeiler ist längst zwecks ›Neubauten‹ abgetragen worden, so daß heute nur noch das aus Bruchstein bestehende Innere dieser Pfeiler erhalten ist.

Nicht allein Fabrizio Plessi, auch

The Electronic Aqueduct *is a direct result of Plessi's study of Roman history on the occasion of his installation in Mainz. In huge dimension, springing the space of the room it is diagonally built into, the replica of a Roman aqueduct contains an electronic waterway. In the first century A.D. the Roman aqueduct in Mainz was built, of which today only a few remains of pillars can be found in situ. The outer square blocks forming the pillars have long been used to build new houses, and today only some of the quarry stones used to fill the insides of the pillars are left.*

Not only Fabrizio Plessi, but the German artist Günther Uecker, too, has occupied

Acquedotto Elettronico del Kunstverein di Heidelberg si inserisce direttamente nel contesto delle riflessioni di Fabrizio Plessi sulla storia romana dell'installazione di Magonza. La ricostruzione dalle dimensioni gigantesche del frammento di acquedotto romano, collocato diagonalmente nella sala, contiene un corso d'acqua elettronico. Dell'acquedotto romano di Magonza, costruito nel I secolo dopo Cristo, sono oggi conservati in situ solamente pochi resti dei pilastri. L'esterno originario dei pilastri romani squadrati è stato da tempo smantellato per essere riutilizzate in nuove costruzioni conservando appena la struttura interna di pietre di cava.

Oltre Fabrizio Plessi anche

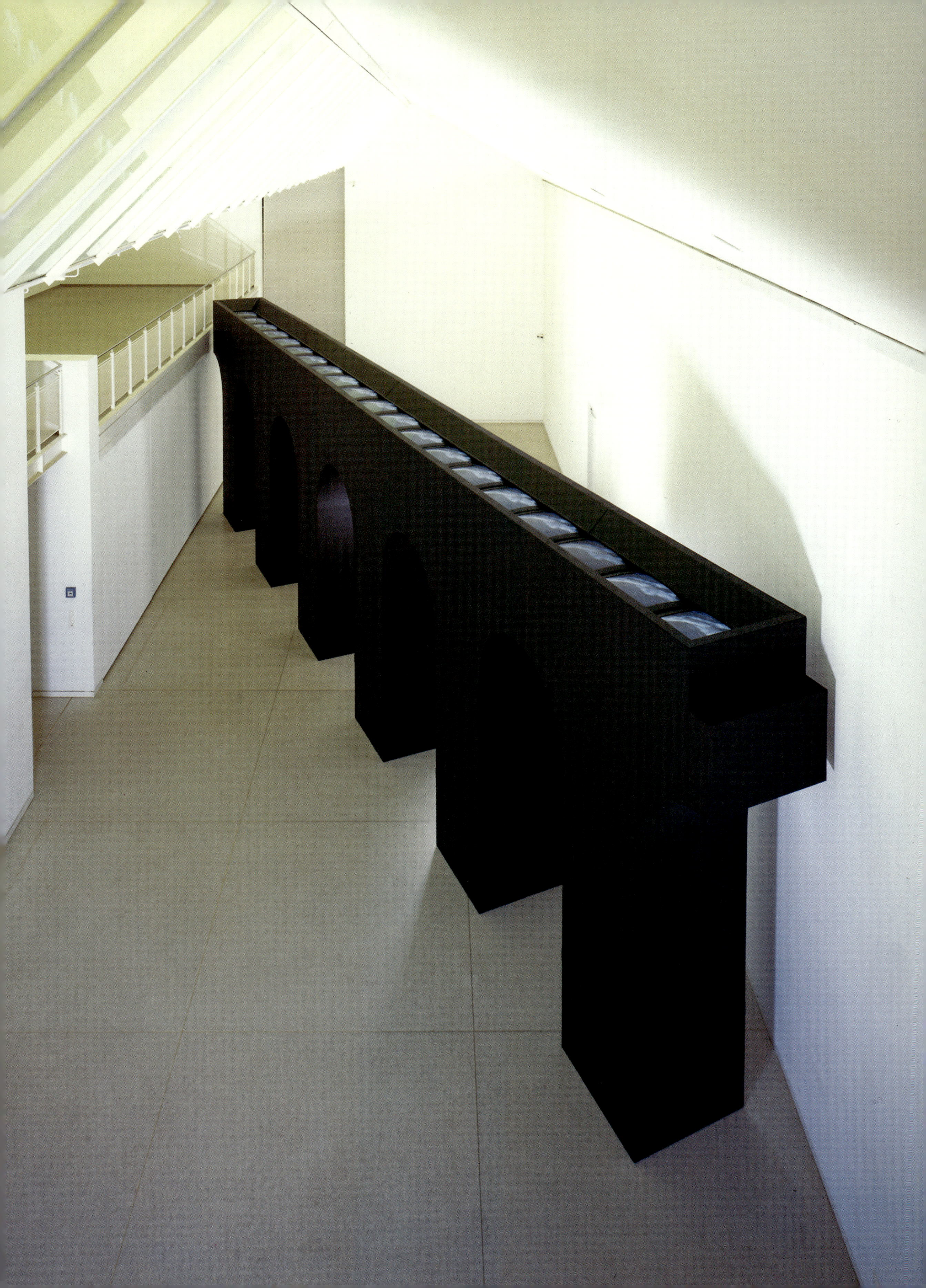

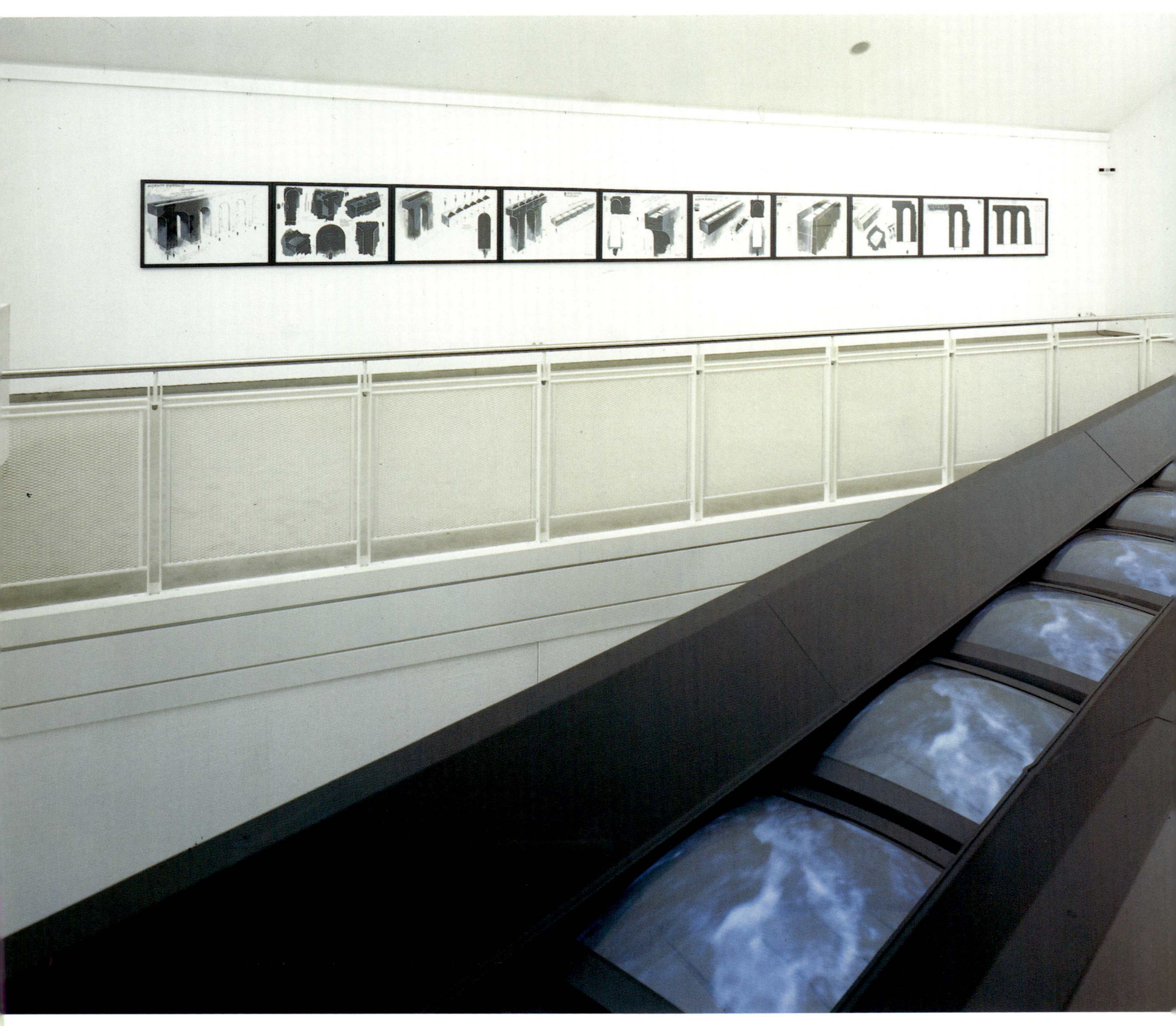

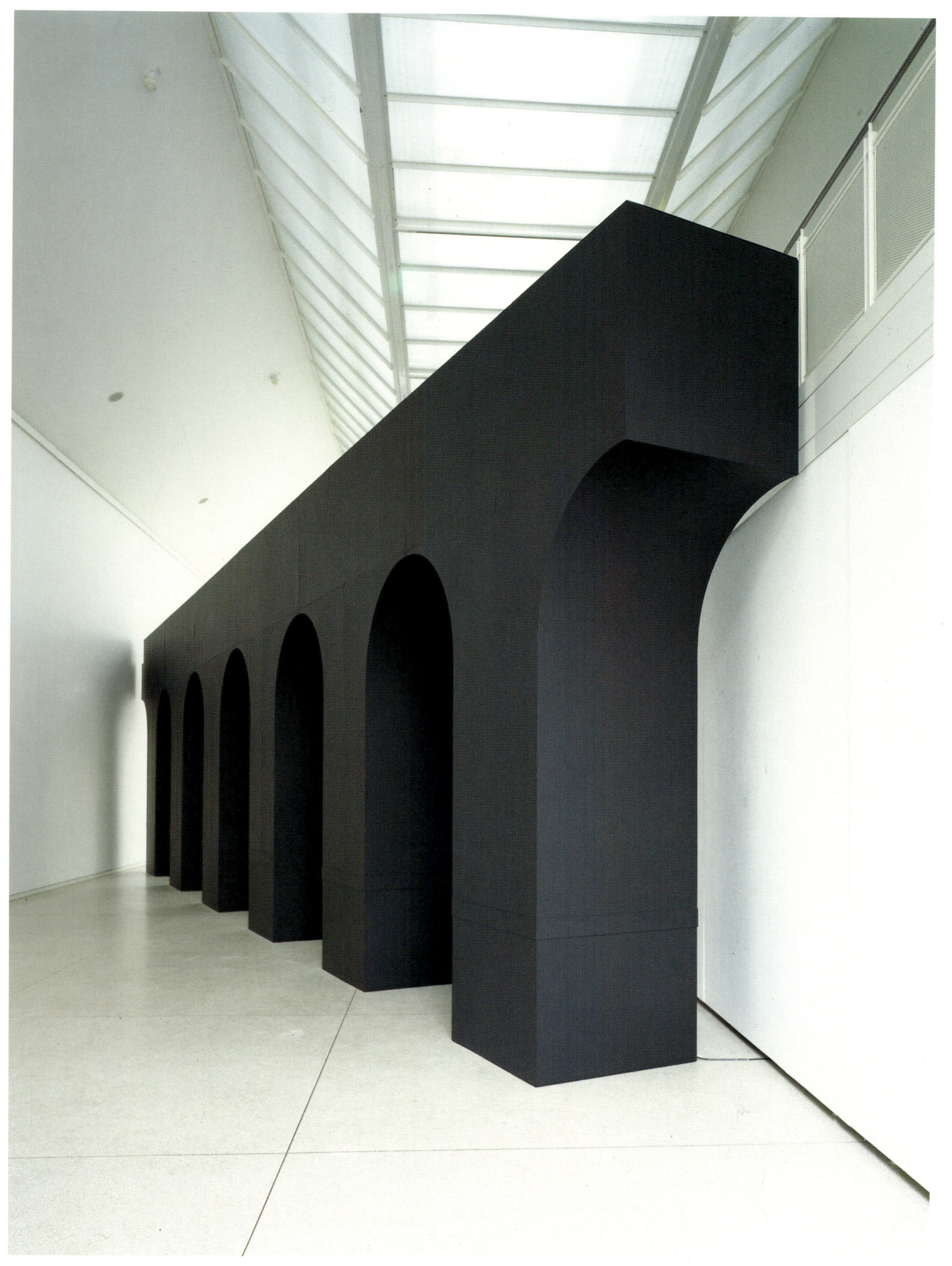

der deutsche Künstler Günther Uecker hat sich mit der ehemaligen römischen Wasserleitung, dem Mainzer Aquädukt, auseinandergesetzt und es zum Thema einer Arbeit gemacht. Den Grund dafür erklärt er mit den Worten: »Mir geht es darum, diese menschlichen Zeichen, die Hinterlassenschaften sind, zu ergründen. Das beweist mir menschliche Anwesenheit über lange Zeiträume und ich glaube für mich, soviel Vergangenheit ich habe, in der Erfaßbarkeit dieser Vergangenheit, in dieser sinnlichen Vergegenwärtigung, soviel Zukunft habe ich auch. Also quantitativ lebe ich aus den Erfahrungen und Erkenntnissen dessen, was mir aus der Vergangenheit her überliefert ist und vergegenwärtige, was der wirkliche hysterische hybrische Lebensaugenblick ist, und das gibt mir Zukunft.« (Uecker, im Ausstellungskatalog *Schatten Schein*, Mainz 1987)

Fabrizio Plessi, dessen großes Thema, neben dem Fluß des Wassers, der Begriff der ›Zeit‹ und des Vergänglichen ist, hat nun ein vergehendes römisches Aquädukt zum Thema einer Videoskulptur gemacht. Ähnlich wie bei Uecker könnte man vermuten, daß Plessi eine Bindung verschiedener Zeiten, eine Harmonisierung von Vergangenheit, Gegenwart und Zukunft herzustellen versucht.

himself with the former Roman waterpipe, the aqueduct in Mainz, and made it the subject of one of his works. He explains the reason for this: "It is my concern to fathom these human signs, which are legacies. These prove to me human presence over a long period of time, and I believe, that as much past I have, in the seizability of this past, in the sensual recalling, that much future I also have. Also, quantitatively I live from the experiences and realisations of that, what has come down to me from the past, and I recall what is the real, hysterical, hybric moment of life, and that gives me future." Günther Uecker, in: catalogue Schatten - Schein, Galerie Dorothea van der Koelen, Mainz 1987)

Fabrizio Plessi, whose major theme is - beside the flow of water - the term of 'time' and transitoriness, has now made a decaying Roman aqueduct the subject of one of his works. Similar as with Uecker one could assume that Plessi tries to create a connection between different ages, a harmonisation of past, present and future.

l'artista tedesco Günther Uecker si è occupato dell'antico acquedotto romano di Magonza eleggendolo tema di una delle sue opere. Egli ne dà così ragione: »Mi interessa indagare tali segni umani, che rappresentano un'eredità e che mi testimoniano la presenza dell'uomo attraverso i tempi. E credo per me stesso che più posseggo il passato, nel senso della intelligibilità e della sua concretizzazione sensuale, più posseggo il futuro. Quantitativamente io vivo dunque delle esperienze e delle conoscenze di quello che mi è stato tramandato dal passato e della cognizione del vero istante isterico e contraddittorio della vita, ed è questo che mi dà futuro.« (Günther Uecker, in: catalogo *Schatten - Schein*, Galerie Dorothea van der Koelen, Magonza 1987)

Fabrizio Plessi il cui grande tema è, oltre il corso dell'acqua, il concetto di ›tempo‹ e di effimero in questa videoscultura elegge come tematica un acquedotto romano fugace. Così come per Uecker, si può supporre per Plessi che egli cerchi di creare un rapporto fra tempi diversi, un'armonizzazione fra passato, presente e futuro.

MOVIMENTI CATODICI BAROCCHI

96005

NAPOLI 1996
FONDAZIONE IDIS
96005.1

NEW YORK 1998
GUGGENHEIM MUSEUM SOHO
96005.2

SAN DIEGO 1998
MUSEUM OF CONTEMPORARY ART LA JOLLA
96005.3

KATHODISCHE BAROCKE
BEWEGUNGEN
Videoinstallation 1996
7 Beichtstühle, aufgehängt mit
Drehmechanismus, je 2 Monitore,
Videorecorder, bespielte
Kassetten, Tonaufzeichnung
je 280 x 100 x 200 cm

CATHODIC BAROQUE MOVEMENTS
Video installation 1996
7 confessionals, constantly
rotating suspension, 2 monitors
each, video recorders, recorded
video cassettes, soundrecording
280 x 100 x 200 cm (each)

MOVIMENTI CATODICI BAROCCHI
Videoinstallazione 1996
7 strutture in legno, macchine
rotanti in movimento, 2 monitors
caduna, vhs, cassette registrate,
sonoro
280 x 100 x 200 cm (caduna)

Beichtstühle in der Kirche
S. Lorenzo in Neapel sind der
Ausgangspunkt gewesen für diese
Videoinstallation mit dem Titel
*Movimenti Catodici Barocchi
(Barocke, kathodische Bewegungen)*. In seiner Installation hat
Fabrizio Plessi die Beichtstühle auf
den Kopf gestellt und an schwingenden Konstruktionen mit einem
sich drehenden Motor aufgehängt.
In die seitlichen Öffnungen sind
Monitore eingebaut, die wildlo-
derndes rotes Feuer zeigen. Wir
kennen die Konstruktion aus Palma
de Mallorca, wo sie als *Fuochi
Fatui (Irrlichter)* in der Fundació
Miró präsentiert waren. Nur hier ist
die Idee quantifiziert, sind zahlreiche weitere Beichtstühle dazu
gekommen und in einem der
Monitore flackert nicht loderndes

*Confessionals in the church
of St. Lorenzo in Naples were
the starting point for this video
installation, entitled* Movimenti
Catodici Barocchi (Baroque
Cathodic Movements). *In his
installation, Fabrizio Plessi has
turned the confessionals upside
down, and hung them suspended
from swinging constructions
with a turning motor. Built into
the openings on the sides, monitors show wildly blazing fire.
We know this construction from
Palma de Mallorca, where they
were presented as* Fuochi Fatui
(will-o'-the-wisp) *at the Fundació Miró. Here, the idea is
quantified, numerous confessionals have been added, and on
one of the monitors, instead of
the flickering fire, we see the*

I confessionali della chiesa di
San Lorenzo a Napoli sono stati
il punto di partenza per questa
videoinstallazione dal titolo
Movimenti Catodici Barocchi.
Nella sua installazione Fabrizio
Plessi ha capovolto i confessionali e li ha appesi ad una costruzione oscillante con motore
rotante. Nelle aperture laterali
sono inseriti i monitors che
rappresentano fuoco rosso
fiammeggiante. Conosciamo la
composizione da *Fuochi Fatui* di
Palma de Mallorca dove fu
presentata alla Fundació Miró,
solo che qui l'idea è quantifica-
ta, sono stati aggiunti ulteriori
confessionali e c'è l'acqua di
uno dei monitors. Il tema di
quest'opera è il contrasto insu-
perabile fra scienza e magia,

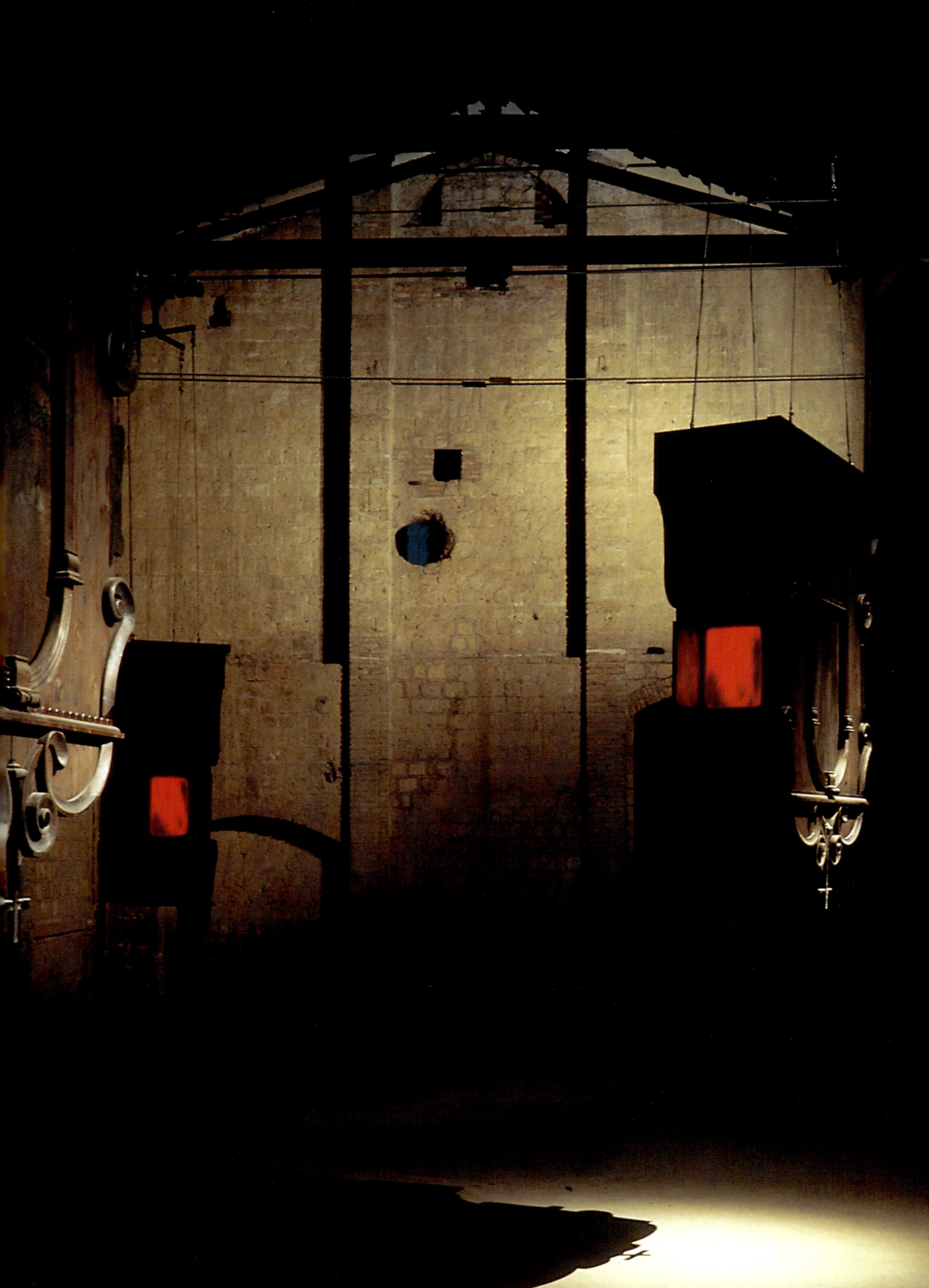

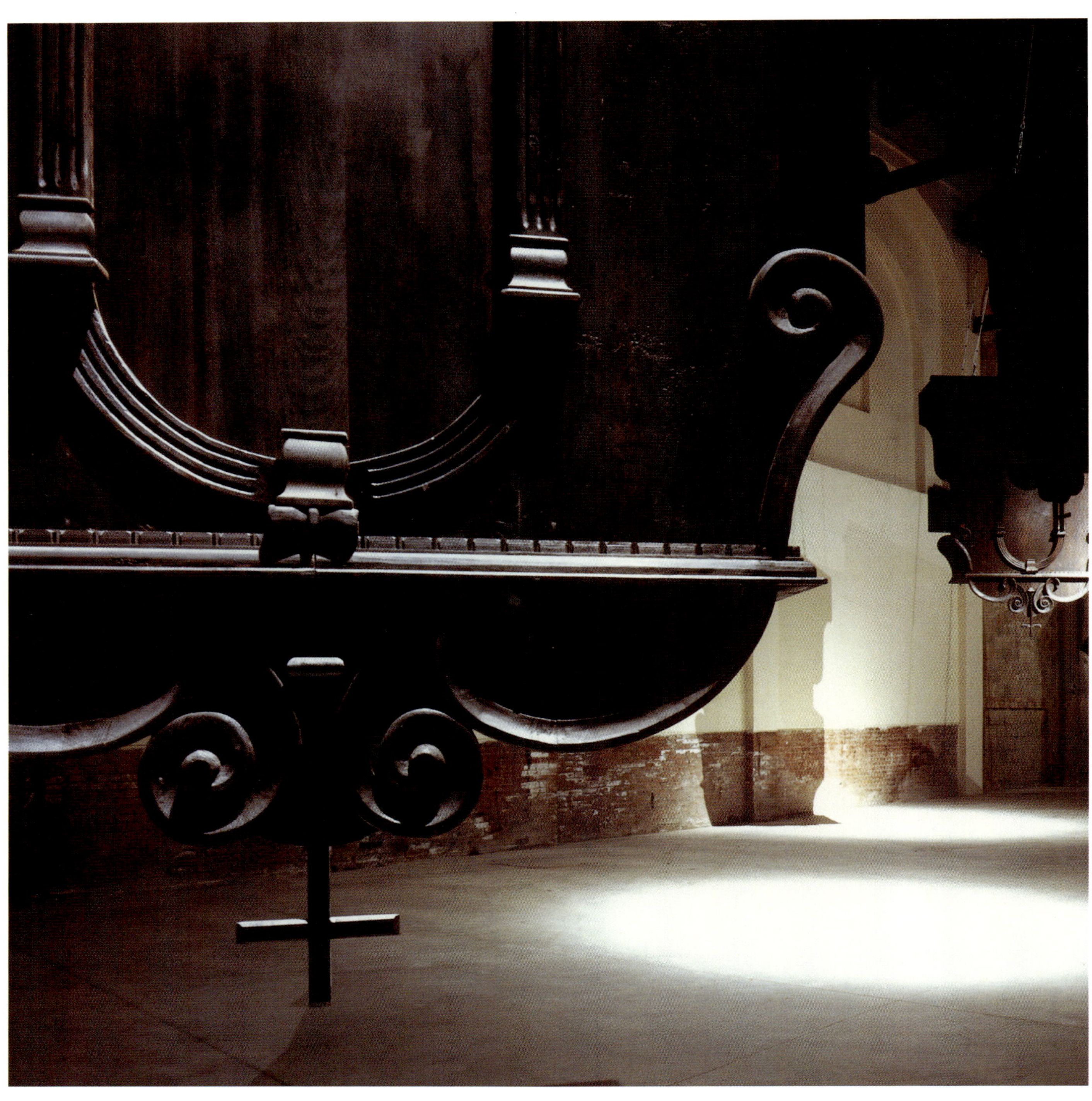

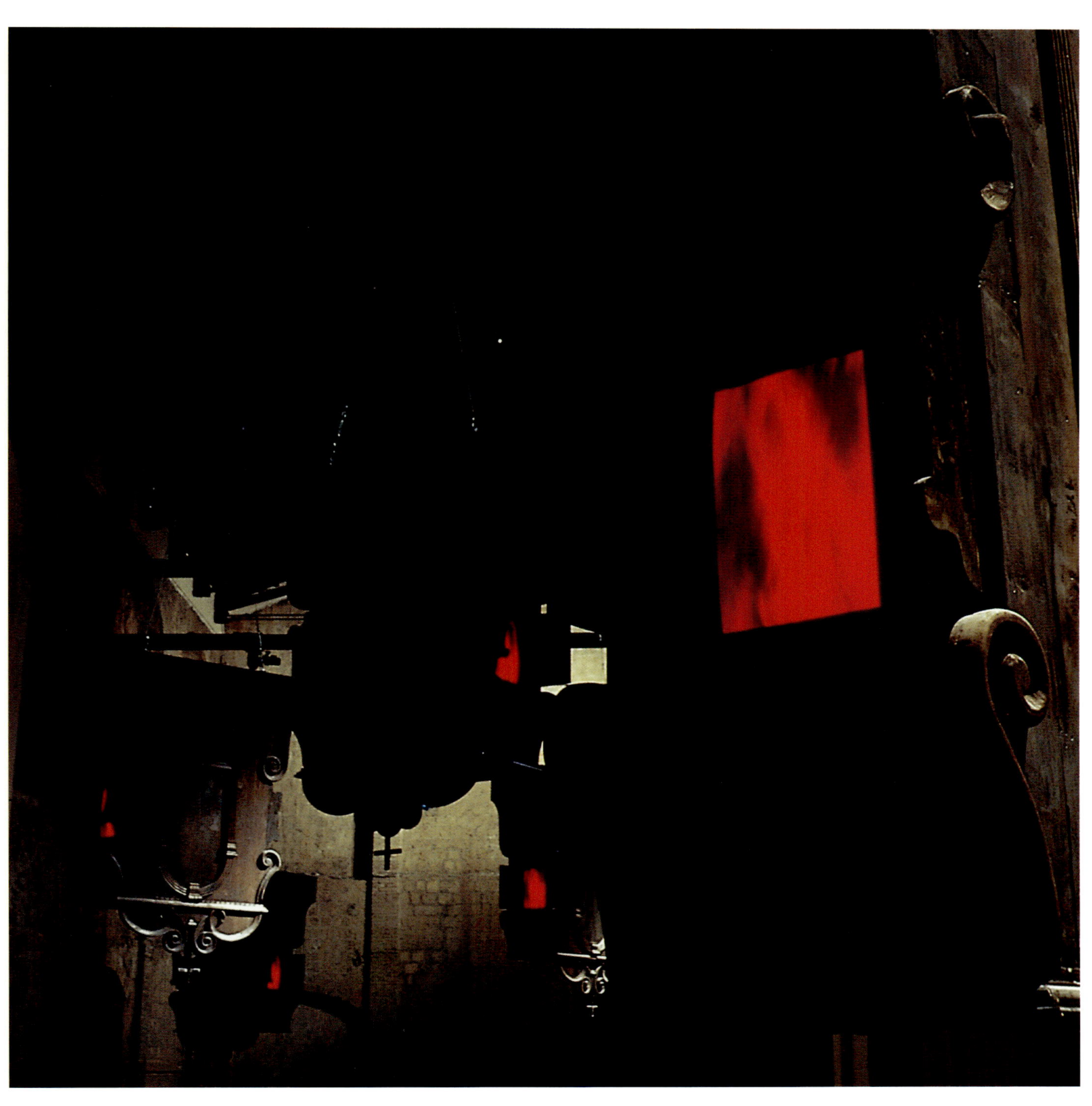

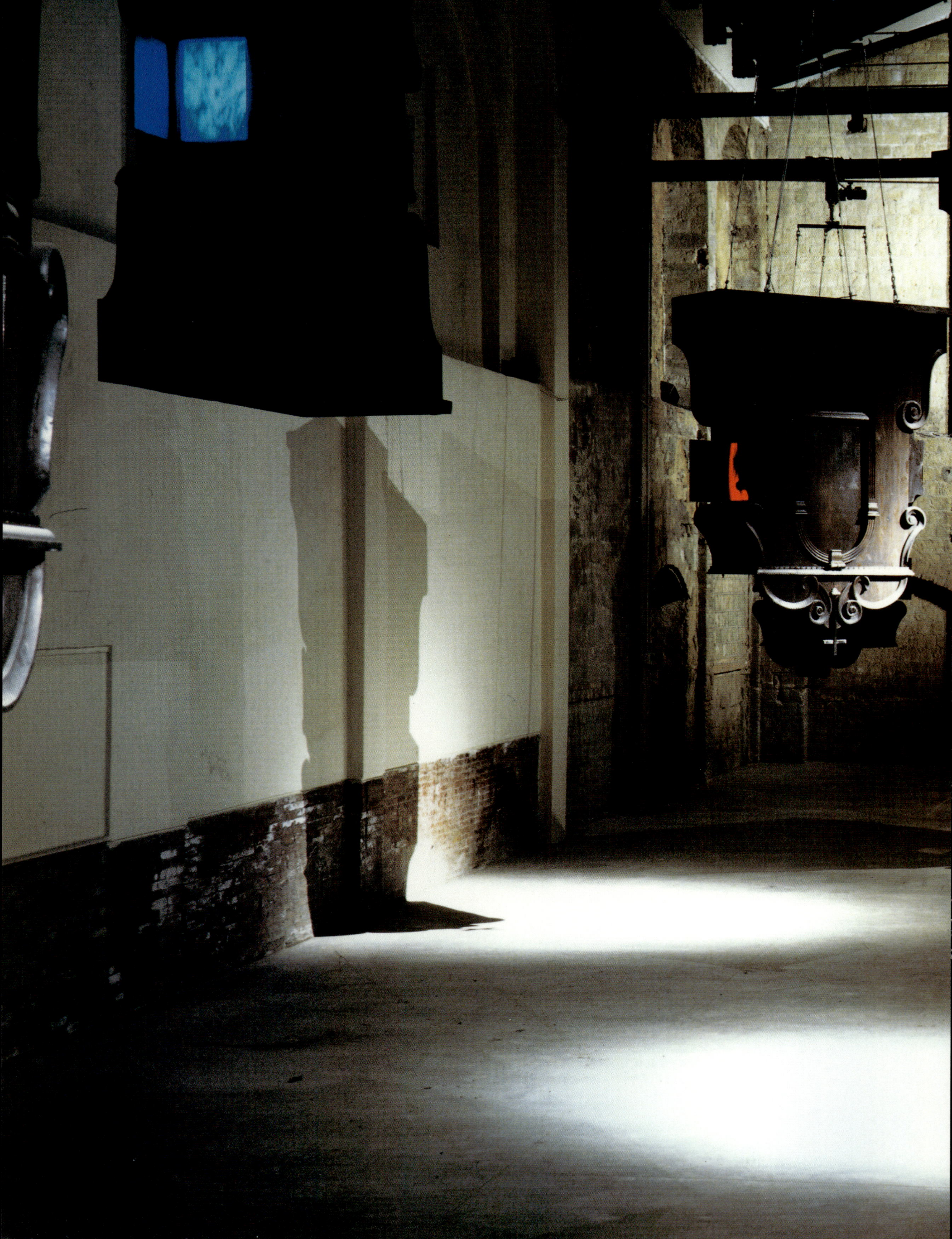

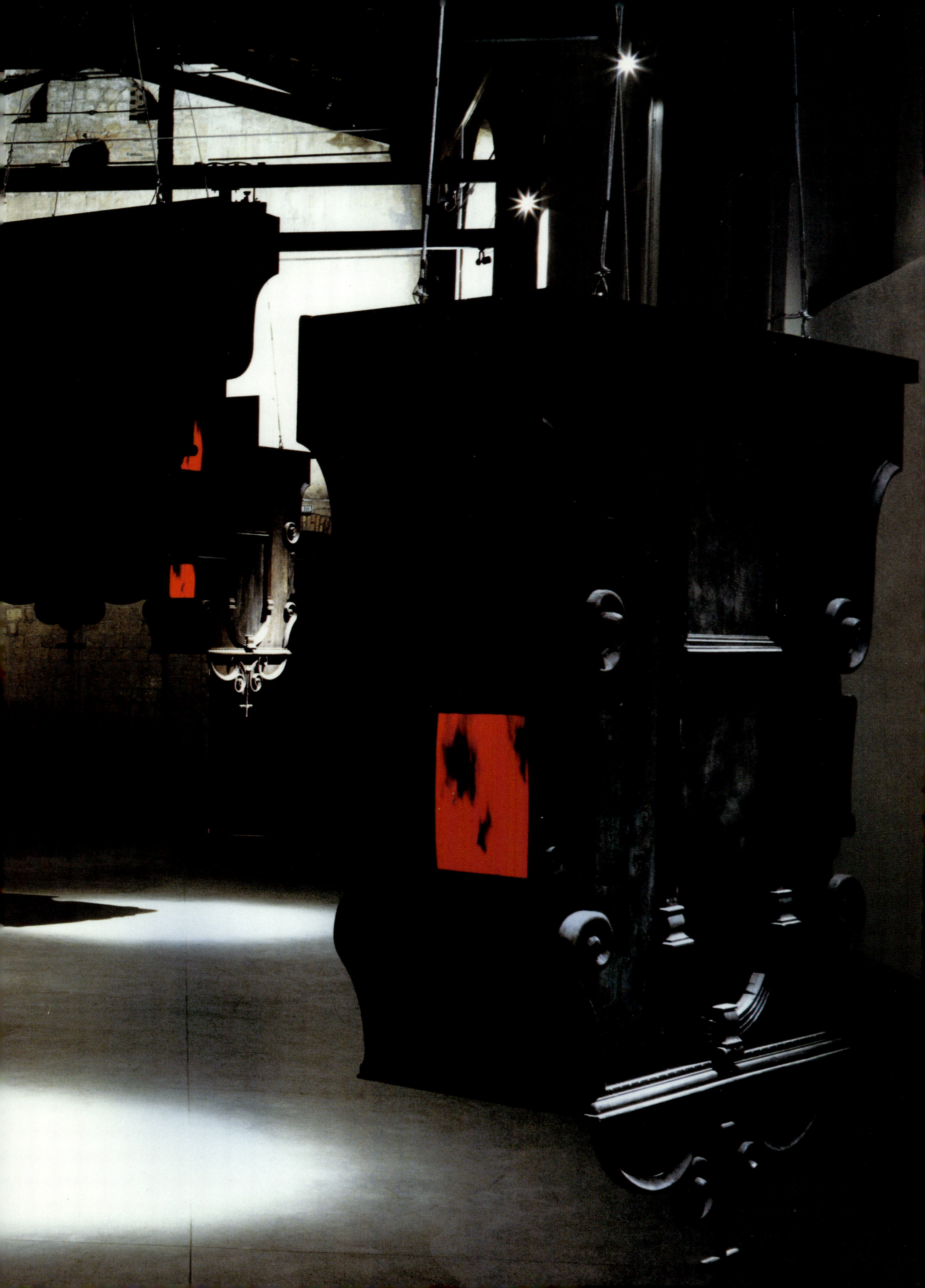

Feuer, sondern fließt rauschendes Wasser. Thematisiert ist in dieser Arbeit der unüberwindliche Gegensatz von Wissenschaft und Magie. Magie, das kann Glaube sein, das kann Religion sein oder auch Kunst. Die scheinbar gesicherten Werte sind wie die Beichtstühle auf den Kopf gestellt. Sie sind verloren gegangen und der im Dunkel gehaltene theatralische Raum unterstreicht noch die Dramatik der Situation. »Künstlerische Kreativität befindet sich im Widerspruch zu bekannten Normen grundsätzlich, sonst ist sie nicht kreativ«, hat Günther Uecker einmal gesagt. Und es wird klar: Die Kunst und der Künstler, sie stellen Fragen, aber sie beantworten sie nicht. Fabrizio Plessi zu seiner Ausstellung: »Die Sünde, die Schuld, das Feuer, düstere Präsenzen, die kopfunter in unterschiedlichen und entgegengesetzten Ellipsen schwingen. Kirchen, Loggien, Gebäude und Portale des 17. Jahrhunderts. Tretet also lärmend ein und nähert euch diesen ›barocken kathodischen Bewegungen‹ ohne Furcht. Da letzten Endes ihr allein der wahre, einzige und antike Motor seid.« (Fabrizio Plessi, in: *Progetti del Mondo*, S. 49)

flow of rushing water. The insurmountable contrast between science and magic is the theme of this work. Magic can be belief, religion, or even art. The seemingly secure values are, like the confessionals, turned upside down. They have been lost, and the theatrically dark room underlines the dramatic situation. "Artistic creativity is in fundamental contradiction of accepted norms, otherwise it is not creative", Günther Uecker once said. And it becomes clear: art and the artist pose questions, but give no answers. Fabrizio Plessi writes on his exposition: "The sin, the guilt, the fire. Sombre presences which swing upside-down in divergent and contrary ellipses. Churches, loggias, buildings and portals from the seventeenth century. Enter boisterously and approach these 'baroque cathodic movements' without fear, because, in the end, you alone are the true, singular and ancient motor." (Fabrizio Plessi, in: Progetti del Mondo, *p. 49)*

magia che può essere fede, può essere religione o anche arte. I valori apparentemente universali sono capovolti come i confessionali, sono persi e l'oscurità dell'ambiente teatrale sottolinea ancora di più la drammaticità della situazione. »La creatività artistica è per principio in contraddizione con le norme accettate, altrimenti non è creatività ...« ha affermato una volta Günther Uecker. E diviene ovvio: l'arte e l'artista pongono quesiti ma non danno risposte. Fabrizio Plessi a proposito della sua mostra: »Il peccato, la colpa, il fuoco. Presenze cupe che ondeggiano a testa in giù con ellittiche diverse e contrarie. Chiese, loggiati, palazzi e portali seicenteschi. Entrate dunque rumorosamente e avvicinatevi senza paura a questi ›Movimenti catodici barocchi‹ perchè solo voi alla fine ne siete il vero, unico ed antico motore.« (Fabrizio Plessi, in: *Progetti del Mondo*, p. 49)

LE CARIATIDI DEI POVERI II

96006

NAPOLI 1996
GALLERIA LUCIO AMELIO
96006.1

DIE KARYATIDEN DER ARMEN II
Videoinstallation 1996
Gebrauchte Koffer, Schnüre,
elektrische Glühlampen,
2 Monitore, Videorecorder,
bespielte Kassetten,
Tonaufzeichnung

THE CARYTIDS OF THE POOR II
Video installation 1996
Used suitcases, electric bulbs,
ropes, 2 monitors, video recorders,
recorded video cassettes,
soundrecording

LE CARIATIDI DEI POVERI II
Videoinstallazione 1996
Vecchie valigie, corda, lampadine,
2 monitors, vhs, cassette
registrate, sonoro

Die zweite Version der *Karyatiden der Armen*, präsentiert bei
Lucio Amelio in Neapel, modifiziert
die ursprüngliche Installation,
indem die Bildmonitore am unteren
Ende jeder Karyatide nicht einen
Ausschnitt des oben gezeigten
Kofferturmes präsentieren, sondern
das von einem Metalldetektor
durchleuchtete Innere eines Kof-
fers, ähnlich der Situation, wie sie
an Flughäfen oder Grenzübergän-
gen im programmierten Videobild
der verborgene Inhalt eines ver-
schlossenen Gepäckstückes zu
sehen ist. Claudia Posca schreibt im
Dortmunder Katalog, zu dem Inhalt:
»Er besteht aus wenigen Dingen,
die die äußere Armseligkeit durch
ein inneres Bild der Armut bestäti-
gen. Wie in der Realität gelten auch
bei der simulierten Durchleuchtung

The second version of Caryatids of the Poor, *presented
by Lucio Amelio in Naples,
modifies the original installation; the monitors at the lower
end of each* Caryatid *do not
show a section of the tower of
suitcases above but the inside of
a suitcase x-rayed with a metal
detector, similar to the situation at airports and border-
crossings, where the contents of
a closed suitcase are visible on
programmed video screens.
Claudia Posca writes in the
catalogue in Dortmund: "It
consists of few things that
confirm the outer poverty with
an inward image of poverty. As
in reality, intimacy and individuality of humans have no
value in the simulation of*

La seconda versione di
Cariatidi dei Poveri, presentata
da Lucio Amelio a Napoli, modifica l'installazione originaria
mostrando nei monitors in basso
di ciascuna cariatide non più un
particolare delle valigie disposte
in alto, ma l'interno di una
valigia ripreso da un metaldetector, così come negli areoporti
o ai confini dove l'immagine
programmata di un video fa
intravedere il contenuto nascosto di un bagaglio chiuso. Di
tale contenuto così si esprime
Claudia Posca nel catalogo di
Dortmund: »Esso consiste di
poche cose che confermano la
miseria esterna attraverso
l'immagine interna della povertà. Così come nella realtà,
anche durante il simulato esame

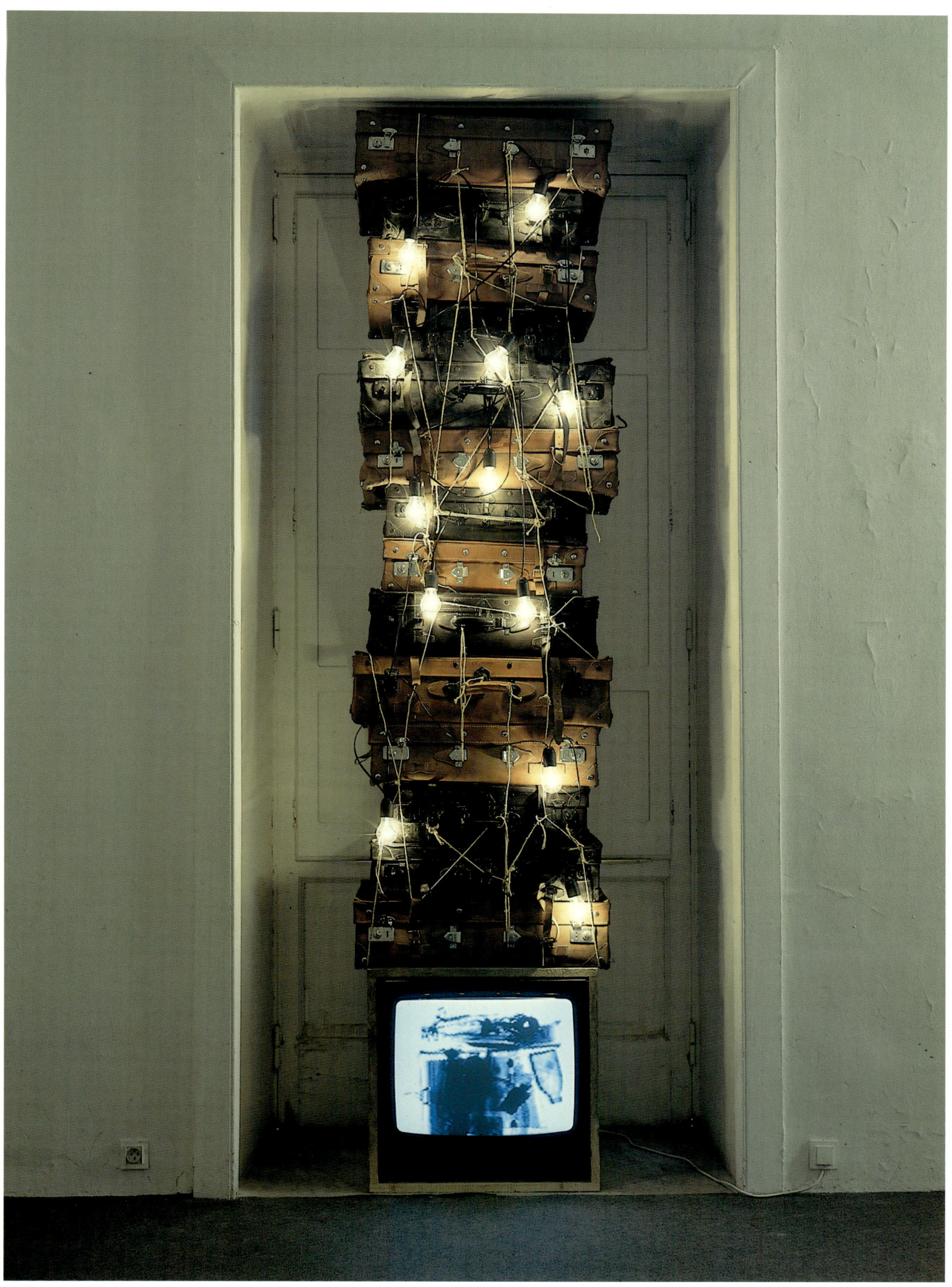

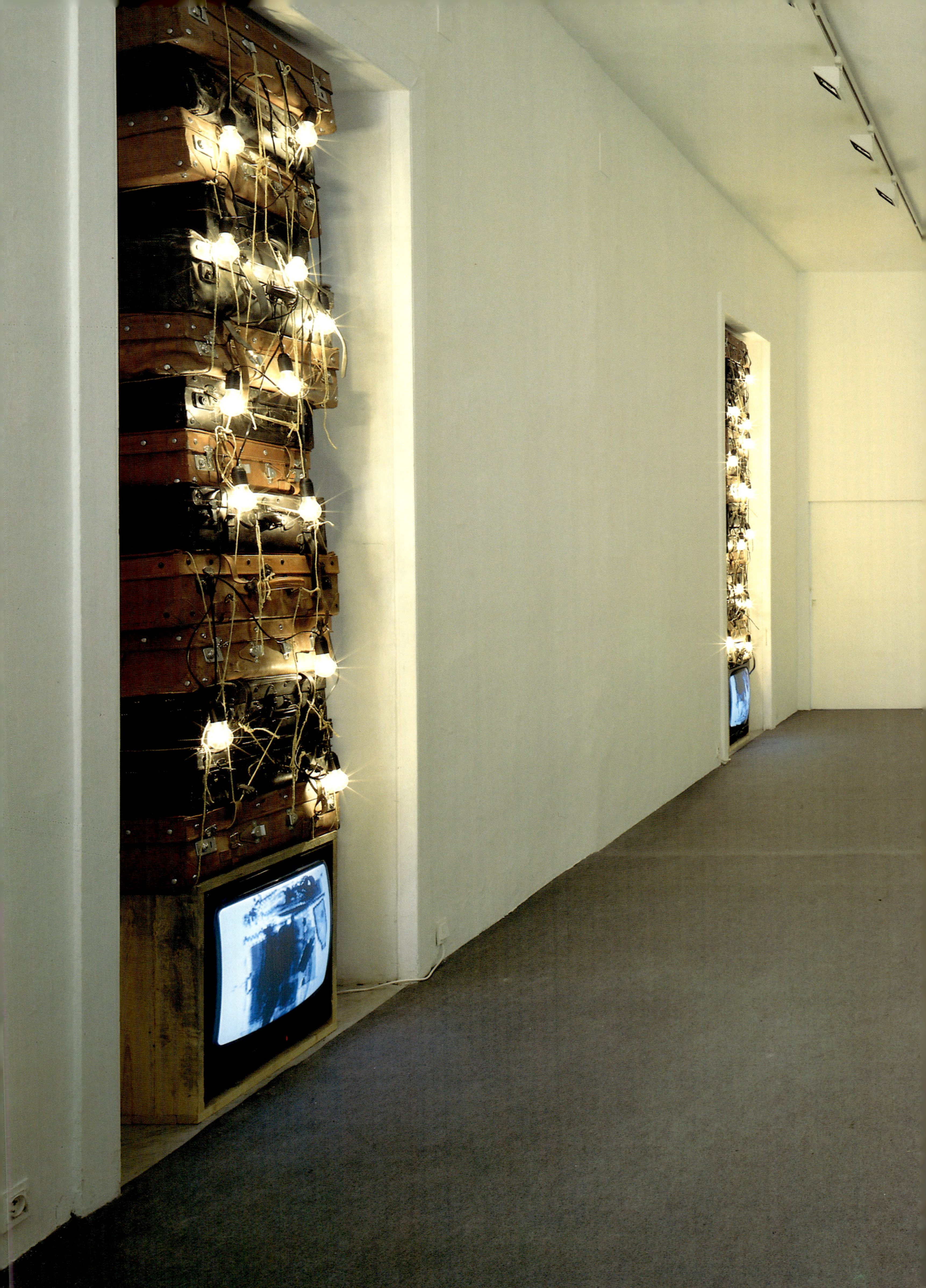

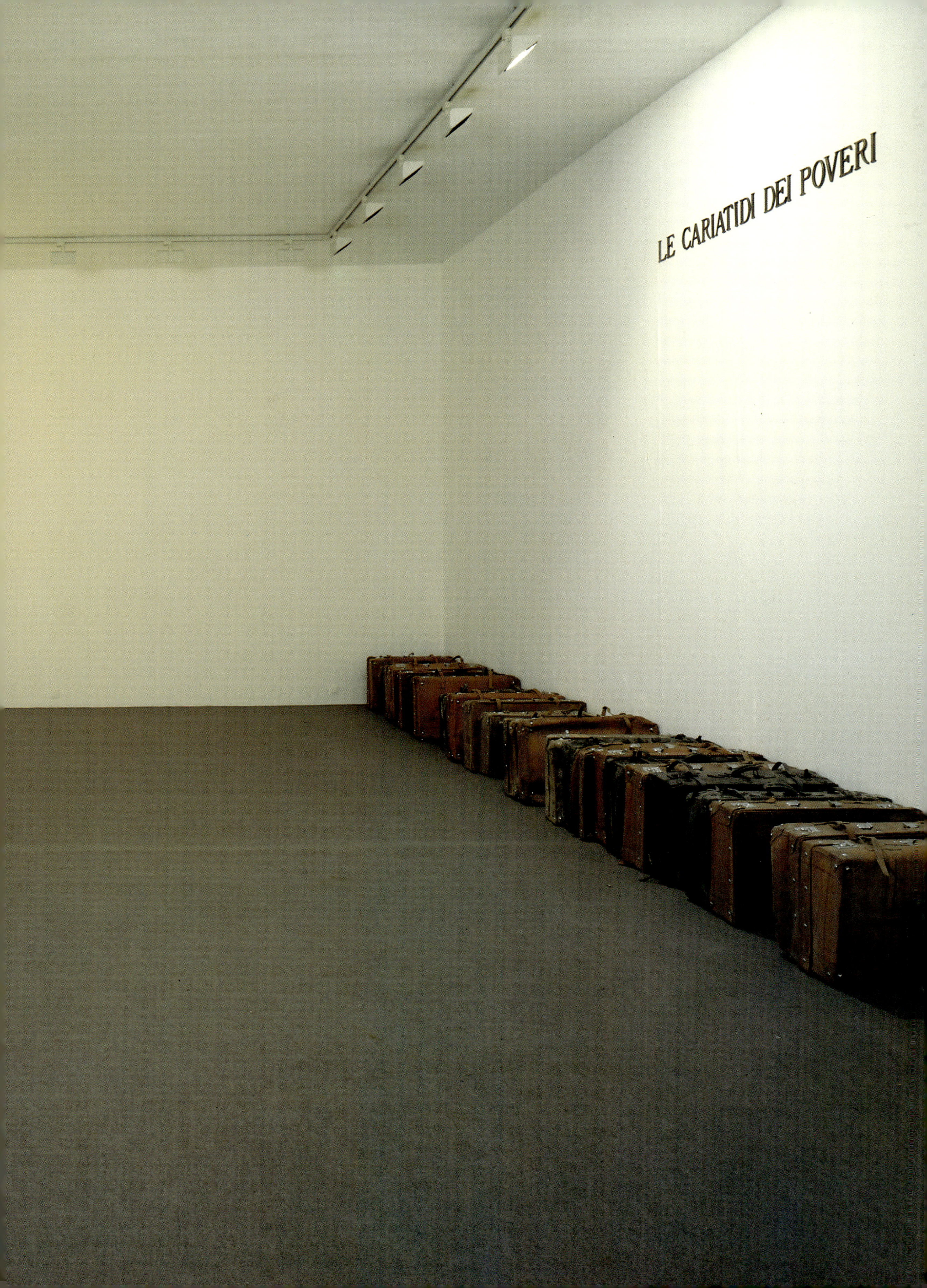

LE CARIATIDI DEI POVERI

Intimität und Individualität des Menschen nicht.« (Katalog Museum am Ostwall, Dortmund 1993, S. 185)

Neben den gewaltigen, schillernden, eindrucksvollen, barockenen, großartigen Videoinstallationen Plessis gibt es immer wieder einen Rückgriff auf ›Arte Povera‹-Elemente, ob nun in dem frühen *Arco Liquido* oder in den zahlreichen Schrankkonstruktionen, ob die Verwendung von angeschwemmtem Treibholz oder wie in dieser Installation die gebrauchten alten Koffer, alle diese Elemente, die oftmals als ›Objets trouvés‹ oder ›Readymades‹ eingesetzt werden, betonen den Aspekt der ›Arte Povera‹ und rücken diesen Künstler gelegentlich in die Nähe von Jannis Kounellis oder Mario Merz. Ganz bewußt sucht Plessi immer wieder die Rückbindung zu diesen einfachen, klaren Materialien, die nicht von sich aus schön oder erhaben sind, aber durch das Kunstwerk ihre Veredelung erfahren.

Die ›Arte Povera‹, die Kunst, die bewußt mit unprätentiösen Materialien umgeht, soll dazu dienen, komplexe Bezüge oder Zusammenhänge zu thematisieren, ohne durch das einzelne Objekt und die Faszination des Objektes zu sehr von dem übergeordneten Inhalt oder dem Gemeinten abgelenkt zu werden. Sie entstand in den 60er Jahren in Italien, breitete sich aber sehr schnell über ganz Europa aus und öffnete in dem fortschreitenden methodischen Präzisierungsprozeß der ›Minimal Art‹ und später der ›Konzept Art‹ in gewisser Weise die Tür.

screening processes." (catalogue Museum am Ostwall, Dortmund 1993, p. 185)

Beside the enormous, glittering, impressive, baroque and great video installations by Plessi there are always refernces to 'Arte Povera' elements, whether in the early Arco Liquido, or in the numerous cabinet constructions, the use of driftwood washed ashore or, as in this installation, the old, used suitcases - all these elements that are often employed as 'objets trouvés' or 'ready-mades' stress the aspect of 'Arte Povera', and sometimes bring the artist close to Jannis Kounellis and Mario Merz. Consciously, Plessi again and again looks for the reassurance found in these clear, simple materials, not beautiful or gracious in themselves, yet finding their refinement in the work of art.

'Arte Povera', that art that intentionally applies unpretentious materials, serves to examine complex relations and connections without being too much distracted from the content or the intention by a single object and its fascination. It was first practised in Italy in the sixties, but soon spread all over Europe and, in the ongoing process of methodical preciseness, in a way opened the door for 'Minimal Art' and, later, 'Concept art'.

ai raggi non contano l'intimità e l'individualità dell'uomo.« (catalogo Museum am Ostwall, Dortmund 1993, p. 185)

Accanto alle potenti, cangianti, impressionanti e imponenti videoinstallazioni dal carattere barocco Plessi spesso attinge a elementi dell'Arte Povera. L'*Arco Liquido* degli esordi, le numerose costruzioni degli armadi, la legna galleggiante riportata a riva o, come in quest'installazione, le vecchie valigie usate, tutti elementi che, inseriti come ›objets trouvés‹ o ›readymades‹, sottolineano l'aspetto dell'Arte Povera e avvicinano l'artista all'opera di Jannis Kounellis o Mario Merz. In maniera mirata Plessi cerca il richiamo di questi semplici materiali, che in sè non sono né belli né sublimi ma che vengono nobilitati dall'opera d'arte.

L'Arte Povera, l'arte che volutamente impiega materiali senza pretese, serve a tematizzare rapporti e contesti complessi senza voler deviare l'attenzione, attraverso un oggetto singolo o attraverso il suo fascino, dal contenuto e dal messaggio principale. Essa nacque in Italia negli anni sessanta per estendersi però presto in tutta l'Europa e aprì le porte in un certo modo attraverso un processo continuo di precisazione metodica alla ›Minimal Art‹ e, più tardi, alla ›Concept Art‹.

MOSAICO LIQUIDO

97001

VENEZIA 1997
COLLEZIONE PRIVATA
97001.1

FLÜSSIGES MOSAIK
Videoskulptur 1997
Stahlgehäuse mit schwenkbaren
Türen, 5 Monitore, Videorecorder,
bespielte Kassetten,
Tonaufzeichnung

LIQUID MOSAIC
Video sculpture 1997
Steel case, two doors, 5 monitors,
video recorder, recorded video
cassettes, soundrecording

MOSAICO LIQUIDO
Videoscultura 1997
Struttura di ferro nero con due
porte, 5 monitors, vhs, cassette
registrate, sonoro

Mosaico Liquido zeigt das flüssige Mosaik aus der Mainzer Installation *Fluß der Geschichte* nun in einer Vertikalen, in den Raum eines venezianischen Palazzo gestellt. Ein schrankartiges Gebilde mit zwei Türen, die sich schließen lassen, erlaubt Einblicke auf das fließende Geschehen, das sich wie ein Kaleidoskop von Augenblick zu Augenblick verändert, die alten Strukturen zerstörend und zugleich neue Strukturen schaffend. Die ganze Bewegung wird begleitet von einem Geräusch, das den Vorgang des Fließens und der Veränderung auch akustisch hörbar werden läßt, selbst wenn man den Schrank schließen würde und das Bild verborgen wäre. Ein geheimnisvoller Ton im Hintergrund, das Fließen des Wassers, gerät in Gleichklang und Harmonie mit den fließenden Kanälen Venedigs.

Mosaico Liquido *shows the liquid mosaic from the installation in Mainz, the* River of History, *now in a vertical version, placed into the room of a Venetian palace. A cabinet-like structure with two doors that can be closed allows insight into the liquid occurrences that change, like a kaleidoscope, from one moment to the next, destroying the old structures, creating new ones at the same time. All this movement is accompanied by sounds that make the process of flowing and change audible, even if one would close the cabinet, and the image were hidden. A sound full of secrets in the background, the flowing water, reaches unison and harmony with the channels flowing through Venice.*

Mosaico Liquido ripropone il mosaico dell'installazione *Il Fiume della Storia* di Magonza, qui però in una verticale disposta nella sala di un palazzo veneziano. Una costruzione simile ad un armadio a due ante che si possono chiudere consente la visione dell'evento fluente, che muta come un caleidoscopio da un momento all'altro distruggendo vecchie strutture e creandone nuove. Tutto il movimento è accompagnato da un rumore che, anche se si chiudessero le ante e svanisse l'immagine, rende acusticamente percettibile il momento dello scorrere e del cambiamento. Un suono misterioso nel sottofondo, il corso dell'acqua, si sintonizza e si armonizza con i canali di Venezia.

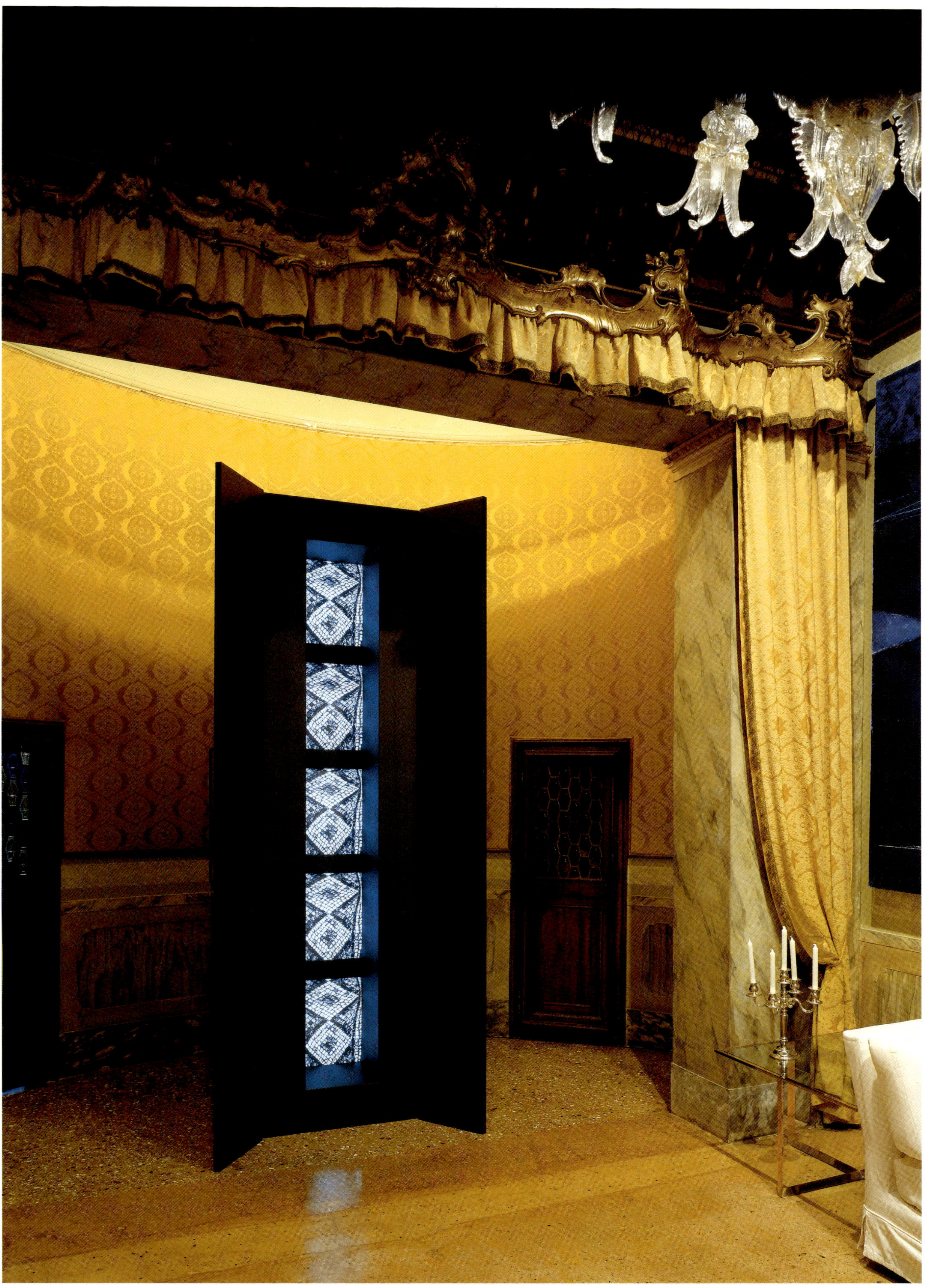

L'ARCA DELL'ARTE

98001

WIEN 1998
Kunsthistorisches Museum
98001.1

FLOSS DER KUNST
Videoskulptur 1998
Stahlrahmen, kontinuierlich
drehendaufgehängt, antike Bilder-
rahmen, Windmaschine, Segeltuch,
Diaprojektion, 28 Monitore,
2 Videorecorder, Kassetten,
Tonaufzeichnung

RAFT OF ARTS
Video sculpture 1998
Steel structure, constantly rotating
suspension, antique picture frames,
wind machine, sail, slide
projection, 28 monitors, 2 video
recorders, recorded video cassettes,
soundrecording

L'ARCA DELL'ARTE
Videoscultura 1998
Struttura di ferro, macchina
rotante, macchina di vento, vela,
cornici antichi, proiezione di
diapositive, 28 monitors, vhs,
cassette registrate, sonoro

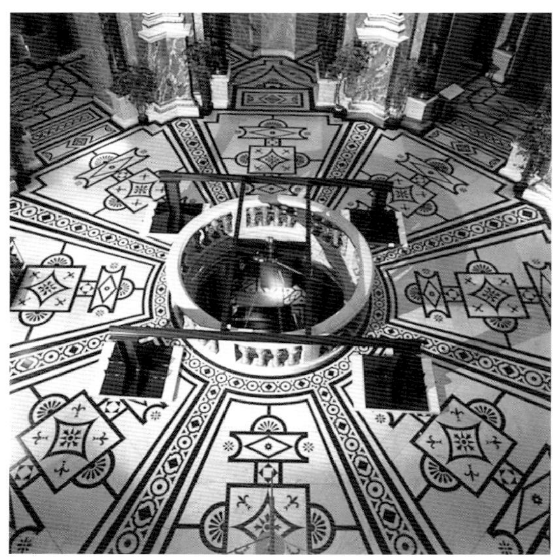

L'Arca del Arte (Das Floß der Kunst), ausgestellt im Kunsthistori-schen Museum in Wien, läßt einen deutlichen Bezug zur Kunstge-schichte erkennen. Das *Floß der Medusa* von Theodore Gericault von 1817 hat sicher Pate gestanden für dieses jüngste Werk von Fabri-zio Plessi. Schon das Gemälde von Gericault, das eine zeitgenössische Schiffskatastrophe mit realistischer Dramatik gestaltete und in Form und Inhalt ›nur‹ ein aktuelles Tagesgeschehen anstelle eines ›bedeutenden‹ Inhaltes im Sinne eines Historienbildes darstellte, war in seiner Größe von etwa fünf mal sieben Metern ein riesiges Werk; wird jedoch von Plessis Videoinstallation in den Ausmaßen noch übertroffen.

Ein Floß, hier als Stahlkonstruk-

L'Arca del Arte (The Raft of Art), exhibited in the Museum of the History of Art, shows a clear reference to art history. Theodo-re Gericault's Medusa's raft has certainly been model for this, the latest work by Fabrizio Plessi. Gericault's painting, depicting a catastrophe at sea in realistic drama, and, in form and content, showing only an actual event of that day and time, instead of an 'important' theme in the sense of a historic painting was, in its size of about five by seven metres, a huge work, surpassed, however, in its dimension by Plessi's video installation.

A raft, here executed in steel, swims on electric water (on monitors) and transports,

L'Arca dell'Arte, esposta al Kunsthistorisches Museum di Vienna, rivela un forte collega-mento con la storia dell'arte. *L'Arca di Medusa* di Theodore Gericault del 1817 ha fatto sicuramente da padrino a quest'opera più recente di Fabrizio Plessi. Il dipinto di Gericault che con drammaticità realistica raffigura il naufragio di una nave nella forma e nel contenuto di un avvenimento del giorno anziché nel contenu-to ›significativo‹ di un dipinto di storia era giá, con le sue misure di cinque per sette metri, un'opera monumentale, ma viene ancora superato nelle misure dalla videoinstallazione di Plessi.

Un'arca, qui realizzata in una

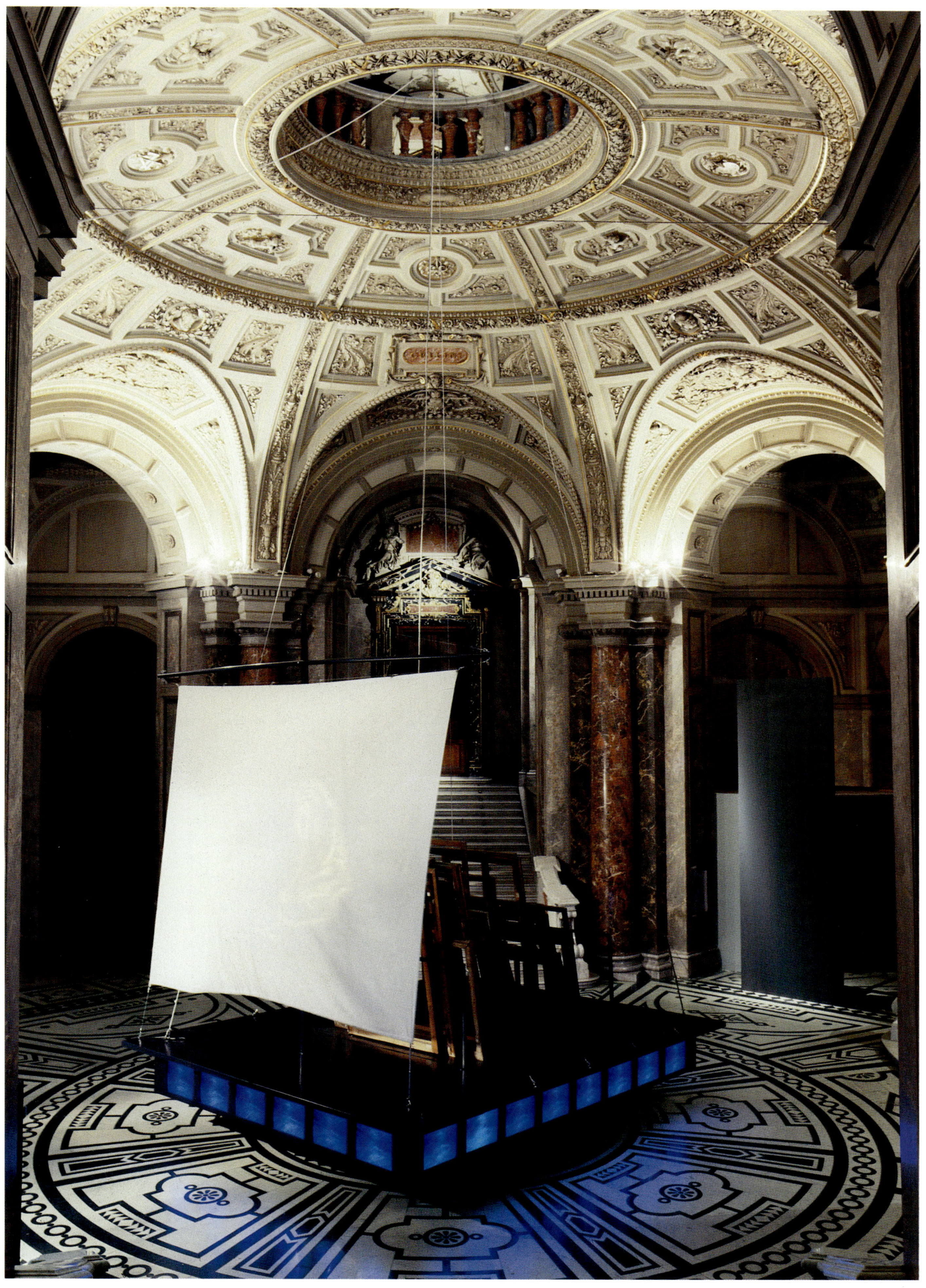

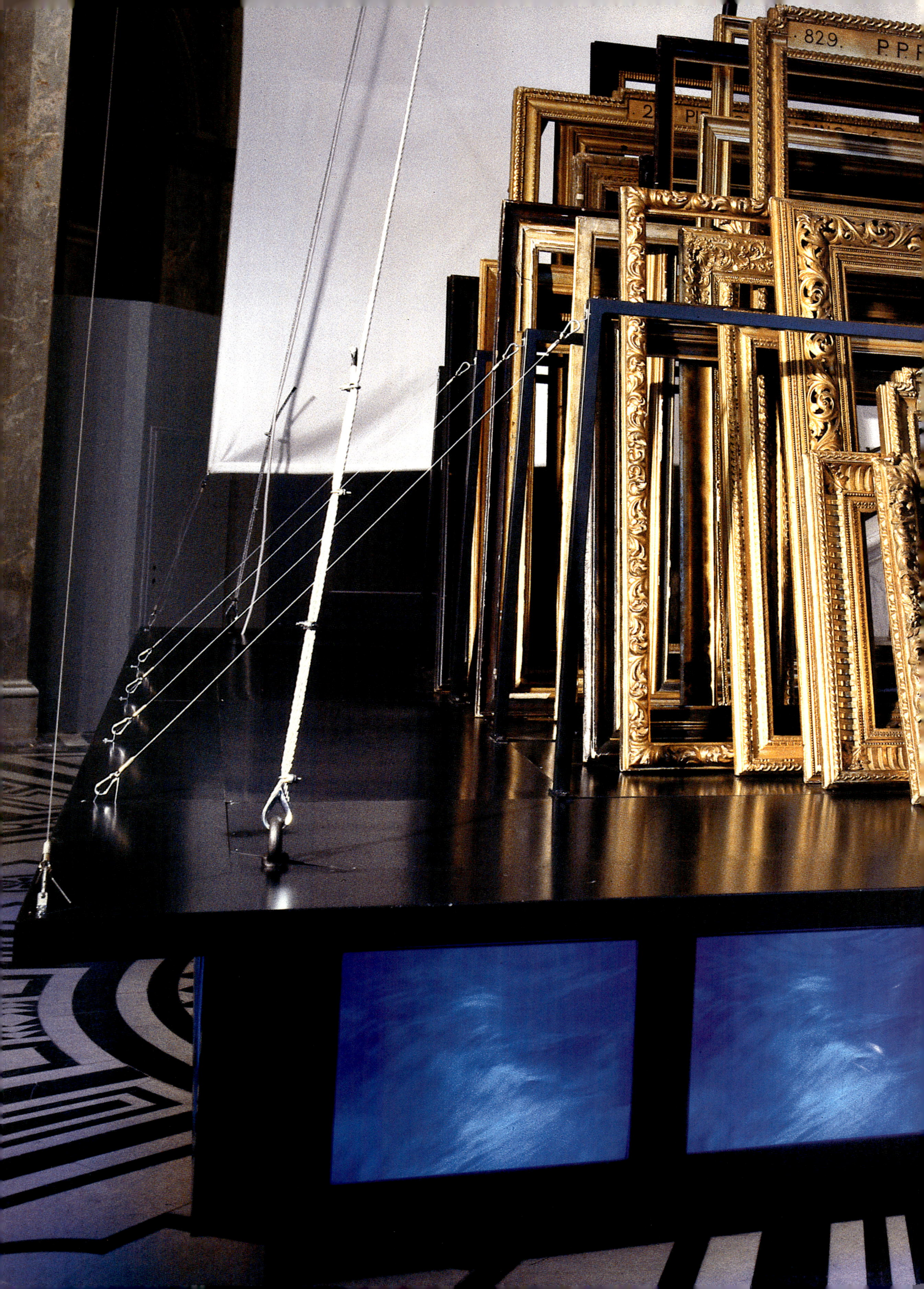
. 829.   P.P.F

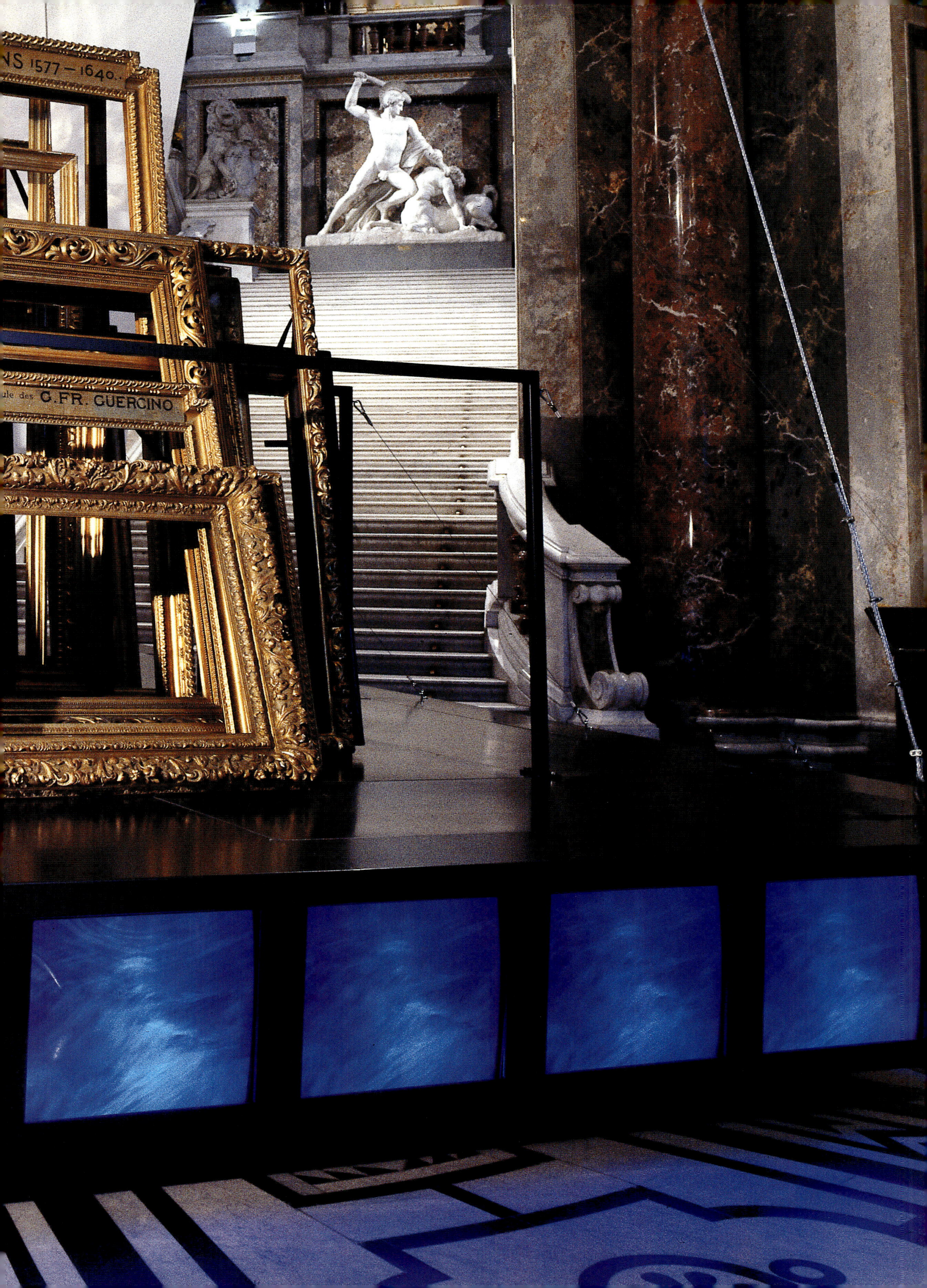
NS 1577 – 1640.
ule des G.FR. GUERCINO

tion ausgeführt, schwimmt auf einem elektronischen Wasser (in Monitoren) und transportiert anstelle von Passagieren leere, antike Bilderrahmen. Die potentiell zu diesen Rahmen gehörenden Bilder sind nur virtuell vorhanden: Sie erscheinen in wechselnden Abständen in Form von Diaprojektionen auf dem Segel. Das Segel ist dabei von einer Windmaschine aufgebläht, die auf dem Floß selbst mitgeführt wird. Die ganze Konstruktion ist aufgehängt, schwebt über den Köpfen der Betrachter und dreht sich langsam im Kreis, so, als würde ein Wind das Floß in irgendeine Richtung vorantreiben. Das Ganze ist völlig autark, da das Floß das (elektronische) Wasser, auf dem es treibt, ebenso wie den Wind, der es ›antreibt‹, mit sich führt.

Wenn Fabrizio Plessi sich seit Beginn der 90er Jahre zunehmend mit Geschichte auseinandersetzt und diese mehr und mehr in seine Videoskulpturen integriert hat, so geht er hier bei dieser Videoinstallation noch einen Schritt weiter, indem er ein deutliches Zitat aus der Kunstgeschichte verwendet und in seine Bildsprache transformiert. So werden geschichtliche Bindungen hergestellt, die zeitüberdauernd sind und damit retrospektiv und prospektiv zugleich.

Dorothea van der Koelen

instead of passengers, empty antique frames. The pictures potentially belonging to these frames are only virtually present: they appear at varying intervals in form of slide projections on the sail. The sail is filled with wind from a wind machine, carried along on the raft. The whole construction is hung up, suspended above the spectators' heads, slowly revolving as if wind would drive the raft forward in some direction. The whole is completely self-sufficient, because the raft carries the (electronic) water on which it floats as well as the wind that 'moves' it.

When, from the beginning of the nineties, Fabrizio Plessi turns more and more to history, and includes it in his video installations and sculptures, he takes a further step with this video installation by using a direct quote from the history of art, translating it into his language. In this way, historic relations are created that are timeless, being retrospective and prospective at the same time.

Dorothea van der Koelen
Translation: Heinz Bartkowski

struttura di ferro, si muove sull'acqua elettronica (dei monitors) e trasporta in luogo dei passeggeri antiche cornici vuote. I dipinti potenziali delle cornici esistono solo in modo virtuale e appaiono sulla vela ad intervalli differenti in forma di diaproiezioni. La vela è gonfiata da un ventilatore collocato sull'arca stessa. L'insieme è sospeso al di sopra delle teste degli spettatori e ruota lentamente come se un vento spingesse in qualche modo l'arca. Tutta l'installazione è autarchica in quanto l'arca porta con sè l'acqua elettronica, sulla quale si muove, e il vento che la spinge.

Dall'inizio degli anni novanta Fabrizio Plessi si occupa in maniera crescente della storia integrandola sempre di più nelle sue videoinstallazioni e videos-culture, ma in quest'opera compie un ulteriore passo trasformando una citazione della storia dell'arte in un linguaggio figurativo proprio. Così si creano collegamenti storici che si collocano al di sopra del tempo, risultando di conseguenza retrospettivi e prospettici al tempo stesso.

Dorothea van der Koelen
Traduzione: Jörg Schepers

APPENDIX

BIOGRAPHIE

1940
Fabrizio Plessi wird in Reggio Emilia geboren. Nach dem Besuch des musischen Lyzeums studiert er an der Kunstakademie in Venedig, wo er später den Lehrstuhl für Malerei erhält.

1968
Bereits in diesem Jahr ist das Wasser das Hauptthema seiner Arbeiten; er behandelt es in Installationen, Filmen, Videos und Performances.

1970/72
Seine Werke werden im Experimentalpavillon auf der Biennale von Venedig 1970 und auf der Biennale von 1972 ausgestellt.

1975-1983
Plessi zeigt seine Arbeiten bereits in öffentlichen Räumen, etwa im Palazzo dei Diamanti in Ferrara, in der Städtischen Galerie im Lenbachhaus, München, im Internationaal Cultureel Centrum Antwerpen (1975, 1978 und 1980) und im Palais des Beaux Arts in Brüssel (1975 und 1983).

1978
Er wird zur Sonderausstellung *L'Immagine Provocata* der Biennale von Venedig eingeladen.

1980
Er nimmt mit seinem Film *Liquid Movie* am Filmfestival von Venedig teil und erhält den Preis ›Città di Milano‹.

1981
Mit dem in Frankreich produzierten Werk *Underwater* wird er zum Filmfestival von Venedig eingeladen; damit werden erstmals elektronische Mittel in eine Filmbiennale eingeführt.

1982
Plessis gesamtes Videoœuvre wird im Centre Pompidou in Paris gezeigt. Seitdem thematisieren seine Arbeiten die natürliche Umwelt mit den Möglichkeiten des Videos, unter Einbeziehung räumlicher Strukturen. Die illusionistische Beziehung zwischen der Realität des flüssigen Elements und seiner

BIOGRAPHICAL NOTES

1940
Fabrizio Plessi is born in Reggio Emilia. After graduating from the College of Art, he studies at the Academy of Fine Arts in Venice, where he is later appointed professor for painting.

1968
Since this year, water is the primary leitmotif of his work, which includes installations, films, videos and performances.

1970/1972
His works are presented in the experimental pavilion at the Biennale in Venice 1970 and at the Biennale in Venice 1972.

1975-1983
Plessi begins exhibiting his works in various public institutions, including the Palazzo dei Diamanti in Ferrara, the Städtische Galerie im Lenbachhaus in Munich, the Internationaal Cultureel Centrum in Antwerp (1975, 1978 and 1980) and the Palais des Beaux Arts in Brussels (1975 and 1983).

1978
He is invited to participate in the exhibition L'Immagine Provocata *at the Biennale in Venice*

1980
He participates in the Venice Film Festival with his film Liquid Movie, *for which he is awarded the 'Città di Milano'.*

1981
He is invited to participate in the Venice Film Festival with his work Underwater, *produced in France. It's the first time that electronic media are included in a film festival.*

1982
Plessi's complete video œuvre is presented in the Centre Pompidou in Paris. Since then, his works focus on the 'natural environment', exploring the possibilities of video and incorporating three-dimensional structures. The illusionist relationship between the reality and representation of flowing

BIOGRAFIA

1940
Fabrizio Plessi nasce a Reggio Emilia. Compie i suoi studi al Liceo artistico e all'Accademia delle Belle Arti di Venezia dove in seguito sarà titolare della cattedra di pittura.

1968
Già nel quest'anno il tema centrale del suo lavoro e l'acqua, presente in installazioni, films, videotapes e performances.

1970/72
Le sue opere vengono esposte al padiglione sperimentale della Biennale di Venezia nel 1970 e alla successiva Biennale del 1972.

1975-1983
Plessi ha già presentato le sue opere in spazi pubblici come il Palazzo dei Diamanti di Ferrara, la Städtische Galerie im Lenbachhaus di Monaco, l'Internationaal Cultureel Centrum di Anversa (1975-1978-1980) e il Palais des Beaux Arts di Bruxelles (1975, 1983).

1978
È invitato alla Biennale di Venezia per la fotografia nella mostra speciale *L'Immagine Provocata.*

1980
Partecipa al Festival del Cinema di Venezia con il film *Liquid Movie* vincendo il Premio ›Città di Milano‹.

1981
Plessi è invitato al Festival del Cinema di Venezia con *Underwater*, una produzione francese: il mezzo elettronico viene così ammesso a una biennale cinematografica.

1982
La sua completa opera video viene presentata al Centre Pompidou, Beaubourg di Parigi. Da quest'anno in poi, i suoi lavori toccano da vicino la natura ambientale delle possibilità del video, incorporando strutture tridimensionali. Il rapporto illusionistico fra rappresentazione e

Darstellung wird durch die extremen technischen Möglichkeiten der mechanischen und elektronischen Wiedergabe noch verstärkt.

1984
Plessis Installationen werden auf der 41. Biennale von Venedig und im Musée d'Art Contemporain in Villeneuve d'Ascq (Lille) gezeigt.

1985
In der Rotonda della Besana in Mailand präsentiert Plessi seine erste große Retrospektive in Italien (*Plessi - Video Going*, Katalog Electa), sie gilt als die erste italienische Ausstellung zum Thema raumbezogene Videoinstallationen.

1986
Plessi vertritt Italien auf der 42. Biennale von Venedig, für die er eine seiner wichtigsten Arbeiten, *Bronx*, schafft.

1987
Plessi zeigt auf der documenta 8 in Kassel seine monumentale Installation *Roma*, die ihn endgültig international bekannt macht. Im selben Jahr wird er in Bologna mit dem internationalen Preis ›L'immagine elettronica‹ ausgezeichnet. Ebenfalls 1987 entwirft er das Bühnenbild für Enzo Cosimis Ballett *Sciame*, das das Festival von Rovereto eröffnet, und zeigt anläßlich des Festivals von Avignon eine große Schau seiner Videoinstallationen in Cavaillon.

1988
Im Museo Español de Arte Cotemporáneo in Madrid findet eine große Retrospektive mit vierzehn Installationen statt. Im selben Jahr ist im Palacio Sástago in Zaragoza die Ausstellung *Palacio Electrónico* zu sehen. Ebenfalls 1988 stellt Plessi in der Neuen Galerie in Linz (Österreich) eine Serie von Videoinstallationen mit dem Titel *Videoland - Videolinz* aus. Zur Eröffnung des Centro per l'Arte Contemporaneo Luigi Pecci in Prato entsteht außerdem die Arbeit *Roma II*. In den Jahren 1987 und 1988 entwirft er die Ausstattung für das Fernsehprogramm ›Immagina‹ bei RAI Uno.

elements is additionally intensified by the extreme technical possibilities of mechanical and electronic reproduction.

1984
Plessi's installations are exhibited at the XLI Biennale in Venice and the Musée d'Art Contemporain in Villeneuve d'Ascq (Lille).

1985
In the Rotonda della Besana in Milan, Plessi presents his first large-scale retrospective in Italy (Plessi - Video Going, catalogue by Electa). This is the first Italian exhibition on the theme of environmental video installations.

1986
He represents Italy at the XLII Biennale in Venice, for which he creates Bronx, one of his most important video instaallations.

1987
Plessi exhibits his monumental installation Roma at the documenta 8 in Kassel, as a result of which he ultimately attains international acclaim. In the same year, he is awarded the international prize 'L'immagine elettronica' in Bologna. He also designs the scenery for Enzo Cosimi's ballet Sciame, which inaugurates the festival of Rovereto. Also in 1987, a comprehensive exhibition of his video installations is presented in Cavaillon as part of the festival of Avignon.

1988
A large-scale retrospective with fourteen installations is presented in the Museo Español de Arte Contemporáneo in Madrid. In the same year, the exhibition Palacio Electrónico takes place in the Palacio Sástago in Zaragoza. Also in 1988, Plessi exhibits a series of video installations with the title Videoland - Videolinz in the Neue Galerie in Linz (Austria). For the opening of the Centro per l'Arte Contemporanea Luigi Pecci in Prato, he creates the work Roma II. In 1987 and 1988, he designs the sets for the television program 'Immagina', produced by RAI Uno.

realtà dell'elemento liquido compare amplificato nelle estreme possibilità tecnologiche della riproduzione meccanica ed elettronica.

1984
Le sue installazioni vengono esposte nel alla XLI Biennale di Venezia e al Musée d'Art Contemporain di Villeneuve d'Ascq (Lille).

1985
Plessi presenta la sua prima grande antologica in Italia (*Plessi - Video Going*, catalogo Electa) alla Rotonda della Besana di Milano, che si può considerare la prima mostra di videoinstallazioni ambientali in Italia.

1986
Rappresenta l'Italia alla XLII Biennale di Venezia e crea per l'occasione una delle sue opere più significative: *Bronx*.

1987
Alla ›documenta 8‹ di Kassel Plessi presenta la monumentale installazione *Roma* che lo rende definitivamente noto a livello internazionale. A Bologna vince il premio internazionale ›L'immagine elettronica‹ e crea le scenografie per la coreografia di Enzo Cosimi *Sciame*, che inaugura il Festival di Rovereto. Dello stesso anno è l'ampia rassegna delle sue videoinstallazioni a Cavaillon in occasione del Festival d'Avignone.

1988
A Madrid al Museo Español de Arte Contemporáneo è presente con una grande retrospettiva di ben quattordici installazioni. Dello stesso anno è la mostra *Palacio Electrónico* al Palacio Sástago di Zaragoza. Sempre nel 1988 espone alla Neue Galerie di Linz una serie di videoinstallazioni dal titolo *Videoland - Videolinz*. A Prato inoltre in quell'anno per l'inaugurazione del Centro per l'Arte Contemporanea Luigi Pecci, crea l'opera *Roma II*. Durante il 1987 e il 1988 si occupa delle scenografie del programma televisivo ›Immagina‹ per la RAI Uno a Roma.

1989
Plessi wird vom Kölnischen Kunstverein zu der Ausstellung *Video-Skulptur* mit einem radikal neuen Werk, *Materia Prima*, eingeladen. Im selben Jahr finden die große Ausstellung *Videosal* im Palau Solleric in Palma de Mallorca und die Ausstellung *Movimenti Catodici* im Palazzo dei Diamanti in Ferrara statt. Im selben Jahr nimmt er an der Ausstellung *Borealis* im Louisiana Museum in Humlebaek (Dänemark) teil und an *Artek*, der Biennale von Nagoya Japan). Während dieses Jahres entwirft er das Bühnenbild und die Kostüme für die Oper *The Fall of Icarus* (Choreographie: Frederic Flamand, Musik: Michael Nyman) an der Opéra Nationale ›La Monnaie‹ in Brüssel. Im Auftrag von Prato Trade entsteht die monumentale elektronische Mühle *Tempo Liquido* für das Centro Pecci in Prato.

1990
Anläßlich seines 50. Geburtstags widmet ihm seine Geburtsstadt Reggio Emilia eine große Retrospektive im Museum, auf dem Foro Boario und auf dem großen Platz der Cavallerizza, wo Plessi zum erstenmal seine *Armadi* ausstellt.

1991
Für das Museum moderner Kunst, Stiftung Ludwig in Wien entsteht die große Arbeit *Roma II*. Aus demselben Jahr stammt die Installation *Porfido a Pergine* eigens für das Schloß. In Palma de Mallorca, in der Stiftung ›Sa Nostra‹, findet eine umfassende, der Typologie der Insel und ihren Materialien gewidmete Ausstellung von Fotografien und großen Projekten statt.

1992
Plessi arbeitet erneut mit Frederic Flamand zusammen; es entsteht das elektronische Bühnenbild für das Werk *Titanic*, das in den imposanten Räumen des Musée de l'Industrie in Charleroi gezeigt wird. Im selben Jahr leitet er für die UNESCO einen Workshop zum Thema ›Babel‹, an dem zwanzig junge Künstler aus verschiedenen Ländern teilnehmen.

1989
Plessi is invited by the Kölnischer Kunstverein (Cologne) to the exhibition Video-Skulptur, *for which he creates the radical new work* Materia Prima. *In the same year, the large-scale exhibition* Videosal *is presented in the Palau Solleric in Palma de Mallorca, followed by the exhibition* Movimenti Catodici *in the Palazzo dei Diamanti in Ferrara. Also in 1989, Plessi participates in the exhibition* Borealis *in the Louisiana Museum in Humlebaek (Denmark), as well as in* Artek, *the Biennial of Nagoya (Japan). During this year, he designs the scenery and costumes for the opera* The Fall of Icarus *(choreography by Frederic Flamand, music by Michael Nyman), presented in the Opéra Nationale 'La Monnaie' in Brussels. Commissioned by Prato Trade, he creates the monumental electronic water mill* Tempo Liquido *for the Centro Pecci in Prato.*

1990
On the occasion of his fiftieth birthday, his hometown of Reggio Emilia honours him with a large retrospective in the municipal museum, on the Foro Boario, and on the large public square Cavallerizza, where Plessi exhibits his Armadi *for the first time.*

1991
The large work Roma II *is created for the Museum Moderner Kunst, Stiftung Ludwig, Vienna. Also the installation* Porfido a Pergine *is created specially for the palace in Pergine. In Palma de Mallorca, a comprehensive exhibition dedicated to the typology and materials of the island and including photographs and large-scale projects takes place in the foundation 'Sa Nostra'*

1992
Plessi collaborates once again with Frederic Flamand, creating the electronic scenery for Titanic, *which is presented in the impressive space of the Musée de l'Industrie in Charleroi. In the same year, he conducts a workshop for UNESCO on the theme of 'Babel', in which twenty young artists from various countries participate.*

1989
Plessi è invitato alla mostra *Video-Skulptur* al Kunstverein di Colonia con una nuova creazione radicale dal titolo *Materia Prima*. Dello stesso anno sono la grande mostra *Videosal* al Palau Solleric di Palma de Mallorca e la mostra *Movimenti Catodici* al Palazzo dei Diamanti di Ferrara. Sempre nel 1989 partecipa alla mostra *Borealis* al Louisiana Museum di Humlebaek in Danimarca e ad *Artek*, Biennale di Nagoya, in Giappone. Durante questo anno disegna le scenografie e i costumi per l'opera *The Fall of Icarus* in collaborazione con Frederic Flamand per le coreografie e Michael Nyman per la musica, produzione dell'Opéra Nationale ›La Monnaie‹ di Bruxelles. Crea il monumentale mulino elettronico *Tempo Liquido*, commissionato da Prato Trade per il Centro Pecci di Prato.

1990
Iin occasione del suo cinquantesimo compleanno la sua città natale Reggio Emilia gli dedica una grande antologica nel museo, nel Foro Boario e nell'ampio spazio della Cavallerizza dove Plessi presenta per la prima volta i suoi *Armadi*.

1991
Crea la grande installazione *Roma II* per il Museum moderner Kunst, Stiftung Ludwig di Vienna. Dello stesso anno è l'installazione *Porfido a Pergine* espressamente studiata per il castello, e la complessa mostra di fotografie e grandi progetti alla fondazione ›Sa Nostra‹ di Palma de Mallorca dedicata alla tipologia dell'isola e a i suoi materiali.

1992
Crea le scenografie elettroniche per la seconda collaborazione con Frederic Flamand *Titanic*, presentato nello spettacolare spazio del Musée de l'Industrie di Charleroi. Dirige un work-shop per l'UNESCO con la partecipazione di venti giovani artisti internazionali sul tema ›Babele‹.

1993

Nach einer Indienreise entsteht die Videoinstallation *Bombay-Bombay* für das Museum Ludwig in Köln. Das Museum am Ostwall in Dortmund widmet Plessi eine große Retrospektive, in der zwölf historische Videoinstallationen gezeigt werden. Für das Caffè Florian in Venedig, entsteht anläßlich der Biennale die Auftragsarbeit *Cristalli Liquidi*. Für das berühmte Live-Konzert von Luciano Pavarotti im New Yorker Central Park entstehen die elektronischen Bühnenbilder. In der Fundació Miró in Barcelona wird Plessis Ausstellung *Bombay-Bombay* eröffnet, und es entsteht die monumentale Videoinstallation *Liquid Time*, die von Philips für die Messe in Berlin produziert und vom Zentrum für Kunst und Medientechnologie in Karlsruhe erworben wird. Von der UNESCO in Paris wird Plessi mit der Miró-Medaille ausgezeichnet.

1994

Er arbeitet zum drittenmal zusammen mit Frederic Flamand: Für die Oper *Ex Machina* werden unter Plessis Leitung elektronische und virtuelle Bühnenbilder von den Studenten der Kunsthochschule für Medien in Köln realisiert. Er wird zur internationalen Sonderausstellung auf der Biennale von São Paulo in Brasilien eingeladen und zeigt in der Neuen Galerie in Linz eine Ausstellung mit Zeichnungen und Projekten auf Papier aus den Jahren 1976-1993.

1994-1995

Plessi gestaltet die elektronische Ausstattung für das Programm ›Studio Moor‹ des deutschen Fernsehsenders Premiere mit Videoinstallationen, die sich jeden Monat ändern.

1995

Ex Machina wird auf der Biennale von Venedig anläßlich deren hundertjährigen Bestehens gezeigt. Im selben Jahr entstehen zwei neue Videoinstallationen für die Fundació Pilar i Joan Miró in Palma de Mallorca, die *Fuochi Fatui*, von denen eine direkt in Mirós Atelier zwischen seinen Arbeiten zu sehen ist. 1995 findet ferner eine große Übersichtsausstellung in der

---

1993

After a journey to India, the video installation Bombay-Bombay *is created for the Museum Ludwig in Cologne. In the same year, the Museum am Ostwall in Dortmund honours him with a large retrospective, in which twelve historical video installations are presented. Also created is* Cristalli Liquidi, *a work commissioned by the Caffè Florian in Venice and presented in the café on the occasion of the Biennale. In the same year, the electronic stage design is created for the famous live concert of Luciano Pavarotti in Central Park in New York. Plessi's exhibition* Bombay-Bombay *is opened in the Fundació Miró in Barcelona. The monumental video installation* Liquid Time *is produced by Philips for the trade fair in Berlin and later acquired by the Centre for Art and Media Technology in Karlsruhe. Plessi is awarded the Miró Medal from the UNESCO in Paris.*

1994

He collaborates for the third time with Frederic Flamand: For the opera Ex Machina, *electronic and virtual scenery is created by the students of the Academy for Media Arts in Cologne, under Plessi's supervision. He is invited to participate in an international exhibition at the Biennial in São Paulo, Brazil. In the same year, an exhibition takes place in the Neue Galerie in Linz (Austria) which includes drawings and projects on paper from 1976 - 1993.*

1994-1995,

Plessi designs the electronic scenery for the television program 'Studio Moor', produced by the German broadcasting company Premiere. Each month, a new video installation is created.

1995

Ex Machina *is presented in Venice, on the occasion of 100th anniversary of the Biennale. In the same year, two new video installations, the* Fuochi Fatui, *are created for the Fundació Miró in Palma de Mallorca. One of these is presented in Miró's studio alongside works by the late artist. Also in 1995, a large-scale retrospective exhibition takes place in the Rocca Paolina in*

1993

Dopo un viaggio in India nasce nel la videoinstallazione *Bombay-Bombay* per il Museo Ludwig di Colonia. Dello stesso anno è la vasta antologica *Plessi - Retrospektive* che il Museum am Ostwall di Dortmund gli dedica con dodici videoinstallazioni storiche. Sempre del 1993 è *Cristalli Liquidi* opera commissionata ed esposta al Caffè Florian di Venezia in occasione della Biennale. Per il celebre concerto live di Luciano Pavarotti al Central Park di New York, Plessi crea le scenografie elettroniche. Si inaugura a Barcellona alla Fundació Joan Miró la mostra *Bombay-Bombay* e la monumentale videoinstallazione *Liquid Time* prodotta dalla Philips per la Fiera di Berlino ed acquistata dal Zentrum für Kunst und Medientechnologie di Karlsruhe. Sempre nel 1993 Plessi viene insignito della medaglia ›Miró‹ dell'UNESCO a Parigi.

1994

Collabora per la terza volta con Frederic Flamand all'opera *Ex Machina* con le scenografie elettroniche e virtuali realizzate sotto la sua direzione dagli studenti della Kunsthochschule für Medien di Colonia. È invitato alla Mostra speciale internazionale della Bienal de São Paulo in Brasile. Nello stesso anno è la mostra di disegni storici e progetti su carta dal 1976 al 1993, presso la Neue Galerie di Linz.

1994-1995

Fabrizio Plessi crea le scenografie elettroniche per la trasmissione ›Studio Moor‹ del canale televisivo tedesco Premiere, con videoinstallazioni che cambiano ogni mese.

1995

L'opera *Ex Machina* è invitata come evento speciale alla Biennale di Venezia del Centenario. Sempre nel 1995 crea le due videoinstallazioni *Fuochi Fatui* per la Fundació Pilar i Joan Miró a Palma de Mallorca, di cui una è ambientata eccezionalmente nello studio stesso di Miró, tra le sue opere. Ancora del 1995 è la sua grande antologica alla Rocca Paolina

Rocca Paolina in Perugia statt, für die Plessi die monumentale Videoinstallation *L'Anima della Pietra* schafft.

1996
Es entstehen einige seiner bisher aufwendigsten und bedeutensten Installationen, darunter: *Il Fiume della Storia* für das Landesmuseum in Mainz, *Fez-Fez* für das Mausoleum in Graz, *Acquedotto Elettronico* für den Heidelberger Kunstverein und *Mysterium Wein* für das Historische Museum der Pfalz in Speyer. Anläßlich der Eröffnung der ›Città della scienza‹ (Stadt der Wissenschaft) der IDIS Stiftung schafft Plessi in Neapel die eindrucksvolle Videoskulptur *Movimenti Catodici Barocchi*.

1997
Bei Dumont erscheint das bedeutende Buch *Plessi, Progetti del Mondo*, das 40 Reisen des Künstlers gewidmet ist, Grundlagen seiner Ideen für Videoinstallationen. Das Buch wird erstmals in der Peggy Guggenheim Stiftung in Venedig, während der Vernissage der Biennale, vorgestellt.

1998
Neben dem Projekt *Arca dell'Arte*, eigens für das Kunsthistorische Museum in Wien geschaffen, findet eine große Einzelausstellung im Guggenheim Museum SoHo in New York statt, die im Herbst vom La Jolla Museum of Contemporary Art in San Diego übernommen und 1999 als Wanderausstellung in anderen wichtige amerikanischen Museen zu sehen sein wird.

Seit 1990 ist Plessi Professor für ›Humanisierung der Technologien‹ an der Kunsthochschule für Medien in Köln und seit 1994 Inhaber des neuen Lehrstuhls ›Elektronische Szenographie‹ ebendort.

Plessi lebt und arbeitet in Venedig.

Perugia, for which Plessi creates the monumental video installation L'Anima della Pietra.

1996
He creates some of his most complex and imposing installations, among them: Il Fiume della Storia *for the Landesmuseum in Mainz,* Fez-Fez *for the Mausoleum in Graz,* Acquedotto Elettronico *for the Kunstverein in Heidelberg and* Wine Mystery *for the Historisches Museum der Pfalz in Speyer. The spectacular video sculpture* Movimenti Catodici Barocchi *was created by Plessi on the occasion of the inauguration of 'Città della scienza' (City of Science), established by IDIS Foundation.*

1997
Dumont publishes the great book Plessi, Progetti del Mondo, *dedicated to 40 travels of the artist, which originated just as many ideas for video installations. The volume is introduced at Peggy Guggenheim Foundation in Venice, at the opening of the Biennale.*

1998
In addition to the project Arca dell'Arte, *that was specially created for the Kunsthistorisches Museum in Vienna, the programm for this year includes a huge one man show at Guggenheim Museum SoHo in New York. In autumn the San Diego Museum of Contemporary Art La Jolla will take over this exhibition and in 1999 it will itinerate to several important American museums.*

Since 1990, Plessi holds the chair of professor for the 'Humanisation of technologies' at the Academy of Media Arts in Cologne; and since 1994, he is also professor for 'Electronic Scenography' at the same academy.

Plessi lives and works in Venice.

di Perugia per la quale crea la monumentale videoinstallazione *L'Anima della Pietra*.

1996
Crea alcune delle più complesse ed imponenti installazioni tra lui: *Il Fiume della Storia* per il Landesmuseum di Mainz, *Fez-Fez* per il Mausoleum di Graz, *Acquedotto Elettronico* per il Kunstverein di Heidelberg e *Mysterium Wein* per l'Historisches Museum der Pfalz a Speyer. Infine, sempre del 1996 è la spettacolare videoscultura *Movimenti Catodici Barocchi* che Plessi crea a Napoli in occasione dell'apertura della città della scienza alla fondazione IDIS.

1997
Per le edizioni Dumont, esce il grande libro *Plessi, Progetti del Mondo* dedicato a quaranta viaggi che hanno suscitato all'artista idee per altretante videoinstallazioni. Il volume è presentato in anteprima alla Fondazione Peggy Guggenheim di Venezia durante la vernice della Biennale.

1998
Oltre all'*Arca dell'Arte* appositamente creata per il Kunsthistorisches Museum di Vienna, nel 1998 è in programma una sua vasta personale al Guggenheim Museum SoHo di New York che proseguirà in autunno per il Museum of Contemporary Art La Jolla di San Diego in California. La mostra itinerante nel 1999 toccherà altri importanti musei americani.

Dal 1990 è professore di ›Umanizzazione delle tecnologie‹ alla Kunsthochschule für Medien di Colonia e dal 1994 è titolare della nuova cattedra di ›Scenografie elettroniche‹ presso la stessa istituzione.

Fabrizio Plessi vive e lavora a Venezia.

AUSSTELLUNGEN (AUSWAHL)
SELECTED SHOWS
MOSTRE (SELEZIONE)

1962
Venezia (I) · Galleria Il Canale
Trento (I) · Galleria Argentario

1963
Bologna (I) · Galleria 2000

1964
Venezia (I) · Galleria Gritti
London (GB) · St. Martin's Gallery
Treviso (I) · Galleria Giraldo

1965
Milano (I) · Galleria Sebastiani
Torino (I) · Galleria Il Punto

1967
Bologna (I) · Galleria De Foscherari
Houston, Tx (USA) · Austin State
College
Venezia (I) · Galleria Il Cavallino
Macerata (I) · Galleria L'Arco

1969
Padova (I) · Galleria La Chiocciola
Lecco (I) · Galleria Stefanoni

1970
Vicenza (I) · Galleria Ghelfi
Houston, Tx (USA) · Austin State
College

1971
Roma (I) · Galleria Piattelli
Milano (I) · Galleria Vinciana
Torino (I) · Galleria Il Punto
Brescia (I) · Galleria S. Michele
Bergamo (I) · Galleria Modi

1972
London (GB) · D.M. Gallery
Milano (I) · Studio Soldano
Varazze (I) · Galleria Carbini
Paris (F) · Galerie Lara Vincy
Bruxelles (B) · Galerie Alexandre

1973
Milano (I) · Galleria Vinciana
Paris (F) · Galerie Lara Vincy
Mantova (I) · Galleria Il Chiodo
Pavia (I) · Università, Collegio Cairoli

1974
Padova (I) · Galleria La Chiocciola
Milano (I) · Centro Rizzoli
Freiburg (D) · Galerie Regio
Treviso (I) · Museo Casa da Noal
Roma (I) · Studio Condotti
Ferrara (I) · Museo Palazzo dei
Diamanti
Strasbourg (F) · Galerie Expression
München (D) · Städtische Galerie im
Lenbachhaus
Madrid (E) · Grupo Quince
Udine (I) · Galleria Plurima
Paris (F) · Galerie Lara Vincy
Hertogenbosch (NL) · De Moriaan
Museum

1975
Alessandria (I) · Comune di Alessandria
Amsterdam (NL) · Jurka Galerie
Torino (I) · Galleria Centro
Bruxelles (B) · Galerie Micha: *Christo,
Oppenheim, Plessi*
Roma (I) · Festival: *Beat '72*
Genova (I) · Galleria Cesarea
Trieste (I) · Galleria Tommaseo
Bruxelles (B) · Palais des Beaux-Arts
Antwerpen (B) · Internationaal
Cultureel Centrum - ICC
Mantova (I) · Galleria Il Chiodo
Paris (F) · 9ᵉ Biennale
Neuenkirchen (D) · Galerie Falazik

1976
New York, Ny (USA) · James Yu Gallery
Udine (I) · Galleria Plurima
Bremen (D) · Festival: *Pro Musica Nova*
Karlsruhe (D) · Badischer Kunstverein
Bologna (I) · Arte Fiera with Galerie
Lara Vincy and Studio Soldano
New York, Ny (USA) · Intermedia
Foundation
Genova (I) · Anagalleria Opera
Como (I) · *Autunno Musicale*
Milano (I) · Studio Marconi

1977
Kiel (D) · Kunsthalle zu Kiel
Ferrara (I) · Sala Polivalente
Padova (I) · Images 70
Bochum (D) · Galerie Inge Baecker
Hagen (D) · Karl Ernst Osthaus
Museum
Venezia (I) · Palazzo delle Prigioni
Cesena (I) · Comune di Cesena
Essen (D) · Folkwang Museum
Cervia (I) · Magazzini del Sale

Paris (F) · Musée d'Art Moderne de la
Ville de Paris
Milano (I) · Studio Marconi
Bruxelles (B) · Palais des Beaux-Arts

1978
Aachen (D) · Neue Galerie Sammlung
Ludwig
Antwerpen (B) · Internationaal
Cultureel Centrum - ICC
Milano (I) · Galleria Vinciana
Ferrara (I) · Sala Polivalente
Liubljana (SLO) · Mala Galerija
Genève (CH) · Galerie Gaetan
Milano (I) · Studio d'Ars
Venezia (I) · Palazzo Grassi
Treviso (I) · Chiesa di S. Teonisto:
L'Acqua e l'Estasi
Karlsruhe (D) · Badischer Kunstverein
Paris (F) · Galerie Lara Vincy
Venezia (I) · IXL Biennale di Venezia

1979
München (D) · Städtische Galerie im
Lenbachhaus
La Spezia (I) · Comune di La Spezia
New York, Ny (USA) · The Kitchen
Lucca (I) · Galleria Guerrieri
Prato (I) · Teatro Magnolfi
Kraków (PL) · Galeria Pawilon
Duisburg (D) · Wilhelm Lehmbruck
Museum
Venezia (I) · Palazzo Grassi
Aachen (D) · Neue Galerie Sammlung
Ludwig
Ferrara (I) · Sala Polivalente
Essen (D) · Folkwang Museum
Firenze (I) · Studio Il Moro

1980
Berlin (D) · Akademie der Künste
Wien (A) · Modern Art Galerie
München (D) · Dany Keller Galerie
Milano (I) · Palazzo Reale
Bremen (D) · Festival: *Pro Musica
Nova*
La Spezia (I) · Comune di La Spezia
Rotterdam (NL) · Rotterdamse
Kunststichting
Milano (I) · Studio Marconi
Linz (A) · Neue Galerie der Stadt Linz
Antwerpen (B) · Internationaal
Cultureel Centrum - ICC
Venezia (I) · XL Biennale di Venezia
Bonn (D) · Rheinisches
Landesmuseum
Utrecht (NL) · Centraal Museum

1981
Milano (I) · Centro Ricerca per il
Teatro - CRT
Lyon (F) · Frigo: *Water Wind*
Lyon (F) · Performance Festival:
Canubis
Venezia (I) · Biennale Internazionale
Cinema
Martina Franca (I) · Teatro d'Artista
Heidelberg (D) · Heidelberger
Kunstverein
Milano (I) · *Cinema Lirico*
Montréal (CAN) · Festival International
Cinéma
Salerno (I) · Festival Cinema
Milano (I) · La Triennale
Padova (I) · Museo Civico
Asolo (I) · Festival Cinema d'Arte
Ferrara (I) · Sala Polivalente

1982
Treviso (I) · Palazzo Scotti
Paris (F) · Galerie Lara Vincy
Montecatini (I) · Festival Cinema
Oberhausen (D) · Kurzfilm-Festival
Paris (F) · Centre Georges Pompidou
Salsomaggiore (I) · *Festival Cinema*
Pistoia (I) · Centro Marino Marini
Lyon (F) · Performance Festival:
Au fil des fleuves
Ravenna (I) · Festival Cinema
Venezia (I) · Biennale Cinema
Lyon (F) · Elac
Milano (I) · *Teatro Lirico*
Edinburgh (GB) · Richard de Marco
Gallery
Caen (F) · *Mixage*
Napoli (I) · Banco S. Spirito
Ferrara (I) · Sala Polivalente

1983
Bruxelles (B) · Palais des Beaux-Arts
Bologna (I) · Arte Fiera
Charleroi (B) · Palais des Beaux Arts
Bologna (I) · Galleria d'Arte Moderna
Milano (I) · Teatro Poliziano
Paris (F) · Galerie Lara Vincy
Salsomaggiore (I) · Incontri Cinema
Heidelberg (D) · Heidelberger
Kunstverein
Montecatini (I) · Festival Cinema
San Sebastián (E) · Festival Cinema
Trieste (I) · Centro Culturale Planetario
München (D) · Städtische Galerie im
Lenbachhaus: *Aktuell '83*
Grenoble (F) · Musée de Grenoble

1984
Marl (D) · Skulpturenmuseum
Glaskasten
Villeneuve d'Ascq (F) · Musée du Nord
Ferrara (I) · Galleria d'Arte Moderna
Freiburg (D) · Kunstverein Freiburg
Venezia (I) · XLI Biennale di Venezia
Tokyo (J) · Image Forum
Locarno (CH) · Festival
Bologna (I) · Galleria d'Arte Moderna:
Immagine Elettronica

1985
Milano (I) · Rotonda della Besana:
Plessi Video Going

1986
Bologna (I) · Galleria d'Arte Moderna
Barcelona (E) · Metronom
London (GB) · ICA
Venezia (I) · XLII Biennale di Venezia:
Bronx
Roma (I) · XI Quadriennale d'Arte
Trieste (I) · Centro Culturale Planetario
Hannover (D) · Art Ware
Ferrara (I) · Sala Polivalente: *U-Tape*

1987
Bologna (I) · Arte Fiera
Ravenna (I) · Pinacoteca Comunale:
Disegnata
Torino (I) · Mole Antonelliana:
Lo Specchio e il Doppio
Bari (I) · Convento Santa Scolastica:
Notturna
Linz (A) · *Ars Electronica*
Tokyo (J) · *Electrovision '87*
Kassel (D) · documenta 8: *Roma*
Cavaillon (F) · Centre Culturel: *Festival
d'Avignon*
München (D) · Art Forum Thomas:
Documenta
Rovereto (I) · Teatro Zandonai: *Sciame*
Nice (F) · Galerie des Ponchettes:
Médias audiovisuels
Bologna (I) · Galleria d'Arte Moderna:
Videoland
Roma (I) · RAI: *Mare Orizzontale*

1988
Madrid (E) · Museo Español de Arte
Contemporáneo: *Videocruz*
Prato (I) · Museo d'Arte Contemporaneo
Luigi Pecci: *Roma II*
Venezia (I) · Museo Correr: *Canal d'Oro*
Valencia (E) · Sala Ateneo Mercant
Zaragoza (E) · Palacio de Sástago:

Plessi - Palacio Electrónico
Linz (A) · Neue Galerie der Stadt Linz:
Videoland - Videolinz
Tielt (B) · Galerie de Gryse
Umag (SLO) · Galerija Dante
Ljubljana (SLO) · Moderna Galerija

1989
Bologna (I) · Arte Fiera
Palma de Mallorca (E) · Palau Solleric
Verona (I) · Studio la Città II
Ferrara (I) · Museo Palazzo dei
Diamanti
Köln (D) · Kölnischer Kunstverein
Humlebaek (DK) · Louisiana Museum:
Borealis 4
Berlin (D) · Neuer Berliner
Kunstverein
Prato (I) · Museo d'Arte Contem-
poraneo Luigi Pecci: *Tempo Liquido*
Nagoya (J) · Biennale: *Artec '89*
Zürich (CH) · Kunsthaus Zürich
Köln (D) · Internationaler Kunstmarkt
Art Cologne 23'89
Bruxelles (B) · Opera Nationale La
Monnaie: *The Fall of Icarus*
Genève (CH) · Galerie Blancpain
Stepczynski

1990
Reggio Emilia (I) · Civici Musei:
Antològica
Frankfurt (D) · Förderverein
Schöneres Frankfurt
Genova (I) · Palazzo Bignole
Roma (I) · Galleria L'Isola
Venezia (I) · Galleria Totem
Trento (I) · Galleria Civica di Arte
Contemporanea
Prato (I) · Museo d'Arte
Contemporaneo Luigi Pecci
Venezia (I) · Studio Barnabò

1991
Madrid (I) · International Art Fair
Dortmund (D) · Museum am Ostwall
Nürnberg (D) · Museum Industrie-
kultur: *Unter Null*
Hamburg (D) · Weißer Raum
Bern (CH) · Galerie Feldmann
Marburg (D) · Kunsthalle
Palma de Mallorca (E) · Centre de
Cultura Sa Nostra
Trento (I) · Galleria Paola Stelzer
Pergine (I) · Castello di Pergine
Wien (A) · Musem Moderner Kunst
Stiftung Ludwig

1992
Berlin (D) · Akademie der Künste
Bruxelles (B) · Artiscope
København (DK) · Charlottenburg
Cagliari (I) · Museo d'Arte
Contemporanea
Maribor (SLO) · Umetnostna Galerija
Barcelona (E) · Fundació Joan Miró
Graz (A) · Haus der Architektur
Charleroi (B) · Musée de l'Industrie:
Titanic

1993
Hamburg (D) · Deichtorhallen: *Mediale*
Köln (D) · Museum Ludwig
Venezia (I) · Caffè Florian
Dortmund (D) · Museum am Ostwall:
Retrospektive
Barcelona (E) · Fundació Joan Miró
Berlin (D) · IFA 93 / Philips: *Liquid Time*
Karlsruhe (D) · Zentrum für Kunst und
Medientechnologie

1994
Chemnitz (D) · Städtische Kunst-
sammlungen: *Agricola*
Bruxelles (B) · Cirque Royal
Charleroi (B) · Charleroi/Danses:
Ex Machina
Mons (F) · Grand Hornu
Hamburg (D) · Weißer Raum
São Paulo (BRA) · Bienal de São Paulo
Köln (D) · Galerie Teutloff
Linz (A) · Neue Galerie der Stadt Linz:
Fabrizio Plessi - Hundert Zeichnungen
London (GB) · Queen Elisabeth Hall

1995
Kraichtal (A) · Ursula Blickle Stiftung
Krems (A) · Kunsthalle
Hongkong (HK) · Art Center
Venezia (I) · XLVI Biennale de Venezia:
Ex Machina
Strasbourg (F) · Musée d'Art Moderne
et Contemporain: *Der Rhein - Le Rhin -
De Waal*
Palma de Mallorca (E) · Fundació Pilar
i Joan Miró
Perugia (I) · Rocca Paolina
Bonn (D) · Rheinisches Landesmuseum:
Der Rhein - Le Rhin - De Waal
Bologna (I) · Museo La Salara
Lyon (F) · Biennale de Lyon
Paris (F) · Galerie Pièce Unique

1996
Palma de Mallorca (E) · La Llonja

Speyer (D) · Historisches Museum der
Pfalz: *Mysterium Wein*
Nijmegen (NL) · Museum
Commanderie van Sint Jan:
Der Rhein - Le Rhin - De Waal
Mainz (D) · Landesmuseum Mainz:
Museum der Medien
Köln (D) · Museum Ludwig
Graz (A) · Mausoleum: *Fez in Graz*
Heidelberg (D) · Heidelberger Kunst-
verein: *Acquedotto Elettronico*
Den Haag (NL) · City Hall
Napoli (I) · Fondazione IDIS:
Movimenti Catodici Barocchi
Napoli (I) · Fondazione Lucio Amelio:
Le Cariatidi dei Poveri

1997
Kaufbeuren (D) · Kunsthaus: *Fez-Fez*
Bruxelles (B) · Halles de Schaerbeek:
Icare - Titanic - Ex Machina
Paderborn (D) · Kaiserpfalz:
Stad(t)t-Art
München (D) · Justizpalast:
Bombay-Bombay
Karlsruhe (D) · Zentrum für Kunst
und Medientechnologie - ZKM
Leverkusen (D) · Museum Schloß
Morsbroich: *Museum vitale*
Luxembourg (L) · Casino
Luxembourg, Forum d'Art
Bologna (I) · Galleria d'Arte Moderna
Venezia (I) · Fondazione Peggy
Guggenheim: *Presentazione
›Progetti del Mondo‹*
Rovigo/Treviso (I) · Teatro Comunale:
Memos

1998
Bologna (I) · Arte Fiera: *Progetti del
Guggenheim SoHo*
Wien (A) · Kunsthistorisches Museum:
L'Arca dell'Arte
New York, NY (USA) · Guggenheim
Museum SoHo
Rottenburg a. Neckar (D) · Kultur-
verein Zehntscheuer: *Fez-Fez*
São Paulo (BRA) · Fundação SECS,
Pompeia: *Deposito dell'Arte*
San José (Costa Rica) · Museo de Arte
y Diseño
Mainz (D) · Galerie Dorothea van der
Koelen: *Fez-Fez*
San Diego, CA (USA) · Museum of
Contemporary Art, La Jolla
Augsburg (D) · Städtische Kunst-
sammlungen Augsburg

VIDEO-BÄNDER
VIDEO TAPES
VIDEO

Travel, 30 min, black & white,
    production: Galleria d'Arte
    Moderna, Ferrara 1974
Acquabiografico, 30 min, black &
    white, production: Galleria d'Arte
    Moderna, Ferrara 1974
Liquid Piece, 30 min, black & white,
    production: ICC, Antwerpen 1975
Camminare sull'acqua, 20 min, black
    & white, production: Instituto
    Franco Tedesco 1975
Taglia acqua - Fatelo da voi, 30 min,
    black & white, production: Galerie
    Lara Vincy, Paris 1975
Vibrations, 20 min, black & white,
    production: Galleria d'Arte
    Moderna, Ferrara 1976
Hollywater, 16 min, black & white,
    production: Galleria d'Arte
    Moderna, Ferrara 1976
Water Percussion, 20 min, black &
    white, production: Environmedia,
    Milano 1976
A morte Venezia!, 30 min, black &
    white, production: Galleria d'Arte
    Moderna, Ferrara 1976
Two and Two, 30 min, black & white,
    production: Galleria d'Arte
    Moderna, Ferrara 1977
Splash!, 60 min, black & white,
    production: Detra / Crad /
    Tuttifrutti, Ravenna 1977
Liquid Time, 30 min, black & white,
    production: Folkwang Museum,
    Essen 1977
Liquid Time Performances, 30 min,
    production: ICC, Antwerpen, Neue
    Galerie, Aachen 1978
Tempo Liquido, 60 min, black & white,
    production: ICC, Antwerpen, Neue
    Galerie, Aachen 1978
Tempo Liquido, 45 min, production:
    The Kitchen, New York 1979
Water Face, 45 min, production: Neue
    Galerie, Aachen 1979
Naufragio, 30 min, production:
    La dip / ca, Vègia 1979
Tam-tam, 60 min, black & white,
    production: Folkwang Museum,
    Essen 1979
Tam-tam, 60 min, production: Modern
    Art Galerie, Wien 1980

Underwater (sequence):
  1 Water Colour
  2 Water Man
  3 Hard Water
  4 Water Wind
  5 Hollywater
  6 Double Movie
  7 Wipers
  8 Wreck
  9 Water Fire
  10 Dirty Movie
  11 Liquid Movie
  12 Water Art,
  Faits Divers System, production:
  Frigo, Lyon 1980
Water Fan, 12 min, production: Centro
  Video Arte, Ferrara 1982
Up down, 12 min, production: Centro
  Video Arte, Ferrara 1982
Surf Control, 12 min, production:
  Centro Video Arte, Ferrara 1982
Vide-eau, by Fabrizio Plessi and
  Gilbert Perlain, 15 min, production:
  Musée d'Art Moderne, Villeneuve
  d'Ascq 1984
Backwater, 16 min, production: Centro
  Video Arte, Ferrara 1984
Ex Machina, 45 1/2 min, production:
  Kunsthochschule für Medien,
  Köln 1984
Plessi Video Going, by Felice Pesoli,
  production: Bip-Bip - Studio
  Equatore, Milano 1986
Plessi, production: Centro Video Arte,
  Ferrara 1987
Plessi - Poesie aus Wasser und Video,
  45 min, production: Renate and
  Wolfgang Liebenwein, 1988
Plessi - Selection by Immagina, by
  Rannuccio Sodi, production: RAI
  Uno, Roma 1991
Plessi, by Danilo Eccher, 18 min,
  production: Sirio Film and Galleria
  Arte Contemporanea, Trento 1992
Plessi - L'Anima della Pietra, by Carlo
  Ansaloni, 16 min, production:
  Comune di Perugia, Perugia 1995
Plessi, by Katrin Ritterling, 6 min,
  production: Kulturweltspiegel,
  Köln 1998

BIBLIOGRAPHIE (AUSWAHL)
SELECTED BIBLIOGRAPHY
BIBLIOGRAFIA (SELEZIONE)

Tonio Toniato, cat. Galleria Il Canale,
  Venezia 1962
Mario De Luigi, cat. Galleria 2000,
  Bologna 1963
Silvio Branzi, Guiseppe Marchiori,
  Toni Toniato: *Plessi*, cat. Galleria
  Griti, Edizioni Eventu, Venezia 1964
Gillo Dorfles, cat. Galleria Sebastiani,
  Milano 1965
Emilio Tadini, cat. Galleria Il Punto,
  Torino 1965
Guiseppe Marchiori, cat. Galleria Il
  Cavallino, Venezia 1967
Guiseppe Marchiori, Toni Toniato:
  Plessi, cat. Galleria De Foscherari,
  Bologna 1968
Umbro Apollonio: *Venezianische
  Malerei*, cat. Neue Galerie der Stadt
  Linz, Linz 1970
Catalogue XXXV Biennale d'Arte di
  Venezia (padiglione sperimentale),
  Venezia 1970
Umbro Apollonio, Luciano Caramel,
  Dietrich Mahlow: *Ricerca e
  progettazione*, La Biennale d'Arte di
  Venezia, Venezia 1970
Enrico Crispolti: *Plessi*, cat. Galleria
  Piattelli, Roma 1970
Roberto Sanesi, Enrico Crispolti, cat.
  Galleria Viniciana, Milano 1972
Roberto Sanesi, cat. D.M. Gallery,
  London 1972
Toni Toniato, cat. XXXVI Biennale
  d'Arte di Venezia, Venezia 1972
Pierre Restany, cat. Galerie Lara
  Vincy, Paris 1973
Pierre Restany, Roberto Sanesi: *Plessi -
  Acquabiografico*, Edizioni Galleria
  Vinciana, Milano 1973
Fabrizio Plessi - L'humidité, cat.
  Galerie Lara Vincy, Jean Petithory,
  Paris 1973
Armin Zweite: *Plessi*, cat. Städtische
  Galerie im Lenbachhaus,
  München 1974
Plessi - Travel, cat. Galerie Lara Vincy,
  Paris 1974
Alfred Olderaan: *Plessi*, cat.
  De Moriaan Museum,
  's-Hertogenbosch 1974
Armin Zweite, cat. Galleria Centro,
  Torino 1975

Jean-Pierre van Tieghem, cat.
  Internationaal Cultureel Centrum -
  ICC, Antwerpen 1975
Plessi, cat. 9ᵉ Biennale de Paris,
  Paris 1975
Enrico Crispolti, Marisa Vescovo:
  Plessi, cat. Comune di Alessandria,
  Alessandria 1975
Gillo Dorfles, Eberhard Freitag, Jens
  Christian Jensen: *Plessi*, cat. Kunst-
  halle zu Kiel, Kiel 1977
Guiseppe Marchiori: *Plessi. Water
  Drawings*, Edizioni Ravagnan, 1977
Gillo Dorfles: *Plessi - azioni/films,
  interventi, videotapes, performances*,
  Mastrogiacomo Editore, Images 70,
  Padova 1977
Luigina Bortolatto: *Metafisica del
  quotidiano*, cat. S. Teonisto,
  Treviso 1978
Pierre Restany: *Venerezia*, cat. Palazzo
  Grassi, Venezia 1978
Luigi Carluccio: *L'immagine
  provocata*, cat. XXXIX Biennale
  d'Arte di Venezia, Venezia 1978
Fabrizio Plessi - Liquid Geometry,
  La Nuova Foglio Editrice,
  Macerata 1978
Gillo Dorfles: *Geometria Liquida*, cat.
  Galerie Lara Vincy, Paris 1978
Georg F. Schwarzbauer: *Kubisch &
  Plessi - Konzerte, Video,
  Performances, Installationen*, cat.
  Neue Galerie Sammlung Ludwig,
  Aachen, Internationaal Cultureel
  Centrum - ICC, Antwerpen 1979
Siegfried Salzmann: *Plessi - Reflecting
  Water*, (Documentation of Duisburg
  installation at Bertasee) Edizioni
  Canova, Treviso 1980
Lola Bonora: *Forme scenografiche
  della televisione*, cat. La Triennale,
  Milano 1981
Internazionale del Cinema, cat.
  Biennale Internazionale del
  Cinema, Venezia 1981
Wulf Herzogenrath: *Videokunst in
  Deutschland 1963-1982*,
  Hamburg 1982
Internazionale del Cinema, cat.
  Biennale Internazionale del
  Cinema, Venezia 1982
Aktuell '83, cat. Städtische Galerie im
  Lenbachhaus, München 1983
Morando Morandini: *Plessi -
  Underwater*, Mastrogiacomo
  Editore, Images 70, Padova 1983

Vittorio Fagone, Hans Gercke, Thierry Raspail: *Plessi - Water Video Projects,* cat. Heidelberger Kunstverein, Palazzo dei Priori, Volterra, Musée de Grenoble, Skulpturenmuseum Glaskasten, Marl, Musée du Nord, Villeneuve d'Ascq, Palazzo dei Diamanti, Ferrara, Kunstverein Freiburg, Freiburg 1983

Catalogue XLI Biennale d'Arte di Venezia, Electa Editrice, Milano 1984

Vittorio Fagone, Maurizio Calvesi, Lola Bonora, Massimo Cacciari, Felix Zdanek et al.: *Plessi - Video Going,* cat. Rotonda della Besana, Electa Editrice, Milano 1985

Lola Bonora: *Install Video Side,* cat. Galleria d'Arte Moderna, L'Immagine Elettronica, Bologna 1986

Jolanda Padilla: *Plessi - Videoland,* cat. Centre Culturel, Cavaillon 1987

Catalogue documenta 8, Kassel 1987

David Galloway: *Kunst und Elektronik,* Econ Verlag, Düsseldorf 1987

Guiseppe Bartolucci: *Plessi - Sciame,* Teatro Zandonai, Rovereto 1987

Achille Bonito Oliva: *Plessi - Videocruz,* cat. Museo Español de Arte Contemporaneo, Madrid 1987

Amnon Barzel: *Europa Oggi,* Museo d'Arte Contemporaneo Luigi Pecci, Prato, Electa Editrice, Milano 1988

Jesa Denegri: *Plessi,* cat. Galerie Dante, Umag 1988

Achille Bonito Oliva: *Il tallone d'Achille,* Feltrinelli Editrice, Milano 1988

José Lebrero Stäls: *Plessi - La máquina domada,* cat. Palacio de Sástago, Zaragoza 1988

Peter Baum: *Plessi - Videoland / Videolinz,* cat. Neue Galerie der Stadt Linz, Linz 1988

Achille Bonito Oliva: *Borealis 4,* cat. Louisiana Museum, Humlebaek 1989

Maurizio Calvesi: *Plessi - La Stanza Fragile,* cat. Galerie Blancpain-Stepczynski, Genève 1989

Wulf Herzogenrath, Edith Decker: *Videoskulptur retrospektiv und aktuell 1963-1989,* Dumont, Köln 1989

Pedro Lombardia, Santiago B. Olmo: *Plessi - Videosal,* cat. Palau Solleric, Palma de Mallorca 1989

Amnon Barzel: *Fabrizio Plessi,* cat. Galleria L'Isola, Roma 1990

Danilo Eccher, Agnes Kohlmeyer: *Gilardi - Plessi,* cat. Galleria Civica di Arte Contemporanea, Trento 1990

Omar Calabrese, Achille Bonito Oliva, Lola Bonora: *Plessi,* cat. Civici Musei, Comune di Reggio Emilia, Edizioni Canova, Treviso 1990

María Lluïsa Borràs, Magdalena Aguiló Victory: *Fabrizio Plessi a Mallorca,* cat. Sa Nostra, Palma de Mallorca 1991

Viana Conti: *Fabrizio Plessi,* cat. Galleria Paola Stelzer, Galleria Il Cenacolo, Trento 1991

Lóránd Hegyi, Amnon Barzel, Peter Baum, Robert Reitbauer: *Plessi,* cat. Museum Moderner Kunst Stiftung Ludwig, Wien 1991

Rosa Maria Malet, Heinrich Klotz: *Moving Image,* cat. Fundació Joan Miró, Barcelona 1992

Ingo Bartsch: *Plessi Retrospektive 1976-1993,* cat. Museum am Ostwall, Dortmund 1993

Gert Kaiser, Dirk Matejovski: *Kultur und Technik im 21. Jahrhundert,* Campus Verlag, 1993

Pierre Restany et al.: *Plessi - Cristalli Liquidi,* cat. Caffè Florian, Venezia 1993

Marc Scheps, Evelyn Weiss: *Fabrizio Plessi. Bombay-Bombay,* cat. Museum Ludwig, Köln, Edizioni Canova, Treviso; Catalan version: Rosa Maria Malet, Fundació Miró, Barcelona, 1993

Michel Baudson: *Plessi - Flamand. Icare, Titanic, Ex Machina,* Charleroi/Danses, Charleroi, Plan K, Bruxelles 1994

Peter Baum: *Plessi,* cat. Neue Galerie der Stadt Linz, Linz 1995

Lola Bonora: *Centro Videoarte 1974-1994,* Comune di Ferrara, Corbo Editore, 1995

Hans Gercke: *Fabrizio Plessi - Rovina Elettronica,* cat. Ursula Blickle Stiftung, Kraichtal 1995

Jörg Schepers, Giorgio Bonomi, Lola Bonora, Wulf Herzogenrath: *Fabrizio Plessi - La Rocca Elettronica,* cat. Rocca Paolina, Provincia di Perugia, Perugia 1995

Die Kunst des 20. Jahrhunderts, Museum Ludwig, Taschen Verlag, Köln 1996

Giesela Fiedler-Bender, Edith Decker-Phillips: *Fabrizio Plessi. Il Fiume della Storia,* cat. Landesmuseum, Mainz 1996

Thierry Raspail, Thierry Prat, Georges Rey: *3ᵉ Biennale de Lyon,* cat. Réunion des Musées Nationaux, 1996

Thomas Wegner, Wulf Herzogenrath: *Art Medial,* cat. La Llonja, Govern Balear, Palma de Mallorca 1996

Boris von Brauchitsch: *Fabrizio Plessi Fez-Fez,* cat. Kunsthaus Kaufbeuren, Kaufbeuren 1997

Gérard A Goodrow: *Plessi - Progetti del Mondo,* Dumont, Köln 1997

Heinrich Klotz: *Contemporary Art - The Collection of ZKM,* Zentrum für Kunst und Medientechnologie, Karlsruhe 1997

Wilfried Seipel: *L'Arca dell'Arte,* cat. Kunsthistorisches Museum, Wien 1998

Dorothea van der Koelen: *Fabrizio Plessi. Opus Video Sculpture,* Catalogue Raisonné, Chorus-Verlag, Mainz - München 1998

1988 Madrid, Museo Español de Arte
Contemporaneo
1993 Dortmund, Museum am Ostwall
1997 Karlsruhe, Zentrum für Kunst
und Medientechnologie (ZKM)
1998 New York, Guggenheim
Museum SoHo
1998 San Diego, Museum of
Contemporary Art La Jolla

85004
WATER DESERT
Deserto d'Acqua
Wasserwüste
exhibited:
1990 Venezia, Studio Barnabó
1993 Dortmund, Museum am Ostwall
1995 Perugia, Rocca Paolina

87001
WINNER
Vincitore
Sieger
exhibited:
1987 Ferrara, Museo Palazzo dei
Diamanti
1989 Palma de Mallorca, Palau
Solleric
1989 Nagoya, Biennale Nagoya
1995 Perugia, Rocca Paolina

87002
ROMA
Rom
Rome
exhibited:
1987 Kassel, documenta 8
1987 München, Art Forum R. Thomas

87003
VIDEOLAND
exhibited:
1987 Cavaillon, Centre Culturel
1987 Bologna, Galleria d'Arte
Moderna
1987 Roma, RAI 1, ›Immagina‹
1988 Linz, Neue Galerie der Stadt

88001
VIDEOCRUZ
Video Croce
Videokreuz
Video Cross
exhibited:
1988 Madrid, Museo Español de Arte
Contemporaneo
1988 Roma, RAI 1, ›Immagina‹

88002
CANAL D'ORO
Goldener Kanal
Golden Canal
exhibited:
1988 Venezia, Museo Correr

88003
ROMA II
Rom II
Rome II
exhibited:
1988 Prato, Museo d'Arte
Contemporanea ›Luigi Pecci‹
1991 Wien, Museum Moderner
Kunst, Stiftung Ludwig
1993 Dortmund, Museum am
Ostwall
1995 Perugia, Rocca Paolina
1998 New York, Guggenheim
Museum SoHo
1998 San Diego, Museum of
Contemporary Art La Jolla

88004
IL PESO DEL MONDO
Die Last der Welt
The Burden of the World
exhibited:
1988 Stift Wilhering, Neue Galeri
der Stadt Linz

88005
ROMA III
Rom III
Rome III
exhibited:
1988 Roma, RAI 1, ›Immagina‹
1990 Reggio Emilia, Museo Civico
d'Arte Moderna

88006
ROMA IV
Rom IV
Rome IV
exhibited:
1988 Zaragoza, Palacio de Sástago

88007
PALACIO ELECTRÓNICO
Palazzo Elettronico
Elektronischer Palast
Electronic Palace
exhibited:
1988 Zaragoza, Palacio de Sástago

88008
COLATORAO
exhibited:
1988 Zaragoza, Palacio de Sástago

89001
GEOMETRIA LIQUIDA
Flüssige Geometrie
Liquid Geometry
exhibited:
1989 Ferrara, Museo Palazzo dei
Diamanti
1989 Bologna, Arte Fiera
1993 Dortmund, Museum am
Ostwall
1995 Perugia, Rocca Paolina
1997 Köln, Baukunst
1997 Leverkusen, Museum Schloß
Morsbroich
1998 Köln, Gerling Konzern

89002
TEMPO LIQUIDO
Flüssige Zeit
Liquid Time
exhibited:
1989 Prato, Museo d'Arte
Contemporanea ›Luigi Pecci‹
1995 Perugia, Rocca Paolina

89003
CROSS
Croce
Kreuz
exhibited:
1989 Ferrara, Museo Palazzo dei
Diamanti

89004
LA STANZA FRAGILE
Zerbrechlicher Raum
Fragil Cabinet
exhibited:
1989 Genève, Galerie Blancpain
Stepczynski

89005
MATERIA PRIMA
Rohstoff
Raw Material
exhibited:
1989 Köln, Kölnischer Kunstverein

89006
L'ARMADIO DELL'ARTE
Schrank der Kunst
Cabinet of Art

exhibited:
1989 Palma de Mallorca, Palau
Solleric
1990 Reggio Emilia, Museo Civico
d'Arte Moderna
1993 Dortmund, Museum am Ostwall

89007
L'ARMADIO DI MARMO
Schrank des Marmors
Cabinet of Marble
exhibited:
1989 Palma de Mallorca, Palau
Solleric
1990 Reggio Emilia, Museo Civico
d'Arte Moderna

89008
LA MÁQUINA SALADA
La Macchina Salata
Salzmaschine
Salt Machine
exhibited:
1989 Palma de Mallorca, Palau
Solleric
1993 Dortmund, Museum am Ostwall

89009
L'ARMADIO DEI SASSI
Schrank der Steine
Cabinet of Stones
exhibited:
1989 Verona, Studio La Citta
1990 Reggio Emilia, Museo Civico
d'Arte Moderna
1990 Roma, Galleria L'Isola
1993 Dortmund, Museum am Ostwall
1995 Köln, Galerie Dorothea van der
Koelen, Art Cologne
1997 Paderborn, Kaiserpfalz

90001
FOR SALE
Vendita
Ausverkauf
exhibited:
1990 Reggio Emilia, Museo Civico
d'Arte Moderna

90002
LA STANZA DEL MARE
Meeresraum
Sea Room
exhibited:
1990 Reggio Emilia, Museo Civico
d'Arte Moderna
1990 Trento, Galleria Civica di Arte

Contemporanea
1991 Hamburg, Weißer Raum
1992 København, Charlottenburg
1997 Karlsruhe, Zentrum für Kunst
und Medientechnologie (ZKM)

90003
L'ARMADIO DELL'ARCHITETTO
Schrank des Architekten
The Architect's Cabinet
exhibited:
1990 Reggio Emilia, Museo Civico
d'Arte Moderna
1991 Wien, Museum Moderner
Kunst, Stiftung Ludwig
1991 Marburg, Marburger
Kunstverein
1993 Dortmund, Museum am
Ostwall
1997 Luxembourg, Casino
Luxembourg, Forum d'Art
Contemporain

90004
L'ARMADIO DELLA LUCE
Schrank des Lichts
Cabinet of Light
exhibited:
1990 Reggio Emilia, Museo Civico
d'Arte Moderna

90005
L'ARMADIO DELLA PAGLIA
Schrank mit Stroh
Cabinet of Straw
exhibited:
1990 Reggio Emilia, Museo Civico
d'Arte Moderna
1990 Trento, Galleria Civica di Arte
Contemporanea

90006
WORK IN PROGRESS
Lavoro nel Progresso
In Arbeit
exhibited:
1990 Reggio Emilia, Museo Civico
d'Arte Moderna

90007
COME ERAVAMO (OMAGGIO A PAIK)
Wie wir gewesen sind
(Hommage à Paik)
The Way We Were (Homage to Paik)
exhibited:
1990 Reggio Emilia, Museo Civico
d'Arte Moderna

90008
L'ARMADIO DI WASSERWAGEN
Schrank des Wasserwagens
Cabinet of the Water Car
exhibited:
1990 Reggio Emilia, Museo Civico
d'Arte Moderna
1995 Hamburg, Premiere Studio
Moore

90009
L'ARMADIO DELLE SCATOLE
Schrank der Schachteln
Cabinet of Boxes
exhibited:
1990 Reggio Emilia, Museo Civico
d'Arte Moderna

90010
L'ARMADIO DELLA LEGNA
Schrank des Holzes
Cabinet of Wood
exhibited:
1990 Reggio Emilia, Museo Civico
d'Arte Moderna

90011
L'ARMADIO DI BRONX
Schrank der Bronx
Cabinet of Bronx
exhibited:
1990 Reggio Emilia, Museo Civico
d'Arte Moderna
1996 Köln, Galerie Dorothea van der
Koelen, Art Cologne
1997 Luxembourg, Casino
Luxembourg, Forum d'Art
Contemporain

90012
PROIBITO
Verboten
Prohibited
exhibited:
1990 Roma, Galleria L'Isola
1993 Dortmund, Museum am Ostwall

90013
LA CARIATIDE DELL'ARCHITETTO
Die Karyatide des Architekten
The Architect's Carytid
exhibited:
1990 Venezia, Galleria Totem
1993 Barcelona, Fundació Joan Miró
1997 Karlsruhe, Zentrum für Kunst
und Medientechnologie (ZKM)

91001
CAIRO-CAIRO
Kairo-Kairo
exhibited:
1991 Trento, Galleria Paola Stelzer

91002
MEDITERRANEA
Mittelmeer
Mediterranean
exhibited:
1991 Cagliari, Galleria d'Arte
Moderna

91003
PORFIDO A PERGINE
Porphyr in Pergine
Porphyry at Pergine
exhibited:
1991 Pergine, Castello di Pergine

92001
MATERIA PRIMA II
Urmaterie
Primeval Matter
exhibited:
1992 Maribor, Umetnostna Galerija
1997 Bologna, Galleria d'Arte
Moderna

92002
DIE KARYATIDEN DER ARMEN
Le Cariatide dei Poveri
The Carytids of the Poor
exhibited:
1992 Graz, Haus der Architektur
1993 Dortmund, Museum am Ostwall
1995 Mainz, Galerie Dorothea van
der Koelen
1995 Basel, Galerie Dorothea van
der Koelen, Art Basel
1995 Perugia, Rocca Paolina

92003
DER RAUM DER WÖRTER
La Stanza delle Parole
Room of Words
exhibited:
1992 Berlin, Akademie der Künste
1993 Dortmund, Museum am Ostwall

93001
BOMBAY-BOMBAY
exhibited:
1993 Köln, Museum Ludwig
1993 Barcelona, Fundació Joan Miró
1997 München, Justizpalast

93002
CRISTALLI LIQUIDI
Flüssige Kristalle
Liquid Crystals
exhibited:
1993 Venezia, Caffè Florian
1998 New York, Guggenheim Museum
1998 San Diego, Museum of
Contemporary Art La Jolla

93003
LIQUID TIME
Tempo Liquido II
Flüssige Zeit II
exhibited:
1993 Berlin, Philips
1997 Karlsruhe, Zentrum für Kunst
und Medientechnologie (ZKM)

94001
PARIS-PARIS
exhibited:
1994 Hamburg, Weißer Raum
1996 Palma de Mallorca, La Llonja

95001
ROVINA ELETTRONICA
Elektronische Ruine
Electronic Ruin
exhibited:
1995 Kraichtal, Ursula Blickle Stiftung
1996 Köln, Museum Ludwig

95002
IN VINO VERITAS
exhibited:
1995 Krems, Kunsthalle Krems

95003
RHEIN-RAUM
La Stanza del Reno
Rhine Room
exhibited:
1995 Bonn, Rheinisches Landesmuseum
1995 Strasbourg, Musée d'Art Moderne et Contemporain
1996 Nijmegen, Museum
Commanderie van Sint Jan

95004
FUOCO FATUO
Irrlicht
Ignis Fatuus
exhibited:
1995 Palma de Mallorca, Fundació
Pilar i Joan Miró

95005
FUOCHI FATUI
Irrlichter
Ignes Fatui
exhibited:
1995 Palma de Mallorca, Fundació
Pilar i Joan Miró

95006
DEPOSITO DELL'ARTE
Kunst-Depot
Art Deposit
exhibited:
1995 Perugia, Rocca Paolina
1998 São Paulo, Fundação SECS,
Pompeia

95007
GLI ARMADI DEL CAOS
Die Schränke des Chaos
Cabinets of the Chaos
exhibited:
1995 Perugia, Rocca Paolina

95008
CRISTALLO LIQUIDO
Flüssiges Kristall
Liquid Crystal
exhibited:
1995 Perugia, Rocca Paolina
1996 Wien

95009
BOMBAY-BOMBAY II
exhibited:
1995 Perugia, Rocca Paolina

95010
L'ANIMA DELLA PIETRA
Die Seele des Steins
Soul of the Stone
exhibited:
1995 Perugia, Rocca Paolina
1996 Den Haag, City-Hall

95011
BOMBAY-BOMBAY III
exhibited:
1995 Bologna, Museo La Salara

95012
LE DUE ANIME DELLA MATERIA
Die zwei Seelen der Materie
The two Souls of Matter
exhibited:
1995 Paris, Galerie Pièce Unique

96001
MYSTERIUM WEIN
Misterio Vino
Wine Mystery
exhibited:
1996 Speyer, Historisches Museum
der Pfalz

96002
IL FIUME DELLA STORIA
Fluß der Geschichte
River of History
exhibited:
1996 Mainz, Landesmuseum Mainz

96003
FEZ-FEZ
exhibited:
1996 Graz, Kirche ›Mausoleum‹
1997 Kaufbeuren, Kunsthaus
1998 Linz, Neue Galerie der Stadt
1998 Rottenburg am Neckar,
Kulturverein Zehntscheuer
1998 Mainz, Galerie Dorothea van
der Koelen

96004
ACQUEDOTTO ELETTRONICO
Elektronisches Aquädukt
Electronic Aqueduct
exhibited:
1996 Heidelberg, Heidelberger
Kunstverein

96005
MOVIMENTI CATODICI BAROCCHI
Kathodische barocke Bewegungen
Cathodic Baroque Movements
exhibited:
1996 Napoli, Fondazione IDIS
1998 New York, Guggenheim Museum
1998 San Diego, Museum of
Contemporary Art La Jolla

96006
LE CARIATIDI DEI POVERI II
Die Karyatiden der Armen II
The Carytids of the Poor II
exhibited:
1996 Napoli, Galleria Lucio Amelio

97001
MOSAICO LIQUIDO
Flüssiges Mosaik
Liquid Mosaic
exhibited:
1997 Venezia, Collezione privata

98001
L'ARCA DELL'ARTE
Floß der Kunst
Raft of Arts
exhibited:
1998 Wien, Kunsthistorisches
Museum

TITEL REGISTER
TITLE REGISTER
REGISTRO TITOLO

TITEL REGISTER (ITALIENISCH)
TITLE REGISTER (ITALIAN)
REGISTRO TITOLO (ITALIANO)

PRÄSENTATIONSREGISTER
PRESENTATION REGISTER
REGISTRO DEI PRESENTAZIONI

1986
Bologna · Galleria d'Arte Moderna:
Reflecting Water 79001

Venezia · XLII Biennale di Venezia:
Bronx 85003

1987
Bologna · Galleria d'Arte Moderna:
Mare di Marmo 85002
Videoland 87003

Cavaillon · Centre Culturel:
Bronx 85003
Videoland 87003

Ferrara · Museo Palazzo dei Diamanti:
Winner 87001

Kassel · documenta 8:
Roma 87002

München · Art Forum R. Thomas:
Roma 87002

Roma · RAI 1, ›Immagina‹:
Mare Orizzontale 76001
Liquid Gravity Center 82001
Casablanca 84004
Bronx 85003
Videoland 87003

1988
Ferrara · Museo Palazzo dei Diamanti:
Arco Liquido 81001

Linz · Neue Galerie der Stadt:
Mare Orizzontale 76001
Wasserwagen 81005
Videoland 87003

Madrid · Museo Español de Arte
Contemporaneo:
Mare Orizzontale 76001
Liquid Gravity Center 82001
Water Wind IV 84002
Bronx 85003
Videocruz 88001

Prato · Museo d'Arte Contemporanea
›Luigi Pecci‹:
Roma II 88003

Roma · RAI 1, ›Immagina‹:
Wasserwagen 81005
Videocruz 88001
Roma III 88005

Stift Wilhering:
Il Peso del Mondo 88004

Venezia · Museo Correr:
Canal d'Oro 88002

Zaragoza · Palacio de Sástago:
Mare di Marmo 85002
Roma IV 88006
Palacio Electrónico 88007
Colatorao 88008

1989
Bologna · Arte Fiera:
Geometria Liquida 89001

Ferrara · Museo Palazzo dei Diamanti:
Geometria Liquida 89001
Cross 89003

Genève · Galerie Blancpain
Stepczynski:
La Stanza Fragile 89004

Humlebaek · Louisiana Museum:
Mare di Marmo 85002

Köln · Kölnischer Kunstverein:
Materia Prima 89005

Nagoya · Biennale Nagoya:
Winner 87001

Palma de Mallorca · Palau Solleric:
Arco Liquido 81001
Winner 87001
L'Armadio dell'Arte 89006
L'Armadio di Marmo 89007
La Máquina Salada 89008

Prato · Museo d'Arte Contemporanea
›Luigi Pecci‹:
Tempo Liquido 89002

Verona · Studio La Citta:
L'Armadio dei Sassi 89009

1990
Reggio Emilia · Museo Civico d'Arte
Moderna:
Roma III 88005
L'Armadio dell'Arte 89006
L'Armadio di Marmo 89007
L'Armadio dei Sassi 89009
For Sale 90001
La Stanza del Mare 90002
L'Armadio dell'Architetto 90003
L'Armadio della Luce 90004
L'Armadio della Paglia 90005
Work in Progress 90006
Come Eravamo 90007
L'Armadio di Wasserwagen 90008
L'Armadio delle Scatole 90009

L'Armadio della Legna 90010
L'Armadio di Bronx 90011

Roma · Galleria L'Isola:
L'Armadio dei Sassi 89009
Proibito 90012

Trento · Galleria Civica di Arte
Contemporanea:
La Stanza del Mare 90002
L'Armadio della Paglia 90005

Venezia · Studio Barnabò:
Water Desert 85004

Venezia · Galleria Totem:
La Cariatide dell'Architetto 90013

1991
Cagliari · Galleria d'Arte Moderna:
Mediterranea 91002

Hamburg · Weißer Raum:
La Stanza del Mare 90002

Marburg · Marburger Kunstverein:
L'Armadio dell'Architetto 90003

Pergine · Castello di Pergine:
Porfido a Pergine 91003

Trento · Galleria Paola Stelzer:
Cairo-Cairo 91001

Wien · Museum Moderner Kunst,
Stiftung Ludwig:
Roma II 88003
L'Armadio dell'Architetto 90003

1992
Barcelona · Fundació Joan Miró:
Wasserwagen 81005

Berlin · Akademie der Künste:
Der Raum der Wörter 92003

Graz · Haus der Architektur:
Die Karyatiden der Armen 92002

København · Charlottenburg:
La Stanza del Mare 90002

Maribor · Umetnostna Galerija:
Materia Prima II 92001

1993
Barcelona · Fundació Joan Miró:
La Cariatide dell'Architetto 90013
Bombay-Bombay 93001

Berlin · Philips:
Liquid Time 93003